FINANCIAL ACCOUNTING
International Financial Reporting Standards

Eighth Edition

Walter T. Harrison Jr.
Baylor University

Charles T. Horngren
Stanford University

C. William (Bill) Thomas
Baylor University

Themin Suwardy
Singapore Management University

Boston   Columbus   Indianapolis   New York   San Francisco   Upper Saddle River
Amsterdam   Cape Town   Dubai   London   Madrid   Milan   Munich   Paris   Montreal   Toronto
Delhi   Mexico City   Sao Paulo   Sydney   Hong Kong   Seoul   Singapore   Taipei   Tokyo

Published in 2011 by
Pearson Education South Asia Pte Ltd
23/25 First Lok Yang Road, Jurong
Singapore 629733

Publishing Director: *Joy Tan*
Acquisitions Editor: *Laura Dent*
Senior Editor: *Lo Hwei Shan*
Project Editor: *Rachel Lee*
Prepress Executive: *Kimberly Yap*

Pearson Education offices in Asia: *Bangkok, Beijing, Hong Kong, Jakarta, Kuala Lumpur, Manila, New Delhi, Seoul, Singapore, Taipei, Tokyo*

If you purchased this book within the United States or Canada you should be aware that it has been imported without the approval of the Publisher or the Author.

Printed in Singapore

4 3 2 1
13 12 11 10

ISBN 13   978-981-06-8457-0
ISBN 10   981-06-8457-6

www.pearsonglobaleditions.com

For our wives,

Nancy, Joan, Mary Ann and Febrita

About the Authors

Walter T. Harrison, Jr. is professor emeritus of accounting at the Hankamer School of Business, Baylor University. He received his BBA from Baylor University, his MS from Oklahoma State University, and his PhD from Michigan State University.

Professor Harrison, recipient of numerous teaching awards from student groups as well as from university administrators, has also taught at Cleveland State Community College, Michigan State University, the University of Texas, and Stanford University.

A member of the American Accounting Association and the American Institute of Certified Public Accountants, Professor Harrison has served as chairman of the Financial Accounting Standards Committee of the American Accounting Association, on the Teaching/Curriculum Development Award Committee, on the Program Advisory Committee for Accounting Education and Teaching, and on the Notable Contributions to Accounting Literature Committee.

Professor Harrison has lectured in several foreign countries and published articles in numerous journals, including *Journal of Accounting Research*, *Journal of Accountancy*, *Journal of Accounting and Public Policy*, *Economic Consequences of Financial Accounting Standards*, *Accounting Horizons*, *Issues in Accounting Education*, and *Journal of Law and Commerce*.

He is co-author of *Financial & Managerial Accounting*, second edition, 2009 and *Accounting*, eighth edition, 2009 (with Charles T. Horngren and M. Suzanne Oliver), published by Pearson Prentice Hall. Professor Harrison has received scholarships, fellowships, and research grants or awards from PricewaterhouseCoopers, Deloitte & Touche, the Ernst & Young Foundation, and the KPMG Foundation.

Charles T. Horngren is the Edmund W. Littlefield professor of accounting, emeritus, at Stanford University. A graduate of Marquette University, he received his MBA from Harvard University and his PhD from the University of Chicago. He is also the recipient of honorary doctorates from Marquette University and DePaul University.

A certified public accountant, Horngren served on the Accounting Principles Board for six years, the Financial Accounting Standards Board Advisory Council for five years, and the Council of the American Institute of Certified Public Accountants for three years. For six years he served as a trustee of the Financial Accounting Foundation, which oversees the Financial Accounting Standards Board and the Government Accounting Standards Board.

Horngren is a member of the Accounting Hall of Fame.

A member of the American Accounting Association, Horngren has been its president and its director of research. He received its first annual Outstanding Accounting Educator Award.

The California Certified Public Accountants Foundation gave Horngren its Faculty Excellence Award and its Distinguished Professor Award. He is the first person to have received both awards.

The American Institute of Certified Public Accountants presented its first Outstanding Educator Award to Horngren.

Horngren was named Accountant of the Year, in Education, by the national professional accounting fraternity, Beta Alpha Psi.

Professor Horngren is also a member of the Institute of Management Accountants, from whom he has received its Distinguished Service Award. He was a member of the institute's Board of Regents, which administers the Certified Management Accountant examinations.

Horngren is the author of these other accounting books published by Pearson Prentice Hall: *Cost Accounting: A Managerial Emphasis*, thirteenth edition, 2008 (with Srikant Datar and George Foster); *Introduction to Financial Accounting*, ninth edition, 2006 (with Gary L. Sundem and John A. Elliott); *Introduction to Management Accounting*, fourteenth edition, 2008 (with Gary L. Sundem and William Stratton); *Financial & Managerial Accounting*, second edition, 2009 and *Accounting*, eighth edition, 2009 (with Walter T. Harrison, Jr. and M. Suzanne Oliver).

Horngren is the consulting editor for Pearson Prentice Hall's Charles T. Horngren Series in Accounting.

Charles William (Bill) Thomas is the KPMG/Thomas L. Holton Chair, the J. E. Bush Professor of Accounting, and a Master Teacher at Baylor University. A Baylor University alumnus, he received both his BBA and MBA there and went on to earn his PhD from The University of Texas at Austin.

With primary interests in the areas of financial accounting and auditing, Bill Thomas has served as the J.E. Bush Professor of Accounting since 1995 and the KPMG/Thomas L. Holton Chair since 2006. He has been a member of the faculty of the Accounting and Business Law Department of the Hankamer School of Business since 1971, and served as chair of the department from 1983 until 1995. He was recognized as an Outstanding Faculty Member of Baylor University in 1984 and Distinguished Professor for the Hankamer School of Business in 2002. Dr. Thomas has received several awards for outstanding teaching, including the Outstanding Professor in the Executive MBA Programs in 2001, 2002, and 2006. In 2004, he received the designation as Master Teacher, an honor that has only been bestowed on 21 persons since the University's inception in 1845.

Thomas is the author of textbooks in auditing and financial accounting, as well as many articles in auditing, financial accounting and reporting, taxation, ethics and accounting education. His scholarly work focuses on the subject of fraud prevention and detection, as well as ethical issues among accountants in public practice. His most recent publication of national prominence is "The Rise and Fall of the Enron Empire" which appeared in the April 2002 *Journal of Accountancy*, and which was selected by Encyclopedia Britannica for inclusion in its *Annals of American History*. He presently serves as both technical and accounting and auditing editor of *Today's CPA*, the journal of the Texas Society of Certified Public Accountants, with a circulation of approximately 28,000.

Thomas is a certified public accountant in Texas. Prior to becoming a professor, Thomas was a practicing accountant with the firms of KPMG, LLP, and BDO Seidman, LLP. He is a member of the American Accounting Association, the American Institute of Certified Public Accountants, and the Texas Society of Certified Public Accountants.

Themin Suwardy is the Associate Dean (Curriculum and Teaching) and MPA Programme Director at School of Accountancy, Singapore Management University. Prior to joining academia, Themin was an auditor with KPMG Peat Marwick.

Besides his teaching and administrative duties at the University, Themin is the faculty champion of a number of SMU IT projects, notably *Virtual Canvas* (MIS Asia's 2006 Best IT Enabler in Education) and *HeuCampus*. He has created many e-learning objects in Accounting and was a recipient of the 2004 Hewlett-Packard Mobile Technology for Teaching Grant Initiative. At SMU, he received the School of Accountancy's 2005 Outstanding Teacher award, 2006 SMU Most Innovative Teacher awards, 2008 Best MBA Teacher (Core) award. Themin's book on *Understanding Financial Statements: A Case-Based Approach* (also published by Pearson) provides examples from 60 companies around the world to help students bridge the gap between theories and financial reporting real-world practices.

Themin is actively involved in various professional bodies and organizations, including the Institute of Certified Public Accountants of Singapore (ICPAS), CPA Australia, The Institute of Internal Auditors, and International Association for Accounting Education and Research (IAAER). Themin has also conducted workshops and corporate training for CPA Australia, Singapore Institute of Directors, Singapore Airlines, DFS, and National Institute of Education. His main research areas include financial reporting and analysis, corporate governance, accounting education with emphasis on technologically-enabled pedagogy.

Brief Contents

Contents

Chapter 4
Internal Control & Cash   231

Chapter 5
Short-Term Investments & Receivables   289

Chapter 6
Inventory & Cost of Goods Sold   341

Chapter 7

PPE & Intangibles   407

Chapter 8

Liabilities   469

Chapter 9

Shareholders' Equity   537

Chapter 10

Long-Term Investments & International Operations   607

Chapter 11

The Income Statement & the Statement of Changes in Equity   661

Chapter 12
The Statement of Cash Flows   711

Chapter 13
Financial Statement Analysis   783

With
Financial Accounting
Student Text, Study Resources,
and MyAccountingLab
students will have more
"I get it!"
moments!

Students will "get it" anytime, anywhere

Students understand (or "get it") right after you do a problem in class. Once they leave the classroom, however, students often struggle to complete the homework on their own. This frustration can cause students to quit on the material altogether and fall behind in the course, resulting in an entire class falling behind as the instructor attempts to keep everyone on the same page.

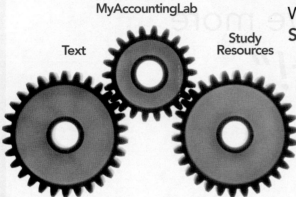

With the *Financial Accounting,* Eighth Edition, **Student Learning System,** all the features of the student textbook, study resources, and online homework system are designed to work together to provide students with the consistency, repetition, and high level of detail that will keep both instructors and students on track, providing more "I get it!" moments inside and outside the classroom.

Replicating the Classroom Experience with Demo Doc Examples

The Demo Doc examples consist of entire problems, worked through step-by-step, from start to finish, narrated with the kind of comments that instructors would say in class. The Demo Docs are available in the accounting cycle chapters of the text and in the study guide. In addition to the printed Demo Docs, Flash-animated versions are available so that students can watch the problems as they are worked through while listening to the explanations and details. Demo Docs will aid students when they are trying to solve exercises and problems on their own, duplicating the classroom experience outside of class.

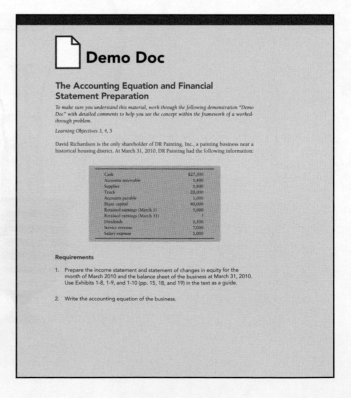

with the Student Learning System!

Consistency, Repetition, and a High Level of Detail Throughout the Learning Process

The concepts, materials, and practice problems are presented with clarity and consistency across all mediums—textbook, study resources, and online homework system. No matter which platform students use they will continually experience the same look, feel, and language, minimizing confusion and ensuring clarity.

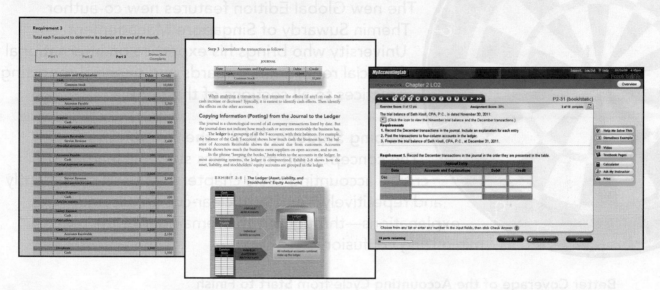

Experiencing the Power of Practice with MyAccountingLab: www.myaccountinglab.com

MyAccountingLab is an online homework system that gives students more "I get it!" moments through the power of practice. With MyAccountingLab, students can

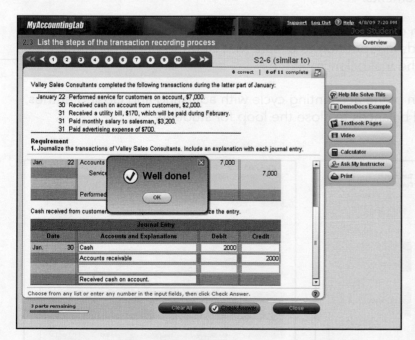

- Work on problems assigned by the instructor that are either exact matches or algorithmic versions of the end-of-chapter material.
- Use the Study Plan for self-assessment and customized study outlines.
- Use the Help Me Solve This for a step-by-step tutorial.
- View the Demo Docs example to see an animated demonstration of where the numbers came from.
- Watch a video to see additional information pertaining to the lecture.
- Open textbook pages to find the material they need to get help on specific problems.

Financial Accounting helps students

Financial Accounting helps students "nail" the accounting cycle up front in order to increase success and retention later on.

The new Global Edition features new co-author Themin Suwardy of Singapore Management University who brings his expertise on international financial reporting standards and financial reporting practices to all sections of the book.

Helping Students "Nail" the Accounting Cycle
The concepts and mechanics students learn in the critical accounting cycle chapters are used consistently and repetitively—and with clear-cut details and explanations—throughout the remainder of the text, minimizing confusion.

Better Coverage of the Accounting Cycle from Start to Finish
Chapter 1 introduces the accounting cycle with a brief financial statement overview, using the financial statements of Carrefour. This first exposure to accounting explores financial statements in depth, familiarizes students with using real business data, and points out basic relationships between the different types of statements.

Chapter 2 continues the discussion of the accounting cycle by explaining how to analyze and record basic transactions, and builds in repetition to ensure that students understand the fundamentals when they prepare the trial balance.

Chapter 3 concludes the discussion of the accounting cycle with adjusting and closing entries, and preparation of the related trial balances to close the loop for students.

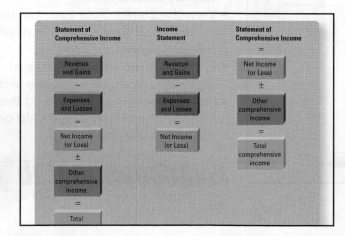

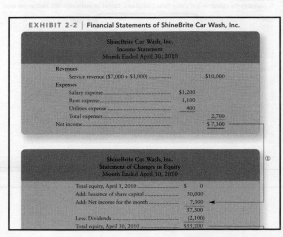

EXHIBIT 2-2 | Financial Statements of ShineBrite Car Wash, Inc.

"nail" the accounting cycle!

Consistency, Repetition, and a High Level of Detail

Throughout the text, the core concepts and mechanics are brought together using consistent language, format, and formulas. Students also receive thorough explanations and details that show the meaning behind each concept and how to do the computation following it, providing an in-depth understanding of the fundamentals.

Whether it's the first transaction or the last, students perform the analysis in the same way, thus reinforcing their understanding, reducing the level of confusion and frustration, and helping them capture those "I get it!" moments.

For example, in Chapter 2 students see the impact of transactions and how the transactions are eventually summarized into the income statement, statement of retained earnings, and balance sheet.

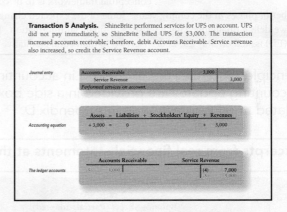

A **Mid-Chapter Summary Problem** provides a stopping point for students—it gives them an opportunity to repeat the entire process again, using data from a different company, to make sure they've "got it." The **End-of-Chapter Summary Problem** closes out the chapter and allows students to practice the process again and really "nail" these fundamental skills.

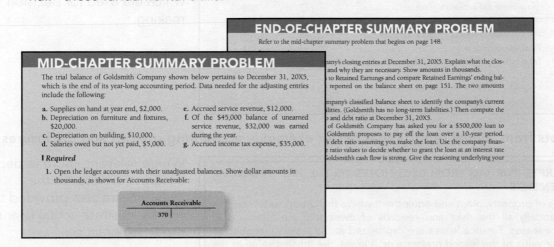

New to the Eighth Edition

Integrated Coverage of International Financial Reporting Standards (IFRS)

This text has been substantially rewritten as an IFRS textbook, rather than just add-on material to a US-GAAP textbook. Students and instructors will continue to benefit from the pedagogical approaches of an established accounting textbook.

TECHNICAL UPDATE

In October 2004, the IASB and FASB began a joint project to develop an improved, common conceptual framework that builds on their existing frameworks as part of their convergence project. The new conceptual framework is to be completed in a number of phases in the coming years. Some of the expected changes will impact how we define qualitative characteristics of financial information. The Exposure Draft (ED) issued on May 29, 2008 lists two fundamental qualitative characteristics (rel-

The next now starts with a more detailed coverage of the accounting framework and how financial statements provide information for decision making. Selected references are made to IFRSs to get students accustomed to the way

principles and rules are expressed in accounting standards. More technical details and relevant accounting updates are provided in a side box for students and instructors. A list of resources related to IFRSs is available in Appendix D.

Excerpts from real financial statements at the start of every chapter

Nestlé SA
Balance Sheets (Partial, adapted)
As at December 31

(In millions CHF, Swiss Franc)	2008	2007
1 Cash and cash equivalents	5,835	6,594
2 Short-term investments*	1,296	2,902
3 Trade and other receivables	13,442	14,890
4 Inventories	9,342	9,272
5 Prepayment and accrued income	627	805
6 Other current assets	2,506	1,307
7 Total current assets	33,048	35,770
8 Total non-current assets	73,167	79,591
9 Total assets	106,215	115,361
* Includes "held for trading" amounting to	854	1,510

Each chapter starts with excerpts of financial statements of real companies around the world, all prepared under IFRS. Students are exposed to theories and concepts of accounting they learn are reflected in financial statements, which are used for decision making.

Excerpts from annual reports that better exemplify accounting policies and disclosures

EXCERPTS (PARTIAL) FROM CSL'S NOTES TO THE 2009 FINANCIAL STATEMENTS

Leases of property, plant and equipment where the Group, as lessee, has substantially all the risks and rewards of ownership are classified as finance leases. Finance leases are capitalized at the lease's inception at the fair value of the leased property or, if lower, the present value of the minimum lease payments. The corresponding rental obligations, net of finance charges, are included in interest bearing liabilities and borrowings. Eash lease payment is allocated between the liability and finance cost. The finance cost is charged to the income statement over the lease period so as to produce a constant periodic rate of interest on the remaining balance of the liability for each period. The property, plant

Where relevant, more in-depth excerpts of notes to the accounts are also provided to further illustrate actual financial reporting practices.

New and Updated Content on Ethics

Sound ethical judgment is important for every major financial decision—which is why this text provides consistent ethical reinforcement in every chapter. And, with Bill Thomas' expertise, a new decision-making model is introduced in Chapter 1 and applied to each of the end-of-chapter cases.

Ethical Issues in Accrual Accounting

Accrual accounting provides some ethical challenges that cash accounting avoids. For example, suppose that in 2008, Starbucks Corporation prepays a $3 million advertising campaign to be conducted by a large advertising agency. The advertisements are scheduled to run during December, January, and February. In this case, Starbucks is buying an asset, a prepaid expense.

Suppose Starbucks pays for the advertisements on December 1 and the ads start running immediately. Starbucks should record one-third of the expense ($1 million) during the year ended December 31, 2008, and two-thirds ($2 million) during 2009.

Suppose 2008 is a great year for Starbucks—net income is better than expected. Starbucks' top managers believe that 2009 will not be as profitable. In this case, the company has a strong incentive to expense the full $3 million during 2008 in order to report all the advertising expense in the 2008 income statement. This unethical

Extended Coverage of Cash Flows

The current economy has created a shift in how we view money—specifically, cash. Cash flow is the lifeblood of any business, so in the Eighth Edition of *Financial Accounting*, coverage of Cash Flows has been increased and highlighted in Chapters 4–10 so that students can easily see the connections and understand the significance.

CASH FLOW · REPORTING SHAREHOLDERS' EQUITY TRANSACTIONS

Statement of Cash Flows

Many of the transactions we've covered are reported on the statement of cash flows. Equity transactions are *financing* activities because the company is dealing with its owners. Financing transactions that affect both cash and equity fall into three main categories:

- issuance of shares
- treasury shares
- dividends

Issuances of Shares. During 2007, Alibaba.com's IPO generated a significant cash inflow to the company, amounting to close to RMB 3 billion. This is as a financ-

New Fraud Coverage

In an age of public scandals, understanding fraud is a key component of *Financial Accounting*. Chapter 4 now includes the concept of fraud, and introduces students to the "fraud triangle" (motivation, opportunity, and rationalization) and a discussion of internal controls as the primary way companies prevent fraud.

For example, **Cooking the Books** sections highlight real fraud cases in relevant sections throughout the text, giving students real-life business context. Examples include the following:

- Satyam Computers (Chapter 4)
- Crazy Eddie (Chapters 6 and 8)
- WorldCom and Waste Management (Chapter 7)
- Enron (Chapters 8, 9, and 10)

COOKING THE BOOKS
by Improper Capitalization
WorldCom

It is one thing to accidentally capitalize a plant asset but quite another to do it intentionally, thus deliberately understating expenses and overstating net income. One well-known company committed one of the biggest financial statement frauds in history.

In 2002, WorldCom, Inc., was one of the largest telecommunications service providers in the world. The company had grown rapidly from a small, regional telephone company in 1983 to a giant corporation in 2002 by acquiring an ever-increasing number of other such companies. But 2002 was a bad year for WorldCom, as well as for many others in the "telecom" industry. The United States was reeling from the effects of a deep economic recession spawned by the "bursting dot-com bubble" in 2000 and intensified by the terrorist attacks on the World Trade Center and the U.S. Pentagon in 2001. Wall Street was looking high and low for positive signs, pressuring public companies to keep profits trending upward in order to support share prices, without much success, at least for the honest companies.

Hallmark Features

Summary Problems and Solutions appear in both the middle and end-of-chapter sections, providing students with additional guided learning. By presenting these problems and solutions twice in one chapter, this text breaks up the information, enabling students to absorb and master the material in more manageable pieces.

END-OF-CHAPTER SUMMARY PROBLEM

Refer to the mid-chapter summary problem that begins on page 148.

❙ Required

1. Make Goldsmith Company's closing entries at December 31, 20X5. Explain what the closing entries accomplish and why they are necessary. Show amounts in thousands.
2. Post the closing entries to Retained Earnings and compare Retained Earnings' ending balance with the amount reported on the balance sheet on page 151. The two amounts should be the same.

MID-CHAPTER SUMMARY PROBLEM

The trial balance of Goldsmith Company shown below pertains to December 31, 20X5, which is the end of its year-long accounting period. Data needed for the adjusting entries include the following:

a. Supplies on hand at year end, $2,000.
b. Depreciation on furniture and fixtures, $20,000.
c. Depreciation on building, $10,000.
d. Salaries owed but not yet paid, $5,000.
e. Accrued service revenue, $12,000.
f. Of the $45,000 balance of unearned service revenue, $32,000 was earned during the year.
g. Accrued income tax expense, $35,000.

❙ Required

1. Open the ledger accounts with their unadjusted balances. Show dollar amounts in thousands, as shown for Accounts Receivable:

Accounts Receivable	
370	

STOP & THINK...

1. A customer pays Starbucks $100 on March 15 for coffee to be served at a party in April. Has Starbucks earned revenue on March 15? When will Starbucks earn the revenue?
2. Starbucks pays $4,500 on July 1 for store rent for the next 3 months. Has Starbucks incurred an expense on July 1?

Answers:

1. No. Starbucks has received the cash but will not deliver the coffee until later. Starbucks earns the revenue when it gives the goods to the customer.

Stop & Think sections relate concepts to everyday life so that students can see the immediate relevance.

Demo Docs in the accounting cycle chapters offer fully worked-through problems that weave computation and concepts together in a step-by-step format, helping students understand the "how" and "why." Additional Demo Docs, including animated versions, are available in the study guide and in **MyAccountingLab**.

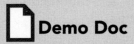 **Demo Doc**

Debit/Credit Transaction Analysis

Demo Doc: To make sure you understand this material, work through the following demonstration "demo doc" with detailed comments to help you see the concept within the framework of a worked-through problem.

Learning Objectives 1, 2, 3, 4

On September 1, 2008, Michael Moe incorporated Moe's Mowing, Inc., a company that provides mowing and landscaping services. During the month of September, the business incurred the following transactions:

a. To begin operations, Michael deposited $10,000 cash in the business's bank account. The business received the cash and issued common stock to Michael.

b. The business purchased equipment for $3,500 on account.

c. The business purchased office supplies for $800 cash.

d. The business provided $2,600 of services to a customer on account.

e. The business paid $500 cash toward the equipment previously purchased on account in transaction b.

f. The business received $2,000 in cash for services provided to a new customer.

g. The business paid $200 cash to repair equipment.

h. The business paid $900 cash in salary expense.

i. The business received $2,100 cash from a customer on account.

j. The business paid cash dividends of $1,500.

Decision Guidelines in the end-of-chapter material summarize the chapter's key terms, concepts, and formulas in the context of business decisions. Not only does this help students read more actively in the question and answer format, but it also reinforces how the accounting information they are learning is used to make decisions in business.

DECISION GUIDELINES

USING THE CURRENT RATIO AND THE DEBT RATIO

In general, a *high* current ratio is preferable to a low current ratio. *Increases* in the current ratio improve financial position. By contrast, a *low* debt ratio is preferable to a high debt ratio. Improvement is indicated by a *decrease* in the debt ratio.

No single ratio gives the whole picture about a company. Therefore, lenders and investors use many ratios to evaluate a company. Let's apply what we have learned. Suppose you are a loan officer at Bank One, and Starbucks Corporation has asked you for a $20 million loan to launch a new blend of coffee. How will you make this loan decision? The Decision Guidelines show how bankers and investors use two key ratios.

USING THE CURRENT RATIO

Decision	Guidelines
How can you measure a company's ability to pay current liabilities with current assets?	$$\text{Current ratio} = \frac{\text{Total current assets}}{\text{Total current liabilities}}$$
Who uses the current ratio for decision making?	*Lenders and other creditors,* who must predict whether a borrower can pay its current liabilities. *Stockholders,* who know that a company that cannot pay its debts is not a good investment because it may go bankrupt. *Managers,* who must have enough cash to pay the company's current liabilities.
What is a good value of the current ratio?	Depends on the industry: A company with strong cash flow can operate successfully with a low current ratio of, say, 1.10–1.20. A company with weak cash flow needs a higher current ratio of, say, 1.30–1.50. Traditionally, a current ratio of 2.00 was considered ideal. Recently, acceptable values have decreased as companies have been able to operate more efficiently; today, a current ratio of 1.50 is considered strong. Cash-rich companies like Starbucks and Yum! Brands can operate with a current ratio below 1.0.

MyAccountingLab®

NEW! End-of-Chapter Material Integrated with MyAccountingLab at www.myaccountinglab.com

Students need practice and repetition in order to successfully learn the fundamentals of financial accounting. *Financial Accounting,* Eighth Edition, now contains an additional set of exercises in the text for professors to choose from. Also available in **MyAccountingLab** are three static alternatives for all exercises and problems, as well as algorithmic versions, providing students with unlimited practice. In addition, IFRS coverage has been added so students can see how IFRS will impact decisions in accounting. (For more information, visit **www.myaccountinglab.com**.)

End-of-Chapter Materials include Quick Check multiple-choice review questions, short exercises, A and B exercises and problems, serial and challenge exercises, multiple-choice quiz questions, decision cases, ethical cases, Focus on Financials (with real financial statements), and group projects.

Student Resources

Study Guide with Demo Docs and Working Papers

This chapter-by-chapter learning aid helps students get the maximum benefit from their study time. For each chapter there is an explanation of each Learning Objective; additional Demo Docs; Quick Practice, True/False, and Multiple Choice questions; Quick Exercises; and a Do It Yourself question, all with solutions. Electronic working papers are also included.

www.myaccountinglab.com

MyAccountingLab is Web-based tutorial and assessment software for accounting that gives students more "I get it!" moments. MyAccountingLab provides students with a personalized interactive learning environment where they can complete their course assignments with immediate tutorial assistance, learn at their own pace, and measure their progress.

In addition to completing assignments and reviewing tutorial help, students have access to the following resources in MyAccountingLab:

- The Flash-based eBook
- Study Guide
- Audio and Student PowerPoints
- Working Papers
- Flashcards

Student Resource Web site: www.pearsonglobaleditions.com/harrison

- General Ledger Student Data Files
- Working Papers
- Excel in Practice

Instructor Resources

The primary goal of the Instructor Resources is to help instructors deliver their course with ease, using any delivery method—traditional, self-paced, or online.

www.myaccountinglab.com

MyAccountingLab is Web-based tutorial and assessment software for accounting that not only gives students more "I get it!" moments, but also provides instructors the flexibility to make technology an integral part of their course. And, because practice makes perfect, **MyAccountingLab** offers exactly the same end-of-chapter material found in the text with algorithmic options that instructors can assign for homework. **MyAccountingLab** also replicates the text's exercises and problems with journal entries and financial statements so that students are familiar and comfortable working with the material.

Instructor's Manual

The Instructor's Manual, available electronically or in print, offers course-specific content including a guide to available resources, a road map for using **MyAccountingLab**, a first-day handout for students, sample syllabi, and guidelines for teaching an online course, as well as content-specific material including chapter overviews, teaching outlines, student summary handouts, lecture outline tips, assignment grids, ten-minute quizzes, and more!

Instructor Resource Center: www.pearsonglobaleditions.com/harrison

For your convenience, many of our instructor supplements are available for download from the textbook's catalog page or your **MyAccountingLab** account. Available resources include the following:

- Solutions Manual containing the fully worked-through and accuracy-checked solutions for every question, exercise, and problem in the text
- Test Item File with TestGen Software providing over 1,600 multiple choice, true/false, and problem-solving questions correlated by Learning Objective and difficulty level as well as AACSB and AICPA standards
- Data and Solution Files—General Ledger
- Working Papers and Solutions
- Instructor's Manual
- Excel in Practice
- Image Library

Changes to this Edition

Students and instructors will benefit from a variety of new content and features in the Global Edition of *Financial Accounting: International Financial Reporting Standards*. To reflect the most recent developments in the economy and in the accounting industry, the following content additions or changes have been made:

Each chapter features **new Company Spotlights** from different countries and industries, which helps to broaden students' general knowledge of businesses. Companies featured include Carrefour, De Beers, Marks & Spencer, Lenovo, Philips and Nokia. Students will see extracts of IFRS-compliant financial statements and notes to the accounts of many companies throughout the text. Key terms have also been changed to reflect the more common practices and words used in the international accounting standards.

The first chapter has been completely rewritten to introduce the **IFRS Framework for Preparation and Presentation of Financial Statements**. It sets the foundation for students' understanding of the principle based approach of International Financial Reporting Standards. Chapter 1 helps students see financial statements as outputs of an accounting system, on which a variety of users rely on to make their decisions. A new appendix (D) was added with a table highlighting the IFRS coverage topic by topic and other additional resources for further review of relevant accounting standards.

With the recent changes and events in the economy, educating students on the importance of **ethics and ethical decision making** is critical. The discussion of ethics in accounting has been updated and moved to Chapter 1, placing greater emphasis on the importance of ethics at the very beginning of the text. The Global Edition also introduces an expanded decision-making model in Chapter 1 and integrates the model throughout the entire text with economic, legal, and ethical dimensions. The Ethical Cases in the end-of-chapter material have been rewritten to unify and better integrate coverage on this important topic so that the material is reinforced consistently in every chapter.

In an age of public scandals, understanding **fraud** is a key component of financial accounting. Chapter 4 now includes the concept of fraud, and introduces students to the "fraud triangle" (motivation, opportunity, and rationalization) that leads to the discussion of internal controls as the primary way that companies prevent fraud—which has also been updated. The discussion of fraud in Chapter 4 also lays the foundation for the new Cooking the Books sections (found in appropriate chapters later on in the book), which add real-life relevance and interest to otherwise dry accounting concepts by presenting real-world fraud cases such as Satyam Computers (Chapter 4), Crazy Eddie (Chapters 6 and 8), WorldCom and Waste Management (Chapter 7), and Enron (Chapters 8, 9, and 10).

Discussions on **receivables impairment** in Chapter 5 have been significantly updated. Whilst IFRS does not allow the use of Last-in First-Out method, it has been retained in Chapter 6 to help students understand the impact of accounting policies on financial statements. Chapter 7 has been updated to include the revaluation model under *IAS16* and intangibles assets under *IAS38*.

To help students understand accounting topics that are currently impacting **the global economy**, Chapter 11 includes a new discussion on quality of earnings, revenue recognition, and fraud. The quality of earnings section focuses on evaluating a company's financial position to help in decision making, which students will need when they enter the workforce. There is also an expanded discussion on the elements of the income statement and revenue recognition.

Understanding **cash flows** is a critical concept for students in today's economy, which is why there is a new and increased emphasis on the use of cash flow information in selected chapters. By highlighting this coverage from chapter to chapter, this edition helps students make the connection between cash and other accounting concepts so that they understand the significance of cash flow is the lifeblood of a business. Analysis of cash flow is further improved through a new section on cash flow patterns in Chapter 12 and cash flow ratios in Chapter 13.

To keep examples and data current and accurate, all **financial statements** for the companies covered have been updated to include the latest available financial statements. All real company financial data now refers to 2007, 2008 and 2009. An integrated Focus on Financials, featuring Nokia, runs through every chapter, so students can develop their analytical skills and see examples of statements and accounting practices that are as current as possible. Extracts of Nokia's financial statements are included in Appendix A.

To provide students with more opportunities to practice important concepts, and to provide instructors with additional choices of material to assign, all of the **end-of-chapter content** has been revised, including the following:

- 100% of values and dates in the end-of-chapter questions are new.
- A new set of "B" exercises has been added in every chapter, giving students more opportunities to practice important concepts.
- Every end-of-chapter question in the Assess Your Progress sections is now available in **MyAccountingLab** for students to complete and receive immediate tutorial feedback and help when they need it. Alternative, static exercises and problems were also added in **MyAccountingLab** (www.myaccountinglab.com) to give students and instructors more options for assignments and practice.

ACKNOWLEDGMENTS

In revising previous editions of *Financial Accounting*, we had the help of instructors from across the country who have participated in online surveys, chapter reviews, and focus groups. Their comments and suggestions for both the text and the supplements have been a great help in planning and carrying out revisions, and we thank them for their contributions.

Financial Accounting, Eighth Edition

Revision Plan Reviewers

Elizabeth Ammann, Lindenwood University
Brenda Anderson, Brandeis University
Patrick Bauer, DeVry University, Kansas City
Amy Bourne, Oregon State University
Elizabeth Brown, Keene State College
Scott Bryant, Baylor University
Marci Butterfield, University of Utah
Dr. Paul Clikeman, University of Richmond
Sue Counte, Saint Louis Community College-Meramec
Julia Creighton, American University
Sue Cullers, Buena Vista University
Betty David, Francis Marion University
Peter DiCarlo, Boston College
Allan Drebin, Northwestern University
Carolyn Dreher, Southern Methodist University
Emily Drogt, Grand Valley State University
Dr. Andrew Felo, Penn State Great Valley
Dr. Caroline Ford, Baylor University
Clayton Forester, University of Minnesota
Timothy Gagnon, Northeastern University
Marvin Gordon, University of Illinois at Chicago
Anthony Greig, Purdue University
Dr. Heidi Hansel, Kirkwood Community College
Michael Haselkorn, Bentley University
Mary Hollars, Vincennes University
Grace Johnson, Marietta College
Celina Jozsi, University of South Florida
John Karayan, Woodbury University
Robert Kollar, Duquesne University
Elliott Levy, Bentley University
Joseph Lupino, Saint Mary's College of California
Anthony Masino, Queens University / NC Central
Lizbeth Matz, University of Pittsburgh, Bradford
Mary Miller, University of New Haven
Scott Miller, Gannon University
Dr. Birendra (Barry) K. Mishra, University of California, Riverside
Lisa Nash, Vincennes University

Rosemary Nurre, College of San Mateo
Stephen Owen, Hamilton College
Rama Ramamurthy, College of William and Mary
Barb Reeves, Cleary University
Anwar Salimi, California State Polytechnic University, Pomona
Philippe Sammour, Eastern Michigan University
Albert A Schepanski, University of Iowa
Lily Sieux, California State University, East Bay
Vic Stanton, Stanford University
Martin Taylor, University of Texas at Arlington
Vincent Turner, California State Polytechnic University, Pomona
Craig Weaver, University of California, Riverside
Betsy Willis, Baylor University
Dr. Jia Wu, University of Massachusetts, Dartmouth
Barbara Yahvah, University of Montana-Helena

Chapter Reviewers

Florence Atiase, University of Texas at Austin
Amy Bourne, Oregon State University
Rada Brooks, University of California, Berkeley
Marci Butterfield, University of Utah
Carolyn Dreher, Southern Methodist University
Lisa Gillespie, Loyola University, Chicago
Mary Hollars, Vincennes University
Constance Malone Hylton, George Mason University
Barry Mishra, University of California, Riverside
Virginia Smith, Saint Mary's College of California
Betsy Willis, Baylor University

Supplements Authors

Excel in Practice Templates: Jennie Mitchell, Saint Mary-of-the-Woods College
Excel Data Files: Jennie Mitchell, Saint Mary-of-the-Woods College
General Ledger Templates: Jamie McCracken, Saint Mary-of-the-Woods College

Instructor's Manual: Denise Wooten, Erie Community
   College–North
PowerPoints: Courtney Baillie, Nebraska
   Wesleyan University
Study Guide: Helen Brubeck, San Jose State University
Solutions Manual: Richard J. Pettit, Mountain
   View College
Test Item File: Sandra Augustine, Hilbert College

Supplements Reviewers

Linda Abernathy, Kirkwood Community College
Brenda Bindschatel, Green River Community College
Allan Sheets, International Business College
Richard J. Pettit, Mountain View College

Previous Edition

Online Reviewers

Lucille Berry, Webster University, MO
Patrick Bouker, North Seattle Community College
Michael Broihahn, Barry University, FL
Kam Chan, Pace University
Hong Chen, Northeastern Illinois University
Charles Coate, St. Bonaventure University, NY
Bryan Church, Georgia Tech at Atlanta
Terrie Gehman, Elizabethtown College, PA
Brian Green, University of Michigan at Dearborn
Chao-Shin Liu, Notre Dame
Herb Martin, Hope College, MI
Bruce Maule, College of San Mateo
Michelle McEacharn, University of Louisiana at Monroe
Bettye Rogers-Desselle, Prairie View A&M University, TX
Norlin Rueschhoff, Notre Dame
William Schmul, Notre Dame
Arnie Schnieder, Georgia Tech at Atlanta
J. B. Stroud, Nicholls State Univesity, LA
Bruce Wampler, Louisiana State University, Shreveport
Myung Yoon, Northeastern Illinois University
Lin Zeng, Northeastern Illinois University

Focus Group Participants

Ellen D. Cook, University of Louisiana at Lafayette
Theodore D. Morrison III, Wingate University, NC
Alvin Gerald Smith, University of Northern Iowa

Carolyn R. Stokes, Frances Marion University, SC
Suzanne Ward, University of Louisiana at Lafayette

Chapter Reviewers

Kim Anderson, Indiana University of Pennsylvania
Peg Beresewski, Robert Morris College, IL
Helen Brubeck, San Jose State University, CA
Mark Camma, Atlantic Cape Community College, NJ
Freddy Choo, San Francisco State University, CA
Laurie Dahlin, Worcester State College, MA
Ronald Guidry, University of Louisiana at Monroe
Ellen Landgraf, Loyola University, Chicago
Nick McGaughey, San Jose State University, CA
Mark Miller, University of San Francisco, CA
Craig Reeder, Florida A&M University
Brian Stanko, Loyola University, Chicago
Marcia Veit, University of Central Florida
Ronald Woan, Indiana University of Pennsylvania

Online Supplement Reviewers

Shawn Abbott, College of the Siskiyous, CA
Sol Ahiarah, SUNY College at Buffalo (Buffalo State)
M. J. Albin, University of Southern Mississippi
Gary Ames, Brigham Young University, Idaho
Walter Austin, Mercer University, Macon GA
Brad Badertscher, University of Iowa
Sandra Bailey, Oregon Institute of Technology
Barbara A. Beltrand, Metropolitan State University, MN
Jerry Bennett, University of South
   Carolina–Spartanburg
John Bildersee, New York University, Stern School
Candace Blankenship, Belmont University, TN
Charlie Bokemeier, Michigan State University
Scott Boylan, Washington and Lee University, VA
Robert Braun, Southeastern Louisiana University
Linda Bressler, University of Houston Downtown
Carol Brown, Oregon State University
Marcus Butler, University of Rochester, NY
Kay Carnes, Gonzaga University, WA
Brian Carpenter, University of Scranton, PA
Sandra Cereola, James Madison University, VA
Hong Chen, Northeastern Illinois University
Shifei Chung, Rowan University, NJ
Bryan Church, Georgia Tech

Charles Christy, Delaware Tech and Community College, Stanton Campus

Carolyn Clark, Saint Joseph's University, PA

Dianne Conry, University of California State College Extension–Cupertino

John Coulter, Western New England College

Donald Curfman, McHenry County College, IL

Alan Czyzewski, Indiana State University

Bonita Daly, University of Southern Maine

Patricia Derrick, George Washington University

Charles Dick, Miami University

Barbara Doughty, New Hampshire Community Technical College

Carol Dutton, South Florida Community College

James Emig, Villanova University, PA

Ellen Engel, University of Chicago

Alan Falcon, Loyola Marymount University, CA

Janet Farler, Pima Community College, AZ

Andrew Felo, Penn State Great Valley

Ken Ferris, Thunderbird College, AZ

Lou Fowler, Missouri Western State College

Lucille Genduso, Nova Southeastern University, FL

Frank Gersich, Monmouth College, IL

Bradley Gillespie, Saddleback College, CA

Brian Green, University of Michigan–Dearborn

Konrad Gunderson, Missouri Western State College

William Hahn, Southeastern College, FL

Jack Hall, Western Kentucky University

Gloria Halpern, Montgomery College, MD

Kenneth Hart, Brigham Young University, Idaho

Al Hartgraves, Emory University

Thomas Hayes, University of North Texas

Larry Hegstad, Pacific Lutheran University, WA

Candy Heino, Anoka-Ramsey Community College, MN

Anit Hope, Tarrant County College, TX

Thomas Huse, Boston College

Fred R. Jex, Macomb Community College, MI

Beth Kern, Indiana University, South Bend

Hans E. Klein, Babson College, MA

Willem Koole, North Carolina State University

Emil Koren, Hillsborough Community College, FL

Dennis Kovach, Community College of Allegheny County–North Campus

Ellen Landgraf, Loyola University Chicago

Howard Lawrence, Christian Brothers University, TN

Barry Leffkov, Regis College, MA

Chao Liu, Notre Dame University

Barbara Lougee, University of California, Irvine

Heidemarie Lundblad, California State University, Northridge

Anna Lusher, West Liberty State College, WV

Harriet Maccracken, Arizona State University

Carol Mannino, Milwaukee School of Engineering

Aziz Martinez, Harvard University, Harvard Business School

Cathleen Miller, University of Michigan–Flint

Frank Mioni, Madonna University, MI

Bruce L. Oliver, Rochester Institute of Technology

Charles Pedersen, Quinsigamond Community College, MA

George Plesko, Massachusetts Institute of Technology

David Plumlee, University of Utah

Gregory Prescott, University of South Alabama

Craig Reeder, Florida A&M University

Darren Roulstone, University of Chicago

Angela Sandberg, Jacksonville State University, AL

George Sanders, Western Washington University, WA

Betty Saunders, University of North Florida

Arnie Schneider, Georgia Tech

Gim Seow, University of Connecticut

Itzhak Sharav, CUNY–Lehman Graduate School of Business

Gerald Smith, University of Northern Iowa

James Smith, Community College of Philadelphia

Beverly Soriano, Framingham State College, MA

J. B. Stroud, Nicholls State University, LA

Al Taccone, Cuyamaca College, CA

Diane Tanner, University of North Florida

Howard Toole, San Diego State University

Bruce Wampler, Louisiana State University, Shreveport

Frederick Weis, Claremont McKenna College, CA

Frederick Weiss, Virginia Wesleyan College

Allen Wright, Hillsborough Community College, FL

Tony Zordan, University of St. Francis, IL

Supplement Authors and Preparers

Excel templates: Al Fisher, Community College of Southern Nevada; Jiwei Wang, Singapore Management University

General Ledger templates: Lanny Nelms, the Landor Group; Jiwei Wang, Singapore Management University

Instructor's Manual: Jiwei Wang, Singapore Management University

Powerpoints: Jiwei Wang, Singapore Management University

Solutions Manual preparer: Diane Colwyn; Jiwei Wang, Singapore Management University

Study Guide: Helen Brubeck, San Jose State University; Jiwei Wang, Singapore Management University

Test Item File: Calvin Fink; Jiwei Wang, Singapore Management University

Working Papers, Essentials of Excel: Dr. L. Murphy Smith, Texas A&M University; Dr. Katherine T. Smith

Videos: Beverly Amer, Northern Arizona University; Lanny Nelms, The Landor Group

The author would like to thank the following faculty members at Baylor University who provided valuable input for improvements in various sections of the eighth edition of this text: Suzanne Abbe, Jane Baldwin, Scott Bryant, Gia Chevis, Carie Ford, DavidHurtt, Becky Jones, and Betsy Willis. The author would like to extend special thanks to Dr. Marty Stuebs, who helped develop the model for ethical decision-making introduced in Chapter 1 and used in problems throughout the remainder of the eighth edition.

International Reviewers

Hetty Barnes, Central University of Technology
Mark Bliss, Hong Kong Polytechnic
Rick Cuijpers, Maastricht University
David Goodwin, Abu Dhabi University
Sawsan Halbouni, University of Sharjah
Helmi Hammami, Qatar University
Nahariah Jaffar, Multimedia University Malaysia
Ann Jorissen, University of Antwerp
Chng Chee Kiong, National University of Singapore
Adele Maree, University of Pretoria
Teye Marra, Rijksuniversiteit Grongingen
Can Sigma Mugan, Middle East Technical University
Azhar Abdul Rahman, Universiti Utara Malaysia
Filip Roodhooft, Katholieke Universiteit Leuven
Mohammed Talha, King Fahd University of Petroleum and Minerals
Albert Tsang, Chinese University of Hong Kong
Harshini Siriwardane, Nanyang Techonological University
Gretha Steenkamp, University of Stellenbosch

Picture Credits

Acknowledgements

The authors would like to acknowledge and thank the following companies and organizations for allowing permission to reproduce/adapt respective materials:

Alibaba.com
Amex Products Inc
Berkshire Hathaway Inc
Bloomberg
Bossini International Holdings Ltd
Carrefour S.A.
Creative Technology Ltd
CSL Ltd
De Beers Group Ltd
Deloitte
Dell Inc
DP World Ltd

Frontier Oil Corporation
Lenovo Group Ltd
Marks & Spencer Group PLC
Nestlé S.A.
Qantas Nokia Corporation
Royal Philips Electronics Inc
Vivendi S.A.
Pactiv Corporation
Reuters
Sincere Watch Ltd
Singapore Airlines

Annual reports, including the financial statements and notes to the financial statements, should be read in its entirety. Excerpts provided in this textbook are intended for teaching and learning purposes. Copyright of these excerpts remain with the original copyright holders. Readers are encouraged to obtain the full annual reports for a complete picture of the respective companies' financial position and financial performance. Summarized data, tables and charts are produced based on information available publicly.

Whilst every reasonable effort has been made to obtain permissions from the copyright holders, we have been unsuccessful in some instances. The author has then proceeded to include some materials and hope that these few companies will take the author's liberty in good faith, taking into account that the materials are available publicly and credited appropriately.

Picture Credits

Chapter 1: Carrefour S.A., p. 1
Chapter 2: The Boots Group Ltd., p. 61
Chapter 3: DP World Ltd., p. 135
Chapter 4: Flickr/World Economic Forum/Toast studio/Maxdus LV, p. 237
Chapter 5: Nestlé S.A., p. 289
Chapter 6: Photo1/RosUkrEnergo/Connell/Bloor/Photo/Vladimir Oschumikov, p. 341
Chapter 7: Lenovo Group Ltd., p. 397
Chapter 8: GSL Ltd., p. 469
Chapter 9: Alibaba.com, p. 533
Chapter 10: Vivendi S.A., p. 607
Chapter 11: Marks & Spencer Group PLC, p. 669
Chapter 12: Royal Philips Electronics Inc., p. 717
Chapter 13: Nielar Corporation, p. 785

Appendix C Map: IASC/IFRS Foundation, p. 878

Acknowledgements

The authors would like to acknowledge and thank the following companies and organizations for allowing permission to reproduce their respective materials:

Alibaba.com
Apex Products Inc.
Berkshire Hathaway Inc.
Bloomberg
Bostan International Holding Ltd.
Carrefour S.A.
Creative Technology Ltd
GSL Ltd.
DP Services Group Ltd.
Deloitte
Dell Inc.
DP World Ltd

Premier Oil Corporation
Lenovo Group Ltd
Marks & Spencer Group PLC
Nestlé S.A.
Omnia Mobile Corporation
Royal Philips Electronics Inc.
Vivendi S.A.
Pacific Corporation
Reuters
Sincere Watch Ltd
Singapore Airlines

Annual reports, including the financial statements and notes to the financial statements, should be read in its entirety. Excerpts provided in this textbook are intended solely for teaching and learning purposes. Copyright of these excerpts remains with the original copyright holders. Readers are encouraged to obtain the full annual reports for a complete picture of the respective companies' financial position and financial performance. Summarized data tables and charts are produced based on information available publicly.

While every reasonable effort has been made to obtain permissions from the copyright holders, we have been unsuccessful in some instances. The author has then proceeded to contact some materials and hope that these few companies will take the authors' efforts in good faith taking due account that the materials are available publicly and credited appropriately.

Prologue

Accounting Careers: Much More Than Counting Things

What kind of career can you have in accounting? Almost any kind you want. A career in accounting lets you use your analytical skills in a variety of ways, and it brings both monetary and personal rewards.

Accounting as an art is widely believed to have been invented by Fra Luca Bartolomeo de Pacioli, an Italian mathematician and Franciscan friar in the 16th Century. Pacioli was a close friend of Leonardo da Vinci, and collaborated with him on many projects.

Accounting as the profession we know today has its roots in the Industrial Revolution during the 18th and 19th centuries, mostly in England. However, accounting did not attain the stature of other professions such as law, medicine, or engineering until early in the 20th Century. Professions are distinguished from trades by the following characteristics: (1) a unifying body of technical literature; (2) standards of competence; (3) codes of professional conduct; and (4) dedication to service to the public.

Today's accountants obtain years of formal education at the college level which, for most, culminates in taking a very rigorous professional exam that qualifies them to hold the designation *certified public accountant* (CPA). There are other professional designations that accountants may obtain as well, each with its own professional exam and set of professional standards. Examples are certified management accountant (CMA), certified internal auditor (CIA), and certified fraud examiner (CFE).

WHERE ACCOUNTANTS WORK

Where can you work as an accountant? There are four kinds of employers.

Public Practice

You can work for a public accounting firm, which could be a large international firm or a variety of medium to small-sized firms. Within the CPA firm, you can specialize in areas such as audit, tax, or consulting. In this capacity, you'll be serving as an external accountant to many different clients. At present, the largest six international firms are Deloitte, Ernst &Young, KPMG, PricewaterhouseCoopers, Grant Thornton, and RSM McGladrey. However, there are many other firms with international and national scope of practice. Most CPAs start their career at a large CPA firm. From there, they move on to obtain positions of leadership in the corporate finance world, industry, or just about anywhere there is a demand for persons who like solving complex problems.

Managerial Accounting

Instead of working for a wide variety of clients, you can work within one corporation or nonprofit enterprise. Your role may be to analyze financial information and communicate that information to managers, who use it to plot strategy and make decisions. You may be called upon to help allocate corporate resources or improve financial performance. For example, you might do a cost-benefit analysis to help decide whether to acquire a company or build a factory. Or you might describe the financial implications of choosing one strategy over another. You might work in areas such as internal auditing, financial management, financial reporting, treasury management, and tax planning. The highest position in management accounting is the chief financial officer (CFO) position, with some CFOs rising to become chief executive officers (CEOs).

Government and Not-for-Profit Entities

As an accountant, you might work for the government—federal, state, or local. Like your counterparts in public accounting and business, your role as a government accountant includes responsibilities in the areas of auditing, financial reporting, and management accounting. You'll evaluate how government agencies are being managed. You may advise decision makers on how to allocate resources to promote efficiency. Many countries have agencies that hires CPAs to investigate the financial aspects of white-collar crime. You might find yourself working for tax authorities, national accounting or audit agencies, security commissions or stock exchanges, ministry of finance or treasury, or even the parliament.

As an accountant, you might also decide to work in the not-for-profit sector. Colleges, universities, public and private primary and secondary schools, hospitals, and charitable organizations all have accounting functions. Accountants for these types of entities prepare financial statements as well as budgets and projections. Most have special training in accounting standards specially designed for work in the not-for-profit sector.

Education

Finally, you can work at a college or university, advancing the thought and theory of accounting and teaching future generations of new accountants. On the research side of education, you might study how companies use accounting information. You might develop new ways of categorizing financial data, or study accounting practices in different countries. You then publish your ideas in journals and books and present them to colleagues at meetings around the world. On the education side, you can help others learn about accounting and give them the tools they need to be their best.

CPA: THREE LETTERS THAT SPEAK VOLUMES

When employers see the CPA designation, they know what to expect about your education, knowledge, abilities, and personal attributes. They value your analytic skills and extensive training. Your CPA credential gives you a distinct advantage in the job market and instant credibility and respect in the workplace. It's a plus when dealing with other professionals such as bankers, attorneys, auditors, and federal regulators. In addition, your colleagues in private industry tend to defer to you when dealing with complex business matters, particularly those involving financial management.[1]

THE HOTTEST GROWTH AREAS IN ACCOUNTING

Recent legislations, such the US Sarbanes-Oxley Act of 2002, or similar legislations in many other parts of the world, have brought rising demand for accountants of all kinds. In addition to strong overall demand, certain areas of accounting are especially hot.[2]

Sustainability Reporting

Sustainability reporting involves reporting on an organization's performance with respect to health, safety, and environmental (HSE) issues. As businesses take a greater interest in environmental issues, CPAs are getting involved in reporting on such matters as employee health, on-the-job accident rates, emissions of certain pollutants, spills, volumes of waste generated, and initiatives to reduce and minimize such incidents and releases. Utilities, manufacturers, and chemical companies are particularly affected by environmental issues. As a result, they turn to CPAs to set up a preventive system to ensure compliance and avoid future claims or disputes or to provide assistance once legal implications have arisen.

Corporate social responsibility reporting (CSR) is similar to HSE reporting but with a broadened emphasis on social matters such as ethical labor practices, training, education, and diversity of workforce and corporate philanthropic initiatives. Most of the world's largest corporations have extensive CSR initiatives.

Assurance Services

Assurance services are services provided by a CPA that improve the quality of information, or its context, for decision makers. Such information can be financial or non-financial, and it can be about past events or about ongoing processes or systems. This broad concept includes audit and attestation services and is distinct from consulting because it focuses primarily on improving information rather than on providing advice or installing systems. You can use your analytical and information-processing expertise by providing assurance services in areas ranging from electronic commerce to elder care, comprehensive risk assessment, business valuations, entity performance measurement, and information systems quality assessment.

Information Technology Services

Companies can't compete effectively if their information technology systems don't have the power or flexibility to perform essential functions. Companies need accountants with strong computer skills who can design and implement advanced systems to fit a company's specific needs and to find ways to protect and insulate data. CPAs skilled in software research and development (including multimedia technology) are also highly valued.

International Accounting

Globalization means that cross-border transactions are becoming commonplace. Countries in Eastern Europe and Latin America, which previously had closed economies, are opening up and doing business with new trading partners. The passage of the North American Free Trade Agreement (NAFTA) and the General Agreement on Tariffs and Trade (GATT) facilitates trade, and the economic growth in areas such as the Pacific Rim further brings greater volumes of trade and financial flows. Organizations need accountants who understand international trade rules, accords, and laws; cross-border merger and acquisition issues; and foreign business customs, languages, cultures, and procedures.

Forensic Accounting

Forensic accounting is in growing demand after scandals such as the collapse of Enron and WorldCom, which are featured in this text. Forensic accountants look at a company's financial records for evidence of criminal activity. This could be anything from securities fraud to overvaluation of inventory to money laundering and improper capitalization of expenses.

Whether you seek a career in business, government, the not-for-profit sector, or a charity, **accounting** has a career for you. Every organization, from the smallest mom-and-pop music retailer to the biggest government in the world, needs accountants to help manage its resources. Global trade demands accountability, and ever-more complex tax laws mean an ever-increasing need for the skills and services of accountants.

ENDNOTES

[1] http://www.startheregoplaces.com/news/news_half5.asp.

[2] AICPA, the American Institute of Certified Public Accountants, http://www.aicpa.org.

1

Conceptual Framework and Financial Statements

SPOTLIGHT: Carrefour

The **Carrefour** Group has grown to become one of the world's leading distribution groups. It is the largest retailer in Europe, and the second largest worldwide, with more than 15,500 stores in 35 countries, employing close to half a million employees. Carrefour operates four main grocery store formats: hypermarkets, supermarkets, hard discount and convenience stores. Carrefour has total assets of €52,082 million as at December 31, 2008, which was financed by liabilities of €41,130 and equity of €10,952 million, respectively.

As you would expect, Carrefour sells a lot of items, anything from groceries and household products, to apparel and consumer electronics. In fact, Carrefour's total sales revenue in the financial year ended December 31, 2008 was €86,967 million. After deducting cost of sales and other expenses, Carrefour's 2008 net income was €1,539 million. From its operating activities, Carrefour generated cash flows of about €4,887 million. Taking into account its investing and financing activities, the net cash flow generated by the Carrefour group for 2008 was €1,153 million.

These terms may be foreign to you now, but after you read this chapter, you will gain more understanding of financial statements. Welcome to the world of accounting!

Carrefour Group
Consolidated Income Statement (Adapted)
Financial Year Ended December 31

(In millions € Euros)	2008	2007
1 Net sales	86,967	82,149
2 Other income..	1,258	1,147
3 Total income	88,225	83,296
4 Cost of sales...	(68,709)	(64,609)
5 Gross margin	19,516	18,686
6 Sales, general and administrative expenses..................	(14,355)	(13,673)
7 Depreciation, amortization and provisions	(1,861)	(1,723)
8 Non-recurring income and expenses	(524)	47
9 Earnings before interest and tax..............................	2,776	3,338
10 Finance costs..	(562)	(526)
11 Income tax..	(743)	(867)
12 Other income items...	68	474
13 Net income	1,539	2,479

Each chapter of this book begins with adapted extracts of an actual financial statement. In this chapter, it's the Consolidated Income Statement of Carrefour. The core of financial accounting revolves around the following basic financial statements:

- Statement of Comprehensive Income (more commonly called Income Statement)
- Statement of Financial Position (more commonly called Balance Sheet)
- Statement of Cash Flows
- Statement of Changes in Equity

Financial statements are the business documents that companies use to report the results of their activities to various user groups, which can include managers, investors, creditors, and regulatory agencies. In turn, these parties use the reported information to make a variety of decisions, such as whether to invest in or loan money to the company. To learn accounting, you must learn to focus on decisions. In this chapter we explain generally accepted accounting principles, their underlying assumptions, principles, and concepts, and the bodies responsible for issuing accounting standards. We discuss the judgment process that is necessary to make good accounting decisions. We also discuss the contents of the four basic financial statements that report the results of those decisions. In later chapters, we will explain in more detail how to construct the financial statements, as well as how user groups typically use the information contained in them to make business decisions.

LEARNING OBJECTIVES

1 **Use** accounting vocabulary

2 **Learn** underlying concepts, assumptions and principles of accounting

3 **Apply** the accounting equation to business organizations

4 **Evaluate** business operations

5 **Use** information in financial statements to make business decisions, which are informed by economic, legal, and ethical guidelines

> For more practice and review of accounting cycle concepts, use ACT, the Accounting Cycle Tutorial, online at www.myaccountinglab.com. Margin logos like this one, directing you to the appropriate ACT section and material, appear throughout Chapters 1, 2, and 3. When you enter the tutorial, you'll find three buttons on the opening page of each chapter module. Here's what the buttons mean: **Tutorial** gives you a review of the major concepts, **Application** gives you practice exercises, and **Glossary** reviews important terms.

BUSINESS DECISIONS

The Carrefour Group's managers make lots of decisions. Which is selling faster, household products, apparel, groceries or consumer electronics? Are branded goods bringing in more profits than in-house brands? Should Carrefour further expand into the United States or Asia? Accounting information helps companies make these decisions.

Take a look at Carrefour's Consolidated Income Statement on page 2. Let's start with the "bottom line", or net income or net profit (line 13). Net income is the excess of revenues over expenses. You can see that Carrefour earned a €1,539 million profit in the year ended December 31, 2008. That's good news because it means that Carrefour had €1,539 million more revenues than expenses for the year. However, the global financial crisis has clearly impacted some parts of Carrefour's operations, as its 2008 net income was 38% lower than the results achieved in 2007. This seems to be caused by some "non-recurring income and expenses" (line 8) which will need further investigation. Hopefully, this will turn out to be a one-off expense and net income will improve again in subsequent years.

Suppose you have €10,000 to invest. What information would you need before deciding to invest Carrefour? Let's see how accounting works!

ACCOUNTING IS THE LANGUAGE OF BUSINESS

OBJECTIVE

1 Use accounting vocabulary

Accounting is an information system. It measures business activities, processes data into reports, and communicates results to decision makers who will make decisions that will impact the business activities. Indeed, accounting is "the language of business". The better you understand the language, the better you can manage your finances as well as those of your business.

Don't confuse bookkeeping and accounting. Bookkeeping is a mechanical part of accounting, just as arithmetic is a part of mathematics. Exhibit 1-1 illustrates the flow of accounting information and helps illustrate accounting's role in business. The accounting process begins and ends with people making decisions.

EXHIBIT 1-1 | The Flow of Accounting Information

Two Kinds of Accounting: Financial Accounting and Management Accounting

Both *external* and *internal users* of accounting information exist. We can therefore classify accounting into two branches. **Financial accounting** provides information for decision makers outside the **entity**, such as investors, creditors, government agencies, and the public. This textbook focuses on financial accounting.

Management accounting provides information for managers of Carrefour. Examples of management accounting information include budgets, forecasts, and projections that are used in making strategic decisions of the entity. Managers of an entity have the ability to determine the form and content of financial information in order to meet its own need. Internal information must still be accurate and relevant for the decision needs of managers.

You may be doing this course as an accounting student or non-accounting student. Regardless of your eventual career ambitions, knowledge of accounting will help you understand how organizations operate. Many accounting graduates work in professional accounting services, typically with the public accounting firms. These firms offer various services to the business and government sectors, such as audit and assurance, taxation advice, consultancy and advisory. Those who venture into the corporate world may work in various accounting functions, from treasury and finance, to internal audit and risk management. Even if you are not an accounting student, in almost all lines of work and industry, you will have to make decisions in your day-to-day activities, most of which will require you to understand, prepare or work within constraints of some form of financial reports and budgets. On an individual level, you may also find that accounting helps you manage your own finances and investments better.

Organizing a Business

Accounting is used in every type of business. A business generally takes one of the following forms:

- proprietorship
- partnership
- corporation

Exhibit 1-2 compares ways to organize a business.

EXHIBIT 1-2 | The Various Forms of Business Organization

	Proprietorship	Partnership	Corporation
1. *Owner(s)*	Proprietor—one owner	Partners—two or more owners	Shareholders—generally many owners
2. *Personal liability of owner(s) for business debts*	Proprietor is personally liable	General partners are personally liable; limited partners are not	Shareholders are *not* personally liable

Proprietorship. A **proprietorship** has a single owner, called the proprietor. **Dell** started out in the college dorm room of Michael Dell, the owner. Proprietorships tend to be small retail stores or solo providers of professional services – physicians, attorneys, or accountants. Legally, the business is the proprietor, and the proprietor is personally liable for all the business's debts. But for accounting purposes, a proprietorship is a distinct entity, separate from its proprietor. Thus, the business records should not include the proprietor's personal finances.

Partnership. A **partnership** has two or more parties as co-owners, and each owner is a partner. Individuals, corporations, partnerships, or other types of entities can be partners. Income and loss of the partnership "flows through" to the partners and they recognize it based on their agreed-upon percentage interest in the business. The partnership is not a taxpaying entity. Instead, each partner takes a proportionate share of the entity's taxable income and pays tax according to that partner's individual or corporate rate. Many retail establishments, professional service firms (law, accounting, etc.), real estate, and oil and gas exploration companies operate as partnerships. Many partnerships are small or medium-sized, but some are gigantic, with thousands of partners. Partnerships are governed by agreement, usually spelled out in writing in the form of a contract between the partners. General partnerships have mutual agency and unlimited liability, meaning that each partner may conduct business in the name of the entity, and can make agreements that legally bind all partners without limit for the partnership's debts. Partnerships are therefore quite risky, because an irresponsible partner can create large debts for the other general partners without their knowledge or authorization. This feature of general partnerships has spawned the creation of limited-liability partnerships (LLPs).

A *limited-liability partnership* is one in which a wayward partner cannot create a large liability for the other partners. In LLPs, each partner is liable for partnership debts only up to the extent of his or her investment in the partnership, plus his or her proportionate share of the liabilities. Each LLP, however, must have one general partner with unlimited liability for all partnership debts.

Corporation.   A **corporation** is a business owned by the **shareholders**, who own shares representing ownership in the corporation. One of the major advantages of doing business in the corporate form is the ability to raise large sums of capital from issuance of shares to the public. All types of entities (individuals, partnerships, corporations, or other types) may be shareholders in a corporation. Even though proprietorships and partnerships are more numerous, corporations transact much more business and are larger in terms of assets, income, and number of employees. Most well-known companies, such as Carrefour Group, **Starbucks**, **Google**, **Toyota**, and **Nokia**, are corporations. Their full names usually indicate that they are structured as a company. The most common labels include Corporation, Incorporated, or simply Company. This depends very much on the local and legal practices in the country of incorporation. For example, in Australia you often see Pty Ltd (proprietary limited), in UK you will see PLC (public limited company), in Germany AG (Aktiengesellschaft), in Italy SpA (società per azioni), Malaysia Sdn Bhd (Sendirian Berhad), in Belgium SA (Société Anonyme), in Brazil Ltda (Sociedade Limitada), etc.

A corporation is formed under the relevant legislation in the country. Unlike proprietorships and partnerships, a corporation is legally distinct from its owners. The corporation is like an artificial person and possesses many of the same rights that a person has. The shareholders have no personal obligation for the corporation's debts and have limited liability. Ultimate control of a corporation rests with the shareholders, who generally get one vote for each share they own. In general, shareholders elect the board of directors, which sets policy and appoints management officers such as the chief executive officer (CEO), chief operating officer (COO) and chief financial officer (CFO), and other key functions as necessary.

Accounting Standards

In science, we assign numerals to represent properties of material systems according to scientific laws that govern those properties. For example, we can measure size of an object, temperature of a room, speed of a car, and so on. Similarly, in accounting, we assign monetary amounts to represent elements of financial statements in accordance to some accounting standards. Accounting standards are necessary because without them, users of financial statements would have to learn the basis of accounting for each company, making comparisons to other companies' financial statements difficult.

Unfortunately, unlike scientific laws which apply throughout the universe, accounting rules tend to vary in different jurisdictions. Until recently, one of the major challenges of conducting global business has been the fact that different countries have adopted different accounting standards for business transactions. Historically, the major developed countries (United States, United Kingdom, Japan, Germany, etc.) have all had their own versions of accounting standards (usually referred to in general as GAAP, **Generally Accepted Accounting Principles**). As investors seek to compare financial results across entities from different countries, they have had to restate and convert accounting data from one country to the next in order to make them comparable. This takes time and can be expensive, especially in a globalised world with multinationals operating across many countries.

The solution to this problem lies with the International Accounting Standards Board (IASB) and **International Financial Reporting Standards** (IFRSs). The IASB (www.iasb.org) was formed in 2001 to replace the International Accounting

Standards Committee (IASC) with the objective of developing a single set of high quality, understandable and enforceable accounting standards to help participants in the world's capital markets and other users make economic decisions. Whilst IASB now pronounces IFRSs, previously issued International Accounting Standards (IASs) by the IASC continue to remain effective. This is why in your study of accounting, you will see some standards labeled IAS or IFRS. Collectively, they are simply referred to as IFRSs. In addition, these standards may be relabeled somewhat differently in different countries. For example, in Singapore, they are called FRS (Financial Reporting Standards), in Australia, they are labeled AASB after its national Australian Accounting Standards Board, in South Africa, they are called GRAP (Generally Recognized Accounting Principles), and so forth. Throughout this book, we will make references to accounting standards by their original IAS and IFRS numbers and titles. You can access the IFRSs from www.iasb.org/IFRSs/IFRS.htm. If you are interested in comparisons between your local accounting standards and IFRS, you can refer to www.iasplus.com/country/compare.htm. Appendix D, at the back of this textbook, contains a listing of IFRSs and some other useful resources.

These standards are now being used by most countries around the world. Since its inception, over 100 countries around the world has either required or permitted the use of IFRSs for financial reporting. The IASB and United States' Financial Accounting Standards Board (FASB) have also signed a Memorandum of Understanding outlining their commitment to the convergence of US Generally Accepted Accounting Principles (US GAAP) and IFRSs. As this gains momentum, you can expect to hear more about the adoption and use of IFRSs, as well as global harmonization of accounting standards, in the future. When you do, the most important things to remember will be that these changes will be beneficial for financial statement users in the long run, and that most of what you learned in this accounting course will still apply.

The advantages to adopting one common set of standards are clear. Companies in jurisdictions that have mandated or allowed the use of IFRS compliant standards, such as Australia, Hong Kong, United Arab Emirates, Europe, and eventually United States, will have financial statements that are more comparable with each other. It will be far easier for investors and other financial statement users to evaluate information of various companies in the same industries from across the globe, and companies will only have to prepare one set of financial statements, instead of multiple versions. Thus, in the long run, global use of IFRS should significantly reduce costs of doing global business.

THE CONCEPTUAL FRAMEWORK

A **conceptual framework** lays the foundation for resolving the "big" issues in accounting. You can think of it as the "Why, Who, What, How" of financial reporting. The *IFRS Framework for the Preparation of Presentation of Financial Statements* prescribes the nature, function and boundaries within which financial accounting and reporting operate.

The *IFRS Framework's* focus is on **general purpose financial statements**, which are prepared and presented (at least) annually and are directed toward the common information needs of a wide range of financial statement users. Many of these users rely on the financial statements as their major source of financial information and such financial statements should, therefore, be prepared and presented with

OBJECTIVE

2 **Learn** underlying concepts, assumptions, and principles of accounting

their needs in view. Special purpose financial reports, such as computations for taxation purposes, are outside the scope of the *IFRS Framework*. Exhibit 1-3 gives an overview of the IFRS conceptual framework.

EXHIBIT 1-3 | **Conceptual Framework of Accounting**

Objective	**Provide information to various user groups that is useful for their economic decision making**	
Qualitative Characteristics	Understand-ability · Reliability · Relevance · Comparability	
Constraints	Timeliness · Balance between qualitative characteristics · Benefits versus Cost	
Assumptions	Accrual Accounting · Going Concern	
Elements	Assets · Liabilities · Equity · Income · Expenses	

Why is Financial Reporting Important?

The *IFRS Framework* states that the objective of financial statements is to provide information about the financial position, performance and changes in financial position of an entity that is useful to a wide range of users in making economic decisions. Users evaluate financial statements to make decisions such as whether or not to make additional investment into the entity, provide credit and financing, or assess management's performance.

Who are the Users of Accounting Information?

Different users make different types of economic decisions, based on their relationship with the entity. In your personal and professional life, you are very likely to assume any of these user roles. Here are some examples of users that may be interested in Carrefour's financial statements:

- Investors of Carrefour would want to know if they are getting adequate returns for the risks they are taking when they invest in the company. They may decide to increase, hold or decrease their ownership of Carrefour by buying or selling Carrefour shares in the stock exchange.
- Employees of Carrefour may be interested in its financial information for many reasons. Job security, salary increments, and compensation bonuses are usually worse off when a company has declining profits, or worse, experiences losses.

- Creditors, such as bankers or other financial institutions, may need to decide if they will grant Carrefour additional loans for its expansion plans. They would want to know if Carrefour has the ability to service the interest payments and eventually repay the loan principal.

- Suppliers and trade creditors often grant credit terms to its customers. They would want to know that Carrefour will be able to pay their invoices as and when they become due.

- It is unlikely that retail customers would demand financial information before buying merchandise from Carrefour. However, for other situations where customers have long-term involvement with the entity, customers want to be assured of the continuance of the entity it deals with. For example, if Carrefour is going to buy a fleet of delivery trucks, it would want to be assured that the car company will exist in the future to service or provide replacement parts for the delivery trucks.

- Government and its agencies are interested in various aspects of a business, for example, tax collection and allocation of grants or subsidies. Listed companies would also need to comply with the stock exchange's disclosure requirements or "listing rules".

- And with increasing expectations of corporate social responsibility, members of the public may be interested in Carrefour's executive remuneration, health and safety issues, or even environmental impact of its business operations.

The *IFRS Framework* assumes that since investors are providers of risk capital to the entity, the provision of financial statements that meet their needs will likely meet most of the needs of other users.

What Makes Accounting Information Useful?

The *IFRS Framework* uses the term **qualitative characteristics** to describe the attributes that make the information provided in financial statements useful to users. The four principal qualitative characteristics are understandability, relevance, reliability and comparability.

Understandability

We discussed earlier that accounting is the language of business. And just like any language, you will need some basic knowledge before you can carry a conversation, read or write. Understandability means that accounting information must be sufficiently transparent so that it makes sense to users of the information. The framework assumes that users have a reasonable knowledge of business, economic activities and accounting, and a willingness to study the information with reasonable diligence. Thus, whilst you may not have the knowledge right now, by the end of this course, you will be able to understand accounting vocabulary and use accounting information for decision making.

Relevance

To be relevant, information must be capable of making a difference to the decision maker, having predictive or feedback value. Thus, the manner by which information on past transactions and events is presented may directly influence the predictive value and feedback value of the information. For example, Carrefour's Income Statement, line 8, showed a "non-recurring expense" of €524 million. This separation helps readers estimate how much recurring profit Carrefour is expected to make in the next financial year. Carrefour's future financial statements will also allow users to confirm or correct their prior assessments based on prior years' financial statements.

The degree of relevance may be influenced by the nature and **materiality** of the information. For example, Carrefour's finance costs (line 10 on Carrefour's Income Statement) is a required disclosure item, regardless of its amount. Materiality means that the information must be important enough to the user so that, if it were omitted or erroneously declared, it would make a difference to the user's decision. Only information that is material needs to be separately disclosed (listed or discussed) in the financial statements. Immaterial items are not required to be disclosed separately and may be combined with other information. Materiality thus depends on the size of the item or error judged in the particular circumstances of its omission or misstatement.

Reliability

Any information that is not reliable is rarely useful. How then do we know when information is reliable? In general, information is reliable if it is complete, free from material error or bias, prudent, and can be expected to faithfully represent the economic substance of the underlying event or transaction (regardless of the legal form of such event or transaction). Carrefour's Income Statement can be relied upon if it exhibits these characteristics.

Comparability

Users usually compare financial statements of an entity over a period of time in order to identify trends in its financial position and performance. Thus, it is important that the basis of preparation and presentation remains comparable over time. For example, the comparison between Carrefour's sales in 2007 and 2008 only makes sense if you know that there has been no material change in the way sales are recognized in the financial statements. Similarly, you may want to compare Carrefour's performance to another retailer, and in doing so you would want to be sure that net sales is derived in the same way for both companies before drawing any conclusion. Comparability does not mean uniformity, nor continuing to use the same accounting principles and policies when more relevant and reliable alternative exists.

What Constraints do we Face in Providing Useful Information?

In providing information that can be useful to our users, we face a number of constraints: timeliness, balance between qualitative characteristics, and benefits versus costs. Timeliness means that the information must be made available to users early enough to help them make decisions, thus making the information more relevant to their needs. In doing this, it is often necessary to report information before all aspects of a transaction are known, which may reduce the degree of reliability.

This example of timeliness as a compromising factor between providing reliable yet relevant information is an illustration of the need to balance, or trade-off between, the four qualitative characteristics. Let's look at another potential conflict. Suppose Carrefour has been reporting its Net Sales using some assumptions on possible return of goods from customers. In light of the financial crisis, perhaps this set of assumptions is no longer relevant. What should Carrefour do? Continue to use the same (but no longer relevant) assumptions for the sake of comparability or use new assumptions for better relevance (but less comparable)?

Accounting information is costly to produce, and the cost should not exceed the expected benefits to users. The responsibility for preparing accounting information lies with the management and thus, managers must exercise sound judgment in determining whether the information is sufficiently material and not excessively costly to warrant separate disclosure.

What are our Assumptions in Financial Reporting?

The *IFRS Framework* states that in order meet the objectives financial reporting, there are assumptions we need to make. Firstly, that we prepare our financial statements on an **accrual basis**. In short, this means that transactions and other events are recognized when they occur and not when cash is received or paid. We will explore more about accrual accounting in Chapter 3.

In measuring and reporting accounting information, we also assume that the entity will continue to operate long enough to use existing assets—land, buildings, equipment and supplies—for its intended purposes. In other words, the business has neither the intention nor the need to liquidate or curtail materially the scale of its operations. This is called the **going concern** assumption which would normally apply to most entities. This is how a business can buy assets with expectations to derive benefits from the use of the assets beyond the current financial period. An entity that is not continuing would be accounted for very differently from one that is a going concern.

What Exactly are We Accounting for?

Carrefour's financial statements tell us how the business is performing and where it stands. But how do we arrive at the financial statements? Let's examine the elements of financial statements, which are the building blocks on which these statements rest:

- **Assets** are economic resources controlled by the entity which are expected to produce future economic benefits to the entity. Examples of assets include cash, inventory, account receivables (money owed to the entity by its debtors), machinery, equipment and properties.
- **Liabilities** are present obligations of the entity which are expected to result in an outflow of economic benefits from the entity. Examples of liabilities include bank loans, account payables (money owed by the entity to its creditors) and other obligations.
- **Equity** the residual interest in the entity's assets after deducting the entity's liabilities and represents shareholder's residual claim to the entity's assets. You will find two major sub-parts in the equity section: **share capital** and **retained earnings**. Share Capital is the amount shareholders have invested in the entity (usually in the form of shares) and Retained Earnings is the amount earned by income-producing activities and kept for use in the business.
- **Income** is increases in economic benefits during an accounting period (i.e. increases in assets or decreases in liabilities) that result in an increase in equity, other than those related to transactions with shareholders. The *IFRS Framework* further separates Income into **revenue** and **gains**. Revenue arises from the ordinary course of business (such as sales revenue), whereas gains may or may not be in the ordinary course of business (such as gain on disposal of a subsidiary).
- **Expenses** are decreases in economic benefits during an accounting period (i.e. decreases in assets or increases in liabilities) that result in a decrease in equity, other than those related to transaction with shareholders. Similarly, expenses can be incurred in the ordinary course of business (such as salaries and wages, rent expense), whereas **losses** may or may not be in ordinary course of business (losses suffered because of natural disasters).

The *IFRS Framework* also provides guidance on when to recognize these elements of financial statements. It states that when an item that meets the definition of an of element of financial statement, it is recognized if (a) it is probable that any future economic benefit associated with the item will flow to or from the entity; and (b) the item has a cost or value that can be measured with reliability.

Information about financial position (assets, liabilities and equity) is primarily provided in a **Balance Sheet**, whereas information about financial performance (income and expenses) is primarily provided in an **Income Statement**. We will examine financial statements later in this chapter.

TECHNICAL UPDATE

In October 2004, the IASB and FASB began a joint project to develop an improved, common conceptual framework that builds on their existing frameworks as part of their convergence project. The new conceptual framework is to be completed in a number of phases in the coming years. Some of the expected changes will impact how we define qualitative characteristics of financial information. The Exposure Draft (ED) issued on May 29, 2008 lists two fundamental qualitative characteristics (relevance and faithful representation), supported by four enhancing qualitative characteristics (comparability, verifiability, timeliness, and understandability) and constrained by materiality and costs.

Now that you have a basic understanding of the *IFRS Framework*, let's see how the elements of financial statements are interconnected and reported.

OBJECTIVE

3 Apply the accounting equation to business organizations

THE ACCOUNTING EQUATIONS

The basic **accounting equation** shows the relationship among assets, liabilities, and equity. Assets appear on the left side and liabilities and owners' equity on the right. The accounting equation can be written as Assets = Liabilities + Equity, or alternatively, Assets – Liabilities = Equity. As Exhibit 1-4 shows, the two sides must be equal. In this example, the entity's assets of $1,000 are financed by liabilities of $600 and equity of $400.

EXHIBIT 1-4 | The Accounting Equation (1)

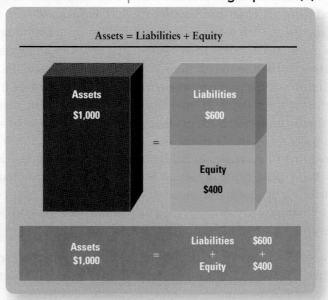

A second accounting equation relates to the calculation of profits earned by an entity during a financial period. Profit is simply Income (Revenue and Gains) less Expenses (Expenses and Losses). Exhibit 1-5 shows that a profit of $200 resulted from total revenue of $500 and expenses of $300. When total revenues exceed total expenses, the result is called **net income**, or **net profit**. When expenses exceed revenues, the result is a **net loss**. In accounting, the word "net" refers to an amount after a subtraction. Net income is thus the profit left over after subtracting expenses and losses from revenues and gains.

EXHIBIT 1-5 | **The Accounting Equation (2)**

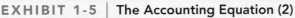

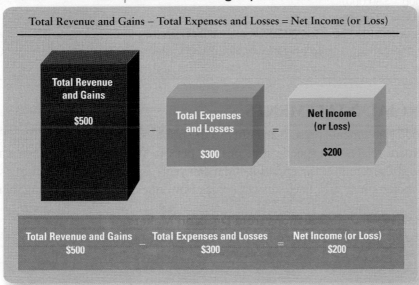

Recall that the *IFRS Framework* states that income increases equity, whereas expenses decrease equity. This is usually shown as an increase to retained earnings for net income or a decrease to retained earnings for net loss. A successful business may pay **dividends** to shareholders as a return on their investments, usually in the form of cash. Dividends are recorded as direct reductions of retained earnings. Remember that just as capital contribution from shareholders to the company is not income, dividend distribution is not an expense and will never affect net income. Exhibit 1-6 shows the movement in retained earnings over an accounting period.

EXHIBIT 1-6 | **The Components of Retained Earnings**

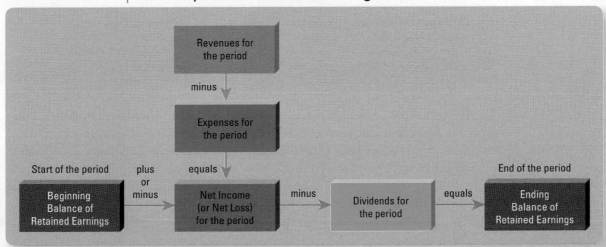

STOP & THINK...

1. If the assets of a business are $240,000 and the liabilities are $80,000, how much is the owners' equity?
2. If the owners' equity in a business is $160,000 and the liabilities are $130,000, how much are the assets?
3. A company reported monthly revenues of $129,000 and expenses of $85,000. What is the result of operations for the month?
4. If the beginning balance of retained earnings is $100,000, revenue is $75,000, expenses total $50,000, and the company pays a $10,000 dividend, what is the ending balance of retained earnings?

Answers:

1. $160,000 ($240,000 − $80,000)
2. $290,000 ($160,000 + $130,000)
3. Net income of $44,000 ($129,000 − $85,000); revenues minus expenses
4. $115,000 [$100,000 beginning balance + net income $25,000 ($75,000 − $50,000) − dividends $10,000]

FINANCIAL STATEMENTS

OBJECTIVE

4 Evaluate business operations

The financial statements present an entity to the public in financial terms. Each financial statement relates to a specific date or time period. What would investors want to know about Carrefour at the end of its financial year? Exhibit 1-7 lists four questions decision makers may ask. Each answer comes from one of the financial statements.

EXHIBIT 1-7 | Questions from Decision Makers

Question	Financial Statement	Answer
1. How well did the company perform during the year?	Statement of Comprehensive Income (which consists of two parts: the traditional Income Statement plus Other Comprehensive Income)	Revenues − Expenses Net income (or Net loss) ± Other Comprehensive Income = Total Comprehensive Income
2. Why did the company's equity change during the year?	Statement of Changes in Equity	Beginning Equity + Total Comprehensive Income − Dividends ± Capital Transactions with owners = Ending Equity
3. What is the company's financial position at financial year end?	Statement of Financial Position (usually called Balance Sheet)	Assets = Liabilities + Equity
4. How much cash did the company generate and spend during the year?	Statement of Cash Flows	Operating Cash Flows ± Investing Cash Flows ± Financing Cash Flows = Net Cash Flows

To learn how to use financial statements, let's work through Carrefour's statements for 2008 financial year (ended December 31, 2008). For your first reading of financial statements, we have simplified some of the items in the financial statements. You will get to see more detailed disclosures as you progress in your study of financial accounting. The following diagram shows how the data flows from one financial statement to the next. The order is important.

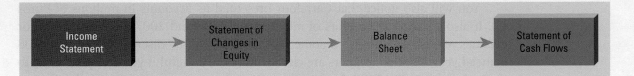

We begin with the Income Statement in Exhibit 1-8.

EXHIBIT 1-8 | Carrefour's Income Statement

<table>
<tr><td colspan="3" align="center">Carrefour Group
Consolidated Income Statement (Adapted)
Financial Year Ended December 31</td></tr>
<tr><td>(In millions € Euros)</td><td>2008</td><td>2007</td></tr>
<tr><td>1 Net sales</td><td>86,967</td><td>82,149</td></tr>
<tr><td>2 Other income</td><td>1,258</td><td>1,147</td></tr>
<tr><td>3 Total income</td><td>88,225</td><td>83,296</td></tr>
<tr><td>4 Cost of sales</td><td>(68,709)</td><td>(64,609)</td></tr>
<tr><td>5 Gross margin</td><td>19,516</td><td>18,686</td></tr>
<tr><td>6 Sales, general and administrative expenses</td><td>(14,355)</td><td>(13,673)</td></tr>
<tr><td>7 Depreciation, amortization and provisions</td><td>(1,861)</td><td>(1,723)</td></tr>
<tr><td>8 Non-recurring income and expenses</td><td>(524)</td><td>47</td></tr>
<tr><td>9 Earnings before interest and tax</td><td>2,776</td><td>3,338</td></tr>
<tr><td>10 Finance costs</td><td>(562)</td><td>(526)</td></tr>
<tr><td>11 Income tax</td><td>(743)</td><td>(867)</td></tr>
<tr><td>12 Other income items</td><td>68</td><td>474</td></tr>
<tr><td>13 Net income</td><td>1,539</td><td>2,479</td></tr>
</table>

The Income Statement Shows a Company's Financial Performance

The Income Statement, (part of **Statement of Comprehensive Income**), reports revenues and expenses for the period. The bottom line is net income or net loss for the period. At the top of Exhibit 1-8 is the company's name, Carrefour Group. On the second line is the term "Consolidated Income Statement". Carrefour Group is actually made up of several corporations that are owned by a common group of shareholders. Commonly controlled corporations like this are required to combine, or consolidate, all of their revenues, expenses, assets, liabilities, and shareholders' equity, and to report them all as one.

The dates of Carrefour's Consolidated Income Statement are for "Financial Year Ended December 31, 2008 and 2007". In this case, the financial year is the same as calendar year, and this happens to be the most common financial period for most companies. But you will also see many other companies using different year end dates. For example, **Wal-Mart** uses 31 January as its fiscal year end, **Lenovo** uses 31 March, **FedEx** uses 31 May and **Steinhoff** (South Africa) uses 30 June. Other companies use a 52- or 53-week financial periods ending nearest to a particular date, for example, **Ahold NV** (Netherlands) uses the Sunday nearest to December 31 as its year end.

You will also notice that Carrefour presented its accounts in millions of Euros (€). It also presented two years of information, 2008 and 2007, to show trends for revenues, expenses, and net income. We shall focus our discussions on the 2008 financial year, but the numbers are clearly more meaningful if you compare them to what was achieved in 2007. Let's examine the Income Statement in more detail.

Revenues.   Carrefour showed two kinds of revenue: net sales and other income. Revenues (lines 1, 2, and 3) do not always carry the word "revenue" in their titles. For example, net sales revenue is often abbreviated as net sales. Net sales means sales revenue after subtracting all the goods customers have returned to the company. Other revenue consists principally of financial and travel services, rental income, franchise fees, etc. You can't quite figure this out from the Income Statement, but the information is disclosed in the Carrefour's Notes to the Accounts, which gives additional information about accounting policies, breakdown of totals, etc. You will see examples of Notes to the Accounts in later chapters. Carrefour's total income (net sales plus other income) has increased from €83,296 to €88,225 million, an increase of close to €5 billion, which is a remarkable achievement given the global financial crisis in 2008.

Expenses.   Similarly, not all expenses have the word "expense" in their title. For example, Carrefour's largest expense is for cost of sales (line 4). Another title for this expense is cost of goods sold (or COGS). This expense represents the direct cost of making sales. This includes Carrefour's cost of the merchandise it sold to customers. For example, suppose a merchandise costs Carrefour $30, and this merchandise was sold for $75. Sales revenue is $75, and cost of goods sold is $30. Cost of goods sold is the major expense of merchandising entities such as **The Bodyshop**, **OSIM**, and **Marks & Spencer**. The difference between total income and cost of sales is called gross margin (line 5). Whilst total income has risen by €5 billion, cost of sales has risen in a higher proportion, thus gross margin only grew by €830 million in 2008.

Carrefour has some other expenses:

- Selling, general and administrative expenses (line 6) are the costs of everyday operations that are not directly related to merchandise purchases. Many expenses may be included in this category, including labor costs, property rentals, maintenance and repairs, fees, advertising, consumables and other general expenses. These expenses amounted to €14,355 million in 2008.
- Depreciation, amortization and provisions (line 7) largely relate to the systematic allocation of costs or benefits consumed from long-lived assets such as property, plant and equipment (PPE). You will learn more about these items in subsequent chapters. A total charge of €1,861 million related to depreciation, amortization and provisions were included in the determination of 2008's net income.
- Non-recurring income and expenses (line 8) was a slightly unusual item. In 2007, this was a positive number, adding to the bottom line, whereas in 2008, this item was an expense and reduces the net income. A further examination of

this item in Carrefour's Notes to the Account shows that this relate to some impairment charge (more on this in Chapter 7) of Carrefour's GV operations in Italy and restructuring costs. This line was separately shown because Carrefour wanted to increase the predictive value of the net income. Some companies would label this type of non-recurring items as "exceptional items".

■ Finance costs, or interest expense (line 10) was €562 million for 2008. This is Carrefour's cost of borrowing money. For Carrefour, interest revenue (€382 million) has been netted against interest expense (€945 million). Companies sometimes offset items like interest income and interest expense against each other and show only the difference (in this case the larger item is interest expense, and so the net amount appears as an expense).

■ Income tax expense (line 11) is the expense levied on Carrefour's, income by the tax authorities. Carrefour's tax expense was lower in 2008 (€743 million) than 2007 (€867 million), most likely due to the lower net income in 2008. Taxation rules can be complicated, and taxable income is not always equal to net income. We will discuss this a little further in Chapter 8.

■ Carrefour's bottom line (line 13) showed a net income of €1,539 million, a decrease of €940 million from 2007's net income.

IAS1 – Presentation of Financial Statements (revised 2007, effective January 1, 2009) has introduced some changes that would affect how financial statements are presented. This standard may or may not be effective yet in your country. The key changes in the revised *IAS1* are:

Names of Financial Statements

Officially, the new terminologies are Statement of Financial Position, Statement of Comprehensive Income, Statement of Changes in Equity and Statement of Cash Flows. However, the Standard allows other titles to be used. You may find that some companies will continue to use the more common names such as Balance Sheet.

Statement of Comprehensive Income and Statement of Changes in Equity

IAS1 requires that only transactions with owners (in their capacity as owners) are presented in the Statement of Changes in Equity. All other non-owner changes in equity are now presented in the Statement of Comprehensive Income, which can be shown as a single statement (i.e. Statement of Comprehensive Income) or two statements (Income Statement, followed by Statement of Comprehensive Income which will begin with the net profit or loss from the Income Statement).

For simplicity, we shall continue to use the term Balance Sheet for Statement of Financial Position and Income Statement to refer to the first portion of the Statement of Comprehensive Income. We shall discuss more of this distinction later in Chapter 11.

Now, let's examine the Statement of Changes in Equity.

The Statement of Changes in Equity Shows a Company's Transactions with its Owners

Recall that the equity is the owner's residual interest in the entity after deducting liabilities. Profits that a company generates ultimately belong to the owners of the company. Shareholders are happy when their wealth in the company increases. In 2008, Carrefour generated profit of €1,539 million. Let's see how this is reflected in its **Statement of Changes in Equity**.

EXHIBIT 1-9 | Carrefour's Statement of Changes in Equity

Carrefour Group
Consolidated Statement of Changes in Equity (Adapted)
Financial Year Ended December 31, 2007 and 2008

(In millions € Euros)	Total Equity
1 Shareholder equity as of December 31, 2006	10,503
2 Net income	2,479
3 Dividends	(821)
4 Reclassifications and other reserves	(391)
5 Shareholder equity as of December 31, 2007	11,770
6 Net income	1,539
7 Dividends	(927)
8 Reclassifications and other reserves	(1,430)
9 Shareholder equity as of December 31, 2008	10,952

Carrefour started the 2007 financial year with the 2006 ending balance of total equity (line 1) of €10,503 million. Net income or net loss flows from the Income Statement to the Statement of Changes in Equity (lines 2 and 6 in Exhibit 1-9). Take a moment to trace this amount from one statement to the other. You can see that net income increases total equity, and if you have any net losses, it will decrease total equity.

After a company earns its net income, its board of directors decides if the company should to pay a dividend to the shareholders. Corporations are not obligated to pay dividends unless their boards decide to pay (i.e. declare) them. Usually, companies who are in development stages or growth mode elect not to pay dividends, opting instead to plough the money back into the company to expand operations or purchase property, plant and equipment. Established companies usually have regular earnings (and cash) to pay dividends. Dividends decrease retained earnings because they represent a distribution of a company's assets (usually cash) to its shareholders. Carrefour paid dividends amounting to €821 and €927 million to its shareholders (lines 3 and 7).

Lines 4 and 8 contain items that are beyond our scope right now (for example, this is where Carrefour accounts for the impact of fluctuations of foreign currency, fair value changes in financial instruments, etc). At the end of the 2008 financial year, Carrefour's total equity stood at €10,952 million.

Sometimes you will also see companies issuing or buying back shares in their Statement of Changes in Equity. This is not the case with Carrefour as it did not issue nor cancel any shares in 2007 and 2008.

Lines 4 and 8 are what *IAS1* calls "non-owner changes in equity". When the revised *IAS1* is adopted by Carrefour, these items will be shown in the Statement of Comprehensive Income (after net income). Lines 2 and 6 will thus be "total comprehensive income" rather than "net income".

The Balance Sheet Shows a Company's Financial Position

A company's Balance Sheet, also called the **Statement of Financial Position**, reports three group of items: assets (lines 1—10), liabilities (lines 11—19), and shareholders' equity (lines 20—22). Carrefour's Consolidated Balance Sheet, shown in Exhibit 1-10, are dated December 31, 2007 and 2008, as financial position is always for a specific point in time, unlike an Income Statement which covers a period of time.

EXHIBIT 1-10 | Carrefour's Balance Sheet

Carrefour Group Consolidated Balance Sheets (Adapted) As at December 31		
(In millions € Euros)	2008	2007
Assets		
1 Cash and cash equivalents	5,317	4,164
2 Trade receivables	2,919	3,424
3 Inventories	6,891	6,867
4 Other current assets	4,723	4,252
5 Total current assets	19,850	18,707
6 Property, plant and equipment	14,809	14,751
7 Intangible assets	12,418	12,847
8 Other non-current assets	5,005	5,627
9 Total non-current assets	32,232	33,225
10 Total assets	52,082	51,932
Liabilities		
11 Trade payable	17,276	17,077
12 Tax payable	1,467	1,193
13 Borrowings—short-term	2,709	3,247
14 Other current liabilities	6,953	7,103
15 Total current liabilities	28,405	28,620
16 Borrowing—long-term	9,506	8,276
17 Other non-current liabilities	3,219	3,266
18 Total non-current liabilities	12,725	11,542
19 Total liabilities	41,130	40,162
Shareholders' Equity		
20 Capital	1,762	1,762
21 Retained earnings, reserves and others	9,190	10,008
22 Total shareholders' equity	10,952	11,770
23 Total liabilities and shareholders' equity	52,082	51,932

Before we proceed, let's just make sure Carrefour's accounting equation is correct. At December 31, 2008, it has total assets of €52,082 million (line 10), which is financed by total liabilities of €41,130 million (line 19) and equity of €10,952 million (line 22). Assets = Liabilities + Equity. This relationship will always remain true at all times.

Assets. There are two main categories of assets: current and non-current (sometimes referred to as long-term) assets. **Current assets** are assets that are expected to be converted to cash, sold, or consumed during the next 12 months or within the business' operating cycle. Current assets typically include cash, short-term investments, receivables (also called debtors), merchandise inventory, and prepaid expenses. Carrefour's total current assets at December 31, 2008 are €19,850 million (line 5). Typically, current assets are presented in some order of liquidity. In this adapted example, they are presented in decreasing order of liquidity for ease of discussion. Let's examine each current asset that Carrefour holds:

- All companies have cash. **Cash** is the liquid asset that's the medium of exchange, and cash equivalents include money-market accounts or other financial instruments that are easily convertible to cash. Carrefour owns €5,317 million in cash and cash equivalents at December 31, 2008 (line 1).
- Account receivables are amounts the company expects to collect from its debtors. Carrefour has trade receivables totalling €2,919 million (line 2). Sometimes you may see some companies use the term "debtors" to describe account receivables. Often, companies will also distinguish between trade and other receivables. Trade receivables are usually amount due from customers, in the context of trading activities. We'll discuss accounts receivable further in Chapter 5. Occasionally, you may see the term notes receivable, which are amounts a company expects to collect from a party who has signed a promissory note to that company and therefore owes it money. Carrefour doesn't own any notes receivable.
- Merchandise **inventory** (line 3) is the company's largest current asset. For a merchandiser like Carrefour, this is to be expected. Inventory of €6,891 million represents 35% of Carrefour's total current assets. We will discuss how to account for inventory and its related Cost of Goods Sold (in the Income Statement) in Chapter 6.
- For simplicity, we have summarized other current assets into one line (line 4). Typically, this could include items such as prepaid expenses, loans to employees, etc. Prepaid expenses or prepayments represent amounts paid in advance for advertisements, rent, insurance, and supplies. Prepaid expenses are current assets because Carrefour will benefit from these expenditures in the next financial year. We will discuss more about prepayments and accruals in Chapter 3.

The main categories of long-term or non-current assets are **property, plant and equipment (PPE)** (line 6) and intangible assets (line 7). Non-current assets may indicate long-term investments and other long-term assets. We will examine PPE and intangibles in greater detail in Chapter 7, and long-term investments in Chapter 10. Let's have a quick look at what non-current assets Carrefour has on its Balance Sheet:

- Net Property, Plant, and Equipment (PPE, sometimes also called fixed assets) of €14,809 million (line 6) includes Carrefour's land, buildings, equipment, fixtures, fittings and installations, etc. PPE is Carrefour's largest asset (almost half of total non-current assets or 28% of total assets). PPE conveys economic benefits over its useful lives, and their acquisition costs are allocated systematically throughout their useful lives. This process is called depreciation. The cumulative amounts that have been previously allocated are called accumulated depreciation. Carrefour's Notes to the Accounts (you will need to obtain the full annual report from Carrefour's website) show that the gross PPE was €30,402 million and accumulated depreciation was €15,593 million as at December 31, 2008.
- Intangibles are assets with no physical form, such as patents, trademarks, and goodwill. Carrefour has €12,418 million of intangibles, mostly in the form of goodwill on acquisitions of subsidiaries.
- Again, for simplicity, we have combined various other non-current assets into one account (line 8). These include investment properties (which are not accounted for as PPE), deferred tax assets, and other non-current financial assets.

Overall, Carrefour reports total assets of €52,082 million at December 31, 2008 (line 10).

Liabilities.   Liabilities are also divided into current and non-current categories. Current liabilities (lines 11—14) are obligations or debts payable within one year or within Carrefour's operating cycle. **Current liabilities** typically include accounts such as accounts payable, taxes payable, and other liabilities like short-term notes payable, and salaries/wages payable. Non-current liabilities are obligations that are likely to require an outflow of economic benefits after one year:

- Account payables (line 10) are the amount due to Carrefour's creditors, most likely suppliers of its merchandise inventory. This amounts to €17,276 million, clearly Carrefour's largest current liability. Similar to receivables, sometimes you will see companies further classifying Payables into trade payables (or Creditors), note payable, and other payables.
- Tax payable (line 11) of €1,467 million is the amount due to various tax authorities.
- Carrefour has total borrowings of €12,215 million, of which €2,709 million is due within the next financial year (line 13) and €9,506 million long-term debt due beyond the next financial year (line 16). Whilst you see two line items on the Balance Sheet, it does not necessarily mean that Carrefour has two separate borrowings. Even if Carrefour only has one financing arrangement, as long as there is some amount due in the next financial year, it will disclose the current portion separately from the non-current portion.

- Other liabilities (line 14 and 17) comprise provisions, pre-collected revenue (or unearned revenue), and deferred tax liabilities.

Overall, Carrefour reports total liabilities of €41,130 million at December 31, 2008 (line 19). You may notice earlier that the total assets were €52,082 million. This means that almost 80% of Carrefour's assets are financed by liabilities.

Accounting Cycle Tutorial Balance Sheet Accounts

Shareholders' Equity. Earlier you have seen the reconciliation of movement in total equity in the last two financial years (Exhibit 1-9). You can check that the total equity of €10,952 million (line 22) in Exhibit 1-10 is the same total as Exhibit 1-9 (line 9). Carrefour's equity consists of:

- Capital. **Paid-in capital** (sometimes labeled share capital or simply, capital) of €1,762 million (line 20). Remember we said there was no additional capital issued or shares bought back during 2008 in the Statement of Changes in Equity? Well, the Balance Sheet confirms that capital has not changed from 2007 to 2008.
- Depending on where the company's is legally registered, some jurisdictions practice a "par value" system, whereas others do not use par values. In situations where a company has par values for its shares, you are likely to see par values of share capital separated from the additional capital paid above par value (usually labeled share premium, additional paid-in capital, or capital in excess of par).
- Retained earnings, reserves and others totaled €9,190 million (line 22). Recall our earlier discussions on retained earnings (Exhibit 1-6, page 13). Retained earnings records the earnings of the entity less the dividends it pays out. In Carrefour's Balance Sheet, it has been combined with a few other items (various reserves and non-controlling interests). The detailed breakdown of the other items is beyond our scope for now. We will explore more in Chapter 9.

Last but not least, the Statement of Cash Flows is the fourth required financial statement.

THE STATEMENT OF CASH FLOWS SHOWS A COMPANY'S CASH RECEIPTS AND PAYMENTS

Companies engage in three basic types of activities: **operating activities**, **investing activities** and **financing activities**. The **statement of cash flows** reports cash flows under each of these activities. Think about the cash flows (receipts and payments) in each category:

- Companies operate by selling goods and services to customers. Operating activities result in net income or net loss, and they either increase or decrease cash. The Income Statement tells us whether the company is profitable but this does not necessarily mean the company has been able to generate cash from operations. Sooner or later, to be successful, a company will need to bring in cash from its operations. For now, we will calculate cash flow from operating activities as an adjusting (line 3 in Exhibit 1-11 below) to net income.

- Companies also invest in non-current assets such as Property, Plant and Equipment. You saw earlier that Carrefour's largest asset is its PPE of €14,809 million. Both purchases and sales of long-term assets are investing cash flows. Cash flows from investing activities show a company's investments into its production capacity.

- Companies need money for financing. Financing comes from both equity owners and borrowings. Carrefour's cash flows from financing activities would include any issuance of shares, repurchase of shares, as well as proceeds and repayments of borrowings.

Have a look at Carrefour's simplified Statement of Cash Flows below in Exhibit 1-11. We will examine the components of various cash flow activities in greater detail in Chapter 12.

EXHIBIT 1-11 | Carrefour's Statement of Cash Flows

Carrefour Group Consolidated Statements of Cash Flows (Adapted) Financial Year Ended December 31		
(In millions € Euros)	2008	2007
1 Cash flows from operating activities:		
2 Net income	1,539	2,479
3 Reconciliation to cash flow from operation	3,348	1,433
4 Cash flow from operating activities	4,887	3,912
5 Cash flows from investing activities	(2,596)	(3,491)
6 Cash flows from financing activities	(1,028)	46
7 Impact of currency fluctuations	(110)	0
8 Net cash flows	1,153	467
9 Cash and cash equivalents at beginning of the year	4,164	3,697
10 Cash and cash equivalents at end of the year	5,317	4,164

Overall, Carrefour's cash increased by about €1,153 million during 2008 (line 8) and ended the year at €5,317 million (line 10). Trace ending cash back to the balance sheet in Exhibit 1-10 (line 1). Cash links the Statement of Cash Flows to the balance sheet.

Let's now summarize the relationships that link the financial statements.

RELATIONSHIPS AMONG THE FINANCIAL STATEMENTS

OBJECTIVE

5 Use information in financial statements to make business decisions, which are informed by economic, legal, and ethical guidelines

Accounting Cycle Tutorial Glossary

Accounting Cycle Tutorial Glossary Quiz

Exhibit 1-12 summarizes the relationships among the financial statements of ABC Company for 2010. These statements are summarized with all amounts assumed for the illustration. Study the exhibit carefully because these relationships apply to all organizations. Specifically, note the following:

1. The Income Statement for the year ended December 31, 2010
   a. Reports revenues and expenses of the year. Revenues and expenses are reported only on the income statement.
   b. Reports net income if total revenues exceed total expenses. If expenses exceed revenues, there is a net loss.

2. The Statement of Changes in Equity for the year ended December 31, 2010
   a. Opens with the beginning equity balance.
   b. Adds net income (or subtracts net loss). Net income comes directly from the Income Statement (arrow ① in Exhibit 1-12).
   c. Subtracts dividends.
   d. Reports the equity balance at the end of the year.

3. The Balance Sheet at December 31, 2010, end of the accounting year
   a. Reports assets, liabilities, and equity at the end of the year. Only the balance sheet reports assets and liabilities.
   b. Reports that assets equal the sum of liabilities plus equity. This balancing feature follows the accounting equation and gives the balance sheet its name.
   c. Reports total equity, which comes from the Statement of Changes in Equity (arrow ② in Exhibit 1-12).

4. The Statement of Cash Flows for the year ended December 31, 2010
   a. Reports cash flows from operating, investing, and financing activities. Each category results in net cash provided (an increase) or used (a decrease).
   b. Reports whether cash increased (or decreased) during the year. The statement shows the ending cash balance, as reported on the balance sheet (arrow ③ in Exhibit 1-12).

EXHIBIT 1-12 | **Relationships Among the Financial Statements**

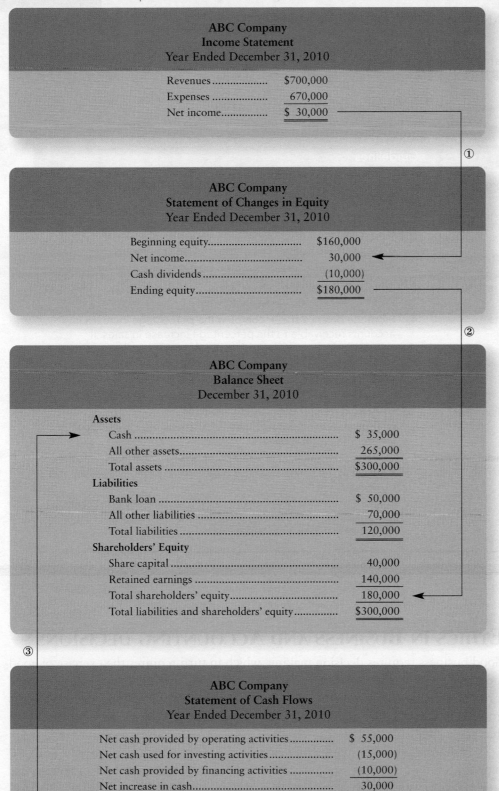

ABC Company
Income Statement
Year Ended December 31, 2010

Revenues	$700,000
Expenses	670,000
Net income	$ 30,000

①

ABC Company
Statement of Changes in Equity
Year Ended December 31, 2010

Beginning equity	$160,000
Net income	30,000
Cash dividends	(10,000)
Ending equity	$180,000

②

ABC Company
Balance Sheet
December 31, 2010

Assets

Cash	$ 35,000
All other assets	265,000
Total assets	$300,000

Liabilities

Bank loan	$ 50,000
All other liabilities	70,000
Total liabilities	120,000

Shareholders' Equity

Share capital	40,000
Retained earnings	140,000
Total shareholders' equity	180,000
Total liabilities and shareholders' equity	$300,000

③

ABC Company
Statement of Cash Flows
Year Ended December 31, 2010

Net cash provided by operating activities	$ 55,000
Net cash used for investing activities	(15,000)
Net cash provided by financing activities	(10,000)
Net increase in cash	30,000
Cash balance, December 31, 2009	5,000
Cash balance, December 31, 2010	$ 35,000

Accounting Cycle Tutorial Applications
Cottage Kitchen

Accounting Cycle Tutorial Applications
Marwood Homes

DECISION GUIDELINES

IN EVALUATING A COMPANY, WHAT DO DECISION MAKERS LOOK FOR?

These Decision Guidelines illustrate how people use financial statements. Decision Guidelines appear throughout the book to show how accounting information aids decision making.

Suppose you are considering an investment in Carrefour. How do you proceed? Where do you get the information you need? What do you look for?

Decision	Guidelines
1. Can the company sell its products?	1. Sales revenue on the income statement. Are sales growing or falling?
2. What are the main income measures to watch for trends?	2. a. Gross profit (Sales – Cost of goods sold) b. Operating income (Gross profit – Operating expenses) c. Net income (bottom line of the income statement) All three income measures should be increasing over time.
3. What percentage of sales revenue ends up as profit?	3. Divide net income by sales revenue. Examine the trend of the net income percentage from year to year.
4. Can the company collect its receivables?	4. From the balance sheet, compare the percentage increase in accounts receivable to the percentage increase in sales. If receivables are growing much faster than sales, collections may be too slow, and a cash shortage may result.
5. Can the company pay its a. Current liabilities? b. Current and long-term liabilities?	5. From the balance sheet, compare a. Current assets to current liabilities. Current assets should be somewhat greater than current liabilities. b. Total assets to total liabilities. Total assets must be somewhat greater than total liabilities.
6. Where is the company's cash coming from? How is cash being used?	6. On the cash-flows statement, operating activities should provide the bulk of the company's cash during most years. Otherwise, the business will fail. Examine investing cash flows to see if the company is purchasing long-term assets—property, plant and equipment and intangibles (this usually signals potential growth).

ETHICS IN BUSINESS AND ACCOUNTING DECISIONS

Good business requires decision making, which in turn requires the exercise of good judgment, both at the individual and corporate levels. For example, you may work for or eventually run a company like **Starbucks** that has decided to devote 5 cents from every cup of coffee sold to helping save the lives of AIDS victims in Africa. Can that be profitable in the long run?

Perhaps as an accountant, you may have to decide whether to record a $50,000 expenditure for a piece of equipment as an asset on the balance sheet or an expense on the income statement. Alternatively, as a sales manager for a company like **SAP**, you may have to decide whether $25 million of goods and services delivered to customers in 2010 would be more appropriately recorded as revenue in 2010 or 2011.

IFRSs are "principles-based", as opposed to US GAAP that are more "rules-based". This put greater emphasis on the importance of judgment in determining the appropriate accounting recognition, measurement and presentation. Depending on the type of business, the facts and circumstances surrounding accounting decisions may not always make them clear cut, and yet the decision may determine whether the company shows a profit or a loss in a particular period! What are the factors that influence business and accounting decisions, and how should these factors be weighed? Generally, three factors influence business and accounting decisions: economic, legal, and ethical.

The economic factor states that the decision being made should maximize the economic benefits to the decision maker. Based on most economic theory, every rational person faced with a decision will choose the course of action that maximizes his or her own welfare, without regard to how that decision impacts others. In summary, the combined outcome of each person acting in his or her own self-interest will maximize the benefits to society as a whole.

The legal factor is based on the proposition that free societies are governed by laws. Laws are written to provide clarity and to prevent abuse of the rights of individuals or society. Democratically enacted laws both contain and express society's collective moral standards. Legal analysis involves applying the relevant laws to each decision, and then choosing the action that complies with those laws. A complicating factor for a global business may be that what is legal in one country might not be legal in another. In that case, it is usually best to abide by the laws of the most restrictive country.

The ethical factor recognizes that while certain actions might be both economically profitable and legal, they may still not be right. Therefore, most companies, and many individuals, have established standards for themselves to enforce a higher level of conduct than that imposed by law. These standards govern how we treat others and the way we restrain our selfish desires. This behavior and its underlying beliefs are the essence of ethics. **Ethics** are shaped by our cultural, socioeconomic, and religious backgrounds. An ethical analysis is needed to guide judgment for making decisions.

The decision rule in an ethical analysis is to choose the action that fulfills ethical duties – responsibilities of the members of society to each other. The challenge in an ethical analysis is to identify specific ethical duties and stakeholders to whom you owe these duties. As with legal issues, a complicating factor in making global ethical decisions may be that what is considered ethical in one country is not considered ethical in another.

Among the questions you may ask in making an ethical analysis are:

- *Which options are most honest, open, and truthful?*
- *Which options are most kind, compassionate, and build a sense of community?*
- *Which options create the greatest good for the greatest number of stakeholders?*
- *Which options result in treating others as I would want to be treated?*

Ethical training starts at home and continues throughout our lives. It is reinforced by the teaching that we receive in our churches, temples, synagogues, or mosques; the schools we attend; and by the persons we associate with and by the company we keep. A thorough understanding of ethics requires more study than we can accomplish in this book. However, remember that when making accounting decisions, do not leave your ethics at the door!

DECISION GUIDELINES

DECISION FRAMEWORK FOR MAKING ETHICAL JUDGMENTS

Weighing tough ethical judgments in business and accounting requires a decision framework. Answering the following four questions will guide you through tough decisions:

Decision	Guidelines
1. What is the issue?	1. The issue will usually deal with making a judgment about an accounting measurement or disclosure that results in economic consequences, often to numerous parties.
2. Who are the stakeholders, and what are the consequences of the decision to each?	2. Stakeholders are anyone who might be impacted by the decision—you, your company, and potential users of the information (investors, creditors, regulatory agencies). Consequences can be economic, legal, or ethical in nature.
3. Weigh the alternatives.	3. Analyze the impact of the decision on all stakeholders, using economic, legal, and ethical criteria. Ask "Who will be helped or hurt, whose rights will be exercised or denied, and in what way?"
4. Make the decision and be prepared to deal with the consequences.	4. Exercise the courage to either defend the decision or to change it, depending on its positive or negative impact. How does your decision make you feel afterward?

To simplify, we might ask three questions:

1. Is the action legal? If not, steer clear, unless you want to go to jail or pay monetary damages to injured parties. If the action is legal, go on to questions (2) and (3).
2. Who will be affected by the decision and how? Be as thorough about this analysis as possible, and analyze it from all three standpoints (economic, legal, and ethical).
3. How will this decision make me feel afterward? How would it make me feel if my family reads about it in the newspaper?

In later chapters throughout the book, we will apply this model to different accounting decisions.

In the business setting, ethics work best when modeled "from the top." **Ethisphere Institute** (www.ethisphere.com) has recently established the Business Ethics Leadership Alliance (BELA), aimed at "reestablishing ethics as the foundation of everyday business practices". BELA members agree to embrace and uphold four core values that incorporate ethics and integrity into all their practices: (1) Legal compliance; (2) Transparency; (3) Conflict identification; and (4) Accountability. Each year, Ethisphere Institute publishes a list of the World's Most Ethical Companies. The 2010 list includes corporations like **IKEA**, **L'Oreal**, **Westpac Banking Corporation**, **Accenture**, Hewlett-Packard, **Kao** and **Phillips**. As you begin to make your decisions about future employers, put these companies on your list! It's easier to act ethically when those you work for recognize the importance of ethics in business practices. These companies have learned from experience that, in the long run, ethical conduct pays big rewards, not only socially, morally, and spiritually, but economically as well!

END-OF-CHAPTER SUMMARY PROBLEM

ShineBrite Car Wash, Inc., began operations on April 1, 2010. During April, the business provided services for customers. It is now April 30, and investors wonder how well ShineBrite performed during its first month. The investors also want to know the company's financial position at the end of April and its cash flows during the month.

The following data are listed in alphabetical order. Prepare the ShineBrite financial statements at the end of April 2010.

Accounts payable	$ 1,800	Land	$18,000
Accounts receivable	2,000	Payments of cash:	
Adjustments to reconcile net		Acquisition of land	40,000
income to net cash provided		Dividends	2,100
by operating activities	(3,900)	Rent expense	1,100
Cash balance at beginning of April	0	Retained earnings at beginning	
Cash balance at end of April	?	of April	0
Cash receipts:		Retained earnings at end of April	?
Issuance (sale) of shares to owners	50,000	Salary expense	1,200
Sale of land	22,000	Service revenue	10,000
Share capital	50,000	Supplies	3,700
		Utilities expense	400

Requirements

1. Prepare the income statement, the statement of changes in equity, and the statement of cash flows for the month ended April 30, 2010, and the balance sheet at April 30, 2010. Draw arrows linking the statements.
2. Answer the following questions:
   a. How well did ShineBrite perform during its first month of operations?
   b. Where does ShineBrite stand financially at the end of April?

Answers

Requirement 1
Financial Statements of ShineBrite Car Wash, Inc.

ShineBrite Car Wash, Inc.
Income Statement
Month Ended April 30, 2010

Revenue:		
Service revenue		$10,000
Expenses:		
Salary expense	$1,200	
Rent expense	1,100	
Utilities expense	400	
Total expenses		2,700
Net income		$ 7,300

①

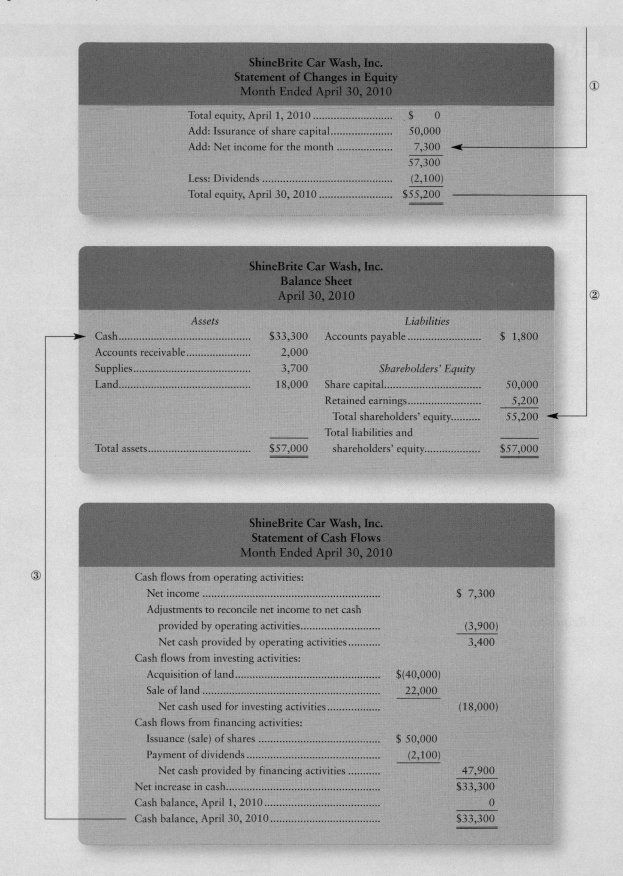

① **ShineBrite Car Wash, Inc.**
Statement of Changes in Equity
Month Ended April 30, 2010

Total equity, April 1, 2010	$ 0
Add: Issurance of share capital.....................	50,000
Add: Net income for the month	7,300
	57,300
Less: Dividends	(2,100)
Total equity, April 30, 2010	$55,200

② **ShineBrite Car Wash, Inc.**
Balance Sheet
April 30, 2010

Assets		*Liabilities*	
Cash..	$33,300	Accounts payable	$ 1,800
Accounts receivable......................	2,000		
Supplies...	3,700	*Shareholders' Equity*	
Land...	18,000	Share capital.................................	50,000
		Retained earnings.........................	5,200
		Total shareholders' equity..........	55,200
		Total liabilities and	
Total assets....................................	$57,000	shareholders' equity..................	$57,000

③ **ShineBrite Car Wash, Inc.**
Statement of Cash Flows
Month Ended April 30, 2010

Cash flows from operating activities:		
Net income		$ 7,300
Adjustments to reconcile net income to net cash		
provided by operating activities...........................		(3,900)
Net cash provided by operating activities...........		3,400
Cash flows from investing activities:		
Acquisition of land...	$(40,000)	
Sale of land	22,000	
Net cash used for investing activities.................		(18,000)
Cash flows from financing activities:		
Issuance (sale) of shares	$ 50,000	
Payment of dividends...	(2,100)	
Net cash provided by financing activities		47,900
Net increase in cash...		$33,300
Cash balance, April 1, 2010.......................................		0
Cash balance, April 30, 2010.....................................		$33,300

❙ Requirement 2

    a. ShineBrite performed rather well in April. Net income was $7,300—very good in relation to service revenue of $10,000. The company was able to pay cash dividends of $2,100.

    b. ShineBrite ended April with cash of $33,300. Total assets of $57,000 far exceed total liabilities of $1,800. Shareholders' equity of $55,200 provides a good cushion for borrowing. The business's financial position at April 30, 2010, is strong.

REVIEW THE FINANCIAL STATEMENTS

Quick Check (Answers are given on page 56.)

1. All of the following statements are true except one. Which statement is false?
   a. The organization that formulates IFRSs is the International Accounting Standards Board.
   b. Users of financial information are limited to shareholders of the company.
   c. Professional accountants are held to a high standard of ethical conduct.
   d. Bookkeeping is only a part of accounting.

2. Which of the following items are qualitative characteristics of financial information?
   a. Going concern and accrual accounting
   b. Relevance and reliability
   c. Materiality and Cost-benefits
   d. Assets and Liabilities

3. The accounting equation can be expressed as:
   a. Assets = Liabilities – Owners' Equity
   b. Assets + Liabilities = Owners' Equity
   c. Assets – Liabilities = Owners' Equity
   d. Owners' Equity - Assets = Liabilities

4. The nature of an asset is best described as:
   a. an economic resource that's expected to benefit future operations.
   b. something with physical form that's valued at cost in the accounting records.
   c. something owned by a business that has a ready market value.
   d. an economic resource representing cash or the right to receive cash in the future.

5. Which financial statement covers a period of time?
   a. Balance sheet   c. Statement of cash flows
   b. Income statement   d. Both b and c

6. How would net income be most likely to affect the accounting equation?
   a. Increase assets and increase liabilities
   b. Decrease assets and decrease liabilities
   c. Increase liabilities and decrease shareholders' equity
   d. Increase assets and increase shareholders' equity

7. During the year, EcoWash, Inc., has $120,000 in revenues, $50,000 in expenses, and $4,000 in dividend payments. Shareholders' equity changed by:
   a. +$66,000   c. –$66,000
   b. +$70,000   d. +$74,000

8. EcoWash in question 7 had a:
   a. net loss of $50,000.
   b. net income of $70,000.
   c. net income of $66,000.
   d. net income of $120,000.

9. Rochester Corporation holds cash of $11,000 and owes $27,000 on accounts payable. Rochester has accounts receivable of $40,000, inventory of $34,000, and land that cost $55,000. How much are Rochester's total assets and liabilities?

	Total assets	Liabilities
a.	$129,000	$27,000
b.	$27,000	$140,000
c.	$140,000	$27,000
d.	$140,000	$93,000

10. Which item(s) is (are) reported on the balance sheet?
    a. Inventory
    b. Accounts payable
    c. Retained earnings
    d. All of the above

11. During the year, McKenna Company's shareholders' equity increased from $38,000 to $50,000. McKenna earned net income of $18,000. How much in dividends did McKenna declare during the year?
    a. $0 (no dividends were paid)
    b. $6,000
    c. $12,000
    d. $7,000

12. Javis Company had total assets of $340,000 and total shareholders' equity of $130,000 at the beginning of the year. During the year assets increased by $70,000 and liabilities increased by $25,000. Shareholders' equity at the end of the year is:
    a. $95,000.
    b. $175,000.
    c. $200,000.
    d. $155,000.

13. Which of the following is a true statement about International Financial Reporting Standards?
    a. They are more exact (contain more rules) than U.S. generally accepted accounting principles.
    b. They are not being applied anywhere in the world yet, but soon will be.
    c. They are converging gradually with U.S. standards.
    d. They are not needed for U.S. businesses since the United States already has the strongest accounting standards in the world.

14. Which of the following is the most accurate statement regarding ethics as applied to decision making in accounting?
    a. Ethics involves making difficult choices under pressure, and should be kept in mind in making every decision, including those involving accounting.
    b. Ethics has no place in accounting, since accounting deals purely with numbers.
    c. It is impossible to learn ethical decision making, since it is just something you decide to do or not to do.
    d. Ethics is becoming less and less important as a field of study in business.

Accounting Vocabulary

accounting (p. 3) The information system that measures business activities, processes that information into reports and financial statements, and communicates the results to decision makers.

accounting equation (p. 12) The most basic relationship in accounting: Assets = Liabilities + Equity. Also Revenue – Expenses = Profit (Loss).

accrual basis (p. 14) Business transactions and other events are recognized when they occur and not when cash is received or paid.

asset (p. 11) An economic resource that is expected to be of benefit in the future.

balance sheet (p. 12) List of an entity's assets, liabilities, and owners' equity as at a specific date. Also called the statement of financial position.

cash (p. 20) Money or any medium of exchange that a bank accepts at face value.

conceptual framework (p. 7) the basic objective, principles and assumptions guiding the presentation and preparation of general purpose financial statements.

corporations (p. 6) A business owned by shareholders. A corporation is a legal entity, an "artificial person" in the eye of the law.

current asset (p. 20) An asset that is expected to be converted to cash, sold, or consumed during the next 12 months.

current liability (p. 21) A debt due to be paid within one year.

dividends (p. 13) Distributions (usually in the form of cash) by a corporation to its shareholders.

entity (p. 4) An organization or a section of an organization that, for accounting purposes, stands apart from other organizations and individuals as a separate economic unit.

equity (p. 11) The claim of the owners of a business to the assets of the business. Also called owners' equity, shareholders' equity or net assets.

ethics (p. 27) Standards of right and wrong that transcend economic and legal boundaries. Ethical standards deal with the way we treat others and restrain our own actions because of the desires, expectations, or rights of others, or with our obligations to them.

expenses (p. 11) Decrease in equity that results from operations; the cost of doing business; opposite of revenues.

financial accounting (p. 4) The branch of accounting that provides information to people outside the firm.

financial statements (p. 2) Business documents that report financial information about a business entity to decision makers.

financing activities (p. 22) Activities that obtain from investors and creditors the cash needed to launch and sustain the business; a section of the statement of cash flows.

gains (p. 11) usually separated from revenues. Part of income and result in an increase in equity.

general purpose financial statements (p. 7) The common set of financial statements prepared for all users of financial statements.

generally accepted accounting principles (GAAP) (p. 6) Accounting guidelines, usually in reference to US standards as formulated by the Financial Accounting Standards Board. By 2014, US GAAP is expected to converge with IFRS.

going concern (p. 11) An assumption that an entity will remain in operation for the foreseeable future.

income (p. 11) Increases in equity from revenue and gains.

income statement (p. 12) A financial statement listing an entity's revenues, expenses, and net income or net loss for a specific period. Part of Statement of Comprehensive Income.

International Financial Reporting Standards (IFRS) (p. 6) Accounting guidelines, formulated by the International Accounting Standards Board (IASB).

inventory (p. 20) The merchandise that a company hold for sale to customers.

investing activities (p. 22) Activities that increase or decrease the long-term assets available to the business; a section of the statement of cash flows.

liability (p. 11) An economic obligation payable to an individual or an organization outside the business.

losses (p. 11) usually separated from expenses, results in a reduction in equity.

management accounting (p. 4) The branch of accounting that generates information for the internal decision makers of a business, such as top executives.

materiality (p. 10) the importance or significant of information that may change the user's final assessment of a situation.

net income (p. 13) Excess of total revenues over total expenses. Also called net earnings or net profit.

net loss (p. 13) Excess of total expenses over total revenues.

net profit (p. 13) Another name for net income.

operating activities (p. 22) Activities that create revenue or expense in the entity's major line of business; a section of the statement of cash flows.

paid-in capital (p. 21) The amount of shareholders' equity that shareholders have contributed to the corporation.

partnership (p. 5) An association of two or more persons who co-owns a business for profit.

property, plant and equipment or PPE (p. 20) Long-lived assets, such as land, buildings, and equipment, used in the operation of the business. Also called fixed assets.

proprietorship (p. 5) A business with a single owner.

retained earnings (p. 11) The amount of shareholders' equity that the corporation has earned through profitable operation that has been retained in the business (not distributed back to shareholders).

revenue (p. 11) Increase in retained earnings from delivering goods or services to customers or clients.

share capital (p. 11) Proof of ownership in a company. Amount invested by owners into the business through share ownership.

shareholder (p. 6) A person who owns shares in a corporation.

statement of cash flows (p. 22) Reports cash receipts and cash payments classified according to the entity's major activities: operating, investing, and financing.

statement of changes in equity (p. 17). Provides a reconciliation of the movement of equity items during a financial period. Affected share issuance, share cancellation, net income (or net loss) and dividends paid.

statement of comprehensive income (p. 15) Net Profit (loss) for the period plus other comprehensive income.

statement of financial position (p. 19) Another name for the balance sheet.

ASSESS YOUR PROGRESS

Short Exercises

S1-1 (*Learning Objective 3: Using the accounting equation*) Suppose you manage a Pizza Sauce restaurant. Identify the missing amount for each situation:

	Total Assets	=	Total Liabilities	+	Shareholders' Equity
a.	$?		$130,000		$210,000
b.	250,000		70,000		?
c.	190,000		?		80,000

S1-2 (*Learning Objective 5: Making ethical judgments*) Good business and accounting practices require the exercise of good judgment. How should ethics be incorporated into making accounting judgments? Why is ethics important?

S1-3 (*Learning Objective 1: Organizing a business*) A Healthy Planet, Inc., needs funds, and Mary Barry, the president, has asked you to consider investing in the business. Answer the following questions about the different ways that Barry might organize the business. Explain each answer.

    a. What forms of organization will enable the owners of A Healthy Planet to limit their risk of loss to the amounts they have invested in the business?

    b. What form of business organization will give Barry the most freedom to manage the business as she wishes?

    c. What form of organization will give creditors the maximum protection in the event that A Healthy Planet fails and cannot pay its debts?

S1-4 (*Learning Objective 2: Applying accounting assumptions*) Daniel Newman is chairman of the board of Quality Food Brands, Inc. Suppose Mr. Newman has just founded Quality Food Brands, and assume that he treats his home and other personal assets as part of Quality Food Brands. Answer these questions about the evaluation of Quality Food Brands, Inc.

    1. Which accounting principle governs this situation?

    2. How can the proper application of this accounting concept give Newman and others a realistic view of Quality Food Brands, Inc.? Explain in detail.

S1-5 (*Learning Objective 2: Understanding Conceptual Framework*) Identify the accounting assumption, principle or qualitative characteristic that best applies to each of the following situations:

    a. At the height of the financial crisis, there were speculations that Lehman Brothers would not be able to meet its obligations before it eventually filed for bankruptcy on September 15, 2008.

    b. ComfortDelgro, a Singapore-based transportation company, has been using an 8-year lifespan on the road worthiness of its fleet of buses. Better maintenance and servicing have allowed the company to use its buses for a period of 12 years.

    c. Toyota wants to determine which division of the company – Toyota or Lexus – is more profitable.

    d. You are about to report your net income for the year. It looks like a record breaking year, sales are expected to top $10 million mark for the first time. However, you were uncertain if you have actually delivered the goods ordered by one customer on December 30, 2010 totaling $500,000.

S1-6 (*Learning Objective 3: Using the accounting equation*)

1. Use the accounting equation to show how to determine the amount of a company's owners' equity. How would your answer change if you were analyzing your own household or a single Burger King's outlet?
2. If you know the assets and the owners' equity of a business, how can you measure its liabilities? Give the equation.

S1-7 (*Learning Objective 1: Defining key accounting terms*) Accounting definitions are precise, and you must understand the vocabulary to properly use accounting. Sharpen your understanding of key terms by answering the following questions:

1. How do the assets and owners' equity of Microsoft Corporation differ from each other? Which one (assets or owners' equity) must be at least as large as the other? Which one can be smaller than the other?
2. How are Microsoft's liabilities and owners' equity similar? Different?

S1-8 (*Learning Objective 1: Classifying assets, liabilities, and owners' equity*) Consider Target, a large retailer. Classify the following items as an Asset (A), a Liability (L), or Shareholders' Equity (S) for Target:

a. ____ Accounts payable
b. ____ Share capital
c. ____ Supplies
d. ____ Retained earnings
e. ____ Land
f. ____ Prepaid expenses
g. ____ Accounts receivable
h. ____ Long-term debt
i. ____ Merchandise inventory
j. ____ Notes payable
k. ____ Expenses payable
l. ____ Equipment

S1-9 (*Learning Objectives 1, 4: Using accounting vocabulary; using the income statement*)

1. Identify the two basic categories of items on an income statement.
2. What do we call the bottom line of the income statement?

S1-10 (*Learning Objective 4: Preparing an income statement*) Call Anywhere Wireless, Inc., began 2010 with total assets of $130 million and ended 2010 with assets of $165 million. During 2010 Call Anywhere earned revenues of $94 million and had expenses of $23 million. Call Anywhere paid dividends of $13 million in 2010. Prepare the company's income statement for the year ended December 31, 2010, complete with an appropriate heading.

S1-11 (*Learning Objective 4: Preparing a statement of changes in equity*) Roam Corp. began 2010 with retained earnings of $210 million and share capital of $100 million. Revenues during the year were $380 million and expenses totaled $250 million. Roam declared dividends of $43 million. What was the company's ending balance of retained earnings? To answer this question, prepare Roam's statement of changes in equity for the year ended December 31, 2010, complete with its proper heading.

S1-12 (*Learning Objective 4: Preparing a balance sheet*) At December 31, 2010, Tommer Products has cash of $12,000, receivables of $5,000, and inventory of $42,000. The company's equipment totals $82,000. Tommer owes accounts payable of $17,000, and long-term notes payable of $78,000. Share capital amounts to $14,800.

Prepare Tommer's balance sheet at December 31, 2010, complete with its proper heading. Use the accounting equation to compute retained earnings.

S1-13 (*Learning Objective 4: Preparing a statement of cash flows*) Lanos Medical, Inc., ended 2009 with cash of $25,000. During 2010, Lanos earned net income of $95,000 and had adjustments to reconcile net income to net cash provided by operations totaling $20,000 (this is a negative amount).

Lanos paid $35,000 to purchase equipment during 2010. During 2010, the company paid dividends of $15,000.

Prepare Lanos' statement of cash flows for the year ended December 31, 2010, complete with its proper heading.

S1-14 *(Learning Objectives 1, 4: Using accounting vocabulary; identifying items with the appropriate financial statement)* Suppose you are analyzing the financial statements of Murphy Radiology, Inc. Identify each item with its appropriate financial statement, using the following abbreviations: Income statement (IS), Statement of Changes in Equity (SCE), Balance sheet (BS), and Statement of cash flows (SCF). Three items appear on two financial statements, and one item shows up on three statements.

a. ____ Dividends
b. ____ Salary expense
c. ____ Inventory
d. ____ Sales revenue
e. ____ Retained earnings
f. ____ Net cash provided by operating activities
g. ____ Net income

h. ____ Cash
i. ____ Net cash used for financing activities
j. ____ Accounts payable
k. ____ Share capital
l. ____ Interest revenue
m. ____ Long-term debt
n. ____ Increase or decrease in cash

S1-15 *(Learning Objectives 2, 4: Applying accounting concepts, assumptions and principles to explain business activity)* Apply your understanding of the relationships among the financial statements to answer these questions.

a. How can a business earn large profits but have a small balance of retained earnings?
b. Give two reasons why a business can have a steady stream of net income over a six-year period and still experience a cash shortage.
c. If you could pick a single source of cash for your business, what would it be? Why?
d. How can a business lose money several years in a row and still have plenty of cash?

Exercises

All of the A and B exercises can be found within MyAccountingLab, an online homework and practice environment. Your instructor may ask you to complete these exercises using MyAccountingLab.

(Group A)

E1-16A *(Learning Objective 3, 4: Using the accounting equation; evaluating business operations)* Compute the missing amount in the accounting equation for each company (amounts in billions):

	Assets	Liabilities	Owners' Equity
Fresh Produce	$?	$ 9	$17
Hudson Bank	29	?	15
Pet Lovers	21	10	?

Which company appears to have the strongest financial position? Explain your reasoning.

E1-17A *(Learning Objectives 3, 4: Using the accounting equation; evaluating business operations)* Hombran Doughnuts has current assets of $290 million; property, plant and equipment of $490 million; and other assets totaling $150 million. Current liabilities are $150 million and long-term liabilities total $310 million.

▌ Requirements

1. Use these data to write Hombran Doughnuts' accounting equation.
2. How much in resources does Hombran have to work with?
3. How much does Hombran owe creditors?
4. How much of the company's assets do the Hombran shareholders actually own?

E1-18A (*Learning Objectives 3, 4: Using the accounting equation; evaluating business operations*)   Nelson, Inc.'s comparative balance sheet at January 31, 2011, and 2010, reports (in millions):

	2011	2010
Total assets	$39	$31
Total liabilities	10	9

I Requirements

Three situations about Nelson's issuance of shares and payment of dividends during the year ended January 31, 2011, follow. For each situation, use the accounting equation and the statement of changes in equity to compute the amount of Nelson's net income or net loss during the year ended January 31, 2011.

1. Nelson issued $11 million of shares and paid no dividends.
2. Nelson issued no shares but paid dividends of $11 million.
3. Nelson issued $55 million of shares and paid dividends of $32 million.

E1-19A (*Learning Objective 3: Using the accounting equation*) Answer these questions about two companies.

1. Clay, Inc., began the year with total liabilities of $50,000 and total shareholders' equity of $80,000. During the year, total assets increased by 35%. How much are total assets at the end of the year?
2. EastWest Airlines Ltd. began the year with total assets of $100,000 and total liabilities of $7,000. Net income for the year was $25,000, and dividends were zero. How much is shareholders' equity at the end of the year?

E1-20A (*Learning Objectives 4, 5: Evaluating business operations; making business decisions*) Assume Facebook is expanding into Ireland. The company must decide where to locate and how to finance the expansion. Identify the financial statement where these decision makers can find the following information about Facebook, Inc. In some cases, more than one statement will report the needed data.

a. Share capital
b. Income tax payable
c. Dividends
d. Income tax expense
e. Ending balance of retained earnings
f. Total assets
g. Long-term debt
h. Revenue

i. Cash spent to acquire the building
j. Selling, general, and administrative expenses
k. Adjustments to reconcile net income to net cash provided by operations
l. Ending cash balance
m. Current liabilities
n. Net income

E1-21A (*Learning Objectives 3, 4: Using the accounting equation; preparing a balance sheet*) Amounts of the assets and liabilities of Ellen Samuel Banking Company, as of January 31, 2010, are given as follows. Also included are revenue and expense figures for the year ended on that date (amounts in millions):

■ spreadsheet

Total revenue	$ 37.8	Investment assets	$169.6
Receivables	0.9	Property and equipment, net	1.9
Current liabilities	151.1	Other expenses	6.9
Share capital	14	Retained earnings, beginning	8.6
Interest expense	0.8	Retained earnings, ending	?
Salary and other employee expenses	17.7	Cash	2.1
Long-term liabilities	2.8	Other assets	14.4

I Requirement

1. Prepare the balance sheet of Ellen Samuel Banking Company at January 31, 2010. Use the accounting equation to compute ending retained earnings.

■ **spreadsheet**

E1-22A *(Learning Objective 4: Preparing an income statement and a statement of changes in equity)* This exercise should be used with Exercise 1-21A. Refer to the data of Ellen Samuel Banking Company in Exercise 1-21A.

I Requirements

1. Prepare the income statement of Ellen Samuel Banking Company, for the year ended January 31, 2010.
2. What amount of dividends did Ellen Samuel declare during the year ended January 31, 2010? Hint: Prepare a statement of changes in equity.

E1-23A *(Learning Objective 4: Preparing a statement of cash flows)* Lucky, Inc., began 2010 with $87,000 in cash. During 2010, Lucky earned net income of $410,000, and adjustments to reconcile net income to net cash provided by operations totaled $70,000, a positive amount. Investing activities used cash of $420,000, and financing activities provided cash of $72,000. Lucky ended 2010 with total assets of $260,000 and total liabilities of $115,000.

I Requirement

1. Prepare Lucky, Inc.'s statement of cash flows for the year ended December 31, 2010. Identify the data items given that do not appear on the statement of cash flows. Also identify the financial statement that reports the unused items.

E1-24A *(Learning Objective 4: Preparing an income statement and a statement of changes in equity)* Assume an Earl Copy Center ended the month of July 2010 with these data:

Payments of cash:			
Acquisition of equipment	$420,000	Cash balance, June 30, 2010	$ 0
Dividends	4,800	Cash balance, July 31, 2010	10,900
Retained earnings		Cash receipts:	
June 30, 2010	0	Issuance of shares	
Retained earnings		to owners	69,500
July 31, 2010	?	Rent expense	2,200
Utilities expense	10,000	Share capital	69,500
Adjustments to reconcile		Equipment	420,000
net income to net cash		Office supplies	14,800
provided by operations	2,200	Accounts payable	17,000
Salary expense	167,000	Service revenue	543,200

I Requirement

1. Prepare the income statement and the statement of changes in equity of Earl Copy Center, Inc., for the month ended July 31, 2010.

E1-25A *(Learning Objective 4: Preparing a balance sheet)* Refer to the data in Exercise 1-24A.

I Requirement

1. Prepare the balance sheet of Earl Copy Center, Inc., for July 31, 2010.

E1-26A *(Learning Objective 4: Preparing a statement of cash flows)* Refer to the data in Exercises 1-24A and 1-25A.

I *Requirement*

1. Prepare the statement of cash flows of Earl Copy Center, Inc., for the month ended July 31, 2010. Also explain the relationship among income statement, statement of changes in equity, balance sheet, and statement of cash flows.

E1-27A *(Learning Objectives 4, 5: Evaluating a business; advising a business)* This exercise should be used in conjunction with Exercises 1-24A through 1-26A.

The owner of Earl Copy Center seeks your advice as to whether he should cease operations or continue the business. Complete the report giving him your opinion of net income, dividends, financial position, and cash flows during his first month of operations. Cite specifics from the financial statements to support your opinion. Conclude your memo with advice on whether to stay in business or cease operations.

writing assignment ■

(Group B)

E1-28B *(Learning Objectives 3, 4: Using the accounting equation; evaluating business operations)*   Compute the missing amount in the accounting equation for each company (amounts in billions):

	Assets	Liabilities	Owners' Equity
DJ Video Rentals	$?	$ 8	$18
Ernie's Bank	34	?	14
Hudson Gift and Cards	20	12	?

Which company appears to have the strongest financial position? Explain your reasoning.

E1-29B *(Learning Objectives 3, 4: Using the accounting equation; evaluating business operations)*   Tinman Doughnuts has current assets of $270 million; property, plant and equipment of $470 million; and other assets totaling $110 million. Current liabilities are $110 million and long-term liabilities total $370 million.

I *Requirements*

1. Use these data to write Tinman's accounting equation.
2. How much in resources does Tinman have to work with?
3. How much does Tinman owe creditors?
4. How much of the company's assets do the Tinman shareholders actually own?

E1-30B *(Learning Objectives 3, 4: Using the accounting equation; evaluating business operations)*   Winkler, Inc.'s comparative balance sheet at January 31, 2011, and 2010, reports (in millions):

	2011	2010
Total assets	$38	$24
Total liabilities	11	1

❙ Requirements

Three situations about Winkler's issuance of shares and payment of dividends during the year ended January 31, 2011, follow. For each situation, use the accounting equation and the statement of changes in equity to compute the amount of Winkler's net income or net loss during the year ended January 31, 2011.

1. Winkler issued $15 million of shares and paid no dividends.
2. Winkler issued no shares but paid dividends of $11 million.
3. Winkler issued $90 million of shares and paid dividends of $35 million.

E1-31B *(Learning Objective 3: Applying the accounting equation)* Answer these questions about two companies.

1. Sapphire, Inc., began the year with total liabilities of $90,000 and total shareholders' equity of $35,000. During the year, total assets increased by 30%. How much are total assets at the end of the year?
2. Southbound Airlines Ltd. began the year with total assets of $95,000 and total liabilities of $47,000. Net income for the year was $26,000, and dividends were zero. How much is shareholders' equity at the end of the year?

E1-32B *(Learning Objectives 4, 5: Evaluating business operations; making business decisions)* Assume Lesley, Inc., is expanding into Sweden. The company must decide where to locate and how to finance the expansion. Identify the financial statement where these decision makers can find the following information about Lesley, Inc. In some cases, more than one statement will report the needed data.

a. Share capital
b. Net income
c. Current liabilities
d. Share capital
e. Income tax payable
f. Ending balance of retained earnings
g. Revenue
h. Ending cash balance
i. Dividends
j. Total Assets
k. Long-term debt
l. Selling, general, and administrative expenses
m. Cash spent to acquire the building
n. Adjustments to reconcile net income to net cash provided by operations

■ **spreadsheet**

E1-33B *(Learning Objectives 3, 4: Using the accounting equation; preparing a balance sheet)* Amounts of the assets and liabilities of Eliza Bennet Banking Company, as of May 31, 2010, are given as follows. Also included are revenue and expense figures for the year ended on that date (amounts in millions):

Total revenue	$ 33.5	Investment assets	$169.8
Receivables	0.2	Property and equipment, net	1.6
Current liabilities	155.1	Other expenses	6.6
Share capital	14.9	Retained earnings, beginning	8.6
Interest expense	0.4	Retained earnings, ending	?
Salary and other employee expenses	17.5	Cash	2.7
Long-term liabilities	2.3	Other assets	14.9

❙ Requirement

1. Prepare the balance sheet of Eliza Bennet Banking Company at May 31, 2010. Use the accounting equation to compute ending retained earnings

■ **spreadsheet**

E1-34B *(Learning Objective 4: Preparing an income statement and a statement of changes in equity)* This exercise should be used with Exercise 1-33B.

❙ Requirements

1. Prepare the income statement of Eliza Bennet Banking Company, for the year ended May 31, 2010.

2. What amount of dividends did Eliza Bennet declare during the year ended May 31, 2010? Hint: Prepare a statement of changes in equity.

E1-35B *(Learning Objective 4: Preparing a statement of cash flows)* Fortune, Inc., began 2010 with $83,000 in cash. During 2010, Fortune earned net income of $440,000, and adjustments to reconcile net income to net cash provided by operations totaled $60,000, a positive amount. Investing activities used cash of $390,000, and financing activities provided cash of $65,000. Fortune ended 2010 with total assets of $300,000 and total liabilities of $120,000.

❙ Requirement

1. Prepare Fortune, Inc.'s statement of cash flows for the year ended December 31, 2010. Identify the data items given that do not appear on the statement of cash flows. Also identify the financial statement that reports each unused items.

E1-36B *(Learning Objective 4: Preparing an income statement and a statement of changes in equity)* Assume a Carson Copy Center ended the month of July 2011 with these data:

Payments of cash:				
Acquisition of equipment	$410,000	Cash balance, June 30, 2011	$	0
Dividends	4,100	Cash balance, July 31, 2011		9,500
Retained earnings		Cash receipts:		
June 30, 2011	0	Issuance of shares		
Retained earnings		to owners		54,200
July 31, 2011	?	Rent expense		2,900
Utilities expense	10,800	Share capital		54,200
Adjustments to reconcile		Equipment		410,000
net income to net cash		Office supplies		15,000
provided by operations	2,900	Accounts payable		17,900
Salary expense	162,000	Service revenue		542,200

❙ Requirement

1. Prepare the income statement and the statement of changes in equity of Carson Copy Center, Inc., for the month ended July 31, 2011.

E1-37B *(Learning Objective 4: Preparing a balance sheet)* Refer to the data in Exercise 1-36B.

❙ Requirement

1. Prepare the balance sheet of Carson Copy Center, Inc., at July 31, 2011.

E1-38B *(Learning Objective 4: Preparing a statement of cash flows)* Refer to the data in Exercises 1-36B and 1-37B.

❙ Requirement

1. Prepare the statement of cash flows of Carson Copy Center, Inc., for the month ended July 31, 2011. Also explain the relationship among income statement, statement of changes in equity, balance sheet, and statement of cash flows.

E1-39B *(Learning Objectives 4, 5: Evaluating a business; advising a business)* This exercise should be used in conjunction with Exercises 1-36B through 1-38B.

writing assignment ■

The owner of Carson Copy Center now seeks your advice as to whether he should cease operations or continue the business. Complete the report giving him your opinion of net income, dividends, financial position, and cash flows during his first month of operations. Cite specifics from the financial statements to support your opinion. Conclude your memo with advice on whether to stay in business or cease operations.

Quiz

Test your understanding of the financial statements by answering the following questions. Select the best choice from among the possible answers given.

Q1-40 The *primary* objective of financial reporting is to provide information
a. useful for making investment and credit decisions.
b. about the profitability of the enterprise.
c. to the federal government.
d. on the cash flows of the company.

Q1-41 Which type of business organization provides the least amount of protection for bankers and other creditors of the company?
a. Partnership
b. Proprietorship
c. Corporation
d. Both a and b

Q1-42 Assets are usually reported at their
a. historical cost.
b. current market value.
c. appraised value.
d. none of the above (fill in the blank).

Q1-43 During March, assets increased by $19,000 and liabilities increased by $6,000. Shareholders' equity must have
a. increased by $13,000.
b. decreased by $13,000.
c. increased by $25,000.
d. decreased by $25,000.

Q1-44 The amount a company expects to collect from customers appears on the
a. statement of cash flows.
b. balance sheet in the current assets section.
c. income statement in the expenses section.
d. balance sheet in the shareholders' equity section.

Q1-45 All of the following are current assets except
a. Inventory.
b. Sales Revenue.
c. Cash.
d. Accounts Receivable.

Q1-46 Revenues are
a. decreases in liabilities resulting from paying off loans.
b. increases in paid-in capital resulting from the owners investing in the business.
c. increases in retained earnings resulting from selling products or performing services.
d. all of the above.

Q1-47 The financial statement that reports revenues and expenses is called the
a. statement of cash flows.
b. income statement.
c. statement of changes in equity.
d. balance sheet.

Q1-48 Another name for the balance sheet is the
a. statement of financial position
b. statement of operations.
c. statement of profit and loss.
d. statement of earnings.

Q1-49 Pinker Corporation began the year with cash of $30,000 and a computer that cost $25,000. During the year Pinker earned sales revenue of $135,000 and had the following expenses: salaries, $57,000; rent, $11,000; and utilities, $4,000. At year-end Pinker's cash balance was down to $18,000. How much net income (or net loss) did Pinker experience for the year?
a. ($12,000)
b. $135,000
c. $63,000
d. $123,000

Q1-50 Advanced Instruments had retained earnings of $155,000 at December 31, 2009. Net income for 2010 totaled $100,000, and dividends for 2010 were $25,000. How much retained earnings should Advanced report at December 31, 2010?
a. $255,000
b. $180,000
c. $230,000
d. $155,000

Q1-51 Net income appears on which financial statement(s)?
a. Income statement
b. Statement of changes in equity
c. Balance sheet
d. Both a and b

Q1-52 Cash paid to purchase a building appears on the statement of cash flows among the
a. Shareholders' equity.
b. Investing activities.
c. Financing activities.
d. Operating activities.

Q1-53 The shareholders' equity of Diakovsky Company at the beginning and end of 2010 totaled $15,000 and $20,000, respectively. Assets at the beginning of 2010 were $27,000. If the liabilities of Diakovsky Company increased by $9,000 in 2010, how much were total assets at the end of 2010? Use the accounting equation.
a. $45,000
b. $34,000
c. $50,000
d. $41,000

Q1-54 Robbin Company had the following on the dates indicated:

	12/31/10	12/31/09
Total assets	$740,000	$510,000
Total liabilities	290,000	190,000

Robbin had no share transactions in 2010 and, thus, the change in shareholders' equity for 2010 was due to net income and dividends. If dividends were $55,000, how much was Robbin's net income for 2010? Use the accounting equation and the statement of changes in equity.
a. $185,000
b. $245,000
c. $155,000
d. $215,000

Problems

All of the following A and B problems can be found within MyAccountingLab, an online homework and practice environment. Your instructor may ask you to complete these problems using MyAccountingLab.

(Group A)

P1-55A (*Learning Objectives 1, 2, 4: Applying accounting vocabulary, concepts, and principles; evaluating business operations*) Assume that the A division of Smith Corporation experienced the following transactions during the year ended December 31, 2011:

  a. Suppose division A supplied copy products for a customer for the discounted price of $252,000. Under normal conditions they would have provided these services for $300,000. Other revenues totaled $52,000.

  b. Salaries cost the division $21,000 to provide these services. The division had to pay employees overtime occasionally. Ordinarily the salary cost for these services would have been $18,000.

c. All other expenses totaled $247,000 for the year. Income tax expense was 35% of income before tax.

d. The A division has two operating subdivisions: basic retail and special contracts. Each subdivision is accounted for separately to indicate how well each is performing. However the A division combines the statements of all subdivisions to show results for the A division as a whole.

e. Inflation affects the amounts that the A division must pay for copy machines. To show the effects of inflation, net income would drop by $4,000.

f. If the A division were to go out of business, the sale of its assets would bring in $147,000 in cash.

Requirements

1. Prepare the A division's income statement for the year ended December 31, 2011.
2. For items a through f, identify the accounting concept, assumption, or principle that provides guidance in accounting for the item. State how you have applied the concept or principle in preparing the income statement.

P1-56A (*Learning Objectives 3, 4: Using the accounting equation; evaluating business operations*) Compute the missing amount (?) for each company—amounts in millions.

	Sapphire Corp.	Lance Co.	Branch Inc.
Beginning			
Assets.....................................	$83	$35	$?
Liabilities	47	23	2
Share capital......................	2	2	1
Retained earnings...............	?	10	4
Ending			
Assets.....................................	$?	$54	$8
Liabilities	49	34	?
Share capital......................	2	?	1
Retained earnings...............	33	?	?
Income statement			
Revenues............................	$221	$?	$18
Expenses	213	152	?
Net income.........................	?	?	?
Retained Earnings			
Beginning retained earnings	$34	$10	$ 4
+ Net income.........................	?	10	3
− Dividends..........................	(9)	(2)	(3)
= Ending retained earnings....	$33	$18	$ 4

At the end of the year, which company has the:

- Highest net income?
- Highest percent of net income to revenues?

P1-57A (*Learning Objectives 3, 4, 5: Using the accounting equation; preparing a balance sheet; making decisions*) The manager of Headlines, Inc., prepared the company's balance sheet while the accountant was ill. The balance sheet contains numerous errors. In particular, the manager knew that the balance sheet should balance, so he plugged in the shareholders' equity amount needed to achieve this balance. The shareholders' equity amount is *not* correct. All other amounts are accurate.

Headlines, Inc. Balance Sheet For the Month Ended June 30, 2010			
Assets		**Liabilities**	
Cash..	$ 8,000	Notes receivable......................	$ 13,000
Equipment...............................	39,500	Interest expense......................	1,800
Accounts payable....................	5,000	Office supplies.........................	1,000
Utilities expense......................	1,700	Accounts receivable................	2,600
Advertising expense................	500	Note payable...........................	55,500
Land..	77,000	Total.......................................	73,900
Salary expense.........................	4,000	**Shareholders' Equity**	
		Shareholders' equity..............	61,800
Total assets.............................	$135,700	Total liabilities.......................	$135,700

I Requirements

1. Prepare the correct balance sheet and date it properly. Compute total assets, total liabilities, and shareholders' equity.
2. Is Headlines actually in better (or worse) financial position than the erroneous balance sheet reports? Give the reason for your answer.
3. Identify the accounts listed on the incorrect balance sheet that should not be reported on the balance sheet. State why you excluded them from the correct balance sheet you prepared for Requirement 1. On which financial statement should these accounts appear?

P1-58A (*Learning Objectives 2, 4, 5: Preparing a balance sheet; applying the entity assumption; making business decisions*) Sandy Healey is a realtor. She organized the business as a corporation on April 16, 2011. The business received $95,000 cash from Healey and issued shares to Healey. Consider the following facts as of April 30, 2011.

a. Healey has $16,000 in her personal bank account and $71,000 in the business bank account.
b. Healey owes $1,000 on a personal charge account with The Loft.
c. Healey acquired business furniture for $41,000 on April 25. Of this amount, the business owes $33,000 on accounts payable at April 30.
d. Office supplies on hand at the real estate office total $11,000.
e. Healey's business owes $36,000 on a note payable for some land acquired for a total price of $110,000.
f. Healey's business spent $24,000 for a Realty Universe franchise, which entitles her to represent herself as an agent. Realty Universe is a national affiliation of independent real estate agents. This franchise is a business asset.
g. Healey owes $140,000 on a personal mortgage on her personal residence, which she acquired in 2003 for a total price of $340,000.

I Requirements

1. Prepare the balance sheet of the real estate business of Sandy Healey Realtor, Inc., at April 30, 2011.
2. Does it appear that the realty business can pay its debts? How can you tell?
3. Identify the personal items given in the preceding facts that should not be reported on the balance sheet of the business.

■ **spreadsheet**

P1-59A *(Learning Objectives 4, 5: Preparing an income statement, a statement of changes in equity and a balance sheet; using accounting information to make decisions)* The assets and liabilities of Post Maple, Inc., as of December 31, 2010, and revenues and expenses for the year ended on that date follow.

Land.....................	$ 8,200	Equipment.........................	$ 33,000
Note payable.....................	28,000	Interest expense.................	4,200
Property tax expense...........	1,900	Interest payable.................	1,200
Rent expense.....................	14,000	Accounts payable	11,000
Accounts receivable.............	24,000	Salary expense...................	34,000
Service revenue..................	145,000	Building............................	126,000
Supplies............................	2,200	Cash................................	15,000
Utilities expense	3,000	Share capital.....................	1,300

Beginning retained earnings was $117,000, and dividends totaled $38,000 for the year.

I Requirements

1. Prepare the income statement of Post Maple, Inc., for the year ended December 31, 2010.
2. Prepare the company's statement of changes in equity for the year.
3. Prepare the company's balance sheet at December 31, 2010.
4. Analyze Post Maple, Inc., by answering these questions:
   a. Was Post Maple profitable during 2010? By how much?
   b. Did retained earnings increase or decrease? By how much?
   c. Which is greater, total liabilities or total equity? Who owns more of Post Maple's assets, creditors of the company or the Post Maple's shareholders?

P1-60A *(Learning Objective 4: Preparing a statement of cash flows)* The following data come from the financial statements of The Water Sport Company for the year ended May 31, 2011 (in millions):

Purchases of property,		Other investing cash	
plant and equipment	$ 3,515	payments............................	$ 180
Net income...........................	3,030	Accounts receivable...............	500
Adjustments to reconcile net		Payment of dividends	290
income to net cash provided		Share capital.........................	4,850
by operating activities	2,370	Issuance of shares..................	170
Revenues.............................	59,200	Sales of property, plant	
Cash, beginning of year........	275	and equipment	30
end of year	1,890	Retained earnings..................	12,990
Cost of goods sold...............	37,450		

I Requirements

1. Prepare a cash flow statement for the year ended May 31, 2011. Not all items given appear on the cash flow statement.
2. What activities provided the largest source amount of cash? Is this a sign of financial strength or weakness?

P1-61A (*Learning Objective 4: Analyzing a company's financial statements*) Summarized versions of Cora Corporation's financial statements are given for two recent years.

	2010	2009
Income Statement	**(In Thousands)**	
Revenues	$ k	$15,750
Cost of goods sold	11,030	a
Other expenses	1,220	1,170
Income before income taxes	1,580	1,830
Income taxes (35% tax rate)	l	641
Net income	$ m	$ b
Statement of Changes in Equity		
Beginning balance	$ n	$ 3,070
Shares bought back	(20)	0
Net income	o	c
Dividends	(98)	(120)
Ending balance	$ p	$ d
Balance Sheet		
Assets:		
Cash	$ q	$ e
Property, plant and equipment	1,600	1,725
Other assets	r	10,184
Total assets	$ s	$13,239
Liabilities:		
Current liabilities	$ t	$ 5,650
Notes payable and long-term debt	4,350	3,380
Other liabilities	50	70
Total liabilities	$ 9,350	$ f
Shareholders' Equity:		
Share capital	$ 390	$ 410
Retained earnings	u	g
Total shareholders' equity	v	4,139
Total liabilities and shareholders' equity	$ w	$ h
Cash Flow Statement		
Net cash provided by operating activities	$ x	$ 950
Net cash used in investing activities	(230)	(300)
Net cash used in financing activities	(560)	(540)
Increase (decrease) in cash	(90)	i
Cash at beginning of year	y	1,220
Cash at end of year	$ z	$ j

❙ Requirement

1. Determine the missing amounts denoted by the letters.

(Group B)

P1-62B (*Learning Objectives 1, 2, 4: Applying accounting vocabulary, concepts, and principles to the income statement; evaluating business operations*) Assume that the A division of Perez Corporation experienced the following transactions during the year ended December 31, 2011:

   a. Suppose division A supplied copy products for a customer for the discounted price of $263,000. Under normal conditions they would have provided these services for $296,000. Other revenues totaled $55,000.

b. Salaries cost the division $24,000 to provide these services. The division had to pay employees overtime occasionally. Ordinarily the salary cost for these services would have been $18,100.

c. All other expenses, excluding income taxes, totaled $235,000 for the year. Income tax expense was 33% of income before tax.

d. The A division has two operating subdivisions: basic retail and special contracts. Each division is accounted for separately to indicate how well each is performing. However, the A division combines the statements of all subdivisions to show results for the A division as a whole.

e. Inflation affects the amounts that the A division must pay for copy machines. To show the effects of inflation, net income would drop by $1,000.

f. If A division were to go out of business, the sale of its assets would bring in $145,000 in cash.

❚ Requirements

1. Prepare the A division's income statement for the year ended December 31, 2011.
2. For items a through f, identify the accounting concept or principle that provides guidance in accounting for the item described. State how you have applied the concept or principle in preparing the income statement.

P1-63B (*Learning Objective 3, 4: Using the accounting equation; evaluating business operations*) Compute the missing amount (?) for each company—amounts in millions.

	Diamond Corp.	Lally Co.	Bryant Inc.
Beginning			
Assets..................................	$82	$25	$?
Liabilities	48	21	5
Share capital........................	3	2	1
Retained earnings...............	?	2	2
Ending			
Assets..................................	$?	$43	$10
Liabilities	50	34	?
Share capital........................	3	?	1
Retained earnings...............	30	?	?
Income statement			
Revenues.............................	$223	$?	$26
Expenses	215	159	?
Net income..........................	?	?	?
Retained Earnings			
Beginning retained earnings	$31	$ 2	$ 2
+ Net income........................	?	7	4
– Dividends..........................	(9)	(2)	(3)
= Ending retained earnings....	$30	$ 7	$ 3

Which company has the:

- Highest net income?
- Highest percent of net income to revenues?

P1-64B (*Learning Objectives 3, 4, 5: Using the accounting equation; preparing a balance sheet; making decisions*) The manager of News Maker, Inc., prepared the company's balance sheet while the accountant was ill. The balance sheet contains numerous errors. In particular, the manager knew that the balance sheet should balance, so he plugged in the shareholders' equity amount needed to achieve this balance. The shareholders' equity amount is *not* correct. All other amounts are accurate.

News Maker, Inc.
Balance Sheet
For the Month Ended November 30, 2010

Assets		Liabilities	
Cash...	$ 7,500	Notes receivable........................	$ 14,500
Equipment................................	39,000	Interest expense........................	1,600
Accounts payable.....................	4,000	Office supplies..........................	900
Utilities expense......................	1,700	Accounts receivable.................	3,400
Advertising expense................	400	Note payable............................	55,000
Land...	82,000	Total	75,400
Salary expense.........................	4,500	**Shareholders' Equity**	
		Shareholders' equity	63,700
Total assets..............................	$139,100	Total liabilities	$139,100

Requirements

1. Prepare the correct balance sheet and date it properly. Compute total assets, total liabilities, and shareholders' equity.
2. Is News Maker in better (or worse) financial position than the erroneous balance sheet reports? Give the reason for your answer.
3. Identify the accounts that should *not* be reported on the balance sheet. State why you excluded them from the correct balance sheet you prepared for Requirement 1. On which financial statement should these accounts appear?

P1-65B (*Learning Objectives 2, 4, 5: Preparing a balance sheet; applying the entity assumption; making business decisions*) Jeana Hart is a realtor. She organized her business as a corporation on September 16, 2011. The business received $95,000 from Hart and issued shares to Hart. Consider these facts as of September 30, 2011.

    a. Hart has $15,000 in her personal bank account and $70,000 in the business bank account.

    b. Hart owes $2,000 on a personal charge account with The Gap.

    c. Hart acquired business furniture for $45,000 on September 25. Of this amount, the business owes $31,000 on accounts payable at September 30.

    d. Office supplies on hand at the real estate office total $7,000.

    e. Hart's business owes $36,000 on a note payable for some land acquired for a total price of $116,000.

    f. Hart's business spent $29,000 for a Realty Region franchise, which entitles her to represent herself as an agent. Realty Region is a national affiliation of independent real estate agents. This franchise is a business asset.

    g. Hart owes $140,000 on a personal mortgage on her personal residence, which she acquired in 2003 for a total price of $360,000.

Requirements

1. Prepare the balance sheet of the real estate business of Jeana Hart Realtor, Inc., at September 30, 2011.
2. Does it appear that the realty business can pay its debts? How can you tell?
3. Identify the personal items given in the preceding facts that should not be reported on the balance sheet of the business.

■ **spreadsheet**

P1-66B (*Learning Objectives 4, 5: Preparing an income statement, a statement of changes in equity, and a balance sheet; using accounting information to make decisions*) The assets and liabilities of Post Shrub as of December 31, 2010, and revenues and expenses for the year ended on that date follow.

Land....................................	$ 9,000	Equipment...........................	$ 36,000
Note payable......................	33,000	Interest expense..................	4,950
Property tax expense...........	1,900	Interest payable..................	1,100
Rent expense......................	13,500	Accounts payable	14,000
Accounts receivable.............	26,000	Salary expense....................	38,000
Service revenue...................	144,000	Building.............................	129,000
Supplies.............................	2,000	Cash..................................	15,000
Utilities expense	3,200	Share capital......................	16,450

Beginning retained earnings was $112,000, and dividends totaled $42,000 for the year.

❙ Requirements

1. Prepare the income statement of Post Shrub, Inc., for the year ended December 31, 2010.
2. Prepare the company's statement of changes in equity for the year.
3. Prepare the company's balance sheet at December 31, 2010.
4. Analyze Post Shrub, Inc., by answering these questions:
   a. Was Post Shrub profitable during 2010? By how much?
   b. Did retained earnings increase or decrease? By how much?
   c. Which is greater, total liabilities or total equity? Who owns more of Post Shrub's assets, creditors of the company or Post Shrub's shareholders?

P1-67B (*Learning Objective 4: Preparing a statement of cash flows*) The following data come from the financial statements of The High Tide Company at the year ended May 31, 2011 (in millions).

Purchases of property,		Other investing cash	
plant and equipment	$ 3,480	payments............................	$ 170
Net income...........................	3,030	Accounts receivable................	500
Adjustments to reconcile net		Payment of dividends.............	285
income to net cash provided		Share capital..........................	4,830
by operating activities	2,390	Issuance of shares..................	190
Revenues...............................	59,400	Sales of property, plant	
Cash, beginning of year........	200	and equipment	25
end of year	1,900	Retained earnings..................	13,000
Cost of goods sold...............	37,550		

❙ Requirements

1. Prepare a cash flows statement for the year ended May 31, 2011. Not all the items given appear on the cash flows statement.
2. Which activities provided the largest amount of cash? Is this a sign of financial strength or weakness?

P1-68B (*Learning Objective 4: Analyzing a company's financial statements*) Summarized versions of Espinola Corporation's financial statements follow for two recent years.

	2011	2010
Income Statement	(In Thousands)	
Revenues	$ k	$15,250
Cost of goods sold	11,070	a
Other expenses	1,280	1,230
Income before income taxes	1,500	1,830
Income taxes (35% tax rate)	l	641
Net income	$ m	$ b
Statement of Changes in Equity		
Beginning balance	$ n	$ 3,260
Shares bought back	(80)	0
Net income	o	c
Dividends	(84)	(140)
Ending balance	$ p	$ d
Balance Sheet		
Assets:		
Cash	$ q	$ e
Property, plant and equipment	2,100	1,750
Other assets	r	10,404
Total assets	$ s	$13,419
Liabilities:		
Current liabilities	$ t	$ 5,690
Notes payable and long-term debt	4,300	3,340
Other liabilities	60	80
Total liabilities	$ 9,250	$ f
Shareholders' Equity:		
Share capital	$ 460	$ 540
Retained earnings	u	g
Total shareholders' equity	v	4,309
Total liabilities and shareholders' equity	$ w	$ h
Cash Flows Statement		
Net cash provided by operating activities	$ x	$ 850
Net cash used in investing activities	(240)	(325)
Net cash used in financing activities	(560)	(490)
Increase (decrease) in cash	(90)	i
Cash at beginning of year	y	1,230
Cash at end of year	$ z	$ j

❙ Requirement

1. Complete Espinola Corporation's financial statements by determining the missing amounts denoted by the letters.

APPLY YOUR KNOWLEDGE

Decision Cases

Case 1. *(Learning Objectives 1, 2, 5: Using financial statements to evaluate a loan request)* Two businesses, Blue Skies Corp., and Open Road, Inc., have sought business loans from you. To decide whether to make the loans, you have requested their balance sheets.

Blue Skies Corp.
Balance Sheet
August 31, 2011

Assets		Liabilities	
Cash.....................................	$ 5,000	Accounts payable	$ 50,000
Accounts receivable...............	10,000	Notes payable	80,000
Furniture...............................	15,000	Total liabilities	130,000
Land.....................................	75,000	**Owners' Equity**	
Equipment............................	45,000	Owners' equity...................	20,000
		Total liabilities and	
Total assets...........................	$150,000	owners' equity................	$150,000

Open Road, Inc.
Balance Sheet
August 31, 2011

Assets		Liabilities	
Cash..	$ 5,000	Accounts payable	$ 6,000
Accounts receivable...................	10,000	Note payable...........................	9,000
Merchandise inventory..............	15,000	Total liabilities	15,000
Building....................................	35,000	**Shareholders' Equity**	
		Shareholders' equity................	50,000
		Total liabilities and	
Total assets..............................	$65,000	shareholders' equity..............	$65,000

❙ Requirement

1. Using only these balance sheets, to which entity would you be more comfortable lending money? Explain fully, citing specific items and amounts from the respective balance sheets. (Challenge)

Case 2. *(Learning Objectives 2, 5: Analyzing a company as an investment)* A year out of college, you have $10,000 to invest. A friend has started GrandPrize Unlimited, Inc., and she asks you to invest in her company. You obtain the company's financial statements, which are summarized at the end of the first year as follows:

Grand Prize Unlimited, Inc. Income Statement Year Ended Dec. 31, 2010	
Revenues..................	$100,000
Expenses	80,000
Net income...............	$ 20,000

Grand Prize Unlimited, Inc. Balance Sheet Dec. 31, 2010			
Cash........................	$ 6,000	Liabilities	$ 60,000
Other assets.............	100,000	Equity.....................	46,000
		Total liabilities	
Total assets..............	$106,000	and equity	$106,000

Visits with your friend turn up the following facts:

a. Revenues and receivables of $40,000 were overlooked and omitted.

b. Software costs of $50,000 were recorded as assets. These costs should have been expenses. GrandPrize Unlimited paid cash for these expenses and recorded the cash payment correctly.

c. The company owes an additional $10,000 for accounts payable.

▌Requirements

1. Prepare corrected financial statements.
2. Use your corrected statements to evaluate GrandPrize Unlimited's results of operations and financial position. (Challenge)
3. Will you invest in Grand Prize Unlimited? Give your reason. (Challenge)

Ethical Issue

You are studying frantically for an accounting exam tomorrow. You are having difficulty in this course, and the grade you make on this exam can make the difference between receiving a final grade of B or C. If you receive a C, it will lower your grade point average to the point that you could lose your academic scholarship. An hour ago, a friend, also enrolled in the course but in a different section under the same professor, called you with some unexpected news. In her sorority test files, she has just found a copy of an old exam from the previous year. In looking at the exam, it appears to contain questions that come right from the class notes you have taken, even the very same numbers. She offers to make a copy for you and bring it over.

You glance at your course syllabus and find the following: "You are expected to do your own work in this class. Although you may study with others, giving, receiving, or obtaining information pertaining to an examination is considered an act of academic dishonesty, unless such action is authorized by the instructor giving the examination. Also, divulging the contents of an essay or objective examination designated by the instructor as an examination is considered an act of academic dishonesty. Academic dishonesty is considered a violation of the student honor code, and will subject the student to disciplinary procedures, which can include suspension from the University." Although you have heard a rumor that fraternities and sororities have cleared their exam files with professors, you are not sure.

❙ Requirements

1. What is the ethical issue in this situation?
2. Who are the stakeholders? What are the possible consequences to each?
3. Analyze the alternatives from the following standpoints: (a) economic, (b) legal, and (c) ethical.
4. What would you do? How would you justify your decision? How would your decision make you feel afterward?
5. How is this similar to a business situation?

Focus on Financials: ■ Nokia Corporation

This and similar cases in succeeding chapters are based on the consolidated financial statements of **Nokia Corporation.** As you work with Nokia, throughout this course, you will develop the ability to use the financial statements of actual companies.

❙ Requirements

Refer to the Nokia's consolidated financial statements in Appendix A at the end of the book. You may find that the information is overwhelming for now, but try to spot the key principles that we have discussed in this chapter.

1. Suppose you own shares in Nokia. If you could pick one item on the company's Consolidated Income Statement to increase year after year, what would it be? Why is this item so important? Did this item increase or decrease during 2008? Is this good news or bad news for the company?
2. What was Nokia's largest expense each year? In your own words, explain the meaning of this item. Give specific examples of items that make up this expense.
3. Investors are vitally interested in a company's sales and profits, and its trends of sales and profits over time. Consider Nokia's sales and net income during the period from 2006 through 2008. What do you think happened to Nokia's sales and bottom lines in these periods? Can you offer a possible explanation for these changes?
4. Use the Consolidated Balance Sheets of Nokia in Appendix A to answer these questions: At the end of 2008, how much in total resources did Nokia have to work with? How much did the company owe? How much of its assets did the company's shareholders actually own? Use these amounts to write Nokia's accounting equation at December 31, 2008.
5. Examine retained earnings in the Statements of Changes in Equity. What caused retained earnings to decrease during 2008? Did Nokia pay any dividends to its owners during the year?
6. How much cash did Nokia have at the beginning of the most recent year? How much cash did Nokia have at the end of the year?

Group Projects

Project 1. As instructed by your professor, obtain the annual report of a well-known company.

❙ *Requirements*

1. Take the role of a loan committee of ABN-Amro, a large banking company headquartered in Amsterdam, Netherlands. Assume the company has requested a loan from ABN-Amro. Analyze the company's financial statements and any other information you need to reach a decision regarding the largest amount of money you would be willing to lend. Go as deeply into the analysis and the related decision as you can. Specify the following:
   a. The length of the loan period—that is, over what period will you allow the company to pay you back?
   b. The interest rate you will charge on the loan. Will you charge the prevailing interest rate, a lower rate, or a higher rate? Why?
   c. Any restrictions you will impose on the borrower as a condition for making the loan.

Note: The long-term debt note to the financial statements gives details of the company's existing liabilities.

2. Write your group decision in a report addressed to the bank's board of directors. Limit your report to two double-spaced word-processed pages.
3. If your professor directs, present your decision and your analysis to the class. Limit your presentation to 10 to 15 minutes.

Project 2. You are the owner of a company that is about to "go public"—that is, issue its shares to outside investors. You wish to make your company look as attractive as possible to raise $1 million of cash to expand the business. At the same time, you want to give potential investors a realistic picture of your company.

❙ *Requirements*

1. Design a booklet to portray your company in a way that will enable outsiders to reach an informed decision as to whether to buy some of your shares. The booklet should include the following:
   a. Name and location of your company.
   b. Nature of the company's business (be as detailed as possible).
   c. How you plan to spend the money you raise.
   d. The company's comparative income statement, statement of changes in equity, balance sheet, and statement of cash flows for two years: the current year and the preceding year. Make the data as realistic as possible with the intent of receiving $1 million.
2. Word-process your booklet, not to exceed five pages.
3. If directed by your professor, make a copy for each member of your class. Distribute copies to the class and present your case with the intent of interesting your classmates in investing in the company. Limit your presentation to 10 to 15 minutes.

For online homework, exercises, and problems that provide you with immediate feedback, please visit www.myaccountinglab.com.

Quick Check Answers

1. *b*
2. *b*
3. *c*
4. *a*
5. *d*
6. *d*
7. *a* ($120,000 − $50,000 − $4,000 = $66,000)
8. *b* ($120,000 − $50,000 = $70,000)
9. *c* Total assets = $140,000 ($11,000 + $40,000 + $34,000 + $55,000). Liabilities = $27,000.
10. *d*
11. *b* $38,000 + Net income ($18,000) − Dividends = $50,000; Dividends = $6,000
12. *b*

	Assets =	Liabilities +	Equity
Beginning	$340,000 =	$210,000* +	$130,000
Increase	70,000 =	25,000 +	45,000*
Ending	$410,000* =	$235,000* +	$175,000*

*Must solve for these amounts.

13. *c*
14. *a*

Demo Doc

The Accounting Equation and Financial Statement Preparation

To make sure you understand this material, work through the following demonstration "Demo Doc" with detailed comments to help you see the concept within the framework of a worked-through problem.

Learning Objectives 3, 4, 5

David Richardson is the only shareholder of DR Painting, Inc., a painting business near a historical housing district. At March 31, 2010, DR Painting had the following information:

Cash	$27,300
Accounts receivable	1,400
Supplies	1,800
Truck	20,000
Accounts payable	1,000
Share capital	40,000
Retained earnings (March 1)	5,000
Retained earnings (March 31)	?
Dividends	1,500
Service revenue	7,000
Salary expense	1,000

Requirements

1. Prepare the income statement and statement of changes in equity for the month of March 2010 and the balance sheet of the business at March 31, 2010. Use Exhibits 1-8, 1-9, and 1-10 (pp. 15, 18, and 19) in the text as a guide.

2. Write the accounting equation of the business.

Demo Doc Solutions

Requirement 1

Prepare the income statement, statement of changes in equity, and balance sheet of the business. Use Exhibits 1-8, 1-9, and 1-10 (pp. 15, 18, and 19) in the text as a guide.

Part 1	Part 2	Demo Doc Complete

Income Statement

The income statement is the first statement to prepare because the other financial statements rely upon the net income number calculated on the income statement.

The income statement reports the profitability of the business. To prepare an income statement, begin with the proper heading. A proper heading includes the name of the company (DR Painting, Inc.), the name of the statement (Income Statement), and the time period covered (Month Ended March 31, 2010). Notice that we are reporting income for a period of time, rather than at a single date.

The income statement lists all revenues and expenses. It uses the following formula to calculate net income:

$$\text{Revenues} - \text{Expenses} = \text{Net income}$$

First, you should list revenues. Second, list the expenses. After you have listed and totaled the revenues and expenses, subtract the total expenses from total revenues to determine net income or net loss. A positive number means you earned net income (revenues exceeded expenses). A negative number indicates that expenses exceeded revenues, and this is a net loss.

DR Painting's total Service Revenue for the month was $7,000. The only expense is Salary Expense of $1,000. On the income statement, these would be reported as follows:

DR Painting, Inc. Income Statement Month Ended March 31, 2010		
Revenue:		
Service revenue		$7,000
Expenses:		
Salary expense	$1,000	
Total expenses		1,000
Net income		$6,000

Note that the result is a net income of $6,000 ($7,000 − $1,000 = $6,000). You will also report net income on the statement of changes in equity, which comes next.

Statement of Changes in Equity

The statement of changes in equity shows the changes in total equity of the entity for a period of time. To prepare a statement of changes in equity, begin with the proper heading. A proper heading includes the name of the company (DR Painting, Inc.), the name of the statement (Statement of Changes in Equity), and the time period covered (Month Ended March 31, 2010). As with the income statement, we are reporting the changes in equity for a period of time, rather than at a single date.

Start the body of the statement of changes in equity with the total equity at the beginning of the period (March 1). If there is any additional capital contributed by the owners, we would list the addition to equity here. Note that the total equity will include both the share capital and beginning balance of retained earnings. Then list net income. Observe that the amount of net income comes directly from the income statement. Following net income you will list the dividends declared and paid, which reduce total equity. Finally, total all amounts and compute the total equity at the end of the period.

The share capital of $40,000 was given in the question, and since there is no additional information on any additional issuance of capital, we can assume that both the beginning and ending share capital is $40,000. Beginning Retained Earnings of $5,000 was given in the problem. Net income of $6,000 comes from the income statement and is added. Dividends of $1,500 are deducted. On the statement of changes in equity, these amounts are reported as follows:

DR Painting, Inc. Statement of Changes in Equity Month Ended March 31, 2010	
Beginning total equity, March 1, 2010	$ 45,000
Add: Net income	6,000
	51,000
Less: Dividends	(1,500)
Ending total equity, March 31, 2010	$ 49,500

Note that Retained Earnings has a balance of $9,500 ($5,000 plus net income of $6,000 less dividends of $1,500) at March 31, 2010. You will also report Retained Earning's ending balance on the balance sheet, which you prepare last.

Balance Sheet

The balance sheet reports the financial position of the business at a moment in time. To prepare a balance sheet, begin with the proper heading. A proper heading includes the name of the company (DR Painting, Inc.), the name of the statement (Balance Sheet), and the time of the ending balances (March 31, 2010). Unlike the income statement and statement of changes in equity, we are reporting the financial position of the company at a specific date rather than for a period of time.

The balance sheet lists all assets, liabilities, and equity of the business, with the accounting equation verified at the bottom.

To prepare the body of the balance sheet, begin by listing assets. Then list all the liabilities and shareholders' equity. Notice that the balance sheet is organized in the same order as the accounting equation. The amount of Retained Earnings comes directly from the ending balance on your statement of changes in equity. You should then total both sides of the balance sheet to make sure that they are equal. If they are not equal, then you must correct an error.

In this case, assets accounts include cash of $27,300, accounts receivable of $1,400, $1,800 worth of supplies, and the truck, valued at $20,000. The only liability is accounts payable of $1,000. Shareholders' equity consists of share capital of $40,000, and the updated retained earnings of $9,500, for a total of $49,500 which was calculated in the statement of changes of equity.

DR Painting, Inc. Balance Sheet March 31, 2010				
Assets			**Liabilities**	
Cash	$27,300		Accounts payable	$ 1,000
Accounts receivable	1,400			
Supplies	1,800		**Shareholders' Equity**	
Truck	20,000		Share capital	40,000
			Retained earnings	9,500
			Total shareholders' equity	49,500
			Total liabilities and	
Total assets	$50,500		shareholders' equity	$50,500

Assets   = Liabilities + Shareholders' Equity

Requirement 2

Write the accounting equation of the business

Part 1	**Part 2**	Demo Doc Complete

In this case, asset accounts total $50,500. Liabilities total $1,000—the balance of Accounts Payable, and shareholder's equity is $49,500. This gives us a total for liabilities and equity of $50,500 ($1,000 + $49,500).

The accounting equation is:

Assets of $50,500 = Liabilities of $1,000 + Shareholders' Equity of $49,500

Part 1	Part 2	**Demo Doc Complete**

2

Transaction Analysis

SPOTLIGHT: De Beers

"A diamond is forever". It is probably one of the most successful marketing slogans in the world. De Beers has used this slogan since 1948 and it symbolizes all the glitter and sparkles that are associated with diamonds.

De Beers was established in 1888 and is the world's leading diamond company with unrivalled expertise in the exploration, mining and marketing of diamonds. From its mining operations across Botswana, Namibia, South Africa and Canada, De Beers produces and markets approximately 40% of the world's supply of rough diamonds.

How does De Beers determine the amount of its revenues, expenses, and net income? Like all other companies, De Beers has a comprehensive accounting system. De Beers' Income Statement is given at the start of this chapter. The Income Statement shows that during financial year ended December 31, 2008, De Beers made over US$6,888 million of sales and earned net income of US$90 million. Where did those figures come from? We will discover that companies, including De Beers, record their transactions based on a double-entry accounting system.

De Beers SA
Income Statement (Adapted)
Financial Year Ended December 31

(In millions USD)	2008
Total sales	$6,888
Cost of sales	5,525
Gross profit	1,363
Operating expenses:	
Exploration, research and development	232
Sorting and marketing	266
Group technical services and corporate overheads	319
Total operating expenses	817
Operating income	546
Other income and losses	282
Income before interest and income taxes	838
Net finance charges	240
Tax expense	304
Once-off items	204
Net income	$ 90

Chapter 1 introduced the financial statements. Chapter 2 will show you how companies actually record the transactions that eventually become part of the financial statements.

LEARNING OBJECTIVES

1 Analyze transactions

2 Understand how accounting works

3 Record transactions in the journal

4 Construct a trial balance

5 Analyze transactions using only T-accounts

> For more practice and review of accounting cycle concepts, use ACT, the Accounting Cycle Tutorial, online at **www.myaccountinglab.com**. Margin logos like this one, directing you to the appropriate ACT section and material, appear throughout Chapters 1, 2, and 3. When you enter the tutorial, you'll find three buttons on the opening page of each chapter module. Here's what the buttons mean: **Tutorial** gives you a review of the major concepts, **Application** gives you practice exercises, and **Glossary** reviews important terms.

TRANSACTIONS

Business activity is all about transactions. A **transaction** is any event that has a financial impact on the business and can be measured reliably. For example, De Beers sells diamonds, borrows money, and repays the loan—three separate transactions.

But not all events qualify as transactions. De Beers' diamonds may be featured in a trade magazine and motivate jewelers to buy diamonds. The magazine article may create lots of new business for De Beers, but no transaction occurs until someone actually buys a De Beers diamond. A transaction must occur before De Beers records anything.

Transactions provide objective information about the financial impact on a company. Every transaction has two sides:

- You give something.
- You receive something.

In accounting we always record both sides of a transaction. And we must be able to measure the financial impact of the event on the business before recording it as a transaction.

THE ACCOUNT

As we saw in Chapter 1, the accounting equation expresses the basic relationships of accounting:

$$\text{Assets} = \text{Liabilities} + \text{Shareholders' (Owners') Equity}$$

For each asset, each liability, and each element of shareholders' equity, we use a record called the account. An **account** is the record of all the changes in a particular asset, liability, or shareholders' equity during a period. The account is the basic summary device of accounting. Before launching into transaction analysis, let's review the accounts that a company such as De Beers, uses.

Assets

Assets are economic resources that provide a future benefit for a business. Most firms use the following asset accounts:

Cash.   Cash means money and any medium of exchange including bank account balances, paper currency, coins, certificates of deposit, and cheques.

Accounts Receivable.   De Beers like most other companies, sells its goods and services and receives a promise for future collection of cash. The Accounts Receivable account holds these amounts.

Notes Receivable.   De Beers may receive a note receivable from a customer, who signed the note promising to pay De Beers. A note receivable is similar to an account receivable, but a note receivable is more binding because the customer signed the note. Notes receivable usually specify an interest rate.

Inventory.   De Beers' most important asset is its inventory—the diamonds it sells to customers. Other titles for this account include *Stocks* and *Merchandise Inventory*.

Prepaid Expenses.   De Beers pays certain expenses in advance, such as insurance and rent. A prepaid expense or *payments* is an asset because the payment provides a *future* benefit for the business. Prepaid Rent, Prepaid Insurance, and Supplies are examples prepaid expenses.

Land.   The Land account shows the cost of the land De Beers uses in its operations.

Buildings. The costs of De Beers' office building, manufacturing plant, and the like appear in the Buildings account.

Equipment, Furniture, and Fixtures. De Beers has a separate asset account for each type of equipment, for example, Manufacturing Equipment and Office Equipment. The Furniture and Fixtures account shows the cost of these assets, which are similar to equipment.

Most companies report their land, buildings, equipment, furniture, fixtures and other non-current physical assets under the heading Property, Plant and Equipment (PPE).

Liabilities

Recall that a *liability* is an obligation to pay an individual or organisation. A payable is always a liability. The most common types of liabilities include:

Accounts Payable. The Accounts Payable account is the direct opposite of Accounts Receivable. De Beers' promise to pay a debt arising from a credit purchase of inventory or from a utility bill appears in the Accounts Payable account.

Notes Payable. A note payable is the opposite of a note receivable. The Notes Payable account includes the amounts De Beers must *pay* because De Beers signed notes promising to pay a future amount. Notes payable, like notes receivable, also carry interest.

Accrued Liabilities. An **accrued liability** is a liability for an expense you have not yet paid. Interest Payable and Salary Payable are accrued liability accounts for most companies. Income Tax Payable is another accrued liability.

Shareholders' (Owners') Equity

The owners' claims to the assets of a corporation are called *shareholders' equity* or simply *equity*. A corporation such as De Beers, uses Shares Capital, Retained Earnings, and Dividends accounts to record the various components of shareholders' equity. In a proprietorship, there is a single capital account. For a partnership, each partner has a separate capital account.

Share Capital. The Share Capital account shows the owners' investment in the corporation. De Beers receives cash and issues shares to its shareholders. A company's ordinary share capital is its most basic element of equity. All corporations have ordinary shares. We will examine other forms of share capital in Chapter 9.

STOP & THINK. . .

Name two things that (1) increase De Beers' shareholders' equity and (2) decrease De Beers' shareholders' equity.

Answer:
(1) Increases in equity: Issuance of share capital and net income (revenue greater than expenses).
(2) Decreases in equity: Dividends and net loss (expenses greater than revenue).

Retained Earnings. The Retained Earnings account shows the cumulative net income earned by De Beers over the company's lifetime, minus its cumulative net losses and dividends.

Dividends. Dividends are optional; they are *declared* by the board of directors (may require, shareholders' approval at the corporation's **Annual General Meeting**). After profitable operations, the board of directors of De Beers may (or may not) declare and pay a cash dividend. The corporation may keep a separate account titled *Dividends*, which indicates a decrease in Retained Earnings for the financial year.

Revenues. The increase in shareholders' equity from delivering goods or services to customers is called *revenue*. The company uses as many revenue accounts as needed. De Beers uses a Sales Revenue account for revenue earned by selling its products. De Beers may also use a Service Revenue account for the revenue it earns by providing services to customers. A lawyer provides legal services for clients and also uses a Service Revenue account. A business that loans money to an outsider needs an Interest Revenue account. If the business rents a building to a tenant, the business needs a Rent Revenue account.

Expenses. The cost of operating a business is called *expense*. Expenses *decrease* shareholders' equity, the opposite effect of revenues. A business needs a separate account for each type of expense, such as Cost of Goods Sold, Salary Expense, Rent Expense, Advertising Expense, Insurance Expense, Utilities Expense, and Income Tax Expense. Businesses strive to minimize expenses and thereby maximize net income. The level of details captured in the accounting system depends on the information needs of the business.

ACCOUNTING FOR BUSINESS TRANSACTIONS
Example: ShineBrite Car Wash, Inc.

To illustrate the accounting for transactions, let's return to ShineBrite Car Wash, Inc. In Chapter 1's End-of-Chapter Problem, Van Gray opened ShineBrite Car Wash, Inc., in April 2010.

> OBJECTIVE
>
> **1** **Analyze** transactions

We consider 11 events and analyze each in terms of its effect on ShineBrite Car Wash. We begin by using the accounting equation. Impact of revenue and expense transactions are taken directly to equity. In the second half of this chapter, we record transactions using the journal and ledger of the business.

Transaction 1. Gray and a few friends invest $50,000 to open ShineBrite Car Wash, and the business issues ordinary share capital to the shareholders. The effect of this transaction on the accounting equation of ShineBrite Car Wash, Inc. is a receipt of cash and issuance of ordinary share capital, as follows:

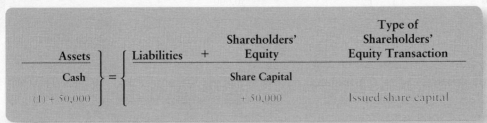

Assets		Liabilities	+	Shareholders' Equity	Type of Shareholders' Equity Transaction
Cash	=			Share Capital	
(1) + 50,000				+ 50,000	Issued share capital

Every transaction's net amount on the left side of the equation must equal the net amount on the right side. The first transaction increases both the cash and the share capital of the business. To the right of the transaction we write "issued share capital" to show the reason for the increase in shareholders' equity.

Every transaction affects the financial statements of the business, and we can prepare financial statements after one, two, or any number of transactions. For example, ShineBrite Car Wash could report the company's Balance Sheet after its first transaction, shown here.

ShineBrite Car Wash, Inc.
Balance Sheet
April 1, 2010

Assets		Liabilities	
Cash..........................	$50,000	None	
		Shareholders' Equity	
		Share capital....................................	$50,000
		Total shareholders' equity.............	50,000
		Total liabilities and	
Total assets................	$50,000	shareholders' equity......................	$50,000

This balance sheet shows that the business holds cash of $50,000 and owes no liabilities. The company's equity (ownership) is denoted as *share capital* on the Balance Sheet. A bank would look favorably on this balance sheet because the business has $50,000 cash and no debt—a strong financial position.

As a practical matter, most entities report their financial statements at the end of the accounting period—not after each transaction. But an accounting system can produce statements whenever managers need to know where the business stands.

Transaction 2. ShineBrite purchases land for a new location and pays cash of $40,000. The effect of this transaction on the accounting equation is:

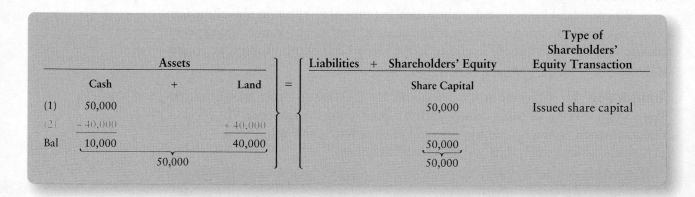

The purchase increases one asset (Land) and decreases another asset (Cash) by the same amount. After the transaction is completed, ShineBrite has cash of $10,000, land of $40,000, and no liabilities. Shareholders' equity is unchanged at $50,000. Note that total assets must always equal total liabilities plus equity

Transaction 3. The business buys supplies on account, agreeing to pay $3,700 within 30 days. This transaction increases both the assets and the liabilities of the business. Its effect on the accounting equation follows.

	Assets						Liabilities	+	Shareholders' Equity
	Cash	+	Supplies	+	Land		Accounts Payable	+	Share Capital
Bal	10,000				40,000				50,000
(3)			+ 3,700			=	+ 3,700		
Bal	10,000		3,700		40,000		3,700		50,000
			53,700					53,700	

The new asset is Supplies, and the liability is an Account Payable. ShineBrite signs no formal promissory note, so the liability is an account payable, not a note payable.

Transaction 4.   ShineBrite earns $7,000 of service revenue by providing services for customers. The business collects the cash. The effect on the accounting equation is an increase in the asset Cash and an increase in Retained Earnings, as follows:

	Assets						Liabilities	+	Shareholders' Equity			Type of Shareholders' Equity Transaction
	Cash	+	Supplies	+	Land		Accounts Payable	+	Share Capital	+	Retained Earnings	
Bal	10,000		3,700		40,000	=	3,700		50,000			
(4)	+ 7,000										+ 7,000	Service revenue
Bal	17,000		3,700		40,000		3,700		50,000		7,000	
			60,700						60,700			

To the right we record "Service revenue" to show where the $7,000 of increase in Retained Earnings came from.

Transaction 5.   ShineBrite performs service on account, which means that ShineBrite lets some customers pay later. ShineBrite earns revenue but doesn't receive the cash immediately. In transaction 5, ShineBrite cleans a fleet of **UPS** delivery trucks, and UPS promises to pay ShineBrite $3,000 within one month. This promise is an account receivable—an asset—of ShineBrite Car Wash. The transaction record follows.

	Assets								Liabilities	+	Shareholders' Equity			Type of Shareholders' Equity Transaction
	Cash	+	Accounts Receivable	+	Supplies	+	Land		Accounts Payable	+	Share Capital	+	Retained Earnings	
Bal	17,000				3,700		40,000	=	3,700		50,000		7,000	
(5)			+ 3,000										+ 3,000	Service revenue
Bal	17,000		3,000		3,700		40,000		3,700		50,000		10,000	
			63,700								63,700			

It's performing the service that earns the revenue—not collecting the cash. Therefore, ShineBrite records revenue when it performs the service—regardless of whether ShineBrite receives cash now or later.

Transaction 6.   During the month, ShineBrite Car Wash pays $2,700 for the following expenses: equipment rent, $1,100; employee salaries, $1,200; and utilities, $400. The effect on the accounting equation is as follows:

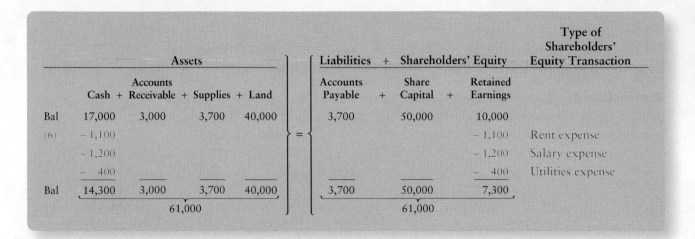

	Assets					Liabilities	+	Shareholders' Equity			Type of Shareholders' Equity Transaction
	Cash +	Accounts Receivable +	Supplies +	Land		Accounts Payable	+	Share Capital +	Retained Earnings		
Bal	17,000	3,000	3,700	40,000		3,700		50,000	10,000		
(6)	− 1,100								− 1,100		Rent expense
	− 1,200				=				− 1,200		Salary expense
	− 400								− 400		Utilities expense
Bal	14,300	3,000	3,700	40,000		3,700		50,000	7,300		
			61,000					61,000			

The expenses decrease ShineBrite's Cash and Retained Earnings. List each expense separately to keep track of its amount.

Transaction 7.   ShineBrite pays $1,900 on account, which means to pay off an account payable. In this transaction ShineBrite pays the store from which it purchased supplies in transaction 3. The transaction decreases Cash and also decreases Accounts Payable as follows:

	Assets					Liabilities	+	Shareholders' Equity		
	Cash +	Accounts Receivable +	Supplies +	Land		Accounts Payable	+	Share Capital +	Retained Earnings	
Bal	14,300	3,000	3,700	40,000	=	3,700		50,000	7,300	
(7)	− 1,900					− 1,900				
Bal	12,400	3,000	3,700	40,000		1,800		50,000	7,300	
			59,100					59,100		

Transaction 8.   Van Gray, the major shareholder of ShineBrite Car Wash, paid $30,000 to remodel his home. This event is a personal transaction of the Gray family. It is not recorded by the ShineBrite Car Wash business. We focus solely on the business entity, not on its owners. This transaction illustrates the entity assumption from Chapter 1.

Transaction 9.   In transaction 5, ShineBrite performed services for UPS on account. The business now collects $1,000 from UPS. We say that ShineBrite *collects the cash on account*, which means that ShineBrite will record an increase in Cash and a decrease in

Accounts Receivable. This is not service revenue because ShineBrite already recorded the revenue in transaction 5. The effect of collecting cash on account is:

	Assets							Liabilities	+	Shareholders' Equity		
	Cash	+	Accounts Receivable	+	Supplies	+	Land	Accounts Payable	+	Share Capital	+	Retained Earnings
Bal	12,400		3,000		3,700		40,000 $=$	1,800		50,000		7,300
(9)	+ 1,000		− 1,000									
Bal	13,400		2,000		3,700		40,000	1,800		50,000		7,300
				59,100						59,100		

Transaction 10. ShineBrite sells some land for $22,000, which is the same amount that ShineBrite paid for the land. ShineBrite receives $22,000 cash, and the effect on the accounting equation is as follows:

	Assets							Liabilities	+	Shareholders' Equity		
	Cash	+	Accounts Receivable	+	Supplies	+	Land	Accounts Payable	+	Share Capital	+	Retained Earnings
Bal	13,400		2,000		3,700		40,000 $=$	1,800		50,000		7,300
(10)	+ 22,000						− 22,000					
Bal	35,400		2,000		3,700		18,000	1,800		50,000		7,300
				59,100						59,100		

Note that the company did not sell all its land; ShineBrite still owns $18,000 worth of land.

Transaction 11. ShineBrite Car Wash declares a dividend and pays the shareholders $2,100 cash. The effect on the accounting equation is as follows:

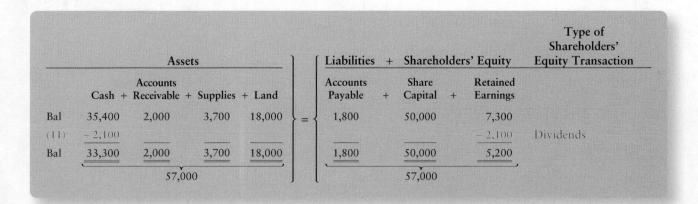

	Assets				Liabilities	+	Shareholders' Equity			Type of Shareholders' Equity Transaction
	Cash +	Accounts Receivable +	Supplies +	Land	Accounts Payable	+	Share Capital	+	Retained Earnings	
Bal	35,400	2,000	3,700	18,000 $=$	1,800		50,000		7,300	
(11)	− 2,100								− 2,100	Dividends
Bal	33,300	2,000	3,700	18,000	1,800		50,000		5,200	
		57,000					57,000			

The dividend decreases both the Cash and the Retained Earnings of the business. *But dividends are not an expense*, because they are transactions with owners of the business.

Transactions and Financial Statements

Exhibit 2-1 summarizes the 11 preceding transactions. Panel A gives the details of the transactions, and Panel B shows the transaction analysis. As you study the exhibit, note that every transaction maintains the equality:

Assets = Liabilities + Shareholders' Equity

Exhibit 2-1 provides the data for ShineBrite Car Wash's financial statements:

EXHIBIT 2-1 | Transaction Analysis: ShineBrite Car Wash, Inc.

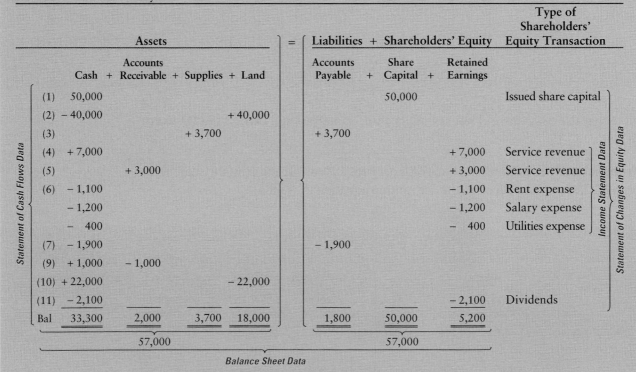

PANEL A—Transaction Details

(1) Received $50,000 cash and issued shares to the owners
(2) Paid $40,000 cash for land
(3) Bought $3,700 of supplies on account
(4) Received $7,000 cash from customers for service revenue earned
(5) Performed services for a customer on account, $3,000
(6) Paid cash expenses: rent, $1,100; employee salary, $1,200; utilities, $400

(7) Paid $1,900 on the account payable created in transaction 3
(8) Major shareholder paid personal funds to remodel home, *not* a transaction of the business
(9) Received $1,000 on account
(10) Sold land for cash at the land's cost of $22,000
(11) Declared and paid a dividend of $2,100 to the shareholders

PANEL B—Transaction Analysis

	Assets				=	Liabilities	+	Shareholders' Equity		Type of Shareholders' Equity Transaction
	Cash	Accounts Receivable	Supplies	Land		Accounts Payable		Share Capital	Retained Earnings	
(1)	50,000							50,000		Issued share capital
(2)	−40,000			+40,000						
(3)			+3,700			+3,700				
(4)	+7,000								+7,000	Service revenue
(5)		+3,000							+3,000	Service revenue
(6)	−1,100								−1,100	Rent expense
	−1,200								−1,200	Salary expense
	−400								−400	Utilities expense
(7)	−1,900					−1,900				
(9)	+1,000	−1,000								
(10)	+22,000			−22,000						
(11)	−2,100								−2,100	Dividends
Bal	33,300	2,000	3,700	18,000		1,800		50,000	5,200	
		57,000						57,000		

Statement of Cash Flows Data

Income Statement Data

Statement of Changes in Equity Data

Balance Sheet Data

- *Income Statement* data appear as revenues and expenses under Retained Earnings. The revenues increase retained earnings; the expenses decrease retained earnings.
- The *Balance Sheet* data are composed of the ending balances of the assets, liabilities, and shareholders' equities shown at the bottom of the exhibit. The accounting equation shows that total assets ($57,000) equal total liabilities plus shareholders' equity ($57,000).
- The *Statement of Changes in Equity* reconciles the movements in equity for the period. Issuance of share capital and net income increases total equity, whereas dividends decrease equity. Ending equity is the final result.
- Data for the *Statement of Cash Flows* are aligned under the Cash account. Cash receipts increase cash, and cash payments decrease cash.

Exhibit 2-2 on the following page shows the ShineBrite Car Wash financial statements at the end of April, the company's first month of operations. Follow the flow of data to observe the following:

1. The Income Statement reports revenues, expenses, and either a net income or a net loss for the period. During April, ShineBrite earned net income of $7,300. Compare ShineBrite's Income Statement with that of De Beers, at the beginning of the chapter. The Income Statement includes only two types of accounts: revenues and expenses.

2. The Statement of Changes in Equity starts with the beginning balance of equity, which is zero for a new business. Add share capital contribution net income for the period (arrow ①), subtract dividends, and compute the ending balance of equity ($55,200).

3. The balance sheet lists the assets, liabilities, and shareholders' equity of the business at the end of the period. Included in shareholders' equity is retained earnings, which can be seen from the Statement of Changes in Equity (arrow ②).

EXHIBIT 2-2 | **Financial Statements of ShineBrite Car Wash, Inc.**

ShineBrite Car Wash, Inc.
Income Statement
Month Ended April 30, 2010

Revenues		
Service revenue ($7,000 + $3,000)		$10,000
Expenses		
Salary expense..	$1,200	
Rent expense...	1,100	
Utilities expense	400	
Total expenses...		2,700
Net income..		$ 7,300

①

ShineBrite Car Wash, Inc.
Statement of Changes in Equity
Month Ended April 30, 2010

Total equity, April 1, 2010	$ 0	
Add: Issuance of share capital	50,000	
Add: Net income for the month	7,300	
	57,300	
Less: Dividends	(2,100)	
Total equity, April 30, 2010	$55,200	

②

ShineBrite Car Wash, Inc.
Balance Sheet
April 30, 2010

Assets		Liabilities	
Cash..	$33,300	Accounts payable	$ 1,800
Accounts receivable................	2,000	**Shareholders' Equity**	
Supplies..................................	3,700	Share Capital.................................	50,000
Land..	18,000	Retained earnings...........................	5,200
		Total shareholders' equity............	55,200
Total assets.............................		Total liabilities and	
	$57,000	shareholders' equity.....................	$57,000

Let's put into practice what you have learned thus far.

MID-CHAPTER SUMMARY PROBLEM

Shelly Herzog opens a research service near a college campus. She names the corporation Herzog Researchers, Inc. During the first month of operations, July 2010, the business engages in the following transactions:

a. Herzog Researchers, Inc., issues its ordinary shares to Shelly Herzog, who invests $25,000 to open the business.

b. The company purchases on account office supplies costing $350.

c. Herzog Researchers pays cash of $20,000 to acquire a lot next to the campus. The company intends to use the land as a building site for a business office.

d. Herzog Researchers performs research for clients and receives cash of $1,900.

e. Herzog Researchers pays $100 on the account payable it created in transaction b.

f. Herzog pays $2,000 of personal funds for a vacation.

g. Herzog Researchers pays cash expenses for office rent ($400) and utilities ($100).

h. The business sells a small parcel of the land for its cost of $5,000.

i. The business declares and pays a cash dividend of $1,200.

I Requirements

1. Analyze the preceding transactions in terms of their effects on the accounting equation of Herzog Researchers, Inc. Use Exhibit 2-1, Panel B as a guide.
2. Prepare the Income Statement, Statement of Changes in Equity, and Balance Sheet of Herzog Researchers, Inc., after recording the transactions. Draw arrows linking the statements.

Answers

I Requirement 1

PANEL B—Analysis of Transactions

	Assets			=	Liabilities	+	Shareholders' Equity		Type of Shareholders' Equity Transaction
	Cash	+	Office Supplies	+	Land		Accounts Payable	+	Share Capital	+	Retained Earnings	
(a)	+ 25,000								+ 25,000			Issued share capital
(b)			+ 350				+ 350						
(c)	– 20,000				+ 20,000								
(d)	+ 1,900										+ 1,900	Service revenue
(e)	– 100						– 100						
(f)	Not a transaction of the business											
(g)	– 400										– 400	Rent expense
	– 100										– 100	Utilities expense
(h)	+ 5,000				– 5,000								
(i)	– 1,200										– 1,200	Dividends
Bal	10,100		350		15,000		250		25,000		200	
		25,450							25,450			

	Assets	=	Liabilities	+	Shareholders' Equity
Accounting equation	+ 1,000	=	0	+	0
	− 1,000				

	Cash				Accounts Receivable		
The ledger accounts	(1)	50,000	(2)	40,000	(5)	3,000	(9)	1,000
	(4)	7,000	(6)	2,700				
	(9)	1,000	(7)	1,900				

Transaction 10 Analysis. The business sold land for its cost of $22,000, receiving cash. The asset cash increased; debit Cash. The asset land decreased; credit Land.

Journal entry	Cash	22,000	
	Land		22,000
	Sold land.		

	Assets	=	Liabilities	+	Shareholders' Equity
Accounting equation	+ 22,000	=	0	+	0
	− 22,000				

	Cash				Land		
The ledger accounts	(1)	50,000	(2)	40,000	(2)	40,000	(10)	22,000
	(4)	7,000	(6)	2,700				
	(9)	1,000	(7)	1,900				
	(10)	22,000						

Transaction 11 Analysis. ShineBrite Car Wash paid its shareholders cash dividends of $2,100. Credit Cash for the payment. The transaction also decreased shareholders' equity and requires a debit to an equity account. Therefore, debit Dividends.

Journal entry	Dividends	2,100	
	Cash		2,100
	Declared and paid dividends.		

	Assets	=	Liabilities	+	Shareholders' Equity
Accounting equation	− 2,100	=	0	−	2,100 (Dividends)

The ledger accounts

Cash				Dividends	
(1)	50,000	(2)	40,000	(11)	2,100
(4)	7,000	(6)	2,700		
(9)	1,000	(7)	1,900		
(10)	22,000	(11)	2,100		

Accounts After Posting to the Ledger

Exhibit 2-11 shows the accounts after all transactions have been posted to the ledger. Group the accounts under assets, liabilities, and equity.

Each account has a balance, denoted as Bal, which is the difference between the account's total debits and its total credits. For example, the Accounts Payable's balance of $1,800 is the difference between the credit ($3,700) and the debit ($1,900). Cash has a debit balance of $33,300.

A horizontal line separates the transaction amounts from the account balance. If an account's debits exceed its total credits, that account has a debit balance, as for Cash. If the sum of the credits is greater, the account has a credit balance, as for Accounts Payable.

Accounting Cycle Tutorial Application 1—Xpert Driving School

Accounting Cycle Tutorial Application 2—Small Business Services

EXHIBIT 2-11 | ShineBrite Car Wash's Ledger Accounts After Posting

Assets		=	Liabilities		+	Shareholders' Equity	

Cash

(1)	50,000	(2)	40,000
(4)	7,000	(6)	2,700
(9)	1,000	(7)	1,900
(10)	22,000	(11)	2,100
Bal	33,300		

Accounts Payable

(7)	1,900	(3)	3,700
		Bal	1,800

Share Capital

		(1)	50,000
		Bal	50,000

Dividends

(11)	2,100	
Bal	2,100	

Accounts Receivable

(5)	3,000	(9)	1,000
Bal	2,000		

Revenue

Service Revenue

		(4)	7,000
		(5)	3,000
		Bal	10,000

Expenses

Rent Expense

(6)	1,100	
Bal	1,100	

Supplies

(3)	3,700	
Bal	3,700	

Salary Expense

(6)	1,200	
Bal	1,200	

Land

(2)	40,000	(10)	22,000
Bal	18,000		

Utilities Expense

(6)	400	
Bal	400	

THE TRIAL BALANCE

A **trial balance** lists all accounts with their balances—assets first, then liabilities and shareholders' equity. The trial balance summarizes all the account balances for the financial statements and shows whether total debits equal total credits. A trial balance

OBJECTIVE

4 Construct a trial balance

■ *transposition* (writing $2,100 as $1,200). The accounts would be out of balance by $900 ($2,100 − $1,200 = $900). Dividing $900 by 9 yields $100. Trace all amounts on the trial balance back to the T-accounts. Dividends (balance of $2,100) is the misstated account.

Chart of Accounts

As you know, the ledger contains the accounts grouped under these headings:

1. Balance sheet accounts: Assets, Liabilities, and Shareholders' Equity
2. Income statement accounts: Revenues and Expenses

Organizations use a **chart of accounts** to list all their accounts and account numbers. Account numbers usually have two or more digits. Asset account numbers may begin with 1, liabilities with 2, shareholders' equity with 3, revenues with 4, and expenses with 5. The second, third, and higher digits in an account number indicate the position of the individual account within the category. For example, Cash may be account number 101, which is the first asset account. Accounts Payable may be number 201, the first liability. All accounts are numbered by using this system.

Organizations with many accounts use lengthy account numbers. For example, the chart of accounts of De Beers, may use ten-digit account numbers. The chart of accounts for ShineBrite Car Wash appears in Exhibit 2-13. The gap between account numbers 111 and 141 leaves room to add another category of receivables, for example, Notes Receivable, which may be numbered 121.

EXHIBIT 2-13 | **Chart of Accounts—ShineBrite Car Wash, Inc.**

Balance Sheet Accounts		
Assets	**Liabilities**	**Shareholders' Equity**
101 Cash	201 Accounts Payable	301 Share Capital
111 Accounts Receivable	231 Notes Payable	311 Dividends
141 Office Supplies		312 Retained Earnings
151 Office Furniture		
191 Land		

	Income Statement Accounts (Part of Shareholders' Equity)	
	Revenues	**Expenses**
	401 Service Revenue	501 Rent Expense
		502 Salary Expense
		503 Utilities Expense

Appendix C to this book gives two expanded charts of accounts that you will find helpful as you work through this course. The first chart lists the typical accounts that a *service* corporation, such as ShineBrite Car Wash, would have after a period of growth. The second chart is for a *merchandising* corporation, one that sells a product instead of a service.

The Normal Balance of an Account

An account's *normal balance* falls on the side of the account—debit or credit—where increases are recorded. The normal balance of assets is on the debit side, so assets are *debit-balance accounts*. Conversely, liabilities and shareholders' equity usually have a credit balance, so these are *credit-balance accounts*. Exhibit 2-14 illustrates the normal balances of all the assets, liabilities, and shareholders' equities, including revenues and expenses.

EXHIBIT 2-14 | Normal Balances of the Accounts

Assets...	Debit	
Liabilities		Credit
Shareholders' Equity—overall		Credit
Share capital		Credit
Retained earnings.............................		Credit
Dividends...	Debit	
Revenues..		Credit
Expenses	Debit	

As explained earlier, shareholders' equity usually contains several accounts. Dividends and expenses carry debit balances because they represent decreases in shareholders' equity. In total, the equity accounts show a normal credit balance.

Account Formats

So far we have illustrated accounts in a two-column T-account format, with the debit column on the left and the credit column on the right. Another format has four *amount* columns, as illustrated for the Cash account in Exhibit 2-15. The first pair of amount columns are for the debit and credit amounts of individual transactions. The last two columns are for the account balance. This four-column format keeps a running balance in the two right columns.

Accounting Cycle Tutorial
The Journal, the Ledger, and the Trial Balance

EXHIBIT 2-15 | Account in Four-Column Format

Account: Cash					Account No. 101
				Balance	
Date	Item	Debit	Credit	Debit	Credit
2010					
Apr 2	Share Capital	50,000		50,000	
3	Land		40,000	10,000	

Analyzing Transactions Using Only T-Accounts

Businesspeople must often make decisions without the benefit of a complete accounting system. For example, the managers of De Beers may consider borrowing $100,000 to buy equipment. To see how the two transactions [(a) borrowing cash and (b) buying equipment] affect De Beers, the manager can go directly to T-accounts, as follows:

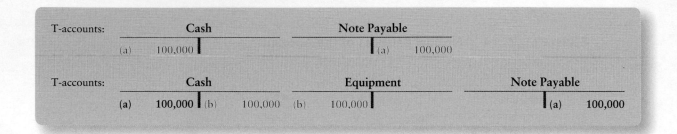

This informal analysis shows immediately that De Beers will add $100,000 of equipment and a $100,000 note payable. Assuming that De Beers began with zero balances, the equipment and note payable transactions would result in the following balance sheet (date assumed for illustration only):

De Beers
Balance Sheet
September 12, 2010

Assets		Liabilities	
Cash..................................	$ 0	Note payable............................	$100,000
Equipment......................	100,000		
		Shareholders' Equity	0
		Total liabilities and	
Total assets......................	$100,000	shareholders' equity..............	$100,000

Companies don't actually keep records in this shortcut fashion. But a decision maker who needs information quickly may not have time to journalize, post to the accounts, take a trial balance, and prepare the financial statements. A manager who knows accounting can analyze the transaction and make the decision quickly.

Now apply what you've learned. Study the Decision Guidelines, which summarize the chapter.

Accounting Cycle Tutorial Application
Constanza Architect

DECISION GUIDELINES

HOW TO MEASURE RESULTS OF OPERATIONS AND FINANCIAL POSITION

Any entrepreneur must determine whether the venture is profitable. To do this, he or she needs to know its results of operations and financial position. If the Oppenheimer family (who owns 40% of De Beers) wants to know whether the business is making money, the Guidelines that follow will help them.

Decision	Guidelines
Has a transaction occurred?	If the event affects the entity's financial position and can be reliably recorded—Yes. If either condition is absent—No.
Where to record the transaction?	In the *journal*, the chronological record of transactions
How to record an increase or decrease in the following accounts?	Rules of *debit* and *credit*:

	Increase	Decrease
Assets	Debit	Credit
Liabilities	Credit	Debit
Shareholders' equity...............	Credit	Debit
Revenues.................................	Credit	Debit
Expenses	Debit	Credit
Dividends...............................	Debit	Credit

Decision	Guidelines
Where to store all the information for each account?	In the *ledger*, the book of accounts
Where to list all the accounts and their balances?	In the *trial balance*
Where to report the:	
Results of operations?	In the *income statement* (Revenues − Expenses = Net income or net loss)
Financial position?	In the *balance sheet* (Assets = Liabilities + Shareholders' equity)

END-OF-CHAPTER SUMMARY PROBLEM

The trial balance of Calderon Service Center, Inc., on March 1, 2010, lists the entity's assets, liabilities, and shareholders' equity on that date.

	Balance	
Account Title	**Debit**	**Credit**
Cash......................................	$26,000	
Accounts receivable...............	4,500	
Accounts payable		$ 2,000
Share capital..........................		10,000
Retained earnings...................		18,500
Total	$30,500	$30,500

During March, the business completed the following transactions:

a. Borrowed $45,000 from the bank, with Calderon signing a note payable in the name of the business.

b. Paid cash of $40,000 to a real estate company to acquire land.

c. Performed service for a customer and received cash of $5,000.

d. Purchased supplies on credit, $300.

e. Performed customer service and earned revenue on account, $2,600.

f. Paid $1,200 on account.

g. Paid the following cash expenses: salaries, $3,000; rent, $1,500; and interest, $400.

h. Received $3,100 on account.

i. Received a $200 utility bill that will be paid next week.

j. Declared and paid dividend of $1,800.

I Requirements

1. Open the following accounts, with the balances indicated, in the ledger of Calderon Service Center, Inc. Use the T-account format.
   - Assets—Cash, $26,000; Accounts Receivable, $4,500; Supplies, no balance; Land, no balance
   - Liabilities—Accounts Payable, $2,000; Note Payable, no balance
   - Shareholders' Equity—Share Capital, $10,000; Retained Earnings, $18,500; Dividends, no balance
   - Revenues—Service Revenue, no balance
   - Expenses—(none have balances) Salary Expense, Rent Expense, Interest Expense, Utilities Expense

2. Journalize the preceding transactions. Key journal entries by transaction letter.

3. Post to the ledger and show the balance in each account after all the transactions have been posted.

4. Prepare the trial balance of Calderon Service Center, Inc., at March 31, 2010.

5. To determine the net income or net loss of the entity during the month of March, prepare the income statement for the month ended March 31, 2010. List expenses in order from the largest to the smallest.

Answers

❙ Requirement 1

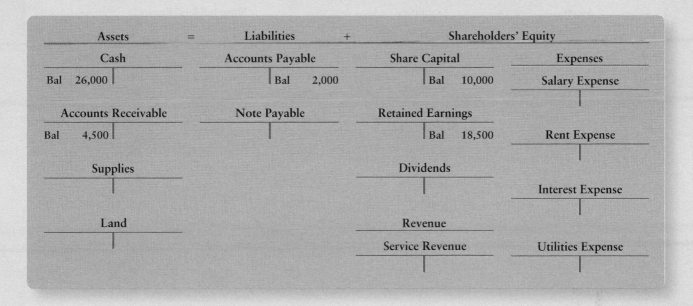

❙ Requirement 2

Accounts and Explanation	Debit	Credit	Accounts and Explanation	Debit	Credit
a. Cash...	45,000		g. Salary Expense	3,000	
Note Payable		45,000	Rent Expense	1,500	
Borrowed cash on note payable.			Interest Expense	400	
b. Land...	40,000		Cash		4,900
Cash		40,000	Paid cash expenses.		
Purchased land for cash.			h. Cash...	3,100	
c. Cash..	5,000		Accounts Receivable		3,100
Service Revenue		5,000	Received on account.		
Performed service and received cash.			i. Utilities Expense............................	200	
d. Supplies......................................	300		Accounts Payable....................		200
Accounts Payable...............		300	Received utility bill.		
Purchased supplies on account.			j. Dividends.....................................	1,800	
e. Accounts Receivable................	2,600		Cash		1,800
Service Revenue		2,600	Declared and paid dividends.		
Performed service on account.					
f. Accounts Payable	1,200				
Cash		1,200			
Paid on account.					

❚ Requirement 3

| Assets | | | = | Liabilities | | | + | Shareholders' Equity | | |

Cash					Accounts Payable				Share Capital				Expenses		
Bal	26,000	(b)	40,000	(f)	1,200	Bal	2,000		Bal	10,000		**Salary Expense**		
(a)	45,000	(f)	1,200			(d)	300					(g)	3,000	
(c)	5,000	(g)	4,900			(i)	200		**Retained Earnings**			Bal	3,000	
(h)	3,100	(j)	1,800			Bal	1,300							
Bal	31,200								Bal	18,500		**Rent Expense**		

Accounts Receivable					Note Payable				Dividends			(g)	1,500	
Bal	4,500	(h)	3,100			(a)	45,000		(j)	1,800		Bal	1,500	
(e)	2,600					Bal	45,000		Bal	1,800				
Bal	4,000											**Interest Expense**		

Supplies									Revenue			(g)	400	
(d)	300								**Service Revenue**			Bal	400	
Bal	300													
										(c)	5,000	**Utilities Expense**		

Land										(e)	2,600	(i)	200	
(b)	40,000									Bal	7,600	Bal	200	
Bal	40,000													

❚ Requirement 4

Calderon Service Center, Inc.
Trial Balance
March 31, 2010

	Balance	
Account Title	Debit	Credit
Cash...	$31,200	
Accounts receivable................	4,000	
Supplies...................................	300	
Land...	40,000	
Accounts payable		$ 1,300
Note payable...........................		45,000
Share capital...........................		10,000
Retained earnings...................		18,500
Dividends	1,800	
Service revenue.......................		7,600
Salary expense........................	3,000	
Rent expense...........................	1,500	
Interest expense......................	400	
Utilities expense	200	
Total	$82,400	$82,400

❙ Requirement 5

Calderon Service Center, Inc. Income Statement Month Ended March 31, 2010		
Revenue		
Service revenue.................		$7,600
Expenses		
Salary expense.................	$3,000	
Rent expense...................	1,500	
Interest expense..............	400	
Utilities expense	200	
Total expenses....................		5,100
Net income........................		$2,500

REVIEW TRANSACTION ANALYSIS

Quick Check (Answers are given on page 120.)

1. A debit entry to an account
   a. increases liabilities.
   b. increases assets.
   c. increases shareholders' equity.
   d. both a and c.

2. Which account types normally have a credit balance?
   a. Revenues
   b. Liabilities
   c. Expenses
   d. Both a and b

3. An attorney performs services of $900 for a client and receives $100 cash with the remainder on account. The journal entry for this transaction would
   a. debit Cash, debit Service Revenue, credit Accounts Receivable.
   b. debit Cash, debit Accounts Receivable, credit Service Revenue.
   c. debit Cash, credit Service Revenue.
   d. debit Cash, credit Accounts Receivable, credit Service Revenue.

4. Accounts Payable had a normal beginning balance of $1,600. During the period, there were debit postings of $300 and credit postings of $900. What was the ending balance?
   a. $1,000 credit
   b. $2,200 debit
   c. $2,200 credit
   d. $1,000 debit

5. The list of all accounts with their balances is the
   a. balance sheet.
   b. journal.
   c. trial balance.
   d. chart of accounts.

6. The basic summary device of accounting is the
   a. account.
   b. ledger.
   c. trial balance.
   d. journal.

7. The beginning Cash balance was $9,000. At the end of the period, the balance was $11,000. If total cash paid out during the period was $25,000, the amount of cash receipts was
   a. $27,000.
   c. $23,000.
   b. $45,000.
   d. $5,000.

8. In a double-entry accounting system
   a. half of all the accounts have a normal credit balance.
   b. liabilities, owners' equity, and revenue accounts all have normal debit balances.
   c. a debit entry is recorded on the left side of a T-account.
   d. both a and c are correct.

9. Which accounts appear on which financial statement?

	Balance sheet	*Income statement*
a.	Receivables, land, payables	Revenues, supplies
b.	Cash, revenues, land	Expenses, payables
c.	Cash, receivables, payables	Revenues, expenses
d.	Expenses, payables, cash	Revenues, receivables, land

10. A doctor purchases medical supplies of $760 and pays $380 cash with the remainder on account. The journal entry for this transaction would be which of the following?
    a. Supplies
          Cash
            Accounts Payable
    c. Supplies
          Accounts Payable
          Cash
    b. Supplies
          Accounts Payable
          Cash
    d. Supplies
          Accounts Receivable
          Cash

11. Which is the correct sequence for recording transactions and preparing financial statements?
    a. Ledger, trial balance, journal, financial statements
    b. Financial statements, trial balance, ledger, journal
    c. Ledger, journal, trial balance, financial statements
    d. Journal, ledger, trial balance, financial statements

12. The error of posting $300 as $30 can be detected by
    a. totaling each account's balance in the ledger.
    b. dividing the out-of-balance amount by 2.
    c. examining the chart of accounts.
    d. dividing the out-of-balance amount by 9.

Accounting Vocabulary

account (p. 63) The record of the changes that have occurred in a particular asset, liability, or shareholders' equity during a period. The basic summary device of accounting.

accrued liability (p. 64) A liability for an expense that has not yet been paid by the company.

chart of accounts (p. 88) List of a company's accounts and their account numbers.

credit (p. 75) The right side of an account.

debit (p. 75) The left side of an account.

journal (p. 78) The chronological accounting record of an entity's transactions.

ledger (p. 79) The book of accounts and their balances.

posting (p. 79) Copying amounts from the journal to the ledger.

transaction (p. 62) Any event that has a financial impact on the business and can be measured reliably.

trial balance (p. 85) A list of all the ledger accounts with their balances.

ASSESS YOUR PROGRESS

Short Exercises

S2-1 (*Learning Objective 1: Explaining an asset versus an expense*) Brian Horton opened a software consulting firm that immediately paid $8,000 for a computer. Was Horton's computer an expense of the business? If not, explain.

S2-2 (*Learning Objective 1: Analyzing the effects of transactions*) Young Software began with cash of $13,000. Young then bought supplies for $1,800 on account. Separately, Young paid $4,000 for a computer. Answer these questions.

    a. How much in total assets does Young have?
    b. How much in liabilities does Young owe?

S2-3 (*Learning Objectives 1, 2: Analyzing transactions; understanding how accounting works*) Hannah Lyle, MD, opened a medical practice. The business completed the following transactions:

Aug 1	Lyle invested $31,000 cash to start her medical practice. The business issued ordinary shares to Lyle.
1	Purchased medical supplies on account totaling $9,200.
2	Paid monthly office rent of $3,000.
3	Recorded $10,000 revenue for service rendered to patients, received cash of $2,000, and sent bills to patients for the remainder.

After these transactions, how much cash does the business have to work with? Use a T-account to show your answer.

S2-4 (*Learning Objective 1: Analyzing transactions*) Refer to Short Exercise 2-3. Which of the transactions of Hannah Lyle, MD, increased the total assets of the business? For each transaction, identify the asset that was increased.

S2-5 (*Learning Objective 1: Analyzing transactions*) Capri Design specializes in imported clothing. During May, Capri completed a series of transactions. For each of the following items, give an example of a transaction that has the described effect on the accounting equation of Capri Design.

    a. Increase one asset and decrease another asset.
    b. Decrease an asset and decrease owners' equity.
    c. Decrease an asset and decrease a liability.
    d. Increase an asset and increase owners' equity.
    e. Increase an asset and increase a liability.

S2-6 (*Learning Objectives 2, 3: Understanding how accounting works; journalizing transactions*) After operating for several months, architect Gwen Markum completed the following transactions during the latter part of July:

Jul 15	Borrowed $34,000 from the bank, signing a note payable.
22	Performed service for clients on account totaling $8,500.
28	Received $6,500 cash on account from clients.
29	Received a utility bill of $700, an account payable that will be paid during August.
31	Paid monthly salary of $3,100 to employee.

Journalize the transactions of Gwen Markum, Architect. Include an explanation with each journal entry.

S2-7 (*Learning Objectives 2, 3: Understanding how accounting works; journalizing transactions; posting*) Architect David Delorme purchased supplies on account for $2,000. Later Delorme paid $500 on account.

1. Journalize the two transactions on the books of David Delorme, architect. Include an explanation for each transaction.
2. Open a T-account for Accounts Payable and post to Accounts Payable. Compute the balance and denote it as Bal.
3. How much does the Delorme business owe after both transactions? In which account does this amount appear?

S2-8 (*Learning Objectives 2, 3: Understanding how accounting works; journalizing transactions; posting*) Orman Unlimited performed service for a client who could not pay immediately. Orman expected to collect the $5,200 the following month. A month later, Orman received $2,400 cash from the client.

1. Record the two transactions on the books of Orman Unlimited. Include an explanation for each transaction.
2. Post to these T-accounts: Cash, Accounts Receivable, and Service Revenue. Compute each account balance and denote as Bal.

S2-9 (*Learning Objective 4: Preparing and using a trial balance*) Assume that Old Boardwalk reported the following summarized data at December 31, 2010. Accounts appear in no particular order; dollar amounts are in millions.

Other liabilities	$ 5	Revenues	$37
Cash	6	Other assets	13
Expenses	27	Accounts payable	1
Shareholders' equity	3		

Prepare the trial balance of Old Boardwalk at December 31, 2010. List the accounts in their proper order. How much was Old Boardwalk's net income or net loss?

S2-10 (*Learning Objective 4: Using a trial balance*) Redberry's trial balance follows.

Redberry, Inc.
Trial Balance
December 31, 2010

	Balance	
Account Title	Debit	Credit
Cash	$ 7,500	
Accounts receivable	12,000	
Supplies	5,000	
Equipment	24,000	
Land	52,000	
Accounts payable		$ 21,000
Note payable		32,000
Share capital		7,000
Retained earnings		9,000
Service revenue		63,000
Salary expense	23,000	
Rent expense	7,500	
Utilities expense	1,000	
Total	$132,000	$132,000

Compute these amounts for the business:

1. Total assets
2. Total liabilities
3. Net income or net loss during December

S2-11 (*Learning Objective 4: Using a trial balance*) Refer to Redberry's trial balance in Short Exercise 2-10. The purpose of this exercise is to help you learn how to correct three common accounting errors.

Error 1. Slide. Suppose the trial balance lists Land as $5,200 instead of $52,000. Recompute column totals, take the difference, and divide by 9. The result is an integer (no decimals), which suggests that the error is either a transposition or a slide.

Error 2. Transposition. Assume the trial balance lists Accounts Receivable as $21,000 instead of $12,000. Recompute column totals, take the difference, and divide by 9. The result is an integer (no decimals), which suggests that the error is either a transposition or a slide.

Error 3. Mislabeling an item. Assume that Redberry accidentally listed Accounts Receivable as a credit balance instead of a debit. Recompute the trial balance totals for debits and credits. Then take the difference between total debits and total credits, and divide the difference by 2. You get back to the original amount of Accounts Receivable.

S2-12 (*Learning Objective 2: Using key accounting terms*) Accounting has its own vocabulary and basic relationships. Match the accounting terms at left with the corresponding definition or meaning at right.

____ 1. Debit	A. The cost of operating a business; a decrease in
____ 2. Expense	shareholders' equity
____ 3. Net income	B. Always a liability
____ 4. Ledger	C. Revenues – Expenses
____ 5. Posting	D. Grouping of accounts
____ 6. Normal balance	E. Assets – Liabilities
____ 7. Payable	F. Record of transactions
____ 8. Journal	G. Always an asset
____ 9. Receivable	H. Left side of an account
____ 10. Owners' equity	I. Side of an account where increases are recorded
	J. Copying data from the journal to the ledger

S2-13 (*Learning Objective 5: Analyzing transactions without a journal*) Seventh Investments, Inc., began by issuing ordinary shares for cash of $140,000. The company immediately purchased computer equipment on account for $100,000.

1. Set up the following T-accounts of Seventh Investments, Inc.: Cash, Computer Equipment, Accounts Payable, Share Capital.
2. Record the first two transactions of the business directly in the T-accounts without using a journal.
3. Show that total debits equal total credits.

Exercises

All of the A and B exercises can be found within MyAccountingLab, an online homework and practice environment. Your instructor may ask you to complete these exercises using MyAccountingLab.

MyAccountingLab

(Group A)

E2-14A (*Learning Objectives 1, 2: Analyzing transactions*) Assume M. Crew opened a store in Dallas, starting with cash and ordinary shares of $94,000. Melissa Farino, the store manager, then signed a note payable to purchase land for $88,000 and a building for $123,000. Farino also paid $60,000 for equipment and $8,000 for supplies to use in the business.

writing assignment ■

Suppose the home office of M. Crew requires a weekly report from store managers. Write Farino's memo to the home office to report on her purchases. Include the store's balance sheet as the final part of your memo. Prepare a T-account to compute the balance for Cash.

E2-15A *(Learning Objective 1: Analyzing transactions)* The following selected events were experienced by either Solution Seekers, Inc., a corporation, or Paul Flynn, the major shareholder. State whether each event (1) increased, (2) decreased, or (3) had no effect on the total assets of the business. Identify any specific asset affected.

    a. Received $9,200 cash from customers on account.
    b. Flynn used personal funds to purchase a swimming pool for his home.
    c. Sold land and received cash of $65,000 (the land was carried on the company's books at $65,000).
    d. Borrowed $60,000 from the bank.
    e. Made cash purchase of land for a building site, $90,000.
    f. Received $25,000 cash and issued shares to a shareholder.
    g. Paid $70,000 cash on accounts payable.
    h. Purchased equipment and signed a $101,000 promissory note in payment.
    i. Purchased merchandise inventory on account for $17,000.
    j. The business paid Flynn a cash dividend of $5,000.

E2-16A *(Learning Objective 1: Analyzing transactions; using the accounting equation)* Harry Samson opened a medical practice specialising in surgery. During the first month of operation (March), the business, titled Harry Samson, Professional Corporation (P.C.), experienced the following events:

Mar	6	Samson invested $42,000 in the business, which in turn issued its ordinary shares to him.
	9	The business paid cash for land costing $25,000. Samson plans to build an office building on the land.
	12	The business purchased medical supplies for $16,000 on account.
	15	Harry Samson, P.C., officially opened for business.
	15–31	During the rest of the month, Samson treated patients and earned service revenue of $7,700, receiving cash for half the revenue earned.
	15–31	The business paid cash expenses: employee salaries, $900; office rent, $900; utilities, $200.
	31	The business sold supplies to another physician for cost of $200.
	31	The business borrowed $18,000, signing a note payable to the bank.
	31	The business paid $1,100 on account.

❚ Requirements

    1. Analyze the effects of these events on the accounting equation of the medical practice of Harry Samson, P.C.
    2. After completing the analysis, answer these questions about the business.
        a. How much are total assets?
        b. How much does the business expect to collect from patients?
        c. How much does the business owe in total?
        d. How much of the business's assets does Samson really own?
        e. How much net income or net loss did the business experience during its first month of operations?

E2-17A *(Learning Objectives 2, 3: Understanding how accounting works; journalizing transactions)* Refer to Exercise 2-16A.

❚ Requirement

    1. Record the transactions in the journal of Harry Samson, P.C. List the transactions by date and give an explanation for each transaction.

E2-18A (*Learning Objectives 2, 3: Understanding how accounting works; journalizing transactions*) Harris Tree Cellular, Inc., completed the following transactions during April 2010, its first month of operations:

■ **general ledger**

Apr	1	Received $19,100 and issued ordinary shares.
	2	Purchased $300 of office supplies on account.
	4	Paid $14,700 cash for land to use as a building site.
	6	Performed service for customers and received cash of $2,700.
	9	Paid $200 on accounts payable.
	17	Performed service for ShipEx on account totaling $1,000.
	23	Collected $200 from ShipEx on account.
	30	Paid the following expenses: salary, $1,300; rent, $500.

❚ Requirement

1. Record the transactions in the journal of Harris Tree Cellular, Inc. Key transactions by date and include an explanation for each entry.

E2-19A (*Learning Objectives 3, 4: Posting to the ledger; preparing and using a trial balance*) Refer to Exercise 2-18A.

■ **general ledger**

❚ Requirements

1. After journalizing the transactions of Exercise 2-18A, post the entries to the ledger, using T-accounts. Key transactions by date. Date the ending balance of each account April 30.
2. Prepare the trial balance of Harris Tree Cellular, Inc., at April 30, 2010.
3. How much are total assets, total liabilities, and total shareholders' equity on April 30?

E2-20A (*Learning Objectives 2, 3: Understanding how accounting works; journalizing transactions*) The first seven transactions of Fournier Advertising, Inc., have been posted to the company's accounts as follows:

Cash				Supplies			Equipment		Land	
(1)	10,200	(3)	6,000	(4) 500	(5) 150	(6)	5,100		(3)	30,000
(2)	6,900	(6)	5,100							
(5)	150	(7)	100							

Accounts Payable			Note Payable			Share Capital	
(7) 100	(4) 500			(2)	6,900	(1)	10,200
				(3)	24,000		

❚ Requirement

1. Prepare the journal entries that served as the sources for the seven transactions. Include an explanation for each entry. As Fournier moves into the next period, how much cash does the business have? How much does Fournier owe in total liabilities?

E2-21A (*Learning Objective 4: Preparing and using a trial balance*) The accounts of Deluxe Deck Service, Inc., follow with their normal balances at June 30, 2010. The accounts are listed in no particular order.

Account	Balance	Account	Balance
Share Capital...................	$ 8,400	Dividends........................	$ 6,100
Accounts payable.............	4,400	Utilities expense..............	2,100
Service revenue................	22,400	Accounts receivable..........	15,900
Land................................	29,800	Delivery expense..............	700
Note payable....................	10,500	Retained earnings.............	25,600
Cash...............................	8,500	Salary expense.................	8,200

I Requirements

1. Prepare the company's trial balance at June 30, 2010, listing accounts in proper sequence, as illustrated in the chapter. For example, Accounts Receivable comes before Land. List the expense with the largest balance first, the expense with the next largest balance second, and so on.

2. Prepare the financial statement for the month ended June 30, 2010, that will tell the company the results of operations for the month.

E2-22A (*Learning Objective 4: Correcting errors in a trial balance*) The trial balance of Carver, Inc., at September 30, 2010, does not balance:

Cash	$ 4,500	
Accounts receivable	13,100	
Inventory	16,600	
Supplies	200	
Land	52,000	
Accounts payable		$11,900
Share capital		47,500
Service revenue		30,500
Salary expense	1,700	
Rent expense	1,100	
Utilities expense	900	
Total	$90,100	$89,900

The accounting records hold the following errors:

a. Recorded a $400 cash revenue transaction by debiting Accounts Receivable. The credit entry was correct.

b. Posted a $3,000 credit to Accounts Payable as $300.

c. Did not record utilities expense or the related account payable in the amount of $500.

d. Understated Share Capital by $500.

e. Omitted Insurance Expense of $3,000, from the trial balance.

I Requirement

1. Prepare the correct trial balance at September 30, 2010, complete with a heading. Journal entries are not required.

E2-23A (*Learning Objective 5: Recording transactions without a journal*) Set up the following T-accounts: Cash, Accounts Receivable, Office Supplies, Office Furniture, Accounts Payable, Share Capital, Dividends, Service Revenue, Salary Expense, and Rent Expense. Record the following transactions directly in the T-accounts without using a journal. Use the letters to identify the transactions.

a. Linda Oxford opened a law firm by investing $12,000 cash and office furniture valued at $8,600. Organized as a corporation, the business issued ordinary shares to Oxford.

b. Paid monthly rent of $1,000.

c. Purchased office supplies on account, $700.

d. Paid employees' salaries of $2,000.

e. Paid $300 of the account payable created in Transaction c.

f. Performed legal service on account, $8,100.

g. Declared and paid dividends of $2,900.

E2-24A (*Learning Objective 4: Preparing and using a trial balance*) Refer to Exercise 2-23A.

writing assignment ■

1. After recording the transactions in Exercise 2-23A, prepare the trial balance of Linda Oxford, Attorney, at May 31, 2010. Use the T-accounts that have been prepared for the business.

2. How well did the business perform during its first month? Compute net income (or net loss) for the month.

(Group B)

E2-25B (*Learning Objectives 1, 2: Analyzing transactions*) Assume T. Crew opened a store in San Diego, starting with cash and ordinary shares of $90,000. Barbara Breen, the store manager, then signed a note payable to purchase land for $91,000 and a building for $120,000. Breen also paid $62,000 for equipment and $13,000 for supplies to use in the business.

writing assignment ■

Suppose the home office of T. Crew requires a weekly report from store managers. Write Breen's memo to the head office to report on her purchases. Include the store's balance sheet as the final part of your memo. Prepare a T-account to compute the balance for Cash.

E2-26B (*Learning Objective 1: Analyzing transactions*) The following selected events were experienced by either Simple Solutions, Inc., a corporation, or Bob Gallagher, the major shareholder. State whether each event (1) increased, (2) decreased, or (3) had no effect on the total assets of the business. Identify any specific asset affected.

a. Received $30,000 cash and issued shares to a shareholder.
b. Purchased equipment for $75,000 cash.
c. Paid $10,000 cash on accounts payable.
d. Gallagher used personal funds to purchase a flat screen TV for his home.
e. Purchased land for a building site and signed an $80,000 promissory note to the bank.
f. Received $17,000 cash from customers for services performed.
g. Sold land and received a note receivable of $55,000 (the land was carried on the company's books at $55,000).
h. Earned $25,000 in revenue for services performed. The customer promises to pay Simple Solutions in one month.
i. Purchased supplies on account for $5,000.
j. The business paid Gallagher a cash dividend of $4,000.

E2-27B (*Learning Objective 1: Analyzing transactions; using the accounting equation*) Kyle Cohen opened a medical practice specialising in surgery. During the first month of operation (July), the business, titled Kyle Cohen, Professional Corporation (P.C.), experienced the following events:

Jul	6	Cohen invested $44,000 in the business, which in turn issued its ordinary shares to him.
	9	The business paid cash for land costing $31,000. Cohen plans to build an office building on the land.
	12	The business purchased medical supplies for $1,700 on account.
	15	Kyle Cohen, P.C., officially opened for business.
	15–31	During the rest of the month, Cohen treated patients and earned service revenue of $7,600, receiving cash for half the revenue earned.
	15–31	The business paid cash expenses: employee salaries, $800; office rent, $800; utilities, $300.
	31	The business sold supplies to another physician for cost of $400.
	31	The business borrowed $16,000, signing a note payable to the bank.
	31	The business paid $700 on account.

I Requirements

1. Analyze the effects of these events on the accounting equation of the medical practice of Kyle Cohen, P.C.
2. After completing the analysis, answer these questions about the business.
   a. How much are total assets?
   b. How much does the business expect to collect from patients?
   c. How much does the business owe in total?
   d. How much of the business's assets does Cohen really own?
   e. How much net income or net loss did the business experience during its first month of operations?

E2-28B (*Learning Objectives 2, 3: Understanding how accounting works; journalizing transactions*) Refer to Exercise 2-27B.

❙ Requirement

1. Record the transactions in the journal of Kyle Cohen, P.C. List the transactions by date and give an explanation for each transaction.

E2-29B (*Learning Objectives 2, 3: Understanding how accounting works; journalizing transactions*) Green Tree Cellular, Inc., completed the following transactions during April 2010, its first month of operations:

Apr	1	Received $19,600 and issued ordinary shares.
	2	Purchased $900 of office supplies on account.
	4	Paid $14,600 cash for land to use as a building site.
	6	Performed service for customers and received cash of $2,500.
	9	Paid $200 on accounts payable.
	17	Performed service for UPS on account totaling $1,200.
	23	Collected $900 from UPS on account.
	30	Paid the following expenses: salary, $1,900; rent, $1,400.

❙ Requirement

1. Record the transactions in the journal of Green Tree Cellular, Inc. Key transactions by date and include an explanation for each entry.

E2-30B (*Learning Objectives 3, 4: Posting to the ledger; preparing and using a trial balance*) Refer to Exercise 2-29B.

❙ Requirements

1. Post the entries to the ledger, using T-accounts. Key transactions by date. Date the ending balance of each account April 30.
2. Prepare the trial balance of Green Tree Cellular, Inc., at April 30, 2010.
3. How much are total assets, total liabilities, and total shareholders' equity on April 30?

E2-31B (*Learning Objectives 2, 3: Understanding how accounting works; journalizing transactions*) The first seven transactions of Portman Advertising, Inc., have been posted to the company's accounts as follows:

Cash					Supplies				Equipment				Land	
(1)	9,700	(3)	5,000	(4)	500	(5)	80	(6)	6,000			(3)	30,000	
(2)	6,700	(6)	6,000											
(5)	80	(7)	90											

Accounts Payable				Note Payable			Share Capital		
(7)	90	(4)	500	(2)	6,700		(1)	9,700	
				(3)	25,000				

❙ Requirement

1. Prepare the journal entries that served as the sources for the seven transactions. Include an explanation for each entry. As Portman moves into the next period, how much cash does the business have? How much does Portman owe in total liabilities?

E2-32B (*Learning Objective 4: Preparing and using a trial balance*) The accounts of Grand Pool Service, Inc., follow with their normal balances at June 30, 2010. The accounts are listed in no particular order.

Account	Balance	Account	Balance
Share Capital....................	$ 8,000	Dividends.........................	$ 6,300
Accounts payable.............	4,500	Utilities expense	1,600
Service revenue.................	22,800	Accounts receivable...........	13,300
Land................................	29,400	Delivery expense	200
Note payable....................	10,500	Retained earnings..............	24,600
Cash................................	9,400	Salary expense..................	8,200

I Requirements

1. Prepare the company's trial balance at June 30, 2010, listing accounts in proper sequence, as illustrated in the chapter. For example, Accounts Receivable comes before Land. List the expense with the largest balance first, the expense with the next largest balance second, and so on.
2. Prepare the financial statement for the month ended June 30, 2010, that will tell the company the results of operations for the month.

E2-33B (*Learning Objective 4: Correcting errors in a trial balance*) The trial balance of Farris, Inc., at June 30, 2010, does not balance.

Cash......................................	$ 4,100	
Accounts receivable...............	13,300	
Inventory...............................	16,500	
Supplies................................	700	
Land.....................................	53,000	
Accounts payable		$12,400
Share capital.........................		47,800
Service revenue......................		31,900
Salary expense......................	2,200	
Rent expense........................	600	
Utilities expense	300	
Total.....................................	$90,700	$92,100

The accounting records hold the following errors:

    a. Recorded a $200 cash revenue transaction by debiting Accounts Receivable. The credit entry was correct.
    b. Posted a $2,000 credit to Accounts Payable as $200.
    c. Did not record utilities expense or the related account payable in the amount of $300.
    d. Understated Share Capital by $100.
    e. Omitted Insurance Expense of $3,300, from the trial balance.

I Requirement

1. Prepare the correct trial balance at June 30, 2010, complete with a heading. Journal entries are not required.

E2-34B *(Learning Objective 5: Recording transactions without a journal)* Set up the following T-accounts: Cash, Accounts Receivable, Office Supplies, Office Furniture, Accounts Payable, Share Capital, Dividends, Service Revenue, Salary Expense, and Rent Expense. Record the following transactions directly in the T-accounts without using a journal. Use the letters to identify the transactions.

a. Linda Conway opened a law firm by investing $11,000 cash and office furniture valued at $9,100. Organized as a corporation, the business issued ordinary shares to Conway.
b. Paid monthly rent of $1,200.
c. Purchased office supplies on account, $700.
d. Paid employee salaries of $2,200.
e. Paid $300 of the accounts payable created in Transaction c.
f. Performed legal service on account, $8,300.
g. Declared and paid dividends of $2,100.

E2-35B *(Learning Objective 4: Preparing and using a trial balance)* Refer to Exercise 2-34B.

❙ Requirements

1. Prepare the trial balance of Linda Conway, Attorney, at January 31, 2010. Use the T-accounts that have been prepared for the business.
2. How well did the business perform during its first month? Compute net income (or net loss) for the month.

Serial Exercise

Exercise 2-36 begins an accounting cycle exercise that will be completed in Chapter 3.

■ general ledger

E2-36 *(Learning Objectives 2, 3, 4: Recording transactions; preparing a trial balance)* Jerome Smith, Certified Public Accountant, operates as a professional corporation (P.C.). The business completed these transactions during the first part of March, 2010:

Mar	2	Received $7,000 cash from Smith, and issued ordinary shares to him.
	2	Paid monthly office rent, $600.
	3	Paid cash for a Dell computer, $2,400, with the computer expected to remain in service for five years.
	4	Purchased office furniture on account, $7,500, with the furniture projected to last for five years.
	5	Purchased supplies on account, $500.
	9	Performed tax service for a client and received cash for the full amount of $1,200.
	12	Paid utility expenses, $300.
	18	Performed consulting service for a client on account, $2,100.

❙ Requirements

1. Journalize the transactions. Explanations are not required.
2. Post to the T-accounts. Key all items by date and denote an account balance on March 18, 2010, as Bal.
3. Prepare a trial balance at March 18, 2010. In the Serial Exercise of Chapter 3, we add transactions for the remainder of March and will require a trial balance at March 31.

Challenge Exercises

E2-37 *(Learning Objective 5: Computing financial statement amounts)* The manager of Pierce Furniture needs to compute the following amounts.

a. Total cash paid during October.
b. Cash collections from customers during October. Analyze Accounts Receivable.
c. Cash paid on a note payable during October. Analyze Notes Payable.

Here's the additional data you need to analyze the accounts:

	Balance		
			Additional Information
Account	Sep 30	Oct 31	for the Month of October
1. Cash..............................	$11,000	$ 6,000	Cash receipts, $83,000
2. Accounts Receivable.......	28,000	26,000	Sales on account, $47,000
3. Notes Payable	15,000	23,000	New borrowing, $24,000

Requirement

1. Prepare a T-account to compute each amount, *a* through *c*.

E2-38 (*Learning Objectives 1, 4: Analyzing transactions; using a trial balance*) The trial balance of Circle 360, Inc., at October 31, 2010, does not balance.

Cash.....................................	$ 4,400	Share capital........................	$20,700
Accounts receivable.............	6,800	Retained earnings................	7,800
Land....................................	34,000	Service revenue....................	9,000
Accounts payable	6,300	Salary expense.....................	3,200
Note payable.......................	5,400	Advertising expense.............	1,000

Requirements

1. How much out of balance is the trial balance? Determine the out-of-balance amount. The error lies in the Accounts Receivable account. Add the out-of-balance amount to, or subtract it from, Accounts Receivable to determine the correct balance of Accounts Receivable.
2. After correcting Accounts receivable, advise the top management of Circle 360, Inc., on the company's
   a. total assets.
   b. total liabilities.
   c. net income or net loss for October.

E2-39 (*Learning Objective 1: Analyzing transactions*) This question concerns the items and the amounts that two entities, Nashua Co., and Ditka Hospital, should report in their financial statements.

During September, Ditka provided Nashua with medical exams for Nashua employees and sent a bill for $46,000. On October 7, Nashua sent a cheque to Ditka for $34,000. Nashua began September with a cash balance of $57,000; Ditka began with cash of $0.

Requirements

1. For this situation, show everything that both Nashua and Ditka will report on their September and October income statements and on their balance sheets at September 30 and October 31.
2. After showing what each company should report, briefly explain how the Nashua and Ditka data relate to each other.

Quiz

Test your understanding of transaction analysis by answering the following questions. Select the best choice from among the possible answers.

Q2-40 An investment of cash into the business will

a. decrease total liabilities.

b. decrease total assets.

c. have no effect on total assets.

d. increase shareholders' equity.

Q2-41 Purchasing a laptop computer on account will

a. increase total liabilities.

b. have no effect on shareholders' equity.

c. increase total assets.

d. all of the above.

Q2-42 Performing a service on account will

a. increase shareholders' equity.

b. increase total assets.

c. increase total liabilities.

d. both a and b.

Q2-43 Receiving cash from a customer on account will

a. increase total assets.

b. decrease liabilities.

c. increase shareholders equity.

d. have no effect on total assets.

Q2-44 Purchasing computer equipment for cash will

a. decrease both total assets and shareholders' equity.

b. increase both total assets and total liabilities.

c. have no effect on total assets, total liabilities, or shareholders' equity.

d. decrease both total liabilities and shareholders' equity.

Q2-45 Purchasing a building for $110,000 by paying cash of $15,000 and signing a note payable for $95,000 will

a. increase both total assets and total liabilities by $95,000.

b. increase both total assets and total liabilities by $110,000.

c. decrease both total assets and total liabilities by $15,000.

d. decrease total assets and increase total liabilities by $15,000.

Q2-46 What is the effect on total assets and shareholders' equity of paying the telephone bill as soon as it is received each month?

	Total assets	Shareholders' equity
a.	No effect	No effect
b.	Decrease	No effect
c.	No effect	Decrease
d.	Decrease	Decrease

Q2-47 Which of the following transactions will increase an asset and increase a liability?

a. Purchasing office equipment for cash

b. Issuing shares

c. Payment of an account payable

d. Buying equipment on account

Q2-48 Which of the following transactions will increase an asset and increase shareholders' equity?

a. Borrowing money from a bank

b. Purchasing supplies on account

c. Performing a service on account for a customer

d. Collecting cash from a customer on an account receivable

Q2-49 Where do we first record a transaction?

a. Journal

b. Trial balance

c. Account

d. Ledger

Q2-50 Which of the following is not an asset account?
a. Salary Expense
b. Service Revenue
c. Share Capital
d. None of the above accounts is an asset.

Q2-51 Which statement is false?
a. Assets are increased by debits.
b. Revenues are increased by credits.
c. Liabilities are decreased by debits.
d. Dividends are increased by credits.

Q2-52 The journal entry to record the receipt of land and a building and issuance of ordinary shares
a. debits Land and credits Share Capital.
b. debits Land and Building and credits Share Capital.
c. debits Land, Building, and Share Capital.
d. debits Share Capital and credits Land and Building.

Q2-53 The journal entry to record the purchase of supplies on account
a. debits Supplies and credits Accounts Payable.
b. credits Supplies and debits Cash.
c. credits Supplies and debits Accounts Payable.
d. debits Supplies Expense and credits Supplies.

Q2-54 If the credit to record the purchase of supplies on account is not posted,
a. expenses will be overstated.
b. liabilities will be understated.
c. shareholders' equity will be understated.
d. assets will be understated.

Q2-55 The journal entry to record a payment on account will
a. debit Cash and credit Expenses.
b. debit Accounts Payable and credit Retained Earnings.
c. debit Accounts Payable and credit Cash.
d. debit Expenses and credit Cash.

Q2-56 If the credit to record the payment of an account payable is not posted,
a. expenses will be understated.
b. liabilities will be understated.
c. cash will be understated.
d. cash will be overstated.

Q2-57 Which statement is false?
a. A trial balance is the same as a balance sheet.
b. A trial balance can verify the equality of debits and credits.
c. A trial balance can be taken at any time.
d. A trial balance lists all the accounts with their current balances.

Q2-58 A business's receipt of a $120,000 building, with a $60,000 mortgage payable, and issuance of $60,000 of cordinary shares will
a. increase shareholders' equity by $60,000.
b. increase assets by $60,000.
c. decrease assets by $60,000.
d. increase shareholders' equity by $120,000.

Q2-59 Gartex, a new company, completed these transactions. What will Gartex's total assets equal?
(1) Shareholders invested $54,000 cash and inventory worth $27,000.
(2) Sales on account, $15,000.
a. $66,000
b. $69,000
c. $96,000
d. $81,000

Problems

All of the A and B problems can be found within MyAccountingLab, an online homework and practice environment. Your instructor may ask you to complete these problems using MyAccountingLab.

(Group A)

writing assignment ▇

P2-60A *(Learning Objective 4: Analyzing a trial balance)* The trial balance of Luxury Specialties, Inc., follows.

Luxury Specialties Trial Balance December 31, 2010		
Cash..	$ 11,000	
Accounts receivable................	48,000	
Prepaid expenses	5,000	
Equipment..............................	239,000	
Building..................................	105,000	
Accounts payable		$108,000
Note payable...........................		90,000
Share capital...........................		35,000
Retained earnings....................		38,000
Dividends................................	19,000	
Service revenue.......................		257,000
Rent expense..........................	28,000	
Advertising expense................	4,000	
Wage expense.........................	61,000	
Supplies expense.....................	8,000	
Total	$528,000	$528,000

Ashley Richards, your best friend, is considering investing in Luxury Specialties, Inc. Ashley seeks your advice in interpreting this information. Specifically, she asks how to use this trial balance to compute the company's total assets, total liabilities, and net income or net loss for the year.

▌Requirement

1. Write a short note to answer Ashley's questions. In your note, state the amounts of Luxury Specialties' total assets, total liabilities, and net income or net loss for the year. Also show how you computed each amount.

P2-61A *(Learning Objective 1: Analyzing transactions with the accounting equation; preparing the financial statements)* The following amounts summarize the financial position of Mason Resources, Inc., on May 31, 2010:

	Assets				=	Liabilities	+	Shareholders' Equity		
	Cash	+	Accounts Receivable	+	Supplies	+	Land	=	Accounts Payable	+	Share Capital	+	Retained Earnings
Bal	1,150		1,350				11,900		7,600		4,400		2,400

During June 2010, Mason Resources completed these transactions:

   a. The business received cash of $9,200 and issued ordinary shares.
   b. Performed services for a customer and received cash of $6,700.
   c. Paid $4,500 on accounts payable.
   d. Purchased supplies on account, $600.
   e. Collected cash from a customer on account, $700.
   f. Consulted on the design of a computer system and billed the customer for services rendered, $2,900.
   g. Recorded the following business expenses for the month: (1) paid office rent—$1,100; (2) paid advertising—$1,000.
   h. Declared and paid a cash dividend of $1,500.

I Requirements

1. Analyze the effects of the preceding transactions on the accounting equation of Mason Resources, Inc.
2. Prepare the income statement of Mason Resources, Inc., for the month ended June 30, 2010. List expenses in decreasing order by amount.
3. Prepare the entity's statement of changes in equity for the month ended June 30, 2010.
4. Prepare the balance sheet of Mason Resources, Inc., at June 30, 2010.

P2-62A *(Learning Objectives 2, 3: Recording transactions; posting)* This problem can be used in conjunction with Problem 2-61A. Refer to Problem 2-61A.

■ **general ledger**

I Requirements

1. Journalize the June transactions of Mason Resources, Inc. Explanations are not required.
2. Prepare T-Accounts for each account. Insert in each T-account its May 31 balance as given (example: Cash $1,150). Then, post the June transactions to the T-Accounts.
3. Compute the balance in each account.

P2-63A *(Learning Objectives 1, 2, 3: Analyzing transactions; understanding how accounting works; journalizing transactions)* Demers Real Estate Co. experienced the following events during the organizing phase and its first month of operations. Some of the events were personal for the shareholders and did not affect the business. Others were transactions of the business.

Nov	4	David Demers, the major shareholder of real estate company, received $100,000 cash from an inheritance.
	5	Demers deposited $57,000 cash in a new business bank account titled Demers Real Estate Co. The business issued ordinary shares to Demers.
	6	The business paid $600 cash for letterhead stationery for the new office.
	7	The business purchased office equipment. The company paid cash of $12,000 and agreed to pay the account payable for the remainder, $8,000, within three months.
	10	Demers sold EVN shares, which he had owned for several years, receiving $76,500 cash from his stockbroker.
	11	Demers deposited the $76,500 cash from sale of the EVN shares in his personal bank account.
	12	A representative of a large company telephoned Demers and told him of the company's intention to transfer $15,500 of business to Demers.
	18	Demers finished a real estate deal for a client and submitted his bill for services, $3,500. Demers expects to collect from the client within two weeks.
	21	The business paid half its account payable on the equipment purchased on November 7.
	25	The business paid office rent of $1,300.
	30	The business declared and paid a cash dividend of $1,900.

❚ Requirements

1. Classify each of the preceding events as one of the following:
   a. A business-related event but not a transaction to be recorded by Demers Real Estate Co.
   b. A business transaction for a shareholder, not to be recorded by Demers Real Estate Co.
   c. A business transaction to be recorded by Demers Real Estate Co.

2. Analyze the effects of the preceding events on the accounting equation of Demers Real Estate Co.

3. Record the transactions of the business in its journal. Include an explanation for each entry.

■ general ledger

P2-64A (*Learning Objectives 2, 3: Understanding how accounting works; analyzing and recording transactions*) During December, Smith Auction Co. completed the following transactions:

Dec	1	Smith received $26,000 cash and issued ordinary shares to the shareholders.
	5	Paid monthly rent, $1,100.
	9	Paid $8,500 cash and signed a $30,000 note payable to purchase land for an office site.
	10	Purchased supplies on account, $1,700.
	19	Paid $600 on account.
	22	Borrowed $20,000 from the bank for business use. Smith signed a note payable to the bank in the name of the business.
	31	Service revenue earned during the month included $12,000 cash and $8,000 on account.
	31	Paid employees' salaries ($2,400), advertising expense ($1,500), and utilities expense ($1,400).
	31	Declared and paid a cash dividend of $6,500.

Smith's business uses the following accounts: Cash, Accounts Receivable, Supplies, Land, Accounts Payable, Notes Payable, Share Capital, Dividends, Service Revenue, Salary Expense, Advertising Expense, and Utilities Expense.

❚ Requirements

1. Journalize each transaction of Smith Auction Co. Explanations are not required.
2. Post to these T-accounts: Cash, Accounts Payable, and Notes Payable.
3. After these transactions, how much cash does the business have? How much in total liabilities does it owe?

■ general ledger

P2-65A (*Learning Objectives 2, 3, 4: Understanding how accounting works; journalizing transactions; posting; preparing and using a trial balance*) During the first month of operations, Simmons Heating and Air Conditioning, Inc., completed the following transactions:

Jan	2	Simmons received $39,000 cash and issued ordinary shares to the shareholders.
	3	Purchased supplies, $200, and equipment, $3,100, on account.
	4	Performed service for a customer and received cash, $1,600.
	7	Paid cash to acquire land, $27,000.
	11	Performed service for a customer and billed the customer, $900. We expect to collect within one month.
	16	Paid for the equipment purchased January 3 on account.
	17	Paid the telephone bill, $170.
	18	Received partial payment from customer on account, $450.
	22	Paid the water and electricity bills, $190.
	29	Received $1,400 cash for servicing the heating unit of a customer.
	31	Paid employee salary, $2,400.
	31	Declared and paid dividends of $3,000.

❚ Requirements

1. Record each transaction in the journal. Key each transaction by date. Explanations are not required.
2. Post the transactions to the T-accounts, using transaction dates as posting references. Label the ending balance of each account Bal, as shown in the chapter.
3. Prepare the trial balance of Simmons Heating and Air Conditioning, Inc., at January 31 of the current year.
4. The manager asks you how much in total resources the business has to work with, how much it owes, and whether January was profitable (and by how much).

P2-66A (*Learning Objectives 4, 5: Recording transactions directly in T-accounts; preparing and using a trial balance*) During the first month of operations (November 2010), Stein Services Corporation completed the following selected transactions:

❚ general ledger

   a. The business received cash of $28,000 and a building valued at $52,000. The corporation issued ordinary shares to the shareholders.
   b. Borrowed $37,300 from the bank; signed a note payable.
   c. Paid $33,000 for music equipment.
   d. Purchased supplies on account, $500.
   e. Paid employees' salaries, $2,500.
   f. Received $1,600 for music service performed for customers.
   g. performed service for customers on account, $3,200.
   h. Paid $100 of the account payable created in Transaction d.
   i. Received an $800 bill for utility expense that will be paid in the near future.
   j. Received cash on account, $1,200.
   k. Paid the following cash expenses: (1) rent, $1,200; (2) advertising, $700.

❚ Requirements

1. Record each transaction directly in the T-accounts without using a journal. Use the letters to identify the transactions.
2. Prepare the trial balance of Stein Services Corporation at November 30, 2010.

(Group B)

P2-67B (*Learning Objective 4: Analyzing a trial balance*) The trial balance of Advantage Specialties, Inc., follows:

writing assignment ❚

Advantage Specialties, Inc. Trial Balance December 31, 2010		
Cash..	$ 11,000	
Accounts receivable................	49,000	
Prepaid expenses	5,000	
Equipment.............................	234,000	
Building.................................	96,000	
Accounts payable		$102,000
Note payable..........................		95,000
Share capital..........................		34,000
Retained earnings...................		36,000
Dividends...............................	23,000	
Service revenue.......................		252,000
Rent expense..........................	25,000	
Advertising expense................	4,000	
Wage expense.........................	65,000	
Supplies expense.....................	7,000	
Total	$519,000	$519,000

Rebecca Smith, your best friend, is considering making an investment in Advantage Specialties, Inc. Rebecca seeks your advice in interpreting the company's information. Specifically, she asks how to use this trial balance to compute the company's total assets, total liabilities, and net income or net loss for the year.

I Requirement

1. Write a short note to answer Rebecca's questions. In your note, state the amounts of Advantage Specialties' total assets, total liabilities, and net income or net loss for the year. Also show how you computed each amount.

P2-68B (*Learning Objective 1: Analyzing transactions with the accounting equation; preparing the financial statements*) The following amounts summarize the financial position of Rodriguez Resources on May 31, 2010:

	Assets							=	Liabilities	+	Shareholders' Equity		
	Cash	+	Accounts Receivable	+	Supplies	+	Land	=	Accounts Payable	+	Share Capital	+	Retained Earnings
Bal	1,450		1,650				11,500		7,800		4,000		2,800

During June, 2010, the business completed these transactions:

a. Rodriguez Resources received cash of $8,600 and issued shares.
b. Performed services for a customer and received cash of $6,500.
c. Paid $4,700 on accounts payable.
d. Purchased supplies on account, $600.
e. Collected cash from a customer on account, $200.
f. Consulted on the design of a computer system and billed the customer for services rendered, $2,700.
g. Recorded the following expenses for the month: (1) paid office rent—$900; (2) paid advertising—$800.
h. Declared and paid a cash dividend of $2,300.

I Requirements

1. Analyze the effects of the preceding transactions on the accounting equation of Rodriguez Resources, Inc.
2. Prepare the income statement of Rodriguez Resources, Inc., for the month ended June 30, 2010. List expenses in decreasing order by amount.
3. Prepare the statement of changes in equity of Rodriguez Resources, Inc., for the month ended June 30, 2010.
4. Prepare the balance sheet of Rodriguez Resources, Inc., at June 30, 2010.

■ general ledger

P2-69B (*Learning Objectives 2, 3: Understanding how accounting works; journalizing transactions; posting*) This problem can be used in conjunction with Problem 2-68B. Refer to Problem 2-68B.

I Requirements

1. Journalize the transactions of Rodriguez Resources, Inc. Explanations are not required.
2. Prepare T-accounts for each account. Insert in each T-account its May 31 balance as given (example: Cash $1,450). Then, post the June transactions to the T-accounts.
3. Compute the balance in each account.

P2-70B (*Learning Objectives 1, 2, 3: Analyzing transactions; understanding how accounting works; journalizing transactions*) Smith Real Estate Co. experienced the following events during the organizing phase and its first month of operations. Some of the events were personal for the shareholders and did not affect the business. Others were transactions of the business.

Nov	4	John Smith, the major shareholder of real estate company, received $108,000 cash from an inheritance.
	5	Smith deposited $59,000 cash in a new business bank account titled Smith Real Estate Co. The business issued ordinary shares to Smith.
	6	The business paid $500 cash for letterhead stationery for the new office.
	7	The business purchased office equipment. The company paid cash of $12,000 and agreed to pay the account payable for the remainder, $8,500, within three months.
	10	Smith sold DLD shares, which he owned for several years, receiving $74,000 cash from his stockbroker.
	11	Smith deposited the $74,000 cash from sale of the DLD shares in his personal bank account.
	12	A representative of a large company telephoned Smith and told him of the company's intention to transfer $12,500 of business to Smith.
	18	Smith finished a real estate deal for a client and submitted his bill for services, $3,000. Smith expects to collect from the client within two weeks.
	21	The business paid half its account payable for the equipment purchased on November 7.
	25	The business paid office rent of $500.
	30	The business declared and paid a cash dividend of $1,700.

▌ Requirements

1. Classify each of the preceding events as one of the following:
   a. A business-related event but not a transaction to be recorded by Smith Real Estate Co.
   b. A business transaction for a shareholder, not to be recorded by Smith Real Estate Co.
   c. A business transaction to be recorded by the Smith Real Estate Co.
2. Analyze the effects of the preceding events on the accounting equation of Smith Real Estate Co.
3. Record the transactions of the business in its journal. Include an explanation for each entry.

P2-71B *(Learning Objectives 2, 3: Analyzing and recording transactions)* During December, Swanson Auction Co. completed the following transactions:

■ **general ledger**

Dec	1	Swanson received $28,000 cash and issued ordinary shares to the shareholders.
	5	Paid monthly rent, $2,000.
	9	Paid $11,500 cash and signed a $33,000 note payable to purchase land for an office site.
	10	Purchased supplies on account, $1,700.
	19	Paid $800 on account.
	22	Borrowed $18,500 from the bank for business use. Swanson signed a note payable to the bank in the name of the business.
	31	Service revenue earned during the month included $14,500 cash and $4,500 on account.
	31	Paid employees' salaries ($2,100), advertising expense ($1,000), and utilities expense ($1,100).
	31	Declared and paid a cash dividend of $2,000.

Swanson's business uses the following accounts: Cash, Accounts Receivable, Supplies, Land, Accounts Payable, Notes Payable, Share Capital, Dividends, Service Revenue, Salary Expense, Rent Expense, Advertising Expense, and Utilities Expense.

I Requirements

1. Journalize each transaction of Swanson Auction Co. Explanations are not required.
2. Post to these T-accounts: Cash, Accounts Payable, and Notes Payable.
3. After these transactions, how much cash does the business have? How much does it owe in total liabilities?

■ **general ledger**

P2-72B *(Learning Objectives 2, 3, 4: Understanding how accounting works; journalizing transactions; posting; preparing and using a trial balance)* During the first month of operations, O'Shea Plumbing, Inc., completed the following transactions:

Jan	2	O'Shea received $33,000 cash and issued ordinary shares to the shareholders.
	3	Purchased supplies, $400, and equipment, $2,900, on account.
	4	Performed service for a client and received cash, $1,700.
	7	Paid cash to acquire land, $22,000.
	11	Performed service for a customer and billed the customer, $1,100. We expect to collect within one month.
	16	Paid for the equipment purchased January 3 on account.
	17	Paid the telephone bill, $130.
	18	Received partial payment from customer on account, $550.
	22	Paid the water and electricity bills, $150.
	29	Received $1,100 cash for servicing the heating unit of a customer.
	31	Paid employee salary, $2,300.
	31	Declared and paid dividends of $2,900.

I Requirements

1. Record each transaction in the journal. Key each transaction by date. Explanations are not required.
2. Post the transactions to the T-accounts, using transaction dates as posting references.
3. Prepare the trial balance of O'Shea Plumbing, Inc., at January 31 of the current year.
4. The manager asks you how much in total resources the business has to work with, how much it owes, and whether January was profitable (and by how much).

P2-73B *(Learning Objectives, 4, 5: Recording transactions directly in T-accounts; preparing and using a trial balance)* During the first month of operations (March 2010), Silver Entertainment Corporation completed the following selected transactions:

a. The business received cash of $32,000 and a building valued at $52,000. The corporation issued ordinary shares to the shareholders.
b. Borrowed $35,800 from the bank; signed a note payable.
c. Paid $32,000 for music equipment.
d. Purchased supplies on account, $200.
e. Paid employees' salaries, $2,300.
f. Received $1,700 for music service performed for customers.
g. Performed service for customers on account, $2,800.
h. Paid $100 of the account payable created in Transaction d.
i. Received a $900 bill for advertising expense that will be paid in the near future.
j. Received cash on account, $1,600.
k. Paid the following cash expenses: (1) rent, $1,200; (2) advertising, $800.

I Requirements

1. Record each transaction directly in the T-accounts without using a journal. Use the letters to identify the transactions.
2. Prepare the trial balance of Silver Entertainment Corporation, at March 31, 2010.

APPLY YOUR KNOWLEDGE

Decision Cases

Case 1. *(Learning Objectives 4, 5: Recording transactions directly in T-accounts; preparing a trial balance; measuring net income or loss)* A friend named Jay Barlow has asked what effect certain transactions will have on his company. Time is short, so you cannot apply the detailed procedures of journalizing and posting. Instead, you must analyze the transactions without the use of a journal. Barlow will continue the business only if he can expect to earn monthly net income of at least $5,000. The following transactions occurred this month:

- **a.** Barlow deposited $5,000 cash in a business bank account, and the corporation issued ordinary shares to him.
- **b.** Borrowed $5,000 cash from the bank and signed a note payable due within 1 year.
- **c.** Paid $1,300 cash for supplies.
- **d.** Purchased advertising in the local newspaper for cash, $1,800.
- **e.** Purchased office furniture on account, $4,400.
- **f.** Paid the following cash expenses for 1 month: employee salary, $2,000; office rent, $1,200.
- **g.** Earned revenue on account, $7,000.
- **h.** Earned revenue and received $2,500 cash.
- **i.** Collected cash from customers on account, $1,200.
- **j.** Paid on account, $1,000.

I Requirements

1. Set up the following T-accounts: Cash, Accounts Receivable, Supplies, Furniture, Accounts Payable, Notes Payable, Share Capital, Service Revenue, Salary Expense, Advertising Expense, and Rent Expense.
2. Record the transactions directly in the accounts without using a journal. Key each transaction by letter.
3. Prepare a trial balance for Barlow Networks, Inc., at the current date. List expenses with the largest amount first, the next largest amount second, and so on.
4. Compute the amount of net income or net loss for this first month of operations. Why or why not would you recommend that Barlow continue in business?

Case 2. *(Learning Objective 2: Correcting financial statements; deciding whether to expand a business)* Sophia Loren opened an Italian restaurant. Business has been good, and Loren is considering expanding the restaurant. Loren, who knows little accounting, produced the following financial statements for Little Italy, Inc., at December 31, 2011, end of the first month of operations:

Little Italy, Inc. Income Statement Month Ended December 31, 2011	
Sales revenue	$42,000
Share capital	10,000
Total revenue	52,000
Accounts payable	$ 8,000
Advertising expense	5,000
Rent expense	6,000
Total expenses	19,000
Net income	$33,000

Little Italy, Inc. Balance Sheet December 31, 2011	
Assets	
Cash	$12,000
Cost of goods sold (expense)	22,000
Food inventory	5,000
Furniture	10,000
Total Assets	$49,000
Liabilities	
None	
Owners' Equity	$49,000

In these financial statements all *amounts* are correct, except for Owners' Equity. Loren heard that total assets should equal total liabilities plus owners' equity, so she plugged in the amount of owners' equity at $49,000 to make the balance sheet come out even.

I Requirement

1. Sophia Loren has asked whether she should expand the restaurant. Her banker says Loren may be wise to expand if (a) net income for the first month reached $10,000 and (b) total assets are at least $35,000. It appears that the business has reached these milestones, but Loren doubts whether her financial statements tell the true story. She needs your help in making this decision. Prepare a corrected income statement and balance sheet. (Remember that Retained Earnings, which was omitted from the balance sheet, should equal net income for the first month; there were no dividends.) After preparing the statements, give Sophia Loren your recommendation as to whether she should expand the restaurant.

Ethical Issues

Issue 1. Scruffy Murphy is the president and principal shareholder of Scruffy's Bar & Grill, Inc. To expand, the business is applying for a $250,000 bank loan. To get the loan, Murphy is considering two options for beefing up the owners' equity of the business:

> *Option 1.* Issue $100,000 of ordinary shares for cash. A friend has been wanting to invest in the company. This may be the right time to extend the offer.
>
> *Option 2.* Transfer $100,000 of Murphy's personal land to the business, and issue ordinary shares to Murphy. Then, after obtaining the loan, Murphy can transfer the land back to himself and zero out the ordinary shares.

I Requirements

Use the ethical decision model in Chapter 1 to answer the following questions:

1. What is the ethical issue?
2. Who are the stakeholders? What are the possible consequences to each?
3. Analyze the alternatives from the following standpoints (a) economic, (b) legal, and (c) ethical.
4. What would you do? How would you justify your decision? How would your decision make you feel afterward?

Issue 2. Part a. You have received your grade in your first accounting course, and to your amazement, it is an A. You feel the instructor must have made a big mistake. Your grade was a B going into the final, but you are sure that you really "bombed" the exam, which is worth 30% of the final grade. In fact, you walked out after finishing only 50% of the exam, and the grade report says you made 99% on the exam!

I Requirements

1. What is the ethical issue?
2. Who are the stakeholders? What are the possible consequences to each?
3. Analyze the alternatives from the following standpoints: (a) economic, (b) legal, and (c) ethical.
4. What would you do? How would you justify your decision? How would it make you feel afterward?

Part b. Now assume the same facts as above, except that you have received your final grade for the course and the grade is a B. You are confident that you "aced" the final. In fact, you stayed to the very end of the period, and checked every figure twice! You are confident that the instructor must have made a mistake grading the final.

❙ Requirements

1. What is the ethical issue?
2. Who are the stakeholders and what are the consequences to each?
3. Analyze the alternatives from the following standpoints: (a) economic, (b) legal, and (c) ethical.
4. What would you do? How would you justify your decision? How would it make you feel?

Part c. How is this situation like a financial accounting misstatement? How is it different?

Focus on Financials: ■ Nokia Corporation

Refer to **Nokia's** financial statements in Appendix A at the end of the book. Assume that Nokia completed the following selected transactions during 2008.

  a. Made company sales (revenue) of $50,710 million, all on account (debit accounts receivable).
  b. Collected cash on accounts receivable $52,466 million.
  c. Purchased inventories, paying cash of $32,994 million.
  d. Incurred cost of sales in the amount of $33,337 million. Debit the Cost of sales (expense) account. Credit the Inventories account.
  e. Paid in cash operating expenses of $12,827 million.
  f. Collected in cash other income (operating) of $420 million.
  g. Collected non-operating income (net) in cash , $4 million.
  h. Paid in cash income tax expense of $1,081 million.
  i. Paid cash for other assets $6,407 million.

❙ Requirements

1. Set up T accounts for Cash (beginning debit balance of $2,125 million); Accounts Receivable, net of allowances for doubtful accounts (debit balance of $11,200 million); Inventories (debit balance $2,876 million); Other Assets ($0 balance); Net Sales ($0 balance); Cost of Sales ($0 balance); Operating expenses ($0 balance); Other income (operating) ($0 balance); Non-operating income (net) ($0 balance); Income tax expense ($0 balance).
2. Journalize Nokia's transactions a-i. Explanations are not required.
3. Post to the T-accounts, and compute the balance for each account. Key postings by transaction letters a-i.
4. For each of the following accounts, compare your computed balance to Nokia's actual balance as shown on its 2008 income statement or balance sheet in Appendix A. Your amounts should agree to the actual figures.

  a. Cash
  b. Accounts Receivable, net of allowances for doubtful accounts
  c. Inventories
  d. Net Sales
  e. Cost of Sales
  f. Operating Expenses
  g. Other income (operating)
  h. Non-operating income (expenses), net
  i. Income Tax Expense

5. Use the relevant accounts from requirement 4 to prepare a summary income statement for Nokia for 2008. Compare the net income you computed to Nokia's actual net income. The two amounts should be equal.
6. Investors are vitally interested in a company's sales and profits, and its trends of sales and profits over time. Consider Nokia's sales and net income during the period from 2006 through 2008. Compute the percentage increase or decrease in net sales and also net income from 2006 to 2008. Can you offer a possible explanation for these changes?

Group Projects

Project 1. You are promoting a rock concert in your area. Your purpose is to earn a profit, so you need to establish the formal structure of a business entity. Assume you organize as a corporation.

I Requirements

1. Make a detailed list of 10 factors you must consider as you establish the business.
2. Describe 10 of the items your business must arrange to promote and stage the rock concert.
3. Identify the transactions that your business can undertake to organize, promote, and stage the concert. Journalize the transactions, and post to the relevant T-accounts. Set up the accounts you need for your business ledger. Refer to Appendix D at the end of the book if needed.
4. Prepare the income statement, statement of changes in equity, and balance sheet immediately after the rock concert, that is, before you have had time to pay all the business bills and to collect all receivables.
5. Assume that you will continue to promote rock concerts if the venture is successful. If it is unsuccessful, you will terminate the business within three months after the concert. Discuss how to evaluate the success of your venture and how to decide whether to continue in business.

Project 2. Contact a local business and arrange with the owner to learn what accounts the business uses.

I Requirements

1. Obtain a copy of the business's chart of accounts.
2. Prepare the company's financial statements for the most recent month, quarter, or year. You may use either made-up account balances or balances supplied by the owner.

If the business has a large number of accounts within a category, combine related accounts and report a single amount on the financial statements. For example, the company may have several cash accounts. Combine all cash amounts and report a single Cash amount on the balance sheet.

You will probably encounter numerous accounts that you have not yet learned. Deal with these as best you can. The charts of accounts given in Appendix D at the end of the book can be helpful.

For online homework, exercises, and problems that provide you with immediate feedback, please visit www.myaccountinglab.com.

Quick Check Answers

1. *b*	5. *c*	8. *c*	11. *d*
2. *d*	6. *a*	9. *c*	12. *d*
3. *b*	7. *a* ($9,000 + x −	10. *c*	
4. *c* ($1,600 +	25,000 = 11,000;		
900 − 300)	x = 27,000)		

Demo Doc

Debit/Credit Transaction Analysis

To make sure you understand this material, work through the following demonstration "Demo Doc" with detailed comments to help you see the concept within the framework of a worked-through problem.

Learning Objectives 1, 2, 3, 4

On September 1, 2010, Michael Moe incorporated Moe's Mowing, Inc., a company that provides mowing and landscaping services. During the month of September, the business incurred the following transactions:

a. To begin operations, Michael deposited $10,000 cash in the business's bank account. The business received the cash and issued shares to Michael.

b. The business purchased equipment for $3,500 on account.

c. The business purchased office supplies for $800 cash.

d. The business provided $2,600 of services to a customer on account.

e. The business paid $500 cash toward the equipment previously purchased on account in transaction b.

f. The business received $2,000 in cash for services provided to a new customer.

g. The business paid $200 cash to repair equipment.

h. The business paid $900 cash in salary expense.

i. The business received $2,100 cash from a customer on account.

j. The business paid cash dividends of $1,500.

Requirements

1. Create blank T-accounts for the following accounts: Cash, Accounts Receivable, Supplies, Equipment, Accounts Payable, Share Capital, Dividends, Service Revenue, Salary Expense, Repair Expense.

2. Journalize the transactions and then post to the T-accounts. Use the table in Exhibit 2-16 to help with the journal entries.

EXHIBIT 2-16 | The Rules of Debit and Credit

	Increase	Decrease
Assets	debit	credit
Liabilities	credit	debit
Shareholders' Equity	credit	debit
Revenues	credit	debit
Expenses	debit	credit
Dividends	debit	credit

3. Total each T-account to determine its balance at the end of the month.

4. Prepare the trial balance of Moe's Mowing, Inc., at September 30, 2010.

Demo Doc Solutions

Requirement 1

Create blank T-accounts for the following accounts: Cash, Accounts Receivable, Supplies, Equipment, Accounts Payable, Share Capital, Dividends, Service Revenue, Salary Expense, Repair Expense.

Part 1	Part 2	Part 3	Part 4	Demo Doc Complete

Opening a T-account means drawing a blank account that looks like a capital "T" and putting the account title across the top. T-accounts show the additions and subtractions made to each account. For easy reference, the accounts are grouped into assets, liabilities, shareholders' equity, revenue, and expenses (in that order).

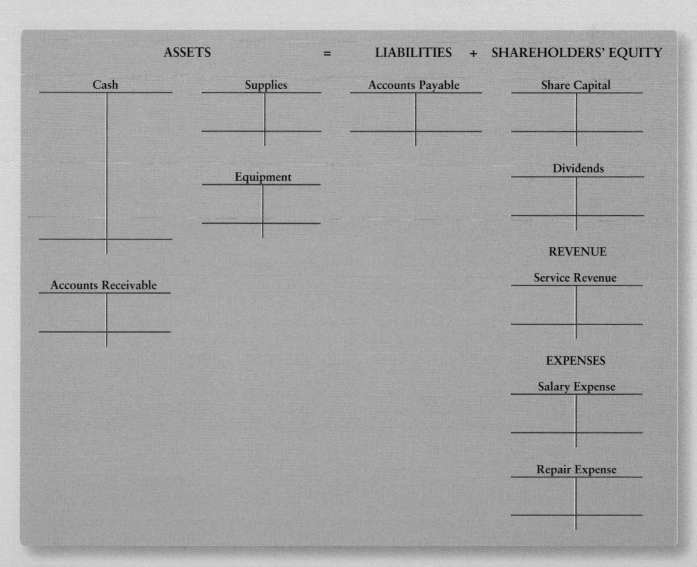

Requirement 2

Journalize the transactions and show how they are recorded in T-accounts.

Part 1	**Part 2**	Part 3	Part 4	Demo Doc Complete

a. To begin operations, Michael deposited $10,000 cash in the business's bank account. The business received the cash and issued shares to Michael.

First, we must determine which accounts are affected by the transaction.

The business received $10,000 cash from its principal shareholder (Michael Moe). In exchange, the business issued shares to Michael. So, the accounts involved are Cash and Share Capital.

Remember that we are recording the transactions of Moe's Mowing, Inc., not the transactions of Michael Moe, the person. Michael and his business are two entirely separate accounting entities.

The next step is to determine what type of accounts these are. Cash is an asset, share capital is part of equity.

Next, we must determine if these accounts increased or decreased. From the business's point of view, Cash (an asset) has increased. Share Capital (equity) has also increased.

Now we must determine if these accounts should be debited or credited. According to the rules of debit and credit (see Exhibit 2-16 on p. 124), an increase in assets is a debit, while an increase in equity is a credit.

So, Cash (an asset) increases, which requires a debit. Share Capital (equity) also increases, which requires a credit.

The journal entry follows ordinary shares.

a.	Cash (Asset ↑; debit)	10,000	
	Share Capital (Equity ↑; credit)		10,000
	Issued ordinary shares.		

The total dollar amounts of debits must always equal the total dollar amounts of credits.

Remember to use the transaction letters as references. This will help as we post entries to the T-accounts.

Each T-account has two sides—one for recording debits and the other for recording credits. To post the transaction to a T-account, simply transfer the amount of each debit to the correct account as a debit (left-side) entry, and transfer the amount of each credit to the correct account as a credit (right-side) entry.

This transaction includes a debit of $10,000 to cash. This means that $10,000 is posted to the left side of the Cash T-account. The transaction also includes a credit of $10,000 to Share Capital. This means that $10,000 is posted to the right side of the Share Capital account, as follows:

Now the first transaction has been journalized and posted. We repeat this process for every journal entry. Let's proceed to the next transaction.

b. The business purchased equipment for $3,500 on account.

The business received equipment in exchange for a promise to pay for the $3,500 cost at a future date. So the accounts involved in the transaction are Equipment and Accounts Payable.

Equipment is an asset and Accounts Payable is a liability.

The asset Equipment has increased. The liability Accounts Payable has also increased.

Looking at Exhibit 2-16, an increase in assets (in this case, the increase in Equipment) is a debit, while an increase in liabilities (in this case, Accounts Payable) is a credit.

The journal entry follows.

b.	Equipment (Asset ↑; debit)	3,500	
	Accounts Payable (Liability ↑; credit)		3,500
	Purchased equipment on account.		

$3,500 is then posted to the debit (left) side of the Equipment T-account. $3,500 is posted to the credit (right) side of Accounts Payable, as follows:

Equipment		Accounts Payable	
b. 3,500		b.	3,500

c. The business purchased office supplies for $800 cash.

The business purchased supplies, paying cash of $800. So the accounts involved in the transaction are Supplies and Cash.

Supplies and Cash are both assets.

Supplies (an asset) has increased. Cash (an asset) has decreased.

Looking at Exhibit 2-16, an increase in assets is a debit, while a decrease in assets is a credit.

So the increase to Supplies (an asset) is a debit, while the decrease to Cash (an asset) is a credit.

The journal entry follows:

c.	Supplies (Asset ↑; debit)	800	
	Cash (Asset ↓; credit)		800
	Purchased supplies for cash.		

$800 is then posted to the debit (left) side of the Supplies T-account. $800 is posted to the credit (right) side of the Cash account, as follows:

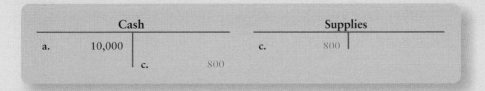

Cash		Supplies	
a. 10,000		c. 800	
	c. 800		

Notice the $10,000 already on the debit side of the Cash account. This came from transaction a.

d. The business provided $2,600 of services to a customer on account.

The business rendered service for a customer and received a promise from the customer to pay us $2,600 cash next month. So the accounts involved in the transaction are Accounts Receivable and Service Revenue.

Accounts Receivable is an asset and Service Revenue is revenue.

Accounts Receivable (an asset) has increased. Service Revenue (revenue) has also increased.

Looking at Exhibit 2-16, an increase in assets is a debit, while an increase in revenue is a credit.

So the increase to Accounts Receivable (an asset) is a debit, while the increase to Service Revenue (revenue) is a credit.

The journal entry follows.

d.	Accounts Receivable (Asset ↑; debit)	2,600	
	Service Revenue (Revenue ↑; credit)		2,600
	Provided services on account.		

$2,600 is posted to the debit (left) side of the Accounts Receivable T-account. $2,600 is posted to the credit (right) side of the Service Revenue account, as follows:

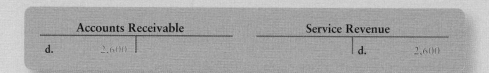

	Accounts Receivable			Service Revenue	
d.	2,600		d.		2,600

e. The business paid $500 cash toward the equipment previously purchased on account in transaction b.

The business paid some of the money that it owed on the purchase of equipment in transaction b. The accounts involved in the transaction are Accounts Payable and Cash.

Accounts Payable is a liability that has decreased. Cash is an asset that has also decreased.

Remember that Accounts Payable shows the amount the business must pay in the future (a liability). When the business pays these creditors, Accounts Payable will decrease because the business will then owe less (in this case, Accounts Payable drops from $3,500—in transaction b—to $3,000).

Looking at Exhibit 2-16, a decrease in liabilities is a debit, while a decrease in assets is a credit.

So Accounts Payable (a liability) decreases, which is a debit. Cash (an asset) decreases, which is a credit.

e.	Accounts Payable (Liability ↓; debit)	500	
	Cash (Asset ↓; credit)		500
	Partial payment on account.		

$500 is posted to the debit (left) side of the Accounts Payable T-account. $500 is posted to the credit (right) side of the Cash account, as follows:

	Cash				Accounts Payable		
a.	10,000					b.	3,500
		c.	800	e.	500		
		e.	500				

Again notice the amounts already in the T-accounts from previous transactions. The reference letters show which transaction caused each amount to appear in the T-account.

f. The business received $2,000 in cash for services provided to a new customer.

The business received $2,000 cash in exchange for mowing and landscaping services rendered to a customer. The accounts involved in the transaction are Cash and Service Revenue.

Cash is an asset that has increased and Service Revenue is revenue, which has also increased.

Looking at Exhibit 2-16, an increase in assets is a debit, while an increase in revenue is a credit.

So the increase to Cash (an asset) is a debit. The increase to Service Revenue (revenue) is a credit.

f.	Cash (Asset ↑; debit)	2,000	
	Service Revenue (Revenue ↑; credit)		2,000
	Provided services for cash.		

$2,000 is then posted to the debit (left) side of the Cash T-account. $2,000 is posted to the credit (right) side of the Service Revenue account, as follows:

	Cash				Service Revenue		
a.	10,000					d.	2,600
		c.	800			f.	2,000
		e.	500				
f.	2,000						

Notice how we keep adding onto the T-accounts. The values from previous transactions remain in their places.

g. The business paid $200 cash to repair equipment.

The business paid $200 cash to have equipment repaired. Because the benefit of the repairs has already been used, the repairs are recorded as Repair Expense. Because the repairs were paid in cash, the Cash account is also involved.

Repair Expense is an expense that has increased and Cash is an asset that has decreased.

Looking at Exhibit 2-16, an increase in expenses calls for a debit, while a decrease in an asset requires a credit.

So Repair Expense (an expense) increases, which is a debit. Cash (an asset) decreases, which is a credit.

g.	Repair Expense (Expense ↑; debit)	200	
	Cash (Asset ↓; credit)		200
	Paid for repairs.		

$200 is then posted to the debit (left) side of the Repair Expense T-account. $200 is posted to the credit (right) side of the Cash account, as follows:

Cash					Repair Expense	
a.	10,000			g.	200	
		c.	800			
		e.	500			
f.	2,000					
		g.	200			

h. The business paid $900 cash for salary expense.

The business paid employees $900 in cash. Because the benefit of the employees' work has already been used, their salaries are recorded as Salary Expense. Because the salaries were paid in cash, the Cash account is also involved.

Salary Expense is an expense that has increased and Cash is an asset that has decreased.

Looking at Exhibit 2-16, an increase in expenses is a debit, while a decrease in an asset is a credit.

In this case, Salary Expense (an expense) increases, which is a debit. Cash (an asset) decreases, which is a credit.

h.	Salary Expense (Expense ↑; debit)	900	
	Cash (Asset ↓; credit)		900
	Paid salary.		

$900 is posted to the debit (left) side of the Salary Expense T-account. $900 is posted to the credit (right) side of the Cash account, as follows:

Cash				Salary Expense		
a.	10,000			h.	900	
		c.	800			
		e.	500			
f.	2,000					
		g.	200			
		h.	900			

i. The business received $2,100 cash from a customer on account.

The business received cash of $2,100 from a customer for services previously provided in transaction d. The accounts affected by this transaction are Cash and Accounts Receivable.

Cash and Accounts Receivable are both assets.

The asset Cash has increased, and the asset Accounts Receivable has decreased.

Remember, Accounts Receivable shows the amount of cash the business has coming from customers. When the business receives cash from these customers, Accounts Receivable will decrease, because the business will have less to receive in the future (in this case, it reduces from $2,600—in transaction d—to $500).

Looking at Exhibit 2-16, an increase in assets is a debit, while a decrease in assets is a credit.

So Cash (an asset) increases, which is a debit. Accounts Receivable (an asset) decreases, which is a credit.

i.		Cash (Asset ↑; debit)	2,100	
		Accounts Receivable (Asset ↓; credit)		2,100
		Received cash on account.		

$2,100 is posted to the debit (left) side of the Cash T-account. $2,100 is posted to the credit (right) side of the Accounts Receivable account, as follows:

Cash				Accounts Receivable		
a.	10,000			d.	2,600	
		c.	800			i.	2,100
		e.	500			
f.	2,000					
		g.	200			
		h.	900			
i.	2,100					

j. The business declared and paid cash dividends of $1,500.

The business paid Michael dividends from the earnings it had retained on his behalf. This caused Michael's ownership interest (equity) to decrease. The accounts involved in this transaction are Dividends and Cash.

Dividends have increased and Cash is an asset that has decreased.

Looking at Exhibit 2-16, an increase in dividends is a debit, while a decrease in an asset is a credit.

Remember that Dividends are a negative element of shareholders' equity. Therefore, when Dividends increase, shareholders' equity decreases. So in this case, Dividends decrease equity with a debit. Cash (an asset) decreases with a credit.

j.	Dividends (Dividends ↑; debit) ↓SE	1,500	
	Cash (Asset ↓; credit)		1,500
	Paid dividends.		

$1,500 is posted to the debit (left) side of the Dividends T-account. $1,500 is posted to the credit (right) side of the Cash account, as follows:

Cash				Dividends	
a.	10,000			j.	1,500
		c.	800		
		e.	500		
f.	2,000				
		g.	200		
		h.	900		
i.	2,100				
		j.	1,500		

Now we can summarize all of the journal entries during the month.

Ref.	Accounts and Explanation	Debit	Credit
a.	Cash	10,000	
	Share Capital		10,000
	Issued share capital.		
b.	Equipment	3,500	
	Accounts Payable		3,500
	Purchased equipment on account.		
c.	Supplies	800	
	Cash		800
	Purchased supplies for cash.		
d.	Accounts Receivable	2,600	
	Service Revenue		2,600
	Provided services on account.		
e.	Accounts Payable	500	
	Cash		500
	Partial payment on account.		
f.	Cash	2,000	
	Service Revenue		2,000
	Provided services for cash.		
g.	Repair Expense	200	
	Cash		200
	Paid for repairs.		
h.	Salary Expense	900	
	Cash		900
	Paid salary.		
i.	Cash	2,100	
	Accounts Receivable		2,100
	Received cash on account.		
j.	Dividends	1,500	
	Cash		1,500
	Paid dividends.		

Requirement 3

Total each T-account to determine its balance at the end of the month.

Part 1	Part 2	**Part 3**	Part 4	Demo Doc Complete

To compute the balance in a T-account (total the T-account), add up the numbers on the debit/left side of the account and (separately) add the credit/right side of the account. The difference between the total debits and the total credits is the account's balance, which is placed on the side that holds the larger total. This gives the balance in the T-account.

For example, for the Cash account, the numbers on the debit/left side total $10,000 + $2,000 + $2,100 = $14,100. The credit/right side = $800 + $500 + $200 + $900 + $1,500 = $3,900. The difference is $14,100 – $3,900 = $10,200. At the end of the period Cash has a debit balance of $10,200. We put the $10,200 at the bottom of the debit side because that was the side that showed the bigger total ($14,100). This is called a debit balance.

An easy way to think of totaling T-accounts is:

Beginning balance in a T-account

+ Increases to the T-account

– Decreases to the T-account

T-account balance (net total)

T-accounts after posting all transactions and totaling each account are as follows:

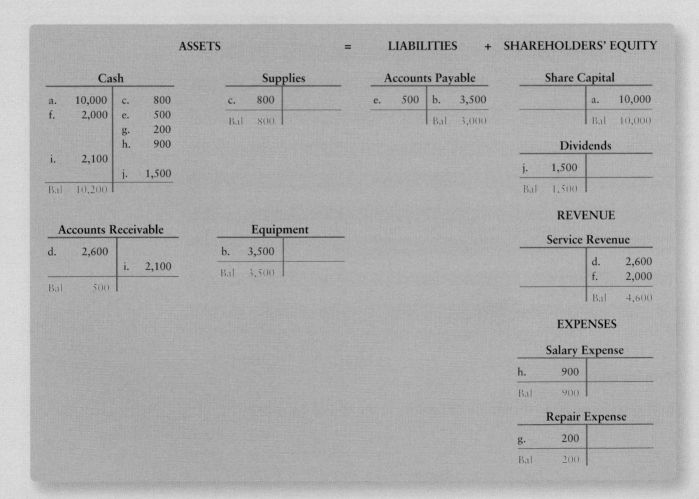

Requirement 4

| Part 1 | Part 2 | Part 3 | **Part 4** | Demo Doc Complete |

The trial balance lists all the accounts along with their balances. This listing is helpful because it summarises all the accounts in one place. Otherwise one must plow through all the T-accounts to find the balance of Accounts Payable, Salary Expense, or any other account.

The trial balance is an *internal* accounting document that accountants and managers use to prepare the financial statements. It's not like the income statement and balance sheet, which are presented to the public.

Data for the trial balance come directly from the T-accounts that we prepared in Requirement 3. A debit balance in a T-account remains a debit in the trial balance, and likewise for credits. For example, the T-account for Cash shows a debit balance of $10,200, and the trial balance lists Cash the same way. The Accounts Payable T-account shows a $3,000 credit balance, and the trial balance lists Accounts Payable correctly.

The trial balance for Moe's Mowing at September 30, 2010, appears as follows. Notice that we list the accounts in their proper order—assets, liabilities, shareholder's equity, revenues, and expenses.

Moe's Mowing, Inc.
Trial Balance
September 30, 2010

		Balance	
		Debit	Credit
Assets	Cash	$10,200	
	Accounts receivable	500	
	Supplies	800	
	Equipment	3,500	
Liabilities	Accounts payable		$ 3,000
Equity	Share capital		10,000
	Dividends	1,500	
Revenues	Service revenue		4,600
Expenses	Salary expense	900	
	Repair expense	200	
	Total	$17,600	$17,600

You should trace each account from the T-accounts to the trial balance.

| Part 1 | Part 2 | Part 3 | Part 4 | **Demo Doc Complete** |

3

Accrual Accounting & Income

SPOTLIGHT: DP World

Have you ever wondered how your supermarket gets its goods from all parts of the world? More likely than not, some form of shipping is involved. Shipping has made the world a truly global market place. With 90% of world trade moving by sea, terminal operators have an unprecedented impact on the smooth running of the global supply chain. Outsourced manufacturing in ever more diverse markets is making that supply chain longer and more complex.

DP World is one of the largest marine terminal operators in the world, with 49 terminals and 12 new developments across 31 countries. At these terminals, cargos of all kind in container boxes are transferred between ocean-going and ground transportation vehicles, from factories to warehouses and eventually retail outlets. In 2009, DP World handled more than 43.8 million TEU (20-foot equivalent container units) across its portfolio from the Americas to Asia.

DP World recorded revenue from operations of USD 2,821 million for the financial year ended December 31, 2009. After deducting cost of sales and expenses, it made a net income of USD 370 million. This was achieved under "accrual basis of accounting". Let's find out more about how accrual accounting works!

DP World Limited
Consolidated Income Statement (Adapted)
Financial Year Ended December 31

(in millions USD)	2009
Revenues from operations	$2,929.2
Cost of sales	(2,064.2)
Gross profit	865.0
General and administration expenses	(305.3)
Other income	22.1
Financial income	85.5
Finance costs	(356.7)
Share of profit of associates and joint ventures	69.3
Profit on sale/termination of business	44.3
Profit before tax	424.2
Income tax	(54.1)
Net income	$ 370.1

This chapter will complete our coverage of the accounting cycle. It will provide the basics of what you need before tackling individual topics such as receivables, inventory, and cash flows.

LEARNING OBJECTIVES

1 **Relate** accrual accounting and cash flows

2 **Apply** the revenue and matching principles

3 **Adjust** the accounts

4 **Prepare** the financial statements

5 **Close** the books

6 **Use** two financial ratios to evaluate a business

For more practice and review of accounting cycle concepts, use ACT, the accounting Cycle Tutorial, online at www.myaccountinglab.com. Margin logos like this one, directing you to the appropriate ACT section and material, appear throughout Chapters 1, 2, and 3. When you enter the tutorial, you'll find three buttons on the opening page of each chapter module. Here's what the buttons mean: **Tutorial** gives you a review of the major concepts, **Application** gives you practice exercises, and **Glossary** reviews important terms.

ACCRUAL ACCOUNTING VERSUS CASH-BASIS ACCOUNTING

Managers want to earn a profit. Investors search for companies whose share prices will increase. Banks seek borrowers who'll pay their debts. Accounting provides the information these people use for decision making. Recall that the *IFRS Framework* makes an assumption that financial reporting is done on accrual basis. Accounting can be based on either the:

- accrual basis, or the
- cash basis.

Accrual accounting records the impact of a business transaction as it occurs. When the business performs a service, makes a sale, or incurs an expense, the accountant records the transaction even if it receives or pays no cash.

Cash basis accounting records only cash transactions—cash receipts and cash payments. Cash receipts are treated as revenues, and cash payments are handled as expenses.

IAS1 – Presentation of Financial Statements requires that an entity prepares its financial statements, with the exception of cash flow information, using accrual accounting. The business records revenues as they are earned and expenses as they are incurred—not necessarily when cash changes hands. Consider a sale on account. Which transaction increases your wealth—making sale of inventory costing $500 for $800 on account, or collecting the $800 cash? Making the sale increases your wealth by $300 because you gave up inventory that cost you $500 and you got a receivable worth $800 in return. Collecting cash later merely swaps your $800 receivable for $800 cash—one asset for another asset. Making the sale is when revenue is earned, not when you collect the cash.

Similarly, suppose DP World paid some office rental in advance of actual occupation. Cash may have been paid, but has DP World actually incurred the expense?

The basic limitation of cash basis accounting is that the cash basis ignores the underlying economic activities (i.e. earning revenue and incurring expenses necessary to earn the revenue). That makes the financial statements purely a record of cash inflows and outflows. While cash basis accounting may still be employed by very small operations, most businesses require a more holistic view of its operations.

Suppose DP World performed shipping services for a client on account. The cash basis does not record the revenue because you received no cash. You may be thinking, "Let's wait until we collect cash and then record the revenue".

What's wrong with this argument? There are two impacts—one on the balance sheet and the other on the income statement.

Balance Sheet Impact.   If DP World fails to record the shipping service on account, the balance sheet reports no account receivable. Why is this inappropriate? The receivable represents a claim to receive cash in the future, which is an asset, and it should appear on the balance sheet. Without this information, assets are understated on the balance sheet.

Income Statement Impact.   The shipping service provides revenue that increases the company's wealth. Cash accounting will ignore this fact and wait until cash is received before the revenue is considered earned. Ignoring the completion of shipping service understates revenue and net income on the income statement.

The take-away lessons from this discussion are as follows:

- Virtually all businesses use the accrual basis of accounting.
- Companies that use the cash basis of accounting do not follow accounting standards. Their financial statements omit important information and thus, less relevant to users of financial statements.

We are not saying that cash flows are not important, they are! However, in measuring financial performance and financial position, accrual accounting gives us a better understanding how companies actually performed during a financial period. We will look at cash flows in more detail in Chapter 12.

Accrual Accounting and Cash Flows

Accrual accounting is more complex—and, in terms of the *IFRS Framework* (Exhibit 1-3), is a more faithful representation of economic reality—than cash basis accounting. To be sure, accrual accounting records cash transactions, such as:

- Collecting cash from customers
- Receiving cash from interest earned
- Paying salaries, rent, and other expenses
- Borrowing money
- Paying off loans
- Issuing shares

But accrual accounting also records *non-cash* transactions, such as:

- Sales on account
- Purchases of inventory on account
- Accrual of expenses incurred but not yet paid
- Depreciation expense
- Usage of prepaid rent, insurance, and supplies
- Earning of revenue when cash was collected in advance

To use accrual accounting, we need to understand a few more concepts and principles. We turn now to the time-period concept, the revenue recognition principle, and the matching principle.

The Time-Period Concept

The only way for a business to know for certain how well it performed is to shut down, sell the assets, pay the liabilities, and return any leftover cash to the owners. This process, called liquidation, means going out of business. Ongoing companies can't close down operations just to measure income! Instead, they need regular progress reports. Accountants, therefore, prepare financial statements for specific periods. The **time-period concept** ensures that accounting information is reported at regular intervals.

IAS1 – Presentation of Financial Statements requires an entity to present a complete set of financial statements (including comparative information, as appropriate) at least annually. This is why you have been looking at extracts of *annual* reports of companies at the start of every chapter.

Companies also prepare financial statements for interim periods of less than a year, such as a month, a quarter (three months), or a half-yearly period (six months). Usually, this is a requirement of the stock exchange where the company is listed. In general, as a company gets larger, it may be subjected to more frequent reporting requirements. Most of the discussions in this text are based on an annual accounting period.

The Revenue Recognition Principle

When should you recognize revenue? In short, when you "earn" the revenue. It sounds simple, but revenue recognition can be a very contentious topic. Think about the things you buy (such as books from **Borders**, your new electronic gadgets from **Samsung**, clothes from **GAP**), the services you consume (your **Time** magazine or **World of Warcraft** or **Xbox Live** subscription, your tuition fees), and ask yourself when do the companies that provide you with these goods or services actually earn your money?

OBJECTIVE

2 **Apply** the revenue and matching principles

The basic guidance on revenue recognition principle comes from *IAS18 – Revenue*. In general, for sale of goods, revenue is recognized when:

- the entity has transferred to the buyer the significant risks and rewards of ownership of the goods;
- the entity retains neither continuing managerial involvement to the degree usually associated with ownership nor effective control over the goods sold;
- the amount of revenue can be measured reliably;
- it is probable that the economic benefits associated with the transaction will flow to the entity; and
- the costs incurred or to be incurred in respect of the transaction can be measured reliably.

Thus, for consumer sales transactions, it is usually at the point of sale, when you hand over your hard earned cash in return for the goods you wish to purchase. Think about how such over the counter purchases would meet the *IAS18* criteria above.

For services, similar principles apply. The only difference is the services you engage may not be consumed at the same time. Revenue is thus earned by reference to a "stage of completion" of the transaction at the balance sheet date. For example, suppose you engaged DP World to make 12 shipments and paid the entire shipping fee in advance on November 1, 2010. Should DP World recognize the entire revenue for the 12 shipments revenue when you sign the contract? No, it shouldn't. DP World only earns the relevant shipping revenue when services are provided. Suppose by the end of the financial year December 31, 2010, DP World shipped a total of eight consignments. It will recognize the revenue for the eight shipments in its income statement and the remaining four as its obligations on its balance sheet. Stage of completion can also be estimated using time period, milestones (such as engineering estimates), or percentage of cost incurred in relation to total costs.

The *amount* of revenue to record is the fair value of the consideration received or receivable taking into account the amount of any trade discounts and volume rebates allowed by the entity. If the shipment fees for your 12 shipments totaled $10,000 and you were given a discount of 10%, DP World should recognize a total of $6,000 at year ended December 31, 2010 and a further $3,000 when the remaining shipments have been performed, say in February 2011.

This revenue recognition example can be depicted in Exhibit 3-1 on the next page.

EXHIBIT 3-1 | When to Record Revenue

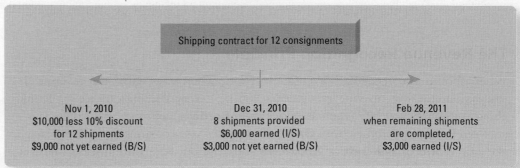

Nov 1, 2010	Dec 31, 2010	Feb 28, 2011
$10,000 less 10% discount for 12 shipments $9,000 not yet earned (B/S)	8 shipments provided $6,000 earned (I/S) $3,000 not yet earned (B/S)	when remaining shipments are completed, $3,000 earned (I/S)

Shipping contract for 12 consignments

So, to conclude, when should you record revenue? After it has been earned—and not before. In most cases, revenue is earned when the business has delivered a good or service to a customer. It has done everything required to earn the revenue by transferring the goods or services to the customer.

TECHNICAL UPDATE

IAS18 also provides additional criteria for recognition of interest income (using effective interest rate method) and dividend income (when the rights to the dividends are established). *IAS18's* Appendix provides additional examples of various revenue recognition scenarios that may interest you.

The Matching Principle

The **matching principle** is the basis for recording and recognizing expenses. The *IFRS Framework* states that expenses recognized in the income statement on the basis of a direct association between the costs incurred and the earning of specific items of income. This process is commonly referred to as the "matching of costs with revenues". Expenses have no future benefit to the company. The matching principle includes two steps:

1. Identify all the expenses incurred during the accounting period.

2. Measure the expenses, and match expenses against the revenues earned.

To *match* expenses against revenues means to subtract expenses from revenues to compute net income or net loss. Exhibit 3-2 illustrates the matching principle.

EXHIBIT 3-2 | The Matching Principle

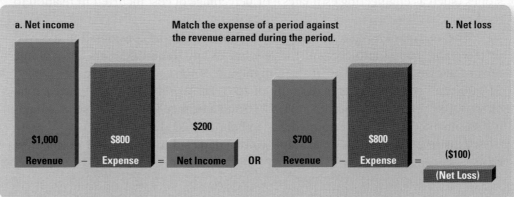

a. Net income

Match the expense of a period against the revenue earned during the period.

b. Net loss

| $1,000 Revenue | − | $800 Expense | = | $200 Net Income | OR | $700 Revenue | − | $800 Expense | = | ($100) (Net Loss) |

STOP & THINK...

1. A customer pays DP World $1,000 on March 15 for a shipment in April. Has DP World earned revenue on March 15? When will DP World earn the revenue?
2. DP World pays $4,500 on July 1 for office rent for the next three months. Has DP World incurred an expense on July 1?

Answers:

1. No. DP World has received the cash but will not perform the shipping services until later. DP World earns the revenue when it has completed the service for the customer.
2. No. DP World has paid cash for rent in advance. There is no expense. This prepaid rent is an asset because DP World has some future economic benefits (i.e. the use of an office space).

Some expenses are paid in cash. Other expenses arise from using up an asset such as supplies. When expenses are incurred but not yet paid, a company has a liability. For example, DP World's salary expense occurs when employees work for the company. DP World may pay the salary expense immediately, or DP World may record a liability for the salary to be paid later. In either case, DP World has salary expense. The critical event for recording an expense is the employees' working for the company, not the payment of cash.

Ethical Issues in Accrual Accounting

Accrual accounting provides some ethical challenges that cash accounting avoids. For example, suppose that late in 2010, DP World prepays a $3 million advertising campaign to be conducted by a large advertising agency. The advertisements are scheduled to run in early 2011 during January, February and March. In this case, DP World is buying an asset, a prepaid expense.

Suppose DP World pays for the advertisements on November 1 and the ads start running immediately. Under accrual accounting, DP World should record two-thirds of the expense ($2 million) during the year ended December 31, 2010, and one-third ($2 million) during 2011.

Suppose financial year 2010 is a great year for DP World—net income is better than expected. DP World's top managers believe that fiscal 2011 will not be as profitable. In this case, the company has a strong incentive to expense the full $3 million during financial year 2010 in order to report all the advertising expense in the 2010 income statement. This questionable action would keep $1 million of advertising expense off the 2011 income statement and make 2011's net income look $1 million better.

UPDATING THE ACCOUNTS: THE ADJUSTING PROCESS

At the end of the period, the business reports its financial statements. This process begins with the trial balance introduced in Chapter 2. We refer to this trial balance as unadjusted because the accounts are not yet ready for the financial statements. In most cases the simple label "Trial Balance" means "unadjusted."

OBJECTIVE

3 Adjust the accounts

Which Accounts Need to Be Updated (Adjusted)?

The shareholders need to know how well ShineBrite Car Wash, Inc., is performing. The financial statements report this information, and all accounts must be up-to-date. That means some accounts must be adjusted. Exhibit 3-3 gives the trial balance of ShineBrite Car Wash, Inc., at June 30, 2010.

EXHIBIT 3-3 | Unadjusted Trial Balance

ShineBrite Car Wash, Inc.
Unadjusted Trial Balance
June 30, 2010

Cash..	$24,800	
Accounts receivable........................	2,200	
Supplies...	700	
Prepaid rent...................................	3,000	
Equipment......................................	24,000	
Accounts payable............................		$13,100
Unearned service revenue		400
Share capital..................................		20,000
Retained earnings...........................		18,800
Dividends.......................................	3,200	
Service revenue..............................		7,000
Salary expense................................	900	
Utilities expense	500	
Total	$59,300	$59,300

This trial balance is unadjusted. That means it's not completely up-to-date. It's not quite ready to be used as the basis for preparing the financial statements.

Cash, Equipment, Accounts Payable, Share Capital, and Dividends are up-to-date and need no adjustment at the end of the period. Why? Because the day-to-day transactions provide all the data for these accounts.

Accounts Receivable, Supplies, Prepaid Rent, and the other accounts are another story. These accounts are not yet up-to-date on June 30. Why? Because certain transactions have not yet been recorded. Consider Supplies. During June, ShineBrite Car Wash used cleaning supplies to wash cars. But ShineBrite didn't make a journal entry for supplies used every time it washed a car. That would waste time and money. Instead, ShineBrite waits until the end of the period and then records the supplies used up during the entire month.

The cost of supplies used up is an expense. An adjusting entry at the end of June updates both Supplies (an asset) and Supplies Expense. We must adjust all accounts whose balances are not yet up-to-date.

Categories of Adjusting Entries

Accounting adjustments fall into three basic categories: deferrals, depreciation, and accruals.

Deferrals. A **deferral** is an adjustment for an item that the business paid or received cash in advance. DP World purchases supplies for use in its operations. During the period, some supplies (assets) are used up and become expenses. At the end of the period, an adjustment is needed to decrease the supplies account for the supplies used up and record the supplies expense. Prepaid rent, prepaid insurance, and all other prepaid expenses require deferral adjustments.

There are also deferral adjustments for liabilities. Companies such as DP World may collect cash from its customers in advance of earning the revenue. When DP World receives cash up front, it has an obligation (i.e. a liability) to provide port and shipping services for its customer. This liability is called Unearned Sales Revenue. Then, when DP World delivers the goods to the customer, it earns Sales Revenue. This earning process requires an adjustment at the end of the period. The adjustment decreases the liability and increases the revenue for the revenue earned. Publishers of magazines such as **Fortune**, and your cell-phone company usually collect cash in advance from their subscribers. They too must make adjusting entries for revenues earned later.

Depreciation. **Depreciation** allocates the cost of an item of Property, Plant and Equipment (PPE) to expense over the asset's useful life. Depreciation is the most common long-term deferral. DP World buys buildings and equipment. As DP World uses the assets, it records depreciation for wear-and-tear and obsolescence. The accounting adjustment records Depreciation Expense and decreases the asset's book value over its life. The process is identical to a deferral-type adjustment; the only difference is the type of asset involved. We will look at other issues related to PPE and depreciation in Chapter 7.

Accruals. An **accrual** is the opposite of a deferral. For an accrued *expense*, DP World records the expense before paying cash. For an accrued revenue, DP World records the revenue before collecting cash.

Salary Expense can create an accrual adjustment. As employees work for DP World Corporation, the company's salary expense accrues with the passage of time. At December 31, 2009, DP World owed employees some salaries to be paid after year end, so DP World recorded Salary Expense and Salary Payable for the amount owed. Other examples of expense accruals include interest expense and income tax expense.

An accrued revenue is a revenue that the business has earned and will collect next year. At year end, DP World must accrue such revenue. The adjustment debits a receivable and credits a revenue. For example, accrual of interest revenue debits Interest Receivable and credits Interest Revenue.

Let's see how the adjusting process actually works for ShineBrite Car Wash at June 30. We start with prepaid expenses.

Prepaid Expenses

A **prepaid expense (or prepayment)** is an expense paid in advance. Therefore, prepaid expenses are assets because they provide a future benefit for the owner. Let's do the adjustments for prepaid rent and supplies.

Prepaid Rent. Companies pay rent in advance. This prepayment creates an asset for the renter, who can then use the rented item in the future. Suppose ShineBrite Car Wash prepays three months' store rent ($3,000) on June 1. The entry for the prepayment of three months' rent debits Prepaid Rent as follows:

Jun 1	Prepaid Rent ($1,000 × 3)	3,000	
	Cash		3,000
	Paid three months' rent in advance.		

The accounting equation shows that one asset increases and another decreases. Total assets are unchanged. Again, we show the impact of revenue and expense transactions directly to equity.

Assets	=	Liabilities	+	Shareholders' Equity
+ 3,000	=	0	+	0
− 3,000				

After posting, the Prepaid Rent account appears as follows:

Prepaid Rent	
Jun 1 3,000	

Throughout June, the Prepaid Rent account carries this beginning balance, as shown in Exhibit 3-3 (p. 142). The adjustment transfers $1,000 from Prepaid Rent to Rent Expense as follows:*

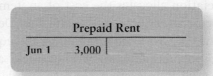

			Adjusting entry a
Jun 30	Rent Expense ($3,000 × 1/3)	1,000	
	Prepaid Rent		1,000
	To record rent expense.		

Both assets and shareholders' equity decrease.

Assets	=	Liabilities	+	Shareholders' Equity	
− 1,000	=	0	+	− 1,000	(rent expense)

After posting, Prepaid Rent and Rent Expense appear as follows:

Prepaid Rent			Rent Expense	
Jun 1 3,000	Jun 30 1,000 →	Jun 30 1,000	
Bal 2,000		Bal 1,000	

This expense illustrates the matching principle. We record an expense in order to measure net income.

Supplies.   Supplies are another type of prepaid expense. On June 2, ShineBrite Car Wash paid cash of $700 for cleaning supplies:

---

*See Exhibit 3-8, page 154, for a summary of adjustments a–g.

Jun 2	Supplies	700	
	Cash		700
	Paid cash for supplies.		

Assets	=	Liabilities	+	Shareholders' Equity
+ 700	=	0	+	0
− 700				

The cost of the supplies ShineBrite used is supplies expense. To measure June's supplies expense, the business counts the supplies on hand at the end of the month. The count shows that $400 of supplies remain. Subtracting the $400 of supplies on hand from the supplies available ($700) measures supplies expense for the month ($300), as follows:

Asset Available During the Period	−	Asset on Hand at the End of the Period	=	Asset Used (Expense) During the Period
$700	−	$400	=	$300

The June 30 adjusting entry debits the expense and credits the asset, as follows:

Adjusting entry b

Jun 30	Supplies Expense ($700 − $400)	300	
	Supplies		300
	To record supplies expense.		

Assets	=	Liabilities	+	Shareholders' Equity	
− 300	=	0	+	− 300	(supplies expense)

After posting, the Supplies and Supplies Expense accounts appear as follows. The adjustment is highlighted for emphasis.

Supplies				Supplies Expense	
Jun 2	700	Jun 30	300 →	Jun 30	300
Bal	400			Bal	300

At the start of July, Supplies has this $400 balance, and the adjustment process is repeated each month.

STOP & THINK. . .

At the beginning of the month, supplies were $5,000. During the month, $7,000 of supplies were purchased. At month's end, $3,000 of supplies are still on hand. What is the:

- adjusting entry?
- ending balance in the Supplies account?

Answer:

Supplies Expense ($5,000 + $7,000 − $3,000)	9,000	
Supplies		9,000
To record supplies used.		

Ending balance of supplies = $3,000 (the supplies still on hand)

Depreciation of Property, Plant and Equipment

Property, Plant and Equipment (PPE) are long-lived tangible assets, such as land, buildings, furniture, and equipment. Sometimes you may see them referred to as fixed assets or plant assets. All PPE but land decline in usefulness, and this decline is an expense. Accountants allocate the cost of each PPE item, except land, over its useful life. Depreciation is the process of allocating cost to expense for PPE. Note that in some countries, land titles are not issued in perpetuity, so in such cases you may see "leasehold land" that are depreciated over the period of the leasehold.

To illustrate depreciation, consider ShineBrite Car Wash. Suppose that on June 2, ShineBrite purchased car-washing equipment on account for $24,000:

Jun 2	Equipment	24,000	
	Accounts Payable		24,000
	Purchased equipment on account.		

Assets	=	Liabilities	+	Shareholders' Equity
+ 24,000	=	+ 24,000	+	0

After posting, the Equipment account appears as follows:

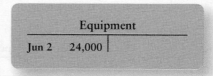

Equipment	
Jun 2 24,000	

ShineBrite records an asset when it purchases equipment. Then, as the asset is used, a portion of the asset's cost is transferred to Depreciation Expense. This is an example of the application of the matching principle. Computerized accounting systems program the depreciation for automatic entry each period.

ShineBrite's equipment will remain useful for five years and then be worthless. One simple way to allocate the amount of depreciation for each year is to divide the cost of the asset ($24,000 in our example) by its expected useful life (five years). This procedure—called the straight-line depreciation method—gives annual depreciation of $4,800. Chapter 7 covers PPE and depreciation in more detail.

> Annual Depreciation = $24,000/5 years = $4,800 per year

Depreciation for June is $400.

> Monthly Depreciation = $4,800/12 months = $400 per month

The Accumulated Depreciation Account.
Depreciation expense for June is recorded as follows:

Adjusting entry c

Jun 30	Depreciation Expense—Equipment	400	
	Accumulated Depreciation—Equipment		400
	To record depreciation.		

Total assets decrease by the amount of the expense:

Assets	=	Liabilities	+	Shareholders' Equity	
– 400	=	0	+	– 400	(depreciation expense)

The Accumulated Depreciation account, not Equipment is credited to preserve the original cost of the asset in the Equipment account. Managers can then refer to the Equipment account if they ever need to know how much the asset cost.

The **Accumulated Depreciation** account shows the sum of all depreciation expense from using the asset. Therefore, the balance in the Accumulated Depreciation account increases over the asset's life.

Accumulated Depreciation is a contra asset account—an asset account with a normal credit balance. A **contra account** has two distinguishing characteristics:

1. It always has a companion account.
2. Its normal balance is opposite that of the companion account.

In this case, Accumulated Depreciation is the contra account to Equipment, so Accumulated Depreciation appears directly after Equipment on the balance sheet. A business carries an accumulated depreciation account for each depreciable asset, for example, Accumulated Depreciation—Building and Accumulated Depreciation—Equipment.

After posting, the PPE accounts of ShineBrite Car Wash are as follows—with the adjustment highlighted:

Equipment		Accumulated Depreciation—Equipment		Depreciation Expense—Equipment	
Jun 3 24,000			Jun 30 400	Jun 30 400	
Bal 24,000			Bal 400	Bal 400	

Book Value.   The net amount of a PPE (cost minus accumulated depreciation) is called that asset's **book value (of a PPE)**, or carrying amount. Exhibit 3-4 shows how ShineBrite would report the book value of its equipment and building at June 30 (the building data are assumed for this illustration).

EXHIBIT 3-4 | **PPE on the Balance Sheet of ShineBrite Car Wash**

ShineBrite Car Wash PPE at June 30		
Equipment..	$24,000	
Less: Accumulated Depreciation	(400)	$23,600
Building..	$50,000	
Less: Accumulated Depreciation	(200)	49,800
Book value of PPE..		$73,400

At June 30, the book value of equipment is $23,600; the book value of the building is $49,800.

STOP & THINK...

What will be the book value of ShineBrite's equipment at the end of July?

Answer:

$24,000 − $400 − $400 = $23,200.

Exhibit 3-5 shows how DP World reports its property, plant and equipment in its annual report. As you can see, DP World reports four categories of PPE. You will find that different companies categorize their PPE differently. Lines 1 to 4 list the four asset categories and their costs, accumulated depreciation and net book value. Line 4 shows that the total cost of PPE is USD 6.03 billion, with accumulated depreciation of USD 1.17 billion, resulting in a net book value of about USD 4.86 billion.

EXHIBIT 3-5 | DP World's Property, Plant and Equipment (Adapted)

As at December 31, 2009 in USD millions			
	Cost	Acc. Depn.	Net Book Value
1 Land and Buildings	$2,677,914	$307,995	$2,369,919
2 Plant and Equipment	2,680,045	853,698	1,826,347
3 Ships	46,638	10,709	35,929
4 Work-in-process	627,005	0	627,005
5 Total	$6,031,602	$1,192,402	$4,859,200

Accrued Expenses

Businesses incur expenses before they pay cash. Consider an employee's salary. DP World's expense and payable will grow as the employee works, so the liability is said to accrue. Another example is interest expense on a note payable. Interest accrues as the clock ticks. The term **accrued expense** refers to a liability that arises from an expense that has not yet been paid.

Companies don't record accrued expenses daily or weekly. Instead, they wait until the end of the period and use an adjusting entry to update each expense (and related liability) for the financial statements. Let's look at salary expense.

Most companies pay their employees at set times. Suppose ShineBrite Car Wash pays its employee a monthly salary of $1,800, half on the 15th and half on the last day of the month. The following calendar for June has the paydays highlighted:

June						
Sun.	Mon.	Tue.	Wed.	Thur.	Fri.	Sat.
						1
2	3	4	5	6	7	8
9	10	11	12	13	14	15
16	17	18	19	20	21	22
23	24	25	26	27	28	29
30						

Assume that if a payday falls on a Sunday, ShineBrite pays the employee on the following Monday. During June, ShineBrite paid its employees the first half-month salary of $900 and made the following entry:

Jun 15	Salary Expense	900	
	Cash		900
	To pay salary.		

Assets	=	Liabilities	+	Shareholders' Equity	
– 900	=	0	+	– 900	(salary expense)

After posting, the Salary Expense account is

Salary Expense	
Jun 15	900

The trial balance at June 30 (Exhibit 3-3, p. 142) includes Salary Expense with its debit balance of $900. Because June 30, the second payday of the month, falls on a Sunday, the second half-month amount of $900 will be paid on Monday, July 1. At June 30, therefore, ShineBrite adjusts for additional salary expense and salary payable of $900 as follows:

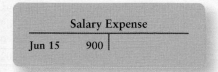

Adjusting entry d

Jun 30	Salary Expense	900	
	Salary Payable		900
	To accrue salary expense.		

An accrued expense increases liabilities and decreases shareholders' equity:

Assets	=	Liabilities	+	Shareholders' Equity	
0	=	+ 900	+	– 900	(salary expense)

After posting, the Salary Payable and Salary Expense accounts appear as follows (adjustment highlighted):

Salary Payable				Salary Expense		
		Jun 30	900	Jun 15	900	
		Bal	900	Jun 30	900	
				Bal	1,800	

The accounts now hold all of June's salary information. Salary Expense has a full month's salary, and Salary Payable shows the amount owed at June 30. All accrued expenses are recorded this way—debit the expense and credit the liability.

Computerized systems usually contain a payroll module. Accrued salaries can be automatically journalized and posted at the end of each period.

Accrued Revenues

Businesses may earn revenue before they receive the cash. A revenue that has been earned but not yet collected is called an **accrued revenue**.

Assume that **FedEx** hires ShineBrite on June 15 to wash FedEx delivery trucks each month. Suppose FedEx will pay ShineBrite $600 monthly, with the first payment on July 15. During June, ShineBrite will earn half a month's fee, $300, for work done June 15 through June 30. On June 30, ShineBrite makes the following adjusting entry:

			Adjusting entry e
Jun 30	Accounts Receivable ($600 × 1/2)	300	
	Service Revenue		300
	To accrue service revenue.		

Revenue increases both total assets and shareholders' equity:

Assets	=	Liabilities	+	Shareholders' Equity	
+ 300	=	0	+	+ 300	(service revenue)

Recall that Accounts Receivable has an unadjusted balance of $2,200, and Service Revenue's unadjusted balance is $7,000 (Exhibit 3-3, p. 142). This June 30 adjusting entry has the following effects (adjustment highlighted):

Accounts Receivable			Service Revenue		
	2,200				7,000
Jun 30	300			Jun 30	300
Bal	2,500			Bal	7,300

All accrued revenues are accounted for similarly—debit a receivable and credit a revenue.

STOP & THINK...

Suppose ShineBrite Car Wash holds a note receivable as an investment. At the end of June, $100 of interest revenue has been earned but not yet received. Journalize the accrued revenue adjustment at June 30.

Answer:

Jun 30	Interest Receivable	100	
	Interest Revenue		100
	To accrue interest revenue.		

Unearned Revenues

Some businesses collect cash from customers before earning the revenue. This creates a liability called **unearned revenue**. Only when the job is completed does the business earn the revenue. Suppose **UPS** engages Shine Brite Car Wash to wash UPS delivery vehicles, agreeing to pay ShineBrite $400 monthly, beginning immediately. If

ShineBrite collects the first amount on June 15, then ShineBrite records this transaction as follows:

Jun 15	Cash	400	
	Unearned Service Revenue		400
	Received cash for revenue in advance.		

Assets	=	Liabilities	+	Shareholders' Equity
400	=	400	+	0

After posting, the liability account appears as follows:

Unearned Service Revenue

	Jun 15	400

Unearned Service Revenue is a liability because ShineBrite is obligated to perform services for UPS. The June 30 unadjusted trial balance (Exhibit 3-3, p. 142) lists Unearned Service Revenue with a $400 credit balance. During the last 15 days of the month, ShineBrite will earn one-half of the $400, or $200. On June 30, ShineBrite makes the following adjustment:

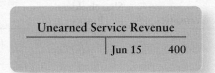
Adjusting entry f

Jun 30	Unearned Service Revenue ($400 × 1/2)	200	
	Service Revenue		200
	To record unearned service revenue that has been earned.		

Assets	=	Liabilities	+	Shareholders' Equity	
0	=	− 200	+	+ 200	(service revenue)

This adjusting entry shifts $200 of the total amount received ($400) from liability to revenue. After posting, Unearned Service Revenue is reduced to $200, and Service Revenue is increased by $200, as follows (adjustment highlighted):

	Unearned Service Revenue			**Service Revenue**	
Jun 30	200	Jun 15	400		7,000
		Bal	200	Jun 30	300
				Jun 30	200
				Bal	7,500

All revenues collected in advance are accounted for this way. An unearned revenue is a liability, not a revenue.

One company's prepaid expense is the other company's unearned revenue. For example, UPS's prepaid expense is ShineBrite Car Wash's liability for unearned revenue.

Exhibit 3-6 diagrams the distinctive timing of prepaids and accruals. Study prepaid expenses all the way across. Then study unearned revenues across, and so on.

EXHIBIT 3-6 | Prepaid and Accrual Adjustments

PREPAIDS—Cash First

	First		Later	
Prepaid expenses	*Pay cash and record an asset:*		*Record an expense and decrease the asset:*	
	Prepaid Expense...... XXX		Expense.............................. XXX	
	Cash...............	XXX	Prepaid Expense.........	XXX
Unearned revenues	*Receive cash and record unearned revenue:*		*Record revenue and decrease unearned revenue:*	
	Cash...................... XXX		Unearned Revenue XXX	
	Unearned Revenue	XXX	Revenue	XXX

ACCRUALS—Cash Later

	First		Later	
Accrued expenses	*Accrue expense and a payable:*		*Pay cash and decrease the payable:*	
	Expense................... XXX		Payable.............................. XXX	
	Payable...........	XXX	Cash...........................	XXX
Accrued revenues	*Accrue revenue and a receivable:*		*Receive cash and decrease the receivable:*	
	Receivable............... XXX		Cash................................. XXX	
	Revenue	XXX	Receivable.................	XXX

The authors thank Professors Darrel Davis and Alfonso Oddo for suggesting this exhibit.

Summary of the Adjusting Process

Two purposes of the adjusting process are to:

- measure income, and
- update the balance sheet.

Therefore, every adjusting entry affects at least one of the following:

- Revenue or expense—to measure income.
- Asset or liability—to update the balance sheet.

Exhibit 3-7 summarizes the basic accounting adjustments at the end of an accounting period.

EXHIBIT 3-7 | Summary of Adjusting Entries

	Type of Account	
Category of Adjusting Entry	Debit	Credit
Prepaid expense..................	Expense	Asset
Depreciation........................	Expense	Contra asset
Accrued expense.................	Expense	Liability
Accrued revenue.................	Asset	Revenue
Unearned revenue...............	Liability	Revenue

Adapted from material provided by Beverly Terry.

Exhibit 3-8 summarizes the adjustments of ShineBrite Car Wash, Inc., at June 30—the adjusting entries we've examined over the past few pages:

- Panel A repeats the data for each adjustment.
- Panel B gives the adjusting entries.
- Panel C on the following page shows the accounts after posting the adjusting entries. The adjustments are keyed by letter.

EXHIBIT 3-8 | The Adjusting Process of ShineBrite Car Wash, Inc.

PANEL A—Information for Adjustments at June 30, 2010	PANEL B—Adjusting Entries
(a) Prepaid rent expired, $1,000.	(a) Rent Expense .... 1,000 Prepaid Rent .... 1,000 To record rent expense.
(b) Supplies used, $300.	(b) Supplies Expense....................................... 300 Supplies.. 300 To record supplies used.
(c) Depreciation on equipment, $400.	(c) Depreciation Expense—Equipment .... 400 Accumulated Depreciation—Equipment 400 To record depreciation.
(d) Accrued salary expense, $900.	(d) Salary Expense .... 900 Salary Payable....................................... 900 To accrue salary expense.
(e) Accrued service revenue, $300.	(e) Accounts Receivable................................. 300 Service Revenue..................................... 300 To accrue service revenue.
(f) Amount of unearned service revenue that has been earned, $200.	(f) Unearned Service Revenue......................... 200 Service Revenue..................................... 200 To record unearned revenue that has been earned.
(g) Accrued income tax expense, $600.	(g) Income Tax Expense .... 600 Income Tax Payable.............................. 600 To accrue income tax expense.

PANEL C—Ledger Accounts

Assets	Liabilities	Shareholders' Equity

Assets

Cash

Bal 24,800 |

Accounts Receivable

2,200	
(e) 300	
Bal 2,500	

Supplies

| 700 | (b) 300 |
| Bal 400 | |

Prepaid Rent

| 3,000 | (a) 1,000 |
| Bal 2,000 | |

Equipment

Bal 24,000 |

Accumulated Depreciation— Equipment

| | (c) 400 |
| | Bal 400 |

Liabilities

Accounts Payable

| | Bal 13,100 |

Salary Payable

| | (d) 900 |
| | Bal 900 |

Unearned Service Revenue

| (f) 200 | 400 |
| | Bal 200 |

Income Tax Payable

| | (g) 600 |
| | Bal 600 |

Shareholders' Equity

Share Capital

| | Bal 20,000 |

Retained Earnings

| | Bal 18,800 |

Dividends

Bal 3,200 |

Revenue

Service Revenue

	7,000
(e)	300
(f)	200
	Bal 7,500

Expenses

Rent Expense

| (a) 1,000 | |
| Bal 1,000 | |

Salary Expense

900	
(d) 900	
Bal 1,800	

Supplies Expense

| (b) 300 | |
| Bal 300 | |

Depreciation Expense—Equipment

| (c) 400 | |
| Bal 400 | |

Utilities Expense

| Bal 500 | |

Income Tax Expense

| (g) 600 | |
| Bal 600 | |

Exhibit 3-8 includes an additional adjusting entry that we have not yet discussed—the accrual of income tax expense. Like individual taxpayers, corporations are subject to income tax. They typically accrue income tax expense and the related income tax payable as the final adjusting entry of the period. Obviously, taxation systems vary from country to country, and we are simplifying tax for now and assuming that income tax payable is $600. We will treat income tax expense like an accrued expense. ShineBrite Car Wash accrues income tax expense with adjusting entry g, as follows:

Adjusting entry g

Jun 30	Income Tax Expense	600	
	Income Tax Payable		600
	To accrue income tax expense.		

The income tax accrual follows the pattern for accrued expenses.

The Adjusted Trial Balance

This chapter began with the unadjusted trial balance (see Exhibit 3-3, p. 142). After the adjustments are journalized and posted, the accounts appear as shown in Exhibit 3-8, Panel C. A useful step in preparing the financial statements is to list the accounts, along with their adjusted balances, on an **adjusted trial balance**. This document lists all the accounts and their final balances in a single place. Exhibit 3-9 shows the adjusted trial balance of ShineBrite Car Wash.

EXHIBIT 3-9 | Adjusted Trial Balance

	ShineBrite Car Wash, Inc. Preparation of Adjusted Trial Balance June 30, 2010						
	Trial Balance		Adjustments		Adjusted Trial Balance		
Account Title	Debit	Credit	Debit	Credit	Debit	Credit	
Cash	24,800				24,800		
Accounts receivable	2,200		(e) 300		2,500		
Supplies	700			(b) 300	400		
Prepaid rent	3,000			(a) 1,000	2,000		
Equipment	24,000				24,000		
Accumulated depreciation—equipment				(c) 400		400	Balance Sheet
Accounts payable		13,100				13,100	(*Exhibit 3-12*)
Salary payable				(d) 900		900	
Unearned service revenue		400	(f) 200			200	
Income tax payable				(g) 600		600	
Share capital		20,000				20,000	
Retained earnings		18,800				18,800	Statement of Changes in Equity
Dividends	3,200				3,200		(*Exhibit 3-11*)
Service revenue		7,000		(e) 300		7,500	
				(f) 200			
Rent expense			(a) 1,000		1,000		
Salary expense	900		(d) 900		1,800		Income Statement
Supplies expense			(b) 300		300		(*Exhibit 3-10*)
Depreciation expense			(c) 400		400		
Utilities expense	500				500		
Income tax expense			(g) 600		600		
	59,300	59,300	3,700	3,700	61,500	61,500	

Accounting Cycle Tutorial Glossary

Note how clearly the adjusted trial balance presents the data. The Account Title and the Trial Balance data come from the trial balance. The two Adjustments columns summarize the adjusting entries. The Adjusted Trial Balance columns then give the final account balances. Each adjusted amount in Exhibit 3-9 is the unadjusted balance plus or minus the adjustments. For example, Accounts Receivable starts with a balance of $2,200. Add the $300 debit adjustment to get Accounts Receivable's ending balance of $2,500. Spreadsheets are very useful for this type of analysis.

PREPARING THE FINANCIAL STATEMENTS

The June financial statements of ShineBrite Car Wash can be prepared from the adjusted trial balance. At the far right, Exhibit 3-9 shows how the accounts are distributed to the financial statements:

OBJECTIVE

4 **Prepare** the financial statements

- The income statement (Exhibit 3-10) lists the revenue and expense accounts.
- The statement of changes in equity (Exhibit 3-11) shows the changes in various components of equity during the period.
- The balance sheet (Exhibit 3-12) reports assets, liabilities, and shareholders' equity.

The arrows in Exhibits 3-10, 3-11, and 3-12 (all on the following page) show the flow of data from one statement to the next.

Why is the income statement prepared first and the balance sheet last?

1. The income statement reports net income or net loss, the result of revenues minus expenses. Revenues and expenses will affect shareholders' equity, hence net income is then transferred to retained earnings. The first arrow tracks net income.

2. The statement of changes in equity reflects the increase in retained earnings from the income statement and records the payment of dividends. If there was any additional capital contribution from owners, it would also be reflected in this statement. The ending balance of equity from Exhibit 3-11 is carried to the balance sheet in Exhibit 3-12 as shown by the second arrow.

EXHIBIT 3-10 | Income Statement

ShineBrite Car Wash, Inc.
Income Statement
Month Ended June 30, 2010

Revenues:		
Service revenue		$7,500
Expenses:		
Salary expense	$1,800	
Rent expense...........................	1,000	
Utilities expense	500	
Depreciation expense..............	400	
Supplies expense	300	4,000
Income before tax		3,500
Income tax expense.....................		600
Net income.....................		$2,900

EXHIBIT 3-11 | Statement of Changes in Equity

ShineBrite Car Wash, Inc.
Statement of Changes in Equity
Month Ended June 30, 2010

Total equity, May 31, 2010	$38,800
Add: Net income	2,900
	21,700
Less: Dividends	(3,200)
Total equity, June 30, 2010	$38,500

①

EXHIBIT 3-12 | Balance Sheet

ShineBrite Car Wash, Inc.
Balance Sheet
June 30, 2010

②

Assets			Liabilities		
Cash.............................		$24,800	Accounts payable		$13,100
Accounts receivable.......		2,500	Salary payable..........................		900
Supplies..........................		400	Unearned service revenue		200
Prepaid rent....................		2,000	Income tax payable		600
Equipment.....................	$24,000		Total liabilities		14,800
Less: Accumulated					
depreciation........	(400)	23,600	**Shareholders' Equity**		
			Share capital............................		20,000
			Retained earnings....................		18,500
			Total shareholders' equity........		38,500
			Total liabilities and		
Total assets....................		$53,300	shareholders' equity..............		$53,300

MID-CHAPTER SUMMARY PROBLEM

The trial balance of Goldsmith Company shown below pertains to December 31, 2010, which is the end of its year-long accounting period. Data needed for the adjusting entries include the following:

a. Supplies on hand at year end, $2,000.

b. Depreciation on furniture and fixtures, $20,000.

c. Depreciation on building, $10,000.

d. Salaries owed but not yet paid, $5,000.

e. Accrued service revenue, $12,000.

f. Of the $45,000 balance of unearned service revenue, $32,000 was earned during the year.

g. Accrued income tax expense, $35,000.

Requirements

1. Open the ledger accounts with their unadjusted balances. Show dollar amounts in thousands, as shown for Accounts Receivable:

Accounts Receivable
370

2. Journalize the Goldsmith Company adjusting entries at December 31, 2010. Key entries by letter, as in Exhibit 3-8, pages 154-155.
3. Post the adjusting entries.
4. Prepare an adjusted trial balance, as shown in Exhibit 3-9, page 156.
5. Prepare the income statement, the statement of changes in equity, and the balance sheet. (At this stage, it is not necessary to classify assets or liabilities as current or long term.) Draw arrows linking these three financial statements.

Goldsmith Company
Trial Balance
December 31, 2010

Cash	$ 198,000	
Accounts receivable	370,000	
Supplies	6,000	
Furniture and fixtures	100,000	
Accumulated depreciation—furniture and fixtures		$ 40,000
Building	250,000	
Accumulated depreciation—building		130,000
Accounts payable		380,000
Salary payable		
Unearned service revenue		45,000
Income tax payable		
Share capital		100,000
Retained earnings		193,000
Dividends	65,000	
Service revenue		286,000
Salary expense	172,000	
Supplies expense		
Depreciation expense—furniture and fixtures		
Depreciation expense—building		
Income tax expense		
Miscellaneous expense	13,000	
Total	$1,174,000	$1,174,000

Answers

▌*Requirements 1 and 3*

(Amounts in thousands)

Assets		**Shareholders' Equity**

Assets

Cash

Bal	198	

Accounts Receivable

	370	
(e)	12	
Bal	382	

Supplies

	6	(a)	4
Bal	2		

Furniture and Fixtures

Bal	100	

Accumulated Depreciation—Furniture and Fixtures

			40
		(b)	20
		Bal	60

Building

Bal	250	

Accumulated Depreciation—Building

			130
		(c)	10
		Bal	140

Liabilities

Accounts Payable

		Bal	380

Salary Payable

		(d)	5
		Bal	5

Unearned Service Revenue

(f)	32		45
		Bal	13

Income Tax Payable

		(g)	35
		Bal	35

Share Capital

		Bal	100

Retained Earnings

		Bal	193

Dividends

Bal	65	

Revenues

Service Revenue

			286
		(e)	12
		(f)	32
		Bal	330

Expenses

Salary Expense

	172	
(d)	5	
Bal	177	

Supplies Expense

(a)	4	
Bal	4	

Depreciation Expense—Furniture and Fixtures

(b)	20	
Bal	20	

Depreciation Expense—Building

(c)	10	
Bal	10	

Income Tax Expense

(g)	35	
Bal	35	

Miscellaneous Expense

Bal	13	

Requirement 2

(a)	Dec 31	Supplies Expense ($6,000 – $2,000)	4,000	
		Supplies		4,000
		To record supplies used.		
(b)	31	Depreciation Expense—Furniture and Fixtures	20,000	
		Accumulated Depreciation—Furniture and Fixtures		20,000
		To record depreciation expense on furniture and fixtures.		
(c)	31	Depreciation Expense—Building	10,000	
		Accumulated Depreciation—Building		10,000
		To record depreciation expense on building.		
(d)	31	Salary Expense	5,000	
		Salary Payable		5,000
		To accrue salary expense.		
(e)	31	Accounts Receivable	12,000	
		Service Revenue		12,000
		To accrue service revenue.		
(f)	31	Unearned Service Revenue	32,000	
		Service Revenue		32,000
		To record unearned service revenue that has been earned.		
(g)	31	Income Tax Expense	35,000	
		Income Tax Payable		35,000
		To accrue income tax expense.		

I Requirement 4

Goldsmith Company
Preparation of Adjusted Trial Balance
December 31, 2010

(Amounts in thousands)	Trial Balance		Adjustments				Adjusted Trial Balance	
Account Title	Debit	Credit	Debit		Credit		Debit	Credit
Cash	198						198	
Accounts receivable	370		(e)	12			382	
Supplies	6				(a)	4	2	
Furniture and fixtures	100						100	
Accumulated depreciation— furniture and fixtures		40			(b)	20		60
Building	250						250	
Accumulated depreciation—building		130			(c)	10		140
Accounts payable		380						380
Salary payable					(d)	5		5
Unearned service revenue		45	(f)	32				13
Income tax payable					(g)	35		35
Share capital		100						100
Retained earnings		193						193
Dividends	65						65	
Service revenue		286			(e)	12		330
					(f)	32		
Salary expense	172		(d)	5			177	
Supplies expense			(a)	4			4	
Depreciation expense— furniture and fixtures			(b)	20			20	
Depreciation expense—building			(c)	10			10	
Income tax expense			(g)	35			35	
Miscellaneous expense	13						13	
	1,174	1,174		118		118	1,256	1,256

▌ Requirement 5

Goldsmith Company
Income Statement
Year Ended December 31, 2010

(Amounts in thousands)

Revenue:		
Service revenue		$330
Expenses:		
Salary expense	$177	
Depreciation expense—furniture and fixtures	20	
Depreciation expense—building............................	10	
Supplies expense	4	
Miscellaneous expense	13	224
Income before tax		106
Income tax expense		35
Net income...		$ 71

①

Goldsmith Company
Statement of Changes in Equity
Year Ended December 31, 2010

(Amounts in thousands)

Total equity, December 31, 2009..........................	$293
Add: Net income	71
	264
Less: Dividends	(65)
Total equity, December 31, 2010..........................	$299

Goldsmith Company
Balance Sheet
December 31, 2010

(Amounts in thousands)

②

Assets			Liabilities		
Cash...		$198	Accounts payable		$380
Accounts receivable.................		382	Salary payable		5
Supplies....................................		2	Unearned service revenue		13
Furniture and fixtures	$100		Income tax payable		35
Less: Accumulated			Total liabilities		433
depreciation.................	(60)	40			
			Shareholders' Equity		
Building...................................	$250		Share capital.................................		100
Less: Accumulated			Retained earnings.........................		199
depreciation.................	(140)	110	Total shareholders' equity............		299
			Total liabilities and		
Total assets..............................		$732	shareholders' equity.................		$732

Which Accounts Need to be Closed?

OBJECTIVE

5 **Close** the books

It is now June 30, the end of the month. Van Gray, the manager, will continue ShineBrite Car Wash into July, August, and beyond. But wait—the revenue and the expense accounts still hold amounts for June. At the end of each accounting period, it is necessary to close the books.

Closing the books means to prepare the accounts for the next period's transactions. The **closing entries** set the revenue, expense, and dividends balances back to zero at the end of the period. The idea is the same as setting the scoreboard back to zero after a game.

Closing is easily handled by computers. Recall that the income statement for a particular year reports only one year's income. For example, 2009 net income for DP World relates exclusively to the year ended December 31, 2009. At each year end, DP World's accountants close the company's revenues and expenses for that year.

Temporary Accounts. Because revenues and expenses relate to a limited period, they are called **temporary accounts**. The Dividends account is also temporary. The closing process applies only to temporary accounts (revenues, expenses, and dividends).

Permanent Accounts. Let's contrast the temporary accounts with the **permanent accounts**: assets, liabilities, and shareholders' equity. The permanent accounts are not closed at the end of the period because they carry over to the next period. Consider Cash, Receivables, Equipment, Accounts Payable, Share Capital, and Retained Earnings. Their ending balances at the end of one period become the beginning balances of the next period.

Closing entries transfer the revenue, expense, and dividends balances to Retained Earnings. Here are the steps to close the books of a company such as DP World or ShineBrite Car Wash:

① Debit each revenue account for the amount of its credit balance. Credit Retained Earnings for the sum of the revenues. Now the sum of the revenues is in Retained Earnings.

② Credit each expense account for the amount of its debit balance. Debit Retained Earnings for the sum of the expenses. The sum of the expenses is now in Retained Earnings.

③ Credit the Dividends account for the amount of its debit balance. Debit Retained Earnings. This entry places the dividends amount in the debit side of Retained Earnings. Remember that dividends are not expenses. Dividends never affect net income.

After closing the books, the Retained Earnings account of ShineBrite Car Wash appears as follows (data from page 158):

Retained Earnings			
		Beginning balance	18,800
Expenses	4,600	Revenues	7,500
Dividends	3,200		
		Ending balance	18,500

Assume that ShineBrite Car Wash closes the books at the end of June. Exhibit 3-13 presents the complete closing process for the business. Panel A gives the closing journal entries, and Panel B shows the accounts after closing.

EXHIBIT 3-13 | Journalizing and Posting the Closing Entries

PANEL A—Journalizing the Closing Entries

Closing Entries

①	Jun 30	Service Revenue..................................	7,500	
		Retained Earnings....................		7,500
②	Jun 30	Retained Earnings.............................	4,600	
		Rent Expense...........................		1,000
		Salary Expense.........................		1,800
		Supplies Expense......................		300
		Depreciation Expense...............		400
		Utilities Expense......................		500
		Income Tax Expense................		600
③	Jun 30	Retained Earnings.............................	3,200	
		Dividends.................................		3,200

PANEL B—Posting to the Accounts

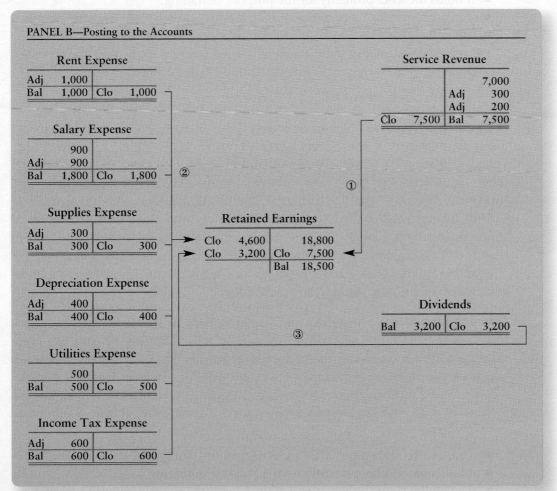

Accounting Cycle Tutorial Adjusting & Closing the Books

Accounting Cycle Tutorial Application—Cottage Kitchen

Accounting Cycle Tutorial Application—Cottage Kitchen 2

Adj = Amount posted from an adjusting entry
Clo = Amount posted from a closing entry
Bal = Balance
As arrow ② in Panel B shows, we can make a compound closing entry for all the expenses.

Classifying Assets and Liabilities Based on Their Liquidity

IAS1 – Presentation of Financial Statement requires that on the balance sheet, assets and liabilities are classified as current or non-current to indicate their relative liquidity. **Liquidity** measures how quickly an item can be converted to cash. Cash is the most liquid asset. Accounts receivable are relatively liquid because cash collections usually follow quickly. Inventory is less liquid than accounts receivable because the company must first sell the goods. Equipment and buildings are even less liquid because these assets are held for use and not for sale. A balance sheet lists assets and liabilities in the order of relative liquidity. Some companies do this in an increasing order of liquidity (i.e. cash first followed by other assets), some do this in reverse order (i.e. cash is shown last).

Current Assets.   As we saw in Chapter 1, **current assets** are the most liquid assets. Cash, Short-Term Investments, Accounts Receivable, Inventory, and Prepaid Expenses are the typical examples of current assets. *IAS1* requires that an entity classify an asset as current when:

- it expects to realize the asset, or intends to sell or consume it, in its normal operating cycle (the time span during which cash is paid for goods and services and these goods and services are sold to bring in cash);
- it holds the asset primarily for the purpose of trading;
- it expects to realize the asset within 12 months after the reporting period; or
- the asset is cash or a cash equivalent unless the asset is restricted from being exchanged or used to settle a liability for at least 12 months after the reporting period.

All other assets are considered non-current.

Non-current Assets.   **Non-current assets** are all assets not classified as current assets. One category of non-current assets is Property, Plant and Equipment (PPE) as you saw earlier in DP World's list of non-current assets in Exhibit 3-5 (page 149). Of these, ShineBrite Car Wash has only Equipment. Long-term Investments and Intangible Assets are also non-current in nature. Intangibles assets (as defined in *IAS38 – Intangible Assets*) are assets an identifiable non-monetary asset without physical substance and include goodwill, trademarks, and brand names arising from merger and acquisitions. We will learn more about non-current assets in Chapter 7 and 10. *IAS1* allows other terminologies besides "non-current", so you may see some companies use the term "long-term" assets as well.

Current Liabilities.   As we saw in Chapter 1, **current liabilities** are obligations that must be paid in the near future. The sooner a liability must be paid, the more pressure it creates. Therefore, the balance sheet usually lists liabilities in the order in which they must be paid. Examples of current liabilities include Accounts Payable, Notes Payable due within one year, Salary Payable, Unearned Revenue, Interest Payable, and Income Tax Payable. *IAS1* requires that an entity classify a liability as current when:

- it expects to settle the liability in its normal operating cycle;
- it holds the liability primarily for the purpose of trading;
- the liability is due to be settled within 12 months after the reporting period; or
- the entity does not have an unconditional right to defer settlement of the liability for at least 12 months after the reporting period.

Similarly, all other liabilities are deemed non-current. Sometimes, you will see companies reporting "current portion of long-term debt" as a current liability. This is because certain portions of a long-term debt (which may be due many years from now) are payable within the next 12 months, and thus disclosed to help readers to better understand the financial obligations faced by the entity in the coming financial year.

Non-Current Liabilities. All liabilities that are not current are classified as **long-term liabilities** or non-current liabilities. Many loans and notes payable are long term. Some notes payable are paid in installments, with the first installment due within one year, the second installment due the second year, and so on. The first installment is a current liability and the remainder is long term.

Let's see how DP World reports these asset and liability categories on its balance sheet.

Reporting Assets and Liabilities: DP World

Exhibit 3-14 on the following page shows a classified balance sheet: The Consolidated Balance Sheet of DP World. A **classified balance sheet** separates current assets from long-term assets and current liabilities from long-term liabilities. You should be familiar with most of DP World's accounts. Study the DP World's balance sheet all the way through—line by line.

FORMATS FOR THE FINANCIAL STATEMENTS

Companies can format their financial statements in different ways.

Balance Sheet Formats

IAS1 does not prescribe a fixed format for balance sheets. For smaller companies, you may find that the Balance Sheet is presented like in an **account format**. The account format lists the assets on the left and the liabilities and shareholders' equity on the right in the same way that a T-account appears, with assets (debits) on the left and liabilities and equity (credits) on the right. Exhibit 3-12 (p. 158) shows an account-format balance sheet for ShineBrite Car Wash.

Most of the time, you will not see balance sheets presented this way in an annual report. It is more likely that it will be shown in a **report format**, which lists the assets at the top, followed by the liabilities and shareholders' equity below. The Consolidated Balance Sheet of DP World in Exhibit 3-14 (p. 168) illustrates the report format. In Exhibit 3-14, the emphasis is on proving that the accounting equation balances, i.e. total assets equal total liabilities plus total equity. Other companies may present balance sheets as proof that total assets less total liabilities equal total equity.

Income Statement Formats

IAS1 requires an entity to present an analysis of expenses recognized in the income statement using a classification based on either their nature or their function within the entity. The choice between the *function* and *nature* of expense method depends on historical and industry factors and the nature of the entity. Both methods have merits for different types of entities and management must select the presentation that in its opinion is the more reliable and more relevant.

EXHIBIT 3-14 | DP World's Balance Sheet

DP World Limited
Balance Sheet (Adapted)
As at 31 December

(in millions USD)	2009
Non-current assets:	
Property, plant and equipment..................................	$ 4,859.2
Intangible assets..	6,598.9
Investment in associates and joint ventures..............	3,453.8
Other investments...	65.3
Other non-current assets...	177.7
Total non-current assets......................................	15,154.9
Current assets:	
Other current assets...	28.4
Inventories...	59.7
Accounts receivable and prepayments......................	807.5
Bank balances and cash	2,910.1
Total current assets..	3,805.7
Total assets	$18,960.6
Non-current liabilities:	
Pension and post-employment benefits	$ 312.3
Interest bearing loans and borrowings.....................	7,474.9
Other non-current liabilities....................................	1,651.6
Total non-current liabilities..................................	9,438.8
Current liabilities:	
Accounts payable and accruals	817.6
Bank overdrafts	11.5
Interest bearing loans and borrowings.....................	483.1
Income tax liabilities...	126.7
Other current liabilities..	45.4
Total current liabilities	1,484.3
Total liabilities	10,923.1
Equity:	
Share capital...	1,660.0
Retained earnings	1,584.8
Other equity items	4,792.6
Total equity..	8,037.4
Total liabilities and equity....................................	$18,960.5

Under the **nature of expenses** format, an entity aggregates its expenses according to their nature (for example, depreciation, cost of materials, transport costs, and employee benefits). Generally the nature method is easier to prepare as it avoids allocation of expenses to the various functions of the entity. A pure nature classification will thus have no Cost of Sales line item. On the other hand, if an entity decided that a **function of expenses** format is more reliable and more relevant, it would classify expenses as part of cost of sales, marketing costs, distribution costs, administrative costs, or other functional groupings. DP World's income statement on the next page uses a function of expenses format. Where line 2 shows Cost of Sales and the resulting Gross Profit on line 3.

EXHIBIT 3-15 | DP World's Income Statement

DP World Limited
Consolidated Income Statement (Adapted)
Year Ended 31 December

(in millions USD)	2009
1 Revenue from operations	$2,929.2
2 Cost of sales	(2,064.2)
3 Gross profit	865.0
4 General and administration expenses	(305.3)
5 Other income	22.1
6 Financial income	85.5
7 Finance costs	(356.7)
8 Share of profits of associates and joint ventures	69.3
9 Profit on sale/termination of business	44.3
10 Profit before tax	424.2
11 Income tax	(54.1)
12 Profit for the year	$ 370.1

Most companies would separate out items that are non-recurring in nature to help financial statement users assess the underlying performance of the business. You saw this earlier with **Carrefour**'s "Non-recurring income and expenses" (Exhibit 1-1, line 8) and DP World's line 9 "Profit on sale/termination of business" is also non-recurring. Many companies also consider it important to report their operating income separately from non-operating income such as interest and dividends. We will discuss the components of the income statement in more detail in Chapter 11.

DP World ends the 2009 financial year with a net income of USD 370 million (line 12). As you have seen throughout this chapter, this income is derived under accural basis of accounting.

USING ACCOUNTING RATIOS

As we've seen, accounting provides information for decision making. A bank considering lending money must make an assessment whether the borrower can repay the loan. If the borrower already has a lot of debt, the probability of repayment may be low. If the borrower owes little, the loan may go through. To analyze a company's financial position, decision makers use ratios computed from various items in the financial statements. Let's see how this process works.

OBJECTIVE

6 Use two financial ratios to evaluate a business

Current Ratio

One of the most widely used financial ratios is the **current ratio**, which divides total current assets by total current liabilities, taken from the balance sheet.

$$\text{Current ratio} = \frac{\text{Total current assets}}{\text{Total current liabilities}}$$

For DP World Exhibit (3-14 on page 168) is as follows:

$$\text{Current ratio} = \frac{\text{Total current assets}}{\text{Total current liabilities}} = \frac{\$3,805.6}{\$1,484.2} = 2.56$$

The current ratio measures the company's ability to pay current liabilities with current assets. A company prefers a high current ratio, which means that the business has plenty of current assets to pay current liabilities. An increasing current ratio from period to period indicates improvement in financial position.

As a rule of thumb, a strong current ratio is 1.50, which indicates that the company has $1.50 in current assets for every $1.00 in current liabilities. A company with a current ratio of 1.50 would probably have little trouble paying its current liabilities. Most successful businesses operate with current ratios between 1.20 and 1.50. A current ratio of 1.00 is considered quite low.

DP World's 2009 current ratio is 2.56. Is this current ratio good or bad? Well, any number or ratio is meaningless unless you give it context. We can, for example, compare the 2009 current ratio to DP World's 2008 current ratio (you will need to obtain the 2008 balance sheet, but for expediency, it's 1.40). This indicates that there has been significant improvement in DP World's ability to pay its current liabilities using its current asset. Another way to make sense of the 1.40 ratio is to compare it to other port operators such as **COSCO** (China), **PSA International** (Singapore), or **Maersk** (Denmark), whose 2009 current ratios were 1.72, 1.06 and 1.07, respectively. Thus, in comparison to other companies in the port business, DP World's current ratio is very strong.

Debt Ratio

A second aid to decision making is the **debt ratio**, which is the ratio of total liabilities to total assets.

$$\text{Debt ratio} = \frac{\text{Total liabilities}}{\text{Total assets}}$$

For DP World (Exhibit 3-14 on page 168),

$$\text{Debt ratio} = \frac{\text{Total liabilities}}{\text{Total assets}} = \frac{\$10,923.1}{\$18,960.5} = 0.58$$

The debt ratio indicates the proportion of a company's assets that is financed with debt. This ratio measures a business's ability to pay both current and long-term debts (total liabilities).

A low debt ratio is safer than a high debt ratio. Why? Because a company with few liabilities has low required debt payments. This company is unlikely to get into financial difficulty. By contrast, a business with a high debt ratio may have trouble paying its liabilities, especially when sales are low and cash is scarce.

DP World's debt ratio of 0.58 (58%) is similar to the other three port operators: such as COSCO (58%), PSA International (58%), or Maersk (54%). The norm for the debt ratio ranges from 40% to 70%, but this may be lower in the future as a result of the financial crisis. DP World's debt ratio is in line with those of its peers.

When a company fails to pay its debts, some of its creditors might be in a position to take the company away from its owners. Most bankruptcies result from high debt ratios. Companies that continue in this pattern are often forced out of business.

How Do Transactions Affect the Ratios?

Companies such as DP World are keenly aware of how transactions affect their ratios. Lending agreements often require that a company make good on its scheduled payments of interests or loan principal repayments. Other loan requirements may include conditions that the company maintains a certain level of current ratio or debt ratio. When a company fails to meet one of these conditions, it is said to default on its lending agreements. The penalty can be severe, such as the lender can requiring immediate payment of the loan. The financial crisis has put many companies in a difficult financial position.

Let's use DP World to examine the effects of some transactions on the company's current ratio and debt ratio. As shown in the preceding section, DP World's ratios are as follows (dollar amounts in USD millions):

$$\text{Current ratio} = \frac{\$3,805.6}{\$1,484.2} = 2.56 \qquad \text{Debt ratio} = \frac{\$10,923.1}{\$18,960.5} = 57.61\%$$

The managers of any company would be concerned about how inventory purchases, payments on account, expense accruals, and depreciation would affect its ratios. Let's see how DP World would be affected by some typical transactions. For each transaction, the journal entry helps identify the effects on the company.

a. Issued shares and received cash of $500 million.

Journal entry:

Cash	500	
Share Capital		500

Cash, a current asset, affects both the current ratio and the debt ratio as follows:

$$\text{Current ratio} = \frac{\$3,805.6 + \$500}{\$1,484.2} = 2.90 \qquad \text{Debt ratio} = \frac{\$10,923.1}{\$18,960.5 + \$500} = 56.13\%$$

The issuance of shares improves both ratios.

b. Paid cash to purchase buildings for $200 million.

Cash, a current asset, decreases, but total assets stay the same. Liabilities are unchanged.

Journal entry:

Buildings	200	
Cash		200

$$\text{Current ratio} = \frac{\$3,805.6 - \$200}{\$1,484.2} = 2.43 \qquad \text{Debt ratio} = \frac{\$10,923.1}{\$18,960.5 + \$200 - \$200} = 57.61\% \text{ no change}$$

A cash purchase of a building decreases the current ratio, but doesn't affect the debt ratio.

c. Performed a $100 million shipping services on account for a grocery chain.

Journal entry:

Accounts Receivable	100	
Shipping Revenue		100

The increase in Accounts Receivable increases current assets and total assets, as follows:

$$\text{Current ratio} = \frac{\$3,805.6 + \$100}{\$1,484.2} = 2.63 \qquad \text{Debt ratio} = \frac{\$10,923.1}{\$18,960.5 + \$100} = 57.31\%$$

A sale on account improves both ratios.

d. Collected the account receivable, $100 million.

Journal entry:

Cash	100	
Accounts Receivable		100

This transaction has no effect on total current assets, total assets, or total liabilities. Both ratios are unaffected.

e. Accrued expenses at year end, $40 million.

Journal entry:

Expenses	40	
Expenses Payable		40

$$\text{Current ratio} = \frac{\$3,805.6}{\$1,484.2 + \$40} = 2.50 \qquad \text{Debt ratio} = \frac{\$10,923.1 + \$40}{\$18,960.5} = 57.82\%$$

As you can see, accruing expenses will decrease both ratios.

f. Recorded depreciation, $80 million.

Journal entry:

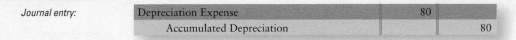

| Depreciation Expense | 80 | |
| Accumulated Depreciation | | 80 |

No current accounts are affected, so only the debt ratio is affected.

$$\text{Current ratio} = \frac{\$3,805.6}{\$1,484.2} = 2.56 \qquad \text{Debt ratio} = \frac{\$10,923.1}{\$18,960.5 - \$80} = 57.85\%$$

Depreciation decreases total assets and therefore hurts the debt ratio.

g. Earned interest revenue and collected cash, $40 million.

Journal entry:

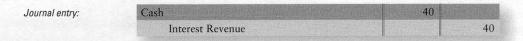

| Cash | 40 | |
| Interest Revenue | | 40 |

Cash, a current asset, affects both the current ratio and the debt ratio as follows:

$$\text{Current ratio} = \frac{\$3,805.6 + \$40}{\$1,484.2} = 2.59 \qquad \text{Debt ratio} = \frac{\$10,923.1}{\$18,960.5 + \$40} = 57.49\%$$

Earning and receiving revenue improve both ratios.

Now, let's wrap up the chapter by seeing how to use the current ratio and the debt ratio for decision making. The Decision Guidelines feature offers some clues.

DECISION GUIDELINES

USING THE CURRENT RATIO AND THE DEBT RATIO

In general, a *high* current ratio is preferable to a low current ratio. *Increases* in the current ratio improve financial position. By contrast, a *low* debt ratio is preferable to a high debt ratio. Improvement is indicated by a *decrease* in the debt ratio.

No single ratio gives the whole picture about a company. Therefore, lenders and investors use many ratios to evaluate a company. Let's apply what we have learned. Suppose you are a loan officer at **Hongkong and Shanghai Banking Corporation (HSBC)**, and DP World has asked you for a $500 million loan to launch a new ship terminal. How will you make this loan decision? The Decision Guidelines show how bankers and investors use two key ratios.

USING THE CURRENT RATIO

Decision	Guidelines
How can you measure a company's ability to pay current liabilities with current assets?	$$\text{Current ratio} = \frac{\text{Total current assets}}{\text{Total current liabilities}}$$
Who uses the current ratio for decision making?	*Lenders and other creditors*, who must predict whether a borrower can pay its current liabilities. *Shareholders*, who know that a company that cannot pay its debts is not a good investment because it may go bankrupt. *Managers*, who must have enough cash to pay the company's current liabilities.
What is a good value of the current ratio?	Depends on the industry: A company with strong cash flow can operate successfully with a low current ratio of, say, 1.10–1.20. A company with weak cash flow needs a higher current ratio of, say, 1.30–1.50. Traditionally, a current ratio of 2.00 was considered ideal. Recently, acceptable values have decreased as companies have been able to operate more efficiently; today, a current ratio of 1.50 is considered strong. Cash-rich companies can operate with a current ratio below 1.0.

USING THE DEBT RATIO

Decision	Guidelines
How can you measure a company's ability to pay total liabilities?	$$\text{Debt ratio} = \frac{\text{Total liabilities}}{\text{Total assets}}$$
Who uses the debt ratio for decision making?	*Lenders and other creditors*, who must predict whether a borrower can pay its debts. *Shareholders*, who know that a company that cannot pay its debts is not a good investment because it may go bankrupt. *Managers*, who must have enough assets to pay the company's debts.
What is a good value of the debt ratio?	Depends on the industry: A company with strong cash flow may operate successfully with a high debt ratio of, say, 0.70–0.80. A company with weak cash flow needs a lower debt ratio of, say, 0.50–0.60. Traditionally, a debt ratio of 0.50 was considered ideal. Until the financial crisis, values have increased as companies have been able to operate more efficiently; today, a normal value of the debt ratio is around 0.4–0.7. This is likely to be lower in the future as credit has become more difficult to obtain, In addition, weaker consumer demands have lowered companies' growth projections and funding needs.

END-OF-CHAPTER SUMMARY PROBLEM

Refer to the Mid-Chapter Summary Problem that begins on page 160. The adjusted trial balance appears on page 163.

▌Requirements

1. Make Goldsmith Company's closing entries at December 31, 2010. Explain what the closing entries accomplish and why they are necessary. Show amounts in thousands.
2. Post the closing entries to Retained Earnings and compare Retained Earnings' ending balance with the amount reported on the balance sheet on page 164. The two amounts should be the same.
3. Prepare Goldsmith Company's classified balance sheet to identify the company's current assets and current liabilities. (Goldsmith has no long-term liabilities.) Then compute the company's current ratio and debt ratio at December 31, 2010.
4. The top management of Goldsmith Company has asked you for a $500,000 loan to expand the business. Goldsmith proposes to pay off the loan over a 10-year period. Recompute Goldsmith's debt ratio assuming you make the loan. Use the company financial statements plus the ratio values to decide whether to grant the loan at an interest rate of 8%, 10%, or 12%. Goldsmith's cash flow is strong. Give the reasoning underlying your decision.

Answers

▌Requirement 1

2010		(In thousands)	
Dec 31	Service Revenue....................................	330	
	Retained Earnings		330
31	Retained Earnings	259	
	Salary Expense		177
	Depreciation Expense—		
	Furniture and Fixtures............................		20
	Depreciation Expense—Building		10
	Supplies Expense		4
	Income Tax Expense		35
	Miscellaneous Expense..............................		13
31	Retained Earnings	65	
	Dividends..		65

▌Explanation of Closing Entries

The closing entries set the balance of each revenue, expense, and Dividends account back to zero for the start of the next accounting period. We must close these accounts because their balances relate only to one accounting period.

▌Requirement 2

Retained Earnings			
			193
Clo	259	Clo	330
Clo	65		
		Bal	199

The balance in the Retained Earnings account agrees with the amount reported on the balance sheet, as it should.

❙ Requirement 3

Goldsmith Company
Balance Sheet
December 31, 2010

(Amounts in thousands)

Assets			Liabilities	
Current assets:			**Current liabilities:**	
Cash		$198	Accounts payable	$380
Accounts receivable		382	Salary payable	5
Supplies		2	Unearned service revenue	13
Total current assets...............		582	Income tax payable	35
Furniture and			Total current liabilities..............	433
fixtures	$100			
Less: Accumulated			*Shareholders' Equity*	
depreciation..................	(60)	40	Share capital...............................	100
Building.....................................	$250		Retained earnings.........................	199
Less: Accumulated			Total shareholders' equity............	299
depreciation..................	(140)	110	Total liabilities and	
Total assets.............................		$732	shareholders' equity..................	$732

$$\text{Current ratio} = \frac{\$582}{\$433} = 1.34 \qquad \text{Debt ratio} = \frac{\$433}{\$732} = 0.59$$

❙ Requirement 4

$$\begin{array}{c}\text{Debt ratio assuming}\\ \text{the loan is made}\end{array} = \frac{\$433 + \$500}{\$732 + \$500} = \frac{\$933}{\$1,232} = 0.76$$

Decision: Make the loan at 10%.

Reasoning: Prior to the loan, the company's financial position and cash flow are strong. The current ratio is in a middle range, and the debt ratio is not too high. Net income (from the income statement) is high in relation to total revenue. Therefore, the company should be able to repay the loan.

The loan will increase the company's debt ratio from 59% to 76%, which is more risky than the company's financial position at present. On this basis, a midrange interest rate appears reasonable—at least as the starting point for the negotiation between Goldsmith Company and the bank.

REVIEW ACCRUAL ACCOUNTING & INCOME

Quick Check (Answers are given on page 216.)

1. On October 1, River Place Apartments received $5,200 from a tenant for four months' rent. The receipt was credited to Unearned Rent Revenue. What adjusting entry is needed on December 31?

a. Unearned Rent Revenue   1,300
    Rent Revenue   1,300

b. Cash   1,300
    Rent Revenue   1,300

c. Rent Revenue   1,300
    Unearned Rent Revenue   1,300

d. Unearned Rent Revenue   3,900
    Rent Revenue   3,900

2. The following normal balances appear on the *adjusted* trial balance of Greenville National Company:

Equipment..	$110,000
Accumulated depreciation, equipment...............	22,000
Depreciation expense, equipment.......................	5,500

The book value of the equipment is

a. $82,500.
b. $66,000.

c. $88,000.
d. $104,500.

3. Details, Inc., purchased supplies for $1,300 during 2010. At year end Details had $800 of supplies left. The adjusting entry should

a. debit Supplies $800.
b. credit Supplies $800.

c. debit Supplies $500.
d. debit Supplies Expense $500.

4. The accountant for Exeter Corp. failed to make the adjusting entry to record depreciation for the current year. The effect of this error is which of the following?

a. Assets, net income, and shareholders' equity are all overstated.
b. Assets and expenses are understated; net income is understated.
c. Net income is overstated and liabilities are understated.
d. Assets are overstated, shareholders' equity and net income are understated.

5. Interest earned on a note receivable at December 31 equals $375. What adjusting entry is required to accrue this interest?

a. Interest Expense   375
    Interest Payable   375

b. Interest Receivable   375
    Interest Revenue   375

c. Interest Payable   375
    Interest Expense   375

d. Interest Expense   375
    Cash   375

6. If a real estate company fails to accrue commission revenue,
   a. revenues are understated and net income is overstated.
   b. assets are understated and net income is understated.
   c. net income is understated and shareholders' equity is overstated.
   d. liabilities are overstated and owners' equity is understated.

7. All of the following statements are true except one. Which statement is false?
   a. A fiscal year ends on some date other than December 31.
   b. The matching principle directs accountants to identify and measure all expenses incurred and deduct them from revenues earned during the same period.
   c. Adjusting entries are required for a business that uses the cash basis.
   d. Accrual accounting produces better information than cash-basis accounting.

8. The account Unearned Revenue is a(n)
   a. asset.   c. revenue.
   b. expense.   d. liability.

9. Adjusting entries
   a. update the accounts.
   b. are needed to measure the period's net income or net loss.
   c. do not debit or credit cash.
   d. all of the above.

10. An adjusting entry that debits an expense and credits a liability is which type?
    a. Depreciation expense   c. Accrued expense
    b. Cash expense   d. Prepaid expense

Use the following data for questions 11 and 12.
Here are key figures from the balance sheet of Geneva, Inc., at the end of 2010 (amounts in thousands):

	December 31, 2010
Total assets (of which 50% are current)	$5,000
Current liabilities	500
Bonds payable (long-term)	1,400
Share capital...	1,000
Retained earnings..	2,100
Total liabilities and shareholders' equity	5,000

11. Geneva's current ratio at the end of 2010 is
    a. 10.00.   c. 1.32.
    b. 1.19.   d. 5.00.

12. Geneva's debt ratio at the end of 2010 is (all amounts are rounded)
    a. 1.32%.   c. 10.00%.
    b. 16%.   d. 38%.

13. On a trial balance, which of the following would indicate that an error has been made?
    a. Accumulated Depreciation has a credit balance.
    b. Salary Expense has a debit balance.
    c. Service Revenue has a debit balance.
    d. All of the above indicate errors.

14. The entry to close Management Fee Revenue would be which of the following?
    a. Management Fee Revenue
           Retained Earnings
    b. Management Fee Revenue does not need to be closed.
    c. Retained Earnings
           Management Fee Revenue
    d. Management Fee Revenue
           Service Revenue

15. Which of the following accounts is not closed?
    a. Dividends
    b. Depreciation Expense
    c. Interest Revenue
    d. Accumulated Depreciation

16. UPS earns service revenue of $800,000. How does this transaction affect UPS's ratios?
    a. Improves the current ratio and doesn't affect the debt ratio
    b. Hurts the current ratio and improves the debt ratio
    c. Hurts both ratios
    d. Improves both ratios

17. Suppose Green Mountain Corporation borrows $20 million on a 20-year note payable. How does this transaction affect Green Mountain's current ratio and debt ratio?
    a. Hurts both ratios
    b. Improves both ratios
    c. Improves the current ratio and hurts the debt ratio
    d. Hurts the current ratio and improves the debt ratio

Accounting Vocabulary

account format (p. 167) A balance-sheet format that lists assets on the left and liabilities and shareholders' equity on the right.

accrual (p. 143) An expense or a revenue that occurs before the business pays or receives cash. An accrual is the opposite of a deferral.

accrual accounting (p. 138) Accounting that records the impact of a business event as it occurs, regardless of whether the transaction affected cash.

accrued expense (p. 149) An expense incurred but not yet paid in cash.

accrued revenue (p. 150) A revenue that has been earned but not yet received in cash.

accumulated depreciation (p. 147) The cumulative sum of all depreciation expense from the date of acquiring a PPE.

adjusted trial balance (p. 156) A list of all the ledger accounts with their adjusted balances.

book value (of a PPE) (p. 148) The asset's cost minus accumulated depreciation.

cash basis accounting (p. 138) Accounting that records only transactions in which cash is received or paid.

classified balance sheet (p. 167) A balance sheet that shows current assets separate from non-current assets, and current liabilities separate from non-current liabilities.

closing the books (p. 164) The process of preparing the accounts to begin recording the next period's transactions. Closing the accounts consists of journalizing and posting the closing entries to set the balances of the revenue, expense, and dividends accounts to zero. Also called closing the accounts.

closing entries (p. 164) Entries that transfer the revenue, expense, and dividends balances from these respective accounts to the Retained Earnings account.

contra account (p. 147) An account that always has a companion account and whose normal balance is opposite that of the companion account.

current asset (p. 166) An asset that is expected to be converted to cash, sold, or consumed during the next 12 months.

current liability (p. 166) A debt due to be paid within one year.

current ratio (p. 169) Current assets divided by current liabilities. Measures a company's ability to pay current liabilities with current assets.

debt ratio (p. 170) Ratio of total liabilities to total assets. States the proportion of a company's assets that is financed with debt.

deferral (p. 124) An adjustment for which the business paid or received cash in advance. Examples include prepaid rent, prepaid insurance, and supplies.

depreciation (p. 143) Allocation of the cost of a PPE to expense over its useful life.

function of expense income statement (p. 168) An income statement that shows Cost of Sales and group expenses into functional categories such as distribution, selling, general and administrative expenses.

liquidity (p. 166) Measure of how quickly an item can be converted to cash.

matching principle (p. 140) The basis for recording expenses. Directs accountants to identify all expenses incurred during the period, to measure the expenses, and to match them against the revenues earned during that same period.

Nature of expense income statement (p. 168) An income statement that lists all the expenses by their nature (e.g. depreciation, purchases of materials, staff costs) without allocation to functional areas.

non-current asset (p. 166) An asset that is not a current asset, also known as long-term asset.

non-current liability (p. 167) A liability that is not a current liability, also known as long-term liability.

operating cycle (p. 166) Time span during which cash is paid for goods and services that are sold to customers who pay the business in cash.

permanent accounts (p. 164) Asset, liability, and shareholders' equity accounts that are not closed at the end of the period.

property, plant and equipment or PPE (p. 146) Long-lived assets, such as land, buildings, and equipment, used in the operation of the business. Sometimes referred to as fixed assets or plant assets.

prepaid expense (p. 143) A category of miscellaneous assets that typically expire or get used up in the near future. Examples include prepaid rent, prepaid insurance, and supplies.

report format (p. 167) A balance-sheet format that lists assets at the top, followed by liabilities and shareholders' equity below.

revenue principle (p. 139) The basis for recording revenues; tells accountants when to record revenue and the amount of revenue to record.

temporary accounts (p. 164) The revenue and expense accounts that relate to a limited period and are closed at the end of the period are temporary accounts. For a corporation, the Dividends account is also temporary.

time-period concept (p. 139) Ensures that accounting information is reported at regular intervals.

unearned revenue (p. 151) A liability created when a business collects cash from customers in advance of earning the revenue. The obligation is to provide a product or a service in the future.

ASSESS YOUR PROGRESS

Short Exercises

S3-1 (*Learning Objective 1: Linking accrual accounting and cash flows*) St. Pierre Corporation made sales of $960 million during 2010. Of this amount, St. Pierre collected cash for all but $25 million. The company's cost of goods sold was $270 million, and all other expenses for the year totaled $300 million. Also during 2010, St. Pierre paid $370 million for its inventory and $285 million for everything else. Beginning cash was $105 million. St. Pierre's top management is interviewing you for a job and they ask two questions:

a. How much was St. Pierre's net income for 2010?

b. How much was St. Pierre's cash balance at the end of 2010?

You will get the job only if you answer both questions correctly.

S3-2 (*Learning Objective 1: Linking accrual accounting and cash flows*) Capeside Corporation began 2010 owing notes payable of $3.9 million. During 2010 Capeside borrowed $2.3 million on notes payable and paid off $2.0 million of notes payable from prior years. Interest expense for the year was $1.8 million, including $0.1 million of interest payable accrued at December 31, 2010.

Show what Capeside should report for these facts on the following financial statements:

1. Income statement
   a. Interest expense
2. Balance sheet
   a. Notes payable
   b. Interest payable

writing assignment ■

S3-3 (*Learning Objectives 1, 2: Linking accrual accounting and cash flows; applying accounting principles*) As the controller of Eden Consulting, you have hired a new employee, whom you must train. She objects to making an adjusting entry for accrued salaries at the end of the period. She reasons, "We will pay the salaries soon. Why not wait until payment to record the expense? In the end, the result will be the same." Write a reply to explain to the employee why the adjusting entry is needed for accrued salary expense.

S3-4 (*Learning Objective 2: Applying the revenue and the matching principles*) A large auto manufacturer sells large fleets of vehicles to auto rental companies, such as Acme and Harris. Suppose Acme is negotiating with the auto manufacturer to purchase 950 vehicles. Write a short paragraph to explain to the auto manufacturer when the company should, and should not, record this sales revenue and the related expense for cost of goods sold. Mention the accounting principles that provide the basis for your explanation.

writing assignment ■

S3-5 (*Learning Objective 2: Applying accounting concepts and principles*) Write a short paragraph to explain in your own words the concept of depreciation as used in accounting.

writing assignment ■

S3-6 (*Learning Objective 2: Applying accounting concepts and principles*) Identify the accounting concept or principle that gives the most direction on how to account for each of the following situations:

a. Salary expense of $35,000 is accrued at the end of the period to measure income properly.

b. May has been a particularly slow month, and the business will have a net loss for the second quarter of the year. Management is considering not following its customary practice of reporting quarterly earnings to the public.

c. A physician performs a surgical operation and bills the patient's insurance company. It may take four months to collect from the insurance company. Should the physician record revenue now or wait until cash is collected?

d. A construction company is building a highway system, and construction will take five years. When should the company record the revenue it earns?

e. A utility bill is received on December 28 and will be paid next year. When should the company record utility expense?

S3-7 (*Learning Objective 3: Adjusting prepaid expenses*) Answer the following questions about prepaid expenses:

a. On March 1, Blue & Green Travel prepaid $4,800 for six months' rent. Give the adjusting entry to record rent expense at March 31. Include the date of the entry and an explanation. Then post all amounts to the two accounts involved, and show their balances at March 31. Blue & Green Travel adjusts the accounts only at March 31, the end of its fiscal year.

b. On December 1, Blue & Green Travel paid $900 for supplies. At March 31, Blue & Green Travel has $700 of supplies on hand. Make the required journal entry at March 31. Then post all amounts to the accounts and show their balances at March 31.

S3-8 (*Learning Objectives 1, 3: Recording depreciation; linking accrual accounting and cash flows*) Suppose that on January 1 Georgetown Golf Company paid cash of $80,000 for computers that are expected to remain useful for four years. At the end of four years, the computers' values are expected to be zero.

1. Make journal entries to record (a) purchase of the computers on January 1 and (b) annual depreciation on December 31. Include dates and explanations, and use the following accounts: Computer Equipment; Accumulated Depreciation—Computer Equipment; and Depreciation Expense—Computer Equipment.
2. Post to the accounts and show their balances at December 31.
3. What is the computer equipment's book value at December 31?

S3-9 (*Learning Objective 2: Applying the matching principle and the time-period concept*) During 2010, Northwest Airlines paid salary expense of $38.3 million. At December 31, 2010, Northwest accrued salary expense of $2.8 million. Northwest then paid $1.8 million to its employees on January 3, 2011, the company's next payday after the end of the 2010 year. For this sequence of transactions, show what Northwest would report on its 2010 income statement and on its balance sheet at the end of 2010.

S3-10 *(Learning Objective 3: Accruing and paying interest expense)* Resort Travel borrowed $80,000 on October 1 by signing a note payable to Texas First Bank. The interest expense for each month is $500. The loan agreement requires Resort to pay interest on December 31.

1. Make Resort's adjusting entry to accrue monthly interest expense at October 31, at November 30, and at December 31. Date each entry and include its explanation.
2. Post all three entries to the Interest Payable account. You need not take the balance of the account at the end of each month.
3. Record the payment of three months' interest at December 31.

S3-11 *(Learning Objective 3: Accruing and receiving cash from interest revenue)* Return to the situation in Short Exercise 3-10. Here you are accounting for the same transactions on the books of Texas First Bank, which lent the money to Resort Travel.

1. Make Texas First Bank's adjusting entry to accrue monthly interest revenue at October 31, at November 30, and at December 31. Date each entry and include its explanation.
2. Post all three entries to the Interest Receivable account. You need not take the balance of the account at the end of each month.
3. Record the receipt of three months' interest at December 31.

writing assignment ■

S3-12 *(Learning Objectives 1, 3: Relating accrual accounting to cash flows; adjusting the accounts)* Write a paragraph to explain why unearned revenues are liabilities instead of revenues. In your explanation, use the following actual example: *The Globe and Trail*, a national newspaper, collects cash from subscribers in advance and later delivers newspapers to subscribers over a one-year period. Explain what happens to the unearned revenue over the course of a year as *The Globe and Trail* delivers papers to subscribers. Into what account does the earned subscription revenue go as *The Globe and Trail* delivers papers? Give the journal entries that The Globe and Trail would make to (a) collect $50,000 of subscription revenue in advance and (b) record earning $50,000 of subscription revenue. Include an explanation for each entry, as illustrated in the chapter.

S3-13 *(Learning Objective 3, 4: Adjusting the accounts; reporting prepaid expenses)* Crow Golf Co. prepaid three years' rent ($24,000) on January 1, 2010. At December 31, 2010, Crow prepared a trial balance and then made the necessary adjusting entry at the end of the year. Crow adjusts its accounts once each year—on December 31.

What amount appears for Prepaid Rent on

 a. Crow's *unadjusted* trial balance at December 31, 2010?
 b. Crow's *adjusted* trial balance at December 31, 2010?

What amount appears for Rent Expense on

 a. Crow's *unadjusted* trial balance at December 31?
 b. Crow's *adjusted* trial balance at December 31?

S3-14 *(Learning Objective 3: Adjusting the accounts)* Bryson, Inc., collects cash from customers two ways:

 a. **Accrued revenue**. Some customers pay Bryson after Bryson has performed service for the customer. During 2010, Bryson made sales of $60,000 on account and later received cash of $45,000 on account from these customers.
 b. **Unearned revenue**. A few customers pay Bryson in advance, and Bryson later performs the service for the customer. During 2010 Bryson collected $7,500 cash in advance and later earned $3,500 of this amount.

Journalize for Bryson

 a. Earning service revenue of $60,000 on account and then collecting $45,000 on account.
 b. Receiving $7,500 in advance and then earning $3,500 as service revenue.

S3-15 (*Learning Objective 4: Preparing the financial statements*) Suppose Vulture Sporting Goods Company reported the following data at March 31, 2010, with amounts in thousands:

Retained earnings, March 31, 2009	$ 2,000	Cost of goods sold	$136,800
Accounts receivable	28,200	Cash	1,300
Net revenues	174,000	Property and equipment, net	6,000
Total current liabilities	53,000	Share capital	27,000
All other expenses	26,000	Inventories	37,000
Other current assets	5,200	Long-term liabilities	12,500
Other assets	28,000	Dividends	0

Use these data to prepare Vulture Sporting Goods Company's income statement for the year ended March 31, 2010; statement of changes in equity for the year ended March 31, 2010; and classified balance sheet at March 31, 2010. Use the report format for the balance sheet. Draw arrows linking the three statements.

S3-16 (*Learning Objective 5: Making closing entries*) Use the Vulture Sporting Goods Company data in Short Exercise 3-15 to make the company's closing entries at March 31, 2010.

Then set up a T-account for Retained Earnings and post to that account. Compare Retained Earnings' ending balance to the amount reported on Vulture's statement of changes in equity and balance sheet. What do you find?

S3-17 (*Learning Objective 6: Computing the current ratio and the debt ratio*) Vulture Sporting Goods reported the following data at March 31, 2010, with amounts adapted in thousands:

Vulture Sporting Goods Company
Income Statement
For the Year Ended March 31, 2010

(Amounts in thousands)

Net revenues	$174,000
Cost of goods sold	136,800
All other expenses	26,000
Net income	$ 11,200

Vulture Sporting Goods Company
Statement of Changes in Equity
For the Year Ended March 31, 2010

(Amounts in thousands)

Beginning equity, March 31, 2009	$29,000
Add: Net income	11,200
Ending equity, March 31, 2010	$40,200

Vulture Sporting Goods Company
Balance Sheet
March 31, 2010

(Amounts in thousands)

ASSETS

Current:

Cash...	$ 1,300
Accounts receivable..............................	28,200
Inventories	37,000
Other current assets	5,200
Total current assets	71,700
Property and equipment, net	6,000
Other assets	28,000
Total assets..	$105,700

LIABILITIES

Total current liabilites	$ 53,000
Long-term liabilities	12,500
Total liabilities	65,500

SHAREHOLDERS' EQUITY

Share capital	27,000
Retained earnings......................................	13,200
Total shareholders' equity..........................	40,200
Total liabilities and shareholders' equity............	$105,700

1. Compute Vulture's current ratio. Round to two decimal places.
2. Compute Vulture's debt ratio. Round to two decimal places.

Do these ratio values look strong, weak, or middle-of-the-road?

S3-18 *(Learning Objective 6: Using the current ratio and the debt ratio)* Refer to the Vulture Sporting Goods Company data in Short Exercise 3-17.

At March 31, 2010, Vulture Sporting Goods Company's current ratio was 1.35 and their debt ratio was 0.62. Compute Vulture's (a) current ratio and (b) debt ratio after each of the following transactions (all amounts in thousands, as in the Vulture financial statements):

1. Vulture earned revenue of $8,000 on account.
2. Vulture paid off accounts payable of $8,000.

When calculating the revised ratios, treat each of the above scenarios independently. Round ratios to two decimal places.

Exercises

(Group A)

E3-19A (*Learning Objective 1: Linking accrual accounting and cash flows*) During 2010 Galaxy Corporation made sales of $4,100 (assume all on account) and collected cash of $4,900 from customers. Operating expenses totaled $1,400, all paid in cash. At year end, 2010, Galaxy customers owed the company $700. Galaxy owed creditors $1,300 on account. All amounts are in millions.

1. For these facts, show what Galaxy reported on the following financial statements:

- Income statement
- Balance sheet

2. Suppose Galaxy had used the cash basis of accounting. What would Galaxy have reported for these facts?

E3-20A (*Learning Objective 1: Linking accrual accounting and cash flows*) During 2010 Prairie Sales, Inc., earned revenues of $580,000 on account. Prairie collected $590,000 from customers during the year. Expenses totaled $480,000, and the related cash payments were $460,000. Show what Prairie would report on its 2010 income statement under the

- **a.** cash basis.
- **b.** accrual basis.

Compute net income under both bases of accounting. Which basis measures net income better? Explain your answer.

E3-21A (*Learning Objectives 1, 2: Using the accrual basis of accounting; applying accounting principles*) During 2010, Carson Network, Inc., which designs network servers, earned revenues of $800 million. Expenses totaled $590 million. Carson collected all but $28 million of the revenues and paid $610 million on its expenses. Carson's top managers are evaluating 2010, and they ask you the following questions:

- **a.** Under accrual accounting, what amount of revenue should Carson Network report for 2010? Is the revenue the $800 million earned or is it the amount of cash actually collected? How does the revenue principle help to answer these questions?
- **b.** Under accrual accounting, what amount of total expense should Carson Network report for 2010—$590 million or $610 million? Which accounting principle helps to answer this question?
- **c.** Which financial statement reports revenues and expenses? Which statement reports cash receipts and cash payments?

■ **general ledger**

E3-22A (*Learning Objectives 1, 3: Journalizing adjusting entries and analyzing their effects on net income; comparing accrual and cash basis*) An accountant made the following adjustments at December 31, the end of the accounting period:

a. Prepaid insurance, beginning, $500. Payments for insurance during the period, $1,500. Prepaid insurance, ending, $1,000.
b. Interest revenue accrued, $1,100.
c. Unearned service revenue, beginning, $1,200. Unearned service revenue, ending, $400.
d. Depreciation, $4,900.
e. Employees' salaries owed for three days of a five-day work week; weekly payroll, $14,000.
f. Income before income tax, $22,000. Income tax rate is 25%.

▌Requirements

1. Journalize the adjusting entries.
2. Suppose the adjustments were not made. Compute the overall overstatement or understatement of net income as a result of the omission of these adjustments.

■ **spreadsheet**

E3-23A (*Learning Objectives 2, 3: Applying the revenue and matching principles; allocating supplies cost between the asset and the expense*) Bird-Bath, Inc., experienced four situations for its supplies. Compute the amounts that have been left blank for each situation. For situations 1 and 2, journalize the needed transaction. Consider each situation separately.

	Situation			
	1	2	3	4
Beginning supplies	$ 100	$ 600	$ 1,400	$ 900
Payments for supplies during the year	?	600	?	700
Total amount to account for	1,400	?	?	1,600
Ending supplies	(200)	(200)	(1,000)	?
Supplies expense	$1,200	$?	$ 1,200	$1,300

■ **general ledger**

E3-24A (*Learning Objective 3: Journalizing adjusting entries*) Jenkins Motor Company faced the following situations. Journalize the adjusting entry needed at December 31, 2010, for each situation. Consider each fact separately.

a. The business has interest expense of $9,500 that it must pay early in January 2011.
b. Interest revenue of $4,500 has been earned but not yet received.
c. On July 1, when we collected $13,600 rent in advance, we debited Cash and credited Unearned Rent Revenue. The tenant was paying us for two years' rent.
d. Salary expense is $1,800 per day—Monday through Friday—and the business pays employees each Friday. This year, December 31 falls on a Wednesday.
e. The unadjusted balance of the Supplies account is $3,300. The total cost of supplies on hand is $1,200.
f. Equipment was purchased at the beginning of this year at a cost of $100,000. The equipment's useful life is five years. There is no residual value. Record depreciation for this year and then determine the equipment's book value.

E3-25A (*Learning Objective 3: Making adjustments in T-accounts*) The accounting records of Fletcher Publishing Company include the following unadjusted balances at May 31: Accounts Receivable, $1,600; Supplies, $600; Salary Payable, $0; Unearned Service Revenue, $900; Service Revenue, $4,800; Salary Expense, $2,500; Supplies Expense, $0.

Fletcher's accountant develops the following data for the May 31 adjusting entries:

a. Supplies on hand, $100
b. Salary owed to employees, $300
c. Service revenue accrued, $800
d. Unearned service revenue that has been earned, $200

Open the foregoing T-accounts with their beginning balances. Then record the adjustments directly in the accounts, keying each adjustment amount by letter. Show each account's adjusted balance. Journal entries are not required.

E3-26A *(Learning Objective 4: Preparing the financial statements)* The adjusted trial balance of Delicious Hams, Inc., follows.

Delicious Hams, Inc.
Adjusted Trial Balance
December 31, 2010

(Amounts in thousands)	Adjusted Trial Balance	
Account	Debit	Credit
Cash	$ 3,800	
Accounts receivable	1,500	
Inventories	1,100	
Prepaid expenses	1,700	
Property, plant and equipment	6,500	
Accumulated depreciation		$ 2,300
Other assets	9,300	
Accounts payable		7,600
Income tax payable		600
Other liabilities		2,200
Share capital		4,700
Retained earnings (beginning, December 31, 2009)		4,700
Dividends	1,500	
Sales revenue		41,400
Cost of goods sold	25,100	
Selling, administrative, and general expenses	10,700	
Income tax expense	2,300	
Total	$63,500	$63,500

❙ Requirement

1. Prepare Delicious Hams, Inc.'s income statement and statement of changes in equity for the year ended December 31, 2010, and its balance sheet on that date.

E3-27A *(Learning Objectives 3, 4: Measuring financial statement amounts; preparing financial statement amounts)* The adjusted trial balances of Dickens Corporation at March 31, 2010, and March 31, 2009, include these amounts (in millions):

	2010	2009
Receivables	$390	$270
Prepaid insurance	190	160
Accrued liabilities payable (for other operating expenses)	730	610

Dickens completed these transactions during the year ended March 31, 2010.

Collections from customers	$20,200
Payment of prepaid insurance	420
Cash payments for other operating expenses	4,100

Compute the amount of sales revenue, insurance expense, and other operating expenses to report on the income statement for the year ended March 31, 2010.

E3-28A (*Learning Objective 4: Reporting on the financial statements*) This question deals with the items and the amounts that two entities, Mother Meghan Hospital (Mother Meghan) and City of Boston (Boston) should report in their financial statements. Fill in the blanks.

I Requirements

1. On July 1, 2010, Mother Meghan collected $6,000 in advance from Boston, a client. Under the contract, Mother Meghan is obligated to perform medical exams for City of Boston employees evenly during the 12 months ending June 30, 2011. Assume you are Mother Meghan.

    Mother Meghan's income statement for the year ended December 31, 2010, will report _____ of $ _____.

    Mother Meghan's balance sheet at December 31, 2010, will report _____ of $ _____.

2. Assume now that you are Boston.

    Boston's income statement for the year ended December 31, 2010, will report _____ of $ _____.

    Boston's balance sheet at December 31, 2010, will report _____ of $ _____.

E3-29A (*Learning Objectives 1, 3: Linking deferrals and cash flows*) Nanofone, the British wireless phone service provider, collects cash in advance from customers. All amounts are in millions of pounds sterling (£), the British monetary unit. Assume Nanofone collected £460 in advance during 2010 and at year end still owed customers phone service worth £110.

I Requirements

1. Show what Nanofone will report for 2010 on its income statement and balance sheet.

2. Use the same facts for Nanofone as in Requirement 1. Further, assume Nanofone reported unearned service revenue of £55 back at the end of 2009. Show what Nanofone will report for 2010 on the same financial statements. Explain why your answer here differs from your answer to Requirement 1.

E3-30A (*Learning Objective 5: Closing the accounts*) Prepare the closing entries from the following selected accounts from the records of Sunnydale Corporation at December 31, 2010:

Cost of services sold	$11,300	Service revenue	$24,000
Accumulated depreciation	40,900	Depreciation expense	4,800
Selling, general, and		Other revenue	300
administrative expenses	6,700	Dividends	600
Retained earnings,		Income tax expense	800
December 31, 2009	2,100	Income tax payable	300

How much net income did Sunnydale earn during 2010? Prepare a T-account for Retained Earnings to show the December 31, 2010, balance of Retained Earnings.

E3-31A (*Learning Objectives 3, 5: Identifying and recording adjusting and closing entries*) The unadjusted trial balance and income statement amounts from the December 31 adjusted trial balance of Draper Production Company follow.

Draper Production Company

Account	Unadjusted Trial Balance		From the Adjusted Trial Balance	
Cash...	14,800			
Prepaid rent.....................................	1,000			
Equipment..	44,000			
Accumulated depreciation...............		3,100		
Accounts payable............................		5,100		
Salary payable.................................				
Unearned service revenue................		9,300		
Income tax payable.........................				
Notes payable, long-term.................		13,000		
Share capital....................................		8,500		
Retained earnings............................		14,100		
Dividends..	1,300			
Service revenue................................		13,600		20,100
Salary expense.................................	4,600		5,100	
Rent expense...................................	1,000		1,300	
Depreciation expense.......................			400	
Income tax expense.........................			1,000	
Total	66,700	66,700	7,800	20,100

Requirement

1. Journalize the adjusting and closing entries of Draper Production Company at December 31. There was only one adjustment to Service Revenue.

E3-32A (*Learning Objectives 4, 6: Preparing a classified balance sheet; using the ratios*) Refer to Exercise 3-31A.

Requirements

1. Use the data in the partial worksheet to prepare Draper Production Company's classified balance sheet at December 31 of the current year. Use the report format. First you must compute the adjusted balance for several of the balance-sheet accounts.
2. Compute Draper Production Company's current ratio and debt ratio at December 31. A year ago, the current ratio was 1.70 and the debt ratio was 0.30. Indicate whether the company's ability to pay its debts—both current and total—improved or deteriorated during the current year.

E3-33A (*Learning Objective 6: Measuring the effects of transactions on the ratios*) Ben Williams Company reported these ratios at December 31, 2010 (dollar amounts in millions):

$$\text{Current ratio} = \frac{\$30}{\$20} = 1.50$$

$$\text{Debt ratio} = \frac{\$30}{\$60} = 0.50$$

Ben Williams Company completed these transactions during 2011:

    a. Purchased equipment on account, $8
    b. Paid long-term debt, $11
    c. Collected cash from customers in advance, $6
    d. Accrued interest expense, $3
    e. Made cash sales, $11

Determine whether each transaction improved or hurt Williams' current ratio and debt ratio.

(Group B)

E3-34B (*Learning Objective 1: Linking accrual accounting and cash flows*) During 2010 Nebula Corporation made sales of $4,800 (assume all on account) and collected cash of $4,900 from customers. Operating expenses totaled $1,100, all paid in cash. At year end, 2010, Nebula customers owed the company $300. Nebula owed creditors $500 on account. All amounts are in millions.

    1. For these facts, show what Nebula reported on the following financial statements:

      • Income statement   • Balance sheet

    2. Suppose Nebula had used the cash basis of accounting. What would Nebula have reported for these facts?

E3-35B (*Learning Objective 1: Linking accrual accounting and cash flows*) During 2010 Mountain Sales, Inc., earned revenues of $510,000 on account. Mountain collected $580,000 from customers during the year. Expenses totaled $470,000, and the related cash payments were $440,000. Show what Mountain would report on its 2010 income statement under the

    a. cash basis.
    b. accrual basis.

Compute net income under both bases of accounting. Which basis measures net income better? Explain your answer.

E3-36B (*Learning Objectives 1, 2: Using the accrual basis of accounting; applying accounting principles*) During 2010 Carlton Network, Inc., which designs network servers, earned revenues of $740 million. Expenses totaled $560 million. Carlton collected all but $24 million of the revenues and paid $580 million on its expenses. Carlton's top managers are evaluating 2010, and they ask you the following questions:

    a. Under accrual accounting, what amount of revenue should Carlton Network report for 2010? Is it the revenue of $740 million earned or is it the amount of cash actually collected? How does the revenue principle help to answer these questions?
    b. Under accrual accounting, what amount of total expense should Carlton report for 2010—$560 million or $580 million? Which accounting principle helps to answer this question?
    c. Which financial statement reports revenues and expenses? Which statement reports cash receipts and cash payments?

E3-37B (*Learning Objectives 1, 3: Journalizing adjusting entries and analyzing their effects on net income; comparing accrual and cash basis*) An accountant made the following adjustments at December 31, the end of the accounting period:

a. Prepaid insurance, beginning, $800. Payments for insurance during the period, $2,400. Prepaid insurance, ending, $1,600.
b. Interest revenue accrued, $1,000.
c. Unearned service revenue, beginning, $1,500. Unearned service revenue, ending, $400.
d. Depreciation, $4,600.
e. Employees' salaries owed for three days of a five-day work week; weekly payroll, $16,000.
f. Income before income tax, $21,000. Income tax rate is 25%.

❙ Requirements
1. Journalize the adjusting entries.
2. Suppose the adjustments were not made. Compute the overall overstatement or understatement of net income as a result of the omission of these adjustments.

E3-38B (*Learning Objectives 2, 3: Applying the revenue and matching principles; allocating supplies cost between the asset and the expense*) Bird-Brain, Inc., experienced four situations for its supplies. Compute the amounts that have been left blank for each situation. For situations 1 and 2, journalize the needed transaction. Consider each situation separately.

	Situation			
	1	2	3	4
Beginning supplies	$ 100	$ 400	$ 1,200	$ 800
Payments for supplies during the year	?	1,000	?	800
Total amount to account for	1,500	?	?	1,600
Ending supplies	(400)	(500)	(700)	?
Supplies Expense	$1,100	$?	$ 1,300	$1,100

E3-39B (*Learning Objective 3: Journalizing adjusting entries*) Folton Motor Company faced the following situations. Journalize the adjusting entry needed at December 31, 2010, for each situation. Consider each fact separately.

a. The business has interest expense of $9,200 that it must pay early in January 2011.
b. Interest revenue of $4,200 has been earned but not yet received.
c. On July 1, when we collected $12,600 rent in advance, we debited Cash and credited Unearned Rent Revenue. The tenant was paying us for two years' rent.
d. Salary expense is $1,900 per day—Monday through Friday—and the business pays employees each Friday. This year, December 31 falls on a Wednesday.
e. The unadjusted balance of the Supplies account is $2,600. The total cost of supplies on hand is $1,200.
f. Equipment was purchased at the beginning of this year at a cost of $160,000. The equipment's useful life is five years. There is no residual value. Record depreciation for this year and then determine the equipment's book value.

E3-40B (*Learning Objective 3: Making adjustments in T-accounts*) The accounting records of Harris Publishing Company include the following unadjusted balances at May 31: Accounts Receivable, $1,200; Supplies, $300; Salary Payable, $0; Unearned Service Revenue, $800; Service Revenue, $4,400; Salary Expense, $1,900; Supplies Expense, $0.

Harris' accountant develops the following data for the May 31 adjusting entries:

a. Supplies on hand, $200
b. Salary owed to employees, $600
c. Service revenue accrued, $800
d. Unearned service revenue that has been earned, $100

Challenge Exercises

E3-50 (*Learning Objective 6: Evaluating the current ratio*) Worthy Hills Corporation reported the following current accounts at December 31, 2010 (amounts in thousands):

Cash..	$1,800
Receivables..	5,300
Inventory...	2,300
Prepaid expenses	1,100
Accounts payable	2,800
Unearned revenue..............................	1,100
Accrued expenses payable	2,000

During 2011, Worthy Hills completed these selected transactions:

- Sold services on account, $8,700
- Depreciation expense, $700
- Paid for expenses, $7,400
- Collected from customers on account, $7,500
- Accrued expenses, $300
- Paid on account, $1,500
- Used up prepaid expenses, $400

Compute Worthy Hills's current ratio at December 31, 2010, and again at December 31, 2011. Did the current ratio improve or deteriorate during 2011? Comment on the level of the company's current ratio.

E3-51 (*Learning Objectives 3, 4: Computing financial statement amounts*) The accounts of Greatbrook Company prior to the year-end adjustments follow.

Cash...	$ 16,600	Share capital.................................	$ 14,000
Accounts receivable.................	7,000	Retained earnings........................	45,000
Supplies....................................	4,200	Dividends......................................	12,000
Prepaid insurance....................	3,400	Service revenue............................	160,000
Building....................................	107,000	Salary expense.............................	34,000
Accumulated depreciation—		Depreciation expense—	
building...............................	15,000	building	
Land...	52,000	Supplies expense..........................	
Accounts payable	6,500	Insurance expense	
Salary payable..........................		Advertising expense.....................	7,600
Unearned service revenue	5,400	Utilities expense	2,100

Adjusting data at the end of the year include which of the following?

a. Unearned service revenue that has been earned, $1,620
b. Accrued service revenue, $32,000
c. Supplies used in operations, $3,600
d. Accrued salary expense, $3,200
e. Prepaid insurance expired, $1,200
f. Depreciation expense—building, $2,500

Rorie Lacourse, the principal shareholder, has received an offer to sell Greatbrook Company. He needs to know the following information within one hour:

a. Net income for the year covered by these data
b. Total assets
c. Total liabilities
d. Total shareholders' equity
e. Prove that Total assets = Total liabilities + Total shareholders' equity after all items are updated.

I Requirement

1. Without opening any accounts, making any journal entries, or using a work sheet, provide Mr. Lacourse with the requested information. The business is not subject to income tax.

Practice Quiz

Test your understanding of accrual accounting by answering the following questions. Select the best choice from among the possible answers given.

Questions 52–54 are based on the following facts:

Frank Dunn began a music business in January 2010. Dunn prepares monthly financial statements and uses the accrual basis of accounting. The following transactions are Dunn Company's only activities during January through April:

Jan 14	Bought music on account for $23, with payment to the supplier due in 90 days.	
Feb 3	Performed a job on account for Jimmy Jones for $38, collectible from Jones in 30 days. Used up all the music purchased on Jan 14.	
Mar 16	Collected the $38 receivable from Jones.	
Apr 22	Paid the $23 owed to the supplier from the January 14 transaction.	

Q3-52 In which month should Dunn record the cost of the music as an expense?
a. January
b. February
c. March
d. April

Q3-53 In which month should Dunn report the $38 revenue on its income statement?
a. January
b. February
c. March
d. April

Q3-54 If Dunn Company uses the *cash* basis of accounting instead of the accrual basis, in what month will Dunn report revenue and in what month will it report expense?

	Revenue	Expense
a.	March	February
b.	February	April
c.	February	February
d.	March	April

Q3-55 In which month should revenue be recorded?
a. In the month that cash is collected from the customer
b. In the month that goods are shipped to the customer
c. In the month that goods are ordered by the customer
d. In the month that the invoice is mailed to the customer

Q3-56 On January 1 of the current year, Bambi Company paid $1,200 rent to cover six months (January–June). Bambi recorded this transaction as follows:

Journal Entry			
Date	Accounts	Debit	Credit
Jan 1	Prepaid Rent	1,200	
	Cash		1,200

Bambi adjusts the accounts at the end of each month. Based on these facts, the adjusting entry at the end of January should include
a. a credit to Prepaid Rent for $1,000.
b. a credit to Prepaid Rent for $200.
c. a debit to Prepaid Rent for $1,000.
d. a debit to Prepaid Rent for $200.

Q3-57 Assume the same facts as in question 3-56. Bambi's adjusting entry at the end of February should include a debit to Rent Expense in the amount of
a. $200.   c. $400.
b. $1,000.   d. $0.

Q3-58 What effect does the adjusting entry in question 3-57 have on Bambi's net income for February?
a. Increase by $200   c. Increase by $400
b. Decrease by $200   d. Decrease by $400

Q3-59 An adjusting entry recorded April salary expense that will be paid in May. Which statement best describes the effect of this adjusting entry on the company's accounting equation?
a. Assets are decreased, liabilities are increased, and shareholders' equity is decreased.
b. Assets are not affected, liabilities are increased, and shareholders' equity is decreased.
c. Assets are decreased, liabilities are not affected, and shareholders' equity is decreased.
d. Assets are not affected, liabilities are increased, and shareholders' equity is increased.

Q3-60 On April 1, 2010, Rural Insurance Company sold a one-year insurance policy covering the year ended April 1, 2011. Rural collected the full $2,700 on April 1, 2010. Rural made the following journal entry to record the receipt of cash in advance:

Journal Entry			
Date	Accounts	Debit	Credit
Apr 1	Cash	2,700	
	Unearned Revenue		2,700

Nine months have passed, and Rural has made no adjusting entries. Based on these facts, the adjusting entry needed by Rural at December 31, 2010, is:

a.	Insurance Revenue	675	
	Unearned Revenue		675
b.	Unearned Revenue	2,025	
	Insurance Revenue		2,025
c.	Insurance Revenue	2,025	
	Unearned Revenue		2,025
d.	Unearned Revenue	675	
	Insurance Revenue		675

Q3-61 The Unearned Revenue account of Super Incorporated began 2010 with a normal balance of $2,000 and ended 2010 with a normal balance of $17,000. During 2010, the Unearned Revenue account was credited for $26,000 that Super will earn later. Based on these facts, how much revenue did Super earn in 2010?

a. $11,000   c. $2,000
b. $28,000   d. $26,000

Q3-62 What is the effect on the financial statements of *recording* depreciation on equipment?
a. Net income is not affected, but assets and shareholders' equity are decreased.
b. Net income and assets are decreased, but shareholders' equity is not affected.
c. Net income, assets, and shareholders' equity are all decreased.
d. Assets are decreased, but net income and shareholders' equity are not affected.

Q3-63 For 2010, Matthews Company had revenues in excess of expenses. Which statement describes Matthews' closing entries at the end of 2010?
a. Revenues will be credited, expenses will be debited, and retained earnings will be credited.
b. Revenues will be debited, expenses will be credited, and retained earnings will be debited.
c. Revenues will be credited, expenses will be debited, and retained earnings will be debited.
d. Revenues will be debited, expenses will be credited, and retained earnings will be credited.

Q3-64 Which of the following accounts would *not* be included in the closing entries?
a. Depreciation Expense   c. Retained Earnings
b. Accumulated Depreciation   d. Service Revenue

Q3-65 A major purpose of preparing closing entries is to
a. zero out the liability accounts.
b. close out the Supplies account.
c. adjust the asset accounts to their correct current balances.
d. update the Retained Earnings account.

Q3-66 Selected data for the Blossom Company follow:

Current assets..............	$ 29,333		Current liabilities	$ 24,800
Long-term assets	187,430		Long-term liabilities	112,738
Total revenues.............	196,651		Total expenses................	169,015

Based on these facts, what are Blossom's current ratio and debt ratio?

Current ratio	Debt ratio
a. 1.633 to 1	0.742 to 1
b. 0.694 to 1	6.815 to 1
c. 1.183 to 1	0.635 to 1
d. 1.633 to 1	0.601 to 1

Q3-67 Unadjusted net income equals $7,500. Calculate what net income will be after the following adjustments:
1. Salaries payable to employees, $660
2. Interest due on note payable at the bank, $100
3. Unearned revenue that has been earned, $950
4. Supplies used, $300

Q3-68 Salary Payable at the beginning of the month totals $28,000. During the month salaries of $126,000 were accrued as expense. If ending Salary Payable is $15,000, what amount of cash did the company pay for salaries during the month?

a. $124,000   c. $126,000
b. $139,000   d. $154,000

Problems

> All of the A and B problems can be found within MyAccountingLab, an online home-work and practice environment. Your instructor may ask you to complete these prob-lems using MyAccountingLab.

(Group A)

P3-69A *(Learning Objective 1: Linking accrual accounting and cash flows)* Labear Corporation earned revenues of $41 million during 2011 and ended the year with net income of $5 million. During 2011, Labear collected $23 million from customers and paid cash for all of its expenses plus an additional $5 million for amounts payable at December 31, 2010. Answer these questions about Labear's operating results, financial position, and cash flows during 2011:

▌Requirements

1. How much were Labear's total expenses? Show your work.
2. Identify all the items that Labear will report on its 2011 income statement. Show each amount.
3. Labear began 2011 with receivables of $4 million. All sales are on account. What was the company's receivables balance at the end of 2011? Identify the appropriate finan-cial statement, and show how Labear will report ending receivables in the 2011 annual report.
4. Labear began 2011 owing accounts payable of $8 million. All expenses are incurred on account. During 2011 Labear paid $41 million on account. How much in accounts payable did the company owe at the end of 2011? Identify the appropriate financial state-ment and show how Labear will report accounts payable in its 2011 annual report.

P3-70A *(Learning Objective 1: Comparing cash basis and accrual basis)* Elders Consulting had the following selected transactions in August:

Aug 1	Prepaid insurance for August through December, $500.
4	Purchased software for cash, $800.
5	Performed services and received cash, $700.
8	Paid advertising expense, $500.
11	Performed service on account, $3,500.
19	Purchased computer on account, $1,700.
24	Collected for August 11 service.
26	Paid account payable from August 19.
29	Paid salary expense, $800.
31	Adjusted for August insurance expense (see Aug 1).
31	Earned revenue of $600 that was collected in advance back in July.

▌Requirements

1. Show how each transaction would be handled using the cash basis and the accrual basis.
2. Compute August income (loss) before tax under each accounting method.
3. Indicate which measure of net income or net loss is preferable. Use the transactions on August 11 and August 24 to explain.

writing assignment ▇ **P3-71A** *(Learning Objective 3: Making accounting adjustments)* Journalize the adjusting entry needed on December 31, end of the current accounting period, for each of the follow-ing independent cases affecting Rowling Corp. Include an explanation for each entry.

a. Details of Prepaid Insurance are shown in the account:

Prepaid Insurance		
Jan 1 Bal	900	
Mar 31	3,600	

Rowling prepays insurance on March 31 each year. At December 31, $1,300 is still prepaid.

b. Rowling pays employees each Friday. The amount of the weekly payroll is $6,100 for a five-day work week. The current accounting period ends on Tuesday.

c. Rowling has a note receivable. During the current year, Rowling has earned accrued interest revenue of $400 that it will collect next year.

d. The beginning balance of supplies was $2,700. During the year, Rowling purchased supplies costing $6,400, and at December 31 supplies on hand total $2,200.

e. Rowling is providing services for Orca Investments, and the owner of Orca paid Rowling $12,000 as the annual service fee. Rowling recorded this amount as Unearned Service Revenue. Rowling estimates that it has earned 70% of the total fee during the current year.

f. Depreciation for the current year includes Office Furniture, $3,000, and Equipment, $5,400. Make a compound entry.

P3-72A (*Learning Objectives 3, 4: Preparing an adjusted trial balance and the financial statements*)   Consider the unadjusted trial balance of London, Inc., at December 31, 2010, and the related month-end adjustment data.

London, Inc.
Trial Balance Work Sheet
December 31, 2010

Account	Trial Balance Debit	Trial Balance Credit	Adjustments Debit	Adjustments Credit	Adjusted Trial Balance Debit	Adjusted Trial Balance Credit
Cash	8,900					
Accounts receivable	1,200					
Prepaid rent	2,400					
Supplies	2,500					
Furniture	72,000					
Accumulated depreciation		3,900				
Accounts payable		3,300				
Salary payable						
Share capital		12,000				
Retained earnings		63,110				
Dividends	3,500					
Service revenue		11,000				
Salary expense	2,300					
Rent expense						
Utilities expense	510					
Depreciation expense						
Supplies expense						
Total	93,310	93,310				

P3-75A *(Learning Objective 5: Closing the books; evaluating retained earnings)* The accounts of Spa View Service, Inc., at March 31, 2010, are listed in alphabetical order.

Accounts payable	$14,400	Interest expense	$ 900
Accounts receivable	16,100	Note payable, long term	6,100
Accumulated depreciation—		Other assets	14,400
equipment	6,900	Prepaid expenses	6,000
Advertising expense	10,900	Retained earnings,	
Cash	7,900	March 31, 2009	22,000
Share capital	5,600	Salary expense	17,800
Current portion of note		Salary payable	2,900
payable	1,000	Service revenue	95,000
Depreciation expense	1,700	Supplies	3,600
Dividends	31,200	Supplies expense	4,400
Equipment	41,700	Unearned service revenue	2,700

I Requirements

1. All adjustments have been journalized and posted, but the closing entries have not yet been made. Journalize Spa View's closing entries at March 31, 2010.
2. Set up a T-account for Retained Earnings and post to that account. Then compute Spa View's net income for the year ended March 31, 2010. What is the ending balance of Retained Earnings?
3. Did Retained Earnings increase or decrease during the year? What caused the increase or the decrease?

P3-76A *(Learning Objectives 4, 6: Preparing a classified balance sheet; using the ratios to evaluate the business)* Refer back to Problem 3-75A.

I Requirements

1. Use the Spa View data in Problem 3-75A to prepare the company's classified balance sheet at March 31, 2010. Show captions for total assets, total liabilities, and total liabilities and shareholders' equity.
2. Compute Spa View's current ratio and debt ratio at March 31, 2010, rounding to two decimal places. At March 31, 2009, the current ratio was 1.25 and the debt ratio was 0.20. Did Spa View's ability to pay both current and total debts improve or deteriorate during 2010? Evaluate Spa View's debt position as strong or weak and give your reason.

P3-77A *(Learning Objective 6: Analyzing financial ratios)* This problem demonstrates the effects of transactions on the current ratio and the debt ratio of Hartford Company. Hartford's condensed and adapted balance sheet at December 31, 2010, follows.

	(In millions)
Total current assets	$15.6
Properties, plant, equipment, and other assets	16.1
	$31.7
Total current liabilities	$ 9.6
Total long-term liabilities	5.8
Total shareholders' equity	16.3
	$31.7

Assume that during the first quarter of the following year, 2011, Hartford completed the following transactions:

- **a.** Paid half the current liabilities.
- **b.** Borrowed $6.0 million on long-term debt.
- **c.** Earned revenue, $2.5 million, on account.
- **d.** Paid selling expense of $0.6 million.
- **e.** Accrued general expense of $0.7 million. Credit General Expense Payable, a current liability.
- **f.** Purchased equipment for $4.2 million, paying cash of $1.5 million and signing a long-term note payable for $2.7 million.
- **g.** Recorded depreciation expense of $0.8 million.

❙ Requirements

1. Compute Hartford's current ratio and debt ratio at December 31, 2010. Round to two decimal places.
2. Consider each transaction separately. Compute Hartford's current ratio and debt ratio after each transaction during 2011, that is, seven times. Round ratios to two decimal places.
3. Based on your analysis, you should be able to readily identify the effects of certain transactions on the current ratio and the debt ratio. Test your understanding by completing these statements with either "increase" or "decrease":
   - **a.** Revenues usually _____ the current ratio.
   - **b.** Revenues usually _____ the debt ratio.
   - **c.** Expenses usually _____ the current ratio. (*Note:* Depreciation is an exception to this rule.)
   - **d.** Expenses usually _____ the debt ratio.
   - **e.** If a company's current ratio is greater than 1.0, as it is for Hartford, paying off a current liability will always _____ the current ratio.
   - **f.** Borrowing money on long-term debt will always _____ the current ratio and _____ the debt ratio.

(Group B)

P3-78B (*Learning Objective 1: Linking accrual accounting and cash flows*) Gauge Corporation earned revenues of $33 million during 2010 and ended the year with net income of $6 million. During 2010 Gauge collected cash of $24 million from customers and paid cash for all of its expenses plus an additional $1 million on account for amounts payable at December 31, 2009. Answer these questions about Gauge's operating results, financial position, and cash flows during 2010:

❙ Requirements

1. How much were Gauge's total expenses? Show your work.
2. Identify all the items that Gauge will report on its 2010 income statement. Show each amount.
3. Gauge began 2010 with receivables of $9 million. All sales are on account. What was Gauge's receivables balance at the end of 2010? Identify the appropriate financial statement and show how Gauge will report its ending receivables balance in the company's 2010 annual report.
4. Gauge began 2010 owing accounts payable of $11 million. All expenses are incurred on account. During 2010, Gauge paid $28 million on account. How much in accounts payable did Gauge owe at the end of 2010? Identify the appropriate financial statement and show how Gauge will report accounts payable in its 2010 annual report.

For online homework, exercises, and problems that provide you with immediate feedback, please visit www.myaccountinglab.com.

Quick Check Answers

1. *d*	6. *b*	10. *c*	14. *a*
2. *c*	7. *c*	11. *d*	15. *d*
3. *d*	8. *d*	12. *d*	16. *d*
4. *a*	9. *d*	13. *c*	17. *c*
5. *b*			

Demo Doc

Preparation of Adjusting Entries, Closing Entries, and Financial Statements

To make sure you understand this material, work through the following demonstration "Demo Doc" with detailed comments to help you see the concept within the framework of a worked-through problem.

Learning Objectives 2–5

Cloud Break Consulting, Inc., has the following information at June 30, 2010:

		Account Title	Balance Debit	Balance Credit
		Cloud Break Consulting, Inc. **Unadjusted Trial Balance** **June 30, 2010**		
		Cash	$131,000	
		Accounts receivable	104,000	
		Supplies	4,000	
		Prepaid rent	27,000	
		Land	45,000	
		Building	300,000	
		Accumulated depreciation—building		$155,000
		Accounts payable		159,000
		Unearned service revenue		40,000
		Share capital		50,000
		Retained earnings		52,000
		Dividends	7,000	
		Service revenue		450,000
		Salary expense	255,000	
		Rent expense	25,000	
		Miscellaneous expense	8,000	
		Total	$906,000	$906,000

June 30 is Cloud Break's fiscal year end; accordingly, it must make adjusting entries for the following items:

a. Supplies on hand at year-end, $1,000.

b. Nine months of rent totaling $27,000 were paid in advance on April 1, 2010. Cloud Break has recorded no rent expense yet.

c. Depreciation expense has not been recorded on the building for the 2010 fiscal year. The building has a useful life of 25 years.

d. Employees work Monday through Friday. The weekly payroll is $5,000 and is paid every Friday. June 30, 2010, falls on a Thursday.

e. Service revenue of $15,000 must be accrued.

f. Cloud Break received $40,000 in advance for consulting services to be provided evenly from January 1, 2010 through August 31, 2010. Cloud Break has recorded none of this revenue.

Requirements

1. Open the T-accounts with their unadjusted balances.

2. Journalize Cloud Break's adjusting entries at June 30, 2010, and post the entries to the T-accounts.

3. Total each T-account in the ledger.

4. Journalize and post Cloud Break's closing entries.

5. Prepare Cloud Break's income statement and statement of changes in equity for the year ended June 30, 2010, and the balance sheet at June 30, 2010. Draw arrows linking the three financial statements.

Demo Doc Solutions

Requirement 1

Open the T-accounts with their unadjusted balances.

Part 1	Part 2	Part 3	Part 4	Part 5	Demo Doc Complete

Remember from Chapter 2 that opening a T-account means drawing a blank account that looks like a capital "T" and putting the account title across the top. To help find the accounts later, they are grouped into assets, liabilities, shareholders' equity, revenues, and expenses (in that order). If the account has a starting balance, it **must** appear on the correct side.

Remember that debits are always on the left side of the T-account and credits are always on the right side. This is true for *every* account.

The correct side to enter each account's starting balance is the side of *increase* in the account. This is because we expect all accounts to have a *positive* balance (that is, more increases than decreases).

For assets, an increase is a debit, so we would expect all assets (except contra assets such as Accumulated Depreciation) to have a debit balance. For liabilities and shareholders' equity, an increase is a credit, so we would expect all liabilities and equities (except Dividends) to have a credit balance. By the same reasoning, we expect revenues to have credit balances and expenses and dividends to have debit balances.

The unadjusted balances appearing in the T-accounts are simply the amounts from the starting trial balance.

ASSETS

Cash
Bal 131,000

Accounts Receivable
Bal 104,000

Supplies
Bal 4,000

Prepaid Rent
Bal 27,000

Land
Bal 45,000

Building
Bal 300,000

Accumulated Depreciation—Building
Bal 155,000

LIABILITIES

Accounts Payable
Bal 159,000

Unearned Service Revenue
Bal 40,000

SHAREHOLDERS' EQUITY

Share Capital
Bal 50,000

Retained Earnings
Bal 52,000

Dividends
Bal 7,000

REVENUE

Service Revenue
Bal 450,000

EXPENSES

Salary Expense
Bal 255,000

Rent Expense
Bal 25,000

Miscellaneous Expense
Bal 8,000

Requirement 2

Journalize Cloud Break's adjusting entries at June 30, 2010, and post the entries to the T-accounts.

Part 1	Part 2	Part 3	Part 4	Part 5	Demo Doc Complete

a. Supplies on hand at year-end, $1,000.

On June 30, 2010, the unadjusted balance in the Supplies account was $4,000. However, a count shows that only $1,000 of supplies actually remains on hand. The supplies that are no longer there have been used. When assets/benefits are used, an expense is created.

Cloud Break will need to make an adjusting journal entry in order to report the correct amount of supplies on the balance sheet.

Looking at the Supplies T-account:

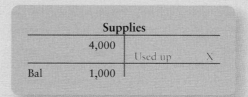

The supplies have decreased because they have been used up. The amount of the decrease is X. X = $4,000 − $1,000 = $3,000.

$3,000 of supplies expense must be recorded to show the value of supplies that have been used.

a.	Jun 30	Supplies Expense ($4,000 − $1,000) (Expense ↑; debit)	3,000	
		Supplies (Asset ↓; credit)		3,000
		To record supplies expense.		

After posting, Supplies and Supplies Expense hold their correct ending balances:

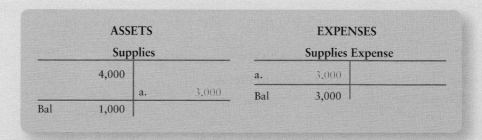

b. Nine months of rent (totalling $27,000) were paid in advance on April 1, 2010. Cloud Break has recorded no rent expense yet.

A prepayment for something, such as for rent or insurance, creates a *future* benefit (an asset) because the business is now entitled to receive the prepaid goods or services. Once those goods or services are received (in this case, once Cloud Break has occupied the building being rented), the benefit expires, and the prepaid cost becomes an expense.

Cloud Break prepaid $27,000 for nine months of rent on April 1. This means that Cloud Break pays $27,000/9 = $3,000 a month for rent. At June 30, Prepaid Rent is adjusted for the amount of the asset that has been used up. Because Cloud Break has occupied the building being rented for three months (April, May, and June), three months of the prepayment have been used. The amount of rent used is 3 × $3,000 = $9,000. Because that portion of the past benefit (asset) has expired, it becomes an expense (in this case, the adjustment transfers $9,000 from Prepaid Rent to Rent Expense).

This means that Rent Expense must be increased (a debit) and Prepaid Rent (an asset) must be decreased (a credit), with the following journal entry:

b.	Jun 30	Rent Expense (Expense ↑; debit)	9,000	
		Prepaid Rent (Asset ↓; credit)		9,000
		To record rent expense.		

Posting places $9,000 in each account, as follows:

	ASSETS				EXPENSES	
	Prepaid Rent				**Rent Expense**	
	27,000				25,000	
		b.	9,000	b.	9,000	
Bal	18,000			Bal	34,000	

c. Depreciation expense has not been recorded on the building for the 2010 fiscal year. The building has a useful life of 25 years.

Depreciation expense per year is calculated as:

$$\text{Depreciation expense per year} = \frac{\text{Original cost of asset}}{\text{Useful life of asset (in years)}}$$

The cost principle compels us to keep the original cost of a PPE in that asset account. Because there is $300,000 in the Building account, we know that this is the original cost of the building. We are told in the question that the building's useful life is 25 years.

$$\text{Depreciation expense per year} = \$300,000/25 \text{ years} = \$12,000 \text{ per year}$$

We will record depreciation of $12,000 in an adjusting journal entry. The journal entry for depreciation expense is *always* the same. Only the dollar amount changes. There is always an increase to Depreciation Expense (a debit) and an increase to the contra asset account of Accumulated Depreciation (a credit).

c.	Jun 30	Depreciation Expense—Building (Expense ↑; debit)	12,000	
		Accumulated Depreciation—Building		
		(Contra Asset ↑; credit)		12,000
		To record depreciation on building.		

	ASSETS					EXPENSES	
	ASSET		**CONTRA ASSET**				
	Building		Accumulated Depreciation—Building			Depreciation Expense—Building	
	300,000				155,000	c.	12,000
				c.	12,000		
Bal	300,000			Bal	167,000	Bal	12,000

The book value of the building is its original cost (the amount in the Building T-account) minus the accumulated depreciation on the building.

Book value of PPE:	
Building...	$300,000
Less: Accumulated depreciation	(167,000)
Book value of the building	$133,000

d. Employees work Monday through Friday. The weekly payroll is $5,000 and is paid every Friday. June 30, 2010, falls on a Thursday.

Salary is an accrued expense. That is, it's a liability that comes from an *expense* that hasn't been paid yet. Most employers pay their employees *after* the work has been done, so the work is a past benefit to the employer. This expense (Salary Expense, in this case) grows until payday.

Cloud Break's employees are paid $5,000 for five days of work. That means they earn $5,000/5 = $1,000 per day. By the end of the day on Thursday, June 30, they have earned $1,000/day × 4 days = $4,000 of salary.

If the salaries have not been paid, then they are pay*able* (or in other words, they are *owed*) and must be recorded as some kind of payable account. You might be tempted to use Accounts Payable, but this account is usually reserved for *bills* received. But employees don't bill employers for their paycheques. The appropriate payable account for salaries is Salary Payable.

The accrual of salary expense creates an increase to Salary Expense (a debit) and an increase to the liability Salary Payable (a credit) of $4,000.

d.	Jun 30	Salary Expense (Expense ↑; debit)		4,000	
		Salary Payable (Liability ↑; credit)			4,000
		To accrue salary expense.			

	EXPENSES				LIABILITIES	
	Salary Expense				Salary Payable	
	255,000				d.	4,000
d.	4,000					
Bal	259,000				Bal	4,000

e. Service revenue of $15,000 must be accrued.

Accrued revenue is another way of saying "accounts receivable" (or receipt in the future). When *accrued* revenue is recorded, it means that accounts receivable are also recorded (that is, the business gave goods or services to customers, but the business has not yet received the cash). The business is entitled to these receivables because the revenue has been earned.

Service Revenue must be increased by $15,000 (a credit) and the Accounts Receivable asset must be increased by $15,000 (a debit).

e.	Jun 30	Accounts Receivable (Asset ↑; debit)	15,000	
		Service Revenue (Revenue ↑; credit)		15,000
		To accrue service revenue.		

ASSETS		REVENUES	
Accounts Receivable		**Service Revenue**	
104,000			450,000
e. 15,000			e. 15,000
Bal 119,000			Bal 465,000

f. Cloud Break received $40,000 in advance for consulting services to be provided evenly from January 1, 2010, through August 31, 2010. Cloud Break has recorded none of this revenue.

Cloud Break received cash in advance for work to be performed in the future. By accepting the cash, Cloud Break also accepted the obligation to perform that work (or provide a refund). In accounting, an obligation is a liability. We call this liability "unearned revenue" because it *will* be revenue (after the work is performed) but it is not revenue *yet*.

The $40,000 collected in advance is still in the Unearned Service Revenue account. However, some of the revenue has been earned as of June 30. Six months of the earnings period have passed (January through June), so Cloud Break has earned six months of the revenue.

The entire revenue-earning period is eight months (January through August), so the revenue earned per month is $40,000/8 = $5,000. The six months of revenue that Cloud Break has earned through the end of June totals $30,000 (6 × $5,000).

So Unearned Service Revenue, a liability, must be decreased by $30,000 (a debit). Because that portion of the revenue is now earned, Service Revenue is increased by $30,000 (a credit).

f.	Jun 30	Unearned Service Revenue (Liability ↓; debit)	30,000	
		Service Revenue (Revenue ↑; credit)		30,000
		To record the earning of service revenue that was		
		collected in advance.		

Essentially, the $30,000 has been shifted from "unearned revenue" to "earned" revenue.

	LIABILITIES		REVENUES	
	Unearned Service Revenue		Service Revenue	
		40,000		450,000
f.	30,000		e.	15,000
			f.	30,000
		Bal 10,000		Bal 495,000

Now we can summarize all of the adjusting journal entries:

Ref.	Date	Accounts and Explanation	Debit	Credit
	2010			
a.	Jun 30	Supplies Expense ($4,000 – $1,000)	3,000	
		Supplies		3,000
		To record supplies expense.		
b.	30	Rent Expense	9,000	
		Prepaid Rent		9,000
		To record rent expense.		
c.	30	Depreciation Expense—Building	12,000	
		Accumulated Depreciation—Building		12,000
		To record depreciation on building.		
d.	30	Salary Expense	4,000	
		Salary Payable		4,000
		To accrue salary expense.		
e.	30	Accounts Receivable	15,000	
		Service Revenue		15,000
		To accrue service revenue.		
f.	30	Unearned Service Revenue	30,000	
		Service Revenue		30,000
		To record the earning of service revenue that was		
		collected in advance.		

Requirement 3

Total each T-account in the ledger.

Part 1	Part 2	**Part 3**	Part 4	Part 5	Demo Doc Complete

After posting all of these entries and totaling all of the T-accounts, we have:

ASSETS		SHAREHOLDERS' EQUITY		EXPENSES	

ASSETS

Cash		Building		Share Capital		Salary Expense	
Bal 131,000		Bal 300,000			Bal 50,000	255,000	
						d. 4,000	
		Accumulated Depreciation—Building		**Retained Earnings**		Bal 259,000	
Accounts Receivable							
104,000			155,000		Bal 52,000	**Supplies Expense**	
e. 15,000			c. 12,000			a. 3,000	
Bal 119,000			Bal 167,000			Bal 3,000	
				Dividends			
Supplies				Bal 7,000		**Rent Expense**	
4,000		**LIABILITIES**				25,000	
	a. 3,000	**Accounts Payable**				b. 9,000	
Bal 1,000			Bal 159,000			Bal 34,000	
Prepaid Rent							
27,000		**Salary Payable**				**Depreciation Expense— Building**	
	b. 9,000		d. 4,000	**REVENUE**		c. 12,000	
Bal 18,000			Bal 4,000	**Service Revenue**		Bal 12,000	
					450,000		
Land		**Unearned Service Revenue**		e. 15,000		**Miscellaneous Expense**	
Bal 45,000			40,000	f. 30,000		Bal 8,000	
		f. 30,000			Bal 495,000		
			Bal 10,000				

Requirement 4

Journalize and post Cloud Break's closing entries.

Part 1	Part 2	Part 3	**Part 4**	Part 5	Demo Doc Complete

We prepare closing entries to (1) clear out the revenue, expense, and dividends accounts to a zero balance in order to get them ready for the next period. They must begin the next period empty so that we can evaluate each period's income separately from all other periods. We also need to (2) update the Retained Earnings account by transferring all revenues, expenses, and dividends into it.

The Retained Earnings balance is calculated each year using the following formula:

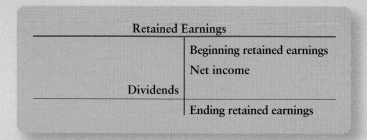

Beginning retained earnings
+ Net income (or − Net loss)
− Dividends paid
= Ending retained earnings

You can see this in the Retained Earnings T-account as well:

Retained Earnings	
	Beginning retained earnings
	Net income
Dividends	
	Ending retained earnings

This formula is the key to preparing the closing entries. We will use this formula, but we will do it *inside* the Retained Earnings T-account.

From the trial balance given in the problem, we know that beginning Retained Earnings is $52,000. The first component of the formula is already in the T-account.

The next component is net income, which is *not* yet in the Retained Earnings account. There is no T-account with net income in it, but we can place all the components of net income into the Retained Earnings account and come out with the net income number at the bottom. Remember:

Revenues − Expenses = Net income

This means that we need to get all of the revenues and expenses into the Retained Earnings account.

a. We start with our revenue T-account (service revenue as shown)

Service Revenue	
	Bal 495,000

In order to clear out all the income statement accounts so that they are empty to begin the next year, the first step is to *debit* each revenue account for the amount of its *credit* balance. Service Revenue has a *credit* balance of $495,000, so to bring that to zero, we need to *debit* Service Revenue for $495,000.

This means that we have part of our first closing entry:

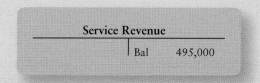

1.	Service Revenue	495,000	
	???		495,000

What is the credit side of this entry? The reason we started with Service Revenue was to help calculate net income in the Retained Earnings account. So the other side of the entry must go to Retained Earnings:

1.		Service Revenue	495,000	
		Retained Earnings		495,000

b. The second step is to *credit* each expense account for the amount of its *debit* balance to bring each expense account to zero. In this case, we have five different expenses:

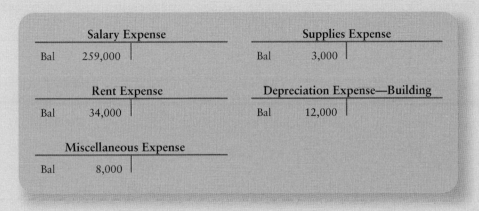

	Salary Expense			Supplies Expense	
Bal	259,000		Bal	3,000	

	Rent Expense			Depreciation Expense—Building	
Bal	34,000		Bal	12,000	

	Miscellaneous Expense	
Bal	8,000	

The sum of all the expenses will go to the debit side of the Retained Earnings account:

2.		Retained Earnings	316,000	
		Salary Expense		259,000
		Supplies Expense		3,000
		Rent Expense		34,000
		Depreciation Expense—Building		12,000
		Miscellaneous Expense		8,000

The last component of the Retained Earnings formula is dividends. There is a Dividends account:

	Dividends	
Bal	7,000	

c. The final step in the closing process is to transfer Dividends to the debit site of the Retained Earnings account. The Dividends account has a *debit* balance of $7,000, so to bring that to zero, we need to *credit* Dividends by $7,000. The balancing debit will go to Retained Earnings:

3.		Retained Earnings	7,000	
		Dividends		7,000

This entry subtracts Dividends from Retained Earnings. Retained Earnings now holds the following data:

Retained Earnings					
				52,000	Beginning retained earnings
Expenses	2.	316,000	1.	495,000	Revenue } Net income
Dividends	3.	7,000			
			Bal	224,000	Ending retained earnings

The formula to update Retained Earnings has now been re-created inside the Retained Earnings T-account.

The following accounts are included in the closing process:

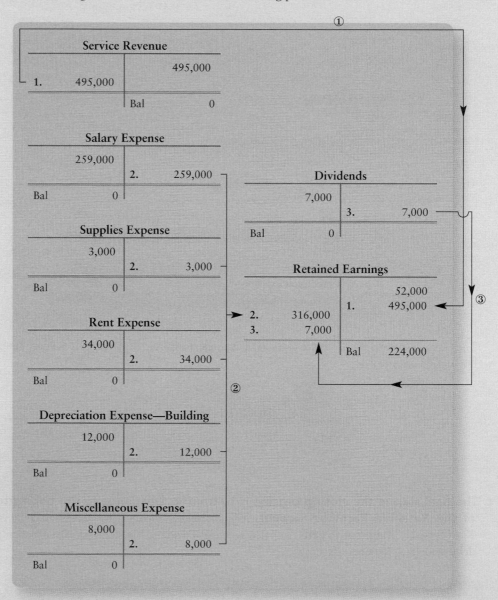

Notice that each temporary account (the Revenues, the Expenses, and Dividends), now has a zero balance.

Requirement 5

Prepare Cloud Break's income statement and the statement of changes in equity for the year ended June 30, 2010, and the balance sheet at June 30, 2010. Draw arrows linking the three financial statements.

Part 1	Part 2	Part 3	Part 4	**Part 5**	Demo Doc Complete

Cloud Break Consulting, Inc.
Income Statement
Year Ended June 30, 2010

Revenue:		
Service revenue		$495,000
Expenses:		
Salary expense	$259,000	
Rent expense	34,000	
Depreciation expense—building	12,000	
Supplies expense	3,000	
Miscellaneous expense	8,000	
Total expenses		316,000
Net income		$179,000

Cloud Break Consulting, Inc.
Statement of Changes in Equity
Year Ended June 30, 2010

Retained earnings, June 30, 2007	$102,000
Add: Net income	179,000
	281,000
Less: Dividends	(7,000)
Total Equity, June 30, 2008	$274,000

Cloud Break Consulting, Inc.
Balance Sheet
June 30, 2010

Assets			Liabilities	
Cash		$131,000	Accounts payable	$159,000
Accounts receivable		119,000	Salary payable	4,000
Supplies		1,000	Unearned service revenue	10,000
Prepaid rent		18,000	Total liabilities	173,000
Land		45,000		
Building	$300,000		**Shareholders' Equity**	
Less: Accumulated			Share capital	50,000
depreciation	(167,000)	133,000	Retained earnings	224,000
			Total shareholders' equity	274,000
			Total liabilities and	
Total assets		$447,000	shareholders' equity	$447,000

RELATIONSHIPS AMONG THE FINANCIAL STATEMENTS

The arrows in these statements show how the financial statements relate to each other. Follow the arrow that takes the ending balance of total equity to the balance sheet.

1. Net income from the income statements is reported as an increase to retained earnings (equity) on the statement of changes in equity. A net loss would be reported as a decrease to retained earnings (equity). Any dividends paid will also reduce retained earnings (equity).

2. The new total equity (and Ending Retained Earnings) from the statement of changes in equity is transferred to the balance sheet.

Part 1	Part 2	Part 3	Part 4	Part 5	Demo Doc Complete

SPOTLIGHT: Satyam Computer Services

January 7, 2009
To the Board of Directors
Satyam Computer Services Ltd.

Dear Board Members,

It is with deep regret, and tremendous burden that I am carrying on my conscience, that I would like to bring the following facts to your notice:

1. The Balance Sheet carries as of September 30, 2008:
   a. Inflated (non-existent) cash and bank balances of 50.40 billion rupees (about USD1.04 billion) as against 53.61 billion reflected in the books.
   b. An accrued interest of 3.76 billion rupees which is non-existent.
   c. An understated liability of 12.30 billion rupees on account of funds arranged by me.
   d. An overstated debtors' position of 4.90 billion rupees (as against 26.51 billion reflected in the books)

2. For the September quarter (Q2) we reported a revenue of 27.00 billion rupees and an operating margin of 6.49 billion rupees (24 percent of revenues) as against the actual revenues of 21.12 billion rupees and an actual operating margin of 610 million rupees (3 percent of revenues). This has resulted in artificial cash and bank balances going up by 5.88 billion rupees in Q2 alone.

The gap in the Balance Sheet has arisen purely on account of inflated profits over a period of last several years (limited only to Satyam standalone, books of subsidiaries reflecting true performance). What started as a marginal gap between actual operating profit and the one reflected in the books of accounts continued to grow over the years. It has attained unmanageable proportions as the size of company operations grew significantly (annualized revenue run rate of 112.76 billion rupees in the September quarter, 2008, and official reserves of 83.92 billion rupees). The differential in the real profits and the one reflected in the books was further accentuated by the fact that the company had to carry additional resources and assets to justify higher level of operations—thereby significantly increasing the costs.

Every attempt made to eliminate the gap failed. As the promoters held a small percentage of equity, the concern was that poor performance would result in a take-over, thereby exposing the gap. It was like riding a tiger, not knowing how to get off without being eaten. Having put these facts before you, I leave it to the wisdom of the board to take the matters forward.

Under the circumstances, I am tendering my resignation as the chairman of Satyam and shall continue in this position only till such time the current board is expanded. My continuance is just to ensure enhancement of the board over the next several days or as early as possible.

I am now prepared to subject myself to the laws of the land and face consequences thereof.

B. Ramalinga Raju
Chairman, Satyam Computer Services Ltd.
Copies marked to:
1. Chairman SEBI
2. Stock Exchanges

Ramalinga Raju's resignation letter shocked the business world in early 2009. You have just read adapted excerpts of the infamous resignation letter, with references to Indian numerical conventions of *crores* (units of ten millions) and *lakhs* (units of one hundred thousands) converted to millions or billions as appropriate.

Satyam Computer Services, headquartered in Hyderabad, India was one of the biggest players in the information technology consultancy, integration and outsourcing business in the world with clients across the globe, including **Nestlé**, **General Motors**, and **General Electric**. In fact, about 185 Fortune 500 companies are clients of Satyam, which employs over 53,000 staff. Satyam was listed on both Bombay Stock Exchange and New York Stock Exchange and had received many awards in the last few years before January 2009. These awards included:

- 2008 Golden Peacock Global Award for Excellence in Corporate Governance (which was subsequently withdrawn)
- 2008 Business Award for corporate social responsibility by UK Trade & Investment India (UKTI)
- 2008 Pinnacle Award (SAP)
- 2007 Competitive Strategy Leadership Award for Offshore Testing Market (Frost & Sullivan)
- 2007 Citizenship Partner of the Year Award (Microsoft)
- 2007 Vision, Impact, Progress (VIP) Award (Computer Associates)
- 2007 Entrepreneur of the Year award for Mr. Raju (Ernst & Young)

How can a company with such supposedly-sterling reputation commit such a fraud? One billion US dollars in cash unaccounted for, operating profit inflated by over 10 times, receivables overstated by over 500%. Satyam's shares went into a freefall immediately following the news, dropping by about 80%, as investors around the world thrashed the company's shares. *Reuters* call it "India's Enron".

Satyam Computer Services
Selected Financial Statement Data (Adapted from various sources)
Income Statement for Quarter Ended September 30, 2008

(In crores, ten million Rupees)	Reported	Admitted
Sales	2,701	2,112
Gross profit	724	
Operating profit	649	61
Balance Sheet as at 30 Sept 2008	Reported	Admitted
Cash	5,361	321
Accounts receivable net	2,651	490
Other receivables	676	300
Total current assets	9,065	
Property, plant and equipment net	1,434	
Goodwill	446	
Total non-current assets	1,996	
Total assets	11,062	
Accounts payable	1,379	
Other current-liabilities	823	2,053
Total current liabilities	2,202	
Long-term debt	488	
Total non-current liabilities	488	
Total liabilities	2,690	
Total equity	8,372	
Total liabilities and equity	11,062	

This chapter begins with a discussion of fraud, its types, and common characteristics. We then discuss internal controls, which are the primary means by which fraud as well as unintentional financial statement errors are prevented. We also discuss how to account for cash. These three topics—fraud, internal control, and cash—go together. Internal controls help prevent fraud. Cash is probably the asset that is most often misappropriated through fraud.

LEARNING OBJECTIVES

1 **Learn** about fraud and how much it costs

2 **Set up** an internal control system

3 **Prepare** and **use** a bank reconciliation

4 **Apply** internal controls to cash receipts and cash payments

5 **Use** a budget to manage cash

FRAUD AND ITS IMPACT

Fraud is an intentional misrepresentation of facts, made for the purpose of persuading another party to act in a way that causes injury or damage to that party. For example, in the chapter opening story, Ramalinga Raju intentionally misstated cash, revenue, receivables and payables in Satyam's financial statements. His actions caused shareholders of Satyam Computer Services to lose billions of dollars. You may have also heard of other "famous" frauds in the last decade: **WorldCom**, **Enron**, **Parmalat**, Bernard Madoff, and unfortunately, the list goes on.

Exhibit 4-1 below gives you another story about **AMEX Products**, which we will discuss throughout this chapter

OBJECTIVE

1 **Learn** about fraud and how much it costs

EXHIBIT 4-1 | Cooking the Books: AMEX Products

The following is adapted from a true story:

"I've never been so shocked in my life!" exclaimed Lee Riffe, manager of the AMEX Products office in Palo Alto, California. "I never thought this could happen to us. We are such a close-knit organization where everyone trusts everyone else. Why, people at AMEX feel like family! I feel betrayed, violated."

Riffe had just returned from the trial of Melissa Price, who had been convicted of embezzling over $600,000 from AMEX over a six-year period. Price had been one of AMEX's most trusted employees for 10 years. A single mom with two teenage daughters, Price had pulled herself up by her own bootstraps, putting herself through community college where she had obtained an associate's degree in accounting. Riffe had hired her as a part-time bookkeeper at AMEX while Price was in college to help her out. She had done such a good job that, when she completed her degree, Riffe asked her to stay on and assigned her the additional role of cashier, in charge of accumulating the daily cash receipts from customers and taking them to the night depository at the bank each day after work. Through the years, he also awarded her what he considered good raises, compensating her at a rate that was generally higher than other employees with her education and experience levels.

Price rapidly became the company's "go-to" financial employee. She was eager to learn, dependable, responsible. In 10 years she never took a day of vacation, choosing instead to take advantage of the company's policy that allowed employees to draw additional compensation for vacation accrued but not taken at the end of each year. Riffe grew to depend on Price more and more each month, as the business grew to serve over 1,000 customers. Price's increased involvement on the financial side of the business freed Riffe to spend his

(continued on the following page)

time working on new business, spending less and less time on financial matters. Riffe had noticed that, in the past few years, Price had begun to wear better clothes and drive a shiny late-model convertible around town. Both of her teenagers also drove late-model automobiles, and the family had recently moved into a new home in an upscale subdivision of the city. Riffe had been pleased that he had contributed to Price's success. But in recent months, Riffe was becoming worried because, in spite of increasing revenues, the cash balances and cash flows from operations at AMEX had been steadily deteriorating, sometimes causing the company difficulty in paying its bills on time.

Price, on the other hand, had felt underappreciated and underpaid for all of her hard work. Having learned the system well, and observing that no one was monitoring her, Price fell into a simple but deadly trap. As cashier, she was in charge of receiving customer payments that came in by mail. Unknown to Riffe, Price had been lapping accounts receivable, an embezzlement scheme nicknamed "robbing Peter to pay Paul". Price began by misappropriating (stealing) some of the customers' cheques, endorsing them, and depositing them to her own bank account. To cover up the shortage in a particular customer's account, Price would apply the collections received later from another customer's account. She would do this just before the monthly statements were mailed to the first customer, so that the customer wouldn't notice when he or she received the statement that someone else's payment was being applied to the amount owed AMEX. Of course, this left the second customer's account short, so Price had to misapply the collection from a third customer to straighten out the discrepancy in the second customer's account. She did this for many customers, over a period of many months, boldly stealing more and more each month. With unlimited access to both cash and customer accounts, and with careful planning and constant diligence, Price became very proficient at juggling entries in the books to keep anyone from discovering her scheme. This embezzlement went on for six years, allowing Price to misappropriate $622,000 from the company. The customer accounts that were misstated due to the fraud eventually had to be written off.

What tipped off Riffe to the embezzlement? Price was involved in an automobile accident and couldn't work for two weeks. The employee covering for Price was swamped with telephone calls from customers wanting to discuss unexplained differences in their billing statements for amounts they could prove had been paid. The ensuing investigation pointed straight to Price, and Riffe turned the case over to the authorities.

Due to Price's scheme, the company had been cheated of $622,000 over several years that it could have used to buy new equipment, expand operations, or pay off debts. AMEX Products has now revamped its internal controls. The company has hired a separate person, with no access to cash, to keep customer accounts receivable records. The company now uses a lock-box system for all cheques received by mail. They are sent to AMEX's bank lock box, where they are gathered by a bank employee and immediately deposited. The remittance advices accompanying the cheques are electronically scanned and forwarded to AMEX's accounts receivable bookkeeper where they are used as the source documents for posting amounts collected from customers. A summary of cash received goes to Riffe, who reviews it for reasonableness and compares it with the daily bank deposit total. Another employee, who has neither cash handling nor customer bookkeeping responsibilities, reconciles AMEX's monthly bank statement, and reconciles the total cash deposited per the daily listings with the total credits to customer accounts receivable. Now Riffe requires every employee to take time off for earned vacation, and rotates other employees through those positions while those employees are away.

Clearly, fraud is a huge problem and that spans across the globe. Recent surveys of large and medium-sized companies in the United States and Canada revealed the following:

- Over 75% of businesses surveyed had experienced fraud;
- Over 50% of companies had experienced six or more instances of fraud in only one year;
- In 2007, companies lost an average of $2.4 million each to fraud (up from $1.7 million each in 2005);
- One out of every five workers indicated personal awareness of fraud in the workplace.

Since small businesses and those in countries outside the United States and Canada were omitted from these surveys, we can be sure that the actual incidence of fraud is even higher! Another recent survey taken by the Association for Certified Fraud Examiners (ACFE) reveals that occupational fraud and abuse in America alone results in losses equal to about 6% of total business revenue. When applied to the U.S. gross domestic product, this means that about $600 billion per year is lost due to fraud, an astonishing $4,500 per employee! If you think that fraud occurs only in the for-profit sector, think again. About 13.4% of the ACFE survey cases are not-for-profit organizations, amounting to about $50 billion in fraud through not-for-profit organizations each year.

Fraud has literally exploded with the expansion of e-commerce via the Internet. In addition, studies have shown that the percentage of losses related to fraud from transactions originating in "third world" or developing countries via the Internet is even higher than in economically-developed countries.

What are the most common types of fraud? What causes fraud? What can be done to prevent it?

There are many types of fraud. Some of the most common types are insurance fraud, forgery, credit card fraud, and identity theft. The two most common types of fraud that impact financial statements are:

- **Misappropriation of assets.** *This type of fraud is committed by employees of an entity who steal money from the company and cover it up* through erroneous entries in the books. The AMEX Products case in Exhibit 4-1 is an example. Other examples of asset misappropriation include employee theft of inventory, bribery or kickback schemes in the purchasing function, or employee overstatement of expense reimbursement requests.
- **Fraudulent financial reporting.** *This type of fraud is committed by company managers who make false and misleading entries in the books*, making financial results of the company appear to be better than they actually are. The purpose of this type of fraud is to deceive investors and creditors into investing or loaning money to the company that they might not otherwise have invested or loaned.

Both of these types of fraud involve making false or misleading entries in the books of the company. We call this "cooking the books". Of these two types, asset misappropriation is the most common, but fraudulent financial reporting is by far the most expensive. Perhaps the two most notorious recent cases involving fraudulent financial reporting involved Enron Corporation in 2001 and WorldCom Corporation in 2002. These two scandals alone rocked the US economy and impacted financial markets across the world. Enron (discussed in Chapter 10) committed fraudulent financial reporting by overstating profits through bogus sales of nonexistent assets with inflated values.

When Enron's banks found out, they stopped loaning the company money to operate, causing it to go out of business almost overnight. WorldCom (discussed in Chapter 7) reported expenses as assets and overstated both profits and assets. The company's internal auditor blew the whistle on WorldCom, resulting in the company's eventual collapse. Sadly, the same international accounting firm, **Arthur Andersen**, had audited both companies' financial statements. Because of these and other failed audits, the once mighty firm of Arthur Andersen was forced to close its doors in 2002.

Each of these frauds, and many others revealed about the same time, involved losses in the billions of dollars and thousands of jobs when the companies went out of business. Widespread media coverage sparked adverse market reaction, loss of confidence in the financial reporting system, and losses through declines in share values that ran in the trillions of dollars! We will discuss some of these cases throughout the remaining chapters of the text as examples of how accounting principles were deliberately misapplied, through cooking the books, in environments characterized by *weak internal controls*.

Exhibit 4-2 explains in graphic form the elements that make up virtually every fraud. We call it the **fraud triangle**.

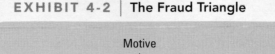

EXHIBIT 4-2 | **The Fraud Triangle**

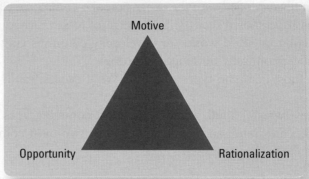

The first element in the fraud triangle is *motive*. This usually results from either critical need or greed on the part of the person who commits the fraud (the perpetrator). Sometimes it is a matter of just never having enough (because some people who commit fraud are already rich by most people's standards). Sometimes it is more about psychological satisfaction, proving that one can "beat the system". Other times, the perpetrator of the fraud might have a legitimate financial need, such as a medical emergency, but he or she uses illegitimate means to meet that need. A recent article in the *Wall Street Journal* indicated that employee theft was on the rise due to economic hard times. In any case, the prevailing attitude on the part of the perpetrator is, "I want it, and someone else has it, so I'm going to do whatever I have to do to get it."

The second element in the fraud triangle is *opportunity*. As in the case of AMEX Products, the opportunity to commit fraud usually arises through weak internal controls. It might be a breakdown in a key element of controls, such as improper *segregation of duties* and/or *improper access to assets*. Or it might result from a weak *control environment*, such as a domineering CEO, a weak or conflicted board of directors, or lax ethical practices, allowing top management to override whatever controls the company has placed in operation for other transactions.

The third element in the triangle is *rationalization*. The perpetrator engages in distorted thinking, such as: "I deserve this;" "Nobody treats me fairly;" "No one will ever know;" "Just this once, I won't let it happen again;" or "Everyone else is doing it."

All three elements of the fraud triangle must be present and take over your decision-making process for fraud to occur. Thieves and robbers have no problems with rationalization nor with motives, all they need is opportunity. You, on the other hand, may have the opportunity to steal money or properties without people knowing, you may have even have a great need for them, but if your moral and ethical values are strong, you will not rationalize the action and will walk away from the opportunity to steal.

Fraud and Ethics

As we pointed out in our decision model for making ethical accounting and business judgments introduced in Chapter 1, the decision to engage in fraud is an act with economic, legal, and ethical implications. The perpetrators of fraud usually do so for their own short-term *economic gain*, while others incur *economic losses* that may far outstrip the gains of the fraudsters. Moreover, fraud is defined by state, federal, and international law as *illegal*. Those who are caught and found guilty of fraud ultimately face penalties which include imprisonment, fines, and monetary damages. Finally, from an *ethical* standpoint, fraud violates the rights of many for the temporary betterment of a few, and for the ultimate betterment of no one. At the end of the day, everyone loses! **Fraud is the ultimate unethical act in business!**

INTERNAL CONTROL

The primary way that fraud, as well as unintentional errors, is prevented, detected, or corrected in an organization is through a proper system of internal control. **Internal control** is a plan of organization and a system of procedures implemented by company management and the board of directors, and designed to accomplish the following five objectives:

1. *Safeguard assets.* A company must safeguard its assets against waste, inefficiency, and fraud. As in the case of AMEX Products, if management fails to safeguard assets such as cash or inventory, those assets will slip away. Most retailers would put in some physical control over their merchandise inventory to prevent shoplifting or employee theft.

2. *Encourage employees to follow company policy.* Everyone in an organization— managers and employees—needs to work toward the same goals. A proper system of controls provides clear policies that result in fair treatment of both customers and employees.

3. *Promote operational efficiency.* Companies cannot afford to waste resources. They work hard to make a sale, and they don't want to waste any of the benefits. If the company can buy something for \$30, why pay \$35? Effective controls minimize waste, which lowers costs and increases profits.

4. *Ensure accurate, reliable accounting records.* Accurate records are essential. Without proper controls, records may be unreliable, making it impossible to tell which part of the business is profitable and which part needs improvement. A business could be losing money on every product it sells—unless it keeps accurate records for the cost of its products.

5. *Comply with legal requirements.* Companies, like people, are subject to laws, such as those of regulatory agencies like the Securities and Exchange Commission or SEC (in the US), stock exchanges, tax authorities, and state, local, and international governing bodies. When companies disobey the law, they are subject to fines, or in extreme cases, their top executives may even go to prison. Effective internal controls help ensure compliance with the law and help avoid of legal difficulties.

How critical are internal controls? They're so important that in some jurisdictions, auditors are required to examine and assess the effectiveness of internal controls of public listed companies. One of the most well-known examples of this requirement is the Sarbanes-Oxley Act (SOX) in the United States.

The Sarbanes-Oxley Act (SOX)

As the Enron and WorldCom scandals unfolded, many people asked, "How can these things happen? If such large companies that we have trusted commit such acts, how can we trust any company to be telling the truth in its financial statements? Where were the auditors?" To address public concerns, the US Congress passed the Sarbanes-Oxley Act of 2002 (SOX). SOX revamped corporate governance in the United States and profoundly affected the way that accounting and auditing is done in public companies. Here are some of the SOX provisions:

1. Public companies must issue an internal control report, and the outside auditor must evaluate and report on the soundness of the company's internal controls.

2. A new body, the Public Company Accounting Oversight Board, has been created to oversee the audits of public companies.

3. An accounting firm may not both audit a public client and also provide certain consulting services for the same client.

4. Stiff penalties await violators—25 years in prison for securities fraud; 20 years for an executive making false sworn statements.

In many other parts of the world, responses to corporate failures, frauds and scandals resulted in similar increased regulatory requirements. In Japan, "J-SOX" (an unofficial term for parts of the Japan's Financial Instruments and Exchange Law) was passed in response to corporate scandals such as **Kanebo**, **Livedoor**, and **Murakami Fund**. In China, the China Securities Regulatory Commission, the National Audit Office, the China Banking Regulatory Commission, and the China Insurance Regulatory Commission jointly announced the Basic Standard for Enterprise Internal Control (also nicknamed "Chinese SOX"). Many other countries have also raised the bar in terms of corporate governance practices. The United Kingdom's Financial Reporting Council is in the process of revising its Combined Code on Corporate Governance. In the European Union, there are various Company Law Directives that regulate company audits, disclosure and governance.

You may be wondering what has all of these internal controls, governance and risk issues have to do with accounting? Simple, accounting matters! The financial information that an accounting system produces are crucial information to capital market participants. Accountants (and auditors), thus have a clear role to play to ensure that the financial information is prepared in accordance with applicable rules, regulations and ethics!

Exhibit 4-3 diagrams the shield that internal controls provide for an organization. Protected by this shield, which provides protection from fraud, waste, and inefficiency, companies can do business in a trustworthy manner that ensures public confidence, an extremely important element in maintaining the stability of financial markets around the world.

How does a business achieve good internal controls? The next section identifies the components of internal control.

EXHIBIT 4-3 | The Shield of Internal Control

The Components of Internal Control

Internal control can be broken down into five components:

OBJECTIVE

2 Set up an internal control system

- Control environment
- Risk assessment
- Information system
- Control procedures
- Monitoring of controls

Exhibit 4-4 (p. 240) diagrams the components of internal control.

Control Environment.   The control environment, symbolized by the roof over the building in Exhibit 4-4, is the "tone at the top" of the business. It starts with the owner and the top managers. They must behave honorably to set a good example for company employees. The owner must demonstrate the importance of internal controls if he or she expects employees to take the controls seriously. A key ingredient in the control environment of many companies is a corporate code of ethics, modeled by top management, which includes such provisions as prohibition against giving or taking bribes or kickbacks from customers or suppliers, prohibition of transactions that involve conflicts of interest, and provisions that encourage good citizenship and corporate social responsibility.

Risk Assessment.   Symbolized by the smoke rising from the chimney, assessment of risks that a company faces offers hints of where mistakes or fraud might arise. A company must be able to identify its business risks, as well as to establish procedures for dealing with those risks to minimize their impacts on the company. For example, Nestlé must take all measures to ensure that its food products do not harm people. Toyota cars should not have faulty parts that could potentially cause motor vehicle accidents. All companies face the risk of bankruptcy. The managements of companies, supported by their boards, have to identify these risks and do what they can to prevent those risks from causing financial or other harm to the company, its employees, its owners, and its creditors.

Information System.   Symbolized by the door of the building, the information system is the means by which accounting information enters and exits. The owner of a business needs accurate information to keep track of assets and measure profits and losses. Every system within the business that processes accounting data should have the ability to capture transactions as they occur, record (journalize) those transactions in an accurate and timely manner, summarize (post) those transactions in the books (ledgers), and report those transactions in the form of account balances or footnotes in the financial statements.

EXHIBIT 4-4 | The Components of Internal Control

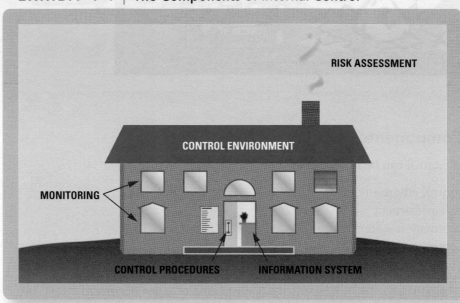

Control Procedures.   Also symbolized by the door, control procedures built into the control environment and information system are the means by which companies gain access to the five objectives of internal controls discussed previously. Examples include proper separation of duties, comparison and other checks, adequate records, proper approvals, and physical safeguards to protect assets from theft. The next section discusses internal control procedures.

Monitoring of Controls.   Symbolized by the windows of the building, monitoring provides "eyes and ears", so that no one person or group of persons can process a transaction completely without being seen and checked by another person or group. With modern computerized systems, much of the monitoring of day-to-day activity is done through controls programmed into a company's information technology. Computer programs dealing with such systems as cash receipts and cash disbursements can be automatically programmed to generate *exception reports* for transactions that exceed certain pre-defined guidelines (such as disbursements in excess of $15,000 in a payroll) for special management scrutiny. In addition, companies hire auditors to monitor their controls. Internal auditors monitor company controls from the inside to safeguard the company's assets, and external auditors test the controls from the outside to ensure that the accounting records are accurate and reliable. Audits are discussed more thoroughly in the next section.

INTERNAL CONTROL PROCEDURES

Whether the business is AMEX Products, **De Beers**, or a **Carrefour** store, every major class of transactions needs to have the following internal control procedures.

Smart Hiring Practices and Separation of Duties

In a business with good internal controls, no important duty is overlooked. Each person in the information chain is important. The chain should start with hiring. Background checks should be conducted on job applicants. Proper training and supervision, as well as paying competitive salaries, helps ensure that all employees are sufficiently competent for their jobs. Employee responsibilities should be clearly laid out in position descriptions. For example, the **treasurer**'s department should be in charge of cash handling, as well as signing and approving cheques. Warehouse personnel should be in charge of storing and keeping track of inventory. With clearly assigned responsibilities, all important jobs get done.

In processing transactions, smart management *separates three key duties: asset handling, record keeping, and transaction approval.* For example, in the case of AMEX Products, separation of the duties of cash handling from record keeping for customer accounts receivable would have removed Melissa Price's incentive to engage in fraud, because it would have made it impossible for her to have lapped accounts receivable if another employee had been keeping the books. Ideally, someone else should also review customer accounts for collectability and be in charge of writing them off if they become completely uncollectible.

The accounting department should be completely separate from the operating departments, such as production and sales. What would happen if sales personnel, who were compensated based on a percentage of the amount of sales they made, approved the company's sales transactions to customers? Sales figures could be inflated and might not reflect the eventual amount collected from customers.

At all costs, accountants must not handle cash, and cash handlers must not have access to the accounting records. If one employee has both cash-handling and accounting duties, that person can steal cash and conceal the theft. This is what happened at AMEX Products.

For companies that are *too small* to hire separate persons to do all of these functions, the key to good internal control is *getting the owner involved*, usually by approving all large transactions, making bank deposits, or reconciling the monthly bank account.

Comparisons and Compliance Monitoring

No person or department should be able to completely process a transaction from beginning to end without being cross-checked by another person or department. For example, separate divisions of the treasurer's department should be responsible for depositing daily cash receipts in the bank. The **controller**'s department should be responsible for recording customer collections to individual customer accounts receivable. A third employee (perhaps the person in the controller's department who reconciles the bank statement) should compare the treasurer department's daily records of cash deposited with the total collections posted to individual customer accounts by the accounting department.

One of the most effective tools for monitoring compliance with management's policies is the use of **operating budgets** and **cash budgets**. A **budget** is a quantitative financial plan that helps control day-to-day management activities. Management may prepare these budgets on a yearly, quarterly, monthly, or on a more frequent basis. Operating budgets are budgets of future periods' net income. They are prepared by line item of the income statement. Cash budgets, discussed in depth later in this chapter, are budgets of future periods' cash receipts and cash disbursements. Often these budgets are "rolling," being constantly updated by adding a time period a year away while dropping the time period that has just passed. Computer systems are programmed to prepare exception reports for data that are out of line with expectations. This data can include variances for each account from budgeted amounts. Department managers are required to explain the variances, and to take corrective actions in their operating plans to keep the budgets in line with expectations. This is an example of the use of **exception reporting**.

To validate the accounting records and monitor compliance with company policies, most companies have an audit. An **audit** is an examination of the company's financial statements and its accounting system, including its controls.

Audits can be internal or external. *Internal auditors* are employees of the business. They ensure that employees are following company policies and operations are running efficiently. Internal auditors also determine whether the company is following legal requirements.

External auditors are completely independent of the business. They are hired to determine whether or not the company's financial statements agree with generally accepted accounting principles. Auditors examine the client's financial statements and the underlying transactions in order to form a professional opinion on the accuracy and reliability of the company's financial statements.

Adequate Records

Accounting records provide the details of business transactions. The general rule is that all major groups of transactions should be supported by either hard copy documents or electronic records. Examples of documents include sales invoices, shipping records, customer remittance advices, purchase orders, vendor invoices, receiving reports, and canceled (i.e. paid) cheques. Documents should be pre-numbered to assure completeness of processing and proper transaction cutoff, and to prevent theft and inefficiency. A gap in the numbered document sequence draws attention to the possibility that transactions might have been omitted from processing.

Limited Access

To complement segregation of duties, company policy should limit access to assets only to those persons or departments that have custodial responsibilities. For example, access to cash should be limited to persons in the treasurer's department. Cash receipts might be processed through a lock-box system. Access to inventory should be limited to persons in the company warehouse where inventories are stored, or to persons in the shipping and receiving functions. Likewise, the company should limit access to records to those persons who have record keeping responsibilities. All manual records of the business should be protected by lock and key and electronic records should be protected by passwords. Only authorized persons should have access to certain records. Individual computers in the business should be protected by user identification and password. Electronic data files should be encrypted (processed through a special code) to prevent their recognition if accessed by a "hacker" or other unauthorized person.

Proper Approvals

No transaction should be processed without management's general or specific approval. The bigger the transaction, the more specific approval it should have. For individual small transactions, management might delegate approval to a specific department. For example:

- Sales to customers on account should all be approved by a separate *credit department* that reviews all customers for creditworthiness before goods are shipped to customers on credit. This helps assure that the company doesn't make sales to customers who cannot afford to pay their bills.
- Purchases of all items on credit should be approved by a separate *purchasing department* that specializes in that function. Among other things, a purchasing department should only buy from approved vendors, on the basis of competitive bids, to assure that the company gets the highest quality products for the most competitive prices.
- All personnel decisions, including hiring, firing, and pay adjustments, should be handled by a separate *human resources (HR) department* that specializes in personnel-related matters.

Very large (material) transactions should generally be approved by top management, and may even go to the board of directors.

What's an easy way to remember the basic control procedures for any class of transactions? Look at the first letters of each of the headings in this section:

Smart hiring practices and **S**egregation of duties
Comparisons and compliance monitoring
Adequate records
Limited access to both assets and records
Proper approvals (either general or specific) for each class of transaction

So, if you can remember SCALP and how to apply each of these attributes, you will be able to control and manage your business well!

Information Technology

Accounting systems are relying less on manual procedures and more on information technology (IT) than ever before for record keeping, asset handling, approval, and monitoring, as well as physically safeguarding the assets. For example, retailers such as **Marks & Spencer** and **Woolworths** control inventory by attaching an *electronic sensor* to merchandise. The cashier must remove the sensor before the customer can walk out of the store. If a customer tries to leave the store with the sensor attached, an alarm sounds. According to *Checkpoint Systems*, these devices reduce theft by as much as 50%. *Bar codes* speed checkout at retail stores, performing multiple operations in a single step. When the sales associate scans the merchandise at the register, the computer records the sale, removes the item from inventory, and computes the amount of cash tendered.

When a company employs sophisticated IT, the basic attributes of internal control (SCALP) do not change, but the procedures by which these attributes are implemented change substantially. For example, segregation of duties is often accomplished by separating mainframe computer departments from other user departments (i.e., controller, sales, purchasing, receiving, credit, HR, treasurer) and restricting access to the IT department only to authorized personnel. Within the computer department, programmers should be separated from computer operators and data librarians. Access to sensitive data files is protected by **password** and data encryption. Electronic records must be saved routinely, or they might be written over or erased. Comparisons of data (such as cash receipts with total credits to customer accounts) that might otherwise be done by hand are performed by the computer. Computers can help monitor inventory levels by item, generating a purchase order for the inventory when it reaches a certain level.

The use of computers has the advantage of speed and accuracy (when programmed correctly). However, a computer that is *not* programmed correctly can corrupt *all* the data, making it unusable. It is therefore important to hire experienced and competent people to run the IT department, to restrict access to sensitive data and the IT department only to authorized personnel, to check data entered into and retrieved from the computer for accuracy and completeness, and to test and retest programs on a regular basis to assure data integrity and accuracy.

Safeguard Controls

Businesses keep important documents in *fireproof vaults*. *Burglar alarms* safeguard buildings, and *security cameras* safeguard other property. *Loss-prevention specialists* train employees to spot suspicious activity.

Employees who handle cash are in a tempting position. Many businesses purchase **fidelity bonds** on cashiers. The bond is an insurance policy that reimburses the company for any losses due to employee theft. Before issuing a fidelity bond, the insurance company investigates the employee's background.

Mandatory vacations and *job rotation* improve internal control. Companies move employees from job to job. This improves morale by giving employees a broad view of the business. Also, knowing someone else will do your job next month keeps you honest. AMEX Products didn't rotate employees to different jobs, and it cost the company $622,000.

INTERNAL CONTROLS FOR E-COMMERCE

As businesses and consumers conduct more transactions over the Internet, e-commerce creates its own risks. Hackers may gain access to confidential information such as account numbers and passwords, resulting in lost of confidence in the business. E-commerce pitfalls include the following:

- Stolen credit card numbers
- Computer viruses and Trojan Horses
- Phishing expeditions

Stolen Credit Card Numbers. Suppose you buy music from **iTunes**. To make the purchase, your credit card number must travel through cyberspace. Wireless networks (Wi-Fi) are creating new security hazards. Amateur hacker Carlos Salgado, Jr., used his home computer to steal 100,000 credit card numbers with a combined limit exceeding $1 billion. Salgado was caught when he tried to sell the numbers to an undercover FBI agent.

Computer Viruses and Trojan Horses. A **computer virus** is a malicious program that (a) enters program code without consent and (b) performs destructive actions in the victim's computer files or programs. A **Trojan Horse** is a malicious computer program that hides inside a legitimate program and works like a virus. Viruses can destroy or alter data, make bogus calculations, and infect files. Most firms have found a virus in their system at some point.

Phishing Expeditions. Thieves **phish** by creating bogus Web sites that sound very similar to the original Web sites to spoof and trick visitors, such as ebay-uk.com and BankAmerica.com. The neat-sounding Web site attracts lots of visitors, and the thieves obtain account numbers and passwords from unsuspecting people. The thieves then use the data for illicit purposes.

The Limitations of Internal Control—Costs and Benefits

Unfortunately, most internal controls can be overcome. Collusion—two or more people working together—can beat internal controls. Consider AMEX Products, discussed in Exhibit 4-1. Even if Riffe were to hire a new person to keep the books, if that person had a relationship with Price and if they conspired with each other, they could design a scheme to lap accounts receivable, the same as Price did, and split the take. Other ways to circumvent a good system of internal controls include management override, human limitations such as fatigue and negligence, and gradual deterioration over time due to neglect. Because of the cost/benefit principle, discussed in the next paragraph, internal controls are not generally designed to detect these types of breakdowns. The best a company can do in this regard is to exercise care in hiring honest persons who have no conflicts of interest with existing employees, and to exercise constant diligence in monitoring the system to assure it continues to work properly.

The stricter the internal control system, the more it costs. An overly complex system of internal control can strangle the business with red tape. How tight should the controls be? Internal controls must be judged in light of their costs and benefits. An example of a good cost/benefit relationship: A part-time security guard at a **Wal-Mart** store costs about $28,000 a year. If we can show that on average, each part-time guard prevents about $50,000 of theft then the net savings to Wal-Mart is $22,000. Most people would say the extra guard is well worth the cost!

THE BANK ACCOUNT AS A CONTROL DEVICE

Cash is the most liquid asset because it's the medium of exchange. Cash is easy to conceal and relatively easy to steal. As a result, most businesses create specific controls for cash.

Keeping cash in a bank account helps control cash because banks have established practices for safeguarding customers' money. The documents used to control a bank account include the following:

- Signature card
- Deposit ticket
- Cheque
- Bank statement
- Bank reconciliation

Signature Card

Banks require each authorized person to sign on an account to provide a *signature card*. This helps safeguard against forgery.

Deposit Ticket/Slip

Banks supply standard forms such as *deposit tickets*. The customer fills in the amount of each deposit. As proof of the transaction, the customer keeps a deposit receipt.

Cheque

To pay cash, the depositor can write a **cheque**, which tells the bank to pay the designated party a specified amount. There are three parties to a cheque:

- The maker, or drawer, who signs the cheque
- The payee, to whom the cheque is paid
- The bank on which the cheque is drawn

EXHIBIT 4-5 | **Cheque with Remittance Advice**

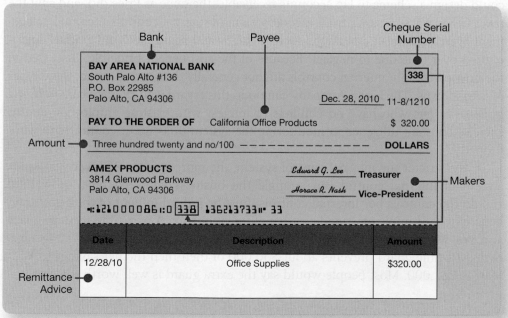

Exhibit 4-5 shows a cheque drawn by AMEX Products, the maker. The cheque has two parts, the cheque itself and the **remittance advice** below. This optional attachment, which may often be scanned electronically, tells the payee the reason for the payment and is used as the source document for posting to proper accounts.

Bank Statement

Banks send monthly statements to customers. A **bank statement** reports what the bank did with the customer's cash. The statement shows the account's beginning and ending balances, cash receipts, and payments. Exhibit 4-6 is the December bank statement of the Palo Alto office of AMEX Products.

EXHIBIT 4-6 | Bank Statement

BANK STATEMENT

BAY AREA NATIONAL BANK

SOUTH PALO ALTO #136 P.O. BOX 22985 PALO ALTO, CA 94306

AMEX Products
3814 Glenwood Parkway
Palo Alto, CA 94306

ACCOUNT 136–213733

DECEMBER 31, 2010

BEGINNING BALANCE	TOTAL DEPOSITS	TOTAL WITHDRAWALS	SERVICE CHARGES	ENDING BALANCE
6,550	4,370	5,000	20	5,900

TRANSACTIONS

DEPOSITS	DATE	AMOUNT
Deposit	12/04	1,150
Deposit	12/08	190
EFT—Receipt of cash dividend	12/17	900
Bank Collection	12/26	2,100
Interest	12/31	30

CHARGES	DATE	AMOUNT
Service Charge	12/31	20

CHEQUES

Number	Amount	Number	Amount	Number	Amount
307	100	333	150	335	100
332	3,000	334	100	336	1,100

OTHER DEDUCTIONS	DATE	AMOUNT
NSF	12/04	50
EFT—Insurance	12/20	400

Electronic funds transfer (EFT) moves cash by electronic communication. It is cheaper to pay without having to mail a cheque, so many people pay their mortgage, rent, utilities, and insurance by EFT.

EXHIBIT 4-7 | Cash Records of AMEX Products

General Ledger:

ACCOUNT Cash				
Date	Item	Debit	Credit	Balance
2010				
Dec 1	Balance			6,550
2	Cash receipt	1,150		7,700
7	Cash receipt	190		7,890
31	Cash payments		6,150	1,740
31	Cash receipt	1,600		3,340

Cash Payments:

Cheque No.	Amount	Cheque No.	Amount
332	$3,000	337	$ 280
333	510	338	320
334	100	339	250
335	100	340	490
336	1,100	Total	$6,150

Bank Reconciliation

There are two records of a business's cash:

1. The bank statement, which shows the cash receipts and payments transacted through the bank. In Exhibit 4-6 the bank shows an ending balance of $5,900 for AMEX Products.

2. The Cash account in the company's general ledger. Exhibit 4-7 on the following page shows that AMEX Products' ending cash balance is $3,340.

The books and the bank statement usually show different cash balances. Differences arise because of a time lag in recording transactions—two examples follow:

- When you write a cheque, you immediately deduct it in your cheque book. But the bank does not subtract the cheque from your account until the bank pays the cheque a few days later, after your payee presents the cheque to his or her own bank (which may be different from your bank). And you immediately add the cash receipt for all your deposits. But it may take a day or two for the bank to add deposits to your balance.
- Your EFT payments and cash receipts are recorded by the bank before you learn of them.

To ensure accurate cash records, you need to update your cash record—either online or after you receive your bank statement. The result of this updating process creates a **bank reconciliation**, which you must prepare. The bank reconciliation explains all differences between your cash records and your bank balance. The person who prepares the bank reconciliation should have no other cash duties. Otherwise, he or she can steal cash and manipulate the reconciliation to conceal the theft.

Preparing the Bank Reconciliation

Here are the items that appear on a bank reconciliation. They all cause differences between the bank balance and the book balance. We call your cash record the "Books."

Bank Side of the Reconciliation

1. Items to show on the *Bank* side of the bank reconciliation include the following:
   a. **Deposits in transit** (outstanding deposits). You have recorded these deposits, but the bank has not. Add deposits in transit on the bank reconciliation.
   b. **Outstanding cheques**. You have recorded these cheques, but the bank has not yet paid them. Subtract outstanding cheques.
   c. **Bank errors.** Correct all bank errors on the Bank side of the reconciliation. For example, the bank may erroneously subtract from your account a cheque written by someone else.

Book Side of the Reconciliation

2. Items to show on the *Book* side of the bank reconciliation include the following:
   a. **Bank collections.** Bank collections are cash receipts that the bank has recorded for your account. But you haven't recorded the cash receipt yet. Many businesses have their customers pay directly to their bank. This is called a *lock-box system* and reduces theft. An example is a bank collecting an account receivable for you. Add bank collections on the bank reconciliation.
   b. **Electronic funds transfers.** The bank may receive or pay cash on your behalf. An EFT may be a cash receipt or a cash payment. Add EFT receipts and subtract EFT payments.
   c. **Service charge.** This cash payment is the bank's fee for processing your transactions. Subtract service charges.
   d. **Interest revenue on your cheque account.** On certain types of bank accounts, you earn interest if you keep enough cash in your account. The bank statement tells you of this cash receipt. Add interest revenue.
   e. **Non-sufficient funds (NSF) cheques.** These are cash receipts from customers for which there are not sufficient funds in their bank to cover the amount. NSF cheques (sometimes called "bounced" cheques) are treated as cash payments on your bank reconciliation. Subtract NSF cheques.
   f. **The cost of printed cheques.** This is usually deducted automatically by the bank and is handled like a service charge. Subtract this cost.
   g. **Book errors.** Correct all book errors on the Book side of the reconciliation. For example, you may have recorded a $150 cheque that you wrote as $510 on your books.

Bank Reconciliation Illustrated. The bank statement in Exhibit 4-6 shows that the December 31 bank balance of AMEX Products is $5,900 (upper right corner). However, the company's Cash account has a balance of $3,340, as shown in Exhibit 4-7. This situation calls for a bank reconciliation. Exhibit 4-8, panel A, on the following page, lists the reconciling items for easy reference, and panel B shows the completed reconciliation.

EXHIBIT 4-8 | Bank Reconciliation

PANEL A—Reconciling Items

Bank side:

1. Deposit in transit, $1,600.
2. Bank error: The bank deducted $100 for a cheque written by another company. Add $100 to the bank balance.
3. Outstanding cheques—total of $1,340.

Cheque No.	Amount
337	$280
338	320
339	250
340	490

Book side:

4. EFT receipt of your dividend revenue earned on an investment, $900.
5. Bank collection of your account receivable, $2,100.
6. Interest revenue earned on your bank balance, $30.
7. Book error: You recorded cheque no. 333 for $510. The amount you actually paid on account was $150. Add $360 to your book balance.
8. Bank service charge, $20.
9. NSF cheque from a customer, $50. Subtract $50 from your book balance.
10. EFT payment of insurance expense, $400.

PANEL B—Bank Reconciliation

AMEX Products
Bank Reconciliation
December 31, 2010

Bank			Books		
Balance, December 31		$5,900	Balance, December 31		$3,340
Add:			Add:		
1. Deposit in transit		1,600	4. EFT receipt of dividend revenue		900
2. Correction of bank error		100	5. Bank collection of account		
		7,600	receivable		2,100
			6. Interest revenue earned on		
			bank balance		30
			7. Correction of book error—		
			overstated our cheque no. 333		360
Less:					6,730
3. Outstanding cheques					
No. 337	$280		Less:		
No. 338	320		8. Service charge	$ 20	
No. 339	250		9. NSF cheque	50	
No. 340	490	(1,340)	10. EFT payment of insurance expense	400	(470)
Adjusted bank balance		$6,260	**Adjusted bank balance**		$6,260

These amounts should agree.

SUMMARY OF THE VARIOUS RECONCILING ITEMS:

BANK BALANCE—ALWAYS

- *Add* deposits in transit.
- *Subtract* outstanding cheques.
- *Add* or *subtract* corrections of bank errors.

BOOK BALANCE—ALWAYS

- *Add* bank collections, interest revenue, and EFT receipts.
- *Subtract* service charges, NSF cheques, and EFT payments.
- *Add* or *subtract* corrections of book errors.

Journalizing Transactions from the Bank Reconciliation. The bank reconciliation is an accountant's tool separate from the journals and ledgers. It does *not* account for transactions in the journal. To get the transactions into the accounts, we must make journal entries and post to the ledger. All items on the *Book* side of the bank reconciliation require journal entries.

The bank reconciliation in Exhibit 4-8 requires AMEX Products to make journal entries to bring the Cash account up-to-date. The numbers in red correspond to the reconciling items listed in Exhibit 4-8, Panel A.

4.	Dec 31	Cash		900	
		Dividend Revenue			900
		Receipt of dividend revenue earned on investment.			
5.	31	Cash		2,100	
		Accounts Receivable			2,100
		Account receivable collected by bank.			
6.	31	Cash		30	
		Interest Revenue			30
		Interest earned on bank balance.			
7.	31	Cash		360	
		Accounts Payable			360
		Correction of cheque no. 333.			
8.	31	Bank Service Charges		20	
		Cash			20
		Bank service charge.			
9.	31	Accounts Receivable		50	
		Cash			50
		NSF cheque returned by bank.			
10.	31	Insurance Expense		400	
		Cash			400
		Payment of monthly insurance.			

The entry for the NSF cheque (entry 9) needs explanation. Upon learning that a customer's $50 cheque to us was not good, we must credit Cash to update the Cash account. Unfortunately, we still have a receivable from the customer, so we must debit Accounts Receivable to reinstate our receivable and try to collect it again!

Online Banking

Online banking allows you to pay bills and view your account electronically. You don't have to wait until the end of the month to get a bank statement. With online banking you can reconcile transactions at any time and keep your account current whenever you wish. Exhibit 4-9 shows a sample page from the account history of a bank account.

MID-CHAPTER SUMMARY PROBLEM

The cash account of Baylor Associates at February 28, 2011, follows.

Cash				
Feb 1	Bal 3,995	Feb 3	400	
6	800	12	3,100	
15	1,800	19	1,100	
23	1,100	25	500	
28	2,400	27	900	
Feb 28	Bal 4,095			

Baylor Associates received the bank statement on February 28, 2011 (negative amounts are in parentheses):

	Bank Statement for February 2011		
Beginning balance			$3,995
Deposits:			
Feb 7		$ 800	
15		1,800	
24		1,100	3,700
Cheques (total per day):			
Feb 8		$ 400	
16		3,100	
23		1,100	(4,600)
Other items:			
Service charge			(10)
NSF cheque from M. E. Crown			(700)
Bank collection of note receivable for the company			1,000
EFT—monthly rent expense			(330)
Interest revenue earned on account balance			15
Ending balance			$3,070

Additional data:
Baylor deposits all cash receipts in the bank and makes all payments by cheque.

I Requirements

1. Prepare the bank reconciliation of Baylor Associates at February 28, 2011.
2. Journalize the entries based on the bank reconciliation.

Answers

▌Requirement 1

Baylor Associates
Bank Reconciliation
February 28, 2011

Bank:		
Balance, February 28, 2011		$3,070
Add: Deposit of February 28 in transit		2,400
		5,470
Less: Outstanding cheques issued on Feb 25 ($500)		
and Feb 27 ($900)		(1,400)
Adjusted bank balance, February 28, 2011		$4,070
Books:		
Balance, February 28, 2011		$4,095
Add: Bank collection of note receivable		1,000
Interest revenue earned on bank balance		15
		5,110
Less: Service charge	$ 10	
NSF cheque	700	
EFT—Rent expense	330	(1,040)
Adjusted book balance, February 28, 2011		$4,070

▌Requirement 2

Feb 28	Cash		1,000	
	Note Receivable			1,000
	Note receivable collected by bank.			
28	Cash		15	
	Interest Revenue			15
	Interest earned on bank balance.			
28	Miscellaneous Expense		10	
	Cash			10
	Bank service charge.			
28	Accounts Receivable		700	
	Cash			700
	NSF cheque returned by bank.			
28	Rent Expense		330	
	Cash			330
	Monthly rent expense.			

INTERNAL CONTROL OVER CASH RECEIPTS

OBJECTIVE

4 **Apply** internal controls to cash receipts and cash payments

Cash requires some specific internal controls because cash is relatively easy to steal and it's easy to convert to other forms of wealth. Moreover, all transactions ultimately affect cash. Let's see how to control cash receipts.

All cash receipts should be deposited for safekeeping in the bank—quickly. Companies receive cash over the counter and through the mail. Each source of cash has its own security measures.

Cash Receipts over the Counter

Exhibit 4-10 illustrates the purchase of products in a grocery store. The point-of-sale terminal provides control over the cash receipts, while also recording the sale and relieving inventory for the appropriate cost of the goods sold. Consider a **Whole Foods Market** store. For each transaction, the Whole Foods sales associate issues a receipt to the customer as proof of purchase. The cash drawer opens when the sales associate enters a transaction, and the machine electronically transmits a record of the sale to the store's main computer. At the end of each shift, the sales associate delivers his or her cash drawer to the office, where it is combined with cash from all other terminals and delivered by armored car to the bank for deposit, as explained in the next section. Later, a separate employee in the accounting department reconciles the electronic record of the sales per terminal to the record of the cash turned in. These measures, coupled with oversight by a manager, discourage theft.

EXHIBIT 4-10 | **Cash Receipts over the Counter**

Point-of-sale terminals also provide effective control over inventory. For example, in a restaurant, these devices track sales by menu item and total sales by cash, type of credit card, gift card redeemed, etc. They create the daily sales journal for that store, which, in turn, interfaces with the general ledger. Managers can use records produced by point-of-sale terminals to cheque inventory levels and compare them against sales records for accuracy. For example, in a restaurant, an effective way to monitor sales of expensive wine is for a manager to perform a quick count of the bottles on hand at the end of the day and compare it with the count at the end of the previous day, plus the record of any purchased. The count at the end of the previous day, plus the record of bottles purchased, minus the count at the end of the current day should equal the amount sold as recorded by the point-of-sale terminals in the restaurant.

An effective control for many chain retail businesses, such as restaurants, grocery stores, or clothing stores, to prevent unauthorized access to cash as well as to allow for more efficient management of cash, is the use of "depository bank accounts." Cash receipts for an individual store are deposited into a local bank account (preferably delivered by armored car for security reasons) on a daily basis. The corporate headquarters arranges for its centralized bank to draft the local depository accounts on a frequent (perhaps daily) basis to get the money concentrated into the company's centralized account, where it can be used to pay the corporation's bills. Depository accounts are "one-way" accounts where the local management may only make deposits. They have no authority to write cheques on the account or take money out of the store's account.

Cash Receipts by Mail

Many companies receive cash by mail, usually from corporate customers and sometimes from retail customers. Exhibit 4-11 shows how companies control cash received by mail. All incoming mail is opened by a mailroom employee. The mailroom then sends all customer cheques to the treasurer, who has the cashier deposit the money in the bank. The remittance advices go to the accounting department for journal entries to Cash and customer accounts receivable. As a final step, the controller compares the following records for the day:

- Bank deposit amount from the treasurer
- Debit to Cash from the accounting department

EXHIBIT 4-11 | Cash Receipts by Mail

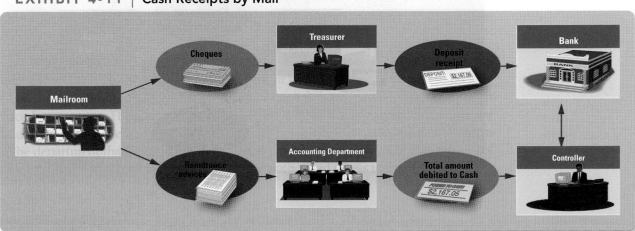

Reporting Cash on the Balance Sheet

Most companies have numerous bank accounts, but they usually combine all cash amounts into a single total called "Cash and Cash Equivalents." **Cash equivalents** include liquid assets such as time deposits, certificates of deposit, and high-grade government securities. These are interest-bearing accounts that can be withdrawn with no penalty, or interest-bearing securities. Slightly less liquid than cash, cash equivalents are sufficiently similar to be reported along with cash. The balance sheet of AMEX Products reported the following:

AMEX Products
Balance Sheet (partial)
For the Year Ended December 31, 2010

Assets	
Cash and cash equivalents.................	$ 6,260
Cash pledged as collateral................	2,000

Compensating Balance Agreements

The Cash account on the balance sheet reports the liquid assets available for day-to-day use. None of the Cash balance is restricted in any way.

Any restricted amount of cash should *not* be reported as Cash on the balance sheet. For example, on the AMEX Products' balance sheet, *cash pledged as collateral* is reported separately because that cash is not available for day-to-day use. Instead, AMEX has pledged the cash as security (collateral) for a loan. If AMEX Products fails to pay the loan, the lender can take the pledged cash. For this reason, the pledged cash is less liquid.

Also, banks often lend money under a compensating balance agreement. The borrower agrees to maintain a minimum balance in an account with the bank at all times. This minimum balance becomes a long-term asset and is therefore not cash in the normal sense.

Suppose AMEX Products borrowed $10,000 at 8% from First Interstate Bank and agreed to keep 20% ($2,000) on deposit at all times. The net result of the compensating balance agreement is that AMEX actually borrowed only $8,000. And by paying 8% interest on the full $10,000, AMEX's actual interest rate is really 10%, as shown here:

$10,000 × 0.08 = $800 interest
$800/$8,000 = 0.10 interest rate

END-OF-CHAPTER SUMMARY PROBLEM

Assume the following situation for PepsiCo, Inc.: PepsiCo ended 2010 with cash of $200 million. At December 31, 2010, Bob Detmer, the CFO of PepsiCo, is preparing the budget for 2011.

During 2011, Detmer expects PepsiCo to collect $26,400 million from customers and $80 million from interest earned on investments. PepsiCo expects to pay $12,500 million for its inventories and $5,400 million for operating expenses. To remain competitive, PepsiCo plans to spend $2,200 million to upgrade production facilities and an additional $350 million to acquire other companies. PepsiCo also plans to sell older assets for approximately $300 million and to collect $220 million of this amount in cash. PepsiCo is budgeting dividend payments of $550 million during the year. Finally, the company is scheduled to pay off $1,200 million of long-term debt plus the $6,600 million of current liabilities left over from 2010.

Because of the growth planned for 2011, Detmer budgets the need for a minimum cash balance of $300 million.

I *Requirement*

1. How much must PepsiCo borrow during 2011 to keep its cash balance from falling below $300 million? Prepare the 2011 cash budget to answer this important question.

Answer

PepsiCo, Inc.
Cash Budget
For the Year Ended December 31, 2011

(In millions)

Cash balance, December 31, 2010		$ 200
Estimated cash receipts:		
Collections from customers		26,400
Receipt of interest		80
Sales of assets		220
		26,900
Estimated cash payments:		
Purchases of inventory	$12,500	
Payment of operating expenses	5,400	
Upgrading of production facilities	2,200	
Acquisition of other companies	350	
Payment of dividends	550	
Payment of long-term debt and other		
liabilities ($1,200 + $6,600)	7,800	(28,800)
Cash available (needed) before new financing		$ (1,900)
Budgeted cash balance, December 31, 2011		(300)
Cash available for additional investments, or		
(New financing needed)		$ (2,200)

PepsiCo. must borrow $2,200 million.

REVIEW INTERNAL CONTROL AND CASH

Quick Check (Answers are given on page 287.)

1. Internal control has its own terminology. On the left are some key internal control concepts. On the right are some key terms. Match each internal control concept with its term by writing the appropriate letter in the space provided. Not all letters are used.

   ___ This procedure limits access to sensitive data.

   ___ This type of insurance policy covers losses due to employee theft.

   ___ Trusting your employees can lead you to overlook this procedure.

   ___ The most basic purpose of internal control.

   ___ Internal control cannot always safeguard against this problem.

   ___ Often mentioned as the cornerstone of a good system of internal control.

   ___ Pay employees enough to require them to do a good job.

   a. Competent personnel
   b. Encryption
   c. Separation of duties
   d. Safeguarding assets
   e. Fidelity bond
   f. Collusion
   g. Firewalls
   h. Supervision
   i. External audits

2. Each of the following is an example of a control procedure, *except*
   a. sound personnel procedures.
   b. a sound marketing plan.
   c. separation of duties.
   d. limited access to assets.

3. Which of the following is an example of poor internal control?
   a. Employees must take vacations.
   b. Rotate employees through various jobs.
   c. The accounting department compares goods received with the related purchase order.
   d. The mailroom clerk records daily cash receipts in the journal.

Lowell Corporation has asked you to prepare its bank reconciliation at the end of the current month. Answer questions 4–8 using the following code letters to indicate how the item described would be reported on the bank reconciliation.
   a. Deduct from the book balance
   b. Does not belong on the bank reconciliation
   c. Add to the bank balance
   d. Deduct from the bank balance
   e. Add to the book balance

4. A cheque for $835 written by Lowell during the current month was erroneously recorded as a $358 payment.

5. A $400 deposit made on the last day of the current month did not appear on this month's bank statement.

6. The bank statement showed interest earned of $65.

7. The bank statement included a cheque from a customer that was marked NSF.

8. The bank statement showed the bank had credited Lowell's account for an $800 deposit made by Lawrence Company.

9. Which of the following reconciling items does not require a journal entry?
   a. Bank service charge   c. NSF cheque
   b. Bank collection of note receivable   d. Deposit in transit

10. A cheque was written for $754 to purchase supplies. The cheque was recorded in the journal as $745. The entry to correct this error would
   a. increase Supplies, $9.   c. decrease Cash, $9.
   b. decrease Supplies, $9.   d. both a. and c.

11. A cash budget helps control cash by
    a. helping to determine whether additional cash is available for investments or new financing is needed.
    b. developing a plan for increasing sales.
    c. ensuring accurate cash records.
    d. all of the above.

Accounting Vocabulary

audit (p. 238) A periodic examination of a company's financial statements and the accounting systems, controls, and records that produce them. Audits may be either external or internal. External audits are usually performed by certified public accountants (CPAs).

bank collections (p. 249) Collection of money by the bank on behalf of a depositor.

bank reconciliation (p. 248) A document explaining the reasons for the difference between a depositor's records and the bank's records about the depositor's cash.

bank statement (p. 247) Document showing the beginning and ending balances of a particular bank account listing the month's transactions that affected the account.

budget (p. 241) A quantitative expression of a plan that helps managers coordinate the entity's activities.

cash budget (p. 241) A budget that projects the entity's future cash receipts and cash disbursements.

cash equivalent (p. 262) Investments such as time deposits, certificates of deposit, or high-grade government securities that are considered so similar to cash that they are combined with cash for financial disclosure purposes on the balance sheet.

cheque (p. 246) Document instructing a bank to pay the designated person or business the specified amount of money.

computer virus (p. 245) A malicious program that enters a company's computer system by e-mail or other means and destroys program and data files.

controller (p. 241) The chief accounting officer of a business.

deposits in transit (p. 249) A deposit recorded by the company but not yet by its bank.

electronic fund transfer (EFT) (p. 247) System that transfers cash by electronic communication rather than by paper documents.

exception reporting (p. 242) Identifying data that is not within "normal limits" so that managers can follow up and take corrective action. Exception reporting is used in operating and cash budgets to keep company profits and cash flow in line with management's plans.

fidelity bond (p. 244) An insurance policy taken out on employees who handle cash.

fraud (p. 233) An intentional misrepresentation of facts, made for the purpose of persuading another party to act in a way that causes injury or damage to that party.

fraud triangle (p. 236) The three elements that are present in almost all cases of fraud. These elements are motive, opportunity, and rationalization on the part of the perpetrator.

fraudulent financial reporting (p. 235) Fraud perpetrated by management by preparing misleading financial statements.

imprest system (p. 260) A way to account for petty cash by maintaining a constant balance in the petty cash account, supported by the fund (cash plus payment tickets) totaling the same amount.

internal control (p. 237) Organizational plan and related measures adopted by an entity to safeguard assets, encourage adherence to company policies, promote operational efficiency, and ensure accurate and reliable accounting records.

lapping (p. 234) A fraudulent scheme to steal cash through misappropriating certain customer payments and posting payments from other customers to the affected accounts to cover it up. Lapping is caused by weak internal controls (i.e., not segregating the duties of cash handling and accounts receivable bookkeeping, allowing the bookkeeper improper access to cash, and not appropriately monitoring the activities of those who handle cash).

lock-box system (p. 234) A system of handling cash receipts by mail whereby customers remit payment directly to the bank, rather than through the entity's mail system.

misappropriation of assets (p. 235) Fraud committed by employees by stealing assets from the company.

non-sufficient funds (NSF) cheque (p. 249) A "hot" cheque, one for which the payer's bank account has insufficient money to pay the cheque. NSF cheques are cash receipts that turn out to be worthless.

operating budget (p. 241) A budget of future net income. The operating budget projects a company's future revenue and expenses. It is usually prepared by line item of the company's income statement.

outstanding cheques (p. 249) A cheque issued by the company and recorded on its books but not yet paid by its bank.

petty cash (p. 260) Fund containing a small amount of cash that is used to pay minor amounts.

phishing (p. 245) Creating bogus Web sites for the purpose of stealing unauthorized data, such as names, addresses, social security numbers, bank account, and credit card numbers.

remittance advice (p. 246) An optional attachment to a cheque (sometimes a perforated tear-off document and sometimes capable of being electronically scanned) that indicates the payer, date, and purpose of the cash payment. The remittance advice is often used as the source documents for posting cash receipts or payments.

treasurer (p. 241) In a large company, the department that has total responsibility for cash handling and cash management. This includes cash budgeting, cash collections, writing cheques, investing excess funds, and making proposals for raising additional cash when needed.

Trojan Horse (p. 245) A malicious program that hides within legitimate programs and acts like a computer virus.

ASSESS YOUR PROGRESS

Short Exercises

S4-1 (*Learning Objective 1: Defining fraud*) Define "fraud." List and briefly discuss the three major components of the "fraud triangle."

S4-2 (*Learning Objective 2: Listing components of internal control*) List the components of internal control. Briefly describe each component.

writing assignment ■

S4-3 (*Learning Objective 2: Explaining and describing characteristics of an effective system of internal control*) Explain why separation of duties is often described as the cornerstone of internal control for safeguarding assets. Describe what can happen if the same person has custody of an asset and also accounts for the asset.

S4-4 (*Learning Objective 2: Identifying internal control characteristics*) Identify the other control procedures usually found in a company's system of internal control besides separation of duties, and tell why each is important.

S4-5 (*Learning Objective 2: Explaining e-commerce internal control pitfalls*) How do computer viruses, Trojan Horses, and phishing expeditions work? How can these e-commerce pitfalls hurt you? Be specific.

S4-6 (*Learning Objective 2: Explaining the role of internal control*) Cash may be a small item on the financial statements. Nevertheless, internal control over cash is very important. Why is this true?

S4-7 (*Learning Objectives 2, 4: Explaining the role of internal control; identifying controls over cash payments*) Crow Company requires that all documents supporting a cheque be cancelled by punching a hole through the packet. Why is this practice required? What might happen if it were not?

S4-8 (*Learning Objective 3: Preparing a bank reconciliation*) The Cash account of Randell Corp. reported a balance of $2,400 at October 31. Included were outstanding cheques totaling $500 and an October 31 deposit of $200 that did not appear on the bank statement. The bank statement, which came from Park Bank, listed an October 31 balance of $3,180. Included in the bank balance was an October 30 collection of $530 on account from a customer who pays the bank directly. The bank statement also shows a $20 service charge, $10 of interest revenue that Randell earned on its bank balance, and an NSF cheque for $40.

Prepare a bank reconciliation to determine how much cash Randell actually has at October 31.

S4-9 (*Learning Objective 3: Recording transactions from a bank reconciliation*) After preparing Randell Corp.'s bank reconciliation in Short Exercise 4-8, make the company's journal entries for transactions that arise from the bank reconciliation. Date each transaction October 31, and include an explanation with each entry.

S4-10 (*Learning Objective 3: Using a bank reconciliation as a control device*) Barbara Smith manages Jones Advertising. Smith fears that a trusted employee has been stealing from the company. This employee receives cash from clients and also prepares the monthly bank reconciliation. To check up on the employee, Smith prepares her own bank reconciliation, as follows:

writing assignment ■

Jones Advertising Bank Reconciliation October 31, 2010				
Bank			**Books**	
Balance, October 31.....................	$4,400	Balance, October 31.....................		$3,920
Add:		Add:		
Deposits in transit	500	Bank collections		900
		Interest revenue		20
Less:		Less:		
Outstanding cheques	(900)	Service charge.........................		(40)
Adjusted bank balance..............	$4,000	Adjusted book balance..............		$4,800

Does it appear that the employee has stolen from the company? If so, how much? Explain your answer. Which side of the bank reconciliation shows the company's true cash balance?

S4-11 (*Learning Objective 4: Applying internal controls over cash receipts*) Greta Cassidy sells memberships to the Phoenix Symphony Association in Phoenix, Arizona. The Symphony's procedure requires Cassidy to write a patron receipt for all memberships sold. The receipt forms are prenumbered. Cassidy is having personal financial problems and she stole $400 received from a customer. To hide her theft, Cassidy destroyed the company copy of the receipt that she gave the patron. What will alert manager Stephanie Stevens that something is wrong?

S4-12 (*Learning Objective 4: Applying internal control over cash payments by cheque*) Answer the following questions about internal control over cash payments:

1. Payment by cheque carries three controls over cash. What are they?
2. Suppose a purchasing agent receives the goods that he purchases and also approves payment for the goods. How could a dishonest purchasing agent cheat his company? How do companies avoid this internal control weakness?

S4-13 (*Learning Objective 5: Using a cash budget*) Briefly explain how a cash budget works and what it accomplishes with its last few lines of data.

writing assignment ■

S4-14 (*Learning Objective 5: Preparing a cash budget*) Crescent Artichoke Growers (CAG) is a major food cooperative. Suppose CAG begins 2010 with cash of $11 million. CAG estimates cash receipts during 2010 will total $104 million. Planned payments will total $93 million. To meet daily cash needs next year, CAG must maintain a cash balance of at least $17 million. Prepare the organization's cash budget for 2010.

writing assignment ■

S4-15 (*Learning Objectives 1, 5: Learning about fraud; making an ethical judgment related to internal controls*) Gretchen Rourke, an accountant for Dublin Limited, discovers that her supervisor, Billy Dunn, made several errors last year. In total, the errors overstated the company's net income by 25%. It is not clear whether the errors were deliberate or accidental. What should Rourke do?

Exercises

MyAccountingLab

All of the Group A and Group B exercises can be found within MyAccountingLab, an online homework and practice environment. Your instructor may ask you to complete these exercises using MyAccountingLab.

(Group A)

writing assignment ■

E4-16A (*Learning Objectives 1, 2: Learning about fraud; identifying internal control weaknesses*) Identify the internal control weakness in the following situations. State how the person can hurt the company.

a. James Mason works as a security guard at SAFETY parking in Detroit. Mason has a master key to the cash box where customers pay for parking. Each night Mason prepares the cash report that shows (a) the number of cars that parked on the lot and (b) the day's cash receipts. Louise Carrington, the SAFETY treasurer, checks Mason's figures by multiplying the number of cars by the parking fee per car. Carrington then deposits the cash in the bank.

b. Elizabeth Fleming is the purchasing agent for Marshfield Golf Equipment. Fleming prepares purchase orders based on requests from division managers of the company. Fleming faxes the purchase order to suppliers who then ship the goods to Marshfield. Fleming receives each incoming shipment and checks it for agreement with the purchase order and the related invoice. She then routes the goods to the respective division managers and sends the receiving report and the invoice to the accounting department for payment.

E4-17A (*Learning Objective 2: Identifying internal control strengths and weaknesses*) The following situations describe two cash payment situations and two cash receipt situations. In each pair, one set of internal controls is better than the other. Evaluate the internal controls in each situation as strong or weak, and give the reason for your answer.

Cash payments:

a. Tim McDermott Construction policy calls for construction supervisors to request the equipment needed for their jobs. The home office then purchases the equipment and has it shipped to the construction site.

b. Gravel & Sand, Inc., policy calls for project supervisors to purchase the equipment needed for jobs. The supervisors then submit the paid receipts to the home office for reimbursement. This policy enables supervisors to get the equipment quickly and keep construction jobs moving.

Cash receipts:

a. At Carlisle Auto Parts, cash received by mail goes straight to the accountant, who debits Cash and credits Accounts Receivable to record the collections from customers. The Carlisle accountant then deposits the cash in the bank.

b. Cash received by mail at Sole Orthopedic Clinic goes to the mail room, where a mail clerk opens envelopes and totals the cash receipts for the day. The mail clerk forwards customer cheques to the cashier for deposit in the bank and forwards the remittance advices to the accounting department for posting credits to customer accounts.

writing assignment ■

E4-18A (*Learning Objectives 1, 2: Learning about fraud; correcting an internal control weakness*) Bobby Flynn served as executive director of Downtown Kalamazoo, an organization created to revitalize Kalamazoo, Michigan. Over the course of 13 years Flynn embezzled

$333,000. How did Flynn do it? By depositing subscriber cash receipts in his own bank account, writing Downtown Kalamazoo cheques to himself, and creating phony entities that Downtown Kalamazoo wrote cheques to.

Downtown Kalamazoo was led by a board of directors comprised of civic leaders. Flynn's embezzlement went undetected until Downtown Kalamazoo couldn't pay its bills.

Give four ways Flynn's embezzlement could have been prevented.

E4-19A (*Learning Objective 3: Classifying bank reconciliation items*) The following items appear on a bank reconciliation:

1. ___ Outstanding cheques
2. ___ Bank error: The bank credited our account for a deposit made by another bank customer.
3. ___ Service charge
4. ___ Deposits in transit
5. ___ NSF cheque
6. ___ Bank collection of a note receivable on our behalf
7. ___ Book error: We debited Cash for $200. The correct debit was $2,000.

Classify each item as (a) an addition to the bank balance, (b) a subtraction from the bank balance, (c) an addition to the book balance, or (d) a subtraction from the book balance.

E4-20A (*Learning Objective 3: Preparing a bank reconciliation*) D. J. Hunter's chequebook lists the following:

Date	Cheque No.	Item	Cheque	Deposit	Balance
6/1					$ 525
4	622	Art Cafe	$ 30		495
9		Dividends received		$ 110	605
13	623	General Tire Co.	35		570
14	624	QuickMobil	68		502
18	625	Cash	55		447
26	626	Woodway Baptist Church	85		362
28	627	Bent Tree Apartments	285		77
30		Paycheque		1,210	1,287

The June bank statement shows

Balance			$525	
Add: Deposits			110	
Debit cheques:	No.	Amount		
	622	$30		
	623	35		
	624	86*		
	625	55	(206)	
Other charges:				
NSF cheque.....................................		$20		
Service charge		10	(30)	
Balance			$399	

*This is the correct amount for cheque number 624.

Requirement

1. Prepare Hunter's bank reconciliation at June 30.

E4-21A *(Learning Objective 3: Preparing a bank reconciliation)* Evan Root operates a bowling alley. He has just received the monthly bank statement at April 30 from City National Bank, and the statement shows an ending balance of $565. Listed on the statement are an EFT rent collection of $320, a service charge of $7, two NSF cheques totaling $115, and an $11 charge for printed cheques. In reviewing his cash records, Root identifies outstanding cheques totaling $602 and an April 30 deposit in transit of $1,790. During April, he recorded a $290 cheque for the salary of a part-time employee as $29. Root's Cash account shows an April 30 cash balance of $1,827. How much cash does Root actually have at April 30?

E4-22A *(Learning Objective 3: Making journal entries from a bank reconciliation)* Use the data from Exercise 4-21 to make the journal entries that Root should record on April 30 to update his Cash account. Include an explanation for each entry.

writing assignment ■

E4-23A *(Learning Objective 4: Evaluating internal control over cash receipts)* McCall stores use point-of-sale terminals as cash registers. The register shows the amount of each sale, the cash received from the customer, and any change returned to the customer. The machine also produces a customer receipt but keeps no record of transactions. At the end of the day, the clerk counts the cash in the register and gives it to the cashier for deposit in the company bank account.

Write a memo to convince the store manager that there is an internal control weakness over cash receipts. Identify the weakness that gives an employee the best opportunity to steal cash and state how to prevent such a theft.

E4-24A *(Learning Objective 4: Evaluating internal control over cash payments)* Green Grass Golf Company manufactures a popular line of golf clubs. Green Grass Golf employs 188 workers and keeps their employment records on time sheets that show how many hours the employee works each week. On Friday the shop foreman collects the time sheets, checks them for accuracy, and delivers them to the payroll department for preparation of paycheques. The treasurer signs the paycheques and returns the cheques to the payroll department for distribution to the employees.

Identify the main internal control weakness in this situation, state how the weakness can hurt Green Grass Golf, and propose a way to correct the weakness.

■ spreadsheet

E4-25A *(Learning Objective 5: Preparing a cash budget)* Cole Communications, Inc., is preparing its cash budget for 2011. Cole ended 2010 with cash of $86 million, and managers need to keep a cash balance of at least $82 million for operations.

Collections from customers are expected to total $11,305 million during 2011, and payments for the cost of services and products should reach $6,167 million. Operating expense payments are budgeted at $2,544 million.

During 2011, Cole expects to invest $1,826 million in new equipment and sell older assets for $118 million. Debt payments scheduled for 2011 will total $603 million. The company forecasts net income of $885 million for 2011 and plans to pay dividends of $347 million.

Prepare Cole Communications' cash budget for 2011. Will the budgeted level of cash receipts leave Cole with the desired ending cash balance of $82 million, or will the company need additional financing? If so, how much?

E4-26A *(Learning Objective 5: Compensating balance agreement)* Assume Lenny's Lanes borrowed $14 million from Greenback Bank and agreed to (a) pay an interest rate of 7.7% and (b) maintain a compensating balance amount equal to 5.7% of the loan. Determine Lenny's Lanes' actual effective interest rate on this loan.

(Group B)

E4-27B (*Learning Objectives 1, 2: Learning about fraud; identifying internal control weaknesses*) Identify the internal control weakness in the following situations. State how the person can hurt the company.

writing assignment ■

   a. Jason Monroe works as a security guard at CITY parking in Dayton. Monroe has a master key to the cash box where customers pay for parking. Each night Monroe prepares the cash report that shows (a) the number of cars that parked on the lot and (b) the day's cash receipts. Linda Cooper, the CITY treasurer, checks Monroe's figures by multiplying the number of cars by the parking fee per car. Cooper then deposits the cash in the bank.

   b. Ashley Adams is the purchasing agent for Superior Golf Equipment. Adams prepares purchase orders based on requests from division managers of the company. Adams faxes the purchase order to suppliers who then ship the goods to Superior. Adams receives each incoming shipment and checks it for agreement with the purchase order and the related invoice. She then routes the goods to the respective division managers and sends the receiving report and the invoice to the accounting department for payment.

E4-28B (*Learning Objective 2: Identifying internal control strengths and weaknesses*) The following situations describe two cash payment situations and two cash receipt situations. In each pair, one set of internal controls is better than the other. Evaluate the internal controls in each situation as strong or weak, and give the reason for your answer.

Cash payments:

   a. Mike Milford Construction policy calls for construction supervisors to request the equipment needed for their jobs. The home office then purchases the equipment and has it shipped to the construction site.

   b. Superior Structures, Inc., policy calls for project supervisors to purchase the equipment needed for jobs. The supervisors then submit the paid receipts to the home office for reimbursement. This policy enables supervisors to get the equipment quickly and keep construction jobs moving.

Cash receipts:

   a. At Cramer Auto Parts, cash received by mail goes straight to the accountant, who debits Cash and credits Accounts Receivable to record the collections from customers. The Cramer accountant then deposits the cash in the bank.

   b. Cash received by mail at Better Vision Eye Clinic goes to the mail room, where a mail clerk opens envelopes and totals the cash receipts for the day. The mail clerk forwards customer cheques to the cashier for deposit in the bank and forwards the remittance slips to the accounting department for posting credits to customer accounts.

E4-29B (*Learning Objectives 1, 2: Learning about fraud; correcting an internal control weakness*) Sam Smith served as executive director of Downtown Scanlon, an organization created to revitalize Scanlon, Minnesota. Over the course of 11 years Smith embezzled $297,000. How did Smith do it? He did it by depositing subscriber cash receipts in his own bank account, writing Downtown Scanlon cheques to himself, and creating phony entities that Downtown Scanlon wrote cheques to.

writing assignment ■

   Downtown Scanlon was led by a board of directors comprised of civic leaders. Smith's embezzlement went undetected until Downtown Scanlon couldn't pay its bills.

   Give four ways Smith's embezzlement could have been prevented.

E4-30B (*Learning Objective 3: Classifying bank reconciliation items*) The following items appear on a bank reconciliation.

Classify each item as (a) an addition to the bank balance, (b) a subtraction from the bank balance, (c) an addition to the book balance, or (d) a subtraction from the book balance.

1. ___ Outstanding cheques
2. ___ Bank error: The bank credited our account for a deposit made by another bank customer.
3. ___ Service charge
4. ___ Deposits in transit
5. ___ NSF cheque
6. ___ Bank collection of a note receivable on our behalf
7. ___ Book error: We debited Cash for $300. The correct debit was $3,000.

E4-31B (*Learning Objective 3: Preparing a bank reconciliation*) D. J. Hill's chequebook and February bank statement show the following:

Date	Cheque No.	Item	Cheque	Deposit	Balance
2/1					$ 515
4	622	Art Cafe	$ 15		500
9		Dividends received		$ 115	615
13	623	General Tire Co.	40		575
14	624	QuickMobil	78		497
18	625	Cash	70		427
26	626	Woodway Baptist Church	85		342
28	627	Bent Tree Apartments	275		67
28		Paycheque		1,215	1,282

Balance			$515	
Add: Deposits			115	
Debit cheques:	No.	Amount		
	622	$15		
	623	40		
	624	87*		
	625	70	(212)	
Other charges:				
NSF cheque....................................		$20		
Service charge		15	(35)	
Balance			$383	

*This is the correct amount for cheque number 624.

❙ Requirement

1. Prepare Hill's bank reconciliation at February 28.

E4-32B (*Learning Objective 3: Preparing a bank reconciliation*) Harry Smith operates a bowling alley. He has just received the monthly bank statement at September 30 from City National Bank, and the statement shows an ending balance of $545. Listed on the statement are an EFT rent collection of $325, a service charge of $8, two NSF cheques totaling $125, and a $10 charge for printed cheques. In reviewing his cash records, Smith identifies outstanding cheques totaling $609 and a September 30 deposit in transit of $1,790. During September, he recorded a $310 cheque for the salary of a part-time employee as $31. Smith's Cash account shows a September 30 cash balance of $1,823. How much cash does Smith actually have at September 30?

E4-33B (*Learning Objective 3: Making journal entries from a bank reconciliation*) Use the data from Exercise 4-32B to make the journal entries that Smith should record on September 30 to update his Cash account. Include an explanation for each entry.

E4-34B (*Learning Objective 4: Evaluating internal control over cash receipts*) Radley stores use point-of-sale terminals as cash registers. The register shows the amount of each sale, the cash received from the customer, and any change returned to the customer. The machine also produces a customer receipt but keeps no record of transactions. At the end of the day, the clerk counts the cash in the register and gives it to the cashier for deposit in the company bank account.

writing assignment ■

Write a memo to convince the store manager that there is an internal control weakness over cash receipts. Identify the weakness that gives an employee the best opportunity to steal cash and state how to prevent such a theft.

E4-35B (*Learning Objective 4: Evaluating internal control over cash payments*) Beautiful Meadows Golf Company manufactures a popular line of golf clubs. Beautiful Meadows Golf employs 173 workers and keeps their employment records on time sheets that show how many hours the employee works each week. On Friday the shop foreman collects the time sheets, checks them for accuracy, and delivers them to the payroll department for preparation of paycheques. The treasurer signs the paycheques and returns the cheques to the payroll department for distribution to the employees.

Identify the main internal control weakness in this situation, state how the weakness can hurt Beautiful Meadows Golf, and propose a way to correct the weakness.

E4-36B (*Learning Objective 5: Preparing a cash budget*) Fallon Communications, Inc., is preparing its cash budget for 2011. Fallon ended 2010 with cash of $82 million, and managers need to keep a cash balance of at least $81 million for operations.

■ spreadsheet

Collections from customers are expected to total $11,307 million during 2011, and payments for the cost of services and products should reach $6,174 million. Operating expense payments are budgeted at $2,545 million.

During 2011, Fallon expects to invest $1,831 million in new equipment and sell older assets for $121 million. Debt payments scheduled for 2011 will total $604 million. The company forecasts net income of $883 million for 2011 and plans to pay dividends of $341 million.

Prepare Fallon Communications' cash budget for 2011. Will the budgeted level of cash receipts leave Fallon with the desired ending cash balance of $81 million, or will the company need additional financing? If so, how much?

E4-37B (*Learning Objective 5: Compensating balance agreement*) Assume Dan's Drums borrowed $19 million from Need It Now Bank and agreed to (a) pay an interest rate of 7.1% and (b) maintain a compensating balance amount equal to 5.8% of the loan. Determine Dan's Drums' actual effective interest rate on this loan.

Challenge Exercises

E4-38 (*Learning Objectives 1, 2, 4: Learning about fraud; evaluating internal controls over cash payments; focusing on ethical considerations*) Susan Healey, the owner of Susan's Perfect Presents, has delegated management of the business to Louise Owens, a friend. Healey drops by to meet customers and check up on cash receipts, but Owens buys the merchandise and handles cash payments. Business has been very good lately, and cash receipts have kept pace with the apparent level of sales. However, for a year or so, the amount of cash on hand has been too low. When asked about this, Owens explains that suppliers are charging more for goods than in the past. During the past year, Owens has taken two expensive vacations, and Healey wonders how Owens can afford these trips on her $59,000 annual salary and commissions.

List at least three ways Owens could be defrauding Healey of cash. In each instance also identify how Healey can determine whether Owens' actions are ethical. Limit your answers to the store's cash payments. The business pays all suppliers by cheque (no EFTs).

E4-39 (*Learning Objective 5: Preparing and using a cash budget*) Dan Davis, the chief financial officer, is responsible for The Furniture Mart's cash budget for 2010. The budget will help Davis determine the amount of long-term borrowing needed to end the year with a cash balance of $130,000. Davis's assistants have assembled budget data for 2010, which the computer printed in alphabetical order. Not all the data items reproduced below are used in preparing the cash budget.

(Assumed Data)	(In thousands)
Actual cash balance, December 31, 2009	$ 130
Budgeted total assets	22,377
Budgeted total current assets	7,976
Budgeted total current liabilities	4,260
Budgeted total liabilities	11,088
Budgeted total shareholders' equity..........................	7,197
Collections from customers	21,800
Dividend payments	317
Issuance of shares...	647
Net income...	1,183
Payment of long-term and short-term debt...............	980
Payment of operating expenses	2,349
Purchases of inventory items	14,545
Purchase of property and equipment.........................	1,528

❙ Requirements

1. Prepare the cash budget of The Furniture Mart, Inc.
2. Compute The Furniture Mart's budgeted current ratio and debt ratio at December 31, 2010. Based on these ratio values, and on the cash budget, would you lend $100,000 to The Furniture Mart? Give the reason for your decision.

Quiz

Test your understanding of internal control and cash by answering the following questions. Answer each question by selecting the best choice from among the answers given.

Q4-40 All of the following are objectives of internal control except
a. to comply with legal requirements.
b. to maximize net income.
c. to ensure accurate and reliable accounting records.
d. to safeguard assets.

Q4-41 All of the following are internal control procedures except
a. Sarbanes-Oxley reforms.
b. electronic devices.
c. assignment of responsibilities.
d. internal and external audits.

Q4-42 Requiring that an employee with no access to cash do the accounting is an example of which characteristic of internal control?

a. Assignment of responsibility

b. Competent and reliable personnel

c. Monitoring of controls

d. Separation of duties

Q4-43 All of the following are controls for cash received over the counter except

a. the cash drawer should open only when the salesclerk enters an amount on the keys.

b. a printed receipt must be given to the customer.

c. the customer should be able to see the amounts entered into the cash register.

d. the sales clerk must have access to the cash register tape.

Q4-44 In a bank reconciliation, an outstanding cheque is

a. deducted from the book balance.

b. added to the bank balance.

c. added to the book balance.

d. deducted from the bank balance.

Q4-45 In a bank reconciliation, a bank collection of a note receivable is

a. deducted from the bank balance.

b. added to the book balance.

c. added to the bank balance.

d. deducted from the book balance.

Q4-46 In a bank reconciliation, an EFT cash payment is

a. deducted from the bank balance.

b. deducted from the book balance.

c. added to the book balance.

d. added to the bank balance.

Q4-47 If a bookkeeper mistakenly recorded a $35 deposit as $53, the error would be shown on the bank reconciliation as a

a. $53 deduction from the book balance.

b. $53 addition to the book balance.

c. $18 deduction from the book balance.

d. $18 addition to the book balance.

Q4-48 If a bank reconciliation included a deposit in transit of $880, the entry to record this reconciling item would include a

a. credit to cash for $880.

b. debit to cash for $880.

c. credit to prepaid insurance for $880.

d. no entry is required.

Q4-49 In a bank reconciliation, interest revenue earned on your bank balance is

a. deducted from the book balance.

b. deducted from the bank balance.

c. added to the bank balance.

d. added to the book balance.

Q4-50 Before paying an invoice for goods received on account, the controller or treasurer should ensure that

a. the company has not already paid this invoice.

b. the company is paying for the goods it ordered.

c. the company is paying for the goods it actually received.

d. all of the above.

Q4-51 The Little French Bakery is budgeting cash for 2011. The cash balance at December 31, 2010, was $6,000. The Little French Bakery budgets 2011 cash receipts at $83,000. Estimated cash payments include $36,000 for inventory, $26,000 for operating expenses, and $19,000 to expand the store. The Little French Bakery needs a minimum cash balance of $15,000 at all times. The Little French Bakery expects to earn net income of $78,000 during 2011. What is the final result of the company's cash budget for 2011?

a. Pay off $14,000 of debt.

b. $7,000 available for additional investments.

c. Must arrange new financing for $7,000.

d. $14,000 available for additional investments.

Problems

MyAccountingLab

> All of the Group A and Group B problems can be found within MyAccountingLab, an online homework and practice environment. Your instructor may ask you to complete these problems using MyAccountingLab.

(Group A)

writing assignment ■

P4-52A (*Learning Objectives 1, 2: Learning about fraud; identifying internal control weaknesses*) Celtic Imports is an importer of silver, brass, and furniture items from Ireland. Eileen Sullivan is the general manager of Celtic Imports. Sullivan employs two other people in the business. Mary McNicholas serves as the buyer for Celtic Imports. In her work McNicholas travels throughout Ireland to find interesting new products. When McNicholas finds a new product, she arranges for Celtic Imports to purchase and pay for the item. She helps the Irish artisans prepare their invoices and then faxes the invoices to Sullivan in the company office.

Sullivan operates out of an office in Boston, Massachusetts. The office is managed by Margaret Sweeney, who handles the mail, keeps the accounting records, makes bank deposits, and prepares the monthly bank reconciliation. Virtually all of Celtic Imports' cash receipts arrive by mail—from sales made to Target, Pier 1 Imports, and Macy's.

Sweeney also prepares cheques for payment based on invoices that come in from the suppliers who have been contacted by McNicholas. To maintain control over cash payments, Sullivan examines the paperwork and signs all cheques.

❙ Requirement

1. Identify all the major internal control weaknesses in Celtic Imports' system and how the resulting action could hurt Celtic Imports. Also state how to correct each weakness.

writing assignment ■

P4-53A (*Learning Objectives 1, 4: Learning about fraud; identifying internal control weakness*) Each of the following situations reveals an internal control weakness:

   a. In evaluating the internal control over cash payments of Framingham Manufacturing, an auditor learns that the purchasing agent is responsible for purchasing diamonds for use in the company's manufacturing process, approving the invoices for payment, and signing the cheques. No supervisor reviews the purchasing agent's work.

   b. Leslie Joyce owns an architectural firm. Joyce's staff consists of 18 professional architects, and Joyce manages the office. Often, Joyce's work requires her to travel to meet with clients. During the past six months, Joyce has observed that when she returns from a business trip, the architecture jobs in the office have not progressed satisfactorily. Joyce learns that when she is away, two of her senior architects take over office management and neglect their normal duties. One employee could manage the office.

   c. J. T. Durfee has been an employee of the City of Maron for many years. Because the city is small, Durfee performs all accounting duties, plus opening the mail, preparing the bank deposit, and preparing the bank reconciliation.

❙ Requirements

1. Identify the missing internal control characteristic in each situation.
2. Identify each firm's possible problem.
3. Propose a solution to the problem.

P4-54A *(Learning Objective 3: Using the bank reconciliation as a control device)* The cash data of Dunlap Automotive for July 2010 follow:

writing assignment ■

■ **spreadsheet**

Cash					Account No. 101
Date	Item	Jrnl. Ref.	Debit	Credit	Balance
Jul 1	Balance				7,900
31		CR6	9,124		17,024
31		CP11		9,087	7,937

Cash Receipts (CR)		Cash Payments (CP)	
Date	Cash Debit	Cheque No.	Cash Credit
Jul 2	$2,771	3113	$1,503
8	516	3114	1,149
10	1,682	3115	1,630
16	871	3116	19
22	352	3117	825
29	924	3118	91
30	2,008	3119	440
Total	$9,124	3120	965
		3121	205
		3122	2,260
		Total	$9,087

Dunlap received the following bank statement on July 31, 2010:

Bank Statement for July 2010

Beginning balance		$ 7,900
Deposits and other additions:		
Jul 1.............................	$ 750 EFT	
4.............................	2,771	
9.............................	516	
12...........................	1,682	
17...........................	871	
22...........................	352	
23...........................	1,250 BC	8,192
Cheques and other deductions:		
Jul 7.............................	$1,503	
13...........................	1,360	
14...........................	407 US	
15...........................	1,149	
18...........................	19	
21...........................	334 EFT	
26...........................	825	
30...........................	91	
30...........................	25 SC	(5,713)
Ending balance....................		$10,379

Explanation: BC—bank collection, EFT—electronic funds transfer, US—unauthorized signature, SC—service charge

Additional data for the bank reconciliation include the following:

a. The EFT deposit was a receipt of monthly rent. The EFT debit was a monthly insurance payment.
b. The unauthorized signature cheque was received from a customer.
c. The correct amount of cheque number 3115, a payment on account, is $1,360. (Dunlap's accountant mistakenly recorded the cheque for $1,630.)

I Requirements

1. Prepare the Dunlap Automotive bank reconciliation at July 31, 2010.
2. Describe how a bank account and the bank reconciliation help the general manager control Dunlap's cash.

■ spreadsheet

P4-55A (*Learning Objective 3: Preparing a bank reconciliation and the related journal entries*) The August 31 bank statement of Dickson Engineering Associates has just arrived from Carolina First Bank. To prepare the Dickson bank reconciliation, you gather the following data:

a. Dickson's Cash account shows a balance of $8,152.71 on August 31.
b. The August 31 bank balance is $8,879.24.
c. The bank statement shows that Dickson earned $15.85 of interest on its bank balance during August. This amount was added to Dickson's bank balance.
d. Dickson pays utilities ($730) and insurance ($280) by EFT.
e. The following Dickson cheques did not clear the bank by August 31:

Cheque No.	Amount
237	$401.00
288	74.82
291	33.25
293	165.55
294	236.00
295	47.75
296	107.85

f. The bank statement includes a deposit of $899.15, collected on account by the bank on behalf of Dickson.
g. The bank statement lists a $5.50 bank service charge.
h. On August 31, the Dickson treasurer deposited $383.54, which will appear on the September bank statement.
i. The bank statement includes a $398.00 deposit that Dickson did not make. The bank added $398.00 to Dickson's account for another company's deposit.
j. The bank statement includes two charges for returned cheques from customers. One is a $185.50 cheque received from a customer with the imprint "Unauthorized Signature." The other is a nonsufficient funds cheque in the amount of $68.15 received from another customer.

I Requirements

1. Prepare the bank reconciliation for Dickson Engineering Associates.
2. Journalize the August 31 transactions needed to update Dickson's Cash account. Include an explanation for each entry.

writing assignment ■

P4-56A (*Learning Objectives 2, 4: Identifying internal control weakness in sales and cash receipts*) Fresh Skin Care makes all sales on credit. Cash receipts arrive by mail, usually within 30 days of the sale. Kate Martin opens envelopes and separates the cheques from the accompanying remittance advices. Martin forwards the cheques to another employee, who makes the daily bank deposit but has no access to the accounting records. Martin sends the remittance advices, which show the amount of cash received, to the accounting department for entry in the accounts receivable. Martin's only other duty is to grant allowances to customers. (An *allowance* decreases the amount that the customer must pay.) When Martin receives a customer cheque for less than the full amount of the invoice, she records the allowance in the accounting records and forwards the document to the accounting department.

❚ Requirement

1. You are a new employee of Fresh Skin Care. Write a memo to the company president identifying the internal control weakness in this situation. State how to correct the weakness.

P4-57A (*Learning Objective 5: Preparing a cash budget and using cash-flow information*) John Watson, chief financial officer of Jasper Wireless, is responsible for the company's budgeting process. Watson's staff is preparing the Jasper cash budget for 2011. A key input to the budgeting process is last year's statement of cash flows, which follows (amounts in thousands):

Jasper Wireless Statement of Cash Flows 2010	
(In thousands)	
Cash Flows from Operating Activities	
Collections from customers	$ 64,000
Interest received	300
Purchases of inventory	(49,000)
Operating expenses	(13,500)
Net cash provided by operating activities	1,800
Cash Flows from Investing Activities	
Purchases of equipment	(4,800)
Purchases of investments	(400)
Sales of investments	500
Net cash used for investing activities	(4,700)
Cash Flows from Financing Activities	
Payment of long-term debt	(400)
Issuance of shares	1,700
Payment of cash dividends	(300)
Net cash provided by financing activities	1,000
Cash	
Increase (decrease) in Cash	(1,900)
Cash, beginning of year	3,400
Cash, end of year	$ 1,500

❚ Requirements

1. Prepare the Jasper Wireless cash budget for 2011. Date the budget simply "2011" and denote the beginning and ending cash balances as "beginning" and "ending." Assume the company expects 2011 to be the same as 2010, but with the following changes:
   a. In 2011, the company expects a 10% increase in collections from customers and a 20% increase in purchases of inventory.
   b. There will be no sales of investments in 2011.
   c. Jasper plans to issue no shares in 2011.
   d. Jasper plans to end the year with a cash balance of $3,800.
2. Does the company's cash budget for 2011 suggest that Jasper is growing, holding steady, or decreasing in size? (Challenge)

(Group B)

P4-58B (*Learning Objectives 1, 2: Learning about fraud; identifying internal control weaknesses*) International Imports is an importer of silver, brass, and furniture items from France. Elaine Spencer is the general manager of International Imports. Spencer employs two other people in the business. Marie Walsh serves as the buyer for International Imports. In her work Walsh travels throughout France to find interesting new products. When Walsh finds a new product, she arranges for International Imports to purchase and pay for the item. She helps the French artisans prepare their invoices and then faxes the invoices to Spencer in the company office.

Spencer operates out of an office in Brooklyn, New York. The office is managed by Donna Durkin, who handles the mail, keeps the accounting records, makes bank deposits, and prepares the monthly bank reconciliation. Virtually all of International Imports' cash receipts arrive by mail—from sales made to Target, Crate and Barrel, and Williams-Sonoma.

Durkin also prepares cheques for payment based on invoices that come in from the suppliers who have been contacted by Walsh. To maintain control over cash payments, Spencer examines the paperwork and signs all cheques.

❙ Requirement

1. Identify all the major internal control weaknesses in International Imports' system and how the resulting action could hurt International Imports. Also state how to correct each weakness.

P4-59B (*Learning Objectives 1, 4: Learning about fraud; identifying internal control weakness*) Each of the following situations reveals an internal control weakness:

Situation a. In evaluating the internal control over cash payments of York Manufacturing, an auditor learns that the purchasing agent is responsible for purchasing diamonds for use in the company's manufacturing process, approving the invoices for payment, and signing the cheques. No supervisor reviews the purchasing agent's work.

Situation b. Rita White owns an architectural firm. White's staff consists of 16 professional architects, and White manages the office. Often, White's work requires her to travel to meet with clients. During the past six months, White has observed that when she returns from a business trip, the architecture jobs in the office have not progressed satisfactorily. White learns that when she is away, two of her senior architects take over office management and neglect their normal duties. One employee could manage the office.

Situation c. M. J. Dowd has been an employee of the City of Northport for many years. Because the city is small, Dowd performs all accounting duties, plus opening the mail, preparing the bank deposit, and preparing the bank reconciliation.

❙ Requirements

1. Identify the missing internal control characteristic in each situation.
2. Identify each firm's possible problem.
3. Propose a solution to the problem.

P4-60B *(Learning Objective 3: Using the bank reconciliation as a control device)* The cash data of Donald Automotive for January 2010 follow:

Cash					Account No. 101
Date	Item	Jrnl. Rcf.	Debit	Credit	Balance
Jan 1	Balance				7,200
31		CR 6	9,127		16,327
31		CP 11		9,983	6,344

	Cash Receipts (CR)		Cash Payments (CP)	
Date	Cash Debit	Cheque No.	Cash Credit	
Jan 2	$2,726	3113	$1,475	
8	572	3114	1,925	
10	1,647	3115	1,530	
16	837	3116	32	
22	436	3117	870	
29	856	3118	132	
30	2,053	3119	493	
Total	$9,127	3120	985	
		3121	219	
		3122	2,322	
		Total	$9,983	

Donald received the following bank statement on January 31, 2010:

Bank Statement for January 2010		
Beginning balance		$ 7,200
Deposits and other additions:		
Jan 1............................	$ 650 EFT	
4............................	2,726	
9............................	572	
12............................	1,647	
17............................	837	
22............................	436	
23............................	1,350 BC	8,218
Cheques and other deductions:		
Jan 7............................	$1,475	
13............................	1,350	
14............................	466 US	
15............................	1,925	
18............................	32	
21............................	331 EFT	
26............................	870	
30............................	132	
30............................	20 SC	(6,601)
Ending balance....................		$ 8,817

Explanation: BC—bank collection, EFT—electronic funds transfer, US—unauthorized signature, SC—service charge

APPLY YOUR KNOWLEDGE

Decision Cases

Case 1. (*Learning Objectives 1, 2, 3: Learning about fraud; using a bank reconciliation to detect a theft*) Environmental Concerns, Inc., has poor internal control. Recently, Oscar Benz, the manager, has suspected the bookkeeper of stealing. Details of the business's cash position at September 30 follow.

    a. The Cash account shows a balance of $10,402. This amount includes a September 30 deposit of $3,794 that does not appear on the September 30 bank statement.

    b. The September 30 bank statement shows a balance of $8,224. The bank statement lists a $200 bank collection, an $8 service charge, and a $36 NSF cheque. The accountant has not recorded any of these items.

    c. At September 30, the following cheques are outstanding:

Cheque No.	Amount
154	$116
256	150
278	853
291	990
292	206
293	145

    d. The bookkeeper receives all incoming cash and makes the bank deposits. He also reconciles the monthly bank statement. Here is his September 30 reconciliation:

Balance per books, September 30..............		$10,402
Add: Outstanding cheques		1,460
Bank collection.................................		200
Subtotal...		12,062
Less: Deposits in transit............................	$3,794	
Service charge	8	
NSF cheque......................................	36	(3,838)
Balance per bank, September 30................		$ 8,224

I Requirement

1. Benz has requested that you determine whether the bookkeeper has stolen cash from the business and, if so, how much. He also asks you to explain how the bookkeeper attempted to conceal the theft. To make this determination, you perform a proper bank reconciliation. There are no bank or book errors. Benz also asks you to evaluate the internal controls and to recommend any changes needed to improve them.

Case 2. (*Learning Objectives 1, 2: Learning about fraud; correcting an internal control weakness*) This case is based on an actual situation experienced by one of the authors. Gilead Construction, headquartered in Topeka, Kansas, built a motel in Kansas City. The construction foreman, Slim Pickins, hired the workers for the project. Pickins had his workers fill out the necessary tax forms and sent the employment documents to the home office.

Work on the motel began on May 1 and ended in December. Each Thursday evening, Pickins filled out a time card that listed the hours worked by each employee during the five-day work-week ended at 5 p.m. on Thursday. Pickins faxed the time sheets to the home office, which prepared the payroll cheques on Friday morning. Pickins drove to the home office after lunch on Friday, picked up the payroll cheques, and returned to the construction site. At 5 p.m. on Friday, Pickins distributed the paycheques to the workers.

    a. Describe in detail the internal control weakness in this situation. Specify what negative result could occur because of the internal control weakness.

    b. Describe what you would do to correct the internal control weakness.

Ethical Issues

For each of the following situations, answer the following questions:

    1. What is the ethical issue in this situation?

    2. What are the alternatives?

    3. Who are the stakeholders? What are the possible consequences to each? Analyze from the following standpoints: (a) economic, (b) legal, and (c) ethical.

    4. Place yourself in the role of the decision maker. What would you do? How would you justify your decision?

Issue 1. Sunrise Bank recently appointed the accounting firm of Smith, Godfroy, and Hannaford as the bank's auditor. Sunrise quickly became one of Smith, Godfroy, and Hannaford's largest clients. Subject to banking regulations, Sunrise must provide for any expected losses on notes receivable that Sunrise may not collect in full.

During the course of the audit, Smith, Godfroy, and Hannaford determined that three large notes receivable of Sunrise seem questionable. Smith, Godfroy, and Hannaford discussed these loans with Susan Carter, controller of Sunrise. Carter assured the auditors that these notes were good and that the makers of the notes will be able to pay their notes after the economy improves.

Smith, Godfroy, and Hannaford stated that Sunrise must record a loss for a portion of these notes receivable to account for the likelihood that Sunrise may never collect their full amount. Carter objected and threatened to dismiss Smith, Godfroy, and Hannaford if the auditor demands that the bank record the loss. Smith, Godfroy, and Hannaford want to keep Sunrise as a client. In fact, Smith, Godfroy, and Hannaford were counting on the revenue from the Sunrise audit to finance an expansion of the firm.

Issue 2. Barry Galvin is executive vice president of Community Bank. Active in community affairs, Galvin serves on the board of directors of The Salvation Army. The Salvation Army is expanding rapidly and is considering relocating. At a recent meeting, The Salvation Army decided to buy 250 acres of land on the edge of town. The owner of the property is Olga Nadar, a major depositor in Community Bank. Nadar is completing a bitter divorce, and Galvin knows that Nadar is eager to sell her property. In view of Nadar's difficult situation, Galvin believes Nadar would accept a low offer for the land. Realtors have appraised the property at $3.6 million.

Issue 3. Community Bank has a loan receivable from IMS Chocolates. IMS is six months late in making payments to the bank, and Jan French, a Community Bank vice president, is assisting IMS to restructure its debt.

French learns that IMS is depending on landing a contract with Snicker Foods, another Community Bank client. French also serves as Snicker Foods' loan officer at the bank. In this capacity, French is aware that Snicker is considering bankruptcy. No one else outside Snicker Foods knows this. French has been a great help to IMS and IMS's owner is counting on French's expertise in loan workouts to advise the company through this difficult process. To help the bank collect on this large loan, French has a strong motivation to alert IMS of Snicker's financial difficulties.

Focus on Financials: ■ Nokia Corporation

Refer to the **Nokia** financial statements in Appendix A at the end of this book. The bank and cash section of the Balance Sheet shows a balance of $1,706 million as of December 31, 2008, and is made up of many different bank accounts, as well as time deposits, certificates of deposit, and perhaps government securities that are equivalent to cash. Suppose Nokia's year-end bank statement for the operating bank account, dated December 31, 2008, has just arrived at company headquarters. Further assume the bank statement shows Nokia's cash balance at $324 million and that Nokia's operating bank account has a balance of $316 million on the books (since this is only one of many bank accounts, it will not be possible to match it to the $1,706 million that is shown).

▌Requirements

1. You must determine the correct balance for cash in the operating bank account on December 31, 2008. Suppose you uncover the following reconciling items (all amounts are assumed and are stated in millions):

   a. Interest earned on bank balance, $1.
   b. Outstanding cheques, $8.
   c. Bank collections of various items, $2.
   d. Deposits in transit, $3.

   Prepare a bank reconciliation to show how Nokia arrived at the correct amount of cash in the operating bank account at December 31, 2008. Journal entries are not required.

2. Look at the bank and cash section. Why did cash change during 2008? (the statement of cash flows holds the answer to this question.) Analyze the five largest individual items on the statement of cash flows (not the summary subtotals such as "net cash provided by operating activities"). For each of the five individual items, state how Nokia's actions affected cash. Show amounts in millions and round to the nearest $1 million.

Group Project

You are promoting a rock concert in your area. Assume you organize as a corporation, with each member of your group purchasing $10,000 of the corporation's shares. Therefore, each of you is risking some hard-earned money on this venture. Assume it is April 1 and that the concert will be performed on June 30. Your promotional activities begin immediately, and ticket sales start on May 1. You expect to sell all of the firm's assets, pay all the liabilities, and distribute all remaining cash to the group members by July 31.

▌Requirements

Write an internal control manual that will help to safeguard the assets of the business. The manual should address the following aspects of internal control:

1. Assign responsibilities among the group members.
2. Authorize individuals, including group members and any outsiders that you need to hire to perform specific jobs.
3. Separate duties among the group and any employees.
4. Describe all documents needed to account for and safeguard the business's assets.

For online homework, exercises, and problems that provide you with immediate feedback, please visit www.myaccountinglab.com

Quick Check Answers

1. *g, e, h, d, f, c, a*   3. *d*   6. *e*   9. *d*
   Unused: *b, i*   4. *a*   7. *a*   10. *d*
2. *b*   5. *c*   8. *d*   11. *a*

5

Short-Term Investments & Receivables

SPOTLIGHT: Nestlé

What comes to mind when you think of **Nestlé**? Do you think of coffee, snacks and other confectionary items? Nestlé is "the world's leading nutrition, health and wellness" company. You might automatically think that inventories are the company's largest current asset. However, as of December 31, 2008, short-term investments and receivables account for about 45% of Nestlé's current assets. In fact, receivables, of about CHF (Swiss Franc) 13.4 billion, are Nestlé's largest current asset.

Another important current asset is short-term investments. As you can see from Nestlé's 2008 balance sheet, Nestlé had about CHF 1.3 billion of short-term investments at the end of 2008. You'll notice that short-term investments are listed on the balance sheet immediately after cash and before receivables. Let's see why.

investments these items may be reported on the income statement as Other revenue, gains, and (losses), as shown in Exhibit 5-2.

EXHIBIT 5-2 | **Reporting Short-Term Investments and the Related Revenues, Gains, and Losses**

Balance sheet		Income statement	
Current assets:..........................		Revenues...........................	$ XXX
Cash....................................	$ XXX	Expenses	XXX
Short-term investments, at		Other revenue, gains	
market value	102,000	and (losses):	
Accounts receivable................	XXX	Interest revenue............	XXX
		Dividend income...........	4,000
		Unrealized gain on	
		investment...............	2,000
		Net income...................	$ XXX

Realized Gains and Losses. A *realized* gain or loss occurs only when the investor sells an investment. This gain or loss is different from the unrealized gain that we reported for Nestlé above. The result may be a:

- Realized gain = Sale price is *greater than* the Investment carrying amount
- Realized loss = Sale price is *less than* the Investment carrying amount

Suppose Nestlé sells its Sony shares during 2011. Remember that we have already updated the Investment in Sony Corp account to $102,000 on December 31, 2010. If the sale price is $98,000, Nestlé makes this journal entry:

2011			
Jan 19	Cash	98,000	
	Loss on Sale of Investments	4,000	
	Investment in Sony Corp		102,000
	Sold investments at a loss.		

Investment in Sony Corp		Loss on Sale of Investments	
100,000		4,000	
2,000	102,000		

Accountants rarely use the word "Realized" in the account title. A gain (or a loss) is understood to be a realized gain (or loss) arising from a sale transaction. Unrealized gains and losses are clearly labeled as *unrealized*. Nestlé would report Gain (or Loss) on Sale of Investments among the "Other" items of the income statement, as shown in Exhibit 5-2.

MID-CHAPTER SUMMARY PROBLEM

The largest current asset on Waverly Corporation's balance sheet is Short-Term Investments. The investments consist of shares in other corporations and cost Waverly $8,660. At the balance sheet date, the fair market value of these securities is $9,000 (amounts in millions).

Suppose Waverly holds the share investments in the hope of selling at a profit within a few months. How will Waverly classify the investments? What will Waverly report on the balance sheet at December 31, 2010? What will Waverly report on its 2010 income statement? Show a T-account for Short-Term Investments.

Answer

These investments in trading securities are *current assets* as reported on the 2010 balance sheet, and Waverly's 2010 income statement will report as follows (amounts in millions):

Balance sheet		Income statement	
Current assets:		Other revenue and expense:	
Cash....................................	$ XX	Unrealized gain on investments	
Short-term investments,		($9,000 – $8,660)	$ 340
at market value	9,000		

Short-Term Investments

8,660	
340	

Suppose Waverly sells the investment in securities for $8,700 in 2011. Journalize the sale and then show the Short-Term Investments T-account as it appears after the sale.

Answer

	(In millions)	
Cash..	8,700	
Loss on Sale of Investments.........	300	
Short-Term Investments..........		9,000
Sold investments at a loss.		

Short-Term Investments

8,660	
340	9,000

ACCOUNTS AND NOTES RECEIVABLE

Receivables are the third most liquid asset—after cash and short-term investments. Most of the remainder of this chapter shows how to account for receivables.

Types of Receivables

Receivables are monetary claims against others. Receivables are acquired mainly by selling goods and services (accounts receivable) and by lending money (notes receivable). The journal entries to record the receivables can be shown as follows:

Performing a Service on Account		Lending Money on a Note Receivable	
Accounts Receivable......................	XXX	Note Receivable..........................	XXX
Service Revenue........................	XXX	Cash..	XXX
Performed a service on account.		*Loaned money to another company.*	

The two major types of receivables are accounts receivable and notes receivable. A business's *accounts receivables* are the amounts collectible from customers from the sale of goods and services. Accounts receivable, which typically classified are *current assets*, are sometimes called *trade receivables, debtors* or *receivables*. The use of the word "trade" is usually to separate receivables (and payables) arising from the selling of goods or provision of services to customers (and buying of goods or services from suppliers) as opposed to non-trade receivables.

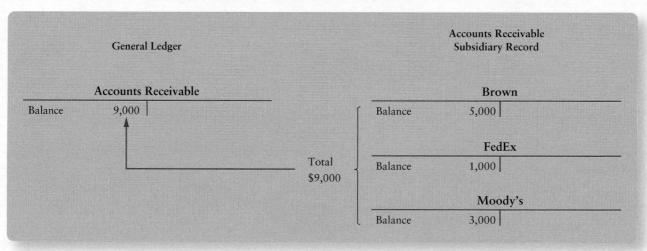

The Accounts Receivable account in the general ledger serves as a *control account* that summarizes the total amount receivable from all customers. Companies also keep a *subsidiary record* of accounts receivable with a separate account for each customer, illustrated as follows:

- *Notes receivable* are more formal contracts than accounts receivable. For a note, the borrower signs a written promise to pay the lender a definite sum at the **maturity** date, plus interest. This is why notes are also called promissory notes. The note may require the borrower to pledge *security* for the loan. This means that the borrower gives the lender permission to claim certain assets, called *collateral*, if the borrower fails to pay the amount due. We cover the details of notes receivable starting on page 306.
- *Other receivables* is a miscellaneous category for all receivables other than accounts receivable and notes receivable. Examples include loans to employees and to related companies.

Internal Controls over Cash Collections on Account

Businesses that sell on credit receive most of their cash receipts from collections of accounts receivable. Internal control over collections on account is important. Chapter 4 discusses control procedures for cash receipts, but another element of internal control deserves emphasis here—the separation of cash-handling and cash-accounting duties. Consider the following case:

Central Paint Company is a small, family-owned business that takes pride in the loyalty of its workers. Most employees have been with Central for 10 or more years. The company makes 90% of its sales on account and receives most of its cash (in the form of cheques) by mail.

The office staff consists of a bookkeeper and an office supervisor. The bookkeeper maintains the general ledger and a subsidiary record of individual customer accounts receivable. The bookkeeper also makes the daily bank deposit.

The supervisor prepares monthly financial statements and any special reports the company needs. The supervisor also takes sales orders from customers and serves as office manager.

Can you identify the internal control weakness here? The problem is that the bookkeeper makes the bank deposit. Remember the **AMEX Products** case in Chapter 4? With this cash-handling duty, the bookkeeper could lap accounts receivable. Alternatively, he or she could steal an incoming customer cheque and write off the customer's account as uncollectible. The customer doesn't complain because the bookkeeper wrote off the customer's account, and Central therefore stops pursuing collection.

How can this weakness be corrected? The supervisor—not the bookkeeper—could open incoming mail and make the daily bank deposit. The bookkeeper should *not* be allowed to handle cash. Only the remittance advices should be forwarded to the bookkeeper to credit customer accounts receivable. Removing cash handling from the bookkeeper and keeping the accounts away from the supervisor separates duties and strengthens internal control.

Using a bank lockbox achieves the same separation of duties. Customers send their payments directly to Central Paint Company's bank, which records cash as the cash goes into Central's bank account. The bank then forwards the remittance advice to Central's bookkeeper, who credits the customer account. No Central Paint employee even touches incoming cash.

How Do We Manage the Risk of Not Collecting?

In Chapters 1 to 4, we used many different companies to illustrate how to account for a business. Chapter 1 began with **Carrefour**, the world's second largest retailer. Whilst most of its sales are in cash, Carrefour still has about €3 billion in receivables. **De Beers**, **DP World**, and Nestlé in this chapter, all hold substantial amounts of receivables from selling goods or providing services on credit.

Selling on credit creates both a benefit and a cost:

- *Benefit*: Customers who cannot pay cash immediately can buy on credit, so sales and profits increase.
- *Cost*: The company cannot collect from some customers. Accountants label this cost **uncollectible-account expense**, **doubtful-account expense**, or **bad-debt expense**.

By selling on credit, companies run the risk of not collecting some receivables. Unfortunately, some customers don't pay their debts. The prospect of failing to collect from a customer provides the biggest challenge in accounting for receivables. The Decision Guidelines address this challenge.

DECISION GUIDELINES

MANAGING AND ACCOUNTING FOR RECEIVABLES

Here are the management and accounting issues a business faces when the company extends credit to customers. For each issue, the Decision Guidelines propose a plan of action. Let's look at a business situation: Suppose you open a health club near your college. Assume you will let customers use the club and bill them for their monthly dues. What challenges will you encounter by extending credit to customers? The main issues in *managing* receivables, along with plans of action, are:

Issues	Plan of Action
1. What are the benefits and the costs of extending credit to customers?	1. Benefit—Increase in sales. Cost—Risk of not collecting.
2. Extend credit only to creditworthy customers.	2. Run a credit check on prospective customers.
3. Separate cash-handling and accounting duties to keep employees from stealing the cash collected from customers.	3. Design the internal control system to separate duties.
4. Pursue collection from customers to maximize cash flow.	4. Keep a close eye on customer pay habits. Send second and third statements to slow-paying customers, if necessary.

The main issues in accounting for receivables, and the related plans of action, are (amounts are assumed):

Issues	Plan of Action
1. Measure and report receivables on the balance sheet at their net realizable value, the amount we expect to collect. This is the appropriate amount to report for receivables.	Report receivables at their net realizable value: **Balance sheet** Receivables.. $1,000 Less: Allowance for uncollectibles............... (80) Receivables, net.. $ 920
2. Measure and report the expense associated with failure to collect receivables. This expense is called *uncollectible-account expense* and is reported on the income statement.	Measure the expense of not collecting from customers: **Income statement** Sales (or service) revenue............................. $8,000 Expenses: Uncollectible-account expense................. 190

These guidelines lead to our next topic, Accounting for Uncollectible Receivables.

ACCOUNTING FOR UNCOLLECTIBLE RECEIVABLES

A company gets an account receivable only when it sells its product or service on credit (on account). You'll recall that the entry to record the earning of revenue on account is (amount assumed)

Accounts Receivable	1,000	
Sales Revenue (or Service Revenue)		1,000
Earned revenue on account.		

Ideally, the company would collect cash for all of its receivables. But unfortunately, this does not happen all the time. How do we account for uncollectible receivables?

Nestlé reported "Trade and other receivables" of CHF 13.4 billion (line 3) on its Balance Sheet at the start of this chapter. Let's see what this comprises.

Gross trade and other receivables	13,886 million
Less allowance for doubtful receivables	444 million
Net trade and other receivables	13,442 million

The allowance for doubtful receivables (CHF 444) represents the amount that Nestlé does not expect to collect. The net amount of the receivables (CHF 13,422) is the amount that Nestlé does expect to collect. This is called the *net receivables* because it's the amount of cash Nestlé expects to realize in cash receipts.

Uncollectible-account expense is an operating expense along with salaries, depreciation, rent, and utilities. You may also see companies label this as *bad debt expense, impairment of receivables expense* or something similar. To measure uncollectible-account expense, accountants use the allowance method or, in certain limited cases, the direct write-off method (p. 305).

Allowance Method

The best way to provide for bad debts is by the allowance method. *IAS39 – Financial Instruments: Recognition and Measurement* stipulates that loans and receivables, like other financial assets, are impaired if, and only if, there is objective evidence of impairment as a result of one or more "loss events" that occurred after their initial recognition. This includes observable data that comes to the attention of the holder of the loans and receivables about the following loss events:

OBJECTIVE

3 Use the allowance method for uncollectible receivables

- Significant financial difficulty of a specific debtor, including possibility of becoming bankrupt.
- A breach of contract by a specific debtor, such as default or inability to make interest and/or principal payments.
- Adverse changes in the number of delayed payments by debtors in general.
- National or local economic conditions that correlate with defaults by debtors in general (e.g. increase in unemployment rates and other adverse changes in industry conditions that affect debtors).

The allowance method thus records collection losses based on estimates developed from the company's collection experience and information about debtors. Nestlé doesn't wait to see which customers will not pay. Instead, Nestlé records the estimated amount as Uncollectible-Account Expense and also sets up an *Allowance for Uncollectible Receivables* account. Other titles for this account are *Allowance for Doubtful Receivables* and *Allowance for Receivables Impairment*. This is a contra account to Accounts Receivable. The allowance shows the amount of the receivables the business expects not to collect.

In Chapter 3 we used the Accumulated Depreciation account to show the amount of a PPE's cost that has been expensed—the portion of the asset whose benefits have been allocated to prior periods. Allowance for Doubtful Debt serves a similar purpose for Accounts Receivable. The allowance shows how much of the receivable is unlikely to be collected. You'll find this diagram helpful (amounts are assumed):

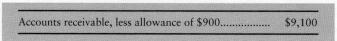

Equipment............................	$100,000	Accounts receivable.....................	$10,000
Less: Accumulated		Less: Allowance for	
depreciation	(40,000)	uncollectible receivables	(900)
Equipment, net....................	60,000	Accounts receivable, net............	9,100

Focus on Accounts Receivable. Customers owe this company $10,000, but it expects to collect only $9,100. The net receivables is therefore $9,100. Another way to report these receivables is

| Accounts receivable, less allowance of $900................. | $9,100 |

You can work backward to determine the full amount of the receivable, $10,000 (net receivables of $9,100 plus the allowance of $900). The income statement reports Uncollectible-Account Expense among the operating expenses, as follows (using assumed figures):

Income statement (partial):	
Expenses:	
Uncollectible-account expense:................	$2,000

STOP & THINK...

Refer to the Nestlé balance sheet on page 290. At December 31, 2008, how much in total did customers owe Nestlé? How much did Nestlé expect *not* to collect? How much did Nestlé expect to collect? What was Nestlé's net receivables?

Answer:

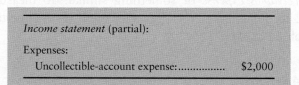

	Millions CHF
Customers owed Nestlé...	$13,886
Nestlé expected not to collect the allowance of	444
Nestlé expected to collect—net receivables.................	$13,442

Notice that, to determine the *total* (gross) amount customers owed, you have to add the amount of the allowance back to the "net receivable" ($13,442 + $444 = $13,866). Although this amount is not shown on the face of financial statements, it is useful for analysis purposes, as shown in the following section.

The best way to estimate uncollectibles uses the company's history of collections from customers and information on "loss events" as suggested by *IAS39* (see page 299). In practice, a popular method for estimating uncollectibles is called aging-of-receivables. The aging method is a balance-sheet approach because it focuses on what should be the most relevant and faithful representation of accounts receivable as of the balance sheet date. In the aging method, individual receivables from specific customers are analyzed based on how long they have been outstanding.

For example, suppose Nestlé's has thousands of account receivables totaling to CHF 13,886. A simplified version of aging method would simply list the status or age of the receivables for the receivables, typically classified into age groups such as "Not yet due", "1-30 days overdue", "31-60 days overdue", and "over 60 days overdue". Nestlé would then apply a percentage (based on its historical collection experience) to these age groups. It may estimate that accounts that are not yet due only has a 1% chance of not being collectible, and those that have been overdue for 1-30 days are more likely to be uncollectible, say 5%, and so forth. The allowance for each age group is thus determined *vertically*, and the totals of these allowances will be what Nestlé will need to provide at the year end. Exhibit 5-3 illustrates a simplified aging method of calculating allowance for uncollectible receivables.

EXHIBIT 5-3 | **Aging the Accounts Receivable of Nestlé**

Receivables	Not yet due	1–30 Days	31–60 Days	Over 60 Days	Total
Age of Account Receivables					
Customer A	400				400
Customer B	100	100			200
Customer C	300	200	600	100	1,200
...	...	...	...	...	...
Totals	11,060	1,363	370	1,093	13,886
Percentage uncollectible	1.0%	5.0%	12.5%	20.0%	
Required allowance	111	68	46	219	444

As you can see, the total desired amount of allowance at the financial year end is calculated to be CHF 444 out of total receivables of CHF 13,886. Whilst we can express this as a percentage, i.e. about 3.2% of the receivables are expected to be impaired or uncollectible, remember that the actual calculation depends on the age groups and the individual percentage uncollectible assigned to each age group.

What is the limitation of the aging method? Well, have a look at Customer C in Exhibit 5–3 above. Let's say Nestlé is now aware of a "loss event" about Customer C, who is very likely to enter bankruptcy. The aging method disregards this fact and only provides an allowance of CHF 108 ($300 \times 1\% + 200 \times 5\% + 600 \times 12.5\% + 100 \times 20\%$) when it is possible that all CHF 1,200 is impaired! If you have assessed each customer's receivable row by row, (i.e. *horizontally* rather than by age group *vertically*), you would have taken into account specific information about each customer in your assessment of receivables impairment.

In practice, a combination of aging and specific customer credit information may be used to determine the required allowance of uncollectible accounts at year end. Nestlé's accounting policies states:

> **EXCERPTS FROM NESTLÉ'S NOTES TO THE 2008 FINANCIAL STATEMENTS**
>
> Allowances for doubtful receivables represent the Group's estimates of losses that could arise from the failure or inability of customers to make payments when due. These estimates are based on the aging of customers' balances, specific credit circumstances and the Group's historical bad receivables experience.

Nestlé also provides the following breakdown of its aging report, similar to our example in Exhibit 5–3.

In millions of CHF	2008
No past due	11,060
Past due 1-30 days	1,363
Past due 31-60 days	370
Past due 61-90 days	242
Past due 91-120 days	144
Past due more than 120 days	707
Allowance for doubtful receivables	(444)
	13,442

Suppose it is December 31, 2008, and Nestlé's receivables show the following before the year-end adjustment (amounts in millions):

Accounts Receivable	Allowance for doubtful receivables
13,886	293

These accounts are not yet ready for the financial statements because the allowance balance has not been adjusted to reflect Nestlé's year-end assessment of the collectability of its receivables. You saw from earlier that the required ending balance of the allowance for doubtful receivables was CHF 444. To update the allowance, Nestlé would make this adjusting entry at year end:

2008			
Dec 31	Uncollectible-Account Expense	151	
	Allowance for doubtful receivables		
	(494 – 293)		151
	Recorded bad debt expense for the year.		

The expense decreases Nestlé's assets and net income, as shown by the accounting equation.

Assets	=	Liabilities	+	Shareholders' Equity
− 151	=	0	+	− 151 (uncollectible account expense)

Now the balance sheet can report the amount that Nestlé expects to collect from customers: 13,442 (13,886 − 444). This is Nestlé's net receivables which you saw on its balance sheet at the start of this Chapter (p. 290).

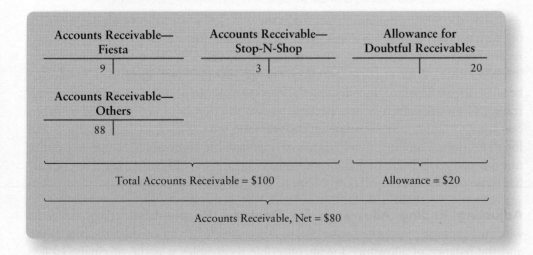

Accounts Receivable		Allowance for Doubtful Receivables		Uncollectible-Account Expense
13,886		Beg Bal	293	151
		Adj	151	
		End Bal	444	

Net accounts receivable, $13,442

Writing Off Uncollectible Accounts.

Assume that at the beginning of 2011 a division of Nestlé had these accounts receivable (amounts in thousands):

Accounts Receivable— Fiesta	Accounts Receivable— Stop-N-Shop	Allowance for Doubtful Receivables
9	3	20

Accounts Receivable— Others		
88		

Total Accounts Receivable = $100   Allowance = $20

Accounts Receivable, Net = $80

Suppose that early in 2011, Nestlé's credit department determines that Nestlé cannot collect from customers Fiesta and Stop–N–Shop. Nestlé then writes off the receivables from these customers with the following entry:

2011			
Jan 31	Allowance for Doubtful receivables	12	
	Accounts Receivable—Fiesta		9
	Accounts Receivable—Stop-N-Shop		3
	Wrote off uncollectible receivables.		

After the write-off, Nestlé's accounts show these amounts:

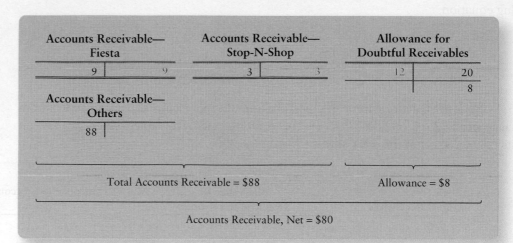

Accounts Receivable—Fiesta		Accounts Receivable—Stop-N-Shop		Allowance for Doubtful Receivables	
9	9	3	3	12	20
					8

Accounts Receivable—Others	
88	

Total Accounts Receivable = $88   Allowance = $8

Accounts Receivable, Net = $80

The receivables are reduced because it is now clear that these amounts will not be collected, and the allowance previously set aside is now "used" by the write-off.

Assets	=	Liabilities	+	Shareholders' Equity
+ 12	=	0	+	0
− 12				

The accounting equation shows that the write-off of uncollectibles has no effect on Nestlé's total assets, no effect on current assets, and no effect on net accounts receivable. Notice that Accounts Receivable, Net is still $80. There is no effect on net income either. Why is there no effect on net income? Net income is unaffected because the write-off of uncollectibles affects no expense account. It is merely a realization of the allowance of uncollectible receivables that has been provided in previous accounting periods. Naturally, at the year end, when Nestlé makes an adjustment for the required amount of allowance of uncollectible receivables, it may recognize more expenses as some of the allowance have been used utilized or used by the earlier write-offs for Fiesta and Stop-N-Shop.

Adjusting Ending Allowance for Doubtful Receivables. Let's continue with this example. Suppose by the end of 2011, Nestlé has receivables totaling $200, and the balance of allowance for uncollectible receivables was the original $20 less the write-offs of $12 = $8. The division also estimated that an appropriate level of allowance for the $200 ending receivables is $30. It will then adjust the allowance for uncollectible receivables to the desired ending balance by recording:

2011			
Dec 31	Uncollectible for Doubtful receivables	22	
	Allowance for Doubtful receivables		
	($30 − $8)		22
	Recorded bad debt expense for the year.		

You can think of the following formula to help you better understand the relationship between uncollectible-account expense, write-offs of receivables and allowance for doubtful receivables accounts.

Recovery of previously written-off receivables. Sometimes, accounts that have been written-off may be partially recovered. This may take place after liquidation of the customer's business. Such recovery can be treated in one of two ways: (1) reverse the write-off entry or (2) decrease bad debt expense, by the amount recovered. Both methods will eventually result in the same bad debt expense at the end of the period when new allowance (and expense) is calculated.

Direct Write-Off Method

There is another, less preferable, way to account for uncollectible receivables. Under the **direct write-off method**, the company waits until a specific customer's receivable proves uncollectible. Then the accountant writes off the customer's account and records Uncollectible-Account Expense, as follows (using assumed data):

2011			
Jan 31	Uncollectible-Account Expense	12	
	Accounts Receivable—Fiesta		9
	Accounts Receivable—Stop-N-Shop		3
	Wrote off bad debts by direct write-off method.		

The direct write-off method is not considered generally accepted accounting for financial statement purposes. It is considered defective because it fails to take into account the possibility of impairment of the receivables at balance sheet date. As a result, receivables are always reported at their full amount, which is more than the business expects to collect. *Assets on the balance sheet may be overstated.* Because of these deficiencies, Nestlé's and virtually all other large companies use the allowance method for preparing their financial statements.

Sometimes you may see the concept of direct write-off method being used for income tax purposes. It is one of several sources of temporary differences that may arise between net income for financial reporting purposes and net income for income tax purposes. We will discuss other differences between book and taxable income in later chapters.

Computing Cash Collections from Customers

A company earns revenue and then collects the cash from customers. For Nestlé and most other companies, there is a time lag between earning the revenue and collecting the cash. Collections from customers are the single most important source of cash for any business. You can compute a company's collections from customers by analyzing its Accounts Receivable account. Receivables typically hold only three types of transactions, as reflected in the five elements of the following Accounts Receivable account balance (amounts assumed):

Accounts Receivable			
Beg Bal (left over from last period)	200	Write-offs of uncollectibles	100[b]
Sales (or service) revenue	1,800[a]	Collections from customers	X = 1,500[c]
End Bal (carries over to next period)	400		

[a] The journal entry that places revenue into the receivable account is

Accounts Receivable	1,800	
Sales (or Service) Revenue		1,800

[b] The journal entry for write-offs is

Allowance for Uncollectibles	100	
Accounts Receivable		100

[c] The journal entry that places collections into the receivable account is

Cash	1,500	
Accounts Receivable		1,500

Suppose you know all these amounts *except* collections from customers. You can compute collections by solving for X in the T-account. The following diagram may help you link the numbers. Collections from customer, X, is therefore $1,500.

Often write-offs are unknown and may be omitted. Then the computation of collections becomes an approximation.

NOTES RECEIVABLE

OBJECTIVE

4 Account for notes receivable

As stated earlier, notes receivable are more formal than accounts receivable. Notes receivable due within one year or less are current assets. Notes due beyond one year are *long-term receivables* and are reported as long-term assets. Some notes receivable are collected in installments. The portion due within one year is a current asset and the remainder is long term. Nestlé may hold a $20,000 note receivable from a customer, but only the $6,000 customer must pay within one year is a current asset of Nestlé.

Before launching into the accounting for notes receivable, let's define some key terms:

Creditor. The party to whom money is owed. The creditor is also called the *lender*.

Debtor. The party that borrowed and owes money on the note. The debtor is also called the *maker* of the note or the *borrower*.

Interest. Interest is the cost of borrowing money. The interest is stated in an annual percentage rate.

Maturity date. The date on which the debtor must pay the note.

Maturity value. The sum of principal and interest on the note.

Principal. The amount of money borrowed by the debtor.

Term. The length of time from when the note was signed by the debtor to when the debtor must pay the note.

There are two parties to a note:

- The *creditor* has a note receivable.
- The *debtor* has a note payable.

Exhibit 5-4 is a typical promissory note.

EXHIBIT 5-4 | A Promissory Note

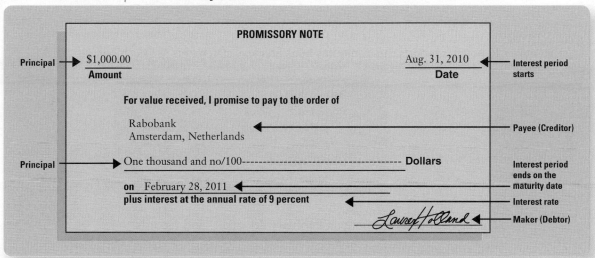

The **principal** amount of the note ($1,000) is the amount borrowed by the debtor, lent by the creditor. This six-month note receivable runs from August 31, 2010, to February 28, 2011, when Lauren Holland (the maker) promises to pay **Rabobank** (the creditor) the principal of $1,000 plus 9% interest. Interest is revenue to the creditor (Rabobank, in this case).

Accounting for Notes Receivable

Consider the promissory note in Exhibit 5-4. After Lauren Holland signs the note, Rabobank gives her $1,000 cash. The bank's entries follow, assuming a December 31 year end for Rabobank:

2010			
Aug 31	Note Receivable—L. Holland	1,000	
	Cash		1,000
	Made a loan.		

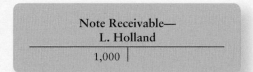

The bank gave one asset, cash, in return for another asset, a note receivable, so total assets did not change.

Rabobank earns interest revenue during September, October, November, and December. At December 31, the bank accrues 9% interest revenue for four months as follows:

2010			
Dec 31	Interest Receivable ($1,000 × 0.09 × 4/12)	30	
	Interest Revenue		30
	Accrued interest revenue.		

The bank's assets and revenues increase.

Rabobank reports these amounts in its financial statements at December 31, 2010:

Balance sheet
Current assets:
    Note receivable $1,000
    Interest receivable................ 30
Income statement
    Interest revenue................... $ 30

The bank collects the note on February 28, 2011, and records

2011			
Feb 28	Cash	1,045	
	Note Receivable—L. Holland		1,000
	Interest Receivable		30
	Interest Revenue ($1,000 × 0.09 × 2/12)		15
	Collected note at maturity.		

This entry zeroes out Note Receivable and Interest Receivable and also records the interest revenue earned in 2011.

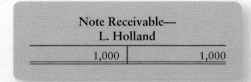

Note Receivable—
L. Holland
| 1,000 | 1,000 |

In its 2011 financial statements the only item that Rabobank will report is the interest revenue of $15 that was earned in 2011. There's no note receivable or interest receivable on the balance sheet because those items were zeroed out when the bank collected the note at maturity.

Three aspects of the interest computation deserve mention:

1. Interest rates are always for an annual period, unless stated otherwise. In this example, the annual interest rate is 9%. At December 31, 2010, Rabobank accrues interest revenue for four months. The interest computation is

Principal	×	Interest Rate	×	Time	=	Amount of Interest
$1,000	×	0.09	×	4/12	=	$30

2. The time element (4/12) is the fraction of the year that the note has been in force during 2010.

3. Interest is often completed for a number of days. For example, suppose you loaned out $10,000 on April 10. The note receivable runs for 90 days and specifies interest at 8%.

   a. Interest starts accruing on April 11 and runs for 90 days, ending on the due date, July 9, as follows:

Month	Number of Days That Interest Accrues
April	20
May	31
June	30
July	9
Total	90

   b. The interest computation is

   $10,000 × 0.08 × 90/365 = $197

Some companies sell goods and services on notes receivable (versus selling on accounts receivable). This often occurs when the payment term extends beyond the customary accounts receivable period of 30 to 60 days.

Suppose that on March 20, 2011, Nestlé sells a large amount of merchandise to Carrefour. Nestlé gets Carrefour's three-month promissory note plus 10% annual interest. At the outset, Nestlé would debit Notes Receivable and credit Sales Revenue.

A company may also accept a note receivable from a trade customer whose account receivable is past due. The company then debits Notes Receivable and credits Accounts Receivable. We would say the company "received a note receivable on account." Now let's examine some strategies to speed up cash flow.

HOW TO SPEED UP CASH FLOW

All companies want speedy cash receipts. Rapid cash flow finances new products, research, and development. Thus, companies such as Nestlé find ways to collect cash quickly. Two common strategies generate cash quickly.

Credit Card or Bankcard Sales

The merchant sells merchandise and lets the customer pay with credit cards such as **American Express**, **VISA** or **MasterCard**. This strategy may increase sales, but the added revenue comes at a cost, which is typically about 2% to 3% of the total amount of the sale. Let's see how credit cards and bankcards work from the seller's perspective.

Suppose **Fujitsu** sells computers for $2,000, and the customer pays with a VISA card. Fujitsu records the sale as follows:

Cash	1,960	
Credit Card Processing Fee	40	
Sales Revenue		2,000
Recorded bankcard sales.		

Assets	=	Liabilities	+	Shareholders' Equity	
+ 1,960	=	0	+	+ 2,000	(sales revenue)
				− 40	(credit card fees)

Nestlé enters the transaction in the credit card machine. The machine, linked to a VISA server, automatically credits Fujitsu's account for a discounted portion, say $1,960, of the $2,000 sale amount. Two percent ($40) goes to VISA. To Fujitsu, the credit card processing fee is an operating expense that reduces Fujitsu's net profit for the year.

Selling (Factoring) Receivables

Nestlé makes some large sales to grocery chains on account, debiting Accounts Receivable and crediting Sales Revenue. Nestlé might then sell these accounts receivable to another business, called a *factor*. The factor earns revenue by paying a discounted price for the receivable and then hopefully collecting the full amount from the customer. The benefit to Nestlé is the immediate receipt of cash. The biggest disadvantage of factoring is that it is often quite expensive, when compared to the costs of retaining the receivable on the books and ultimately collecting the full amount. In addition, the company that factors its receivables may lose control over the collection process and yet be responsible for any bad debts that may arise after the factoring. For these reasons, factoring is often not used by companies who have other less costly means to raise cash, such as short-term borrowing from banks. Factoring may be used by start-up companies with insufficient credit history to obtain loans at a reasonable cost, by companies with weaker credit history, or by companies that are already saddled with a significant amount of debt.

To illustrate selling, or *factoring*, accounts receivable, suppose a company wishes to speed up cash flow and therefore sells $100,000 of accounts receivables, receiving cash of $95,000. The company would record the sale of the receivables as follows:

Cash	95,000	
Financing Expense	5,000	
Accounting Receivable		100,000
Sold accounts receivable.		

Again, Financing Expense is an operating expense, with the same effect as Interest Expense. Discounting a note receivable is similar to selling an account receivable. However, the credit is to Notes Receivable (instead of Accounts Receivable).

Notice the high price (5% of the face amount, or $5,000) the company has had to sacrifice in order to collect the cash immediately, as opposed to waiting 30 to 60 days to collect the full amount. Therefore, if the company can afford to wait, it will probably not engage in factoring in order to collect the full amount of the receivables.

Reporting on the Statement of Cash Flows

Receivables and short-term investments appear on the balance sheet as assets. We saw these in Nestlé's balance sheet at the beginning of the chapter. We've also seen how to report the related revenues, expenses, gains, and losses on the income statement. Because receivable and investment transactions affect cash, their effects must also be reported on the statement of cash flows.

Receivables bring in cash when the business collects from customers. These transactions are reported as *operating* activities on the statement of cash flows because they result from sales operations. Investment transactions show up as *investing activities* on the statement of cash flows. Chapter 12 shows how companies report their cash flows on the statement of cash flows. In that chapter we will see exactly how to report cash flows related to receivables and investment transactions.

USING TWO KEY RATIOS TO MAKE DECISIONS

Investors and creditors use ratios to evaluate the financial health of a company. We introduced the current ratio in Chapter 3. Other ratios, including the **quick** (or *acid-test*) **ratio** and the number of days' sales in receivables, help investors measure liquidity.

Acid-Test (or Quick) Ratio

The balance sheet lists assets in the order of relative liquidity:

1. Cash and cash equivalents

2. Short-term investments

3. Accounts (or notes) receivable

Nestlé's balance sheet in the chapter opening story lists these accounts in order. Managers, shareholders, and creditors care about the liquidity of a company's assets. The current ratio measures ability to pay current liabilities with current assets. A more stringent measure of ability to pay current liabilities is the **acid-test** (or *quick*) **ratio**:

Nestlé 2008

(Swiss Franc in millions, taken from Nestlé balance sheet)

$$\text{Acid-test ratio} = \frac{\text{Cash} + \substack{\text{Short-term} \\ \text{investments}} + \substack{\text{Net current} \\ \text{receivables}}}{\text{Total current liabilities}} = \frac{\$5,835 + \$1,296 + \$13,442}{\$33,223} = 0.62$$

The higher the acid-test ratio, the easier it is to pay current liabilities. Nestlé's acid-test ratio of 0.62 means that it has 62 cents of quick assets to pay each $1 of current liabilities (in this case, it's actually 62 *centimes* for each Swiss Franc). This ratio value is considered reasonably good, but not excellent. Traditionally, companies have wanted an acid-test ratio of at least 1.0 to be safe. The ratio needs to be high enough for safety, but not too high. After all, cash and the other liquid assets don't generate very high rates of return.

What is an acceptable acid-test ratio? The answer depends on the industry. Auto dealers can operate smoothly with an acid-test ratio of 0.20, roughly one-third of Nestlé's quick ratio. How can auto dealers survive with so low an acid-test ratio? The auto manufacturers help finance their dealers' inventory. Most dealers, therefore, have a financial safety net provided through the manufacturers. During the recent business recession, **General Motors'** sales slumped and the company ran dangerously low of cash. One of the many consequences of GM's cash shortage was that it deprived dealerships of these safety nets and put them in jeopardy of bankruptcy and insolvency as well as the company. You can see the "domino effect" of arrangements like this, and why a number of GM dealerships were forced to close, even after GM received about $25 billion in "bailout money" from the United States government.

Days' Sales in Receivables

After a business makes a credit sale, the next step is collecting the receivable. **Days' sales in receivables**, also called the *receivable collection period*, or *days sales outstanding*, tells a company how long it takes to collect its average level of receivables. Shorter is better because cash is coming in quicker. The longer the collection period, the less cash is available to pay bills and expand.

Days' sales in receivables can be computed in two logical steps. First, we can calculate the receivables turnover. The receivable turnover is the number of times average receivables are converted into cash in a year. This is calculated as Sales Revenue divided by Average Receivables. Second, we can convert this number of times into days by dividing 365 by the receivable turnover.

(Dollars in millions, taken from Nestlé's financial statements)

Days' Sales in Receivables		Nestlé
1. Receivable Turnover	$= \dfrac{\text{Sales}}{\text{Average Receivables*}}$	$= \dfrac{109{,}908}{14{,}166} = 7.76 \text{ times}$
2. Days Sales in Receivables	$= 365 / \text{Receivables Turnover} =$	$365/7.76 \quad = 47 \text{ days}$
*Average net receivables	$= \dfrac{\text{Beginning net receivables} + \text{Ending net receivables}}{2}$	$= \dfrac{14{,}890 + 13{,}442}{2} = 14{,}166$

Net sales come from the income statement, and the receivables amounts are taken from the balance sheet. Average receivables is the simple average of the beginning and ending balances.

It takes Nestlé an average of 47 days to collect its receivables. To evaluate Nestlé's collection period of 47 days, we need to compare 47 days to the credit terms that Nestlé's offers customers when the company makes a sale, as well as the number of days on average that creditors typically allow Nestlé to pay them without penalty.

Suppose Nestlé makes sales on "net 30" terms, which means that customers should pay Nestlé within 30 days of the sale. Nestlé's collection period of 47 days is reasonably good in comparison to the ideal measure of 30 days. After all, some customers do drag out their payments. And, as we've seen, some customers don't pay at all. On the other hand, if Nestlé's short-term creditors expect payment of their accounts payable within 30 days, Nestlé might be forced to borrow cash in order to pay its creditors on time, which could prove to be expensive.

Companies watch their collection periods closely. Whenever collections slow down, the business must find other sources of financing, such as borrowing or selling receivables. During recessions, customers may take an even longer time to pay more slowly, and a longer collection period may be unavoidable.

END-OF-CHAPTER SUMMARY PROBLEM

Superior Technical Resources' (STR's) balance sheet at December 31, 2010, reported

	(In millions)
Accounts receivable.....................................	$382
Allowance for doubtful accounts...............	(92)

STR uses the aging method to account for uncollectible receivables.

Requirements

1. How much of the December 31, 2010, balance of accounts receivables did STR expect to collect? Stated differently, what was the net realizable value of STR's receivables?
2. Journalize, without explanations, 2011 entries for STR:
   a. Write-offs of uncollectible accounts receivable totaling $58 million. Prepare a T-account for Allowance for Doubtful Accounts and post to this account. Show its unadjusted balance at December 31, 2011.
   b. December 31, 2011, aging of receivables, which indicates that $47 million of the total receivables of $409 million is uncollectible at year end. Post to Allowance for Doubtful Accounts, and show its adjusted balance at December 31, 2011.
3. Show how STR's receivables and the related allowance will appear on the December 31, 2011, balance sheet.
4. Show what STR's income statement will report for the foregoing transactions.

Answers

Requirement 1

	(In millions)
Net realizable value of receivables ($382 – $92)	$290

Requirement 2

		(In millions)	
a.	Allowance for Doubtful Accounts	58	
	Accounts Receivable		58

Allowance for Doubtful Accounts			
2011 Write-offs	58	Dec 31, 2010	92
		Unadjusted balance at Dec 31, 2011	34

b.	Doubtful-Account Expense ($47 – $34)		13	
	Allowance for Doubtful Accounts			13

Allowance for Doubtful Accounts	
Dec 31, 2011 Unadj bal	34
2011 Expense	13
Dec 31, 2011 Adj bal	47

❙ Requirement 3

	(In millions)
Accounts receivable...............................	$409
Allowance for doubtful accounts...............	(47)

❙ Requirement 4

	(In millions)
Expenses: Doubtful-account expense for 2011.........	$13

REVIEW RECEIVABLES AND INVESTMENTS

Quick Check (Answers are given on page 339.)

1. Henry Funaro Golf Academy held investments in trading securities valued at $40,000 at December 31, 2010. These investments cost Henry Funaro $33,000. What is the appropriate amount for Henry Funaro to report for these investments on the December 31, 2010, balance sheet?
   a. $40,000
   b. $7,000 gain
   c. 33,000
   d. Cannot be determined from the data given

2. Return to Henry Funaro Golf Academy in question 1. What should appear on the Henry Funaro income statement for the year ended December 31, 2010, for the trading securities?
   a. $7,000 unrealized gain
   b. $33,000
   c. $40,000
   d. Cannot be determined from the data given

Use the following information to answer questions 3–7.

Anderson Company had the following information relating to credit sales in 2010.

Accounts receivable 12/31/10	$10,000
Allowance for uncollectible accounts 12/31/10 (before adjustment)	600
Credit sales during 2010	40,000
Cash sales during 2010	15,000
Collections from customers on account during 2010	44,000

3. What is the balance of accounts receivable on December 31, 2011?
   a. $65,000   c. $11,000
   b. $21,000   d. $6,000

4. Uncollectible-account expense for 2010 is $1,600. What is the adjusted balance in the Allowance account at year-end 2010?
   a. $3,800   c. $1,600
   b. $2,200   d. $600

5. If uncollectible accounts are determined by the aging-of-receivables method to be $1,030, the uncollectible account expense for 2010 would be
   a. $1,630.   c. $430.
   b. $600.   d. $1,030.

6. Using the aging-of-receivables method, the balance of the Allowance account after the adjusting entry would be
   a. $600.   c. $1,630.
   b. $1,030.   d. $430.

7. Using the aging-of-receivables method, the net realizable value of accounts receivable on the 12/31/10 balance sheet would be
   a. $8,370.   c. $8,400.
   b. $10,000.   d. $8,970.

8. Accounts Receivable has a debit balance of $2,800, and the Allowance for Uncollectible Accounts has a credit balance of $400. A $90 account receivable is written off. What is the amount of net receivables (net realizable value) after the write-off?
   a. $2,490   c. $2,310
   b. $2,710   d. $2,400

9. Magnolia Corporation began 2010 with Accounts Receivable of $575,000. Sales for the year totaled $2,200,000. Magnolia ended the year with accounts receivable of $725,000. Magnolia's bad-debt losses are minimal. How much cash did Magnolia collect from customers in 2010?
   a. $2,925,000   c. $2,200,000
   b. $2,050,000   d. $2,350,000

10. Neptune Company received a four-month, 9%, $2,800 note receivable on December 1. The adjusting entry on December 31 will
    a. debit Interest Receivable $21.   c. both a and b.
    b. credit Interest Revenue $21.   d. credit Interest Revenue $252.

11. What is the maturity value of a $70,000, 12%, six-month note?
    a. $70,000   c. $65,800
    b. $78,400   d. $74,200

12. If the adjusting entry to accrue interest on a note receivable is omitted, then
    a. assets, net income, and shareholders' equity are understated.
    b. assets are overstated, net income is understated, and shareholders' equity is understated.
    c. liabilities are understated, net income is overstated, and shareholders' equity is overstated.
    d. assets, net income, and shareholders' equity are overstated.

13. Net sales total $803,000. Beginning and ending accounts receivable are $80,000 and $74,000, respectively. Calculate days' sales in receivables.
    a. 35 days   c. 30 days
    b. 36 days   d. 34 days

14. From the following list of accounts, calculate the quick ratio.

Cash..	$ 6,000	Accounts payable	$10,000
Accounts receivable................	9,000	Salary payable..................................	4,000
Inventory.................................	11,000	Notes payable (due in two years)	13,000
Prepaid insurance..................	1,000	Short-term note investments............	3,000

     a. 1.3   c. 1.1
     b. 2.1   d. 1.8

Accounting Vocabulary

acid-test ratio (p. 311) Ratio of the sum of cash plus short-term investments plus net current receivables to total current liabilities. Tells whether the entity can pay all its current liabilities if they come due immediately. Also called the *quick ratio*.

aging-of-receivables (p. 301) A way to estimate bad debts by analyzing individual accounts receivable according to the length of time they have been receivable from the customer.

Allowance for Doubtful Accounts (p. 299) Another name for *Allowance for Uncollectible Accounts*.

Allowance for Uncollectible Accounts (p. 299) The estimated amount of collection losses. Another name for *Allowance for Doubtful Accounts*.

allowance method (p. 299) A method of recording collection losses based on estimates of how much money the business will not collect from its customers.

bad-debt expense (p. 299) Another name for *uncollectible-account expense*.

creditor (p. 306) The party to whom money is owed.

days' sales in receivables (p. 312) Ratio of average net accounts receivable to one day's sales. Indicates how many days' sales remain in Accounts Receivable awaiting collection. Also called the *receivable collection period* or *days sales outstanding*.

debtor (p. 306) The party who owes money.

direct write-off method (p. 305) A method of accounting for bad debts in which the company waits until a customer's

account receivable proves uncollectible and then debits Uncollectible-Account Expense and credits the customer's Account Receivable.

doubtful-account expense (p. 299) Another name for *uncollectible-account expense*.

interest (p. 306) The borrower's cost of renting money from a lender. Interest is revenue for the lender and expense for the borrower.

marketable securities (p. 290) Another name for *short-term investments*.

maturity (p. 296) The date on which a debt instrument must be paid.

maturity date (p. 306) The date on which the debtor must pay the note.

maturity value (p. 307) The sum of principal and interest on the note.

principal (p. 307) The amount borrowed by a debtor and lent by a creditor.

quick ratio (p. 311) Another name for *acid-test ratio*.

receivables (p. 296) Monetary claims against a business or an individual, acquired mainly by selling goods or services and by lending money.

short-term investments (p. 290) Investments that a company plans to hold for one year or less. Also called *marketable securities*.

term (p. 307) The length of time from inception to maturity.

trading securities (p. 291) Share investments that are expected to be sold in the near future with the intent of generating profits on the sale.

uncollectible-account expense (p. 299) Cost to the seller of extending credit. Arises from the failure to collect from credit customers. Also called doubtful-account expense or bad-debt expense.

ASSESS YOUR PROGRESS

Short Exercises

S5-1 (*Learning Objective 1: Reporting trading investments*)   Answer these questions about investments.

1. What is the amount to report on the balance sheet for a trading security?
2. Why is a trading security always a current asset? Explain.

S5-2 (*Learning Objective 1: Accounting for a trading investment*)   Newsome Corp. holds a portfolio of trading securities. Suppose that on November 1, Newsome paid $87,000 for an investment in Quark shares to add to its portfolio. At December 31, the market value of Quark shares is $98,000. For this situation, show everything that Newsome would report on its December 31 balance sheet and on its income statement for the year ended December 31.

S5-3 (*Learning Objective 1: Accounting for a trading investment*)   McCarver Investments purchased Hoffman shares as a trading security on December 18 for $103,000.

1. Suppose the Hoffman shares decreased in value to $96,000 at December 31. Make the McCarver journal entry to adjust the Short-Term Investment account to market value.
2. Show how McCarver would report the short-term investment on its balance sheet and the unrealized gain or loss on its income statement.

S5-4 (*Learning Objective 2: Applying internal controls over the collection of receivables*)   Susan Perry keeps the Accounts Receivable T-account of Abraham & Paige, a partnership. What duty will a good internal control system withhold from Perry? Why?

S5-5 (*Learning Objective 2: Controlling cash receipts from customers*)   As a recent college graduate, you land your first job in the customer collections department of Countryroads Publishing. Zach Peters, the manager, asked you to propose a system to ensure that cash received from customers by mail is handled properly. Draft a short memorandum to explain the essential element in your proposed plan. State why this element is important.

S5-6 (*Learning Objective 3: Applying the allowance method to account for uncollectibles*)
Use the information from the following journal entries of Turning Leaves Furniture Restoration to answer the questions below:

	Journal Entry		
	Accounts	Debit	Credit
1.	Accounts Receivable	1,000,000	
	Sales Revenue		1,000,000
2.	Cash	870,000	
	Accounts Receivable		870,000
3.	Allowance for Uncollectible Accounts	12,000	
	Accounts Receivable		12,000
4.	Uncollectible-Account Expense	40,000	
	Allowance for Uncollectible Accounts		40,000

Requirements

1. Start with Accounts Receivable's beginning balance ($38,000) and then post to the Accounts Receivable T-account. How much do Turning Leaves Furniture Restoration's customers owe the company at December 31, 2011?
2. Start with the Allowance account's beginning credit balance ($12,480) and then post to the Allowance for Uncollectible Accounts T-account. How much of the receivables at December 31, 2011, does Turning Leaves Furniture Restoration expect *not* to collect?
3. At December 31, 2011, how much cash does Turning Leaves Furniture Restoration expect to collect on its accounts receivable?

S5-7 (*Learning Objective 3: Applying the allowance method [aging-of-accounts-receivable] to account for uncollectibles*)   Gray and Dumham, a law firm, started 2010 with accounts receivable of $31,000 and an allowance for uncollectible accounts of $4,000. The 2010 service revenues on account totaled $175,000, and cash collections on account totaled $128,000. During 2010, Gray and Dumham wrote off uncollectible accounts receivable of $2,800. At December 31, 2010, the aging of accounts receivable indicated that Gray and Dumham will not collect $1,850 of its accounts receivable.

Journalize Gray and Dumham's (a) service revenue, (b) cash collections on account, (c) write-offs of uncollectible receivables, and (d) uncollectible-account expense for the year. Explanations are not required. Prepare a T-account for Allowance for Uncollectible Accounts to show your computation of uncollectible-account expense for the year.

S5-8 (*Learning Objective 3: Applying the allowance method to account for uncollectibles*)   Perform the following accounting for the receivables of Evans and Tanner, a law firm, at December 31, 2010.

Requirements

1. Start with the beginning balances for these T-accounts:

   • Accounts Receivable, $97,000   • Allowance for Uncollectible Accounts, $5,000

   Post the following 2010 transactions to the T-accounts:
   a. Service revenue of $698,000, all on account
   b. Collections on account, $722,000
   c. Write-offs of uncollectible accounts, $8,000
   d. Uncollectible-account expense (allowance method), $14,000
2. What are the ending balances of Accounts Receivable and Allowance for Uncollectible Accounts?
3. Show how Evans and Tanner will report accounts receivable on its balance sheet at December 31, 2010.

S5-9 (*Learning Objectives 3, 4: Answering practical questions about receivables*) Answer these questions about receivables and uncollectibles. For the true-false questions, explain any answers that turn out to be false.

1. True or false? Credit sales increase receivables. Collections and write-offs decrease receivables.
2. Which receivables figure, the *total* amount that customers *owe* the company, or the *net* amount the company expects to collect, is more interesting to investors as they consider buying the company's shares? Give your reason.
3. Show how to determine net accounts receivable.
4. True or false? The direct write-off method of accounting for uncollectibles understates assets.
5. California Bank lent $200,000 to Sacramento Company on a six-month, 8% note. Which party has interest receivable? Which party has interest payable? Interest expense? Interest revenue? How much interest will these organizations record one month after Sacramento Company signs the note?
6. When California Bank accrues interest on the Sacramento Company note, show the directional effects on the bank's assets, liabilities, and equity (increase, decrease, or no effect).

S5-10 (*Learning Objective 4: Accounting for a note receivable*) Northend Bank & Trust Company lent $130,000 to Sylvia Peters on a six-month, 9% note. Record the following for bank (explanations are not required):

    a. Lending the money on May 6.
    b. Collecting the principal and interest at maturity. Specify the date.

S5-11 (*Learning Objective 4: Computing note receivable amounts*)

  1. Compute the amount of interest during 2010, 2011, and 2012 for the following note receivable: On April 30, 2010, BCDE Bank lent $170,000 to Carl Abbott on a two-year, 7% note.
  2. Which party has a (an)
    a. note receivable?
    b. note payable?
    c. interest revenue?
    d. interest expense?
  3. How much in total would BCDE Bank collect if Carl Abbott paid off the note early—say, on November 30, 2010?

S5-12 (*Learning Objective 4: Accruing interest receivable and collecting a note receivable*) On August 31, 2010, Nancy Thompson borrowed $2,000 from Green Interstate Bank. Thompson signed a note payable, promising to pay the bank principal plus interest on August 31, 2011. The interest rate on the note is 10%. The accounting year of Green Interstate Bank ends on June 30, 2011. Journalize Green Interstate Bank's (a) lending money on the note receivable at August 31, 2010, (b) accrual of interest at June 30, 2011, and (c) collection of principal and interest August 31, 2011, the maturity date of the note.

S5-13 (*Learning Objective 4: Reporting receivables amounts*) Using your answers to Short Exercise 5-14, show how the Green Interstate Bank will report the following:

    a. Whatever needs to be reported on its classified balance sheet at June 30, 2011.
    b. Whatever needs to be reported on its income statement for the year ended June 30, 2011.
    c. Whatever needs to be reported on its classified balance sheet at June 30, 2012. Ignore Cash.
    d. Whatever needs to be reported on its income statement for the year ended June 30, 2012.

S5-14 (*Learning Objective 5: Evaluating the acid-test ratio and days' sales in receivables*) West Highland Clothiers reported the following amounts in its 2011 financial statements. The 2010 amounts are given for comparison.

		2011		2010
Current assets:				
Cash...		$ 9,700		$ 9,700
Short-term investments................		17,000		14,000
Accounts receivable.....................	$84,000		$77,000	
Less: Allowance for				
uncollectibles......................	(7,100)	76,900	(6,100)	70,900
Inventory....................................		189,000		190,500
Prepaid insurance........................		2,300		2,300
Total current assets		294,900		287,400
Total current liabilities...................		99,000		111,000
Net sales......................................		802,000		736,000

I Requirements

  1. Compute West Highland's acid-test ratio at the end of 2011. Round to two decimal places.

    How does the acid-test ratio compare with the industry average of 0.97?

  2. Compare days' sales in receivables measure for 2011 with the company's credit terms of net 30 days.

S5-15 (*Learning Objectives 2, 3, 5: Reporting receivables and other accounts in the financial statements; using ratios to evaluate a business*)   Norbert Medical Service reported the following items, (amounts in thousands):

Unearned revenues (current)...............	$ 607	Service revenue....................................	$23,653
Allowance for		Other assets...	1,707
doubtful accounts...........................	309	Property, plant and equipment............	25,376
Other expenses....................................	12,559	Operating expense..............................	11,610
Accounts receivable............................	4,467	Cash..	289
Accounts payable	2,255	Notes payable (long term)..................	18,729

I Requirements

1. Classify each item as (a) income statement or balance sheet and as (b) debit balance or credit balance.
2. How much net income (or net loss) did Norbert report for the year?
3. Compute Norbert's quick (acid-test) ratio. Round to two decimal places. Evaluate Norbert Medical Service's liquidity position.

Exercises

All of A and B exercises can be found within MyAccountingLab, an online homework and practice environment. Your instructor may ask you to complete these exercises using MyAccountingLab.

(Group A)

E5-16A (*Learning Objective 1: Accounting for a trading investment*)   Northern Corporation, the investment banking company, often has extra cash to invest. Suppose Northern buys 800 shares of Andy, Inc., at $54 per share. Assume Northern expects to hold the Andy shares for one month and then sell it. The purchase occurs on December 15, 2010. At December 31, the market price per share is $66 per share.

I Requirements

1. What type of investment is this to Northern? Give the reason for your answer.
2. Record Northern's purchase of the Andy shares on December 15 and the adjustment to market value on December 31.
3. Show how Northern would report this investment on its balance sheet at December 31 and any gain or loss on its income statement for the year ended December 31, 2010.

E5-17A (*Learning Objective 1: Reporting a trading investment*)   On November 16, ACA, Inc., paid $95,000 for an investment in the shares of American Pacific Railway (APR). ACA plans to account for these shares as trading securities. On December 12, ACA received a $400 cash dividend from APR. It is now December 31, and the market value of the APR shares is $92,000. For this investment, show what ACA should report in its income statement and balance sheet.

E5-18A (*Learning Objective 1: Accounting for a trading investment*)   Sponsor Corporation reports short-term investments on its balance sheet. Suppose a division of Sponsor completed the following short-term investment transactions during 2010:

2010	
Dec 12	Purchased 600 shares of Disc, Inc., shares for $21,600. Sponsor plans to sell the shares at a profit in the near future.
21	Received a cash dividend of $0.81 per share on the Disc, Inc., investment.
31	Adjusted the investment in Disc, Inc.. Current market value is $27,000. Sponsor still plans to sell the shares in early 2011.
2011	
Jan 16	Sold the Disc, Inc., shares for $35,670.

I *Requirement*

1. Prepare T-accounts for Cash, Short-Term Investment, Dividend Revenue, Unrealized Gain (Loss) on Investment, and Gain on Sale of Investment. Show the effects of Sponsor's investment transactions. Start with a cash balance of $97,000; all the other accounts start at zero.

E5-19A (*Learning Objective 3: Reporting bad debts by the allowance method*) At December 31, 2010, Darci's Travel has an accounts receivable balance of $88,000. Allowance for Doubtful Accounts has a credit balance of $900 before the year-end adjustment. Darci's Travel estimates that doubtful-account expense for the year is equal to 5% of ending receivables. Make the year-end entry to record doubtful-account expense. Show how the accounts receivable and the allowance for doubtful accounts are reported on the balance sheet.

E5-20A (*Learning Objective 3: Using the allowance method for bad debts*) On September 30, Hilly Mountain Party Planners had a $30,000 balance in Accounts Receivable and a $2,000 credit balance in Allowance for Uncollectible Accounts. During October, the store made credit sales of $161,000. October collections on account were $137,000, and write-offs of uncollectible receivables totaled $2,300. The required allowance at year-end is calculated to be $4,000.

I *Requirements*

1. Journalize sales, collections, write-offs of uncollectibles, and uncollectible-account expense by the allowance method during October. Explanations are not required.
2. Show the ending balances in Accounts Receivable, Allowance for Uncollectible Accounts, and *Net* Accounts Receivable at October 31. How much does the store expect to collect?
3. Show how the store will report Accounts Receivable on its October 31 balance sheet.

E5-21A (*Learning Objective 3: Using the direct write-off method for bad debts*) Refer to Exercise 5-20A.

I *Requirements*

1. Record uncollectible-account expense for October by the direct write-off method.
2. What amount of accounts receivable would Hilly Mountain report on its October 31 balance sheet under the direct write-off method? Does it expect to collect the full amount?

E5-22A (*Learning Objective 3: Using the aging approach to estimate bad debts*) At December 31, 2010, before any year-end adjustments, the Accounts Receivable balance of Alpha Company is $210,000. The Allowance for Doubtful Accounts has a $13,500 credit balance. Alpha Company prepares the following aging schedule for Accounts Receivable:

| | Age of Accounts | | | |
Total Balance	1–30 Days	31–60 Days	61–90 Days	Over 90 Days
$210,000	$80,000	$60,000	$40,000	$30,000
Estimated uncollectible	0.6%	4.0%	5.0%	40.0%

■ spreadsheet

I *Requirements*

1. Based on the aging of accounts receivable, is the unadjusted balance of the allowance account adequate? Too high? Too low?
2. Make the entry required by the aging schedule. Prepare a T-account for the allowance.
3. Show how Alpha Company will report Accounts Receivable on its December 31 balance sheet.

E5-23A (*Learning Objective 4: Recording notes receivable and accruing interest revenue*) Record the following note receivable transactions in the journal of Aegean Realty. How much interest revenue did Aegean earn this year? Use a 365-day year for interest computations, and round interest amounts to the nearest dollar.

Sep 1	Loaned $15,000 cash to Carroll Fadal on a one-year, 10% note.
Nov 6	Performed service for Turf Masters, receiving a 90-day, 8% note for $12,000.
16	Received a $4,000, six-month, 11% note on account from Voleron, Inc.
30	Accrued interest revenue for the year.

E5-24A (*Learning Objective 4: Reporting the effects of note receivable transactions on the balance sheet and income statement*) Assume Port City Credit Union completed these transactions:

2010	
Apr 1	Loaned $125,000 to Lee Franz on a one-year, 12% note.
Dec 31	Accrued interest revenue on the Franz note.
2011	
Apr 1	Collected the maturity value of the note from Franz (principal plus interest).

Show what the company would report for these transactions on its 2010 and 2011 balance sheets and income statements.

E5-32B (*Learning Objective 3: Using the direct write-off method for bad debts*) Refer to Exercise 5-31B.

I Requirements

1. Record uncollectible-account expense for May by the direct write-off method.
2. What amount of accounts receivable would Hilltop report on its May 31 balance sheet under the direct write-off method? Does it expect to collect the full amount?

■ **spreadsheet**

E5-33B (*Learning Objective 3: Using the aging approach to estimate bad debts*) At December 31, 2010, before any year-end adjustments, the accounts receivable balance of Digital Electronics Company is $150,000. The allowance for doubtful accounts has a $6,800 credit balance. Digital Electronics Company prepares the following aging schedule for accounts receivable:

		Age of Accounts			
Total Balance		**1–30 Days**	**31–60 Days**	**61–90 Days**	**Over 90 Days**
$150,000		$60,000	$50,000	$30,000	$10,000
Estimated uncollectible		0.6%	4.0%	7.0%	40.0%

I Requirements

1. Based on the aging of accounts receivable, is the unadjusted balance of the allowance account adequate? Too high? Too low?
2. Make the entry required by the aging schedule. Prepare a T-account for the allowance.
3. Show how Digital Electronics Company will report Accounts Receivable on its December 31 balance sheet.

E5-34B (*Learning Objective 4: Recording notes receivable and accruing interest revenue*) Record the following note receivable transactions in the journal of Celtic Realty. How much interest revenue did Celtic earn this year? Use a 365-day year for interest computations, and round interest amounts to the nearest dollar.

Apr	1	Loaned $11,000 cash to Britt Durant on a one-year, 6% note.
Jun	6	Performed service for Putt Masters, receiving a 90-day, 7% note for $14,000.
	16	Received a $3,000, six-month, 12% note on account from Voleron, Inc.
	30	Accrued interest revenue for the year.

E5-35B (*Learning Objective 4: Reporting the effects of note receivable transactions on the balance sheet and income statement*) Assume Tradesmen Credit Union completed these transactions:

2010			
Apr	1	Loaned $50,000 to Leanne Harold on a one-year, 7% note.
Dec	31	Accrued interest revenue on the Harold note.
2011			
Apr	1	Collected the maturity value of the note from Harold (principal plus interest).

Show what the company would report for these transactions on its 2010 and 2011 balance sheets and income statements.

E5-36B (*Learning Objective 5: Using the acid-test ratio and days' sales in receivables to evaluate a company*)   Navajo, Inc., reported the following items at December 31, 2010 and 2009:

Balance Sheets (Summarized)					
	Year End			**Year End**	
	2010	**2009**		**2010**	**2009**
Current assets:			**Current liabilities:**		
Cash..	$ 4,000	$ 10,000	Accounts payable	$ 15,000	$ 16,500
Marketable securities	23,000	12,000	Other current liabilities	105,000	107,000
Accounts receivable, net	56,000	70,000	Long-term liabilities	15,000	16,000
Inventory	192,000	188,000			
Other current assets	6,000	6,000	Shareholders' equity......................	146,000	146,500
Long-term assets					
Total assets.....................................	$281,000	$286,000	Total liabilities and equity..............	$281,000	$286,000
Income Statement (partial):	**2010**				
Sales revenue.............................	$727,000				

Requirement

1. Compute Navajo's (a) acid-test ratio and (b) days' sales in average receivables for 2010. Evaluate each ratio value as strong or weak. Navajo sells on terms of net 30 days.

E5-37B (*Learning Objective 5: Analyzing a company's financial statements*)   Contemporary Co., Inc., the electronics and appliance chain, reported these figures in millions of dollars:

	2011	2010
Net sales...	$572,000	$601,000
Receivables at end of year	3,880	4,810

Requirements

1. Compute Contemporary's average collection period during 2011.
2. Is Contemporary's collection period long or short? Kurzwel Networks takes 36 days to collect its average level of receivables. Damascus, the overnight shipper, takes 35 days. What causes Contemporary's collection period to be so different?

Challenge Exercises

E5-38 (*Learning Objective 2: Determining whether to sell on bankcards*)   Radical Shirt Company sells on credit and manages its own receivables. Average experience for the past three years has been as follows:

	Cash	Credit	Total
Sales	$350,000	$350,000	$700,000
Cost of goods sold	192,500	192,500	385,000
Uncollectible-account expense	—	18,000	18,000
Other expenses	87,500	87,500	175,000

Jack Ryan, the owner, is considering whether to accept bankcards (VISA, MasterCard). Ryan expects total sales to increase by 12% but cash sales to remain unchanged. If Ryan switches to bankcards, the business can save $9,000 on other expenses, but VISA and MasterCard charge 2% on bankcard sales. Ryan figures that the increase in sales will be due to the increased volume of bankcard sales.

❚ Requirement

1. Should Radical Shirt Company start selling on bankcards? Show the computations of net income under the present plan and under the bankcard plan.

E5-39 (*Learning Objective 3: Reconstructing receivables and bad-debt amounts*)   Suppose Diamond, Inc., reported net receivables of $2,586 million and $2,268 million at January 31, 2011, and 2010, after subtracting allowances of $70 million and $64 million at these respective dates. Diamond earned total revenue of $53,333 million (all on account) and recorded doubtful-account expense of $16 million for the year ended January 31, 2011.

❚ Requirement

1. Use this information to measure the following amounts for the year ended January 31, 2011:

    a. Write-offs of uncollectible receivables.
    b. Collections from customers.

Quiz

Test your understanding of receivables by answering the following questions. Select the best choice from among the possible answers given.

Q5-40 United First Bank, the nationwide banking company, owns many types of investments. Assume that United First Bank paid $700,000 for trading securities on December 3. Two weeks later United First Bank received a $37,000 cash dividend. At December 31, these trading securities were quoted at a market price of $705,000. United First Bank's December income statement should report:

a. unrealized loss of $5,000.
b. unrealized loss of $3,000.
c. both a and b.
d. none of the above.

Q5-41 Refer to the United First Bank data in Quiz question 5-40. At December 31, United First Bank's balance sheet should report:

a. dividend revenue of $37,000.
b. short-term investment of $700,000.
c. short-term investment of $705,000.
d. unrealized gain of $5,000.

Q5-42 Under the allowance method for uncollectible receivables, the entry to record uncollectible-account expense has what effect on the financial statements?
a. Decreases owners' equity and increases liabilities
b. Increases expenses and increases owners' equity
c. Decreases assets and has no effect on net income
d. Decreases net income and decreases assets

Q5-43 Vincent Company uses the aging method to adjust the allowance for uncollectible accounts at the end of the period. At December 31, 2010, the balance of accounts receivable is $200,000 and the allowance for uncollectible accounts has a credit balance of $4,000 (before adjustment). An analysis of accounts receivable produced the following age groups:

Current	$160,000
60 days past due.........................	32,000
Over 60 days past due................	8,000
	$200,000

Based on past experience, Vincent estimates that the percentage of accounts that will prove to be uncollectible within the three age groups is 4%, 10%, and 21%, respectively. Based on these facts, the adjusting entry for uncollectible accounts should be made in the amount of
a. $7,280.   c. $16,280.
b. $11,280.   d. $2,000.

Q5-44 Refer to Question 5-43. The net receivables on the balance sheet is _____.

Q5-45 Graham Company uses the aging method in setting its allowance for doubtful receivables. Allowance for doubtful accounts prior to adjustment has a credit balance of $2,000. Management estimates that due to the economic crisis, a higher level of allowance is necessary and decides that a $5,900 allowance is an appropriate amount at the year end. The amount of expense to report on the income statement will be
a. $3,900.   c. $1,000.
b. $5,200.   d. $5,900.

Q5-46 How much interest revenue should Botores accrue on December 31, 2010?
a. $6,000   c. $2,500
b. $3,000   d. Some other amount

Q5-47 If Botores, Inc., fails to make an adjusting entry for the accrued interest,
a. net income will be overstated and liabilities will be understated.
b. net income will be overstated and assets will be overstated.
c. net income will be understated and liabilities will be overstated.
d. net income will be understated and assets will be understated.

Q5-48 How much interest does Botores, Inc., expect to collect on the maturity date (February 1, 2011)?
a. $3,000   c. $2,500
b. $6,000   d. Some other amount

Q5-49 Which of the following accounts will Botores credit in the journal entry at maturity on February 1, 2011, assuming collection in full?
a. Cash   c. Note Payable
b. Interest Payable   d. Interest Receivable

Q5-50 Write the journal entry on the maturity date (February 1, 2011).

Q5-51 Which of the following is included in the calculation of the acid-test ratio?
a. Prepaid expenses and cash   c. Inventory and prepaid expenses
b. Cash and accounts receivable   d. Inventory and short-term investment

Q5-52 A company with net sales of $1,017,000, beginning net receivables of $110,000, and ending net receivables of $120,000, has days' sales in accounts receivable of

a. 38 days.

b. 47 days.

c. 41 days.

d. 44 days.

Q5-53 A company sells on credit terms of "net 30 days" and has days' sales in account receivable of 30 days. Its days' sales in receivables is

a. too high.

b. too low.

c. about right.

d. cannot be evaluated from the data given.

Problems

> All of the A and B problems can be found within MyAccountingLab, an online homework and practice environment. Your instructor may ask you to complete these problems using MyAccountingLab.

(Group A)

P5-54A (*Learning Objective 1: Accounting for a trading investment*)   During the fourth quarter of 2010, Cable, Inc., generated excess cash, which the company invested in trading securities as follows:

2010	
Nov 18	Purchased 900 ordinary shares as an investment in trading securities, paying $12 per share.
Dec 15	Received cash dividend of $0.48 per share on the trading securities.
Dec 31	Adjusted the trading securities to their market value of $8 per share.

❚ Requirements

1. Open T-accounts for Cash (including its beginning balance of $15,000), Short-Term Investments, Dividend Revenue, and Unrealized Gain (Loss) on Investment.
2. Journalize the foregoing transactions and post to the T-accounts.
3. Show how to report the short-term investment on Cable's balance sheet at December 31.
4. Show how to report whatever should appear on Cable's income statement for the year ended December 31, 2010.
5. Cable sold the trading securities for $8,388 on January 12, 2011. Journalize the sale.

writing assignment ❚

P5-55A (*Learning Objective 2: Controlling cash receipts from customers*)   Laptop Delivery, Inc., makes all sales on account. Sarah Carter, accountant for the company, receives and opens incoming mail. Company procedure requires Carter to separate customer cheques from the remittance slips, which list the amounts that Carter posts as credits to customer accounts receivable. Carter deposits the cheques in the bank. At the end of each day she computes the day's total amount posted to customer accounts and matches this total to the bank deposit slip. This procedure ensures that all receipts are deposited in the bank.

❚ Requirement

1. As a consultant hired by Laptop Delivery, Inc., write a memo to management evaluating the company's internal controls over cash receipts from customers. If the system is effective, identify its strong features. If the system has flaws, propose a way to strengthen the controls.

P5-56A (*Learning Objective 3: Accounting for revenue, collections, and uncollectibles*)   This problem takes you through the accounting for sales, receivables, and uncollectibles for Mail Time Corp., the overnight shipper. By selling on credit, the company cannot expect to collect 100% of its accounts receivable. At May 31, 2010, and 2011, respectively, Mail Time Corp. reported the following on its balance sheet (in millions of dollars):

	May 31, 2011	2010
Accounts receivable...	$3,697	$3,434
Less: Allowance for uncollectible accounts..............	(126)	(155)
Accounts receivable, net...	$3,571	$3,279

During the year ended May 31, 2011, Mail Time Corp. earned service revenue and collected cash from customers. Assume uncollectible-account expense for the year was 1% of service revenue and that Mail Time wrote off uncollectible receivables. At year-end Mail Time ended with the foregoing May 31, 2011, balances.

I Requirements

1. Prepare T-accounts for Accounts Receivable and Allowance for Uncollectibles and insert the May 31, 2010, balances as given.
2. Journalize the following assumed transactions of Mail Time Corp. for the year ended May 31, 2011 (explanations are not required):
   a. Service revenue on account, $32,481 million
   b. Collections from customers on account, $31,864 million
   c. Write-offs of uncollectible accounts receivable, $354 million
   d. Uncollectible-account expense, $325 million
3. Post your entries to the Accounts Receivable and the Allowance for Uncollectibles T-accounts.
4. Compute the ending balances for the two T-accounts and compare your balances to the actual May 31, 2011, amounts. They should be the same.
5. Show what Mail Time would report on its income statement for the year ended May 31, 2011.

P5-57A (*Learning Objective 3: Using the aging approach for uncollectibles*)   The September 30, 2011, records of Perfecto Communications include these accounts:

Accounts Receivable.................................	$250,000
Allowance for Doubtful Accounts..............	(8,200)

At year-end (December 31), the company ages its receivables and adjusts the balance in Allowance for Doubtful Accounts to correspond to the aging schedule. During the last quarter of 2011, the company completed the following selected transactions:

Nov 30	Wrote off as uncollectible the $1,400 account receivable from Black Carpets and the $600 account receivable from Old Timer Antiques.
Dec 31	Adjusted the Allowance for Doubtful Accounts and recorded doubtful-account expense at year-end, based on the aging of receivables, which follows.

	Age of Accounts			
Accounts Receivable	1–30 Days	31–60 Days	61–90 Days	Over 90 Days
$232,000	$140,000	$45,000	$18,000	$29,000
Estimated percent uncollectible	0.1%	1%	10%	30%

Requirements

1. Record the transactions in the journal. Explanations are not required.
2. Prepare a T-account for Allowance for Doubtful Accounts and post to that account.
3. Show how Perfecto Communications will report its accounts receivable on its balance sheet as at December 31, 2011.

P5-58A *(Learning Objectives 1, 3, 5: Correcting current asset accounts and recomputing ratios)* Assume Smith & Jones, the accounting firm, advises Ocean Mist Seafood that its financial statements must be changed to conform to accounting standards. At December 31, 2010, Ocean Mist's accounts include the following:

Cash	$ 53,000
Short-term investment in trading securities, at cost	24,000
Accounts receivable	36,000
Inventory	63,000
Prepaid expenses	10,000
Total current assets	$186,000
Accounts payable	$ 67,000
Other current liabilities	39,000
Total current liabilities	$106,000

The accounting firm advised Ocean Mist that

- Cash includes $17,000 that is deposited in a fixed term deposit maturing in 2012.
- The market value of the trading securities is $10,000. Ocean Mist purchased the investments a couple of weeks ago.
- Ocean Mist has been using the direct write-off method to account for uncollectible receivables. During 2010, Ocean Mist wrote off bad receivables of $7,500. Smith & Jones performed an aging of Ocean Mist's receivables, and determined that as at year-end $10,500 are doubtful.
- Ocean Mist reported net income of $92,000 in 2010.

Requirements

1. Restate Ocean Mist's current accounts to conform to GAAP. (Challenge)
2. Compute Ocean Mist's current ratio and acid-test ratio both before and after your corrections.
3. Determine Ocean Mist's correct net income for 2010. (Challenge)

■ **general ledger**

P5-59A *(Learning Objective 4: Accounting for notes receivable and accrued interest revenue)* Healthy Meal completed the following selected transactions.

2010	
Oct 31	Sold goods to Buy Low Foods, receiving a $34,000, three-month, 5.25% note.
Dec 31	Made an adjusting entry to accrue interest on the Buy Low Foods note.
2011	
Jan 31	Collected the Buy Low Foods note.
Feb 18	Received a 90-day, 7.75%, $7,600 note from Dutton Market on account.
19	Sold the Dutton Market note to Amherst Bank, receiving cash of $7,400. (Debit the difference to financing expense.)
Nov 11	Lent $14,600 cash to Street Provisions, receiving a 90-day, 10.00% note.
Dec 31	Accrued the interest on the Street Provisions note.

I Requirements

1. Record the transactions in Healthy Meal's journal. Round interest amounts to the nearest dollar. Explanations are not required.
2. Show what Healthy Meal will report on its comparative classified balance sheet at December 31, 2011, and December 31, 2010.

P5-60A (*Learning Objective 5: Using ratio data to evaluate a company's financial position*) The comparative financial statements of Highland Pools, Inc., for 2011, 2010, and 2009 included the following select data:

■ **spreadsheet**

	(In millions)		
	2011	2010	2009
Balance sheet			
Current assets:			
Cash..	$ 80	$ 70	$ 60
Short-term investments	145	170	120
Receivables, net of allowance for doubtful accounts of $7, $6, and $4, respectively	270	250	240
Inventories	355	345	300
Prepaid expenses	60	30	55
Total current assets	$ 910	$ 865	$ 775
Total current liabilities...................	$ 580	$ 620	$ 690
Income statement			
Net sales	$5,880	$5,130	$4,220

I Requirements

1. Compute these ratios for 2011 and 2010:
   a. Current ratio
   b. Acid-test ratio
   c. Days' sales in receivables
2. Which ratios improved from 2010 to 2011 and which ratios deteriorated? Is this trend favorable or unfavorable?

(Group B)

P5-61B (*Learning Objective 1: Accounting for a trading investment*) During the fourth quarter of 2010, Main St., Inc., generated excess cash, which the company invested in trading securities, as follows:

2010	
Nov 13	Purchased 1,200 ordinary shares as an investment in trading securities, paying $10 per share.
Dec 14	Received cash dividend of $0.48 per share on the trading securities.
Dec 31	Adjusted the securities to their market value of $7 per share.

I Requirements

1. Open T-accounts for Cash (including its beginning balance of $22,000), Short-Term Investment, Dividend Revenue, and Unrealized Gain (Loss) on Investment.
2. Journalize the foregoing transactions and post to the T-accounts.
3. Show how to report the short-term investment on Main St.'s balance sheet at December 31.
4. Show how to report whatever should appear on Main St.'s income statement for the year ended December 31, 2010.
5. Main St. sold the trading securities for $10,512 on January 21, 2011. Journalize the sale.

writing assignment ■

P5-62B (*Learning Objective 2: Controlling cash receipts from customers*) Lakeview Software Solutions makes all sales on account, so virtually all cash receipts arrive in the mail. Larry Higgins, the company president, has just returned from a trade association meeting with new ideas for the business. Among other things, Higgins plans to institute stronger internal controls over cash receipts from customers.

I Requirement

1. Take the role of Larry Higgins, the company president. Write a memo to employees outlining procedures to ensure that all cash receipts are deposited in the bank and that the total amounts of each day's cash receipts are posted to customer accounts receivable.

writing assignment ■

P5-63B (*Learning Objective 3: Accounting for revenue, collections, and uncollectibles*) This problem takes you through the accounting for sales, receivables, and uncollectibles for Dependable Delivery Corp, the overnight shipper. By selling on credit, the company cannot expect to collect 100% of its accounts receivable. At May 31, 2010, and 2011, respectively, Dependable Delivery Corp. reported the following on its balance sheet (in millions of dollars):

	May 31,	
	2011	2010
Accounts receivable...	$3,693	$3,435
Less: Allowance for uncollectible accounts..............	(129)	(156)
Accounts receivable, net...	$3,564	$3,279

During the year ended May 31, 2011, Dependable Delivery Corp. earned sales revenue and collected cash from customers. Assume uncollectible-account expense for the year was 1% of service revenue and Dependable Delivery wrote off uncollectible receivables. At year end, Dependable Delivery ended with the foregoing May 31, 2011 balances.

I Requirements

1. Prepare T-accounts for Accounts Receivable and Allowance for Uncollectibles, and insert the May 31, 2010, balances as given.
2. Journalize the following transactions of Dependable Delivery for the year ended May 31, 2011. (Explanations are not required.)
   a. Service revenue on account, $32,487 million.
   b. Collections from customers on account, $31,877 million.
   c. Write-offs of uncollectible accounts receivable, $352 million
   d. Uncollectible-account expense, $325 million
3. Post to the Accounts Receivable and Allowance for Uncollectibles T-accounts.
4. Compute the ending balances for the two T-accounts and compare your balances to the actual May 31, 2011, amounts. They should be the same.
5. Show what Dependable Delivery should report on its income statement for the year ended May 31, 2011.

■ general ledger

P5-64B (*Learning Objective 3: Using the aging approach for uncollectibles*) The September 30, 2011, records of Image Communications include these accounts:

Accounts Receivable......................................	$260,000
Allowance for Doubtful Accounts..............	(8,100)

At year-end, the company ages its receivables and adjusts the balance in Allowance for Doubtful Accounts to correspond to the aging schedule. During the last quarter of 2011, the company completed the following selected transactions:

Dec 28	Wrote off as uncollectible the $1,500 account receivable from Blue Carpets and the $400 account receivable from Show-N-Tell Antiques.	
Dec 31	Adjusted the Allowance for Doubtful Accounts and recorded doubtful-account expense at year-end, based on the aging of receivables, which follows.	

	Age of Accounts			
Accounts Receivable	1–30 Days	31–60 Days	61–90 Days	Over 90 Days
$230,000	$160,000	$35,000	$14,000	$21,000
Estimated percent uncollectible	0.2%	1%	5%	30%

❚ Requirements

1. Record the transactions in the journal. Explanations are not required.
2. Prepare a T-account for Allowance for Doubtful Accounts and post to that account.
3. Show how Image Communications will report its accounts receivable on its balance sheet as at December 31, 2011.

P5-65B (*Learning Objectives 1, 3, 5: Correcting current asset accounts and recomputing ratios*)   Assume Smith & Jones, the accounting firm, advises Catch of the Day Seafood that its financial statement must be changed to conform to accounting standards. At December 31, 2010, Catch of the Day's accounts include the following:

Cash...	$ 56,000
Short-term trading securities, at cost	18,000
Accounts receivable..	44,000
Inventory...	55,000
Prepaid expenses	16,000
Total current assets	$189,000
Accounts payable...	$ 58,000
Other current liabilities	38,000
Total current liabilities..............................	$ 96,000

The accounting firm advised Catch of the Day that:

- Cash includes $24,000 that is deposited in a fixed term deposit maturing in 2012.
- The market value of the trading securities is $11,000. Catch of the Day purchased the trading securities a couple of weeks ago.
- Catch of the Day has been using the direct write-off method to account for uncollectible receivables. During 2010, Catch of the Day wrote off bad receivables of $5,500. Smith & Jones performed an aging of Catch of the Day's receivables, and determined that as at year-end $14,600 are doubtful.
- Catch of the Day reported net income of $99,000 for 2010.

❚ Requirements

1. Restate Catch of the Day's current accounts to conform to GAAP. (Challenge)
2. Compute Catch of the Day's current ratio and acid-test ratio both before and after your corrections.
3. Determine Catch of the Day's correct net income for 2010. (Challenge)

■ **general ledger**

P5-66B (*Learning Objective 4: Accounting for notes receivable and accrued interest revenue*)   Quick Meals completed the following selected transactions:

2010		
Nov 30	Sold goods to Bragg Market, receiving a $32,000, three-month, 4.00% note.	
Dec 31	Made an adjusting entry to accrue interest on the Bragg Market note.	
2011		
Feb 28	Collected the Bragg Market note.	
Mar 1	Received a 90-day, 8.00%, $7,200 note from Don's Market on account.	
1	Sold the Don's Market note to Chelmsford Bank, receiving cash of $7,000. (Debit the difference to financing expense.)	
Dec 16	Lent $15,400 cash to Stratford Provisions, receiving a 90-day, 9.50% note.	
Dec 31	Accrued the interest on the Stratford Provisions note.	

❙ Requirements

1. Record the transactions in Quick Meals' journal. Round all amounts to the nearest dollar. Explanations are not required.
2. Show what Quick Meals will report on its comparative classified balance sheet at December 31, 2011, and December 31, 2010.

■ **spreadsheet**

P5-67B (*Learning Objective 5: Using ratio data to evaluate a company's financial position*)   The comparative financial statements of Gold Pools, Inc., for 2011, 2010, and 2009 included the following select data:

	(In millions)		
	2011	**2010**	**2009**
Balance sheet			
Current assets:			
Cash...................................	$ 70	$ 80	$ 50
Short-term investments	145	160	110
Receivables, net of allowance for doubtful accounts of $7, $6, and $4, respectively	290	260	230
Inventories	360	345	310
Prepaid expenses	70	10	40
Total current assets.....................	$ 935	$ 855	$ 740
Total current liabilities..................	$ 560	$ 610	$ 680
Income statement			
Net sales	$5,890	$5,150	$4,200

❙ Requirements

1. Compute these ratios for 2011 and 2010:
   a. Current ratio
   b. Acid-test ratio
   c. Days' sales in receivables
2. Which ratios improved from 2010 to 2011 and which ratios deteriorated? Is this trend favorable or unfavorable?

APPLY YOUR KNOWLEDGE

Decision Cases

Case 1. (*Learning Objective 3: Determining allowance for doubtful receivables using the aging method, with and without additional information about loss events*) Two accounting interns, Serene and Joel, were tasked by you, their supervisor to propose the required amount of allowance as at December 31, 2011 for Alyssa Candy Empire (ACE), a distributor of specialty confectionery. Data provided to the two interns include an aging schedule below:

Age of Account Receivables					
Receivables	Not yet due	1–30 Days	31–60 Days	Over 60 Days	Total
Customer A	400				400
Customer B	100	100			200
Customer C	300	200	600	100	1,200
...	...	...	...	...	...
Totals	11,060	1,363	370	1,093	13,886
Percentage uncollectible	1.0%	5.0%	12.5%	20.0%	
Required allowance	111	68	46	219	444

Serene evaluated ACE's historical records of customer defaults and concluded that the likelihood of a receivable becoming bad is correlated to the age of the receivable. She assigned a 1%, 5%, 10% and 20% for each age group of receivables.

Joel took another approach and evaluated the likelihood of receivable impairment customer by customer. His research shows that Customer A is a new customer and since it is not yet overdue, there is only a 1% chance that it will not be collected. Customer B and Customer D are long time customers, and whilst they may pay a little later than the usual credit term of 30 days, the likelihood of not being able to collect their receivables is only 10%. Joel has read that Customer C was not able to make its loan repayments last month. Newspapers articles also point to some worry about Customer C's ability to continue as a growing concern. Joel estimated that it is almost certain that the amount owing would be uncollectible. Customer E, located in another country, has also experienced significant decline in business due to a severe recession in the country. Joel believes that there is a 20% chance that the receivables may be impaired.

Joel and Serene performed their analysis and reported back to you with their recommendations. Whose recommendation will you accept? Why?

Case 2. (*Learning Objective 3: Estimating the collectibility of accounts receivable*) Suppose you work in the loan department of Superior Bank. Dean Young, owner of Dean Young Beauty Aids, has come to you seeking a loan for $500,000 to expand operations. Young proposes to use accounts receivable as collateral for the loan and has provided you with the following information from the company's most recent financial statements:

❙ *Requirement*

1. Analyze the trends of sales, days' sales in receivables, and cash collections from customers for 2011 and 2010. Would you make the loan to Young? Support your decision with facts and figures.

Ethical Issue

Sunnyvale Loan Company is in the consumer loan business. Sunnyvale borrows from banks and loans out the money at higher interest rates. Sunnyvale's bank requires Sunnyvale to submit quarterly financial statements to keep its line of credit. Sunnyvale's main asset is Notes

	2011	2010	2009
	(In thousands)		
Sales	$1,475	$1,001	$902
Cost of goods sold	876	647	605
Gross profit	599	354	297
Other expenses	518	287	253
Net profit or (loss) before taxes	$ 81	$ 67	$ 44
Accounts receivable	$ 128	$ 107	$ 94
Allowance for doubtful accounts	13	11	9

Receivable. Therefore, Uncollectible-Account Expense and Allowance for Uncollectible Accounts are important accounts for the company.

Kimberly Burnham, the company's owner, prefers that net income reflect a steady increase in a smooth pattern, rather than increase in some periods and decrease in other periods. To report smoothly increasing net income, Burnham underestimates Uncollectible-Account Expense in some periods. In other periods, Burnham overestimates the expense. She reasons that the income overstatements roughly offset the income understatements over time.

▌*Requirements*

1. What is the ethical issue in this situation?
2. Who are the stakeholders? What are the possible consequences to each?
3. Analyze the alternatives from the following standpoints: (a) economic, (b) legal, (c) ethical.
4. What would you do? How would you justify your decision?

Focus on Financials: ■ Nokia Corporation

Refer to **Nokia**'s Balance Sheets as well as Note 1- Accounting principles, in Appendix A at the end of this book.

1. Refer to the account in Nokia's balance sheet entitled "accounts receivable, net of allowances for doubtful accounts" What does the "net" mean? How does Nokia determine its allowance for doubtful accounts?
2. How much is the allowance for doubtful accounts in 2008 and 2007? How much was utilised in 2008 and 2007? Do the journal entries for the writing off of uncollectible accounts and the allowance for bad debts in 2008.
3. Look at Note 15- Available-for-sale investments. Note that the 2008 ending balance for current available-for-sale investments totals $5,114 million. Make a T-account for current available-for-sale investments. Record $9,628 million as the balance in the account as at the end of 2007. Using information in the investments section of the consolidated statement of cash flows, record the cash purchases and sales of current available-for-sale investments during 2008. Why doesn't the ending balance equal the amount shown on the balance sheet as of the end of 2008?

Group Project

Jillian Michaels and Dee Childress worked for several years as sales representatives for Xerox Corporation. During this time, they became close friends as they acquired expertise with the company's full range of copier equipment. Now they see an opportunity to put their expertise to work and fulfill lifelong desires to establish their own business. Navarro Community College, located in their city, is expanding, and there is no copy center within five miles of the campus. Business in the area is booming, office buildings and apartments are springing up, and the population of the Navarro section of the city is growing.

Michaels and Childress want to open a copy center, similar to FedEx Kinko's, near the Navarro campus. A small shopping center across the street from the college has a vacancy that would fit their needs. Michaels and Childress each have $35,000 to invest in the business, but they forecast the need for $200,000 to renovate the store and purchase some of the equipment they will need. Xerox Corporation will lease two large copiers to them at a total monthly rental of $6,000. With enough cash to see them through the first six months of operation, they are confident they can make the business succeed. The two women work very well together, and both have excellent credit ratings. Michaels and Childress must borrow $130,000 to start the business, advertise its opening, and keep it running for its first six months.

❚ Requirements

Assume two roles: (1) Michaels and Childress, the partners who will own Navarro Copy Center; and (2) loan officers at Synergy Bank.

1. As a group, visit a copy center to familiarize yourselves with its operations. If possible, interview the manager or another employee. Then write a loan request that Michaels and Childress will submit to Synergy Bank with the intent of borrowing $130,000 to be paid back over three years. The loan will be a personal loan to the partnership of Michaels and Childress, not to Navarro Copy Center. The request should specify all the details of Michaels' and Childress' plan that will motivate the bank to grant the loan. Include a budget for each of the first six months of operation of the proposed copy center.
2. As a group, interview a loan officer in a bank. Write Synergy Bank's reply to the loan request. Specify all the details that the bank should require as conditions for making the loan.
3. If necessary, modify the loan request or the bank's reply in order to reach agreement between the two parties.

Quick Check Answers

1. *a*
2. *a*
3. *d* 6,000 (10,000 + 40,000 − 44,000)
4. *b* ($600 + $1,600)
5. *c* ($1,030 − $600)
6. *b*
7. *d* ($10,000 − $1,030)
8. *d* ($2,800 − $90) − ($400 − $90)
9. *b* ($575,000 + $2,200,000 − $725,000)
10. *c* ($2,800 × 0.09 × 4/12 × 1/4)
11. *d* $70,000 + ($70,000 × 0.12 × 6/12)
12. *a*
13. *a* [($80,000 + $74,000)/2] ÷ ($803,000/365)
14. *a* ($6,000 + $3,000 + $9,000) ÷ ($10,000 + $4,000)

For online homework, exercises, and problems that provide you with immediate feedback, please visit www.myaccountinglab.com.

6

Inventory & Cost of Goods Sold

SPOTLIGHT: Bossini

With close to 1,200 outlets in over 30 countries and regions around the globe, **Bossini** is a leading apparel retailer in the Asia Pacific region.

As a retailer, inventory is an important part of Bossini's operations. Its Balance Sheet showed that, excluding cash, inventories is the second largest asset. Bossini has more inventory than its total non-current assets! In addition, Bossini's biggest expense item on its Income Statement is the cost of the inventory it sold to customers.

Inventory is really at the heart of a retail operation! In this chapter, we will learn about how companies account for their inventory and how its related cost of goods sold.

Bossini International Holdings
Consolidated Balance Sheets (Partial, adapted)
As at June 30

(in thousands HKD, Hong Kong Dollars)	2009	2008
1 Cash and cash equivalents.............................	$ 342,260	$ 310,303
2 Debtors..	55,143	62,519
3 Inventories..	280,987	230,056
4 Bills receivable	9,783	4,923
5 Deposits paid	33,934	26,234
6 Prepayments and other receivables................	43,250	29,167
7 Tax recoverable..	269	134
8 Total current assets	765,626	663,336
9 Property, plant and equipment	178,464	175,767
10 Trademark	1,164	1,164
11 Deferred tax assets	3,290	2,848
12 Deposits paid	62,967	68,430
13 Total non-current assets	245,885	248,209
14 Total assets...	1,011,511	911,545
15 Total liabilities	338,751	256,503
16 Total equity...	672,760	655,042
17 Total liabilities and equity...........................	$1,011,511	$ 911,545

Bossini International Holdings
Consolidated Income Statements (Partial, adapted)
Financial Year Ended June 30

(in thousands HKD, Hong Kong Dollars)	2009	2008
1 Revenues...	$2,254,126	$2,316,869
2 Cost of sales..	(1,141,484)	(1,147,017)
3 Gross profit...	1,112,642	1,169,852
4 Other income...	13,481	11,017
5 Selling and distribution costs........................	(779,144)	(793,917)
6 Administrative expenses...............................	(235,799)	(256,133)
7 Other operating expenses.............................	(51,368)	(41,091)
8 Profit from operations.................................	59,812	89,728
9 Finance costs...	(2,707)	(2,204)
10 Tax	(6,853)	(23,949)
11 Profit for the year.......................................	$ 50,252	$ 63,575

You can see that cost of sales is by far Bossini's largest expense. The title *Cost of Sales* (many companies also use the term *Cost of Goods Sold*) perfectly describes that expense. In short:

- Bossini buys (or manufactures) inventory, an asset carried on the books at cost.
- The goods that Bossini sells are no longer Bossini's assets. The cost of inventory that's sold gets shifted into the expense account, Cost of Sales or Cost of Goods Sold (COGS). We will use both terms interchangeably.

Inventory is the heart of a merchandising business, and cost of goods sold is the most important expense item for a retailer. Gross profit (or gross margin) is the difference between net sales and cost of goods sold. This chapter covers the accounting for inventory and cost of goods sold. It also shows you how to further analyze financial statements. Here we focus on inventory, cost of goods sold and gross profit.

LEARNING OBJECTIVES

1 Account for inventory

2 Understand the various inventory methods

3 Use gross profit percentage and inventory turnover to evaluate operations

4 Estimate inventory by the gross profit method

5 Show how inventory errors affect the financial statements

ACCOUNTING FOR INVENTORY

We begin by showing how the financial statements of a merchandiser such as Bossini, or **Muji**, differ from those of service entities such as **Singapore Airlines** and accounting firms. The financial statements in Exhibit 6-1 (p. 344) highlight how service entities differ from merchandisers (dollar amounts are assumed).

The basic concept of accounting for merchandise inventory can be illustrated with an example. Suppose Bossini has in stock three shirts that cost $30 each. Bossini sells two shirts for $50 each:

- Bossini's balance sheet reports the one shirt that the company still holds in inventory.
- The income statement reports the cost of the two shirts sold, as shown in Exhibit 6-2 (p. 345).

Here is the basic concept of how we identify **inventory**, the asset, from **cost of goods sold**, the expense.

OBJECTIVE

1 Account for inventory

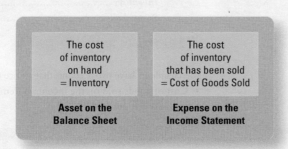

TECHNICAL UPDATE

IAS2 – Inventories defines inventories as assets that are (a) held for sale in the ordinary course of business, (b) in the process of production for such sale; or (c) in the form of materials or supplies to be consumed in the production process or in the rendering of services. This means that inventory could be raw materials, work in process or finished goods.

A retailer is more likely to have only finished goods in its inventory, whereas a manufacturer may have inventories at various stages of completion (from raw materials to finished goods). We shall limit our discussion in this chapter on finished goods, or goods ready for resale; but the principles of accounting for inventory remain the same for all three categories of inventories.

EXHIBIT 6-1 | **Contrasting a Service Company with a Merchandiser**

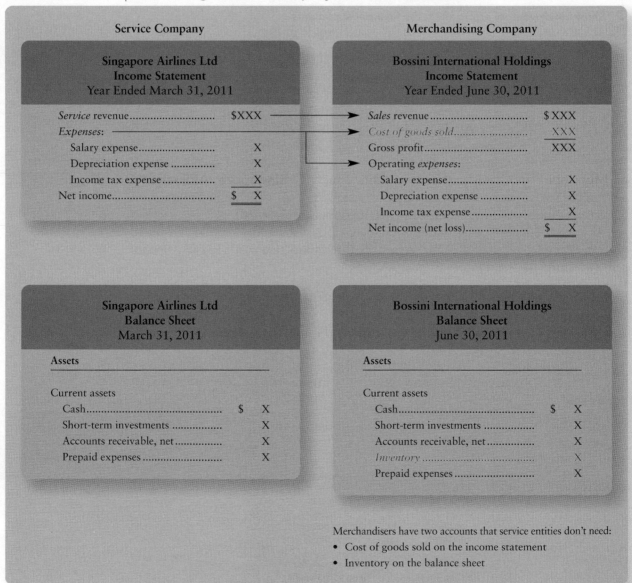

Merchandisers have two accounts that service entities don't need:
- Cost of goods sold on the income statement
- Inventory on the balance sheet

EXHIBIT 6-2 | Inventory and Cost of Goods Sold When Inventory Cost is Constant

Balance Sheet (partial)		Income Statement (partial)	
Current assets		Sales revenue	
Cash...	$XXX	(2 shirts @ sale price of $50 each)	$100
Short-term investments	XXX	Cost of goods sold	
Accounts receivable.................................	XXX	(2 shirts @ cost of $30 each)	60
Inventory (1 shirt @ cost of $30).............	30	Gross profit...	$ 40
Prepaid expenses	XXX		

The cost of the inventory sold shifts from asset to expense when the seller delivers the goods to the buyer. We discussed this in Chapter 3, and looked at the revenue recognition criteria stipulated in *IAS18 – Revenue* (p.139).

Sale Price vs. Cost of Inventory

Note the difference between the sale price of inventory and the cost of inventory. In our example:

- Sales revenue is based on the *sale price* of the inventory sold ($50 per shirt).
- Cost of goods sold is based on the *cost* of the inventory sold ($30 per shirt).
- Inventory on the balance sheet is based on the *cost* of the inventory still on hand ($30 per shirt).

Exhibit 6-2 above shows these items.

Gross profit, also called **gross margin**, is the excess of sales revenue over cost of goods sold. It is called *gross* profit because operating expenses have not yet been subtracted. Exhibit 6-3 shows actual inventory and cost of goods sold adapted from the financial statements of Bossini.

EXHIBIT 6-3 | Bossini's Inventory and Cost of Goods Sold (Cost of Sales)

Bossini International Holdings Consolidated Balance Sheet (Partial, adapted) As at June 30	
(In thousands HKD, Hong Kong Dollars)	2009
1 Cash and cash equivalents.....................................	$342,260
2 Debtors...	55,143
3 Inventories	280,987

Bossini International Holdings
Consolidated Income Statement (Partial, adapted)
Financial Year Ended June 30

(In thousands HKD, Hong Kong Dollars)	2009
1 Revenue	$2,254,126
2 Cost of sales	(1,141,484)
3 Gross profit	$1,112,642

Bossini's inventory of 280,987 represents:

$$\text{Inventory (balance sheet)} = \text{Number of units of inventory } on\ hand \times \text{Cost per unit of inventory}$$

And the cost of goods sold of 1,141,484 represents:

$$\text{Cost of goods sold (income statement)} = \text{Number of units of inventory } sold \times \text{Cost per unit of inventory}$$

Let's see what "units of inventory" and "cost per unit" mean.

Number of Units of Inventory. The number of inventory units on hand is determined from the accounting records, backed up by a physical count of the goods at year end. Companies do not include any goods in their inventory which they hold on **consignment** because those goods belong to another company. But they do include their own inventory that is out on consignment and held by another company. Companies include inventory in transit from suppliers or in transit to customers that, according to shipping terms, legally belong to them as of the year end. Shipping terms, otherwise known as *FOB terms*, indicate who owns the goods at a particular time and, therefore, who must pay for the shipping costs. The term **FOB** stands for *free on board* (or *freight on board*). When the vendor invoice specifies *FOB shipping point* (the most common business practice), legal title to the goods passes from the seller to the purchaser when the inventory leaves the seller's place of business. The purchaser therefore owns the goods while they are in transit and must pay the transportation costs. In the case of goods purchased FOB shipping point, the company purchasing the goods must include goods in transit from suppliers as units in inventory as of the year end. In the case of goods purchased *FOB destination*, title to the goods does not pass from the seller to the purchaser until the goods arrive at the purchaser's receiving dock. Therefore, these goods are not counted in year-end inventory of the purchasing company. Rather, the cost of these goods is included in inventory of the seller until the goods reach their destination.

Cost Per Unit of Inventory. The cost per unit of inventory poses a challenge because companies purchase goods at different prices throughout the year. Which unit costs go into ending inventory? Which unit costs go to cost of goods sold?

Let's have a look at Bossini's inventory policy. There are many terms that you may not quite understand for now, but as we progress through this Chapter, you will hopefully gain a better understanding of the inventory policy.

EXCERPTS FROM BOSSINI'S NOTES TO THE 2009 FINANCIAL STATEMENTS

Inventories

Inventories are stated at the lower of cost and net realizable value. Cost is determined on the first-in, first-out basis and includes all costs of purchase and other costs incurred in bringing the inventories to their present location and condition. Net realizable value is based on estimated selling prices less any estimated costs necessary to make the sale.

The next section shows how different accounting methods determine amounts reported on the balance sheet and the income statement. First, however, you need to understand how inventory accounting systems work.

Accounting for Inventory in the Perpetual System

There are two main types of inventory accounting systems: the periodic system and the perpetual system. The **periodic inventory system**, discussed in more detail in Appendix 6A (p. 401), is used for inexpensive goods. A fabric store or a lumber yard won't keep a running record of every bolt of fabric or every piece of wood. Instead, these stores count their inventory periodically—at least once a year—to determine the quantities on hand. Businesses such as restaurants and hometown nurseries also use the periodic system because the accounting cost of a periodic system is low.

A **perpetual inventory system** uses computer software to keep a running record of inventory on hand. This system achieves control over goods such as Bossini's clothing, furniture, automobiles, jewelry, apparel, and most other types of inventory. Most businesses use the perpetual inventory system.

Even with a perpetual system, a business should still counts the inventory on hand annually. The physical count establishes the correct amount of ending inventory for the financial statements and also serves as a check on the perpetual records. Here is a quick summary of the two main inventory accounting systems.

Perpetual Inventory System	Periodic Inventory System
• Used for all types of goods	• Used for inexpensive goods
• Keeps a running record of all goods bought, sold and on hand	• Does *not* keep a running record of all goods bought, sold and on hand
• Inventory counted at least once a year	• Inventory counted at least once a year

How the Perpetual System Works.   Let's use an everyday situation to show how a perpetual inventory system works. When you check out of a **Carrefour**, a **Marks & Spencer**, or a Bossini store, the sales clerk scans the bar codes on the labels of the items you buy. Exhibit 6-4 illustrates a typical bar code. Suppose you are buying a pair of jeans from Bossini. The bar code on the product label holds lots of information. The optical scanner reads the bar code, and the computer records the sale and updates the inventory records.

EXHIBIT 6-4 | Bar Code for Electronic Scanner

0 72512 06581 5

Recording Transactions in the Perpetual System. All accounting systems record each purchase of inventory. When Bossini makes a sale, two entries are needed in the perpetual system:

- The company records the sale—debits Cash or Accounts Receivable and credits Sales Revenue for the sale price of the goods.
- It also debits Cost of Goods Sold and credits Inventory for the cost of the inventory sold.

Exhibit 6-5 shows the accounting for inventory in a perpetual system. Panel A gives the journal entries and the T-accounts, and Panel B shows the income statement and the balance sheet. All amounts are assumed. (Appendix 6A illustrates the accounting for these same transactions for a periodic inventory system.)

EXHIBIT 6-5 | **Recording and Reporting Inventory—Perpetual System (Amounts Assumed)**

PANEL A—Recording Transactions and the T-accounts (All amounts are assumed)

Journal Entry

1.	Inventory	560,000	
	Accounts Payable		560,000
	Purchased inventory on account.		
2.	Accounts Receivable	900,000	
	Sales Revenue		900,000
	Sold inventory on account.		
	Cost of Goods Sold	540,000	
	Inventory		540,000
	Recorded cost of goods sold.		

Inventory

Beginning balance	100,000*		
Purchases	560,000	Cost of goods sold	540,000
Ending balance	120,000		

*Beginning inventory was $100,000

Cost of Goods Sold

| Cost of goods sold | 540,000 | |

PANEL B—Reporting in the Financial Statements

Income Statement (partial)

Sales revenue	$900,000
Cost of goods sold	540,000
Gross profit	$360,000

Ending Balance Sheet (partial)

Current assets:	
Cash	$ XXX
Short-term investments	XXX
Accounts receivable	XXX
Inventory	120,000
Prepaid expenses	XXX

In Exhibit 6-5, the first entry to Inventory summarizes a lot of detail. The cost of the inventory, $560,000, is the *net* amount of the purchases, is determined as follows (using assumed amounts):

Purchase price of the inventory	$600,000
+ **Freight-in** (the cost to transport the goods from the seller to the buyer)	4,000
− **Purchase returns** for unsuitable goods returned to the seller	(25,000)
− **Purchase allowances** granted by the seller	(5,000)
− **Purchase discounts** for early payment by the buyer	(14,000)
= Net purchases of inventory (Cost to the buyer)	$560,000

Freight-in is the transportation cost, paid by the buyer, under terms FOB shipping point, to move goods from the seller to the buyer. Freight-in is accounted for as part of the cost of inventory. A **purchase return** is a decrease in the cost of inventory because the buyer returned the goods to the seller (vendor). A **purchase allowance** also decreases the cost of inventory because the buyer got an allowance (a deduction) from the amount owed. To document approval of purchase returns, management issues a **debit memorandum** (or debit memo), meaning that accounts payable are reduced (debited) for the amount of the return. The offsetting credit is to inventory as the goods are shipped back to the seller (vendor). Purchase discounts and allowances are usually documented on the final invoice received from the vendor. Throughout this book, we often refer to net purchases simply as Purchases.

A **purchase discount** is a decrease in the buyer's cost of inventory earned by paying quickly. Many companies offer payment terms of "2/10 n/30." This means the buyer can take a 2% discount for payment within 10 days, with the final amount due within 30 days. Another common credit term is "net 30," which tells the customer to pay the full amount within 30 days. In summary:

$$
\begin{aligned}
\text{Net purchases} = \ &\text{Purchases} \\
&- \text{Purchase returns and allowances} \\
&- \text{Purchase discounts} \\
&+ \text{Freight-in}
\end{aligned}
$$

Net sales are computed exactly the same as net purchases, but with no freight-in, as follows:

$$
\begin{aligned}
\text{Net sales} = \ &\text{Sales revenue} \\
&- \text{Sales returns and allowances} \\
&- \text{Sales discounts}
\end{aligned}
$$

Freight-out paid by the *seller*, under shipping terms FOB destination, is not part of the cost of inventory. Instead, freight-out is delivery expense. It's the seller's expense of delivering merchandise to customers.

INVENTORY COSTING

Inventory is an example of an asset for which a manager can decide which accounting method to use. The accounting method selected affects the profits to be reported, the amount of income tax to be paid, and the values of the ratios derived from the balance sheet.

What Goes into Inventory Cost?

The cost of inventory on Bossini's balance sheet represents all the costs that the company incurred to bring its inventory to the point of sale. *IAS2 – Inventories* states that the cost of inventories shall comprise all costs of purchase, costs of conversion and other costs incurred in bringing the inventories to their present location and condition. The costs of purchase of inventories thus comprise the purchase price, import duties and other taxes, and transport, handling and other costs directly attributable to the acquisition of finished goods, materials and services. If an entity receives trade discounts, rebates and other similar items, they are deducted when determining the costs of purchase. As we have seen, inventory's cost includes its basic purchase price, plus freight-in, insurance while in transit, and any fees or taxes paid to get the inventory ready to sell, less returns, allowances, and discounts.

Once the goods are ready for resale, other costs, such as advertising and sales commissions, are *not* included as the cost of inventory. Advertising, sales commissions, and delivery costs are selling expenses that go in the income statement, rather than in the balance sheet.

The Various Inventory Costing Methods

OBJECTIVE

2 Understand the various inventory methods

Determining the cost of inventory is easy when the unit cost remains constant, as in Exhibit 6-2. But the unit cost usually changes. For example, prices often rise. The khakis that cost Bossini $10 in January may cost $14 in June and $18 in October. Suppose Bossini sells 1,000 pair of khakis in November. How many of those khakis cost $10, how many cost $14, and how many cost $18?

To compute cost of goods sold and the cost of ending inventory still on hand, we must assign unit cost to the items. *IAS2 – Inventories* prescribes that cost of inventory items that are not ordinarily interchangeable (and goods or services produced and segregated for specific projects) shall be assigned by using **specific identification** (also known as specific unit) of their individual costs. Cost of other inventories that are ordinarily interchangeable shall be determined using some cost formulas. The common cost formulas (also known as inventory cost assumption) include: first-in, first-out (FIFO), last-in first-out (LIFO) and average cost method. The methods can have very different effects on reported profits in the income statement and inventory on the balance sheet. Therefore, companies select their inventory method with great care. *IAS2* requires an entity to use the same cost formula for all inventories having a similar nature and use to the entity. It is possible to use different cost formulas for inventories with a different nature or use.

TECHNICAL UPDATE

IAS2 – Inventories also allows the *retail inventory method* to be used, as long as they approximate the cost. This method is used by retailers for measuring inventories of large numbers of rapidly changing items with similar margins. The cost of the inventory is determined by reducing the sales value of the inventory by the appropriate percentage gross margin. The percentage used takes into consideration inventory that has been marked down to below its original selling price. As this is an industry specific cost formula, we will not be discussing this method in detail.

In addition, *IAS2 – Inventories* prohibits the use of last-in, last-out (LIFO) cost formula. This is one of the major differences between US and International GAAP. For the purpose of discussions in this Chapter, we will continue to elaborate on LIFO because it provides a good contrast to FIFO, one of the cost formulas allowed under IFRS.

Let's have a look how specific identification and the other cost formulas work.

Specific Identification. Some businesses deal in unique inventory items, such as automobiles, antique furniture, jewelry, and real estate. These businesses cost their inventories at the specific cost of the particular unit. For instance, a **Toyota** dealer may have four vehicles in the showroom—(1) a Camry, (2) a Corolla, (3) a Prius and (4) a Lexus. If the dealer sells the Camry, Prius and Lexus, the cost of goods sold is the costs of the three vehicles (1, 3 and 4) sold. The only item remaining on its balance sheet will be the (2) Corolla. The diagram below illustrates this point.

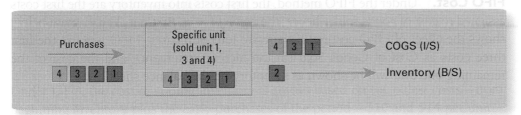

The Hourglass (a specialist luxury watch retailer), **Aspial** (a contemporary fashion jeweler), **Jardine Cycle and Carriage** (automotive retailer) all use the specific identification method.

The specific identification method is also called the specific-unit-cost method. This method is too expensive to use for inventory items that have common characteristics, such as bushels of wheat, gallons of paint, or the casual apparel that Bossini sells.

The other inventory accounting methods—average, FIFO, and LIFO—are fundamentally different. These other methods do not use the specific cost of a particular unit. Instead, they assume different flows of inventory costs. Remember that the goods are interchangeable, and cost formulas are not the same as the physical units. Businesses will always try to sell older units first (to prevent spoilage, obsolescence, etc.) before selling newer units. This is independent of the cost formulas used.

To illustrate average, FIFO, and LIFO costing, we use a common set of data, given in Exhibit 6-6.

EXHIBIT 6-6 | **Inventory Data Used to Illustrate the Various Inventory Costing Methods**

		Inventory		
Beg bal	(10 units @ $10)	100		
Purchases:			Cost of goods sold	
No. 1	(25 units @ $14)	350	(40 units @ ?)	?
No. 2	(25 units @ $18)	450		
End bal	(20 units @ ?)	?		

In Exhibit 6-6, let's assume Bossini began the period with 10 khakis that cost $10 each; hence the beginning inventory was therefore $100. During the period, Bossini bought 50 more khakis (at different prices), sold 40 khakis, and ended the period with 20 khakis, summarized as follows:

Goods Available		Number of Units	Total Cost
Goods available	=	10 + 25 + 25 = 60 units	$100 + $350 + $450 = $900
Cost of goods sold	=	40 units	?
Ending inventory	=	20 units	?

Effects of FIFO, LIFO and Average Cost on Cost of Goods Sold, Gross Profit, and Ending Inventory

In our Bossini khakis example, the cost of inventory rose from $10 to $14 to $18. When inventory unit costs change this way, the various inventory methods produce different cost-of-goods sold figures. Exhibit 6-7 summarizes the income effects (sales—cost of goods sold = gross profit) of the three inventory methods (remember that prices are rising). Study Exhibit 6-7 carefully, focusing on cost of goods sold and gross profit.

EXHIBIT 6-7 | **Income Effects of the FIFO, LIFO, and Average Cost Inventory Methods**

	FIFO	LIFO	Average
Sales revenue (assumed)	$1,000	$1,000	$1,000
Cost of goods sold........................	540 (lowest)	660 (highest)	600
Gross profit.................................	$ 460 (highest)	$ 340 (lowest)	$ 400

Exhibit 6-8 shows the impact of both FIFO and LIFO costing methods on cost of goods sold and inventories during both increasing costs (Panel A) and decreasing costs (Panel B). Study this exhibit carefully; it will help you *really* understand FIFO and LIFO.

EXHIBIT 6-8 | **Cost of Goods Sold and Ending Inventory—FIFO and LIFO; Increasing Costs and Decreasing Costs**

Panel A—When Inventory Costs are Increasing

	Cost of Goods Sold (COGS)	Ending Inventory
FIFO	FIFO COGS is lowest because it's based on the oldest costs, which are low. Gross profit is therefore, the highest.	FIFO ending inventory is highest because it's based on the most recent costs, which are high.
LIFO	LIFO COGS is highest because it's based on the most recent costs, which are high. Gross profit is therefore, the lowest.	LIFO ending inventory is lowest because it's based on the oldest costs, which are low.

Panel B—When Inventory Costs Are Decreasing

	Cost of Goods Sold (COGS)	Ending Inventory
FIFO	FIFO COGS is highest because it's based on the oldest costs, which are high. Gross profit is therefore, the lowest.	FIFO ending inventory is lowest because it's based on the most recent costs, which are low.
LIFO	LIFO COGS is lowest because it's based on the most recent costs which are low. Gross profit is therefore, the highest.	LIFO ending inventory is highest because it's based on the oldest costs, which are high.

Exhibit 6-9, based on an American Institute of Certified Public Accountants (AICPA) survey of 600 companies in 2008, indicates that FIFO remains the most popular inventory method.

EXHIBIT 6-9 | Use of the Various Inventory Methods

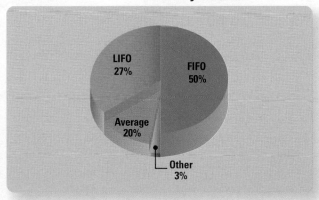

Recall that *IAS2* requires entities to use the same cost formula unless the nature of the inventories is dissimilar. Here's an example from **Sincere Watch**, another specialist luxury watch retailer, on the use of different inventory methods for different inventory items.

EXCERPTS (ADAPTED) FROM SINCERE WATCH'S NOTES TO THE 2008 FINANCIAL STATEMENTS

Inventories
High-end inventories are stated using specific identification method and low-end inventories are stated using weighted average method.

Comparison of the Inventory Methods

Let's compare the average, FIFO, and LIFO inventory methods.

1. Measuring Cost of Goods Sold. How well does each method match inventory expense—cost of goods sold—against revenue? LIFO results in the most realistic net income figure because LIFO assigns the most recent inventory costs to expense. In contrast, FIFO matches old inventory costs against revenue—a poor measure of expense. FIFO income is therefore less realistic than LIFO income.

2. Measuring Ending Inventory. Which method reports the most up-to-date inventory cost on the balance sheet? FIFO. LIFO can value inventory at very old costs because LIFO leaves the oldest prices in ending inventory.

MID-CHAPTER SUMMARY PROBLEM

Suppose a division of **Flextronics** that sells computer microchips has these inventory records for January 2011:

Date		Item	Quantity	Unit Cost	Total cost
Jan	1	Beginning inventory	100 units	$ 8	$ 800
	6	Purchase	60 units	9	540
	21	Purchase	150 units	9	1,350
	27	Purchase	90 units	10	900

Company accounting records show sales of 310 units for revenue of $6,770. Operating expense for January was $1,900.

Requirements

1. Prepare the January income statement, showing amounts for LIFO, average, and FIFO cost. Label the bottom line "Operating income." Round average cost per unit to three decimal places and all other figures to whole-dollar amounts. Show your computations.
2. Suppose you are the financial vice president of Flextronics. Which inventory method will you use if your motive is to
   a. minimize income taxes?
   b. report the highest operating income?
   c. report operating income between the extremes of FIFO and LIFO?
   d. report inventory on the balance sheet at the most current cost?
   e. attain the best measure of net income for the income statement?
   State the reason for each of your answers.

Answers

Requirement 1

Flextronics International Limited
Income Statement for Microchip
Month Ended January 31, 2011

	LIFO	Average	FIFO
Sales revenue..........................	$6,770	$6,770	$6,770
Cost of goods sold.................	2,870	2,782	2,690
Gross profit...........................	3,900	3,988	4,080
Operating expenses	1,900	1,900	1,900
Operating income..................	$2,000	$2,088	$2,180

Cost of goods sold computations:

LIFO: (90 @ $10) + (150 @ $9) + (60 @ $9) + (10 @ $8) = $2,870

Average: 310 × $8.975* = $2,782

FIFO: (100 @ $8) + (60 @ $9) + (150 @ $9) = $2,690

$$*\frac{(\$800 + \$540 + \$1,350 + \$900)}{(100 + 60 + 150 + 90)} = \$8.975$$

I *Requirement 2*

a. Use LIFO to minimize income taxes. Operating income under LIFO is lowest when inventory unit costs are increasing, as they are in this case (from $8 to $10). (If inventory costs were decreasing, income under FIFO would be lowest.)

b. Use FIFO to report the highest operating income. Income under FIFO is highest when inventory unit costs are increasing, as in this situation.

c. Use the average cost method to report an operating income amount between the FIFO and LIFO extremes. This is true in this situation and in others when inventory unit costs are increasing or decreasing.

d. Use FIFO to report inventory on the balance sheet at the most current cost. The oldest inventory costs are expensed as cost of goods sold, leaving in ending inventory the most recent (most current) costs of the period.

e. Use LIFO to attain the best measure of net income. LIFO produces the best matching of current expense with current revenue. The most recent (most current) inventory costs are expensed as cost of goods sold.

ACCOUNTING PRINCIPLES RELATED TO INVENTORY

Comparability Principle

The **comparability principle** states that businesses should use the same accounting methods and procedures from period to period. Consistency enables investors to compare a company's financial statements from one period to the next.

Suppose you are analyzing a company's net income pattern which showed an increase over a two-year period. However, you also noted that the company switched from LIFO to FIFO during that time. Its net income increased dramatically but only because of the change in inventory method. If you did not know of the accounting change, you might believe that the company's income increased due to improved operations, but that's not the case!

The comparability principle does not mean that a company is not permitted to change its accounting methods. However, a company making an accounting change must disclose the effect of the change on net income.

For example, on November 18, 2009, **Frontier Oil Corporation** changed its inventory cost method from FIFO to LIFO and provided this explanation in its press release:

EXCERPTS FROM FRONTIER'S PRESS RELEASE ON NOVEMBER 18, 2009

Frontier Oil Corporation (NYSE:FTO) today announced its intention to change its inventory valuation method to the last-in, first-out (LIFO) method from the first-in, first-out (FIFO) method ... The inventory valuation change will decrease Frontier's reported pre-tax income for the nine months ended September 30, 2009 by approximately $180 million. As a result of lower pre-tax income, the Company believes it will recognize cash tax savings in excess of $60 million for the nine months ended September 30, 2009.

On the other hand, **Pactiv Corporation** changed its inventory cost method from a combination of LIFO and FIFO to exclusively FIFO. Its press release on December 21, 2009 stated the following:

EXCERPTS FROM PACTIV CORP'S PRESS RELEASE ON DEC 21, 2009

Pactiv Corporation (NYSE: PTV) today announced a change in accounting for inventories from a combination of the use of the last in, first out (LIFO) method and first in, first out (FIFO) method to the FIFO method. The company believes the change is preferable because the FIFO method:

- better reflects the current value of inventories.
- provides better matching of sales and expenses, particularly during periods of resin price volatility because the lag between resin price changes and selling price changes will be reduced by approximately two months.
- provides uniformity across all operations with respect to the method of inventory accounting.
- enhances comparability with peers.

In addition, the cash tax deferral benefits of the LIFO accounting method largely have been eliminated by the year-over-year lower resin prices in 2009. This change in accounting method will lower cash tax payments in 2010 by an estimated $8 million. Furthermore, the convergence of U.S. and international accounting standards will likely eliminate LIFO because international accounting standards does not allow its use.

Net Realizable Value

All our previous discussions have focused on the cost aspect of inventory. Regardless of which cost method you are using, there is one additional aspect that is equally important. *IAS2* requires inventories to be measured at the lower of cost and net realizable value (NRV). In other words, once you have determined cost (using specific identification, FIFO or average cost method), you will need to compare the inventory to its NRV. The lower of the two shall be what is reported on the balance sheet. **Net realizable value** is the estimated selling price in the ordinary course of business less the estimated costs of completion and the estimated costs necessary to make the sale.

This evaluation of cost versus NRV is necessary because an entity may not be able to recover the cost of inventory if the goods are damaged or obsolete, or if their selling price has declined below costs. If an inventory is written down to an NRV below cost, the write-down is recognized as an expense in the period of the write-down. Any subsequent reversal is recognized as a reduction in COGS in the period in which the reversal occurs. The exact determination of NRV is not within the scope of this textbook, but an example below would demonstrate the concept of lower of cost and NRV.

Suppose Bossini paid $3,000 for inventory on September 26. By June 30, its financial year-end, $2,000 of the inventory has been sold, and the cost of the remaining inventory is $1,000. Let's further assume that some of these inventories are damaged and no longer suitable for normal sale. Bossini estimates that the net realizable value of these goods to be $400. Bossini's year-end balance sheet must report this inventory at NRV of $400. Exhibit 6-10 on the following page presents the effects of NRV on the balance sheet and the income statement. Before any NRV effect, cost of goods sold is $2,000. An NRV write-down decreases Inventory and increases Cost of Goods Sold, as follows:

Cost of Goods Sold	600	
Inventory		600
Wrote inventory down to realizable value.		

EXHIBIT 6-10 | **Net Realizable Value (NVR) Effects on Inventory and Cost of Goods Sold**

Balance Sheet

Current assets:

Cash	$ XXX
Short-term investments	XXX
Accounts receivable...	XXX
Inventories, net realizable value	
(which is lower than $1,000 cost)	400
Prepaid expenses	XXX
Total current assets	$X,XXX

Income Statement

Sales revenue..	$ XXX
Cost of goods sold ($2,000 + $600)....................	2,600
Gross profit..	$X,XXX

If the NRV of Bossini's inventory had been above cost, it would have made no adjustment for NRV. In that case, simply report the inventory at cost, which is the lower of cost and NRV.

Bossini provided the following disclosure on its determination of NRV (adapted). Note that the 2009 Cost of Sales figures you saw in its income statement included an additional expense for NRV adjustment and conversely, in 2008, there was a deduction from COGS as a result of a reversal of the previously written-down inventory.

EXCERPTS (ADAPTED) FROM BOSSINI'S NOTES TO THE 2009 FINANCIAL STATEMENTS

Allowance for inventories

The management reviews the aging analysis of inventories of the Group at each balance sheet date, and makes provision for obsolete and slow-moving inventory items identified that are no longer suitable for sale. ... In addition, physical count on all inventories is carried out on a periodical basis in order to determine whether allowance need to be made in respect of any obsolete inventories identified. The Group carries out an inventory review at each balance sheet date and makes allowance against obsolete and slow-moving items.

Cost of Sales:

Cost of inventories sold	$1,135,100	$1,154,253
Allowances (write-back of allowance) for inventory	6,384	(7,236)
	1,141,484	1,147,017

INVENTORY AND THE FINANCIAL STATEMENTS

Detailed Income Statement

Exhibit 6-11 provides an example of a detailed income statement, complete with all the discounts and expenses in their proper places. Study it carefully.

EXHIBIT 6-11 | Detailed Income Statement

NightskyTechnology, Inc.
Income Statement
Year Ended December 31, 2011

Sales revenue	$100,000	
Less: Sales discounts	(2,000)	
Sales returns and allowances	(3,000)	
Net sales		$95,000*
Cost of goods sold		45,000
Gross profit		50,000
Operating expenses:		
Selling:		
Sales commission expense	$ 5,000	
Freight-out	1,000	
Other expenses	6,000	12,000
Administrative:		
Salary expense	$ 2,000	
Depreciation expense	2,000	
Other expenses	4,000	8,000
Income before income tax		30,000
Income tax expense (40%)		12,000
Net income		$18,000

*Most companies report only the net sales figure, $95,000.

Analyzing Financial Statements

Owners, managers, and investors use ratios to evaluate a business. Two ratios relate directly to inventory: gross profit percentage and the rate of inventory turnover.

Gross Profit Percentage. Gross profit—sales minus cost of goods sold—is a key indicator of a company's ability to sell inventory at a profit. Merchandisers strive to increase **gross profit percentage**, also called the **gross margin percentage**. Gross profit percentage is mark-up stated as a percentage of sales. Gross profit percentage is computed as follows for Bossini. Data (in thousand HKD) for 2009 was taken from Bossini's financial statements on page 342.

OBJECTIVE

3 Use gross profit percentage and inventory turnover to evaluate operations

$$\text{Gross profit percentage} = \frac{\text{Gross profit}}{\text{Net sales revenue}} = \frac{\$1,112,642}{\$2,254,126} = 0.494 = 49.4\%$$

The gross profit percentage is watched carefully by managers and investors. A 49.4% gross margin means that each dollar of sales generates about 49 cents of gross profit. On average, cost of goods sold consumes 51 cents of each sales dollar for Bossini. For most firms, the gross profit percentage changes little from year to year, so a small downturn may signal trouble. Bossini's gross profit in 2008 was 50.5%, so the company experienced a 1.1% decline in gross margin year over year. In 2008 and 2009, a severe economic recession hit retail sales hard. In order to sell inventories, many retailers have had to cut selling prices, thus reducing gross margins.

Bossini's gross profit percentage of 49% is greater than that of Marks & Spencer (37%) and Carrefour (21%). Exhibit 6-12 graphs the gross profit percentages for these three companies. We will further discuss how to evaluate a company's performance in comparison with its peers in Chapter 11.

EXHIBIT 6-12 | **Gross Profit Percentages of Three Retailers**

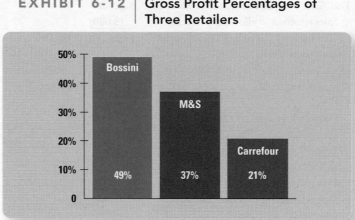

Inventory Turnover. Bossini strives to sell its inventory as quickly as possible because the goods generate no profit until they're sold. The faster the sales, the higher the income, and vice versa, for slow-moving goods. Ideally, a business could operate with zero inventory, but most businesses, especially retailers, must keep some goods on hand. **Inventory turnover**, the ratio of cost of goods sold to average inventory, indicates how rapidly inventory is sold. The 2009 computation for Bossini follows (data in thousand HKD) from Bossini's financial statements (p. 342):

$$\text{Inventory turnover} = \frac{\text{Cost of goods sold}}{\text{Average inventory}} = \frac{\text{Cost of goods sold}}{\left(\dfrac{\text{Beginning}}{\text{inventory}} + \dfrac{\text{Ending}}{\text{inventory}}\right) \div 2}$$

$$= \frac{\$1,141,484}{(\$280,987 + \$230,056)/2} = \begin{array}{c}\text{4.47 times per year}\\ \text{(every 82 days)}\end{array}$$

The inventory turnover statistic shows how many times the company sold (or turned over) its average level of inventory during the year. The turnover can also be expressed in days, called *inventory resident period*, by dividing 365 by the turnover (365/4.47 = 82 days). Inventory turnover varies from industry to industry.

Exhibit 6-13 graphs the rates of inventory turnover for the same three companies. Let's compare Bossini's turnover with that of Marks & Spencer (11.1 times per year, or 32.9 days) and Carrefour (9.99 times per year, or 36.5 days). You can see that Bossini's inventory turnover is significantly lower (i.e. slower) than the other two companies.

EXHIBIT 6-13 | **Inventory Turnover of Three Leading Retailers**

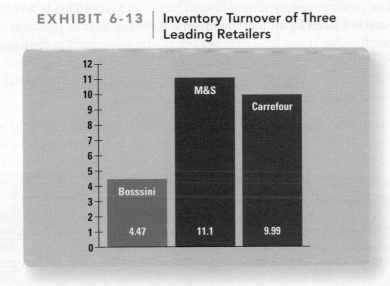

ADDITIONAL INVENTORY ISSUES

Using the Cost-of-Goods-Sold Model

Exhibit 6-14 presents the **cost-of-goods-sold model.** Some may view this model as related to the periodic inventory system. But the cost-of-goods-sold model is used by all companies, regardless of their accounting system. The model is extremely powerful because it captures all the inventory information for an entire accounting period. Study this model carefully (note that all amounts are assumed).

EXHIBIT 6-14 | **The Cost-of-Goods-Sold Model**

Cost of goods sold:

Beginning inventory	$1,200
+ Purchases	6,300
= Goods available.....................	7,500
− Ending inventory....................	(1,500)
= Cost of goods sold..................	$6,000

Bossini uses a perpetual inventory accounting system. Let's see how they can use the cost-of-goods-sold model to manage the business effectively.

1. What's the single most important question for Bossini to address?
   - What merchandise should Bossini offer to its customers? This is a *marketing* question that requires market research. If Bossini continually stock up on the wrong merchandise, sales will suffer and profits will drop.
2. What's the second most important question for Bossini?
   - How much inventory should Bossini buy or produce? **This is an accounting question faced by all merchandisers**. If Bossini buys or produces too much merchandise, it will have to lower prices, the gross profit percentage will suffer, and the company may lose money. Buying or making the right quantity of inventory is critical for success. This question can be answered with the cost-of-goods-sold model. Let's see how it works.

We must rearrange the cost-of-goods-sold formula. Then we can help a Bossini store manager know how much inventory to buy, as follows (using amounts from Exhibit 6-14):

1	Cost of goods sold (based on the plan for the next period).....................	$6,000
2 +	Ending inventory (based on the plan for the next period).......................	1,500
3 =	Goods available as planned...	7,500
4 −	Beginning inventory (actual amount left over from the prior period)......	(1,200)
5 =	Purchases (how much inventory the manager needs to buy)...................	$6,300

In this case, the manager should buy $6,300 of merchandise in order to plan for the upcoming period.

Estimating Inventory by the Gross Profit Method

Often a business must *estimate* the value of its goods. A fire may destroy inventory, and the insurance company requires an estimate of the loss. In this case, the business must estimate the cost of ending inventory because it was destroyed.

The **gross profit method**, also known as the **gross margin method**, is widely used to estimate ending inventory. This method uses the familiar cost-of-goods-sold model (amounts are assumed):

Beginning inventory	$ 4,000
+ Purchases	16,000
= Goods available...	20,000
− Ending inventory.......................................	(5,000)
= Cost of goods sold.....................................	$15,000

For the gross-profit method, we rearrange *ending inventory* and *cost of goods sold* as follows:

Beginning inventory	$ 4,000
+ Purchases	16,000
= Goods available...	20,000
− Cost of goods sold.....................................	(15,000)
= Ending inventory.......................................	$ 5,000

Suppose a fire destroys some of Bossini's inventory. To collect insurance, the company must estimate the cost of the ending inventory lost. Using its *actual gross profit rate* of 49%, you can estimate the cost of goods sold. Then subtract cost of goods sold from goods available to estimate the amount of ending inventory. Exhibit 6-15 shows the calculations for the gross profit method, with new amounts assumed for the illustration.

EXHIBIT 6-15 | Gross Profit Method of Estimating Inventory

Beginning inventory		$ 38,000
Purchases		72,000
Goods available		110,000
Estimated cost of goods sold:		
Net sales revenue	$100,000	
Less estimated gross profit of 49%	(49,000)	
Estimated cost of goods sold		51,000
Estimated cost of *ending inventory* lost		$ 59,000

You can also use the gross profit method to test the overall reasonableness of an ending inventory amount. This method also helps to detect large errors.

STOP & THINK...

Beginning inventory is $70,000, net purchases total $365,000, and net sales are $500,000. With a normal gross profit rate of 40% of sales (cost of goods sold = 60%), how much is ending inventory?

Answer:

$135,000 = [$70,000 + $365,000 − (0.60 × $500,000)]

Effects of Inventory Errors

Inventory errors sometimes occur. An error in ending inventory creates errors for two accounting periods. For example, if ending inventory has been **overstated** by $5,000, cost of goods sold will thus be **understated** by the same amount, resulting in an **overstated** gross profit. In addition, the error in ending inventory in period 1 will also impact the beginning inventory in period 2. In the absence of any further errors, inventory errors counterbalance in two consecutive periods. Why? Period 1's ending inventory becomes period 2's beginning amount. Thus, the period 1 error carries over into period 2, resulting in an **overstated** cost of goods sold, and an **understated** gross profit in period 2.

In Exhibit 6-16 on the following page, we show the effect of the above inventory errors over a 3 years' period, with constant sales and purchases. Had there been no error in period 1, the figures under period 3 are the correct ones. You can compare the figures in period 1 and 2 to those in period 3 for a better understanding of the impact of the inventory errors.

OBJECTIVE

5 Show how inventory errors affect the financial statements

EXHIBIT 6-16 | **Inventory Errors: An Example**

	Period 1 Ending Inventory Overstated by $5,000	Period 2 Beginning Inventory Overstated by $5,000	Period 3 Correct
Sales revenue..	$100,000	$100,000	$100,000
Cost of goods sold:			
Beginning inventory	$10,000	$15,000	$10,000
Purchases	50,000	50,000	50,000
Cost of goods available	60,000	65,000	60,000
Ending inventory........................	(15,000)	(10,000)	(10,000)
Cost of goods sold	45,000	55,000	50,000
Gross profit..	$ 55,000	$ 45,000	$ 50,000
		100,000	

The authors thank Professor Carl High for this example.

Beginning inventory and ending inventory have opposite effects on cost of goods sold (beginning inventory is added; ending inventory is subtracted). Therefore, after two periods, an inventory error washes out (counterbalances). Notice that total gross profit is correct for periods 1 and 2 combined ($100,000) even though each year's gross profit is off by $5,000. The correct gross profit is $50,000 for each period, as shown in Period 3.

We must have accurate information for all periods. Exhibit 6-17 summarizes the effects of inventory accounting errors.

EXHIBIT 6-17 | **Effects of Inventory Errors**

	Period 1		Period 2	
Inventory Error	Cost of Goods Sold	Gross Profit and Net Income	Cost of Goods Sold	Gross Profit and Net Income
Period 1				
Ending inventory **overstated**	Understated	Overstated	Overstated	Understated
Period 1				
Ending inventory **understated**	Overstated	Understated	Understated	Overstated

COOKING THE BOOKS
with Inventory
Crazy Eddie

It is one thing to make honest mistakes in accounting for inventory, but quite another to use inventory to commit fraud. The two most common ways to "cook the books" with inventory are:

1. inserting fictitious inventory, thus overstating quantities; and

2. deliberately overstating unit prices used in the computation of ending inventory amounts.

Either one of these tricks has exactly the same effect on income as inventory errors, discussed in the previous section. The difference is that honest inventory errors are often corrected as soon as they are detected, thus minimizing their impact on income. In contrast, deliberate overstatement of inventories tends to be repeated over and over again throughout the course of months, or even years, thus causing the misstatement to grow ever higher until it is discovered. By that time, it can be too late for the company.

Crazy Eddie, Inc.[1] was a retail consumer electronics store in 1987, operating 43 retail outlets in the New York City area, with $350 million in reported sales and reported profits of $10.5 million. Its stock was a Wall Street "darling," with a collective market value of $600 million. The only problem was that the company's reported profits had been grossly overstated since 1984, the year that the company went public.

Eddie Antar, the company's founder and major shareholder, became preoccupied with the price of his company's shares in 1984. Antar realized that the company, in an extremely competitive retail market in the largest city in the United States, had to keep posting impressive operating profits in order to maintain the upward trend in the company's share price.

Within the first six months, Antar ordered a subordinate to double count about $2 million of inventory in the company's stores and warehouses. Using Exhibits 6-16 and 6-17, you can see that the impact of this inventory overstatement went straight to the "bottom line," overstating profits by the same amount. Unfortunately, the company's auditors failed to detect the inventory overstatement. The following year, emboldened by the audit error, Antar ordered subordinates (now accomplices) to bump the overstatement to $9 million. In addition, he ordered employees to destroy incriminating documents to conceal the inventory shortage. When auditors asked for these documents, employees told them they had been lost. Antar also ordered that the company scrap its sophisticated computerized perpetual inventory system and return to an outdated manual system that was easier to manipulate. The auditors made the mistake of telling Antar which company stores and warehouses they were going to visit in order to observe the year-end physical count of inventory. Antar shifted sufficient inventory to those locations just before the counts to conceal the shortages. By 1988, when the fraud was discovered, the inventory shortage (overstatement) was larger than the total profits the company had reported since it went public in 1984.

In June 1989, Crazy Eddie, Inc., filed for Chapter 11 bankruptcy protection. Later that year, the company closed its stores and sold off its assets. Eddie Antar became a fugitive from justice, moved to Israel, and took an assumed name. He was arrested in 1992, extradited to the United States, and convicted on 17 counts of fraudulent financial reporting in 1993. He was ordered to pay $121 million in restitution to former shareholders and creditors.

A series of missteps by the courts led to a plea bargain agreement in 1996, a condition of which Antar admitted, for the first time, that he had defrauded investors by manipulating the company's accounting records. One of the prosecuting attorneys was quoted as saying, "Crazy Eddie wasn't crazy, just crooked."

▲

The following Decision Guidelines summarize the situations that call for (a) a particular inventory system and (b) the motivation for using each costing method.

---

[1]Michael C. Knapp, *Contemporary Auditing: Real Issues and Cases*, 6th edition, Mason, Ohio: Thomson Southwestern, 2009.

DECISION GUIDELINES

ACCOUNTING FOR INVENTORY

Suppose a **Franc Franc**, a furniture store, stocks two basic categories of merchandise:

- Furniture pieces, such as tables and chairs.
- Small items of low value, near the checkout stations, such as cupholders and coasters.

Jacob Stiles, the store manager, is considering how accounting will affect the business. Let's examine several decisions Stiles must make to properly account for the store's inventory.

Decision	Guidelines	System or Method
Which inventory system to use?	■ Expensive merchandise ■ Cannot control inventory by visual inspection	Perpetual system for the furniture
	■ Can control inventory by visual inspection	Periodic system for the small, low value items
Which costing method to use?	■ Unique inventory items	Specific unit cost for designer furniture because they are unique
	■ Most current cost of ending inventory ■ Maximizes reported income when costs are rising	FIFO
	■ Most current measure of cost of goods sold and net income ■ Minimizes income tax when costs are rising	LIFO (not allowed under IFRS)
	■ Middle-of-the-road approach for income tax and reported income	Average

END-OF-CHAPTER SUMMARY PROBLEM

Town & Country Gift Ideas began 2010 with 60,000 units of inventory that cost $36,000. During 2010, Town & Country purchased merchandise on account for $352,500 as follows:

Purchase 1	(100,000 units costing)	$ 65,000
Purchase 2	(270,000 units costing)	175,500
Purchase 3	(160,000 units costing)	112,000

Cash payments on account totaled $326,000 during the year.

Town & Country's sales during 2010 consisted of 520,000 units of inventory for $660,000, all on account. The company uses the FIFO inventory method.

Cash collections from customers were $630,000. Operating expenses totaled $240,500, of which Town & Country paid $211,000 in cash. Town & Country credited Accrued Liabilities for the remainder. At December 31, Town & Country accrued income tax expense at the rate of 35% of income before tax.

Requirements

1. Make summary journal entries to record Town & Country's transactions for the year, assuming the company uses a perpetual inventory system.
2. Determine the FIFO cost of Town & Country's ending inventory at December 31, 2010 two ways:
   a. Use a T-account.
   b. Multiply the number of units on hand by the unit cost.
3. Show how Town & Country would compute cost of goods sold for 2010. Follow the FIFO example on page 352.
4. Prepare Town & Country's income statement for 2010. Show totals for the gross profit and income before tax.
5. Determine Town & Country's gross profit percentage, rate of inventory turnover, and net income as a percentage of sales for the year. In Town & Country's industry, a gross profit percentage of 40%, an inventory turnover of six times per year, and a net income percentage of 7% are considered excellent. How well does Town & Country compare to these industry averages?

Thurston & Talty need to know the company's gross profit percentage and rate of inventory turnover for 2010 under:

1. FIFO

2. LIFO

Which method makes the business look better on:

3. Gross profit percentage?

4. Inventory turnover?

E6-25A (*Learning Objective 2: Budgeting inventory purchases*) Toys Plus prepares budgets to help manage the company. Toys Plus is budgeting for the fiscal year ended January 31, 2010. During the preceding year ended January 31, 2009, sales totaled $9,300 million and cost of goods sold was $6,500 million. At January 31, 2009, inventory stood at $2,100 million. During the upcoming 2010 year, suppose Toys Plus expects cost of goods sold to increase by 10%. The company budgets next year's ending inventory at $2,400 million.

I *Requirement*

1. One of the most important decisions a manager makes is how much inventory to buy. How much inventory should Toys Plus purchase during the upcoming year to reach its budgeted figures?

■ **spreadsheet**

E6-26A (*Learning Objective 4: Estimating inventory by the gross profit method*)   J R Company began May with inventory of $47,500. The business made net purchases of $30,900 and had net sales of $62,100 before a fire destroyed the company's inventory. For the past several years, J R's gross profit percentage has been 35%. Estimate the cost of the inventory destroyed by the fire. Identify another reason owners and managers use the gross profit method to estimate inventory.

E6-27A (*Learning Objective 5: Correcting an inventory error*) Big Blue Sea Marine Supply reported the following comparative income statement for the years ended September 30, 2010, and 2009:

Big Blue Sea Marine Supply
Income Statements
For the Years Ended September 30, 2010, and 2009

	2010		2009	
Sales revenue		$143,000		$120,000
Cost of goods sold:				
Beginning inventory	$ 14,500		$ 9,000	
Net purchases	74,000		67,000	
Cost of goods available	88,500		76,000	
Ending inventory	(19,000)		(14,500)	
Cost of goods sold		69,500		61,500
Gross profit		73,500		58,500
Operating expenses		28,000		24,000
Net income		$ 45,500		$ 34,500

Big Blue Sea's president and shareholders are thrilled by the company's boost in sales and net income during 2010. Then the accountants for the company discover that ending 2009 inventory was understated by $6,500. Prepare the corrected comparative income statement for the 2-year period, complete with a heading for the statement. How well did Big Blue Sea really perform in 2010, as compared with 2009?

(Group B)

E6-28B (*Learning Objectives 1, 2: Accounting for inventory transactions under FIFO costing*)   Accounting records for Rockford Corporation yield the following data for the year ended December 31, 2010:

Inventory, December 31, 2009..	$ 8,000
Purchases of inventory (on account)...	49,000
Sales of inventory—76% on account; 24% for cash (cost $40,000).........	74,000
Inventory at FIFO, December 31, 2010...	17,000

Ⅰ Requirements

1. Journalize Rockford's inventory transactions for the year under the perpetual system.
2. Report ending inventory, sales, cost of goods sold, and gross profit on the appropriate financial statement.

E6-29B (*Learning Objectives 1, 2: Analyzing inventory transactions under FIFO costing*)   Ron's, Inc.'s inventory records for a particular development program show the following at May 31:

May 1	Beginning inventory	7 units @ $160	=	$1,120
15	Purchase..............................	6 units @ $160	=	960
26	Purchase..............................	11 units @ $170	=	1,870

At May 31, 10 of these programs are on hand. Journalize for Ron's:

1. Total May purchases in one summary entry. All purchases were on credit.
2. Total May sales and cost of goods sold in two summary entries. The selling price was $625 per unit and all sales were on credit. Assume that Ron's uses the FIFO inventory method.
3. Under FIFO, how much gross profit would Ron's earn on these transactions? What is the FIFO cost of Ron's, Inc.'s ending inventory?

E6-30B (*Learning Objective 2: Determining ending inventory and cost of goods sold by four methods*)   Use the data for Ron's, Inc., in Exercise 6-29B to answer the following.

Ⅰ Requirements

1. Compute cost of goods sold and ending inventory using each of the following methods:
   a. Specific unit cost, with five $160 units and five $170 units still on hand at the end.
   b. Average cost.
   c. FIFO.
   d. LIFO.
2. Which method produces the highest cost of goods sold? Which method produces the lowest cost of goods sold? What causes the difference in cost of goods sold?

E6-31B (*Learning Objective 2: Computing the tax advantage of LIFO over FIFO*)   Use the data for Ron's, Inc., in Exercise 6-29B to illustrate Ron's income tax advantage from using LIFO over FIFO. Sales revenue is $8,750, operating expenses are $2,000, and the income tax rate is 32%. How much in taxes would Ron's save by using the LIFO method versus FIFO?

Trigger's gross profit percentage is

a. 46.3.   c. 47.3.
b. 52.7.   d. 57.4.

Q6-57 Shipley Tank Company had the following beginning inventory, net purchases, net sales, and gross profit percentage for the first quarter of 2010:

Beginning inventory, $52,000	Net purchases, $73,000
Net sales revenue, $94,000	Gross profit rate, 50%

By the gross profit method, the ending inventory should be

a. $80,000.   c. $81,000.
b. $78,000.   d. $79,000.

Q6-58 An error understated Regan Corporation's December 31, 2010, ending inventory by $42,000. What effect will this error have on total assets and net income for 2010?

Assets	Net income
a. Understate	No effect
b. No effect	No effect
c. Understate	Understate
d. No effect	Overstate

Q6-59 An error understated Regan Corporation's December 31, 2010, ending inventory by $42,000. What effect will this error have on net income for 2011?

a. Overstate
b. Understate
c. No effect

Problems

> All of the A and B problems can be found within MyAccountingLab, an online homework and practice environment. Your instructor may ask you to complete these problems using MyAccountingLab.

(Group A)

■ **general ledger**

P6-60A *(Learning Objectives 1, 2: Accounting for inventory in a perpetual system using average costing method)* Nice Buy purchases inventory in crates of merchandise; each crate of inventory is a unit. The fiscal year of Nice Buy ends each February 28. Assume you are dealing with a single Nice Buy store in Dallas, Texas. The Dallas store began 2010 with an inventory of 21,000 units that cost a total of $1,050,000. During the year, the store purchased merchandise on account as follows:

April (31,000 units at $51)	$1,581,000
August (51,000 units at $55)	2,805,000
November (61,000 units at $61)	3,721,000
Total purchases	$8,107,000

Cash payments on account totaled $7,707,000. During fiscal year 2010, the store sold 148,000 units of merchandise for $14,208,000, of which $4,900,000 was for cash and the balance was on account. Nice Buy uses the average cost method for inventories. Operating expenses for the year were $3,750,000. Nice Buy paid 70% in cash and accrued the rest as accrued liabilities. The store accrued income tax at the rate of 30%.

I Requirements

1. Make summary journal entries to record the store's transactions for the year ended February 28, 2010. Nice Buy uses a perpetual inventory system.
2. Prepare a T-account to show the activity in the Inventory account.
3. Prepare the store's income statement for the year ended February 28, 2010. Show totals for gross profit, income before tax, and net income.

P6-61A *(Learning Objective 2: Measuring cost of goods sold and ending inventory—perpetual system)* Assume a Tiger Sports outlet store began October 2010 with 48 pairs of running shoes that cost the store $34 each. The sale price of these shoes was $69. During October, the store completed these inventory transactions:

		Units	Unit Cost	Units Sales Price
Oct 3	Sale	11	$34	$69
8	Purchase......	83	35	
11	Sale	37	34	69
19	Sale	6	35	71
24	Sale	38	35	71
30	Purchase......	25	36	

I Requirements

1. The preceding data are taken from the store's perpetual inventory records. Which cost method does the store use? Explain how you arrived at your answer.
2. Determine the store's cost of goods sold for October. Also compute gross profit for October.
3. What is the cost of the store's October 31 inventory of running shoes?

P6-62A *(Learning Objective 2: Computing inventory by three methods—perpetual system)* Fatigues Surplus began October with 72 tents that cost $17 each. During the month, Fatigues Surplus made the following purchases at cost:

Oct 4	103 tents @ $19 = $1,957
19	158 tents @ $21 = 3,318
25	43 tents @ $22 = 946

Fatigues Surplus sold 324 tents and at October 31 the ending inventory consists of 52 tents. The sale price of each tent was $51.

I Requirements

1. Determine the cost of goods sold and ending inventory amounts for October under the average cost, FIFO cost, and LIFO cost. Round average cost per unit four decimal places, and round all other amounts to the nearest dollar.
2. Explain why cost of goods sold is highest under LIFO. Be specific.
3. Prepare Fatigues Surplus' income statement for October. Report gross profit. Operating expenses totaled $5,000. Fatigues Surplus uses average costing for inventory. The income tax rate is 40%.

P6-63A (*Learning Objective 2: Applying the different inventory costing methods—perpetual system*) The records of Bell Aviation include the following accounts for inventory of aviation fuel at December 31 of the current year:

Inventory			
Jan 1	Balance	790 units @ $7.70	$ 6,083
Mar 6	Purchase	320 units @ $7.80	2,496
Jun 22	Purchase	8,350 units @ $8.20	68,470
Oct 4	Purchase	530 units @ $9.20	4,876

Sales Revenue		
Dec 31	9,010 units	$132,447

❙ Requirements

1. Prepare a partial income statement through gross profit under the average, FIFO, and LIFO methods. Round average cost per unit to four decimal places and all other amounts to the nearest dollar.
2. Which inventory method would you use to minimize income tax? Explain why this method causes income tax to be the lowest.

P6-64A (*Learning Objective 2: Applying the net realizable value to inventories—perpetual system*) ELV Trade Mart has recently had lackluster sales. The rate of inventory turnover has dropped, and the merchandise is gathering dust. It is now December 31, 2010, and the current NRV cost of ELV's ending inventory is $75,000 below what ELV actually paid for the goods, which was $220,000. Before any adjustments at the end of the period, the Cost of Goods Sold account has a balance of $770,000.

  a. What accounting action should ELV take in this situation?
  b. Give any journal entry required.
  c. At what amount should ELV report Inventory on the balance sheet?
  d. At what amount should the company report Cost of Goods Sold on the income statement?
  e. Discuss the accounting principle or concept that is most relevant to this situation.

P6-65A (*Learning Objective 3: Using gross profit percentage and inventory turnover to evaluate two companies*) Sprinkle Top and Coffee Shop are both specialty food chains. The two companies reported these figures, in millions:

Sprinkle Top, Inc. Income Statement (Adapted) Years Ended December 31		
(Amounts in millions)	2010	2009
Revenues:		
Net sales	$544	$707
Costs and Expenses:		
Cost of goods sold..	478	594
Selling, general, and administrative expenses..............	60	55

Sprinkle Top, Inc.
Balance Sheet (Adapted)
December 31

(Amounts in millions)	2010	2009
Assets		
Current assets:		
Cash and cash equivalents................	$12	$27
Receivables.....................................	28	40
Inventories	26	36

Coffee Shop Corporation
Income Statement (Adapted)
Years Ended December 31

(Amounts in millions)	2010	2009
Net sales	$7,700	$6,300
Cost of goods sold.............................	3,160	2,604
Selling, general, and administrative expenses.......	2,950	2,390

Coffee Shop Corporation
Balance Sheet (Adapted)
December 31

(Amounts in millions)	2010	2009
Assets		
Current assets:		
Cash and temporary investments................	$313	$172
Receivables, net..........................	230	188
Inventories	627	544

I Requirements

1. Compute the gross profit percentage and the rate of inventory turnover for Sprinkle Top and Coffee Shop for 2010.
2. Based on these statistics, which company looks more profitable? Why? What other expense category should we consider in evaluating these two companies?

P6-66A (*Learning Objectives 1, 4: Estimating inventory by the gross profit method; preparing the income statement*)   Assume Thompson Company, a copy center, lost some inventory in a fire. To file an insurance claim, Thompson Company must estimate its inventory by the gross profit method. Assume that for the past two years that Thompson

■ **spreadsheet**

Company's gross profit has averaged 41% of net sales. Suppose the Thompson Company's inventory records reveal the following data:

Inventory, October 1	$ 57,100
Transactions during October:	
Purchases	490,200
Purchase discounts	11,000
Purchase returns	70,900
Sales	667,000
Sales returns	11,000

I *Requirements*

1. Estimate the cost of the lost inventory, using the gross profit method.
2. Prepare the October income statement for this product through gross profit. Show the detailed computations of cost of goods sold in a separate schedule.

P6-67A (*Learning Objective 3: Determining the amount of inventory to purchase*) Maroney's Convenience Store's income statement and balance sheet reported the following.

Maroney's Convenience Stores
Income Statement
Year Ended December 31, 2009

Sales	$957,000
Cost of sales	720,000
Gross profit	237,000
Operating expenses	114,000
Net income	$123,000

Maroney's Convenience Stores
Balance Sheet
December 31, 2009

Assets		Liabilities	
Cash	$ 44,000	Accounts payable	$ 31,000
Inventories	68,000	Note payable	187,000
Land and		Total liabilities	218,000
buildings, net	273,000	Owner, capital	167,000
		Total liabilities	
Total assets	$385,000	and capital	$385,000

The business is organized as a proprietorship, so it pays no corporate income tax. The owner is budgeting for 2010. He expects sales and cost of goods sold to increase by 6%. To meet customer demand, ending inventory will need to be $76,000 at December 31, 2010. The owner hopes to earn a net income of $154,000 next year.

I *Requirements*

1. One of the most important decisions a manager makes is the amount of inventory to purchase. Show how to determine the amount of inventory to purchase in 2010.
2. Prepare the store's budgeted income statement for 2010 to reach the target net income of $154,000. To reach this goal, operating expenses must decrease by $16,780.

P6-68A (*Learning Objective 5: Correcting inventory errors over a three-year period*) The accounting records of R.B. Video Sales show the data on the following page (in millions). The shareholders are very happy with R.B.'s steady increase in net income.

Auditors discovered that the ending inventory for 2008 was understated by $3 million and that the ending inventory for 2009 was also understated by $3 million. The ending inventory at December 31, 2010, was correct.

	2010	2009	2008
Net sales revenue............................	$39	$36	$33
Cost of goods sold:			
Beginning inventory...................	$ 5	$ 4	$ 3
Net purchases	27	25	23
Cost of goods available..............	32	29	26
Less ending inventory................	(6)	(5)	(4)
Cost of goods sold	26	24	22
Gross profit.................................	13	12	11
Operating expenses.......................	6	6	6
Net income.................................	$ 7	$ 6	$ 5

I Requirements

1. Show corrected income statements for each of the three years.
2. How much did these assumed corrections add to or take away from R.B.'s total net income over the three-year period? How did the corrections affect the trend of net income?
3. Will R.B.'s shareholders still be happy with the company's trend of net income? Give the reason for your answer.

(Group B)

P6-69B (*Learning Objectives 1, 2: Accounting for inventory in a perpetual system using average costing method*)   Best Guy purchases inventory in crates of merchandise; each crate of inventory is a unit. The fiscal year of Best Guy ends each February 28. Assume you are dealing with a single Best Guy store in Denver, Colorado. The Denver store began 2010 with an inventory of 17,000 units that cost a total of $850,000. During the year, the store purchased merchandise on account as follows:

■ **general ledger**

April (33,000 units at $60)...................................	$1,980,000
August (53,000 units at $64)...............................	3,392,000
November (63,000 units at $70)	4,410,000
Total purchases..	$9,782,000

Cash payments on account totaled $9,382,000. During fiscal 2010, the store sold 152,000 units of merchandise for $14,592,000, of which $4,500,000 was for cash and the balance was on account. Best Guy uses the average cost method for inventories. Operating expenses for the year were $2,750,000. Best Guy paid 60% in cash and accrued the rest as accrued liabilities. The store accrued income tax at the rate of 35%.

I Requirements

1. Make summary journal entries to record the store's transactions for the year ended February 28, 2010. Best Guy uses a perpetual inventory system.
2. Prepare a T-account to show the activity in the Inventory account.
3. Prepare the store's income statement for the year ended February 28, 2010. Show totals for gross profit, income before tax, and net income.

Coffee Grind Corporation
Income Statement (Adapted)
Years Ended December 31

(Amounts in millions)	2010	2009
Net sales	$7,171	$6,369
Cost of goods sold	3,190	2,603
Selling, general, and administrative expenses	2,955	2,360

Coffee Grind Corporation
Balance Sheet (Adapted)
December 31

(Amounts in millions)	2010	2009
Assets		
Current assets:		
Cash and temporary investments	$310	$171
Receivables, net	227	193
Inventories	631	546

I Requirements

1. Compute the gross profit percentage and the rate of inventory turnover for Pastry People and Coffee Grind for 2010.
2. Based on these statistics, which company looks more profitable? Why? What other expense category should we consider in evaluating these two companies?

■ **spreadsheet**

P6-75B (*Learning Objectives 1, 4: Estimating inventory by the gross profit method; preparing the income statement*)   Assume Ross Company, a sporting goods store, lost some inventory in a fire. To file an insurance claim, Ross Company must estimate its ending inventory by the gross profit method. Assume that for the past two years, Ross Company's gross profit has averaged 43% of net sales. Suppose Ross Company's inventory records reveal the following data:

Inventory, January 1	$ 57,500
Transactions during January:	
Purchases	490,500
Purchase discounts	12,000
Purchase returns	70,300
Sales	664,000
Sales returns	16,000

I Requirements

1. Estimate the cost of the lost inventory, using the gross profit method.
2. Prepare the January income statement for this product through gross profit. Show the detailed computation of cost of goods sold in a separate schedule.

P6-76B (*Learning Objective 3: Determining the amount of inventory to purchase*)   Dave's Convenience Store's income statement and balance sheet reported the following. The business is organized as a proprietorship, so it pays no corporate income tax. The owner is budgeting for 2010. He expects sales and cost of goods sold to increase by 9%. To meet customer demand, ending inventory will need to be $78,000 at December 31, 2010. The owner hopes to earn a net income of $156,000 next year.

Dave's Convenience Stores
Income Statement
Year Ended December 31, 2009

Sales	$964,000
Cost of sales	722,000
Gross profit	242,000
Operating expenses	110,000
Net income	$132,000

Dave's Convenience Stores
Balance Sheet
December 31, 2009

Assets		Liabilities	
Cash	$ 35,000	Accounts payable	$ 28,000
Inventories	65,000	Note payable...............	193,000
Land and		Total liabilities	221,000
buildings, net	268,000	Owner, capital..............	147,000
		Total liabilities	
Total assets....................	$368,000	and capital	$368,000

Requirements

1. One of the most important decisions a manager makes is the amount of inventory to purchase. Show how to determine the amount of inventory to purchase in 2010.
2. Prepare the store's budgeted income statement for 2010 to reach the target net income of $156,000. To reach this goal, operating expenses must decrease by $2,220.

P6-77B (*Learning Objective 5: Correcting inventory errors over a three-year period*)   The accounting records of Waterville Video Sales show these data (in millions). The shareholders are very happy with Waterville's steady increase in net income.

	2010		2009		2008	
Net sales revenue.............................		$42		$39		$36
Cost of goods sold:						
Beginning inventory....................	$ 10		$ 9		$ 8	
Net purchases	33		31		29	
Cost of goods available..............	43		40		37	
Less ending inventory.................	(11)		(10)		(9)	
Cost of goods sold		32		30		28
Gross profit......................................		10		9		8
Operating expenses..........................		5		5		5
Net income.......................................		$ 5		$ 4		$ 3

Auditors discovered that the ending inventory for 2008 was understated by $2 million and that the ending inventory for 2009 was also understated by $2 million. The ending inventory at December 31, 2010 was correct.

Requirements

1. Show corrected income statements for each of the three years.
2. How much did these assumed corrections add to or take away from Waterville's total net income over the three-year period? How did the corrections affect the trend of net income?
3. Will Waterville's shareholders still be happy with the company's trend of net income? Give the reason for your answer.

APPLY YOUR KNOWLEDGE

Decision Cases

writing assignment ■

Case 1. (*Learning Objectives 1, 2: Assessing the impact of a year-end purchase of inventory*) Duracraft Corporation is nearing the end of its first year of operations. Duracraft made inventory purchases of $745,000 during the year, as follows:

January	1,000 units @	$100.00 =	$100,000
July	4,000	121.25	485,000
November	1,000	160.00	160,000
Totals	6,000		$745,000

Sales for the year are 5,000 units for $1,200,000 of revenue. Expenses other than cost of goods sold and income taxes total $200,000. The president of the company is undecided about whether to adopt the FIFO method or the LIFO method for inventories. The income tax rate is 40%.

❙ Requirements

1. To aid company decision making, prepare income statements under FIFO and under LIFO.
2. Compare the net income under FIFO with net income under LIFO. Which method produces the higher net income? What causes this difference? Be specific.

writing assignment ■

Case 2. (*Learning Objective 2: Assessing the impact of the inventory costing method on the financial statements*) The inventory costing method a company chooses can affect the financial statements and thus the decisions of the people who use those statements.

❙ Requirements

1. Company A uses the LIFO inventory method and discloses its use of the LIFO method in notes to the financial statements. Company B uses the FIFO method to account for its inventory. Company B does *not* disclose which inventory method it uses. Company B reports a higher net income than Company A. In which company would you prefer to invest? Give your reason.
2. Conservatism is an accepted accounting concept. Would you want management to be conservative in accounting for inventory if you were a shareholder or a creditor of a company? Give your reason.

Ethical Issue

During 2010, Vanguard, Inc., changed to the LIFO method of accounting for inventory. Suppose that during 2011, Vanguard changes back to the FIFO method and the following year Vanguard switches back to LIFO again.

❙ Requirements

1. What would you think of a company's ethics if it changed accounting methods every year?
2. What accounting principle would changing methods every year violate?
3. Who can be harmed when a company changes its accounting methods too often? How?

Focus on Financials: ■ Nokia Corporation

The notes to the accounts are part of the financial statements. They provide additional details about accounting policies and further information on numbers reported on the financial statements. This case will help you learn to use a company's inventory notes. Refer to Nokia's consolidated financial statements and related notes in Appendix A at the end of the book and answer the following questions:

❚ Requirements

1. How does Nokia value its inventories? Which cost method does the company use?
2. What would be the effect of Nokia adopting another inventory costing method, assuming rising inventory prices?
3. Three important pieces of inventory information are (a) the cost of inventory on hand, (b) the cost of sales, and (c) the cost of inventory purchases. Identify or compute each of these items for Nokia at the end of 2008.
4. Assume that all inventory purchases were made on account, and that only inventory purchases increased accounts payable. Compute Nokia's cash payments for inventory during 2008.
5. Did Nokia's gross profit percentage on company sales improve or deteriorate in the year ended December 31, 2008, compared to the previous year?
6. Would you rate Nokia's rate of inventory turnover for the years ended December 31, 2008, and December 31, 2007, as fast or slow in comparison to most other companies in its industry? Explain your answer. (2006 inventory: 1,554 million)

Group Project

(*Learning Objective 3: Comparing companies' inventory turnover ratios*) Obtain the annual reports of 10 companies, two from each of five different industries. Most companies' financial statements can be downloaded from their Web sites.

writing assignment ■

1. Compute each company's gross profit percentage and rate of inventory turnover for the most recent two years. If annual reports are unavailable or do not provide enough data for multiple-year computations, you can gather financial statement data from *Moody's Industrial Manual*.
2. For the industries of the companies you are analyzing, obtain the industry averages for gross profit percentage and inventory turnover from Robert Morris Associates, *Annual Statement Studies*; Dun and Bradstreet, *Industry Norms and Key Business Ratios*; or Leo Troy, *Almanac of Business and Industrial Financial Ratios*.
3. How well does each of your companies compare to the other company in its industry? How well do your companies compare to the average for their industry? What insight about your companies can you glean from these ratios?
4. Write a memo to summarize your findings, stating whether your group would invest in each of the companies it has analyzed.

For online homework, exercises, and problems that provide you with immediate feedback, please visit www.myaccountinglab.com.

Quick Check Answers

1. *b*
2. *a*
3. *e*
4. *c* [(15 × $5) + (25 × $8)]
5. *b* (15 × $5) + ($10 × $8)
6. *c* 25 × [($75 + $320 + $90) ÷ 65]
7. *c*
8. *a*
9. *c*
10. *a* ($117,000 − $57,000)
11. *c* ($145,000 + $25,000 − $15,000)
12. *b* ($28,000 + $93,000 + $3,000 − $7,000 − $35,000)
13. *a* ($184,000 − $82,000)/$184,000
14. *b* [$82,000 ÷ ($28,000 + $35,000)/2]
15. *d* $110,000 + $260,000 − [$470,000 × (1 − 0.40)]
16. *a*

APPENDIX 6A

Accounting for Inventory in the Periodic System

In the periodic inventory system, the business keeps no running record of the merchandise. Instead, at the end of the period, the business counts inventory on hand and applies the unit costs to determine the cost of ending inventory. This inventory figure appears on the balance sheet and is used to compute cost of goods sold.

Recording Transactions in the Periodic System

In the periodic system, throughout the period the Inventory account carries the beginning balance left over from the preceding period. The business records purchases of inventory in the Purchases account (an expense). Then, at the end of the period, the Inventory account must be updated for the financial statements. A journal entry removes the beginning balance by crediting Inventory and debiting Cost of Goods Sold. A second journal entry sets up the ending inventory balance, based on the physical count. The final entry in this sequence transfers the amount of Purchases to Cost of Goods Sold. These end-of-period entries can be made during the closing process.

Exhibit 6A-1 illustrates the accounting in the periodic system. After the process is complete, Inventory has its correct ending balance of $120,000, and Cost of Goods Sold shows $540,000.

EXHIBIT 6-A1 | **Recording and Reporting Inventories—Periodic System (Amounts Assumed)**

PANEL A—Recording Transactions and the T-accounts (All amounts are assumed)

1.	Purchases	560,000	
	Accounts Payable		560,000
	Purchased inventory on account.		
2.	Accounts Receivable	900,000	
	Sales Revenue		900,000
	Sold inventory on account.		
3.	End-of-period entries to update Inventory and record Cost of Goods Sold:		
a.	Cost of Goods Sold	100,000	
	Inventory (beginning balance)		100,000
	Transferred beginning inventory to COGS.		
b.	Inventory (ending balance)	120,000	
	Cost of Goods Sold		120,000
	Set up ending inventory based on physical count.		
c.	Cost of Goods Sold	560,000	
	Purchases		560,000
	Transferred purchases to COGS.		

The T-accounts show the following:

Inventory			Cost of Goods Sold	
100,000*	100,000		100,000	120,000
120,000			560,000	
			540,000	

*Beginning inventory was $100,000

PANEL B—Reporting in the Financial Statements

Income Statement (Partial)

Sales revenue..........................		$900,000
Cost of goods sold:		
Beginning inventory...........	$ 100,000	
Purchases..........................	560,000	
Goods available	660,000	
Ending inventory...............	(120,000)	
Cost of goods sold.................		540,000
Gross profit........................		$360,000

Ending Balance Sheet (Partial)

Current assets:	
Cash...	$ XXX
Short-term investments	XXX
Accounts receivable......................	XXX
Inventory	120,000
Prepaid expenses	XXX

Appendix Assignments

Short Exercises

S6A-1 (*Recording inventory transactions in the periodic system*) Saxton Technologies began the year with inventory of $480. During the year, Saxton purchased inventory costing $1,180 and sold goods for $3,200, with all transactions on account. Saxton ended the year with inventory of $610. Journalize all the necessary transactions under the periodic inventory system.

S6A-2 *(Computing cost of goods sold and preparing the income statement—periodic system)*   Use the data in Short Exercise 6A-1 to do the following for Saxton Technologies:

❚ Requirements

1. Post to the Inventory and Cost of Goods Sold accounts.
2. Compute cost of goods sold by the cost-of-goods-sold model.
3. Prepare the income statement of Saxton Technologies through gross profit.

Exercises

All of these exercises can be found within MyAccountingLab, an online homework and practice environment. Your instructor may ask you to complete these exercises using MyAccountingLab.

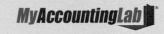

(Group A)

E6A-3A *(Computing amounts for various inventory methods—periodic system)*   Suppose Halton Corporation's inventory records for a particular computer chip indicate the following at July 31:

Jul	1	Beginning inventory	5 units @ $59 = $295
	8	Purchase.................................	3 units @ $59 = 177
	15	Purchase.................................	13 units @ $69 = 897
	26	Purchase.................................	1 units @ $79 = 79

The physical count of inventory at July 31 indicates that seven units of inventory are on hand.

❚ Requirements

Compute ending inventory and cost of goods sold, using each of the following methods:

1. Specific unit cost, assuming two $59 units and five $69 units are on hand
2. Average cost (round average unit cost to the nearest cent)
3. First-in, first-out
4. Last-in, first-out

E6A-4A *(Journalizing inventory transactions in the periodic system; computing cost of goods sold)*   Use the data in Exercise 6A-3A.

❚ Requirements

Journalize the following for the periodic system:

1. Total July purchases in one summary entry. All purchases were on credit.
2. Total July sales in a summary entry. Assume that the selling price was $295 per unit and that all sales were on credit.
3. July 31 entries for inventory. Halton uses LIFO. Post to the Cost of Goods Sold T-account to show how this amount is determined. Label each item in the account.
4. Show the computation of cost of goods sold by the cost-of-goods-sold model.

(Group B)

E6A-5B *(Computing amounts for various inventory methods—periodic system)* Suppose Saxton Corporation's inventory records for a particular computer chip indicate the following at December 31:

Dec	1	Beginning inventory	6 units @ $60 = $360
	8	Purchase.................................	4 units @ $60 = 240
	15	Purchase.................................	13 units @ $70 = 910
	26	Purchase.................................	2 units @ $80 = 160

The physical count of inventory at December 31 indicates that nine units of inventory are on hand.

❙ Requirements

Compute ending inventory and cost of goods sold, using each of the following methods:

1. Specific unit cost, assuming four $60 units and five $70 units are on hand
2. Average cost (round average unit cost to the nearest cent)
3. First-in, first-out
4. Last-in, first-out

E6A-6B *(Journalizing inventory transactions in the periodic system; computing cost of goods sold)* Use the data in Exercise 6A-5B.

❙ Requirements

Journalize the following for the periodic system:

1. Total December purchases in one summary entry. All purchases were on credit.
2. Total December sales in a summary entry. Assume that the selling price was $315 per unit and that all sales were on credit.
3. December 31 entries for inventory. Saxton uses LIFO. Post to the Cost of Goods Sold T-account to show how this amount is determined. Label each item in the account.
4. Show the computation of cost of goods sold by the cost-of-goods-sold model.

Problems

All of these problems can be found within MyAccountingLab, an online homework and practice environment. Your instructor may ask you to complete these problems using MyAccountingLab.

(Group A)

P6A-7A (*Computing cost of goods sold and gross profit on sales—periodic system*) Assume a Watercrest outlet store began July 2010 with 48 units of inventory that cost $16 each. The sale price of these units was $69. During July, the store completed these inventory transactions:

		Units	Unit Cost	Units Sale Price
Jul 3	Sale	19	$16	$69
8	Purchase......	80	17	71
11	Sale	29	16	69
19	Sale	3	17	71
24	Sale	35	17	71
30	Purchase......	22	18	72
31	Sale	4	17	71

I Requirements

1. Determine the store's cost of goods sold for July under the periodic inventory system. Assume the FIFO method.
2. Compute gross profit for July.

P6A-8A (*Recording transactions in the periodic system; reporting inventory items in the financial statements*) Accounting records for Halton Desserts, Inc., yield the following data for the year ended December 31, 2010 (amounts in thousands):

Inventory, December 31, 2009	$ 560
Purchases of inventory (on account)..	2,040
Sales of inventory—70% on account; 30% for cash..	3,400
Inventory at the lower of FIFO cost or NRV, December 31, 2010	680

I Requirements

1. Journalize Halton Desserts' inventory transactions for the year under the periodic system. Show all amounts in thousands.
2. Report ending inventory, sales, cost of goods sold, and gross profit on the appropriate financial statement (amounts in thousands). Show the computation of cost of goods sold.

(Group B)

P6A-9B (*Computing cost of goods sold and gross profit on sales—periodic system*) Assume a Championship outlet store began January 2010 with 50 units of inventory that cost $19 each. The sale price of these units was $71. During January the store completed these inventory transactions:

		Units	Unit Cost	Units Sale Price
Jan 3	Sale	17	$19	$71
8	Purchase......	77	20	73
11	Sale	33	19	71
19	Sale	2	20	73
24	Sale	39	20	73
30	Purchase......	19	21	74
31	Sale	5	20	73

❙ Requirements

1. Determine the store's cost of goods sold for January under the periodic inventory system. Assume the FIFO method.
2. Compute gross profit for January.

P6A-10B (*Recording transactions in the periodic system; reporting inventory items in the financial statements*) Accounting records for Just Desserts, Inc., yield the following data for the year ended December 31, 2010 (amounts in thousands):

Inventory, December 31, 2009	$ 530
Purchases of inventory (on account)...	2,000
Sales of inventory—75% on account, 25% for cash......................................	3,800
Inventory at the lower of FIFO cost or NRV, December 31, 2010	650

❙ Requirements

1. Journalize Just Desserts' inventory transactions for the year under the periodic system. Show all amounts in thousands.
2. Report ending inventory, sales, cost of goods sold, and gross profit on the appropriate financial statement (amounts in thousands). Show the computation of cost of goods sold.

7

PPE & Intangibles

SPOTLIGHT: Lenovo

Prior to its acquisition of the IBM Personal Computing Division in 2005 for USD 1.75 billion, **Lenovo** was already the biggest computer maker in the China market with its own "Legend" brand. Lenovo is now the fourth largest computer maker in the world, and develops, manufactures and markets technology products and services worldwide. To do this, it makes significant investments in its operating and research capacity.

This chapter covers non-current (or long-term) assets to complete our coverage of assets, except for long-term investments in Chapter 10. Let's begin by examining the various types of non-current assets.

Lenovo Group Limited
Consolidated Balance Sheet (Partial, adapted)
As at March 31

(In thousands USD)	2009	2008
1 Total current assets	$3,787,353	$4,705,366
2 Property, plant and equipment	314,142	364,778
3 Prepaid lease payments	5,833	6,099
4 Construction-in-progress..............	47,062	51,237
5 Intangible assets	1,852,861	1,838,368
6 All other non-current assets	301,048	233,999
7 Total non-current assets	2,520,946	2,494,481
8 Total assets................................	$3,787,353	$4,705,366

Property, plant and equipment (line 2):	Cost	Acc. Depn.	Net book value
9 Buildings.....................................	$ 115,948	$ 24,676	$ 91,272
10 Leasehold improvements.............	74,761	40,967	33,794
11 Plant and machinery	226,812	158,975	67,837
12 Furniture and fixtures	43,096	14,624	28,472
13 Office equipment	223,217	131,403	91,814
14 Motor vehicles	2,318	1,365	953
15 Total PPE	$ 686,152	$ 372,010	$ 314,142

Prepaid lease payments (line 3):

16 Prepaid lease payments represents the payment for land use rights held by the Group in the Chinese Mainland under medium leases (less than 50 years not less than 10 years)

Intangible assets (line 5):	Cost	AAIL*	Net book value
17 Goodwill.....................................	$1,296,938	—	$1,296,938
18 Trademarks and trade names	516,352	136,352	380,000
19 Internal use software...................	272,922	102,198	170,724
20 Customer relationships	17,000	17,000	—
21 Patent and technology................	106,620	101,421	5,199
22 Marketing rights	78,337	78,337	—
23 Total intangible assets	$2,288,169	$ 435,308	$1,852,861

*Accumulated Amortization and Impairment losses

LEARNING OBJECTIVES

1 **Determine** the cost of a PPE

2 **Account** for depreciation

3 **Understand** additional issues related to accounting for PPE

4 **Analyze** the effects of a PPE disposal

5 **Account** for natural resources and depletion

6 **Account** for intangible assets and amortization

7 **Report** PPE transactions on the statement of cash flows

TYPES OF NON-CURRENT ASSETS

Businesses use several types of **Property, Plant and Equipment (PPE)**, as shown in Lenovo's balance sheet. Lenovo has PPE totaling USD 314 million (lines 2 and 15), which is further detailed in its notes to accounts into buildings, leasehold improvements, plant and machinery, furniture and fixtures, office equipment and motor vehicles (lines 9—14), each with its own costs and accumulated depreciation (and impairment). The difference between a PPE's cost and its accumulated depreciation is called "the carrying amount" (or net book value):

- **PPE**, sometimes called *fixed assets*, are non-current or long-lived assets that are tangible—for instance, land, buildings, and equipment. They are held for use in the production or supply of goods or services, for rental to others, or for administrative purposes; and are expected to be used during more than one period. The allocation of a PPE's cost over its useful life is called *depreciation*. The amount that has been allocated over the years is called *accumulated depreciation*. Of the PPE items, freehold land is unique. Land that is owned in perpetuity is not depreciated over time because its usefulness does not decrease. In many countries, however, land titles are not issued in perpetuity and usually have a limited tenure, after which the title is returned to the government. This type of land is usually called "leasehold land". Lenovo called this "Prepaid Lease Payments" (line 3, which is further explained in line 16). The primary source of guidance for PPE is *IAS16 – Property, Plant and Equipment*.

- Lenovo has a **Construction in Progress** (line 4) non-current asset. This account is a "placeholder" for assets that are being constructed. Once completed, the cost of the asset that has been accumulated in the Construction in Progress account is then moved to PPE (or Intangible Asset) account.

- **Intangible assets** are identifiable non-monetary assets without physical substance. Non-monetary simply means that the asset is not expressed in fixed or determinable amounts of money. These intangible assets are unique because they do not have any physical form. Lenovo reports a total of USD 1.85 billion of net intangible assets (line 5), comprising goodwill, trademarks and trade names, internal use software, customer relationships, patent and technology, and marketing rights (lines 17—22). Accounting for intangibles is similar in nature to accounting for PPE assets. With the exception of goodwill (and other intangible assets with indefinite useful lives), the cost of intangible assets are also allocated over the assets' respective useful lives. We usually refer to this as amortization. The primary source of guidance for intangible assets is *IAS38 – Intangible Assets*.

- Sometimes, you may also see companies with **Investment Properties** as a non-current asset. These are a specially designated class of properties (land and/or buildings) held to earn rentals or for capital appreciation or both, rather than for usage associated with sales, production or general administrative functions. Investment properties are beyond the scope of this course, but you can refer to *IAS40 – Investment Properties* for additional information. At other times, you may also see companies with **Agriculture** assets such as dairy cattle, trees in a plantation forest, vines or fruit trees. The agriculture or biological assets are accounted for under *IAS41 – Agriculture*.

PPE and intangibles are subject to impairment tests (*IAS36 – Impairment of Assets*) to ensure that the values reported on the balance sheet do not exceed the fair value of the assets.

Accounting for PPE and intangibles has its own terminology. Different names apply to the individual PPE and their corresponding expenses, as shown in Exhibit 7-1.

EXHIBIT 7-1 | PPE & Intangibles Terminology

Asset Account (Balance Sheet)	Related Expense Account (Income Statement)
Property, Plant and Equipment	
Freehold Land	None
Leasehold Land	Depreciation
Buildings, Machinery and Equipment	Depreciation
Furniture and Fixtures	Depreciation
Land Improvements	Depreciation
Natural Resources	Depletion
Intangibles	
Intangibles with finite useful lives	Amortization
Intangibles with indefinite useful lives	None

Before examining the various types of PPE and intangible assets, let's see how we can recognize and measure them.

INITIAL RECOGNITION AND MEASUREMENT OF PPE

Recognition of PPE and Intangible Assets

OBJECTIVE

1 Determine the cost of a PPE

PPE and intangible assets are recognized when they meet their definition and the recognition criteria similar to that of any other assets; it is probable that future economic benefits associated with the item will flow to the entity and the cost of the item can be measured reliably. We will start our discussion with PPE for now and discuss intangible assets later on.

Measurement of PPE on Initial Recognition

Here is a basic working rule for determining the cost of an asset: *The cost of any asset is the sum of all the costs incurred to bring the asset to its intended use.* Specifically, *IAS16* requires that the cost of an item of PPE includes:

- its purchase price, including import duties and non-refundable purchase taxes, after deducting trade discounts and rebates.
- any costs directly attributable to bringing the asset to the location and condition necessary for it to be capable of operating in the manner intended by management.

TECHNICAL UPDATE

There is an additional cost element in *IAS16* that is seldom applicable for most PPE items. *IAS16* requires that the cost of an item of PPE also includes an initial estimate of the costs of dismantling and removing the item and restoring the site on which it is located, the obligation for which an entity incurs either when the item is acquired or as a consequence of having used the item during a particular period for purposes other than to produce inventories during that period. The obligation component of the dismantling cost is accounted as per *IAS37 – Provisions, Contingent Liabilities and Contingent Assets*. Since this is rarely applicable for most assets, we will not discuss this cost component.

IAS16 provides some examples of "directly attributable cost":

- costs of employee benefits arising directly from the construction or acquisition of the item of property, plant and equipment;
- costs of site preparation;
- initial delivery and handling costs;
- installation and assembly costs;
- costs of testing whether the asset is functioning properly, after deducting the net proceeds from selling any items produced while bringing the asset to that location and condition (such as samples produced when testing equipment); and
- professional fees.

Similarly, *IAS16* also provided examples of what should **not** be included in cost of an item of PPE:

- costs of opening a new facility;
- costs of introducing a new product or service (including costs of advertising and promotional activities);
- costs of conducting business in a new location or with a new class of customer (including costs of staff training); and
- administration and other general overhead costs.

Let's apply this recognition and measurement criteria to a number of PPE items.

Land and Land Improvements

The cost of land includes its purchase price (cash plus any note payable given), brokerage commission, survey fees, legal fees, and any property taxes that the purchaser pays. Land cost also includes expenditures for grading and clearing the land and for removing unwanted buildings.

The cost of land does not include the cost of fencing, paving, security systems, and lighting. These are separate PPE—called land improvements—and they are subject to depreciation. Lenovo's balance sheet included a "leasehold improvements" of about USD 75 million dollars (line 10). Recall earlier discussions that Leasehold land simply means that the land title is not in perpetuity.

Suppose Lenovo signs a $300,000 note payable to purchase a parcel of land for a new shipping site. Lenovo also pays $10,000 for real estate commission, $8,000 of back property tax, $5,000 for removal of an old building, a $1,000 survey fee, and $260,000 to pave the parking lot—all in cash. What should Lenovo recognize as the cost of this land?

Purchase price of land......................		$300,000
Add related costs:		
Real estate commission..............	$10,000	
Back property tax........................	8,000	
Removal of building...................	5,000	
Survey fee...................................	1,000	
Total related costs.......................		24,000
Total cost of land...........................		$324,000

Note that the cost to pave the parking lot, $260,000, is *not* included in the land's cost, because the pavement is a land improvement. Lenovo would record the purchase of this land as follows:

Land		324,000	
Note Payable			300,000
Cash			24,000

Assets	=	Liabilities	+	Shareholders' Equity
+ 324,000 − 24,000	=	+ 300,000	+	0

This purchase of land increases both assets and liabilities. There is no effect on equity.[1]

The cost to pave a parking lot ($260,000) would be recorded in a separate account entitled Land Improvements (or Leasehold Improvements if the land title is not in perpetuity). This account includes costs for such other items as driveways, signs, fences, and sprinkler systems. Although these assets are located on the land, they are subject to decay, and their cost should therefore be depreciated. The cost of leasehold improvements should be depreciated over the term of the lease. Most companies call the depreciation on leasehold improvements *amortization*, which is the same concept as *depreciation*.

Buildings, Machinery, and Equipment

The cost of constructing a building includes architectural fees, building permits, contractors' charges, and payments for material, labor, and overhead. If the company constructs its own building, the cost will also include the cost of interest on money borrowed to finance the construction (if the recognition criteria in *IAS23 – Borrowing Costs* are met).

---

[1] We show the accounting equation along with each journal entry—where the accounting equation aids your understanding of the transaction. Impact of revenue and expense transactions are taken directly to equity.

When an existing building (new or old) is purchased, its cost includes the purchase price, brokerage commission, sales and other taxes paid, and all expenditures to repair and renovate the building for its intended purpose.

The cost of Lenovo's manufacturing equipment includes its purchase price (less any discounts), plus transportation from the seller to Lenovo, insurance while in transit, sales and other taxes, purchase commission, installation costs, and any expenditures to test the asset before it's placed in service. The equipment cost will also include the cost of any special platforms. After the asset is up and running, insurance, taxes, and regular maintenance costs are recorded as expenses, not as part of the asset's cost.

Lump-Sum (or Basket) Purchases of Assets

Businesses often purchase several assets as a group, or a "basket", for a single lump-sum amount. For example, Lenovo may pay one price for land and a building but the company must first identify the cost of each asset. The total cost is then divided among the assets according to their relative sales (or market) values. This technique is called the *relative-sales-value method*.

Suppose Lenovo purchases land and a building in Bangkok, Thailand. The building sits on two acres of land, and the combined purchase price of land and building is 95 million Thai Baht or about USD 2,800,000 (for simplicity, we will use USD to account for this transaction). An appraisal indicates that the land's market value is $300,000 and that the building's market value is $2,700,000.

Lenovo first figures the ratio of each asset's market value to the total market value. The total appraised value is $2,700,000 + $300,000 = $3,000,000. Thus, the land, valued at $300,000, is 10% of the total market value. The building's appraised value is 90% of the total. These percentages are then used to determine the cost of each asset, as follows:

Asset	Market (Sales) Value		Total Market Value		Percentage of Total Market Value		Total Cost	Cost of Each Asset
Land	$ 300,000	÷	$3,000,000	=	10%	×	$2,800,000	$ 280,000
Building	2,700,000	÷	3,000,000	=	90%	×	$2,800,000	2,520,000
Total	$3,000,000				100%			$2,800,000

If Lenovo pays cash, the entry to record the purchase of the land and building is

Land	280,000	
Building	2,520,000	
Cash		2,800,000

Assets	=	Liabilities	+	Shareholders' Equity
+ 280,000	=			
+ 2,520,000	=	0	+	0
− 2,800,000	=			

Total assets don't change—they are merely the makeup of Lenovo's assets.

STOP & THINK...

How would Lenovo divide a $120,000 lump-sum purchase price for land, building, and equipment with estimated market values of $40,000, $95,000, and $15,000, respectively?

Answer:

	Estimated Market Value	Percentage of Total Market Value	×	Total Cost	=	Cost of Each Asset
Land..................	$ 40,000	26.7%*	×	$120,000	=	$ 32,040
Building.............	95,000	63.3%	×	$120,000	=	75,960
Equipment.........	15,000	10.0%	×	$120,000	=	12,000
Total................	$150,000	100.0%				$120,000

*$40,000/$150,000 = 0.267, and so on

Subsequent Costs

The PPE recognition criteria in *IAS16* helps us in determining whether an expenditure should be recognized as an asset in the balance sheet or expensed immediately to the income statement. The same criteria also helps us with expenditures subsequent to the initial recognition. Specifically, *IAS16* states that an entity should **not** be recognized in the carrying amount of an item of PPE the costs of the day-to-day servicing which typically comprises the costs of labor and consumables, or small parts of the item. These costs are expensed or charged to the income statement as incurred. The purpose of these expenditures is often described as for the "repairs and maintenance" of the PPE. For example, Lenovo may perform regular maintenance of its motor vehicles. The costs of repainting a Lenovo delivery truck, repairing its dented bumper or worn tires are also expensed immediately.

On the other hand, expenditures that increase the asset's capacity or extend its useful life are called "capital expenditures". For example, the cost of a major overhaul that extends the useful life of a Lenovo truck is a capital expenditure. Capital expenditures are said to be capitalized, which means the cost is added to an asset account and not expensed immediately. Thus, a major decision in accounting for PPE is whether to capitalize or to expense a certain cost.

Continuing with our delivery truck example, Exhibit 7-2 shows the distinction between recognizing the capital expenditures as asset and immediate charging the expenditure as expense for the period.

EXHIBIT 7-2 | **Capital Expenditure or Immediate Expense for Costs Associated with a Delivery Truck**

Record an Asset for Capital Expenditures	Record Repair and Maintenance Asset Expense
Significant or Major repairs:	**Ordinary repairs:**
Major engine overhaul	Repair of transmission or other mechanism
Addition to storage capacity of truck	Oil change, lubrication, and so on
Modification of body for new use	Replacement of tires and windshield,
of truck	or a paint job

TECHNICAL UPDATE

For certain industries, it is possible that certain "repairs and maintenance" may be a necessary precondition to continue to operate the asset. For example, you would want to be sure that any airline you fly with has complied with all the required safety and maintenance checks. These are probably regular major inspections at certain points of the asset's useful life or at preset usage intervals. *IAS16* allows for the capitalization of these major inspections as part of the carrying amount of the item of property.

For example, **Qantas**' 2009 annual report states that: "The standard cost of subsequent major airframe and engine maintenance checks is capitalized and depreciated over the shorter of the scheduled usage period to the next major inspection event or the remaining life of the aircraft. Manpower costs in relation to employees that are dedicated to major modifications to aircraft are capitalized as part of the cost of the modification to which they relate. … All other maintenance costs are expensed … Modifications that enhance the operating performance or extend the useful lives of airframes or engines are capitalized and depreciated over the remaining estimated useful life of the asset."

The distinction between a capital expenditure and an expense requires judgment: Does the cost extend the asset's usefulness or its useful life? If so, record an asset. If the cost merely repairs the asset or returns it to its prior condition, then record an expense.

Most companies expense all small costs, say, below $1,000. For higher costs, they follow the rule we gave above: capitalize costs that extend the asset's usefulness or its useful life, and expense all other costs. A conservative policy is one that avoids overstating assets and profits. A company that overstates its assets may get into trouble and have to defend itself in court.

Accounting errors sometimes occur for PPE costs. For example, a company may:

- expense a cost that should have been capitalized. This error overstates expenses and understates net income in the year of the error.
- capitalize a cost that should have been expensed. This error understates expenses and overstates net income in the year of the error.

COOKING THE BOOKS
by Improper Capitalization
WorldCom

It is one thing to accidentally capitalize an expense as PPE but quite another to do it intentionally, thus deliberately overstating assets, understating expenses, and overstating net income. One well-known company committed one of the biggest financial statement frauds in U.S. history in this way.

In 2002, WorldCom, Inc., was one of the largest telecommunications service providers in the world. The company had grown rapidly from a small, regional telephone company in 1983 to a giant corporation in 2002 by acquiring an ever-increasing number of other such companies. But 2002 was a bad year for WorldCom, as well as for many others in the "telecom" industry. The United States was reeling from the effects of a deep economic recession spawned by the "bursting dot-com bubble" in 2000 and intensified by the terrorist attacks on U.S. soil in 2001. Wall Street was looking high and low for positive signs, pressuring public companies to keep profits trending upward in order to support share prices, without much success, at least for the honest companies.

Bernard J. ("Bernie") Ebbers, WorldCom's chief executive officer, was worried. He began to press his chief financial officer, Scott Sullivan, to find a way to make the company's income statement look healthier. After all legitimate attempts to improve earnings failed, Sullivan concocted a scheme to cook the books.

Like all telecommunications companies, WorldCom had signed contracts with other telephone companies, paying them fees so that WorldCom customers could use their lines for telephone calls and Internet usage. Accounting standards require such fees to be expensed as incurred, rather than capitalized. Overestimating the growth of its business, WorldCom had incurred billions of dollars in such costs, about 15% more than its customers would ever use.

In direct violation of accounting standards, Sullivan rationalized that the excessive amounts WorldCom had spent on line costs would eventually lead to the company's recognizing revenue in future years (thus extending their usefulness and justifying, in his mind, their classification as assets). Sullivan directed the accountants working under him to reclassify line costs as property, plant, and equipment assets, rather than as expenses, and to amortize (spread) the costs over several years rather than to expense them in the periods in which they were incurred. Over several quarters, Mr. Sullivan and his assistants transferred a total of $3.1 billion in such charges from operating expense accounts to property, plant and equipment, resulting in the transformation of what would have been a net loss for all of 2001 and the first quarter of 2002 into a sizeable profit. It was the largest single fraud in U.S. history to that point.

Sullivan's fraudulent scheme was discovered by the company's internal audit staff during a routine spot-check of the company's records for capital expenditures. The staff members reported Sullivan's (and his staff's) fraudulent activities to the head of the company's audit committee and its external auditor, setting in motion a chain of events that resulted in Ebbers' and Sullivan's firing, and the company's eventual bankruptcy. Ebbers, Sullivan, and several of their assistants went to prison for their participation in this fraudulent scheme.

Shareholders of WorldCom lost billions of dollars in share value when the company went down, and more than 500,000 people lost their jobs.

The WorldCom scandal rocked the financial world, causing global stock markets to plummet from lack of confidence. This scandal (as well as others such as Enron) eventually led to the passage of the US Sarbanes-Oxley Act (p. 238).

MEASURING DEPRECIATION ON PPE

As we've seen in previous chapters, PPE are reported on the balance sheet at their carrying amounts or book values, which is:

> Carrying amount of an item PPE = Cost − Accumulated Depreciation

Depreciation is the systematic allocation of the cost of an asset over its useful life. The depreciation process matches the asset's expense against revenue to measure income, as the matching principle directs. Exhibit 7-3 illustrates this concept with an example of an Airbus A330 owned by **Singapore Airlines**.

EXHIBIT 7-3 | Depreciation and the Matching of Expense with Revenue

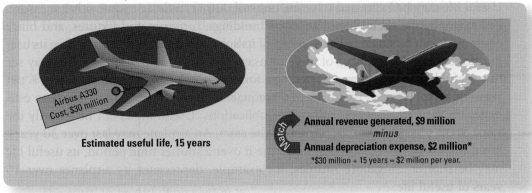

Recall that depreciation expense is charged periodically to the income statement. The cumulative amount of depreciation charged since the initial recognition and measurement of an asset is called accumulated depreciation, which you will find in the balance sheet.

You've just seen what depreciation is. Let's see what depreciation is *not*.

1. **Depreciation is not a process of valuation.** Businesses do *not* record depreciation based on changes in the market value of their PPEs. Instead, businesses allocate the asset's *cost* to the period of its useful life.

2. **Depreciation does not mean setting aside cash to replace assets as they wear out.** Any cash fund is entirely separate from depreciation.

How to Allocate Depreciation

Before we move to the specific depreciation methods, let's make sure we understand the basic concepts and terminologies related to depreciation. To allocate depreciation for a PPE item, we must know three things about the asset:

1. Cost   2. Estimated useful life   3. Estimated residual value

We have discussed cost, which is a known amount. The other two factors must be estimated.

The economic benefits from owning a PPE is consumed by an entity primarily through the use of the PPE in the ordinary course of business over the PPE's useful life. As the allocation of expenses is usually predetermined in advance (we will discuss method of depreciation in the next section), an entity such as Lenovo would have to make an estimate of the useful lives of its buildings, leasehold improvements, plant and machinery, furniture and fixtures, office equipment and motor vehicles. *IAS16* indicates that the following factors ought to be considered in determining an asset's useful life:

- expected usage of the asset;
- expected physical wear and tear, including the necessary repair and maintenance program;
- technical or commercial obsolescence, including a change in the market demand for the product or service output of the asset; and
- legal or similar limits on the use of the asset, such as the expiry dates of Lenovo's leasehold land.

An asset's final book value is its *residual value* ($1,000 in Exhibit 7-5). At the end of its useful life, the asset is said to be *fully depreciated*.

STOP & THINK...

A Lenovo office equipment that cost $10,000, has a useful life of five years, and residual value of $2,000, was purchased on January 1. What is SL depreciation for each year?

Answer:

$1,600 = ($10,000 − $2,000)/5

Units-of-Production Method. In the **units-of-production (UOP) method**, a fixed amount of depreciation is assigned to each *unit of output*, or service, produced by the asset. Depreciable cost is divided by useful life—in units of production—to determine this amount. This per-unit depreciation expense is then multiplied by the number of units produced each period to compute depreciation. Obviously, the Lenovo delivery truck will not stop working just because it has been driving to 100,000 miles. We continue with the same delivery truck as an illustration, but in real life, this method is more likely to be used with assets with technical capacity or unit limitations rather than a delivery truck. The UOP depreciation for the Lenovo truck data in Exhibit 7-4 (p. 418) is

$$\text{Units-of-production depreciation per unit of output} = \frac{\text{Cost} - \text{Residual value}}{\text{Useful life, in units of production}}$$

$$= \frac{\$41,000 - \$1,000}{100,000 \text{ miles}} = \$0.40 \text{ per mile}$$

Assume that Lenovo expects to drive the truck 20,000 miles during the first year, 30,000 during the second, 25,000 during the third, 15,000 during the fourth, and 10,000 during the fifth. Exhibit 7-6 shows the UOP depreciation schedule.

EXHIBIT 7-6 | Units-of-Production Depreciation Schedule

Date	Asset Cost	Depreciation for the Year			Accumulated Depreciation	Asset Carrying Amount
		Depreciation Per Unit*	Number of Units	Depreciation Expense		
1-1-2009	$41,000					$41,000
12-31-2009		$0.40* ×	20,000 =	$ 8,000	$ 8,000	33,000
12-31-2010		0.40 ×	30,000 =	12,000	20,000	21,000
12-31-2011		0.40 ×	25,000 =	10,000	30,000	11,000
12-31-2012		0.40 ×	15,000 =	6,000	36,000	5,000
12-31-2013		0.40 ×	10,000 =	4,000	40,000	1,000

*($41,000 − $1,000)/100,000 miles = $0.40 per mile.

The amount of UOP depreciation varies with the number of units the asset produces in a year. In our example above, we have estimated the usage pattern, but the actual depreciation charge each year will be based on the actual outputs for the year. For example, if the actual miles driven in 2009 were 21,000, the depreciation charge for the year would have been $0.40 x 21,000 = $8,400. UOP depreciation does not depend directly on passage of time, as do the other methods.

Double-Declining-Balance Method. An accelerated depreciation method (or using *IAS16's* terminology, "diminishing balance method") writes off a larger amount of the asset's cost near the start of its useful life than the straight-line method does. **Double-declining-balance (DDB)** is the main accelerated depreciation method and computes annual depreciation by multiplying the asset's declining book value by a constant percentage, which is double (or two times) the straight-line depreciation rate. DDB amounts are computed as follows:

- *First*, compute the straight-line depreciation rate per year. A five-year truck has a straight-line depreciation rate of 1/5, or 20% each year. A 10-year asset has a straight-line rate of 1/10, or 10%, and so on.
- *Second*, multiply the straight-line rate by 2 to compute the DDB rate. For a five-year asset, the DDB rate is 40% (20% × 2). A 10-year asset has a DDB rate of 20% (10% × 2). The DDB rate for the delivery truck in Exhibit 7-4 (p. 418) is:

$$\text{DDB depreciation rate per year} = \frac{1}{\text{Useful life, in years}} \times 2$$

$$= \frac{1}{5 \text{ years}} \times 2$$

$$= 20\% \times 2 = 40\%$$

- *Third*, multiply the DDB rate by the period's beginning asset book value (cost less accumulated depreciation). Under the DDB method, ignore the residual value of the asset in computing depreciation, except during the last year.
- *Fourth*, determine the final year's depreciation amount—that is, the amount needed to reduce asset book value to its residual value. In Exhibit 7-7, the fifth and final year's DDB depreciation is $4,314—book value of $5,314 less the $1,000 residual value. *The residual value should not be depreciated* but should remain on the books until the asset is disposed of.

EXHIBIT 7-7 | **Double-Declining-Balance Depreciation Schedule**

Date	Asset Cost	DDB Rate		Asset Carrying Amount		Depreciation Expense	Accumulated Depreciation	Asset Carrying Amount
				Depreciation for the Year				
1- 1-2009	$41,000							$41,000
12-31-2009		0.40	×	$41,000	=	$16,400	$16,400	24,600
12-31-2010		0.40	×	24,600	=	9,840	26,240	14,760
12-31-2011		0.40	×	14,760	=	5,904	32,144	8,856
12-31-2012		0.40	×	8,856	=	3,542	35,686	5,314
12-31-2013						4,314*	40,000	1,000

*Last-year depreciation is the "plug" amount needed to reduce asset book value (far right column) to the residual amount ($5,314 – $1,000 = $4,314).

The DDB method differs from the other methods in three ways:

1. It is an accelerated depreciation method, so depreciation expenses in the early years are significantly more than in later years.

2. Residual value is ignored initially; first-year depreciation is computed on the asset's full cost.

3. Depreciation expense in the final year is the "plug" amount needed to reduce the asset's book value to the residual amount.

STOP & THINK. . .

What is the DDB depreciation each year for the asset in the Stop & Think on page 420?

Answers:

> Yr. 1: $4,000 ($10,000 × 40%)
> Yr. 2: $2,400 ($6,000 × 40%)
> Yr. 3: $1,440 ($3,600 × 40%)
> Yr. 4: $160 ($10,000 − $4,000 − $2,400 − $1,440 − $2,000 = $160)*
> Yr. 5: $0

*The asset is not depreciated below residual value of $2,000.

Comparing Depreciation Methods

Let's compare the three methods in terms of the yearly amount of depreciation. The yearly amount varies by method, but the total $40,000 depreciable cost is the same under all methods.

	Amount of Depreciation Expense per Year		
Year	Straight-Line	Units-of-Production	Accelerated Method Double-Declining Balance
1	$ 8,000	$ 8,000	$16,400
2	8,000	12,000	9,840
3	8,000	10,000	5,904
4	8,000	6,000	3,542
5	8,000	4,000	4,314
Total	$40,000	$40,000	$40,000

Exhibit 7-8 graphs annual depreciation amounts for the straight-line, units-of-production, and accelerated depreciation (DDB) methods. The graph of straight-line depreciation is flat through time because annual depreciation is the same in all periods. Units-of-production depreciation follows no particular pattern because annual depreciation depends on the actual use of the asset during the year. Accelerated depreciation is greatest in the first year and less in the later years.

EXHIBIT 7-8 | **Depreciation Patterns Through Time**

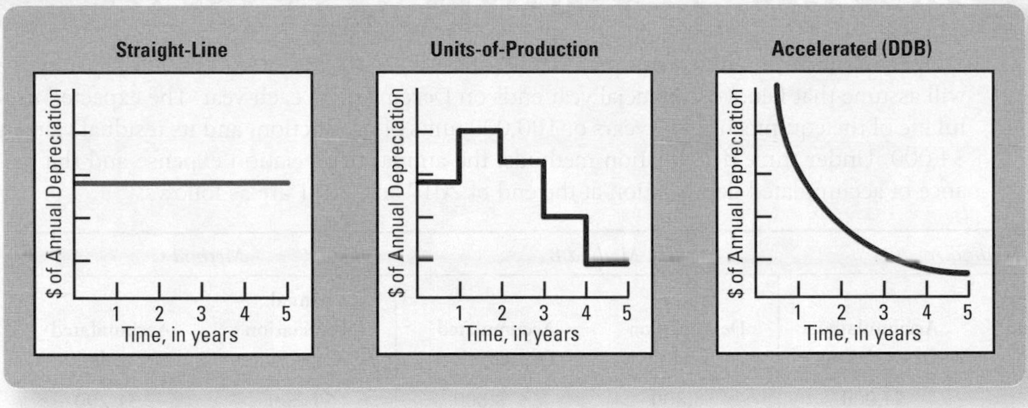

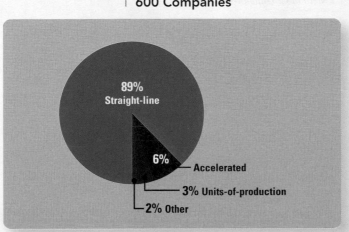

Choosing a Depreciation Method

Clearly, the choice of a depreciation method will impact the profit of any entity. How should an entity choose the "right" depreciation method? *IAS16* requires that the depreciation method chosen ought to reflect the pattern of consumption of the economic benefits embodied in the asset. At every financial year-end, an entity should review the depreciation method, and unless there is a significant change in the pattern of consumption, it should continue to apply the method consistently from period to period.

For PPE assets with a reasonably constant pattern of consumption, the straight-line method best meets the matching principle. The units-of-production method best fits those assets that wear out because of physical use rather than obsolescence. An accelerated method (such as DDB) applies best to assets that generate more revenue earlier in their useful lives and less in later years.

Exhibit 7-9 shows the percentage of companies that use each depreciation method from a survey of Standard & Poor's 600 companies by the American Institute of Certified Public Accountants. Note that a company may use more than one depreciation method from different classes of assets. For reporting in the financial statements, straight-line depreciation is clearly the most popular.

EXHIBIT 7-9 | **Depreciation Methods Used by 600 Companies**

MID-CHAPTER SUMMARY PROBLEM

Suppose Lenovo purchased equipment on January 1, 2010, for $44,000. For simplicity, we will assume that Lenovo's financial year ends on December 31 each year. The expected useful life of the equipment is 10 years or 100,000 units of production, and its residual value is $4,000. Under three depreciation methods, the annual depreciation expense and the balance of accumulated depreciation at the end of 2010 and 2011 are as follows:

	Method A		Method B		Method C	
Year	Annual Depreciation Expense	Accumulated Depreciation	Annual Depreciation Expense	Accumulated Depreciation	Annual Depreciation Expense	Accumulated Depreciation
2010	$4,000	$4,000	$8,800	$ 8,800	$1,200	$1,200
2011	4,000	8,000	7,040	15,840	5,600	6,800

Requirements

1. Identify the depreciation method used in each instance, and show the equation and computation for each. (Round to the nearest dollar.)
2. Assume continued use of the same method through year 2012. Determine the annual depreciation expense, accumulated depreciation, and book value of the equipment for 2010 through 2012 under each method, assuming 12,000 units of production in 2012.

Answers

Requirement 1

Method A: Straight-Line

Depreciable cost = $40,000($44,000 − $4,000)
Each year: $40,000/10 years = $4,000

Method B: Double-Declining-Balance

$$\text{Rate} = \frac{1}{10 \text{ years}} \times 2 = 10\% \times 2 = 20\%$$

2010: 0.20 × $44,000 = $8,800
2011: 0.20 × ($44,000 − $8,800) = $7,040

Method C: Units-of-Production

$$\text{Depreciation per unit} = \frac{\$44,000 - \$4,000}{100,000 \text{ units}} = \$0.40$$

2010: $0.40 × 3,000 units = $1,200
2011: $0.40 × 14,000 units = $5,600

I *Requirement 2*

Method A: Straight-Line

Year	Annual Depreciation Expense	Accumulated Depreciation	Book Value
Start			$44,000
2010	$4,000	$ 4,000	40,000
2011	4,000	8,000	36,000
2012	4,000	12,000	32,000

Method B: Double-Declining-Balance

Year	Annual Depreciation Expense	Accumulated Depreciation	Book Value
Start			$44,000
2010	$8,800	$ 8,800	35,200
2011	7,040	15,840	28,160
2012	5,632	21,472	22,528

Method C: Units-of-Production

Year	Annual Depreciation Expense	Accumulated Depreciation	Book Value
Start			$44,000
2010	$1,200	$ 1,200	42,800
2011	5,600	6,800	37,200
2012	4,800	11,600	32,400

Computations for 2012

Straight-line	$40,000/10 years = $4,000
Double-declining-balance	$28,160 × 0.20 = $5,632
Units-of-production	12,000 units × $0.40 = $4,800

OTHER ISSUES IN ACCOUNTING FOR PPE

OBJECTIVE

2 Understand additional issues related to accounting for PPE

Accounting for PPE may also need to handle issues related to:

- choice of depreciation method may affect income taxes; a different depreciation method may be used for financial reporting versus tax purposes.
- the fact that PPE have long lives, and subsequent better information may change estimates of useful life of assets and residual values.
- alternative models for measurement of PPE subsequent to initial recognition.
- companies that have gains or losses when they sell PPE.

Let's take a brief look at some of these issues.

Depreciation for Tax Purposes

Lenovo and most other companies use straight-line depreciation for reporting to shareholders and creditors on their financial statements. But for tax purposes, they may keep a separate set of depreciation records, depending on the specific tax regulations in various jurisdictions. There are two reasons primary reasons why this is the case.

First, certain jurisdictions may mandate a specific treatment for specific assets. For example, in Singapore, the depreciation of Lenovo's commercial vehicles, such as its delivery trucks, may be used to claim capital allowances (i.e. deductions from taxable income), but the depreciation of non-commercial vehicles, such as motor vehicles for its senior management staff, would not be allowed as a deduction. In other countries, there may be a maximum cap of the depreciable amount allowed for certain assets. Clearly, in order to comply with taxation rules, a different set of depreciation records will be required.

Second, tax regulations could provide alternative depreciation methods or schedules that are more favorable than what is being used for financial reporting. For example, investment in research into "green technologies" may be granted a double tax deduction to encourage companies to make head-way in the fight against climate change. You may have spent $1 million on such research, but you are entitled to claim $2 million as deductions in your tax forms. In other instances, you may be using the straight-line method for financial reporting, but the tax regulations may allow you to use an accelerated method such as DDB for tax reporting.

Suppose you are a Lenovo country manager, and your local tax authority allows an accelerated depreciation method. Why would you prefer accelerated over straight-line depreciation for income-tax purposes? This choice is easy. Accelerated depreciation provides the fastest tax deductions, thus decreasing immediate tax payments. Lenovo can reinvest the tax savings back into the business or pay off interest-bearing debts.

To understand the relationships between cash flow, depreciation, and income tax, recall our depreciation example of a Lenovo delivery truck:

- First-year depreciation is $8,000 under straight-line and $16,400 under double-declining-balance (DDB).
- DDB is permitted for income tax purposes.

EXHIBIT 7-10 | **The Cash-Flow Advantage of Accelerated Depreciation over Straight-Line Depreciation for Income Tax Purposes**

		SL	Accelerated
1	Cash revenue	$400,000	$400,000
2	Cash operating expenses	300,000	300,000
3	Cash provided by operations before income tax	100,000	100,000
4	Depreciation expense (a noncash expense)	8,000	16,400
5	Income before income tax	$ 92,000	$ 83,600
6	Income tax expense (30%)	$ 27,600	$ 25,080
	Cash-flow analysis:		
7	Cash provided by operations before tax	$100,000	$100,000
8	Income tax expense	27,600	25,080
9	Cash provided by operations	$ 72,400	$ 74,920
10	Extra cash available for investment or debt repayment if DDB is used ($74,920 – $72,400)		$ 2,520

You can see that, for income-tax purposes, accelerated depreciation helps conserve cash for the business. That's why virtually all companies will choose accelerated depreciation to compute their income tax, if allowed.

Remember that there are two different "profits", one is the net profit in your financial statements which are prepared in accordance to the applicable financial standards, and the other is taxable income your tax filings which are prepared in accordance to the applicable taxation rules. To understand more about taxation for accounting purposes, you may cover *IAS12 – Income Taxes* in your future courses, but if your interest is on the tax reporting side, you will need to read the various taxation rules and regulations. *IAS12* is beyond our course coverage, but it results in some accounts that you may encounter in many companies: deferred tax assets and deferred tax liabilities. These are due to the difference between net profit (in financial reporting) and taxable income (in tax reporting).

This does not mean that we are "keeping two set of books", which is usually associated with unscrupulous behavior and cheating. We need to maintain two separate schedules because the rules are different, not because we are trying to hide income from the tax authorities!

Depreciation for Partial Years

Companies purchase PPE whenever they need them, not just at the beginning of the year. Therefore, companies must compute depreciation for partial years or whenever they need to report to shareholders (e.g. quarterly or half-yearly reports). Suppose Lenovo purchases a warehouse building on April 1 for $500,000. The building's estimated life is 20 years, and its estimated residual value is $80,000. We will continue to assume that Lenovo's year-end is December 31 for discussion purposes. Let's consider how Lenovo computes depreciation for April through December:

- First, compute depreciation for a full year.
- Second, multiply full-year depreciation by the fraction of the year that you held the asset—in this case, 9/12. Assuming the straight-line method, the year's depreciation for this Lenovo building is $15,750, as follows:

$$\text{Full-year depreciation} \quad \frac{\$500,000 - \$80,000}{20} = \$21,000$$

$$\text{Partial year depreciation} \quad \$21,000 \times 9/12 = \$15,750$$

What if Lenovo bought the asset on April 18? Many businesses record no monthly depreciation on assets purchased after the 15th of the month, and they record a full month's depreciation on an asset bought on or before the 15th. Actual practices may vary from company to company, but in the overall scheme of things, a difference of a few days is not likely to be material for long-lived assets.

Most companies use computerized systems to account for fixed assets. Each depreciable asset has a unique identification number, and the system will automatically calculate the asset's depreciation expense. Accumulated Depreciation will then be automatically updated.

Changes in Estimates of Useful Lives or Residual Values

After an asset is in use, managers may change its useful life on the basis of experience and new information. Lenovo's 2008 annual report contained this disclosure:

EXCERPTS (ADAPTED) FROM LENOVO'S 2008 NOTES TO THE FINANCIAL STATEMENTS

During the year, the estimated useful life of tooling equipment was reviewed and changed from 10-20 years to two years as it reflects the current product life cycle. This change has resulted in an accelerated depreciation charge of approximately US$37 million.

As you can see from the disclosure above, the change to a shorter useful life increased the depreciation charge for the year. This is called a change in accounting estimate (more on *IAS8 – Accounting Policies, Changes in Accounting Estimates and Errors* in Chapter 11). Lenovo recalculated depreciation on the basis of revised useful lives of its tooling equipment. Changes in estimates may also occur for residual values and accounted for similarly.

Assume that Lenovo bought equipment costing $50,000 and that the company originally believed the asset had a 10-year useful life with no residual value. Using the straight-line method, the company would record $5,000 depreciation each year ($50,000/10 years = $5,000). Suppose Lenovo used the asset for four years. Accumulated depreciation reached $20,000, leaving a remaining depreciable book value (cost less accumulated depreciation less residual value) of $30,000 ($50,000 – $20,000). Based on the asset's conditions at the end of year four, management believes the asset will remain useful for 8 more years. The company would spread the remaining depreciable book value over the asset's remaining life as follows:

Asset's remaining depreciable book value	÷	(New) Estimated useful life remaining	=	(New) Annual depreciation
$30,000	÷	8 years	=	$3,750

The yearly depreciation entry based on the new estimated useful life is

Depreciation Expense—Equipment	3,750	
Accumulated Depreciation—Equipment		3,750

Depreciation decreases both assets and equity.

Assets	=	Liabilities	+	Shareholders' Equity	
− 3,750	=	0	+	− 3,750	(depreciation expense)

COOKING THE BOOKS
Through Depreciation

Waste Management

Since PPEs usually involve relatively large amounts and relatively large numbers of assets, sometimes a seemingly subtle change in the way they are accounted for can have a tremendous impact on the financial statements. When these changes are made in order to cook the books, the results can be devastating.

Waste Management, Inc., is North America's largest integrated waste service company, providing collection, transfer, recycling, disposal, and waste-to-energy services for commercial, industrial, municipal, and residential customers from coast to coast.

Starting in 1992, six top executives of the company, including its founder and chairman of the board, its chief financial officer, its corporate controller, its top lawyer, and its vice president of finance, decided that the company's profits were not growing fast enough to meet "earnings targets," which were tied to their executive bonuses. Among several fraudulent financial tactics these top executives employed to cook the books were: (1) assigning unsupported and inflated salvage values to garbage trucks; (2) unjustifiably extending the estimated useful lives of their garbage trucks; and (3) assigning arbitrary salvage values to other fixed assets that previously had no salvage values. All of these tactics had the effect of decreasing the amount of depreciation expense in the income statements and increasing net income by a corresponding amount. While practices like this might seem relatively subtle and even insignificant when performed on an individual asset, remember that there were thousands of trash trucks and dumpsters involved, so the dollar amount grew huge in a short time. In addition, the company continued these practices for five years, overstating earnings by $1.7 billion.

The Waste Management fraud was the largest of its kind in history until the WorldCom scandal, discussed earlier in this chapter. In 1997, the company fired the officers involved and hired a new CEO who ordered a review of these practices, which uncovered the fraud. In the meantime, these dishonest executives had profited handsomely, receiving performance-based bonuses based on the company's inflated earnings, retaining their high-paying jobs, and receiving enhanced retirement benefits. One of the executives took the fraud to another level. Just 10 days before the fraud was disclosed, he enriched himself with a tax benefit by donating inflated company shares to his alma mater to fund a building in his name! Although the men involved were sued for monetary damages, none of them ever went to jail.

When the fraud was disclosed, Waste Management shareholders lost over $6 billion in the market value of their investments when the share price plummeted by more than 33%. The company and these officers eventually settled civil lawsuits for approximately $700 million because of the fraud.

You might ask, "Where were the auditors while this was occurring?" The company's auditor was Arthur Andersen, LLP, whose partners involved on the audit engagement were eventually found to be complicit in the scheme. In fact, a few of the Waste Management officers who perpetrated the scheme had been ex-partners of the audit firm. As it turns out, the auditors actually identified many of the improper accounting practices of Waste Management. However, rather than insisting that the company fix the errors, or risk exposure, they merely "persuaded" management to agree not to repeat these practices in the future, and entered into an agreement with them to write off the accumulated balance sheet overstatement over a period of 10 years. In June 2001, the SEC fined Arthur Andersen $7 million for "knowingly and recklessly issuing false and misleading audit reports" for Waste Management from 1993 through 1996.

In October 2001, immediately on the heels of these disclosures, the notorious Enron scandal broke. Enron, as well as WorldCom, were Arthur Andersen clients at the time. The Enron scandal (discussed in Chapter 10) finally put the firm out of business. Many people felt that, had it not been for Andersen's involvement in the Waste Management affair, the SEC might have been more lenient toward the company in the Enron scandal.

Impairment of PPE

As you probably know, the fight for the next generation format was won by **Sony**'s Blu-ray when **Toshiba** abandoned the HD DVD format in February 2008. Prior to this, Toshiba had experienced significant difficulties over a period of time, **Warner Brothers**, **Wal-Mart**, **Best-Buy** and many others had started to stop the sales of HD DVD, causing a severe drop in demand for HD DVD. Suppose that at the start of the format war, Toshiba had a dedicated factory costing $1 billion that produced HD DVD, which was being depreciated over its estimated useful life of 10 years on a straight-line basis. After three years, the carrying amount of the equipment would have been $700 million. In this scenario, should Toshiba have continued depreciating the factory over 10 years, in light of the significant changes in the market for the outputs of its factory?

This is an example of how an asset may be impaired. *IAS36 – Impairment of Assets* provides guidance on this matter. An asset is impaired when its carrying value is higher than its recoverable amount. **Recoverable amount** is the higher of fair value less cost to sell and value in use. The determination of recoverable amount, and many other aspects of impairment of assets, is beyond an introductory accounting course. However, it is important for you to know the basic concepts of impairment. Many companies in the financial crisis have reported billions of impairment losses. Suppose that when the carrying amount of the factory was $700 million, the recoverable amount was $300 million. Toshiba would then recognize an impairment loss of $400 million with the following journal entry:

Year 3	Impairment Loss on Factory ($700 – $300)	400	
	Accumulated Depreciation and Impairment Loss		400

Both assets (Factory) and equity decrease (through the Loss account). Under IFRS, reversal of impairment losses may be permitted under certain limited circumstances.

Assets	=	Liabilities	+	Shareholders' Equity	
– 30	=	0	+	– 30	(impairment loss)

Measurement Subsequent to Initial Recognition

Under *IAS16*, an entity elects one out of two measurement models for each class of property, which is defined as a grouping of assets of similar nature and use in an entity's operations. For example, Lenovo uses six classes of PPE: Buildings, Leasehold improvements, Plant and machinery, Furniture and fixtures, Office equipment, and Motor vehicles:

- **Cost model:** an item of PPE shall be carried at its cost, less any accumulated depreciation and any accumulated impairment losses. This is similar to what we have discussed in this chapter thus far.
- **Revaluation model:** an item of PPE whose fair value can be measured reliably shall be carried at a revalued amount, being its fair value at the date of the revaluation less any subsequent accumulated depreciation and subsequent accumulated impairment losses. Revaluations shall be made with sufficient regularity to ensure that the carrying amount does not differ materially from that which would be determined using fair value at the balance sheet dates.

TECHNICAL UPDATE The revaluation model is a little more complicated than the cost model. *IAS16* provides additional guidelines on the determination of fair values, the frequency of revaluations, the treatment of revaluation gains and losses, and adjustments to accumulated depreciation. Your instructor may refer you to *IAS16* if additional coverage of the operations of revaluation model is required for your course.

Using Fully Depreciated Assets

A *fully depreciated asset* is one that has reached the end of its estimated useful life. Suppose Lenovo has fully depreciated equipment with zero residual value (cost was $60,000). Lenovo's accounts will appear as follows:

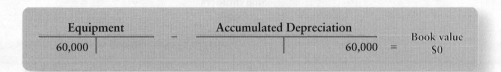

Equipment		Accumulated Depreciation		Book value
60,000	−		60,000 =	$0

The equipment's book value is zero, but that doesn't mean the equipment is worthless. Lenovo may use the equipment for a few more years, but Lenovo will not record any more depreciation on a fully depreciated asset.

When Lenovo disposes of the equipment, Lenovo will remove both the asset's cost ($60,000) and its accumulated depreciation ($60,000) from the books. The next section shows how PPE disposals are accounted.

ACCOUNTING FOR DISPOSAL OF PPE

Eventually, a PPE will cease to serve a company's needs. The asset may wear out or become obsolete. Before accounting for the disposal of the asset, the business should bring depreciation up to date to:

OBJECTIVE

3 **Analyze** the effects of a PPE disposal

- update the asset's final book value; and
- record the expense up to the date of sale.

To account for disposal, remove the asset and its related accumulated depreciation from the books. Suppose the final year's depreciation expense has just been recorded for a machine that cost $60,000 and is estimated to have zero residual value. The machine's accumulated depreciation thus totals $60,000. Assuming that this asset is junked or scrapped, the entry to record its disposal is:

Accumulated Depreciation—Machinery	60,000	
Machinery		60,000
To dispose of a fully depreciated machine.		

Assets	=	Liabilities	+	Shareholders' Equity
+ 60,000 − 60,000	=	0	+	0

There is no gain or loss on this disposal, and there's no effect on total assets, liabilities, or equity.

If assets are junked before being fully depreciated, the company incurs a loss on the disposal. Suppose Lenovo disposes of equipment that cost $60,000. This asset's accumulated depreciation is $50,000, and book value is, therefore, $10,000. Scrapping this equipment results in a loss equal to the book value of the asset, as follows:

Accumulated Depreciation—Equipment	50,000	
Loss on Disposal of Equipment	10,000	
Equipment		60,000
To dispose of equipment.		

Assets	=	Liabilities	+	Shareholders' Equity	
+ 50,000 − 60,000	=	0	+	− 10,000	(loss on disposal of PPE)

Lenovo got rid of an asset with $10,000 book value and received nothing. The result is a $10,000 loss, which decreases both total assets and equity.

The (gain) loss on disposal of equipment is reported as other income (expense) on the income statement. Losses decrease net income exactly as expenses do. Gains increase net income in the same as revenues.

Selling a PPE. Suppose Lenovo sells equipment on September 30, 2012, for $7,300 cash. The equipment cost $10,000 when purchased on January 1, 2009, and has been depreciated straight-line. Lenovo estimated a 10-year useful life and no residual value. Prior to recording the sale, Lenovo accountants must update the asset's depreciation. Partial-year depreciation must be recorded for the asset's depreciation from January 1, 2012 to the sale date. The straight-line depreciation entry at September 30, 2012, is

Sep 30	Depreciation Expense ($10,000/10 years × 9/12)	750	
	Accumulated Depreciation—Equipment		750
	To update depreciation.		

The Equipment account and the Accumulated Depreciation account appear as follows. Observe that the equipment's book value is $6,250 ($10,000 − $3,750).

Equipment				Accumulated Depreciation		
Jan 1, 2009	10,000		−	Dec 31, 2009	1,000	
				Dec 31, 2010	1,000	= Book value
				Dec 31, 2011	1,000	$6,250
				Sep 30, 2012	750	
				Balance	3,750	

The gain on the sale of the equipment for $7,300 is $1,050, computed as follows:

Cash received from sale of the asset		$7,300
Book value of asset sold:		
Cost	$10,000	
Less: Accumulated depreciation	(3,750)	6,250
Gain on sale of the asset.................................		$1,050

The entry to record sale of the equipment is:

Sep 30	Cash	7,300	
	Accumulated Depreciation—Equipment	3,750	
	Equipment		10,000
	Gain on Sale of Equipment		1,050
	To sell equipment.		

This shows that the total assets will increase along with equity—by the amount of the gain.

Assets	=	Liabilities	+	Shareholders' Equity	
+ 7,300					
+ 3,750	=	0	+	1,050	(gain from sale of equipment)
− 10,000					

Gains are recorded as credits. Gains and losses on asset disposals appear on the income statement as Other income (expense), or Other gains (losses).

What if Lenovo sold the same asset on September 30, 2012 for $5,000? Recall that the book value on the date of the sale was $6,250. Thus, a loss of $1,250 on disposal of PPE would be recognized.

Sep 30	Cash	5,000	
	Accumulated Depreciation—Equipment	3,750	
	Loss on Sale of PPE	1,250	
	Equipment		10,000
	To sell equipment.		

Total assets decrease, and equity decreases—by the amount of the loss.

Assets	=	Liabilities	+	Shareholders' Equity	
+ 5,000					
+ 3,750	=	0	+	− 1,250	(loss on sale of equipment)
− 10,000					

This entry is almost identical to a depreciation entry using the units-of-production method.

If 4,500 barrels are removed the next year, that period's depletion is $45,000 (4,500 barrels × $10 per barrel). Accumulated Depletion is a contra account similar to Accumulated Depreciation.

Natural resource assets can be reported on Shell's balance sheet as follows (amounts assumed):

Property, Plant and Equipment:		
Equipment...	$960,000	
Less: Accumulated depreciation	(410,000)	$550,000
Oil..	$340,000	
Less: Accumulated depletion	(140,000)	200,000
Total property, plant and equipment................		$750,000

ACCOUNTING FOR INTANGIBLE ASSETS

OBJECTIVE

5 Account for intangible assets and amortization

As we've seen, *intangible assets* are identifiable, long-lived assets without physical substance. Intangibles are valuable because they carry special rights from patents, copyrights, trademarks, franchises, leaseholds, and goodwill. If you look back at Lenovo's balance sheet on page 408 at the start of this chapter, you may notice that Lenovo's intangible assets (line 5) are by far, its largest component of non-current assets. Of the USD 2.5 billion of total non-current assets, intangibles total USD 1.85 billon or 73%. It is almost six times the total of all Lenovo's tangible PPE assets. Intangibles are the most valuable assets of high-tech companies and those that depend on research and development. Like buildings and equipment, an intangible asset is recorded at its acquisition cost. However, unlike PPE, *IAS38 – Intangible Assets* states that it is unlikely that any subsequent expenditure will be recognized in the carrying amount of an intangible asset.

The choice of cost model or revaluation model is also available for intangible assets, but *IAS38* made it clear that it will be very rare for an entity to be able to use the revaluation model. In our discussions, we will assume that the intangibles will be measured at cost subsequent to acquisition.

The accounting for intangible assets can be a little complicated. After all, it's definitely harder to account for things that have no physical form than those with physical form! We will give you the basics here, but you will likely revisit this topic in greater details in more advanced accounting course. Let's see what *IAS38* says.

Intangible assets fall into two categories:

- Intangibles with *finite lives* that can be measured reliably. We record amortization for these intangibles. **Amortization** expense is the title of the expense associated with intangibles. Amortization works like depreciation and is usually computed on a straight-line basis. The residual value of most intangibles is zero.
- Intangibles with *indefinite lives*. Record no amortization for these intangibles. Instead, check them annually for any loss in value (impairment), and record a loss when it occurs. Goodwill is the most prominent example of an intangible asset with an indefinite life.

As far as intangible assets are concerned, remember that the opposite of finite lives is not infinite lives! In addition, both categories of intangibles are subject to impairment test. Impairment was previously explained in relation to PPE, but the same principles apply. For more details, you may refer to *IAS36 – Impairment of Assets*.

In the following discussions, we illustrate the accounting for both categories of intangibles.

Accounting for Specific Intangibles

Each type of intangible asset is unique, and the accounting can vary from one asset to another. How the asset is acquired, for example through purchase, a business combination (i.e. merger or acquisition of another company) or internally-developed may also impact how the intangible asset is recognized and measured.

Patents.   Patents are granted by a government to give the holder the exclusive right for a certain number of years to produce and sell an invention. The invention may be a specific product or process—for example, **Apple**'s iPad and the Dolby noise-reduction process. Like any other asset, a patent may be purchased. Suppose **Yamaha** pays 15 million JPY (Japanese yen), or about USD 170,000 to acquire a patent on January 1, and the business believes the expected useful life of the patent is five years (not necessarily the entire legal enforceability of the patent). Amortization expense is $34,000 per year ($170,000/5 years). Yamaha records the acquisition and amortization for this patent as follows:

Jan 1	Patents	170,000	
	Cash		170,000
	To acquire a patent.		

Dec 31	Amortization Expense—Patents ($170,000/5)	34,000	
	Accumulated Amortization—Patents		34,000
	To amortize the cost of a patent.		

Alternatively, we can credit the patents account directly (not using an Accumulated Amortization account). Either way, the impact on the accounting equation is the same.

Assets	=	Liabilities	+	Shareholders' Equity	
– 34,000	=	0	+	– 34,000	(amortization expense)

Amortization for an intangible decreases both assets and equity exactly as depreciation does for equipment or a building.

Copyrights.   Copyrights are exclusive rights to reproduce and sell a book, musical composition, film, or other work of art. Copyrights also protect computer software programs, such as **Microsoft**'s Windows® and Excel. Issued by governments, copyrights in certain jurisdictions can extend up to 70 years beyond the author's (composer's, artist's, or programmer's) life. The cost of obtaining a copyright from the government is low, but a company may pay a large sum to purchase an existing copyright from the owner. For example, a publisher may pay the author of a popular novel $1 million or more for the book's copyright.

and development. Under IFRS, costs associated with the creation of intangible assets are classified into *research phase* costs and *development phase* costs. Costs in the research phase are always expensed. However, costs in the development phase are capitalized if the company can demonstrate meeting all of the following six criteria:

- the technical feasibility of completing the intangible asset;
- the intention to complete the intangible asset;
- the ability to use or sell the intangible asset;
- the future economic benefits (e.g. the existence of a market or, if for internal use, the usefulness of the intangible asset);
- the availability of adequate resources to complete development of the asset; and
- the ability to reliably measure the expenditure attributable to the intangible asset during its development.

Like many accounting standards, the separation between research and development phase is one that requires judgment, supported by objective evidence.

Having seen the accounting principles related to intangible assets, let's have a look at part of Lenovo's intangible assets disclosure.

Lenovo Group Limited
Notes to the 2009 Financial Statements
(18 - Intangible Assets, adapted)

(In thousands USD)

1	Operating net book value	$1,838,368
2	Additions	98,222
3	Impairment	(18,526)
4	Amortization	(65,203)
5	Ending net book value	1,852,861

Lenovo's intangible assets consist of goodwill, trademark and trade names, internal use software, customer relationships and marketing rights. This Notes to the Account reconciles the movements in the net book value of these intangibles. You can confirm that line 1 and line 5 above tally with the 2008 and 2009 balances of Lenovo's net intangible assets on its balance sheet (p. 408).

REPORTING PPE TRANSACTIONS ON THE STATEMENT OF CASH FLOWS

OBJECTIVE

6 Report PPE transactions on the statement of cash flows

Three main types of PPE transactions appear on the statement of cash flows:

- acquisitions,
- sales, and
- depreciation (including amortization and depletion).

Acquisitions and disposal of PPE are investing activities. A company invests in PPE. The payments for PPE are investing activities that appear on the statement of cash flows. The sale of PPE results in a cash receipt, as illustrated in Exhibit 7-11, which excerpts data from the Lenovo's statements of cash flows for 2009 and 2008. Depreciation, acquisitions, and sales of PPE are denoted in color (lines 2, 5, and 6).

EXHIBIT 7-11 | Lenovo's Statement of Cash Flows

Lenovo Group Limited
Cash Flow Statement (partial, adapted)
Financial Year Ended March 31

(In thousands USD)	2009	2008
Cash flows from operating activities		
1 Profit (Loss) before taxation	$ (187,945)	$ 512,850
Adjustments to reconcile net income		
to net cash provided by operating activities		
2 Depreciation and amortization	281,112	268,666
3 Other items (summarized)	(190,474)	227,332
4 Net cash generated from (used in) operating activities	(97,307)	1,008,848
Cash flows from investing activities		
5 Purchase of property, plant and equipment	(107,016)	(124,561)
6 Sale of property, plant and equipment.	10,671	4,975
7 Other items (summarized)	528,588	(614,351)
8 Net cash generated from (used in) investing activities	432,243	(733,937)
Cash flows from financing activities		
9 Net cash generated from (used in) financial activities	(116,309)	290,665
Net Cash Flows	218,627	565,576
10 Effects of foreign currency adjustments	(6,668)	22,128
11 Cash and cash equivalent at the beginning of the year	1,651,420	1,063,716
12 Cash and cash equivalent at the end of the year	$1,863,379	$1,651,420

As you can see, the cash components of PPE transactions will be reflected in the statement of cash flows. You may wonder why depreciation and amortization (line 2) is listed in the cash flow from operating activities when it is a non-cash expense. This is a feature of the "indirect method" of preparing statement of cash flows. We will revisit this topic in the full context of the statement of cash flows in Chapter 12.

You can also see that Lenovo's 2009 cash flows were very different from those in 2008. Obviously the financial crisis has had an impact on Lenovo's cash flows. Despite the loss (and negative cash flows from operating activities), Lenovo was still able to increase its cash by $218,627,000. It has a very healthy amount of cash and the company should emerge stronger from the crisis, as compared to its competitors who have less cash to tide over the recession.

DECISION GUIDELINES

PPE AND RELATED EXPENSES

Lenovo Group Limited, like all other companies, must make some decisions about how to account for its property, plant & equipment (PPE) and intangibles. Let's review some of these decisions.

Decision	Guidelines
Capitalize or expense a cost?	General rule: Capitalize all costs that provide *future* benefit for the business such as a new package-handling system. Expense all costs that provide no *future* benefit, such as ordinary repairs to a delivery funds.
Capitalize or expense:	
• Cost associated with a new asset?	Capitalize all costs that bring the asset to its intended use, including asset purchase price, transportation charges, and taxes paid to acquire the asset.
• Cost associated with an existing asset?	Capitalize only those costs that add to the asset's usefulness or to its useful life. Expense all other costs as maintenance or repairs.
Which depreciation method to use:	
• For financial reporting?	Use the method that best matches depreciation expense against the revenues produced by the asset. Most companies use the straight-line method.
• For income tax?	Use the method that produces the fastest tax deductions. Depending on the applicable fax regulations, a company may be able to different depreciation methods for financial reporting and for income-tax purposes.
• How to account for natural resources?	Capitalize the asset's acquisition cost and all later costs that add to the natural resource's future benefit. Then record depletion expense, as computed by the units-of-production method.
• How to account for intangibles?	Capitalize acquisition cost. For intangibles with finite lives, record amortization expense. For intangibles with indefinite lives, do not record amortization. All intangible assets are subject to impairment tests

END-OF-CHAPTER SUMMARY PROBLEM

The figures that follow appear in the *Answers to the Mid-Chapter Summary Problem*, Requirement 2, on page 424.

	Method A: Straight-Line			*Method B: Double-Declining-Balance*		
Financial Year	Annual Depreciation Expense	Accumulated Depreciation	Book Value	Annual Depreciation Expense	Accumulated Depreciation	Book Value
Start			$44,000			$44,000
2009	$4,000	$ 4,000	40,000	$8,800	$ 8,800	35,200
2010	4,000	8,000	36,000	7,040	15,840	28,160
2011	4,000	12,000	32,000	5,632	21,472	22,528

I Requirements

1. Suppose the income tax authorities permitted a choice between these two depreciation methods. Which method would Lenovo select for income-tax purposes? Why?
2. Suppose Lenovo purchased the equipment described in the table on April 1, 2008. Management has depreciated the equipment by using the double-declining-balance method. On October 1, 2011, Lenovo sold the equipment for $27,000 cash.

Record depreciation for 2011 and the sale of the equipment on October 1, 2011.

Answers

I Requirement 1

For tax purposes, most companies select the accelerated method because it results in the most depreciation in the earliest years of the asset's life. Accelerated depreciation minimizes income tax payments in the early years of the asset's life. That maximizes the business's cash at the earliest possible time.

I Requirement 2

Entries to record depreciation to date of sale, and then the sale of the equipment, follow:

2011			
Oct 1	Depreciation Expense—Equipment ($5,632 × 1/2 year)	2,816	
	Accumulated Depreciation—Equipment		2,816
	To update depreciation.		
	Cash	27,000	
Oct 1	Accumulated Depreciation—Equipment		
	($15,840 + $2,816)	18,656	
	Equipment		44,000
	Gain on Sale of Equipment		1,656
	To record sale of equipment.		

REVIEW PPES AND INTANGIBLES

Quick Check (Answers are given on page 468.)

1. Bartman, Inc., purchased a tract of land, a small office building, and some equipment for $1,900,000. The appraised value of the land was $1,380,000, the building $575,000, and the equipment $345,000. What is the cost of the land?
   a. $633,333   c. $1,380,000
   b. $1,140,000   d. None of the above

2. Which statement is false?
   a. Depreciation is a process of allocating the cost of a PPE over its useful life.
   b. Depreciation is based on the matching principle because it matches the cost of the asset with the revenue generated over the asset's useful life.
   c. The cost of a PPE minus accumulated depreciation equals the asset's book value.
   d. Depreciation creates a fund to replace the asset at the end of its useful life.

Use the following data for questions 3–6.

On July 1, 2010, Horizon Communications purchased a new piece of equipment that cost $45,000. The estimated useful life is 10 years and estimated residual value is $5,000.

3. What is the depreciation expense for 2010 if Horizon uses the straight-line method?
   a. $4,000   c. $4,500
   b. $2,000   d. $2,250

4. Assume Horizon Communications purchased the equipment on January 1, 2010. If Horizon uses the straight-line method for depreciation, what is the asset's book value at the end of 2011?
   a. $42,000   c. $32,000
   b. $36,000   d. $37,000

5. Assume Horizon Communications purchased the equipment on January 1, 2010. If Horizon uses the double-declining-balance method, what is depreciation for 2011?
   a. $9,000   c. $16,200
   b. $6,400   d. $7,200

6. Return to Horizon's original purchase date of July 1, 2010. Assume that Horizon uses the straight-line method of depreciation and sells the equipment for $36,500 on July 1, 2014. The result of the sale of the equipment is a gain (loss) of
   a. ($3,500).   c. $2,500.
   b. $7,500.   d. $0.

7. A company bought a new machine for $24,000 on January 1. The machine is expected to last five years and have a residual value of $4,000. If the company uses the double-declining-balance method, accumulated depreciation at the end of year 2 will be
   a. $12,800.   c. $19,200.
   b. $15,360.   d. $16,000.

8. Which of the following is *not* a capital expenditure?
   a. The addition of a building wing   d. Replacement of an old motor with a
   b. A tune-up of a company vehicle   new one in a piece of equipment
   c. A complete overhaul of an air-   e. The cost of installing a piece of
      conditioning system   equipment

9. Which of the following assets is *not* subject to a decreasing book value through depreciation, depletion, or amortization?
   a. Land improvements   c. Intangibles
   b. Goodwill   d. Natural resources

10. Why would a business select an accelerated method of depreciation for tax purposes?
    a. Accelerated depreciation will result higher gain on disposal of PPE than straight-line depreciation.
    b. Accelerated depreciation generates higher depreciation expense immediately, and therefore lowers tax payments in the early years of the asset's life.
    c. Accelerated depreciation is easier to calculate because salvage value is ignored.
    d. Accelerated depreciation generates a greater amount of depreciation over the life of the asset than does straight-line depreciation.
11. A company purchased an oil well for $270,000. It estimates that the well contains 90,000 barrels, has an eight-year life, and no salvage value. If the company extracts and sells 10,000 barrels of oil in the first year, how much depletion expense should be recorded?
    a. $33,750
    b. $135,000
    c. $27,000
    d. $30,000
12. Which item among the following is not an intangible asset?
    a. A copyright
    b. A patent
    c. A trademark
    d. Goodwill
    e. All of the above are intangible assets.

Accounting Vocabulary

accelerated depreciation method (p. 421) A depreciation method that writes off a relatively larger amount of the asset's cost nearer the start of its useful life than the straight-line method does.

amortization (p. 436) The systematic reduction of a lump-sum amount. Expense that applies to intangible assets in the same way depreciation applies to PPE and depletion applies to natural resources.

capital expenditure (p. 414) Expenditure that increases an asset's capacity or efficiency or extends its useful life. Capital expenditures are debited to an asset account.

copyright (p. 437) Exclusive right to reproduce and sell a book, musical composition, film, other work of art, or computer program. Issued by the government, copyrights extend 70 years beyond the author's life.

depletion expense (p. 435) That portion of a natural resource's cost that is used up in a particular period. Depletion expense is computed in the same way as units-of-production depreciation.

depreciable cost (p. 418) The cost of a PPE minus its estimated residual value.

double-declining-balance (DDB) method (p. 421) An accelerated depreciation method that computes annual depreciation by multiplying the asset's decreasing book value by a constant percentage, which is two times the straight-line rate.

estimated residual value (p. 418) Expected cash value of an asset at the end of its useful life. Also called *residual value, scrap value,* or *salvage value.*

estimated useful life (p. 418) Length of service that a business expects to get from an asset. May be expressed in years, units of output, miles, or other measures.

franchises and licenses (p. 438) Privileges granted by a private business or a government to sell a product or service in accordance with specified conditions.

goodwill (p. 438) Excess of the cost of an acquired company over the sum of the market values of its net assets (assets minus liabilities).

impairment (p. 439) The condition that exists when the carrying amount of a long-lived asset exceeds its fair value. Whenever long-term assets have been impaired, they have to be written down to fair market values. Under U.S. GAAP, once impaired, the carrying value of a long-lived asset may never again be increased. Under IFRS, if the fair value of impaired assets recovers in the future, the values may be increased.

intangible assets (p. 409) An asset with no physical form, a special right to current and expected future benefits.

patent (p. 437) A government grant giving the holder the exclusive right for 20 years to produce and sell an invention.

recoverable amount (p. 430) The higher of fair value less cost to sell and value in use. Used in impairment tests.

Property, plant and equipment or PPE (p. 409) Long-lived assets, such as land, buildings, and equipment, used in the operation of the business. Also called *fixed assets* or *plant assets.*

straight-line (SL) method (p. 419) Depreciation method in which an equal amount of depreciation expense is assigned to each year of asset use.

trademark, trade name (p. 438) A distinctive identification of a product or service. Also called a *brand name.*

units-of-production (UOP) method (p. 420) Depreciation method by which a fixed amount of depreciation is assigned to each unit of output produced by the PPE.

ASSESS YOUR PROGRESS

Short Exercises

S7-1 *(Learning Objective 1: Determining cost and book value of a company's PPEs)* Examine Round Rock's assets.

Round Rock Corporation Consolidated Balance Sheets (Partial, Adapted)		
	May 31	
(In millions)	**2011**	**2010**
1 Assets		
2 Current assets		
3 Cash and cash equivalents	$ 2,098	$ 246
4 Receivables, less allowances of $144 and $125..............	2,772	2,610
5 Spare parts, supplies, and fuel......................................	4,670	4,510
6 Prepaid expenses and other...	468	411
7 Total current assets	10,008	7,777
8 Property and equipment, at cost		
9 Aircraft..	2,394	2,394
10 Package handling and ground support equipment..........	12,225	12,139
11 Computer and electronic equipment	28,165	26,115
12 Vehicles..	586	453
13 Facilities and other...	1,435	1,594
14 Total cost..	44,805	42,695
15 Less: Accumulated depreciation	(14,903)	(12,942)
16 Net property and equipment....................................	29,902	29,753
17 Other long-term assets		
18 Goodwill..	724	724
19 Prepaid pension cost	1,341	1,275
20 Intangible and other assets...	324	329
21 Total other long-term assets....................................	2,389	2,328
22 Total assets..	$42,299	$39,858

1. What is Round Rock's largest category of assets? List all 2011 assets in the largest category and their amounts as reported by Round Rock.
2. What was Round Rock's cost of property and equipment at May 31, 2011? What was the book value of property and equipment on this date? Why is book value less than cost?

S7-2 *(Learning Objective 1: Measuring the cost of a PPE)* This chapter lists the costs included for the acquisition of land on pages 411–412. First is the purchase price of the land, which is obviously included in the cost of the land. The reasons for including the other costs are not so obvious. For example, property tax is ordinarily an expense, not part of the cost of an asset. State why the other costs listed are included as part of the cost of the land. After the land is ready for use, will these related costs be capitalized or expensed?

S7-3 (*Learning Objective 1: Determining the cost of individual assets in a lump-sum purchase of assets*)   Foley Distribution Service pays $140,000 for a group purchase of land, building, and equipment. At the time of acquisition, the land has a current market value of $75,000, the building's current market value is $45,000, and the equipment's current market value is $30,000. Journalize the lump-sum purchase of the three assets for a total cost of $140,000. You sign a note payable for this amount.

S7-4 (*Learning Objective 1: Capitalizing versus expensing PPE costs*)   Assume Nation Airlines repaired a Boeing 777 aircraft at a cost of $1.5 million, which Nation paid in cash. Further, assume the Nation accountant erroneously capitalized this expense as part of the cost of the plane.

Show the effects of the accounting error on Nation Airlines' income statement. To answer this question, determine whether revenues, total expenses, and net income were overstated or understated by the accounting error.

S7-5 (*Learning Objective 2: Computing depreciation by three methods—first year only*)   Assume that at the beginning of 2010, SilkAir, a regional airline in Southeast Asia, purchased a used Boeing 737 aircraft at a cost of $53,000,000. SilkAir expects the plane to remain useful for five years (six million miles) and to have a residual value of $5,000,000. SilkAir expects to fly the plane 775,000 miles the first year, 1,275,000 miles each year during the second, third, and fourth years, and 1,400,000 miles the last year.

1. Compute SilkAir's first-year depreciation on the plane using the following methods:
   a. Straight-line
   b. Units-of-production
   c. Double-declining-balance
2. Show the airplane's book value at the end of the first year under each depreciation method.

S7-6 (*Learning Objective 2: Computing depreciation by three methods—third year only*)   Use the SilkAir data in Short Exercise 7-5 to compute SilkAir's third-year depreciation on the plane using the following methods:

   a. Straight-line
   b. Units-of-production
   c. Double-declining balance

S7-7 (*Learning Objective 3: Selecting the best depreciation method for income tax purposes*)   This exercise uses the assumed SilkAir data from Short Exercise 7-5. Assume SilkAir is trying to decide which depreciation method to use for income tax purposes. The company can choose from among the following methods: (a) straight-line, (b) units of production, or (c) double-declining-balance.

1. Which depreciation method offers the tax advantage for the first year? Describe the nature of the tax advantage.
2. How much income tax will SilkAir save for the first year of the airplane's use under the method you selected above as compared with using the straight-line depreciation method? Assume tax rate is 32%. Ignore any earnings from investing the extra cash.

S7-8 (*Learning Objectives 2, 3: Computing partial year depreciation; selecting the best depreciation method*)   Assume that on September 30, 2010, LoganAir, the national airline of Switzerland, purchased an Airbus aircraft at a cost of €45,000,000. LoganAir expects the plane to remain useful for six years (4,500,000 miles) and to have a residual value of €5,400,000. LoganAir will fly the plane 410,000 miles during the remainder of 2010. Compute LoganAir's depreciation on the plane for the year ended December 31, 2010, using the following methods:

   a. Straight-line
   b. Units-of-production
   c. Double-declining-balance

Which method would produce the highest net income for 2010? Which method produces the lowest net income?

S7-9 (*Learning Objectives 2, 3: Computing and recording depreciation after a change in useful life of the asset*) Ten Flags over Georgia paid $100,000 for a concession stand. Ten Flags started out depreciating the building straight-line over 20 years with zero residual value. After using the concession stand for three years, Ten Flags determines that the building will remain useful for only six more years. Record Ten Flags' depreciation on the concession stand for year 4 by the straight-line method.

S7-10 (*Learning Objectives 2, 4: Computing depreciation; recording a gain or loss on disposal*) On January 1, 2010, ABC Airline Service purchased an airplane for $37,700,000. ABC Airline Service expects the plane to remain useful for six years and to have a residual value of $2,900,000. ABC Airline Service uses the straight-line method to depreciate its airplanes. ABC Airline Service flew the plane for three years and sold it on January 1, 2013, for $8,300,000.

1. Compute accumulated depreciation on the airplane at January 1, 2013 (same as December 31, 2012).
2. Record the sale of the plane on January 1, 2013.

S7-11 (*Learning Objective 5: Accounting for the depletion of a company's natural resources*) North Coast Petroleum, the giant oil company, holds reserves of oil and gas assets. At the end of 2010, assume the cost of North Coast Petroleum's mineral assets totaled $120 billion, representing 10 billion barrels of oil in the ground.

1. Which depreciation method is similar to the depletion method that North Coast Petroleum and other oil companies use to compute their annual depletion expense for the minerals removed from the ground?
2. Suppose North Coast Petroleum removed 0.4 billion barrels of oil during 2011. Record depletion expense for the year. Show amounts in billions.
3. At December 31, 2010, North Coast Petroleum's Accumulated Depletion account stood at $38 billion. Report Mineral Assets and Accumulated Depletion at December 31, 2011. Do North Coast Petroleum's Mineral Assets appear to be plentiful or mostly used up? Give your reason.

S7-12 (*Learning Objective 6: Measuring and recording goodwill*) Vector, Inc., dominates the snack-food industry with its Tangy-Chip brand. Assume that Vector, Inc., purchased Concord Snacks, Inc., for $8.8 million cash. The market value of Concord Snacks' assets is $15 million, and Concord Snacks has liabilities of $8 million.

❙ *Requirements*

1. Compute the cost of the goodwill purchased by Vector.
2. Explain how Vector will account for goodwill in future years.

S7-13 (*Learning Objective 6: Accounting for patents and research and development cost*) This exercise summarizes the accounting for patents, which like copyrights, trademarks, and franchises, provide the owner with a special right or privilege. It also covers research and development costs.

Suppose Solar Automobiles Limited paid $600,000 to research and develop a new global positioning system. Solar also paid $350,000 to acquire a patent on a new motor. After readying the motor for production, Solar's sales revenue for the first year totaled $5,200,000. Cost of goods sold was $3,800,000, and selling expenses totaled $480,000. All these transactions occurred during 2010. Solar expects the patent to have a useful life of seven years.

Prepare Solar Automobiles' income statement for the year ended December 31, 2010, complete with a heading. Ignore income tax.

S7-14 (*Learning Objective 7: Reporting investing activities on the statement of cash flows*)   During 2010, Northern Satellite Systems, Inc., purchased two other companies for $16 million. Also during 2010, Northern made capital expenditures of $7 million to expand its market share. During the year, Northern sold its North American operations, receiving cash of $14 million. Overall, Northern reported a net income of $2 million during 2010.

Show what Northern would report for cash flows from investing activities on its statement of cash flows for 2010. Report a total amount for net cash provided by (used in) investing activities.

Exercises

All of the A and B exercises can be found within MyAccountingLab, an online homework and practice environment. Your instructor may ask you to complete these exercises using MyAccountingLab.

(Group A)

E7-15A (*Learning Objective 1: Determining the cost of PPE*)   Ayer Self Storage purchased land, paying $175,000 cash as a down payment and signing a $190,000 note payable for the balance. Ayer also had to pay delinquent property tax of $3,500, title insurance costing $3,000, and $9,000 to level the land and remove an unwanted building. The company paid $59,000 to add soil for the foundation and then constructed an office building at a cost of $650,000. It also paid $55,000 for a fence around the property, $14,000 for the company sign near the property entrance, and $8,000 for lighting of the grounds. Determine the cost of Ayer's land, land improvements, and building.

E7-16A (*Learning Objectives 1, 4: Allocating costs to assets acquired in a lump-sum purchase; disposing of a PPE*)   Deadwood Manufacturing bought three used machines in a $167,000 lump-sum purchase. An independent appraiser valued the machines as shown in the table.

Machine No.	Appraised Value
1	$38,250
2	73,100
3	58,650

What is each machine's individual cost? Immediately after making this purchase, Deadwood sold machine 2 for its appraised value. What is the result of the sale? (Round decimals to three places when calculating proportions, and use your computed percentages throughout.)

E7-17A (*Learning Objective 1: Distinguishing capital expenditures from expenses*)   Assume Candy Corner, Inc., purchased conveyor-belt machinery. Classify each of the following expenditures as a capital expenditure or an immediate expense related to machinery:

    a. Sales tax paid on the purchase price
    b. Transportation and insurance while machinery is in transit from seller to buyer
    c. Purchase price
    d. Installation

E7-44 *(Learning Objective 4: Determining the sale price of property and equipment)* Wilson Corporation reported the following for property and equipment (in millions, adapted):

	Year End	
	2011	**2010**
Property and equipment..................	$24,073	$22,011
Accumulated depreciation................	(13,306)	(12,087)

During 2011, Wilson paid $2,510 million for new property and equipment. Depreciation for the year totaled $1,546 million. During 2011, Wilson sold property and equipment for cash of $48 million. How much was Wilson's gain or loss on the sale of property and equipment during 2011?

E7-45 *(Learning Objectives 2, 3: Determining net income after a change in depreciation method)* Norzani, Inc., has a popular line of sunglasses. Norzani reported net income of $66 million for 2010. Depreciation expense for the year totaled $32 million. Norzani, Inc., depreciates PPE over eight years using the straight-line method and no residual value.

Norzani, Inc., paid $256 million for PPE at the beginning of 2010. Then at the start of 2011, Norzani switched over to double-declining-balance (DDB) depreciation. 2011 is expected to be the same as 2010 except for the change in depreciation method. If Norzani had been using DDB depreciation all along, how much net income can Norzani, Inc., expect to earn during 2011? Ignore income tax.

E7-46 *(Learning Objective 1: Capitalizing versus expensing; measuring the effect of an error)* All French Press (AFP) is a major French telecommunication conglomerate. Assume that early in year 1, AFP purchased equipment at a cost of 8 million euros (€8 million). Management expects the equipment to remain in service for four years and estimated residual value to be negligible. AFP uses the straight-line depreciation method. *Through an accounting error, AFP expensed the entire cost of the equipment at the time of purchase.* Because AFP is operated as a partnership, it pays no income tax.

I Requirements

Prepare a schedule to show the overstatement or understatement in the following items at the end of each year over the four-year life of the equipment:

1. Total current assets
2. Equipment, net
3. Net income

Quiz

Test your understanding of accounting for PPE, natural resources, and intangibles by answering the following questions. Select the best choice from among the possible answers given.

Q7-47 A capital expenditure
a. adds to an asset.
b. is expensed immediately.
c. is a credit like capital (owners' equity).
d. records additional capital.

Q7-48 Which of the following items should be accounted for as a capital expenditure?
a. The monthly rental cost of an office building.
b. Taxes paid in conjunction with the purchase of office equipment.
c. Maintenance fees paid with funds provided by the company's capital.
d. Costs incurred to repair leaks in the building roof.

Q7-49 Suppose you buy land for $2,900,000 and spend $1,200,000 to develop the property. You then divide the land into lots as follows:

Catergory	Sale Price per Lot
10 Hilltop lots	$525,000
10 Valley lots	350,000

How much did each hilltop lot cost you?
a. $246,000
b. $175,715
c. $234,285
d. $410,000

Q7-50 Which statement about depreciation is false?
a. Depreciation should not be recorded in years that the market value of the asset has increased.
b. Depreciation is a process of allocating the cost of an asset to expense over its useful life.
c. A major objective of depreciation accounting is to match the cost of using an asset with the revenues it helps to generate.
d. Obsolescence as well as physical wear and tear should be considered when determining the period over which an asset should be depreciated.

Q7-51 Boston Corporation acquired a machine for $33,000 and has recorded depreciation for two years using the straight-line method over a five-year life and $6,000 residual value. At the start of the third year of use, Boston revised the estimated useful life to a total of 10 years. Estimated residual value declined to $0.

What is the book value of the machine at the end of two full years of use?
a. $13,200
b. $16,800
c. $10,800
d. $22,200

Q7-52 Boston Corporation acquired a machine for $33,000 and has recorded depreciation for two years using the straight-line method over a five-year life and $6,000 residual value. At the start of the third year of use, Boston revised the estimated useful life to a total of 10 years. Estimated residual value declined to $0.

How much depreciation should Boston record in each of the asset's last eight years (that is, year 3 through year 10), following the revision?
a. $13,200
b. $3,300
c. $2,775
d. Some other amount

Q7-53 King Company failed to record depreciation of equipment. How does this omission affect King's financial statements?
a. Net income is overstated and assets are understated.
b. Net income is overstated and assets are overstated.
c. Net income is understated and assets are overstated.
d. Net income is understated and assets are understated.

Q7-54 Jimmy's DVD, Inc., uses the double-declining-balance method for depreciation on its computers. Which item is not needed to compute depreciation for the first year?
a. Original cost
b. Expected useful life in years
c. Estimated residual value
d. All the above are needed.

Q7-55 Which of the following costs is reported on a company's income statement?
a. Land
b. Accumulated depreciation
c. Depreciation expense
d. Accounts payable

P7-64A (*Learning Objectives 1, 2, 3, 4: Recording PPE transactions, exchanges, and changes in useful life*) Carr, Inc., has the following PPE accounts: Land, Buildings, and Equipment, with a separate accumulated depreciation account for each of these except land. Carr completed the following transactions:

Jan 2		Traded in equipment with accumulated depreciation of $65,000 (cost of $136,000) for similar new equipment with a cash cost of $175,000. Received a trade-in allowance of $75,000 on the old equipment and paid $100,000 in cash.
Jun 30		Sold a building that had a cost of $655,000 and had accumulated depreciation of $130,000 through December 31 of the preceding year. Depreciation is computed on a straight-line basis. The building has a 40-year useful life and a residual value of $275,000. Carr received $115,000 cash and a $405,250 note receivable.
Oct 29		Purchased land and a building for a single price of $390,000. An independent appraisal valued the land at $221,100 and the building at $180,900.
Dec 31		Recorded depreciation as follows:
		Equipment has an expected useful life of 5 years and an estimated residual value of 6% of cost. Depreciation is computed on the double-declining-balance method.
		Depreciation on buildings is computed by the straight-line method. The new building carries a 40-year useful life and a residual value equal to 20% of its cost.

I Requirement

1. Record the transactions in Carr, Inc.'s journal.

P7-65A (*Learning Objective 2: Explaining the concept of depreciation*) The board of directors of Gold Structures, Inc., is reviewing the 2010 annual report. A new board member—a wealthy woman with little business experience—questions the company accountant about the depreciation amounts. The new board member wonders why depreciation expense has decreased from $220,000 in 2008 to $204,000 in 2009 to $196,000 in 2010. She states that she could understand the decreasing annual amounts if the company had been disposing of properties each year, but that has not occurred. Further, she notes that growth in the city is increasing the values of company properties. Why is the company recording depreciation when the property values are increasing?

P7-66A (*Learning Objectives 1, 2, 3: Computing depreciation by three methods; identifying the cash-flow advantage of accelerated depreciation for tax purposes*) On January 9, 2010, J.T. Outtahe Co. paid $230,000 for a computer system. In addition to the basic purchase price, the company paid a setup fee of $1,000, $6,000 sales tax, and $28,000 for a special platform on which to place the computer. J.T. Outtahe management estimates that the computer will remain in service for five years and have a residual value of $15,000. The computer will process 30,000 documents the first year, with annual processing decreasing by 2,500 documents during each of the next four years (that is, 27,500 documents in year 2011; 25,000 documents in year 2012; and so on). In trying to decide which depreciation method to use, the company president has requested a depreciation schedule for each of the three depreciation methods (straight-line, units-of-production, and double-declining-balance).

I Requirements

1. For each of the generally accepted depreciation methods, prepare a depreciation schedule showing asset cost, depreciation expense, accumulated depreciation, and asset book value.
2. J.T. Outtahe reports to shareholders and creditors in the financial statements using the depreciation method that maximizes reported income in the early years of asset use. For income tax purposes, the company uses the depreciation method that minimizes income tax payments in those early years. Consider the first year J.T. Outtahe Co. uses the computer. Identify the depreciation methods that meet Outtahe's objectives, assuming the income tax authorities permit the use of any of the methods.

3. Cash provided by operations before income tax is $156,000 for the computer's first year. The income tax rate is 28%. For the two depreciation methods identified in Requirement 2, compare the net income and cash provided by operations (cash flow). Show which method gives the net-income advantage and which method gives the cash-flow advantage.

P7-67A (*Learning Objectives 2, 4, 7: Analyzing PPE transactions from a company's financial statements*)   Floral, Inc., sells electronics and appliances. The excerpts that follow are adapted from Floral's financial statements for 2010 and 2009.

| | February 28, | |
Balance Sheet (dollars in millions)	2010	2009
Assets		
Total current assets	$7,980	$6,900
Property, plant and equipment	4,830	4,199
Less: Accumulated depreciation	2,126	1,726
Goodwill..	558	519

| | Year Ended February 28, | |
Statement of Cash Flows (dollars in millions)	2010	2009
Operating activities:		
Net income	$1,146	$ 981
Noncash items affecting net income:		
Depreciation	460	457
Investing activities:		
Additions to property, plant and equipment................	(707)	(615)

I Requirements

1. How much was Floral's cost of PPE at February 28, 2010? How much was the book value of PPE? Show computations.
2. The financial statements give three evidences that Floral purchased PPE and goodwill during fiscal year 2010. What are they?
3. Prepare T-accounts for Property, Plant and Equipment; Accumulated Depreciation; and Goodwill. Then show all the activity in these accounts during 2010. Label each increase or decrease and give its dollar amount. During 2010, Floral sold PPE that had cost the company $76 million (accumulated depreciation on these assets was $60 million). Assume there were no losses on goodwill during 2010.

P7-68A (*Learning Objective 5: Accounting for natural resources, and the related expense*) Northeastern Energy Company's balance sheet includes the asset Iron Ore. Northeastern Energy paid $2.5 million cash for a lease giving the firm the right to work a mine that contained an estimated 197,000 tons of ore. The company paid $65,000 to remove unwanted buildings from the land and $75,000 to prepare the surface for mining. Northeastern Energy also signed a $37,230 note payable to a landscaping company to return the land surface to its original condition after the lease ends. During the first year, Northeastern Energy removed 33,500 tons of ore, which it sold on account for $35 per ton. Operating expenses for the first year totaled $250,000, all paid in cash. In addition, the company accrued income tax at the tax rate of 32%.

I Requirements

1. Record all of Northeastern Energy's transactions for the year.
2. Prepare the company's income statement for its iron ore operations for the first year. Evaluate the profitability of the company's operations.

P7-69A (*Learning Objectives 4, 7: Reporting PPE transactions on the statement of cash flows*)   At the end of 2009, Solving Engineering Associates (SEA) had total assets of $17.1 billion and total liabilities of $9.7 billion. Included among the assets were property, plant and equipment with a cost of $4.4 billion and accumulated depreciation of $3.2 billion.

SEA completed the following selected transactions during 2010: The company earned total revenues of $26.4 billion and incurred total expenses of $21.2 billion, which included depreciation of $1.9 billion. During the year, SEA paid $1.8 billion for new property, plant and equipment and sold old PPE for $0.3 billion. The cost of the assets sold was $1.1 billion, and their accumulated depreciation was $0.6 billion.

I Requirements

1. Explain how to determine whether SEA had a gain or loss on the sale of old PPE during the year. What was the amount of the gain or loss, if any?
2. Show how SEA would report property, plant and equipment on the balance sheet at December 31, 2010, after all the year's activity. What was the book value of property, plant and equipment?
3. Show how SEA would report its operating activities and investing activities on its statement of cash flows for 2010. Ignore gains and losses.

(Group B)

P7-70B (*Learning Objectives 1, 2, 3: Identifying the elements of a PPE's cost*) Assume Lance Pharmacy, Inc., opened an office in Vero Beach, Florida. Further assume that Lance Pharmacy incurred the following costs in acquiring land, making land improvements, and constructing and furnishing the new sales building:

a.	Purchase price of land, including an old building that will be used for a garage (land market value is $310,000; building market value is $90,000)	$340,000
b.	Landscaping (additional dirt and earth moving)	8,900
c.	Fence around the land	31,000
d.	Attorney fee for title search on the land	400
e.	Delinquent real estate taxes on the land to be paid by Lance Pharmacy	5,800
f.	Company signs at entrance to the property	1,400
g.	Building permit for the sales building	700
h.	Architect fee for the design of the sales building	19,900
i.	Masonry, carpentry, and roofing of the sales building	510,000
j.	Renovation of the garage building	41,900
k.	Interest cost on construction loan for sales building	9,000
l.	Landscaping (trees and shrubs)	6,300
m.	Parking lot and concrete walks on the property	52,900
n.	Lights for the parking lot and walkways	7,000
o.	Salary of construction supervisor (86% to sales building; 10% to land improvements; and 4% to garage building renovations)	41,000
p.	Office furniture for the sales building	79,200
q.	Transportation and installation of furniture	1,100

Assume Lance Pharmacy depreciates buildings over 30 years, land improvements over 15 years, and furniture over eight years, all on a straight-line basis with zero residual value.

I Requirements

1. Show how to account for each of Lance Pharmacy's costs by listing the cost under the correct account. Determine the total cost of each asset.
2. All construction was complete and the assets were placed in service on May 2. Record depreciation for the year ended December 31. Round to the nearest dollar.
3. How will what you learned in this problem help you manage a business?

P7-71B (*Learning Objectives 2, 3: Recording PPE transactions; reporting on the balance sheet*)   Rossi Lakes Resort reported the following on its balance sheet at December 31, 2010:

■ **general ledger**

Property, plant and equipment, at cost:	
Land...	$ 149,000
Buildings	704,000
Less: Accumulated depreciation	(342,000)
Equipment..	401,000
Less: Accumulated depreciation	(268,000)

In early July 2011, the resort expanded operations and purchased additional equipment at a cost of $105,000. The company depreciates buildings by the straight-line method over 20 years with residual value of $89,000. Due to obsolescence, the equipment has a useful life of only 10 years and is being depreciated by the double-declining-balance method with zero residual value.

❙ Requirements

1. Journalize Rossi Lakes Resort's PPE purchase and depreciation transactions for 2011.
2. Report PPE on the December 31, 2011, balance sheet.

P7-72B (*Learning Objectives 1, 2, 3, 4: Recording PPE transactions, exchanges, and changes in useful life*)   Tarrier, Inc., has the following PPE accounts: Land, Buildings, and Equipment, with a separate accumulated depreciation account for each of these except land. Tarrier completed the following transactions:

■ **general ledger**

Jan 2	Traded in equipment with accumulated depreciation of $64,000 (cost of $138,000) for similar new equipment with a cash cost of $179,000. Received a trade-in allowance of $73,000 on the old equipment and paid $106,000 in cash.
Jun 30	Sold a building that had a cost of $645,000 and had accumulated depreciation of $155,000 through December 31 of the preceding year. Depreciation is computed on a straight-line basis. The building has a 40-year useful life and a residual value of $285,000. Tarrier received $135,000 cash and a $350,500 note receivable.
Oct 29	Purchased land and a building for a single price of $340,000. An independent appraisal valued the land at $108,900 and the building at $254,100.
Dec 31	Recorded depreciation as follows: Equipment has an expected useful life of 4 years and an estimated residual value of 4% of cost. Depreciation is computed on the double-declining-balance method. Depreciation on buildings is computed by the straight-line method. The new building carries a 40-year useful life and a residual value equal to 10% of its cost.

❙ Requirement

1. Record the transactions in Tarrier, Inc.'s journal.

P7-73B (*Learning Objective 2: Explaining the concept of depreciation*)   The board of directors of Cooper Structures, Inc., is reviewing the 2010 annual report. A new board member—a wealthy woman with little business experience—questions the company accountant about the depreciation amounts. The new board member wonders why depreciation expense has decreased from $190,000 in 2008 to $174,000 in 2009 to $166,000 in 2010. She states that she could understand the decreasing annual amounts if the company had been disposing of properties each year, but that has not occurred. Further, she notes that growth in the city is increasing the values of company properties. Why is the company recording depreciation when the property values are increasing?

writing assignment ■

P7-74B *(Learning Objectives 1, 2, 3: Computing depreciation by three methods; identifying the cash-flow advantage of accelerated depreciation for tax purposes)* On January 6, 2010, K.P. Scott Co. paid $245,000 for a computer system. In addition to the basic purchase price, the company paid a setup fee of $800, $6,400 sales tax, and $27,800 for a special platform on which to place the computer. K.P. Scott management estimates that the computer will remain in service for five years and have a residual value of $20,000. The computer will process 45,000 documents the first year, with annual processing decreasing by 2,500 documents during each of the next four years (that is, 42,500 documents in 2011; 40,000 documents in 2012; and so on). In trying to decide which dep-reciation method to use, the company president has requested a depreciation schedule for each of the three depreciation methods (straight-line, units-of-production, and double-declining-balance).

▌ Requirements

1. For each of the generally accepted depreciation methods, prepare a depreciation schedule showing asset cost, depreciation expense, accumulated depreciation, and asset book value.
2. K.P. Scott reports to shareholders and creditors in the financial statements using the depreciation method that maximizes reported income in the early years of asset use. For income tax purposes, the company uses the depreciation method that minimizes income tax payments in those early years. Consider the first year K.P. Scott Co. uses the computer. Identify the depreciation methods that meet Scott's objectives, assuming the income tax authorities permit the use of any of the methods.
3. Cash provided by operations before income tax is $155,000 for the computer's first year. The income tax rate is 35%. For the two depreciation methods identified in Requirement 2, compare the net income and cash provided by operations (cash flow). Show which method gives the net-income advantage and which method gives the cash-flow advantage.

P7-75B *(Learning Objectives 2, 4, 7: Analyzing PPE transactions from a company's financial statements)* Parem, Inc., sells electronics and appliances. The excerpts that follow are adapted from Parem's financial statements for 2010 and 2009.

| | February 28, | |
Balance Sheet (dollars in millions)	2010	2009
Assets		
Total current assets	$7,986	$6,901
Property, plant and equipment	4,836	4,198
Less: Accumulated depreciation	2,123	1,727
Goodwill	553	511

| | Year Ended February 28, | |
Statement of Cash Flows (dollars in millions)	2010	2009
Operating activities:		
Net income	$1,147	$ 989
Noncash items affecting net income:		
Depreciation	458	460
Investing activities:		
Additions to property, plant and equipment	(716)	(617)

I *Requirements*

1. How much was Parem's cost of PPE at February 28, 2010? How much was the book value of PPE? Show computations.
2. The financial statements give three evidences that Parem purchased PPE and goodwill during fiscal year 2010. What are they?
3. Prepare T-accounts for Property, Plant and Equipment; Accumulated Depreciation; and Goodwill. Then show all the activity in these accounts during 2010. Label each increase or decrease and give its dollar amount. During 2010, Parem sold PPE that had cost the company $78 million (accumulated depreciation on these assets was $62 million). Assume there were no losses on goodwill during 2010.

P7-76B (*Learning Objective 5: Accounting for natural resources and the related expense*)   South Pacific Energy Company's balance sheet includes the asset Iron Ore. South Pacific Energy paid $2.2 million cash for a lease giving the firm the right to work a mine that contained an estimated 190,000 tons of ore. The company paid $61,000 to remove unwanted buildings from the land and $71,000 to prepare the surface for mining. South Pacific Energy also signed a $24,000 note payable to a landscaping company to return the land surface to its original condition after the lease ends. During the first year, South Pacific Energy removed 31,500 tons of ore, which it sold on account for $31 per ton. Operating expenses for the first year totaled $242,000, all paid in cash. In addition, the company accrued income tax at the tax rate of 25%.

I *Requirements*

1. Record all of South Pacific Energy's transactions for the year.
2. Prepare the company's income statement for its iron ore operations for the first year. Evaluate the profitability of the company's operations.

P7-77B (*Learning Objectives 4, 7: Reporting PPE transactions on the statement of cash flows*)   At the end of 2009, Great Financial Associates (GFA) had total assets of $17.4 billion and total liabilities of $9.9 billion. Included among the assets were property, plant and equipment with a cost of $4.5 billion and accumulated depreciation of $3.3 billion.

GFA completed the following selected transactions during 2010: The company earned total revenues of $26.1 billion and incurred total expenses of $21.0 billion, which included depreciation of $1.9 billion. During the year, GFA paid $1.6 billion for new property, plant and equipment and sold old PPE for $0.4 billion. The cost of the assets sold was $1.2 billion, and their accumulated depreciation was $0.5 billion.

I *Requirements*

1. Explain how to determine whether GFA had a gain or loss on the sale of old PPE during the year. What was the amount of the gain or loss, if any?
2. Show how GFA would report property, plant and equipment on the balance sheet at December 31, 2010, after all the year's activity. What was the book value of property, plant and equipment?
3. Show how GFA would report its operating activities and investing activities on its statement of cash flows for 2010. Ignore gains and losses.

APPLY YOUR KNOWLEDGE

Decision Cases

writing assignment ■

Case 1. (*Learning Objectives 2, 3: Measuring profitability based on different inventory and depreciation methods*) Suppose you are considering investing in two businesses, La Petite France Bakery and Burgers Ahoy!. The two companies are virtually identical, and both began operations at the beginning of the current year. During the year, each company purchased inventory as follows:

Jan	4	10,000 units at $4 =	40,000
Apr	6	5,000 units at $5 =	25,000
Aug	9	7,000 units at $6 =	42,000
Nov	27	10,000 units at $7 =	70,000
Totals		32,000	$177,000

During the first year, both companies sold 25,000 units of inventory.

In early January, both companies purchased equipment costing $150,000 that had a 10-year estimated useful life and a $20,000 residual value. La Petite France uses the inventory and depreciation methods that maximize reported income. By contrast, Burgers uses the inventory and depreciation methods that minimize income tax payments. Assume that both companies' trial balances at December 31 included the following:

Sales revenue.........................	$350,000
Operating expenses...............	50,000

The income tax rate is 40%.

I Requirements

1. Prepare both companies' income statements.
2. Write an investment newsletter to address the following questions: Which company appears to be more profitable? Which company has more cash to invest in promising projects? If prices continue rising over the long term, which company would you prefer to invest in? Why? (Challenge)

writing assignment ■

Case 2. (*Learning Objectives 1, 6: Accounting for PPE and intangible assets*) The following questions are unrelated except that they all apply to PPEs and intangible assets:

1. The manager of Carpet World regularly debits the cost of repairs and maintenance of PPE to Plant and Equipment. Why would she do that, since she knows she is violating GAAP?
2. The manager of Horizon Software regularly buys PPE and debits the cost to Repairs and Maintenance Expense. Why would he do that, since he knows this action violates GAAP?
3. It has been suggested that because many intangible assets have no value except to the company that owns them, they should be valued at $1.00 or zero on the balance sheet. Many accountants disagree with this view. Which view do you support? Why?

Ethical Issue

United Jersey Bank of Princeton purchased land and a building for the lump sum of $6.0 million. To get the maximum tax deduction, the bank's managers allocated 80% of the purchase price to the building and only 20% to the land. A more realistic allocation would have been 60% to the building and 40% to the land.

❙ *Requirements*

1. What is the ethical issue in this situation?
2. Who are the stakeholders? What are the possible consequences to each?
3. Analyze the alternatives from the following standpoints: (a) economic, (b) legal, and (c) ethical.
4. What would you do? How would you justify your decision?

Focus on Financials: ■ Nokia Corporation

Refer to **Nokia**'s Consolidated Financial Statements in Appendix A at the end of the book, and answer the following questions:

❙ *Requirements*

1. Refer to Note 13- Property, plant and equipment. What kinds of assets are included in fixed assets of Nokia?
2. Which depreciation method does Nokia use for reporting to shareholders and creditors in the financial statements? What type of depreciation method does the company probably use for income tax purposes? Why is this method preferable for tax purposes?
3. Depreciation expense is embedded in the expense amounts listed on the income statement. It is reported on the Consolidated Statements of Cash Flows. How much was Nokia's depreciation and amortization expense during 2008? (You can find the figure in Note 9 and Note 32.) Now refer to Note 13. How much was Nokia's accumulated depreciation and amortization at the end of 2008? Explain why accumulated depreciation and amortization exceeds depreciation and amortization expense for the current year.
4. How much did Nokia spend on capital expenditures during 2008? In 2007? Evaluate the trend in these capital expenditures as to whether it conveys good news or bad news for Nokia. Explain.
5. Refer to Note 1- Accounting principles and Note 12- Intangible assets. What are Nokia's intangible assets, and what level of detail does the company provide on them? How does the company account for each of these intangibles over its lifetime?
6. How much impairment did Nokia record for 2008? What do you understand by "impairment", and where would we find the losses attributable to impairment on Nokia's financial statements? Examine carefully Note 7, and describe one event in 2008 that led to impairment of PPE.

Group Project

Visit a local business.

❙ *Requirements*

1. List all its PPE.
2. If possible, interview the manager. Gain as much information as you can about the business's PPE. For example, try to determine the assets' costs, the depreciation method the company is using, and the estimated useful life of each asset category. If an interview is impossible, then develop your own estimates of the assets' costs, useful lives, and book values, assuming an appropriate depreciation method.

3. Determine whether the business has any intangible assets. If so, list them and gain as much information as possible about their nature, cost, and estimated useful lives.

4. Write a detailed report of your findings and be prepared to present your results to the class.

For online homework, exercises, and problems that provide you with immediate feedback, please visit www.myaccountinglab.com.

Quick Check Answers

1. *b* {[$1,380/($1,380 + $575 + $345)] × $1,900 = $1,140}
2. *d*
3. *b* ($45,000 – $5,000)/10 × 6/12 = $2,000)
4. *d* [($45,000 – $5,000)/10 × 2 = $8,000; $45,000 = $8,000 = $37,000]
5. *d* [$45,000 × .2 = $9,000; ($45,000 – $9,000) × .2 = $7,200]
6. *b* [($45,000 – $5,000)/5 × 4 = $16,000; $45,000 – $16,000 = $29,000; $36,500 – $29,000 = gain of $7,500]
7. *b* [$24,000 × 2/5 = $9,600; ($24,000 – $9,600) × 2/5 = $5,760; $9,600 + $5,760 = $15,360]
8. *b*
9. *b*
10. *b*
11. *d* [$270,000 × (3,000/90,000) = $30,000]
12. *e*

8
Liabilities

SPOTLIGHT: CSL

2009 may be remembered as the year of financial meltdown by most people, but it was not the only crisis that affected millions of people. The 2009 H1N1 influenza pandemic caused panic worldwide. Many pharmaceutical companies raced to develop a suitable vaccine, including **CSL Limited**.

To be able to do this, CSL Limited required a significant amount of resources, from physical assets such as research labs and manufacturing plants, to services from its employees and scientists. These resources are, in turn, provided by shareholders and creditors of CSL Limited. Let's see how the various types of liabilities play a role in CSL's ability to offer medicines, anti-venoms, serums and vaccines to the world.

CSL Limited Consolidated Balance Sheet (Partial, adapted) As at June 30		
(in thousands AUD, Australian Dollars)	2009	2008
1 Total current assets	$4,949,048	$2,610,626
2 Total non-current assets	2,417,767	2,084,338
3 Total assets	7,366,815	4,694,964
4 Trade payables	271,835	160,630
5 Accruals and other payables	391,983	284,093
6 Interest-bearing liabilities and borrowings	332,359	128,052
7 Current tax liabilities	101,173	123,018
8 Provisions	126,959	139,525
9 Other current liabilities	1,342	636
10 Total current liabilities	1,225,650	835,954
11 Interest-bearing liabilities and borrowings	385,420	825,134
12 Deferred tax liabilities	108,062	93,677
13 Provisions	38,811	41,553
14 Retirement benefit liabilities	133,894	85,571
15 Other non-current liabilities	12,083	6,950
16 Total non-current liabilities	678,270	1,052,885
17 Total liabilities	1,903,920	1,806,839
18 Total equity	$5,462,895	$2,806,125

This chapter shows how to account for liabilities—both current and long-term. We begin with a refresher on liabilities and then proceed with our discussions on current liabilities.

LEARNING OBJECTIVES

1 **Account** for current liabilities and contingent liabilities

2 **Account** for bonds payable

3 **Measure** interest expense

4 **Understand** the advantages and disadvantages of borrowing

5 **Report** liabilities on the balance sheet

LIABILITIES

You have seen many examples of liability accounts, but let's recall what a liability is. The *IFRS Framework* defines liability as a present obligation which will be settled through an outflow of resources embodying economic benefits. Liabilities are recognized on the balance sheet when it is probable that such an outflow will occur and the amount of which can be measured reliably.

CURRENT LIABILITIES

Current liabilities are obligations due within one year or a company's normal operating cycle (see p. 166-167). Obligations due beyond that period of time are classified as *non-current* or *long-term liabilities*. Lines 4 to 9 are CSL's current liabilities, and lines 11 to 15 are its non-current liabilities.

(see p. 166-167)

Broadly speaking, current liabilities can be classified into two types:

- Those with known amounts.
- Those whose amounts require estimation.

We look first at current liabilities of a known amount.

Current Liabilities of Known Amount

Current liabilities of known amount include accounts payable, short-term notes payable, sales tax payable, accrued liabilities, payroll liabilities, unearned revenues, and current portion of long-term debt.

Accounts Payable. Amounts owed for products or services purchased on account are *accounts payable* or *trade payables*. For example, CSL purchases test tubes and petri dishes on accounts payable. As you can see from its balance sheet, CSL's trade payables (line 4) amounted to $272 million on June 30, 2009. You have also seen many other accounts payable examples in preceding chapters. One of a merchandiser's most common transactions is the credit purchase of inventory. **Carrefour** and **Bossini** buy their inventory on account.

Short-Term Notes Payable. **Short-term notes payable**, a common form of financing, are notes payable due within one year. **DP World** may issue short-term notes payable to borrow cash or to purchase assets. On its notes payable, DP World must accrue interest expense and interest payable at the end of the period. The following sequence of entries covers the purchase of inventory, accrual of interest expense, and payment of a 10% short-term note payable that's due in one year.

2010			
Mar 1	Inventory	8,000	
	Note Payable, Short-Term		8,000
	Purchase of inventory by issuing a note payable.		

This transaction increases both an asset and a liability.

Assets	=	Liabilities	+	Shareholders' Equity
+ 8,000	=	+ 8,000	+	0

DP World's financial year ends each December 31. At year-end, DP World must accrue interest expense at 10% for March through December:

Dec 31	Interest Expense ($8,000 × 0.10 × 9/12)	600	
	Interest Payable		600
	Accrual of interest expense at year-end.		

Liabilities increase and equity decreases because of the expense.

Assets	=	Liabilities	+	Shareholders' Equity	
0	=	+ 600	+	− 600	(interest expense)

The balance sheet at year-end will report the Note Payable of $8,000 and the related Interest Payable of $600 as current liabilities. The income statement will report interest expense of $600.

The following entry records the note's payment at maturity on March 1, 2011:

2011				
Mar 1	Note Payable, Short-Term		8,000	
	Interest Payable		600	
	Interest Expense ($8,000 × 0.10 × 3/12)		200	
	Cash [$8,000 + ($8,000 × 0.10)]			8,800
	Payment of a note payable and interest at maturity.			

The debits zero out the payables and also record DP World's interest expense for January, February, and March 2011.

Sales Tax Payable.   Most countries have some form of consumption tax. This tax is usually called Goods and Services Tax (GST), Value-Added Tax (VAT) or simply sales tax. Retailers collect the tax from customers and thus owe the tax authority for sales tax collected. Suppose one Saturday's sales at an **IKEA** store totaled $200,000. IKEA collected an additional 5% ($10,000) of sales tax. The store would record that day's sales as follows:

Cash ($200,000 × 1.05)		210,000	
Sales Revenue			200,000
Sales Tax Payable ($200,000 × 0.05)			10,000
To record cash sales and the related sales tax.			

Assets, liabilities, and equity all increase—equity because of the revenues.

Assets	=	Liabilities	+	Shareholders' Equity	
+ 210,000	=	+ 10,000	+	+ 200,000	(sales revenue)

When the sales tax payable is remitted to the tax authority, IKEA would perform the following entry. Note that there is no impact on revenue or equity.

Sales tax payable		10,000	
Cash			10,000
To record payment of sales tax.			

Assets	=	Liabilities	+	Shareholders' Equity
− 10,000	=	− 10,000	+	0

Accrued Liabilities (Accrued Expenses).   An **accrued liability** usually results from an expense the business has incurred but not yet paid. Therefore, an accrued expense creates a liability, which explains why it is also called an **accrued expense**. CSL's total accruals and other payables amounted to $392 million on June 30, 2009 (line 5).

For example, CSL's salary expense and salary payable occur as employees work for the company. Interest expense accrues with the passage of time. There are several examples of accrued expenses:

- Salaries and Wages Payable
- Interest Payable
- Income Taxes Payable

Salaries and Wages Payable is the liability for payroll expenses not yet paid at the end of the period. This category includes salaries, wages, and payroll taxes (if any; more on this in the next section) withheld from employee payments. *Interest Payable* is the company's interest payable on notes payable. *Income Taxes Payable* is the amount of income tax the company still owes at year-end. You have seen examples of accruals in Chapter 3.

Payroll Liabilities.   **Payroll**, also called *employee compensation*, is a substantial expense for many companies. For service organizations—such as law firms, real estate companies, and airlines—employee compensation is the major expense, just as cost of goods sold is the largest expense for a merchandising company.

Employee compensation takes many different forms. A *salary* is employee pay stated at a monthly or yearly rate. A *wage* is employee pay stated at an hourly rate. Sales employees earn a *commission*, which is a percentage of the sales the employee has made. A *bonus* is an amount over and above regular compensation. In some jurisdictions, employee's income tax is deducted from employee's salaries as they are paid, or the employer may be required to pay some form of payroll tax. There may be also other kinds of deductions, such as employee's contribution to a provident fund. Salary expense thus represents gross pay (that is, employee pay before subtractions for taxes and other deductions). Your instructor may give you additional information about your local payroll regulations. Accounting for all forms of compensation follows the general pattern illustrated in Exhibit 8-1 (using assumed figures).

EXHIBIT 8-1 | **Accounting for Payroll Expenses and Liabilities**

Salary Expense	10,000	
Employee Income Tax Payable (if applicable)		2,000
Cash (or Salary Payable)		8,000
To record salary expense.		

Unearned Revenues.   *Unearned revenues* are also called *deferred revenues* or *revenues collected in advance*. For all unearned revenue the business has received cash from customers before earning the revenue. The company has a liability—an obligation to provide goods or services to the customer. Let's consider an example.

Thai Airways sells tickets and collects cash in advance. Thai Airways therefore reports Unearned Ticket Revenue for airline tickets sold in advance. Let's see how Thai Airways would account for unearned ticket revenue.

Assume that Thai Airways collects $1,000 for a round-trip ticket from Bangkok (Thailand) to Madrid (Spain) and back. Thai Airways records the cash collection and related liability as follows:

2010			
Dec 15	Cash	1,000	
	Unearned Ticket Revenue		1,000
	Received cash in advance for ticket sales.		

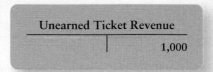

Suppose the customer flies to Madrid late in December. Thai Airways records the revenue earned as follows:

Unearned Ticket Revenue		500	
Ticket Revenue ($1,000 × 1/2)			500
Earned revenue that was collected in advance.			

The liability decreases and the revenue goes up.

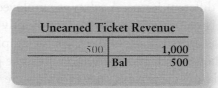
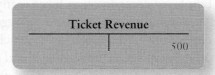

At year-end, Thai Airways reports:

- $500 of unearned ticket revenue (a liability) on the balance sheet
- $500 of ticket revenue on the income statement

The customer returns to Bangkok in January 2011, and Thai Airways records the revenue earned with this journal entry:

2011			
Jan 4	Unearned Ticket Revenue	500	
	Ticket Revenue ($1,000 × 1/2)		500
	Earned revenue that was collected in advance.		

Now the liability balance is zero because Thai Airways has earned all the revenue it collected in advance.

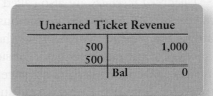

Current Portion of Non-current (or Long-term) Debt. Some long-term debt must be paid in installments. The **current portion of long-term debt** (also called *current maturity* or *current installment*) is the amount of the principal that is payable within one year. At the end of each year, a company reclassifies (from long-term debt to a current liability) the amount of its long-term debt that must be paid next year.

CSI's balance sheet on page 470 at the start of this chapter showed that its interest-bearing liabilities and borrowings consists of a current portion of $332 million (line 6) and a non-current portion of $385 million (line 11). *Long-term debt* refers to long-term notes payable and bonds payable, which we will cover in the second half of this chapter.

Current Liabilities That Must Be Estimated

A business may know that a liability exists but not know its exact amount. The business must report the liability on the balance sheet. Estimated liabilities vary among companies. Let's look first at Provisions for Warranty, a liability account that most merchandisers and manufacturers have.

Provision for Warranty Repairs. Many companies guarantee their products under *warranty agreements*. The warranty period may extend for 90 days to a year for consumer products. For example, automobile companies—**Peugeot Citroën**, **BMW**, and **Toyota**—make provisions for vehicle warranties. Provisions are covered under *IAS37 – Provisions, Contingent Assets and Contingent Liabilities*.

Whatever the warranty's life, the matching principle requires that the company record the *warranty expense* in the same period that the business records sales revenue. After all, the warranty motivates customers to buy products, so the company must record warranty expense. At the time of the sale, however, the company doesn't know which products are defective. The exact amount of warranty expense cannot be known with certainty, so the business must estimate warranty expense and the related liability.

Assume that **Makita Corporation**, which manufactures power tools, made sales of $100,000 subject to product warranties. Assume that in past years between 2% and 4% of products proved defective. Makita could estimate that 3% of sales will require repair or replacement. In this case, Makita would estimate warranty expense of $3,000 ($100,000 x 0.03) for the year and make the following entry:

Warranty Expense	3,000	
Provision for Warranty Repairs		3,000
To accrue warranty expense.		

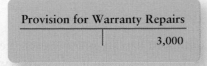

Provision for Warranty Repairs
3,000

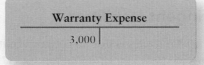

Warranty Expense
3,000

Assume that defects add up to $2,800, and Makita will replace the defective products. Makita then records the following:

Provision for Warranty Repairs	2,800	
Inventory		2,800
To replace defective products sold under warranty.		

Provision for Warranty Repairs		
2,800		3,000
	Bal	200

At the end of the year Makita will report Estimated Warranty Payable of $200 ($3,000 - $2,800) as a current liability. The income statement reports Warranty Expense of $3,000 for the year. Then, next year Makita will repeat this process. The Estimated Warranty Payable account probably won't ever zero out. If Makita paid cash to satisfy the warranty, then the credit would be to Cash rather than to Inventory.

Obviously, provisions are not limited to warranty. Let's have a look at what CSL says about its provisions.

EXCERPTS (ADAPTED) FROM CSL'S NOTES TO THE 2009 FINANCIAL STATEMENTS

Provisions are recognized when the Group has a present or constructive obligation arising from past transactions or events, it is probable that an outflow of resources will be required to settle the obligation and a reliable estimate can be made of the amount of the obligation. ... Provisions recognized reflect management's best estimate of the expenditure required to settle the present obligation at the reporting date. ...

Provisions as at June 30, 2009	Current	Non-current	Total
Employee benefits	$ 73,305	$37,326	$110,631
Restructuring	7,757	–	7,757
Onerous contracts	14,217	–	14,217
Other provisions	31,680	1,485	33,165
Total provisions	$126,959	$38,811	$165,770

As you can see, CSL has provision totaling $165,770 on June 30, 2009, of which $126,959 is current. You can tally these totals to its balance sheet (lines 8 and 13) on page 470 at the start of this Chapter.

Contingent Liabilities

A *contingent liability* is **not** an actual liability. Contingent liability is a disclosure item in the notes to the financial statement. *IAS37* states that a contingent liability arises when:

- there is a possible obligation to be confirmed by a future event that is outside the control of the entity; or
- a present obligation may, but probably will not, require an outflow of resources; or
- a sufficiently reliable estimate of the amount of a present obligation cannot be made.

Examples of contingent liabilities are future obligations that may arise because of lawsuits, tax disputes, or alleged violations of environmental protection laws.

CSL, for example, disclosed the following contingent liability:

EXCERPTS (PARTIAL) FROM CSL'S NOTES TO THE 2009 FINANCIAL STATEMENTS

The group has recently been served with two lawsuits filed in the US courts alleging that the Group and a competitor has conspired to restrict output and artificially increase the price of plasma-derived therapies in the US. Both actions were files by individual, private hotel groups but were filed as class actions. The Group believes these lawsuits are unsupported by fact and without merit and will robustly defend against these suits.

The Group is involved in other litigation in the ordinary course of business. The directors believe that future payment of a material amount in respect of litigation is remote. An estimate of the financial effect of this obligation cannot be calculated as it is not practicable at this stage. The Group has disclaimed liability for, and is vigorously defending, all current material claims and actions that have been made.

It is important to remember that there is no need to report a contingent loss that is unlikely to occur. Instead, wait until new information is available to up the situation. For example, suppose **Del Monte Foods** grows vegetables in Nicaragua, and the Nicaraguan government threatens to confiscate the assets of all foreign companies. Del Monte will report nothing about the contingency if the probability of a loss is considered remote.

The IASB has proposed a new standard to replace *IAS37*. The new IFRS is likely to be issued in late 2010. It is likely that future financial statements of all companies will include more disclosures of both quantitative and qualitative information for contingent liabilities than are presently required.

Are All Liabilities Reported in the Balance Sheet?

The big danger with liabilities is that you may fail to report a large debt on your balance sheet. What is the consequence of missing a large liability? You will definitely understate your liabilities and your debt ratio. By failing to accrue interest on the liability, you'll probably overstate your net income as well. In short, your financial statements will make you look better than you really are. Any such error, if significant, hurts a company's credibility.

Contingent liabilities are very easy to overlook because they aren't actual debts. How would you feel if you owned shares in a company that failed to report a contingency that eventually caused the company to go out of business? If you had known of the contingency, you could have sold the shares and avoided the loss.

COOKING THE BOOKS
with Liabilities
Crazy Eddie, Inc.

Accidentally understating liabilities is one thing, but doing it intentionally is quite another. When unethical management decides to cook the books in the area of liabilities, its strategy is to **deliberately understate recorded liabilities**. This can be done by intentionally under-recording the amount of existing liabilities, or by omitting certain liabilities altogether.

Crazy Eddie, Inc., first discussed in Chapter 6, used *multiple tactics* to overstate its financial position from 1984 through 1987. In addition to overstating inventory (thus understating cost of goods sold and overstating income), the management of the company deliberately *understated accounts payable* by issuing fictitious (false) debit memoranda from suppliers (vendors). A debit memo is issued for goods returned to a vendor, such as Sony. When a debit memorandum is issued, accounts payable are debited (reduced), thus reducing current liabilities and increasing the current ratio. Eventually, expenses are also decreased, and profits are correspondingly increased through reduction of expenses. Crazy Eddie, Inc., issued $3 million of fictitious debit memoranda in 1985, making the company's current ratio and debt ratio look better than they actually were, and eventually overstating profits.

SUMMARY OF CURRENT LIABILITIES

Let's summarize what we've covered thus far. A company can report its current liabilities on the balance sheet as follows:

Accounting, Inc.
Balance Sheet
December 31, 2010

Assets		Liabilities	
Current Assets:		Current liabilities:	
Cash		Accounts payable	
Short-term investments		Salary payable*	
Etc.		Interest payable*	
		Income tax payable*	
Non-current Assets:		Unearned revenue	
PPE		Provision for warranty repairs*	
Intangibles		Notes payable, short-term	
Etc.		Current portion of long-term debt	
		Total current liabilities	
		Long-term liabilities	
		Shareholders' Equity	
		Share capital	
		Retained earnings	
Total assets	$XXX	Total liabilities and shareholders equity	$XXX

*These items are often combined and reported in a single total as "Accrued liabilities" or "Accrued expenses payable."

MID-CHAPTER SUMMARY PROBLEM

Assume that **Estée Lauder** faced the following liability situations at June 30, 2010, the end of the company's fiscal year. Show how Estée Lauder would report these liabilities on its balance sheet at June 30, 2010.

a. Salary expense for the last payroll period of the year was $900,000. Of this amount, employees' withheld income tax totaled $88,000 and employer's payroll taxes were $61,000. These payroll amounts will be paid in early July.

b. On fiscal-year 2010 sales of $400 million, management estimates warranty expense of 2%. One year ago, at June 30, 2009, provision for warranty stood at $3 million. Warranty payments were $9 million during the year ended June 30, 2010.

c. The company pays royalties on its purchased trademarks. Royalties for the trademarks are equal to a percentage of Estée Lauder's sales. Assume that sales in 2010 were $400 million and were subject to a royalty rate of 3%. At June 30, 2010, Estée Lauder owes two-thirds of the year's royalty, to be paid in July.

d. Long-term debt totals $100 million and is payable in annual installments of $10 million each. The interest rate on the debt is 7%, and the interest is paid each December 31.

Answer

Liabilities at June 30, 2010:	
a. Current liabilities:	
Salary payable ($900,000 − $88,000 − $61,000)...............	$ 751,000
Employee income tax payable	88,000
Employer payroll tax payable...	61,000
b. Current liabilities:	
Estimated warranty payable	2,000,000
[$3,000,000 + ($400,000,000 × 0.02) − $9,000,000]	
c. Current liabilities:	
Royalties payable ($400,000,000 × 0.03 × 2/3).................	8,000,000
d. Current liabilities:	
Current installment of long-term debt................................	10,000,000
Interest payable ($100,000,000 × 0.07 × 6/12).................	3,500,000
Long-term debt ($100,000,000 − $10,000,000)....................	90,000,000

LONG-TERM LIABILITIES: BONDS AND NOTES PAYABLE

Large companies such as **Unilever**, **Procter & Gamble**, and **Daimler Chrysler** cannot borrow billions from a single lender. So how do corporations borrow huge amounts? They issue (sell) bonds to the public. **Bonds payable** are groups of notes payable issued to multiple lenders, called bondholders. Unilever needs financing for its operations and can borrow large amounts by issuing bonds to thousands of individual investors, who each lend Unilever a modest amount. Unilever receives the cash it needs, and each investor limits risk by diversifying investments—not putting all the investor's "eggs in one basket". Here we treat bonds payable and notes payable together because their accounting is similar.

Bonds: An Introduction

Each bond payable is, in effect, a note payable. Bonds payable are debts of the issuing company.

Purchasers of bonds receive a bond's certificate, which carries the issuing company's name. The certificate also states the *principal*, which is typically stated in units of $1,000; principal is also called the bond's *face value*, *maturity value*, or *par value*. The bond obligates the issuing company to pay the debt at a specific future time called the *maturity date*.

Interest expense is the rental fee on borrowed money. The bond certificate states the interest rate that the issuer will pay the holder and the dates that the interest payments are due (generally twice a year). Exhibit 8-2 shows an actual bond certificate.

Issuing bonds usually requires the services of a securities firm, such as **Merrill Lynch** (now part of **Bank of America**), to act as the underwriter of the bond issue. The **underwriter** purchases the bonds from the issuing company and resells them to its clients, or it may sell the bonds to its clients and earn a commission on the sale.

EXHIBIT 8-2 | **Bond Certificate (Adapted)**

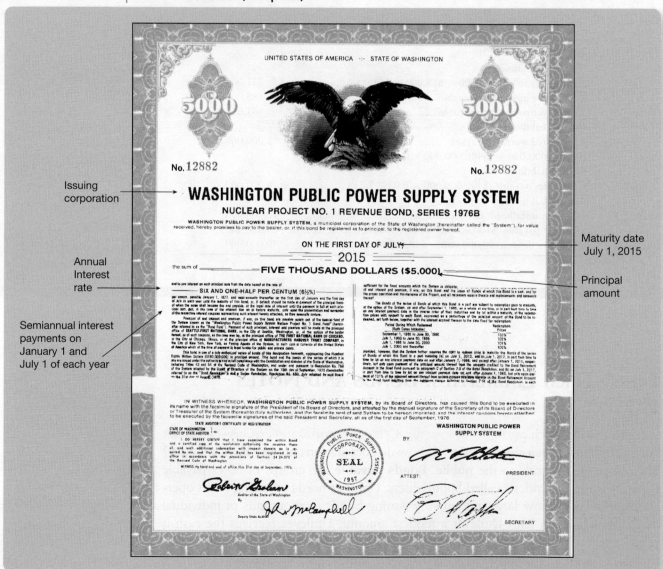

Types of Bonds.   All the bonds in a particular issue may mature at the same time (**term bonds**) or in installments over a period of time (**serial bonds**). Serial bonds are like installment notes payable. Some of Unilever's long-term debts are serial in nature because they are payable in installments.

Secured, or mortgage, bonds give the bondholder the right to take specified assets of the issuer if the company defaults—that is, fails to pay interest or principal. Unsecured bonds, called **debentures**, are backed only by the good faith of the borrower. Debentures carry a higher rate of interest than secured bonds because debentures are riskier investments.

Bond Prices.   Investors may buy and sell bonds through bond markets. Bond prices are quoted at a percentage of their maturity value. For example:

- A $1,000 bond quoted at 100 is bought or sold for $1,000, which is 100% of its face value.
- The same bond quoted at 101.5 has a market price of $1,015 (101.5% of face value = $1,000 × 1.015).
- A $1,000 bond quoted at 88.375 is priced at $883.75 ($1,000 × 0.88375).

Bond Premium and Bond Discount.   A bond issued at a price above its face (par) value is said to be issued at a **premium**, and a bond issued at a price below face (par) value has a **discount**.

Premium on Bonds Payable has a credit balance and Discount on Bonds Payable carries a debit balance. Bond Discount is therefore a contra liability account.

As a bond nears maturity, its market price moves toward par value. Therefore, the price of a bond issued at a:

- premium decreases toward face value.
- discount increases toward face value.

On the maturity date, a bond's market value exactly equals its face value because the company that issued the bond pays that amount to retire the bond.

The Time Value of Money.   A dollar received today is worth more than a dollar to be received in the future. You can invest today's dollar immediately and earn income from it. But if you must wait to receive the dollar, you forgo the interest revenue. Money earns income over time, a fact called the time value of money. Let's examine how the time value of money affects the pricing of bonds.

Assume that a Unilever bond with a face value of $1,000 reaches maturity three years from today and carries no interest. Would you pay $1,000 today to purchase this bond? No, because the payment of $1,000 today to receive the same amount in the future provides you with no income on the investment. Just how much would you pay today to receive $1,000 at the end of three years? The answer is some amount less than $1,000. Let's suppose that you feel $750 is a good price. By investing $750 now to receive $1,000 later, you earn $250 interest revenue over the three years. The issuing company such as Unilever, sees the transaction this way: Unilever will pay you $250 interest to use your $750 for three years.

The amount to invest now to receive more later is called the **present value** of a future amount. In our example, $750 is the present value, and $1,000 is the future amount.

Our $750 bond price is a reasonable estimate. The exact present value of any future amount depends on

1. the amount of the future payment ($1,000 in our example).
2. the length of time from the investment date to the date when the future amount is to be collected (three years).
3. the interest rate during the period (say 10%).

In this case the present value is very close to $750. Present value is always less than the future amount. We discuss how present value is computed in Appendix B at the end of the book.

Bond Interest Rates Determine Bond Prices.   Bonds are always sold at their *market price*, which is the amount investors will pay for the bond. **Market price is the bond's present value**, which equals the present value of the principal payment plus the present value of the cash interest payments. Interest is usually paid semiannually (twice a year). Some companies pay interest annually or quarterly.

Two interest rates work to set the price of a bond:

■ The **stated interest rate**, also called the *coupon rate*, is the interest rate printed on the bond certificate. The stated interest rate determines the amount of cash interest the borrower pays—and the investor receives—each year. Suppose Unilever bonds have a stated interest rate of 9%. Unilever would pay $9,000 of interest annually on each $100,000 bond. Each semiannual payment would be $4,500 ($100,000 × 0.09 × 6/12).

■ The **market interest rate**, or *effective interest rate*, is the rate that investors demand for loaning their money. The market interest rate can fluctuate after issuance of a bond.

A company may issue bonds with a stated interest rate that differs from the prevailing market interest rate. In fact, the two interest rates often differ.

Exhibit 8-3 shows how the stated interest rate and the market interest rate interact to determine the issue price of a bond payable for three separate cases.

EXHIBIT 8-3 | **How the Stated Interest Rate and the Market Interest Rate Interact to Determine the Price of a Bond**

Issue Price of Bonds Payable

Case A:

Stated interest rate on a bond payable	equals	Market interest rate	Therefore,	Price of face (par, or maturity) value
Example: 9%	=	9%	→	*Par: $1,000 bond issued for $1,000*

Case B:

Stated interest rate on a bond payable	less than	Market interest rate	Therefore,	Discount price (price below face value)
Example: 9%	<	10%	→	*Discount: $1,000 bond issued for a price below $1,000*

Case C:

Stated interest rate on a bond payable	greater than	Market interest rate	Therefore,	Premium price (price above face value)
Example: 9%	>	8%	→	*Premium: $1,000 bond issued for a price above $1,000*

Unilever may issue 9% bonds when the market rate is at 10%. Will the Unilever's 9% bonds attract investors in this market? No, because investors can earn 10% on other bonds of similar risk. Therefore, investors will purchase Unilever bonds only at a price less than their face value. The difference between the lower price and face value is a *discount* (Exhibit 8-3). Conversely, if the market interest rate is 8%, Unilever's 9% bonds will be so attractive that investors will pay more than face value to purchase them. The difference between the higher price and face value is a *premium*.

Issuing Bonds Payable at Par (Face Value)

We start with the most straightforward situation—issuing bonds at their par value. There is no premium or discount on these bonds payable.

OBJECTIVE

2 Account for bonds payable

Suppose Unilever has $50,000 of 9% bonds payable that mature in five years. Assume that Unilever issued these bonds at par on January 1, 2010. The issuance entry is:

2010			
Jan 1	Cash	50,000	
	Bonds Payable		50,000
	To issue bonds at par.		

Bonds Payable	
	50,000

Assets and liabilities increase when a company issues bonds payable.

Assets	=	Liabilities	+	Shareholders' Equity
+ 50,000	=	+ 50,000	+	0

Unilever, the borrower, makes a one-time entry to record the receipt of cash and the issuance of bonds. Afterward, investors buy and sell the bonds through the bond markets. These later buy-and-sell transactions between outside investors do *not* involve Unilever at all.

Interest payments occur each January 1 and July 1. Unilever's entry to record the first semiannual interest payment is:

2010			
Jul 1	Interest Expense ($50,000 × 0.09 × 6/12)	2,250	
	Cash		2,250
	To pay semiannual interest.		

The payment of interest expense decreases assets and equity. Bonds payable are not affected.

Assets	=	Liabilities	+	Shareholders' Equity	
− 2,250	=	0	+	− 2,250	(interest expense)

At year-end, Unilever accrues interest expense and interest payable for six months (July through December), as follows:

2010			
Dec 31	Interest Expense ($50,000 × 0.09 × 6/12)	2,250	
	Interest Payable		2,250
	To accrue interest.		

Liabilities increase, and equity decreases.

Assets	=	Liabilities	+	Shareholders' Equity	
0	=	+2,250	+	− 2,250	(interest expense)

On January 1, Unilever will pay the interest, debiting Interest Payable and crediting Cash. Then, at maturity, Unilever pays off the bonds as follows:

2015			
Jan 1	Bonds Payable	50,000	
	Cash		50,000
	To pay bonds payable at maturity.		

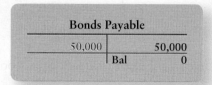

	Bonds Payable	
	50,000	50,000
	Bal	0

Assets	=	Liabilities	+	Shareholders' Equity
− 50,000	=	− 50,000	+	0

Issuing Bonds Payable at a Discount

Market conditions may force a company to issue bonds at a discount. Suppose Unilever issued $100,000 of 9%, five-year bonds when the market interest rate is 10%. The issuance price of the bonds drops, and Unilever receives $96,149[3] at issuance. The transaction is recorded as follows:

2010			
Jan 1	Cash	96,149	
	Discount on Bonds Payable	3,851	
	Bonds Payable		100,000
	To issue bonds at a discount.		

---

[3]Appendix B at the end of this book shows how to determine the price of this bond.

The accounting equation shows that Unilever has a net liability of $96,149—not $100,000.

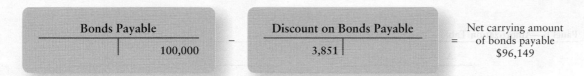

Assets	=	Liabilities	+	Shareholders' Equity
+ 96,149	=	− 3,851	+	0
		+ 100,000		

The bonds payable accounts have a net balance of $96,149 as follows:

Bonds Payable	−	Discount on Bonds Payable	=	Net carrying amount of bonds payable $96,149
100,000		3,851		

Unilever's balance sheet immediately after issuance of the bonds would report the following:

Non-current liabilities:		
Bonds payable, 9%, due 2015	$100,000	
Less: Discount on bonds payable	(3,851)	96,149

Discount on Bonds Payable is a contra account to Bonds Payable, a decrease in the company's liabilities. Subtracting the discount from Bonds Payable yields the *carrying amount* of the bonds. Thus, Unilever's liability is $96,149, which is the amount the company effectively borrowed.

What Is the Interest Expense on These Bonds Payable?

Unilever pays interest on bonds semiannually, which is common practice. Each semi-annual *interest payment* is set by the bond contract and therefore remains the same over the life of the bonds:

OBJECTIVE

3 Measure interest expense

Semiannual interest payment = $100,000 × 0.09 × 6/12
= $4,500

But Unilever's *interest expense* increases as the bonds march toward maturity. Remember: These bonds were issued at a discount.

Panel A of Exhibit 8-4 on the following page repeats the Unilever bond data we've been using. Panel B provides an amortization table that does two things:

- Determines the periodic interest expense (column B)
- Shows the bond carrying amount (column E)

Study the exhibit carefully because the amounts we'll be using come directly from the amortization table. This exhibit shows the *effective-interest method of amortization*, which is required by *IAS39* to measure interest expense.

EXHIBIT 8-4 | Debt Amortization for a Bond Discount

Panel A—Bond Data

Issue date—January 1, 2010	Maturity date—January 1, 2015
Face (par or *maturity*) value—$100,000	Market interest rate at time of issue—10% annually, 5% semiannually
Stated interest rate—9%	Issue price—$96,149
Interest paid—4½% semiannually, $4,500 = $100,000 × 0.09 × 6/12	

Panel B—Amortization Table

	A	B	C	D	E
Semiannual Interest Date	Interest Payment (4½% of Maturity Value)	Interest Expense (5% of Preceding Bond Carrying Amount)	Discount Amortization (B – A)	Discount Account Balance (Preceding D – C)	Bond Carrying Amount ($100,000 – D)
Jan 1, 2010				$3,851	$ 96,149
Jul 1, 2010	$4,500	$4,807	$307	3,544	96,456
Jan 1, 2011	4,500	4,823	323	3,221	96,779
Jul 1, 2011	4,500	4,839	339	2,882	97,118
Jan 1, 2012	4,500	4,856	356	2,526	97,474
Jul 1, 2012	4,500	4,874	374	2,152	97,848
Jan 1, 2013	4,500	4,892	392	1,760	98,240
Jul 1, 2013	4,500	4,912	412	1,348	98,652
Jan 1, 2014	4,500	4,933	433	915	99,085
Jul 1, 2014	4,500	4,954	454	461	99,539
Jan 1, 2015	4,500	4,961*	461	-0-	100,000

*Adjusted for effect of rounding

Notes
- Column A   The semiannual interest payments are constant—fixed by the bond contract.
- Column B   The interest expense each period = the preceding bond carrying amount × the market interest rate.
  Interest expense increases as the bond carrying amount (E) increases.
- Column C   The discount amortization (C) is the excess of interest expense (B) over interest payment (A).
- Column D   The discount balance (D) decreases when amortized.
- Column E   The bond carrying amount (E) increases from $96,149 at issuance to $100,000 at maturity.

Interest Expense on Bonds Issued at a Discount

In Exhibit 8-4, Unilever borrowed $96,149 cash but must pay $100,000 when the bonds mature. What happens to the $3,851 balance of the discount account over the life of the bond issue?

The $3,851 is an additional interest expense to Unilever over and above the stated interest that Unilever pays each six months. Exhibit 8-5 graphs the interest expense and the interest payment on the Unilever bonds over their lifetime. Observe that the semiannual interest payment is fixed—by contract—at $4,500. But the amount of interest expense increases as the discount bond marches upward towards maturity.

EXHIBIT 8-5 | Interest Expense on Bonds Payable Issued at a Discount

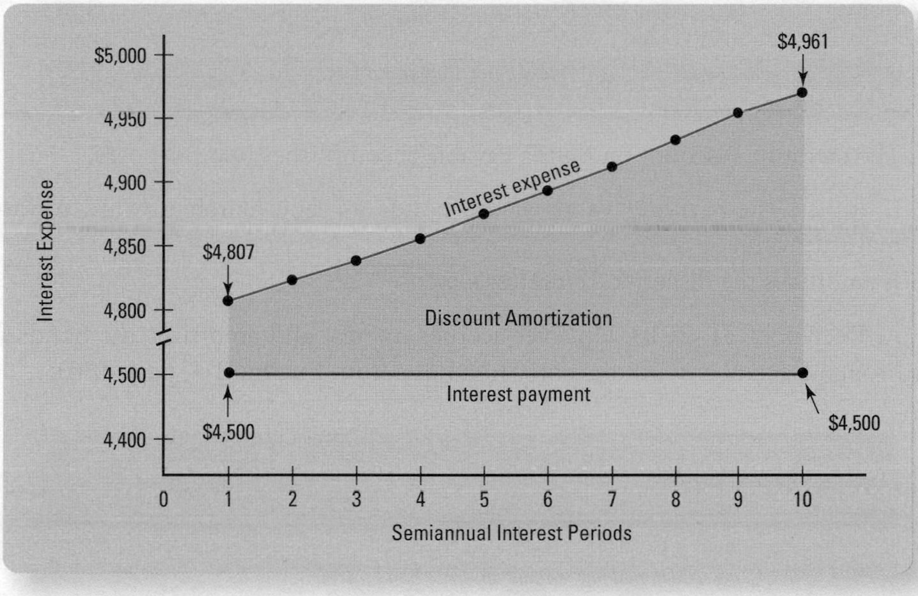

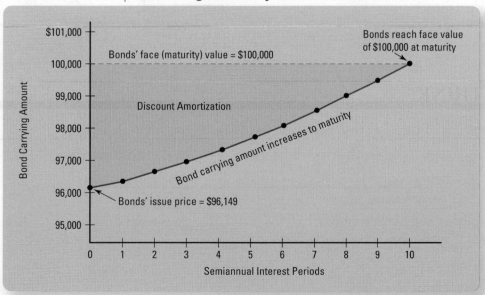

The discount is allocated to interest expense through amortization over the term of the bonds. Exhibit 8-6 illustrates the amortization of the bonds from $96,149 at the start to $100,000 at maturity. These amounts come from Exhibit 8-4, column E (p. 486).

EXHIBIT 8-6 | Amortizing Bonds Payable Issued at a Discount

Now let's see how Unilever would account for these bonds issued at a discount. In our example, Unilever issued its bonds on January 1, 2010. On July 1, Unilever made the first semiannual interest payment. But Unilever's interest expense is greater than its payment of $4,500. Unilever's journal entry to record interest expense and the interest payment for the first 6 months is as follows (with all amounts taken from Exhibit 8-4):

2010			
Jul 1	Interest Expense	4,807	
	Discount on Bonds Payable		307
	Cash		4,500
	To pay semiannual interest and amortize bond discount.		

The credit to Discount on Bonds Payable accomplishes two purposes:

- It adjusts the carrying value of the bonds as they march upward towards maturity value.
- It amortizes the discount to interest expense.

At December 31, 2010, Unilever accrues interest and amortizes the bonds for July through December with this entry (amounts from Exhibit 8-4, page 486):

2010			
Dec 31	Interest Expense	4,823	
	Discount on Bonds Payable		323
	Interest Payable		4,500
	To accrue semiannual interest and amortize bond discount.		

At December 31, 2010, Unilever's bond accounts appear as follows:

Bonds Payable		Discount on Bonds Payable	
	100,000	3,851	307
			323
		Bal 3,221	

Bond carrying amount, $96,779 = $100,000 − $3,221 from Exhibit 8-4, page 486.

STOP & THINK...

What would Unilever's 2010 income statement and year-end balance sheet report for these bonds?

Answer:

Income Statement for 2010		
Interest expense ($4,807 + $4,823)		$ 9,630
Balance Sheet at December 31, 2010		
Current liabilities:		
Interest payable...		$ 4,500
Long-term liabilities:		
Bonds payable...	$100,000	
Less: Discount on bonds payable..............	(3,221)	96,779

At maturity on January 1, 2015, the discount will have been amortized to zero, and the bonds' carrying amount will be face value of $100,000. Unilever will retire the bonds by paying $100,000 to the bondholders.

Partial-Period Interest Amounts

Companies don't always issue bonds at the beginning or the end of their accounting year. They issue bonds when market conditions are most favorable, and that may be on May 16, August 1, or any other date. To illustrate partial-period interest, assume **Fuji-Xerox** issues $100,000 of 8% bonds payable at 96 on August 31, 2010. The market rate of interest was 9%, and these bonds pay semiannual interest on February 28 and August 31 each year. The first few lines of Fuji-Xerox's amortization table are:

Semiannual Interest Date	4% Interest Payment	4½% Interest Expense	Discount Amortization	Discount Account Balance	Bond Carrying Amount
Aug 31, 2010				$4,000	$96,000
Feb 28, 2011	$4,000	$4,320	$320	3,680	96,320
Aug 31, 2011	4,000	4,334	334	3,346	96,654

Fuji-Xerox's accounting year ends on December 31, so at year-end Fuji-Xerox must accrue interest and amortize bond discount for four months (September through December). At December 31, 2010, Fuji-Xerox will make this entry:

2010			
Dec 31	Interest Expense ($4,320 × 4/6)	2,880	
	Discount on Bonds Payable ($320 × 4/6)		213
	Interest Payable ($4,000 × 4/6)		2,667
	To accrue interest and amortize discount at year-end.		

The year-end entry at December 31, 2010, uses 4/6 of the upcoming semiannual amounts at February 28, 2011. This example clearly illustrates the benefit of an amortization schedule.

Issuing Bonds Payable at a Premium

Let's modify the Unilever bond example to illustrate issuance of the bonds at a premium. Assume that Unilever issues $100,000 of five-year, 9% bonds that pay interest semiannually. If the 9% bonds are issued when the market interest rate is 8%, their issue price is $104,100.[4] The premium on these bonds is $4,100, and Exhibit 8-7 on the following page shows how to amortize the bonds by the effective-interest method. In practice, bond premiums are rare because few companies issue their bonds to pay cash interest above the market interest rate. We cover bond premiums for completeness.

Unilever's entries to record issuance of the bonds on January 1, 2010, and to make the first interest payment and amortize the bonds on July 1, are as follows:

2010			
Jan 1	Cash	104,100	
	Bonds Payable		100,000
	Premium on Bonds Payable		4,100
	To issue bonds at a premium.		

---

[4]Appendix B at the end of this book shows how to determine the price of this bond.

At the beginning, Unilever's liability is $104,100—not $100,000. The accounting equation makes this clear.

Assets	=	Liabilities	+	Shareholders' Equity
+ 104,100	=	+ 100,000	+	0
		+ 4,100		

2010				
Jul 1	Interest Expense (from Exhibit 8-7)	4,164	
	Premium on Bonds Payable	336	
	Cash		4,500
	To pay semiannual interest and amortize bond premium.		

EXHIBIT 8-7 | Debt Amortization for a Bond Premium

Panel A—Bond Data

Issue date—January 1, 2010	Maturity date—January 1, 2015
Face (par or *maturity*) value—$100,000	Market interest rate at time of issue—8% annually, 4% semiannually
Stated interest rate—9%	Issue price—$104,100
Interest paid—4½% semiannually, $4,500 = $100,000 × 0.09 × 6/12	

Panel B—Amortization Table

	A	B	C	D	E
Semiannual Interest Date	Interest Payment (4½% of Maturity Value)	Interest Expense (4% of Preceding Bond Carrying Amount)	Premium Amortization (A – B)	Premium Account Balance (Preceding D – C)	Bond Carrying Amount ($100,000 + D)
Jan 1, 2010				$4,100	$ 104,100
Jul 1, 2010	$4,500	$4,164	$336	3,764	103,764
Jan 1, 2011	4,500	4,151	349	3,415	103,415
Jul 1, 2011	4,500	4,137	363	3,052	103,052
Jan 1, 2012	4,500	4,122	378	2,674	102,674
Jul 1, 2012	4,500	4,107	393	2,281	102,281
Jan 1, 2013	4,500	4,091	409	1,872	101,872
Jul 1, 2013	4,500	4,075	425	1,447	101,447
Jan 1, 2014	4,500	4,058	442	1,005	101,005
Jul 1, 2014	4,500	4,040	460	545	100,545
Jan 1, 2015	4,500	3,955*	545	-0-	100,000

*Adjusted for effect of rounding

Notes
- Column A   The semiannual interest payments are constant—fixed by the bond contract.
- Column B   The interest expense each period = the preceding bond carrying amount × the market interest rate. Interest expense decreases as the bond carrying amount (E) decreases.
- Column C   The premium amortization (C) is the excess of interest payment (A) over interest expense (B).
- Column D   The premium balance (D) decreases when amortized.
- Column E   The bond carrying amount (E) decreases from $104,100 at issuance to $100,000 at maturity.

Immediately after issuing the bonds at a premium on January 1, 2010, Unilever would report the bonds payable on the balance sheet as follows:

Non-current liabilities:		
Bonds payable..	$100,000	
Premium on bonds payable	4,100	104,100

A premium is *added* to the balance of bonds payable to determine the carrying amount.

In Exhibit 8-7 Unilever borrowed $104,100 cash but must pay back only $100,000 at maturity. The $4,100 premium is a reduction in Unilever's interest expense over the term of the bonds. Exhibit 8-8 graphs Unilever's interest payments (column A from Exhibit 8-7) and interest expense (column B).

EXHIBIT 8-8 | **Interest Expense on Bonds Payable Issued at a Premium**

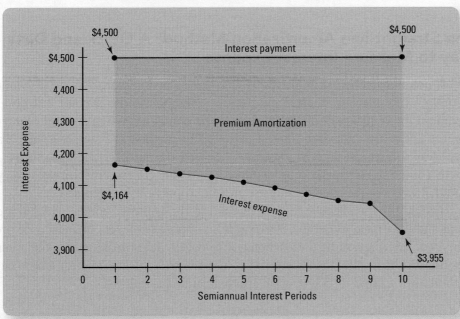

Amortization of the bond's premium decreases interest expense each period over the term of the bonds. Exhibit 8-9 on the following page illustrates the amortization of the bonds from the issue price of $104,100 to a maturity value of $100,000. All amounts are taken from Exhibit 8-7.

EXHIBIT 8-9 | Amortizing Bonds Payable Issued at a Premium

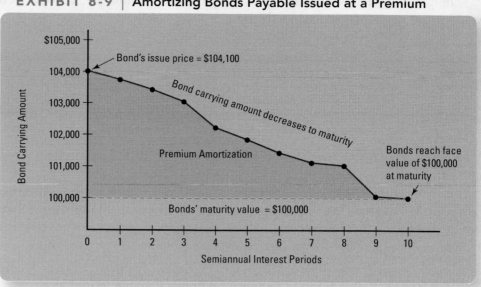

The Straight-line Amortization Method: A Quick and Dirty Way to Measure Interest Expense

Whilst not allowed by *IAS39*, there's a less precise way to amortize bond discount or premium. The effective interest amortization method divides a bond discount (or premium) into equal periodic amounts over the bond's term. The amount of interest expense is the same for each interest period. This method is a simply a "quick and dirty" way to estimate interest expense when you do not have the tools to use the effective interest rate method as required by *IAS39*. Unless otherwise stated, you should always use the effective interest method as previously discussed.

Let's apply the effective interest method to the Unilever bonds issued at a discount and illustrated in Exhibit 8-4 (p. 486). Suppose Unilever's financial vice president is considering issuing the 9% bonds at $96,149. To estimate semiannual interest expense on the bonds, the executive can use the straight-line interest amortization method for the bond discount, as an approximation, as follows:

Semiannual cash interest payment ($100,000 × 0.09 × 6/12)...............	$4,500
+ Semiannual amortization of discount ($3,851 ÷ 10)...........................	385
= Estimated semiannual interest expense...	$4,885

The straight-line interest amortization method uses these same amounts every period over the term of the bonds.

Unilever's entry to record interest and amortization of the bond discount under the straight-line interest amortization method would be:

2010			
Jul 1	Interest Expense	4,885	
	Discount on Bonds Payable		385
	Cash		4,500
	To pay semiannual interest and amortize bond discount.		

Should We Retire Bonds Payable Before Their Maturity?

Normally, companies wait until maturity to pay off, or *retire*, their bonds payable. But companies sometimes retire bonds early. The main reason for retiring bonds early is to relieve the pressure of making high interest payments. Also, the company may be able to borrow at a lower interest rate.

Some bonds are **callable**, which means that the issuer may *call*, or pay off, those bonds at a prearranged price (this is the *call price*) whenever the issuer chooses. The call price is often a percentage point or two above the par value, perhaps 101 or 102. Callable bonds give the issuer the benefit of being able to pay off the bonds whenever it is most favorable to do so. The alternative to calling the bonds is to purchase them in the open market at their current market price.

Unilever has $300 million of debenture bonds outstanding. Assume the unamortized discount is $30 million. Lower interest rates may convince management to pay off these bonds now. Assume that the bonds are callable at 101. If the market price of the bonds is 99, will Unilever call the bonds at 101 or purchase them for 99 in the open market? Market price is the better choice because the market price is lower than the call price. Let's see how to account for an early retirement of bonds payable. Retiring the bonds at 99 results in a loss of $27 million, computed as follows:

	Millions
Par value of bonds being retired..............................	$300
Less: Unamortized discount......................................	(30)
Carrying amount of the bonds being retired............	270
Market price ($300 × 0.99).......................................	297
Loss on retirement of bonds payable.......................	$ 27

Gains and losses on early retirement of bonds payable are usually reported as Other income (loss) on the income statement.

Convertible Bonds and Notes

Some corporate bonds may be converted into the issuing company's share capital. These bonds are called **convertible bonds** (or **convertible notes**). For investors these bonds combine the safety of (a) assured receipt of interest and principal on the bonds with (b) the opportunity for gains on the shares. The conversion feature can be so attractive that investors are willing to accept a lower interest rate than they would on nonconvertible bonds. The lower cash interest payments benefit the issuer. If the market price of the issuing company's shares gets high enough, the bondholders will convert the bonds into shares.

Suppose Unilever has convertible notes payable of $100 million. If Unilever's share price rises high enough, the noteholders will convert the notes into the company's shares. Conversion of the notes payable into shares will decrease Unilever's liabilities and increase its equity.

Assume the noteholders convert the notes into 4 million shares of Unilever shares ($1 par) on May 14. Unilever makes the following entry in its accounting records:

May 14	Notes Payable	100,000,000	
	Share Capital (4,000,000 × $1 par)		4,000,000
	Capital in Excess of Par		96,000,000
	To record conversion of notes payable.		

The accounting equation shows that liabilities decrease and equity goes up.

Assets	=	Liabilities	+	Shareholders' Equity
0	=	− 100,000,000	+	+ 4,000,000
				+ 96,000,000

The carrying amount of the notes ($100 million) ceases to be debt and becomes shareholders' equity. Share Capital is recorded at its *par value*, which is a dollar amount assigned to each share. In this case, the credit to Share Capital is $4,000,000 (4,000,000 shares × $1 par value per share). The extra carrying amount of the notes payable ($96,000,000) is credited to another shareholders' equity account, Capital in Excess of Par. We'll be using this account in various ways in the next chapter.

Financing Operations with Bonds or Shares?

OBJECTIVE

4 Understand the advantages and disadvantages of borrowing

Managers must decide how to get the money they need to pay for assets. There are three main ways to finance operations:

- By retained earnings
- By issuing shares
- By issuing bonds (or notes) payable

Each strategy has its advantages and disadvantages.

1. *Financed by retained earnings* means that the company already has enough cash to purchase the needed assets. There's no need to issue more shares or to borrow money. This strategy is low-risk to the company.

2. *Issuing shares* creates no liabilities or interest expense and is less risky to the issuing corporation. But issuing shares is more costly, as we shall see.

3. *Issuing bonds or notes payable* does not dilute control of the corporation. It often results in higher earnings per share because the earnings on borrowed money can potentially exceed interest expense. But creating more debt increases the risk of the company.

Earnings per share (EPS) is the amount of a company's net income for each of its shares outstanding. EPS is the single most important statistic for evaluating companies because EPS is a standard measure of operating performance that applies to companies of different sizes and from different industries. We will cover EPS in more detail in Chapter 11.

Suppose Unilever needs $500,000 for expansion. Assume Unilever has net income of $300,000 and 100,000 shares outstanding. Its management is considering two financing plans. Plan 1 is to issue $500,000 of 6% bonds payable, and plan 2 is to issue 50,000 shares for $500,000. Its management believes the new cash can be invested in operations to earn income of $200,000 before interest and taxes.

Exhibit 8-10 shows the earnings-per-share advantage of borrowing. As you can see, Unilever's EPS amount is higher if the company borrows by issuing bonds (compare lines 9 and 10). Unilever earns more on the investment ($102,000) than the interest it pays on the bonds ($30,000). This is called **trading on the equity**, or using **leverage**. It is widely used to increase earnings per share.

EXHIBIT 8-10 | **Earnings-Per-Share Advantage of Borrowing**

	Plan 1		Plan 2	
	Borrow $500,000 at 6%		Issue 50,000 Shares of Share Capital for $500,000	
1 Net income before expansion		$300,000		$300,000
2 Expected project income before interest and income tax	$200,000		$200,000	
3 Less interest expense ($500,000 × 0.06)	(30,000)		0	
4 Expected project income before income tax	170,000		200,000	
5 Less income tax expense (40%)	(68,000)		(80,000)	
6 Expected project net income		102,000		120,000
7 Total company net income		$402,000		$420,000
8 Earnings per share after expansion:				
9 Plan 1 Borrow ($402,000/100,000 shares)		$4.02		
10 Plan 2 Issue Shares ($420,000/150,000 shares)				$2.80

In this case borrowing results in higher earnings per share than issuing new shares. Borrowing has its disadvantages, however. Interest expense may be high enough to eliminate net income and lead to losses. Also, borrowing creates liabilities that must be paid during bad years as well as good years. In contrast, a company that issues shares can omit its dividends during a bad year. The Decision Guidelines provide some help in deciding how to finance operations.

DECISION GUIDELINES

FINANCING WITH DEBT OR WITH SHARES

Nando's is the leading chain of Portuguese/Mozambique-themed restaurants, famous for its flame-grilled chicken and "Peri-Peri" sauces. Originated in South Africa, Nando's is now present in over 26 countries and has continued its expansion plan. Suppose Nando's is expanding into a new country or region. Take the role of Fernando Duarte and Robert Brozin, founders of Nando's, and assume you must make some key decisions about how to finance the expansion.

Decision	Guidelines
How will you finance Nando's expansion?	Your financing plan depends on Nando's ability to generate cash flow, your willingness to give up some control of the business, the amount of financing risk you are willing to take, and Nando's credit rating.
Do Nando's operations generate enough cash to meet all its financing needs?	If yes, the business needs little outside financing. There is no need to borrow. If no, the business will need to issue additional shares or borrow the money.
Are you willing to give up some of your control of the business?	If yes, then issue shares to other shareholders, who can vote their shares to elect the company's directors. If no, then borrow from bondholders, or financial institution, who have no vote in the management of the company.
How much financing risk are you willing to take?	If much, then borrow as much as you can, and you may increase Nando's earnings per share. But this will increase the business's debt ratio and the risk of being unable to pay its debts. If little, then borrow sparingly. This will hold the debt ratio down and reduce the risk of default on borrowing agreements. But Nando's earnings per share may be lower than if you were to borrow.
How good is the business's credit rating?	The better the credit rating, the easier it is to borrow on favorable terms. A good credit rating also makes it easier to issue shares. Neither shareholders nor creditors will entrust their money to a company with a bad credit rating.

The Times-Interest-Earned Ratio

We have just seen how borrowing can increase EPS. But too much debt can lead to bankruptcy if the business cannot pay liabilities as they come due. Many companies in the recent financial crisis fell into the debt trap because they leveraged (borrowed) too much, in anticipation of a sustained booming economy, which ran into a crisis eventually.

The **debt ratio** measures the effect of debt on the company's *financial position* but says nothing about the ability to pay interest expense. Analysts use a second ratio—the **times-interest-earned ratio**—to relate income to interest expense. To compute this ratio, we divide *income from operations* (also called *operating income*) by interest expense. This ratio measures the number of times that operating income can *cover* interest expense. The times-interest-earned ratio is also called the **interest-coverage ratio**. A high times-interest-earned ratio indicates ease in paying interest expense; a low value suggests difficulty.

Let's see how CSL performed in this area. For comparison purposes, we will use **Sinovac Biotech Ltd**, a China-based biopharmaceutical company that also produces a H1N1 vaccine amongst many other vaccines, and **GlaxoSmithKline**, one of the leading pharmaceutical companies in the world.

Times–interest-earned ratio	=	$\dfrac{\text{Operating income}}{\text{Interest expense}}$	
CSL (June 30, 2009) in thousands AUD	=	$\dfrac{1{,}431{,}656}{61{,}909}$	= 23.13 times
Sinovac (Dec 31, 2008) in millions GBP	=	$\dfrac{15{,}581}{702}$	= 22.20 times
GlaxoSmithKline (Dec 31, 2008) in millions GBP	=	$\dfrac{7{,}141}{843}$	= 8.47 times

CSL's income from operations covers its interest expense about 23 times, slightly higher than Sinovac's 22 times. In contrast, GSK's times-interest-earned ratio was about eight times. Whilst this is still considered sufficient, it is much lower than CSL and Sinovac.

STOP & THINK...

Which company, CSL, Sinovac or GSK, would you expect to have the higher debt ratio? Compute the two companies' debt ratios to confirm your opinion. Summarized balance sheets of information are as follows.

	Assets	Liabilities	Equity
CSL (30 June 2009, in thousands AUD)	7,366,815	1,903,920	5,462,895
Sinovac (31 Dec 2008, in thousands USD)	83,203	26,304	56,899
GlaxoSmithKline (31 Dec 2008, in millions GBP)	39,393	31,075	8,318

Answer:
Debt ratio can be calculated using Total Assets divided by Total Liabilities.

		CSL		Sinovac		GSK
Debt ratio = $\dfrac{\text{Total liabilities}}{\text{Total assets}}$	=	$\dfrac{19{,}303{,}920}{7{,}366{,}815}$	=	$\dfrac{26{,}304}{31{,}075}$	=	$\dfrac{31{,}075}{39{,}393}$
		= 0.26		= 0.32		= 0.79

As expected, GSK has the higher debt ratio (0.79) as opposed to CSL (0.26) and Sinovac (0.32).

NON-CURRENT LIABILITIES: LEASES AND PENSIONS

A **lease** is a rental agreement in which the tenant (**lessee**) agrees to make rent payments to the property owner (**lessor**) in exchange for the use of the asset. Leasing allows the lessee to acquire the use of a needed asset without having to make the large up-front payment that purchase agreements require.

The balance of the lease liability is now $43,295 less $7,835, or $35,460. In the subsequent period, less and less interest will be charged, and higher portions of the lease payments will go towards reducing the lease liability. This schedule is called a lease amortization schedule, as shown below.

Period	Begin LL	Payment	Interest	Principal	End LL
1	$ 43,295	$ 10,000	$ 2,165	$ 7,835	$ 35,460
2	$ 35,460	$ 10,000	$ 1,773	$ 8,227	$ 27,232
3	$ 27,232	$ 10,000	$ 1,362	$ 8,638	$ 18,594
4	$ 18,594	$ 10,000	$ 930	$ 9,070	$ 9,524
5	$ 9,524	$ 10,000	$ 476	$ 9,524	$ -0-

For the financial year ended June 30, 2009, CSL disclosed the following in regards to its capital leases.

EXCERPTS (PARTIAL) FROM CSL'S NOTES TO THE 2009 FINANCIAL STATEMENTS

Leases of property, plant and equipment where the Group, as lessee, has substantially all the risks and rewards of ownership are classified as finance leases. Finance leases are capitalized at the lease's inception at the fair value of the leased property or, if lower, the present value of the minimum lease payments. The corresponding rental obligations, net of finance charges, are included in interest bearing liabilities and borrowings. Eash lease payment is allocated between the liability and finance cost. The finance cost is charged to the income statement over the lease period so as to produce a constant periodic rate of interest on the remaining balance of the liability for each period. The property, plant and equipment acquired under finance leases are depreciated over the shorter of the asset's useful life and the lease term.

Finance leases (in thousands AUD) Commitments in relation to finance leases are payable as follows:	2009	2008
Not later than one year	$ 5,484	$ 4,900
Later than one year but not later than five years	20,000	17,786
Later than five years	40,709	38,972
Total minimum lease payments	66,193	61,658
Future finance charges	(22,863)	(23,833)
Finance lease liability	43,330	37,825
The present value of finance lease liabilities is as follow:		
Not later than one year	3,229	2,744
Later than one year but not later than five years	12,381	9,962
Later than five years	27,720	25,119
	43,330	37,825
Finance lease – current liability	3,229	2,744
Finance lease – non-current liability	40,101	35,081
	$43,330	$37,825

Do Lessees Prefer Operating Leases or Capital Leases?

Suppose you were the chief financial officer (CFO) of CSL. CSL leases some of its property, plant and equipment. Suppose the leases can be structured either as operating leases or as capital leases. Which type of lease would you prefer for CSL? Why? Consider what would happen to CSL's debt ratio if its operating leases were capitalized, and the related liabilities recognized. Computing CSL's debt ratio two ways (*operating leases* versus reclassifying them as *capital leases*) will make your decision clear (using CSL's actual figures in thousands AUD).

	Operating Leases as Stated	Operating Leases Reclassified as Capital Leases	
Debt ratio $= \dfrac{\text{Total liabilities}}{\text{Total assets}} =$	$\dfrac{\$19,303,920}{\$7,366,815}$	$\dfrac{\$19,303,920 + \$267,756}{\$7,366,815 + \$267,756}$	$= \dfrac{\$21,616,676}{\$7,624,571}$
	$= \quad 0.26$		$= \quad 0.28$

*For simplicity, we did not discount $267,756 to the present value as what was done for capital lease.

You can see that a capital lease increases the debt ratio—by about two percentage points for CSL, but potentially a lot more for other companies. By contrast, notice that operating leases don't affect the debt ratio that's reported on the balance sheet. For this reason, companies prefer operating leases. It is easy to see why CSL's long-term commitment for operating leases, as disclosed in its notes to the financial statements, far outweighs that of its capital lease agreements.

Pensions and Post-retirement Liabilities

Broadly speaking, there are two basic schemes in relation to employees' post-retirement obligations: *defined contribution* and *defined benefits*. In defined contribution schemes, employers contribute a fixed amount of money to an employee's pension (also known as provident, or superannuation) funds. The employer's obligation ends once the contribution has been made. As members of the pension fund, the employees are able to use, invest or withdraw the contribution accumulated, subject to the fund's rules and regulations.

In a defined benefit plan, the employee is promised some post-retirement benefits, usually referred to as **pensions**. Companies may also provide other post-retirement benefits, such as medical insurance for retired former employees. Because employees earn these benefits by their service, the company records pension and retirement-benefit expenses while employees work for the company.

Pensions are one of the most complex areas of accounting, and beyond the scope of this textbook. As employees earn their pensions and the company pays into the pension plan, the plan's assets grow. The obligation for future pension payments to employees also accumulates. At the end of each period, the company compares:

- the fair market value of the assets in the retirement plans—cash and investments—with
- the plans' *accumulated benefit obligation*, which is the present value of promised future payments to retirees.

If the plan assets exceed the accumulated benefit obligation, the plan is said to be *overfunded*. In this case, the asset and obligation amounts are to be reported only in the notes to the financial statements. However, if the accumulated benefit obligation (the liability) exceeds plan assets, the plan is *underfunded*, and the company must report the excess liability amount as a long-term liability on the balance sheet.

You saw at the start of this chapter (p. 470 line 14), CSL has a "Retirement Benefit Liabilities" totaling $133,894. This is CSL's obligation to its various defined benefits post-retirement plans.

EXCERPTS (PARTIAL) FROM CSL'S NOTES TO THE 2009 FINANCIAL STATEMENTS

Surplus/(deficit) for each defined benefit plan on a funding basis

	Plan assets	Accrued benefit	Plan surplus /(deficit)
	$000	$000	$000
Consolidated Group – June 2009			
CSL Pension Plan (Australia)	$ 28,016	$(30,788)	$(2,772)
CSL Bioplasma AG Pension Fund (Switzerland)	263,898	(287,552)	(23,654)
CSL Behring Union Pension Plan (US UPP)	42,079	(56,300)	(14,221)
CSL Behring GmbH Pension Plan (Germany)	–	(76,041)	(76,041)
CSL Pharma GmbH Pension Plan (Germany)	–	(1,560)	(1,560)
CSL Behring KG Pension Plan (Germany)	–	(3,608)	(3,608)
CSL Plasma GmbH Pension Plan (Germany)	–	(125)	(125)
CSL Behring KK Retirement Allowance Plan (Japan)	–	(11,913)	(11,913)
	$333,993	$(467,887)	$(133,894)

REPORTING LIABILITIES

Reporting on the Balance Sheet

OBJECTIVE

5 **Report** liabilities on the balance sheet

This chapter began with the liabilities reported on the consolidated balance sheets of CSL. Exhibit 8-11 reproduces the liabilities section of its balance sheet.

EXHIBIT 8-11 | CSL's Balance Sheet

CSL Limited
Consolidated Balance Sheet (Partial, adapted)
As at June 30

(in thousands AUD, Australian Dollars)	2009	2008
Liabilities:		
Trade payables	$ 271,835	$160,630
Accruals and other payables	391,983	284,093
Interest-bearing liabilities and borrowings	332,358	128,052
Current tax liabilities	101,173	123,018
Provisions	126,959	139,525
Other current liabilities	1,342	636
Total current liabilities	1,225,650	835,954
Interest-bearing liabilities and borrowings	385,420	825,134
Deferred tax liabilities	108,062	93,677
Provisions	38,811	41,553
Retirement benefit liabilities	133,894	85,571
Other non-current liabilities	12,083	6,950
Total non-current liabilities	678,270	1,052,885
Total liabilities	$1,903,920	$1,888,839

Each of these line items have explanatory notes to the financial statements that further detail the breakdown and nature of the liabilities. You saw earlier how Note 26 explains the $133,894 retirement benefit obligations. Similarly, Note 15 provides details of CSL's interest-bearing liabilities and borrowings.

EXCERPTS (PARTIAL) FROM CSL'S NOTES TO THE 2009 FINANCIAL STATEMENTS

Interest-bearing liabilities and borrowings

(in thousands AUD)	2009	2008
Current		
Bank overdrafts - Unsecured	$ 5,905	$ 5,994
Bank loans - Unsecured	305,518	104,001
Senior Unsecured Notes - Unsecured	17,706	15,313
Lease liability - Secured	3,229	2,744
	332,358	128,052
Non-current		
Bank loans - Unsecured	96,468	554,253
Senior Unsecured Notes - Unsecured	248,851	235,800
Lease liability - Secured	40,101	35,081
	$385,420	$825,134

Working back and forth between the financial statements and the related notes is an important part of financial analysis. You now have the tools to understand the liabilities reported on an actual balance sheet.

Reporting the Fair Market Value of Long-Term Debt

IFRS107 – Financial Instruments: Disclosures requires companies to report the fair market value of their financial liabilities. At June 30, 2009, CSL's Note 34 included this excerpt:

EXCERPTS (PARTIAL) FROM CSL'S NOTES TO THE 2009 FINANCIAL STATEMENTS

Fair values

With the exception of certain of the Group's financial liabilities as disclosed in the table below, the remainder of the Group's and the company's financial assets and financial liabilities have a fair value equal to the carrying value of those assets and liabilities as shown in the Group's and company's respective balance sheet. There are no unrecognized gains or losses in respect to any financial asset or financial liability.

Consolidated Group	Carrying Amount	Fair Value	Carrying Amount	Fair Value
	2009	2009	2008	2008
(in thousands AUD)				
Financial Liabilities				
Interest bearing liabilities and borrowings				
Unsecured bank loans	$401,986	$402,227	$658,254	$658,676
Unsecured notes	$266,557	$267,415	$251,113	$252,286

Overall, the fair market value of CSL's interest-bearing liabilities and borrowings is about $669,642 compared to a carrying amount of $668,543. Fair market values of publicly-traded debt are based on quoted market prices, which fluctuate with interest rates and overall market conditions. Therefore, at any one time, fair market values for various obligations can either exceed or be less than their carrying amounts.

Reporting Financing Activities on the Statement of Cash Flows

The CSL consolidated balance sheet (p. 470) shows that the company finances 26% of its operations with debt. Let's examine CSL's financing activities as reported on its statement of cash flows. Exhibit 8-12 is an excerpt from CSL's consolidated statement of cash flows.

EXHIBIT 8-12 | CSL's Statement of Cash Flows

CSL Limited
Consolidated Cash Flow Statement (Partial, adapted)
Financial Year Ended June 30

(in thousands AUD, Australian Dollars)	2009	2008
Cash flow from operating activities	$1,024,824	$689,256
Cash flow from investing activities	(449,529)	(239,121)
Cash flow from financing activities:		
Proceeds from issue of shares	1,859,903	13,099
Dividends paid	(319,492)	(227,431)
Repayment of borrowings	(397,340)	(36,858)
Payment of shares bought back	(54,941)	–
Settlement of finance hedges	(34,004)	26,808
	1,054,126	(225,110)
Net cash flow	$1,629,421	$225,025

We will be looking at the Cash Flow Statement in detail in Chapter 12, but let's just have a quick look at CSL's cash flows from financing activities. During the 2009 financial year, CSL has reduced its borrowings by a significant amount, $397,340. This contributed to the reduction of interest-bearing liabilities and borrowings from $825,134 in 2008 to $385,420 in 2009. CSL ended the 2009 financial year with a very large increase of $1,629,421 net cash flow.

END-OF-CHAPTER SUMMARY PROBLEM

The **Cessna Aircraft Company** has an outstanding issue of 8% convertible bonds that mature in 2018. Suppose the bonds are dated October 1, 2010, and pay interest each April 1 and October 1.

Requirements

1. Complete the following effective-interest amortization table through October 1, 2012.

   Bond Data
   Maturity (face) value—$100,000
   Stated interest rate—8%
   Interest paid—4% semiannually, $4,000 ($100,000 × 0.08 × 6/12)
   Market interest rate at the time of issue—9% annually, 4 1/2% semiannually
   Issue price—93.5

	A	B	C	D	E
			Amortization Table		
Semiannual Interest Date	Interest Payment (4% of Maturity Amount)	Interest Expense (4½% of Preceding Bond Carrying Amount)	Discount Amortization (B – A)	Discount Account Balance (Preceding D – C)	Bond Carrying Amount ($100,000 – D)
10-1-10					
4-1-11					
10-1-11					
4-1-12					
10-1-12					

2. Using the amortization table, record the following transactions:
   a. Issuance of the bonds on October 1, 2010.
   b. Accrual of interest and amortization of the bonds on December 31, 2010.
   c. Payment of interest and amortization of the bonds on April 1, 2011.
   d. Conversion of one-third of the bonds payable into no-par share on October 2, 2012. For no-par share, transfer the bond carrying amount into the Share Capital account. There is no Additional Paid-in Capital account.
   e. Retirement of two-thirds of the bonds payable on October 2, 2012. Purchase price of the bonds was based on their call price of 102.

Answers

Requirement 1

	A	B	C	D	E
Semiannual Interest Date	Interest Payment (4% of Maturity Amount)	Interest Expense (4½% of Preceding Bond Carrying Amount)	Discount Amortization (B – A)	Discount Account Balance (Preceding D – C)	Bond Carrying Amount ($100,000 – D)
10-1-10				$6,500	$93,500
4-1-11	$4,000	$4,208	$208	6,292	93,708
10-1-11	4,000	4,217	217	6,075	93,925
4-1-12	4,000	4,227	227	5,848	94,152
10-1-12	4,000	4,237	237	5,611	94,389

Use this information to answer questions 12–16.

McCabe Corporation issued $550,000 of 7% 10-year bonds. The bonds are dated and sold on January 1, 2011. Interest payment dates are January 1 and July 1. The bonds are issued for $512,408 to yield the market interest rate of 8%. Use the effective-interest method for questions 12–15.

12. What is the amount of interest expense that McCabe Corporation will record on July 1, 2011, the first semiannual interest payment date? (All amounts rounded to the nearest dollar.)
    a. $20,496
    b. $38,500
    c. $19,250
    d. $22,000

13. What is the amount of discount amortization that McCabe Corporation will record on July 1, 2011, the first semiannual interest payment date?
    a. $0
    b. $2,562
    c. $1,246
    d. $1,504

14. What is the total cash payment for interest for each 12-month period? (All amounts rounded to the nearest dollar.)
    a. $22,000
    b. $38,500
    c. $40,993
    d. $44,000

15. What is the carrying amount of the bonds on the January 1, 2012 balance sheet?
    a. $514,950
    b. $513,654
    c. $512,408
    d. $516,167

16. Using effective interest amortization, the carrying amount of McCabe Corporation's bonds at December 31, 2011, is
    a. $513,654.
    b. $512,408.
    c. $514,950.
    d. $516,167.

Accounting Vocabulary

accrued expense (p. 473) An expense incurred but not yet paid in cash. Also called *accrued liability*.

accrued liability (p. 473) A liability for an expense that has not yet been paid. Also called *accrued expense*.

bonds payable (p. 479) Groups of notes payable issued to multiple lenders called *bondholders*.

callable bond (p. 493) Bonds that are paid off early at a specified price at the option of the issuer.

capital lease (p. 499) Lease agreement in which the lessee assumes, in substance, the risks and rewards of asset ownership.

convertible bonds (or notes) (p. 493) Bonds or notes that may be converted into the issuing company's share capital at the investor's option.

current portion of long-term debt (p. 475) The amount of the principal that is payable within one year.

debentures (p. 481) Unsecured bonds—bonds backed only by the good faith of the borrower.

discount (on a bond) (p. 481) Excess of a bond's face (par) value over its issue price.

earnings per share (EPS) (p. 495) Amount of a company's net income per share of its outstanding share capital.

interest-coverage ratio (p. 496) Another name for the *times-interest-earned ratio*.

lease (p. 497) Rental agreement in which the tenant (lessee) agrees to make rent payments to the property owner (lessor) in exchange for the use of the asset.

lessee (p. 497) Tenant in a lease agreement.

lessor (p. 497) Property owner in a lease agreement.

leverage (p. 495) Using borrowed funds to increase the return on equity. Successful use of leverage means earning more income on borrowed money than the related interest expense, thereby increasing the earnings for the owners of the business. Also called *trading on the equity*.

market interest rate (p. 482) Interest rate that investors demand for loaning their money. Also called *effective interest rate.*

operating lease (p. 498) A lease in which the lessee does not assume the risks or rewards of asset ownership.

payroll (p. 473) Employee compensation, a major expense of many businesses.

pension (p. 501) Employee compensation that will be paid during the employee's retirement.

premium (on a bond) (p. 481) Excess of a bond's issue price over its face (par) value.

present value (p. 481) Amount a person would invest now to receive a greater amount at a future date.

serial bonds (p. 481) Bonds that mature in installments over a period of time.

short-term notes payable (p. 471) Note payable due within one year.

stated interest rate (p. 482) Interest rate that determines the amount of cash interest the borrower pays and the investor receives each year.

term bonds (p. 481) Bonds that all mature at the same time for a particular issue.

times-interest-earned ratio (p. 496) Ratio of income from operations to interest expense. Measures the number of times that operating income can cover interest expense. Also called the *interest-coverage ratio.*

trading on the equity (p. 495) Earning more income on borrowed money than the related interest expense, thereby increasing the earnings for the owners of the business. Also called *leverage.*

underwriter (p. 480) Organization that purchases the bonds from an issuing company and resells them to its clients or sells the bonds for a commission, agreeing to buy all unsold bonds.

ASSESS YOUR PROGRESS

Short Exercises

S8-1 (*Learning Objective 1: Accounting for a note payable*) Franklin Sports Authority purchased inventory costing $5,000 by signing an 8% short-term note payable. The purchase occurred on September 30, 2010. Franklin pays annual interest each year on September 30. Journalize the company's (a) purchase of inventory, (b) accrual of interest expense on June 30, 2011, which is the year-end, and (c) payment of the note plus interest on September 30, 2011. (Round your answers to the nearest whole number.)

S8-2 (*Learning Objective 1: Reporting a short-term note payable and the related interest in the financial statements*) This short exercise works with Short Exercise 8-1.

1. Refer to the data in Short Exercise 8-1. Show what the company would report on its balance sheet at June 30, 2011, and on its income statement for the year ended on that date.
2. What single item will the financial statements for the year ended June 30, 2012, report? Identify the financial statement, the item, and its amount.

S8-3 (*Learning Objective 1: Accounting for warranty expense and provision for warranty repairs*) Trekster guarantees automobiles against defects for five years or 55,000 miles, whichever comes first. Suppose Trekster can expect warranty costs during the five-year period to add up to 6% of sales. Assume that a Trekster dealer in Paris, France, made sales of $483,000 during 2010. Trekster received cash for 30% of the sales and took notes receivable for the remainder. Payments to satisfy customer warranty claims totaled $19,000 during 2010.

1. Record the sales, warranty expense, and warranty payments for Trekster.
2. Post to the Provision for Warranty Repairs T-account. The beginning balance was $11,000. At the end of 2010, how much in provision for warranty repairs does Trekster owe to its customers?

S8-4 (*Learning Objective 1: Applying GAAP; reporting warranties in the financial statements*) Refer to the data given in Short Exercise 8-3. What amount of warranty expense will Trekster report during 2010? Which accounting principle addresses this situation? Does

■ spreadsheet

E8-42B *(Learning Objectives 2, 3: Issuing bonds payable (discount); recording interest payments and the related bond amortization)* First Place Sports Ltd. is authorized to issue $1,000,000 of 9%, 10-year bonds payable. On December 31, 2010, when the market interest rate is 10%, the company issues $800,000 of the bonds and receives cash of $750,232. First Place Sports amortizes bonds by the effective-interest method. The semiannual interest dates are June 30 and December 31.

▌*Requirements*

1. Prepare a bond amortization table for the first four semiannual interest periods.
2. Record issuance of the bonds payable on December 31, 2010, the first semiannual interest payment on June 30, 2011, and the second payment on December 31, 2011.

■ spreadsheet

E8-43B *(Learning Objectives 2, 3: Issuing bonds payable (premium); recording interest accrual and payment and the related bond amortization)* On June 30, 2010, the market interest rate is 9%. Team Sports Ltd. issues $3,200,000 of 10%, 10-year bonds payable at 106.5. The bonds pay interest on June 30 and December 31. Team Sports Ltd. amortizes bonds by the effective-interest method.

▌*Requirements*

1. Prepare a bond amortization table for the first four semiannual interest periods.
2. Record the issuance of bonds payable on June 30, 2010, the payment of interest on December 31, 2010, and the payment of interest on June 30, 2011.

■ spreadsheet

E8-44B *(Learning Objective 3: Creating a bond amortization schedule (discount))* Tewksbury Co. issued $720,000 of 11% (0.11), 10-year bonds payable on January 1, 2010, when the market interest rate was 12% (0.12). The company pays interest annually at year-end. The issue price of the bonds was $679,318.

▌*Requirement*

1. Create a spreadsheet model to prepare a schedule to amortize the bonds. Use the effective-interest method of amortization. (Round to the nearest dollar.)

E8-45B *(Learning Objective 2: Recording conversion of notes payable)* Worldview Imaging Ltd. issued $3,600,000 of 9% notes payable on December 31, 2010, at a price of 94. The notes' term maturity is 10 years. After four years, the notes may be converted into Worldview share capital. Each $1,000 face amount of notes is convertible into 60 shares of $1 par share capital. On December 31, 2015, noteholders exercised their right to convert all the notes into share capital.

▌*Requirements*

1. Without making journal entries, compute the carrying amount of the notes payable at December 31, 2015, immediately before conversion. Worldview uses the effective interest method to amortize bonds.
2. All amortization has been recorded properly. Journalize the conversion transaction at December 31, 2015.

E8-46B *(Learning Objective 4: Measuring the times-interest-earned ratio)* Companies that operate in different industries may have very different financial ratio values. These differences may grow even wider when we compare companies located in different countries.

Compare three leading companies on their current ratio, debt ratio, and times-interest-earned ratio. Compute three ratios for Company F, Company L, and Company V.

(Amounts in millions or billions)	Company F	Company L	Company V
Income data			
Total revenues.............................	$9,728	¥7,312	€136,377
Operating income........................	294	229	5,627
Interest expense...........................	43	29	687
Net income.................................	25	12	443
Asset and liability data			
(Amounts in millions or billions)			
Total current assets.....................	433	5,414	147,378
Long-term assets	137	731	61,153
Total current liabilities................	227	2,237	72,600
Long-term liabilities...................	107	2,310	110,907
Shareholders' equity...................	236	1,598	25,024

Based on your computed ratio values, which company looks the least risky?

E8-47B (*Learning Objective 4: Analyzing alternative plans for raising money*)   First Federal Financial Services is considering two plans for raising $600,000 to expand operations. Plan A is to borrow at 5%, and plan B is to issue 100,000 shares of share capital at $6.00 per share. Before any new financing, First Federal Financial Services has a net income of $400,000 and 100,000 shares of share capital outstanding. Assume you own most of First Federal Financial Services existing shares. Its management believes the company can use the new funds to earn additional income of $550,000 before interest and taxes. First Federal Financial Services' income tax rate is 40%.

writing assignment ∎

I Requirements

1. Analyze First Federal Financial Services situation to determine which plan will result in the higher earnings per share.
2. Which plan results in the higher earnings per share? Which plan allows you to retain control of the company? Which plan creates more financial risk for the company? Which plan do, you prefer? Why? Present your conclusion in a memo to First Federal Financial Services' board of directors.

Challenge Exercises

E8-48 (*Learning Objectives 1, 5: Reporting current liabilities*)   The top management of Pratt Marketing Services examines the following company accounting records at August 29, immediately before the end of the year, August 31:

Total current assets	$ 324,700
Noncurrent assets........................	1,067,500
	$1,392,200
Total current liabilities...............	$ 193,400
Noncurrent liabilities	253,400
Owners' equity...........................	945,400
	$1,392,200

Q8-58 A bond with a face amount of $10,000 has a current price quote of 104.885. What is the bond's price?

a. $10,488.50

b. $1,048,850

c. $1,048.85

d. $10,104.89

Q8-59 Bond carrying value equals Bonds Payable

a. minus Premium on Bonds Payable.

b. plus Discount on Bonds Payable.

c. minus Discount on Bonds Payable.

d. plus Premium on Bonds Payable.

e. Both a and b

f. Both c and d

Q8-60 What type of account is *Discount on Bonds Payable* and what is its normal balance?

a. Adjusting amount;   Credit

b. Reversing account;   Debit

c. Contra liability;   Credit

d. Contra liability;   Debit

Questions 61–64 use the following data:

Spring Company sells $200,000 of 12%, 10-year bonds for 96 on April 1, 2010. The market rate of interest on that day is 12.5%. Interest is paid each year on April 1.

Q8-61 The entry to record the sale of the bonds on April 1 would be

a.	Cash	192,000	
	Discount on Bonds Payable	8,000	
	Bonds Payable		200,000
b.	Cash	200,000	
	Discount on Bonds Payable		8,000
	Bonds Payable		192,000
c.	Cash	200,000	
	Bonds Payable		200,000
d.	Cash	192,000	
	Bonds Payable		192,000

Q8-62 Spring Company uses the effective interest amortization method. The amount of interest expense on April 1 of each year will be

a. $24,000.

b. $25,000.

c. $24,800.

d. $32,000.

e. none of these.

Q8-63 Write the adjusting entry required at December 31, 2010.

Q8-64 Write the journal entry requirements at April 1, 2011.

Q8-65 McPartlin Corporation issued $300,000 of 10%, 10-year bonds payable on January 1, 2010, for $236,370. The market interest rate when the bonds were issued was 14%. Interest is paid semiannually on January 1 and July 1. The first interest payment is July 1, 2010. Using the effective-interest amortization method, how much interest expense will McPartlin record on July 1, 2010?

a. $15,500   d. $21,000
b. $15,000   e. $16,546
c. $14,500

Q8-66 Using the facts in the preceding question, McPartlin's journal entry to record the interest expense on July 1, 2010 will include a

a. debit to Bonds Payable.   c. credit to Interest Expense.
b. credit to Discount on Bonds Payable.   d. debit to Premium on Bonds Payable.

Q8-67 Amortizing the discount on bonds payable
a. reduces the semiannual cash payment for interest.
b. is necessary only if the bonds were issued at more than face value.
c. reduces the carrying value of the bond liability.
d. increases the recorded amount of interest expense.

Q8-68 The journal entry on the maturity date to record the payment of $500,000 of bonds payable that were issued at a $50,000 discount includes
a. a debit to Bonds Payable for $500,000.
b. a credit to Cash for $550,000.
c. a debit to Discount on Bonds Payable for $50,000.
d. all of the above.

Q8-69 Is the payment of the face amount of a bond on its maturity date regarded as an operating activity, an investing activity, or a financing activity?

a. Financing activity   b. Investing activity   c. Operating activity

Problems

All of the A and B problems can be found within MyAccountingLab, an online homework and practice environment. Your instructor may ask you to complete these problems using MyAccountingLab.

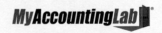

(Group A)

P8-70A (*Learning Objective 1: Measuring current liabilities*)   Big Wave Marine experienced these events during the current year.

   a. Its December revenue totaled $120,000, and in addition, Big Wave collected sales tax of 5%. The tax amount will be sent to the state of Florida early in January.
   b. On August 31, Big Wave signed a six-month, 4% note payable to purchase a boat costing $85,000. The note requires payment of principal and interest at maturity.
   c. On August 31, Big Wave received cash of $2,400 in advance for service revenue. This revenue will be earned evenly over six months.
   d. Revenues of $850,000 were covered by Big Wave's service warranty. At January 1, provision for warranty repairs was $11,600. During the year, Big Wave recorded warranty expense of $34,000 and paid warranty claims of $34,800.
   e. Big Wave owes $70,000 on a long-term note payable. At December 31, 12% interest for the year plus $35,000 of this principal are payable within one year.

❚ Requirement

1. For each item, indicate the account and the related amount to be reported as a current liability on the Big Wave Marine balance sheet at December 31.

P8-71A *(Learning Objective 1: Recording liability-related transactions)* The following transactions of Harmony Music Company occurred during 2010 and 2011:

2010	
Mar 3	Purchased a piano (inventory) for $70,000, signing a six-month, 4% note payable.
May 31	Borrowed $75,000 on a 4% note payable that calls for annual installment payments of $15,000 principal plus interest. Record the short-term note payable in a separate account from the long-term note payable.
Sep 3	Paid the six-month, 4% note at maturity.
Dec 31	Accrued warranty expense, which is estimated at 3.0% of sales of $190,000.
31	Accrued interest on the outstanding note payable.
2011	
May 31	Paid the first installment and interest for one year on the outstanding note payable.

❚ Requirement

1. Record the transactions in Harmony's journal. Explanations are not required.

P8-72A *(Learning Objectives 2, 3: Recording bond transactions (at par); reporting bonds payable on the balance sheet)* The board of directors of Monitors Plus authorizes the issue of $9,000,000 of 10%, five-year bonds payable. The semiannual interest dates are May 31 and November 30. The bonds are issued on May 31, 2010, at par.

❚ Requirements

1. Journalize the following transactions:
   a. Issuance of half of the bonds on May 31, 2010.
   b. Payment of interest on November 30, 2010.
   c. Accrual of interest on December 31, 2010.
   d. Payment of interest on May 31, 2011.
2. Report interest payable and bonds payable as they would appear on the Monitors Plus balance sheet at December 31, 2010.

P8-73A *(Learning Objectives 2, 3, 5: Issuing bonds at a discount; amortizing by the effective interest method; reporting bonds payable on the balance sheet)* On February 28, 2010, Marlin Corp. issues 8%, 10-year bonds payable with a face value of $900,000. The bonds pay interest on February 28 and August 31. Marlin Corp. amortizes bonds by the effective interest method.

❚ Requirements

1. If the market interest rate is 7% when Marlin Corp. issues its bonds, will the bonds be priced at par, at a premium, or at a discount? Explain.
2. If the market interest rate is 9% when Marlin Corp. issues its bonds, will the bonds be priced at par, at a premium, or at a discount? Explain.
3. Assume that the issue price of the bonds is 99. Journalize the following bonds payable transactions.
   a. Issuance of the bonds on February 28, 2010.
   b. Payment of interest and amortization of the bonds on August 31, 2010.
   c. Accrual of interest and amortization of the bonds on December 31, 2010.
   d. Payment of interest and amortization of the bonds on February 28, 2011.
4. Report interest payable and bonds payable as they would appear on the Marlin Corp. balance sheet at December 31, 2010.

P8-74A (*Learning Objectives 2, 3: Accounting for bonds payable at a discount; amortizing by the effective interest method*)

❙ Requirements

1. Journalize the following transactions of Laporte Communications, Inc.:

2010		
Jan	1	Issued $7,000,000 of 9%, 10-year bonds payable at 96.
Jul	1	Paid semiannual interest and amortized bonds by the effective interest method on the 9% bonds payable.
Dec	31	Accrued semiannual interest expense and amortized bonds by the effective interest method on the 9% bonds payable.
2011		
Jan	1	Paid semiannual interest.
2020		
Jan	1	Paid the 9% bonds at maturity.

2. At December 31, 2010, after all year-end adjustments, determine the carrying amount of Laporte Communications bonds payable, net.
3. For the six months ended July 1, 2010, determine for Laporte Communications, Inc.:
   a. Interest expense
   b. Cash interest paid

What causes interest expense on the bonds to exceed cash interest paid?

P8-75A (*Learning Objectives 2, 3, 5: Analyzing a company's long-term debt; reporting long-term debt on the balance sheet (effective-interest method)*)   The notes to the Helping Charities financial statements reported the following data on December 31, Year 1 (end of the fiscal year).

■ spreadsheet

Note 6. Indebtedness		
Bonds payable, 7% due in Year 7	$3,000,000	
Less: Discount..	(138,686)	$2,861,314
Notes payable, 6%, payable in amounts of $55,000 annual installments starting in Year 5...............		330,000

Helping Charities amortizes bonds by the effective-interest method and pays all interest amounts at December 31.

❙ Requirements

1. Answer the following questions about Helping Charities' long-term liabilities:
   a. What is the maturity value of the 7% bonds?
   b. What are Helping Charities' annual cash interest payments on the 7% bonds?
   c. What is the carrying amount of the 7% bonds at December 31, year 1?
2. Prepare an amortization table through December 31, Year 4, for the 7% bonds. The market interest rate on the bonds was 8%. (Round all amounts to the nearest dollar.) How much is Helping Charities' interest expense on the 7% bonds for the year ended December 31, Year 4?
3. Show how Helping Charities would report the 7% bonds payable and the 6% notes payable at December 31, Year 4.

■ spreadsheet

P8-76A (*Learning Objectives 2, 3, 5: Issuing convertible bonds at a discount; amortizing by the effective-interest method; converting bonds; reporting the bonds payable on the balance sheet*)   On December 31, 2010, Mugaboo Corp. issues 7%, 10-year convertible bonds payable with a maturity value of $3,000,000. The semiannual interest dates are June 30 and December 31. The market interest rate is 8%, and the issue price of the bonds is 93.165. Mugaboo Corp. amortizes bonds by the effective-interest method.

I Requirements

1. Prepare an effective-interest method amortization table for the first four semiannual interest periods.
2. Journalize the following transactions:
   a. Issuance of the bonds on December 31, 2010, Credit Convertible Bonds Payable
   b. Payment of interest and amortization of the bonds on June 30, 2011.
   c. Payment of interest and amortization of the bonds on December 31, 2011.
   d. Conversion by the bondholders on July 1, 2012, of bonds with face value of $1,200,000 into 40,000 shares of Mugaboo Corp.'s $1-par share capital.
3. Show how Mugaboo Corp. would report the remaining bonds payable on its balance sheet at December 31, 2012.

writing assignment ■

P8-77A (*Learning Objective 4: Financing operations with debt or with shares*)   Paulus Sporting Goods is embarking on a massive expansion. Assume plans call for opening 25 new stores during the next three years. Each store is scheduled to be 40% larger than the company's existing locations, offering more items of inventory, and with more elaborate displays. Its management estimates that company operations will provide $1.5 million of the cash needed for expansion. Paulus must raise the remaining $6.5 million from outsiders. The board of directors is considering obtaining the $6.5 million either through borrowing or by issuing share capital.

I Requirement

1. Write a memo to Paulus' management discussing the advantages and disadvantages of borrowing and of issuing share capital to raise the needed cash. Which method of raising the funds would you recommend?

P8-78A (*Learning Objectives 4, 5: Reporting liabilities on the balance sheet; calculating the times-interest-earned ratio*)   The accounting records of Barnstable Foods, Inc., include the following items at December 31, 2010:

Mortgage note payable, current	$ 94,000	Accumulated depreciation, equipment	$164,000
Accumulated pension benefit obligation	465,000	Discount on bonds payable (all long-term)	27,000
Bonds payable, long-term	1,200,000	Operating income	400,000
Mortgage note payable, long-term	319,000	Equipment	745,000
Bonds payable, current portion	400,000	Pension plan assets (market value)	405,000
Interest expense	222,000	Interest payable	72,000

I Requirements

1. Show how each relevant item would be reported on the Barnstable Foods, Inc., classified balance sheet, including headings and totals for current liabilities and long-term liabilities.
2. Answer the following questions about Barnstable's financial position at December 31, 2010:
   a. What is the carrying amount of the bonds payable (combine the current and long-term amounts)?
   b. Why is the interest-payable amount so much less than the amount of interest expense?
3. How many times did Barnstable cover its interest expense during 2010?

(Group B)

P8-79B (*Learning Objective 1: Measuring current liabilities*)   Sea Breeze Marine experienced these events during the current year.

    a. December revenue totaled $110,000, and in addition, Sea Breeze collected sales tax of 8%. The tax amount will be sent to the state of Georgia early in January.

    b. On August 31, Sea Breeze signed a six-month, 4% note payable to purchase a boat costing $82,000. The note requires payment of principal and interest at maturity.

    c. On August 31, Sea Breeze received cash of $1,200 in advance for service revenue. This revenue will be earned evenly over six months.

    d. Revenues of $750,000 were covered by Sea Breeze's service warranty. At January 1, provision for warranty repairs was $11,400. During the year, Sea Breeze recorded warranty expense of $30,000 and paid warranty claims of $34,600.

    e. Sea Breeze owes $85,000 on a long-term note payable. At December 31, 10% interest for the year plus $25,000 of this principal are payable within one year.

Requirement

1. For each item, indicate the account and the related amount to be reported as a current liability on the Sea Breeze Marine balance sheet at December 31.

P8-80B (*Learning Objective 1: Recording liability-related transactions*)   The following transactions of Soft Sounds Music Company occurred during 2010 and 2011:

2010	
Mar 3	Purchased a piano (inventory) for $30,000, signing a six-month, 10% note payable.
May 31	Borrowed $75,000 on a 6% note payable that calls for annual installment payments of $15,000 principal plus interest. Record the short-term note payable in a separate account from the long-term note payable.
Sep 3	Paid the six-month, 10% note at maturity.
Dec 31	Accrued warranty expense, which is estimated at 1.5% of sales of $196,000.
31	Accrued interest on the outstanding note payable.
2011	
May 31	Paid the first installment and interest for one year on the outstanding note payable.

Requirement

1. Record the transactions in Soft Sounds Music Company's journal. Explanations are not required.

P8-81B (*Learning Objectives 2, 3: Recording bond transactions (at par); reporting bonds payable on the balance sheet*)   The board of directors of Pictures Plus authorizes the issue of $6,000,000 of 8%, 15-year bonds payable. The semiannual interest dates are May 31 and November 30. The bonds are issued on May 31, 2010, at par.

Requirements

1. Journalize the following transactions:

    a. Issuance of half of the bonds on May 31, 2010.

    b. Payment of interest on November 30, 2010.

    c. Accrual of interest on December 31, 2010.

    d. Payment of interest on May 31, 2011.

2. Report the interest payable and bonds payable as they would appear on the Pictures Plus balance sheet at December 31, 2010.

P8-82B (*Learning Objectives 2, 3, 5: Issuing bonds at a discount; amortizing by the effective interest method; reporting notes payable on the balance sheet*) On February 28, 2010, Mackerel Corp. issues 6%, 20-year bonds payable with a face value of $1,800,000. The bonds pay interest on February 28 and August 31. Mackerel Corp. amortizes bonds by the effective interest method.

❙ Requirements

1. If the market interest rate is 5% when Mackerel Corp. issues its bonds, will the bonds be priced at par, at a premium, or at a discount? Explain.
2. If the market interest rate is 7% when Mackerel Corp. issues its bonds, will the bonds be priced at par, at a premium, or at a discount? Explain.
3. Assume that the issue price of the bonds is 96. Journalize the following bond transactions.
   a. Issuance of the bonds on February 28, 2010.
   b. Payment of interest and amortization of the bonds on August 31, 2010.
   c. Accrual of interest and amortization of the bonds on December 31, 2010, the year-end.
   d. Payment of interest and amortization of the bonds on February 28, 2011.
4. Report interest payable and bonds payable as they would appear on the Mackerel Corp. balance sheet at December 31, 2010.

P8-83B (*Learning Objectives 2, 3: Accounting for bonds payable at a discount; amortizing by the effective interest method*)

❙ Requirements

1. Journalize the following transactions of Lamore Communications, Inc.:

2010		
Jan 1		Issued $4,000,000 of 7%, 10-year bonds payable at 96.
Jul 1		Paid semiannual interest and amortized the bonds by the effective interest method on the 7% bonds payable.
Dec 31		Accrued semiannual interest expense and amortized the bonds by the effective interest method on the 7% bonds payable.
2011		
Jan 1		Paid semiannual interest.
2020		
Jan 1		Paid the 7% bonds at maturity.

2. At December 31, 2010, after all year-end adjustments, determine the carrying amount of Lamore Communications bonds payable, net.
3. For the six months ended July 1, 2010, determine the following for Lamore Communications Inc:
   a. Interest expense   b. Cash interest paid

What causes interest expense on the bonds to exceed cash interest paid?

■ spreadsheet

P8-84B (*Learning Objectives 2, 3, 5: Analyzing a company's long-term debt; reporting the long-term debt on the balance sheet (effective-interest method)*) The notes to the Helpful Charities financial statements reported the following data on December 31, Year 1 (end of the fiscal year):

Note 6. Indebtedness		
Bonds payable, 4% due in Year 7	$6,000,000	
Less: Discount	(304,542)	$5,695,458
Notes payable, 7%, payable in $60,000 annual installments starting in Year 5..............		360,000

Helpful Charities amortizes bonds by the effective-interest method and pays all interest amounts at December 31.

❚ Requirements

1. Answer the following questions about Helpful Charities long-term liabilities:
   a. What is the maturity value of the 4% bonds?
   b. What is Helpful Charities' annual cash interest payment on the 4% bonds?
   c. What is the carrying amount of the 4% bonds at December 31, Year 1?
2. Prepare an amortization table through December 31, Year 4, for the 4% bonds. The market interest rate on the bonds was 5%. Round all amounts to the nearest dollar. How much is Helpful Charities' interest expense on the 4% bonds for the year ended December 31, Year 4?
3. Show how Helpful Charities would report the 4% bonds and the 7% notes payable at December 31, Year 4.

P8-85B (*Learning Objectives 2, 3, 5: Issuing convertible bonds at a discount; amortizing by the effective-interest method; converting bonds; reporting the bonds payable on the balance sheet*)   On December 31, 2010, Rugaboo Corp. issues 9%, 10-year convertible bonds payable with a maturity value of $2,000,000. The semiannual interest dates are June 30 and December 31. The market interest rate is 10%, and the issue price of the bonds is 93.779. Rugaboo Corp. amortizes bonds by the effective-interest method.

■ spreadsheet

❚ Requirements

1. Prepare an effective-interest method amortization table for the first four semiannual interest periods.
2. Journalize the following transactions:
   a. Issuance of the bonds on December 31, 2010, Credit Convertible Bonds Payable
   b. Payment of interest and amortization of the bonds on June 30, 2011.
   c. Payment of interest and amortization of the bonds on December 31, 2011.
   d. Conversion by the bondholders on July 1, 2012, of bonds with face value of $800,000 into 90,000 shares of Rugaboo Corp. $1-par share capital.
3. Show how Rugaboo Corp. would report the remaining bonds payable on its balance sheet at December 31, 2012.

P8-86B (*Learning Objective 4: Financing operations with debt or with shares*)   Fitzpatrick Sporting Goods is embarking on a massive expansion. Assume plans call for opening 30 new stores during the next four years. Each store is scheduled to be 45% larger than the company's existing locations, offering more items of inventory, and with more elaborate displays. Its management estimates that company operations will provide $1.75 million of the cash needed for expansion. Fitzpatrick must raise the remaining $7 million from outsiders. The board of directors is considering obtaining the $7 million either through borrowing or by issuing share capital.

writing assignment ■

❚ Requirement

1. Write a memo to Fitzpatrick's management discussing the advantages and disadvantages of borrowing and of issuing share capital to raise the needed cash. Which method of raising the funds would you recommend?

P8-87B (*Learning Objectives 4, 5: Reporting liabilities on the balance sheet; calculating the times-interest-earned ratio*)   The accounting records of Brilliant Foods, Inc., include the following items at December 31, 2010:

Mortgage note payable, current	$ 95,000	Accumulated depreciation, equipment	$165,000
Accumulated pension benefit obligation	460,000	Discount on bonds payable (all long-term)	23,000
Bonds payable, long-term	200,000	Operating income	360,000
Mortgage note payable, long-term	313,000	Equipment	746,000
Bonds payable, current portion	500,000	Pension plan assets (market value)	410,000
Interest expense	224,000	Interest payable	72,000

I *Requirements*

1. Show how each relevant item would be reported on the Brilliant Foods, Inc., classified balance sheet, including headings and totals for current liabilities and long-term liabilities.
2. Answer the following questions about Brilliant's financial position at December 31, 2010:
   a. What is the carrying amount of the bonds payable (combine the current and long-term amounts)?
   b. Why is the interest-payable amount so much less than the amount of interest expense?
3. How many times did Brilliant cover its interest expense during 2010?

APPLY YOUR KNOWLEDGE

Decision Cases

Case 1. (*Learning Objective 2: Exploring an actual bankruptcy*) In 2002, **Enron Corporation** filed for Chapter 11 bankruptcy protection, shocking the business community: How could a company this large and this successful go bankrupt? This case explores the causes and the effects of Enron's bankruptcy.

At December 31, 2000, and for the four years ended on that date, Enron reported the following (amounts in millions):

Balance Sheet (summarized)			
Total assets			$65,503
Total liabilities			54,033
Total shareholders' equity			11,470
Income Statements (excerpts)			
	2000	**1999**	**1998**	**1997**
Net income	$979*	$893	$703	$105

*Operating income = $1,953
Interest expense = $838

Unknown to investors and lenders, Enron also controlled hundreds of partnerships that owed vast amounts of money. These special-purpose entities (SPEs) did not appear on the Enron financial statements. Assume that the SPEs' assets totaled $7,000 million and their liabilities stood at $6,900 million; assume a 10% interest rate on these liabilities.

During the four-year period up to December 31, 2000, Enron's share price shot up from $17.50 to $90.56. Enron used its escalating share price to finance the purchase of the SPEs by guaranteeing lenders that Enron would give them Enron shares if the SPEs could not pay their loans.

In 2001, the SEC launched an investigation into Enron's accounting practices. It was alleged that Enron should have been including the SPEs in its financial statements all along. Enron then restated net income for the years up to 2000, wiping out nearly $600 million of total net income (and total assets) for this four-year period. Enron's share price tumbled, and the guarantees to the SPEs' lenders added millions to Enron's liabilities (assume the full amount of the SPEs' debt). To make matters worse, the assets of the SPEs lost much of their value; assume that their market value is only $500 million.

I *Requirements*

1. Compute the debt ratio that Enron reported at the end of 2000. Recompute this ratio after including the SPEs in Enron's financial statements. Also compute Enron's times-interest-earned ratio both ways for 2000. Assume that the changes to Enron's financial position occurred during 2000.
2. Why does it appear that Enron failed to include the SPEs in its financial statements? How do you view Enron after including the SPEs in the company's financial statements? (Challenge)

Case 2. *(Learning Objective 4: Analyzing alternative ways of raising $5 million)* Business is going well for **Park 'N Fly**, the company that operates remote parking lots near major airports. The board of directors of this family-owned company believes that Park 'N Fly could earn an additional $1.5 million income before interest and taxes by expanding into new markets. However, the $5 million that the business needs for growth cannot be raised within the family. The directors, who strongly wish to retain family control of the company, must consider issuing securities to outsiders. The directors are considering three financing plans.

Plan A is to borrow at 6%. Plan B is to issue 100,000 shares of share capital. Plan C is to issue 100,000 shares of non-voting, $3.75 preference shares ($3.75 is the annual dividend paid on each share of preference shares).[5] Park 'N Fly presently has net income of $3.5 million and 1 million shares of share capital outstanding. The company's income tax rate is 35%.

I Requirements

1. Prepare an analysis to determine which plan will result in the highest earnings per share of share capital.
2. Recommend a plan to the board of directors. Give your reasons.

Ethical Issues

Issue 1.   Microsoft Corporation is the defendant in numerous lawsuits claiming unfair trade practices. Microsoft has strong incentives not to disclose these contingent liabilities. However, accounting standards require that companies report their contingent liabilities.

I Requirements

1. Why would a company prefer not to disclose its contingent liabilities?
2. Identify the parties involved in the decision and the potential consequences to each.
3. Analyze the issue of whether to report contingent liabilities from lawsuits from the following standpoints:
    a. economic
    b. legal
    c. ethical

Issue 2.   When Is a Lease a Capital Idea? Laurie Gocker, Inc., entered into a lease arrangement with Nathan Morgan Leasing Corporation for an industrial machine. Morgan's primary business is leasing. The cash purchase price of the machine is $1,000,000. Its economic life is six years.

Gocker's balance sheet reflects total assets of $10 million and total liabilities of $7.5 million. Among the liabilities is a $2.5 million long-term note outstanding at Last National Bank. The note carries a restrictive covenant that requires the company's debt ratio to be no higher than 75%. The company's revenues have been falling of late and the shareholders are concerned about profitability.

Gocker and Morgan are engaging in negotiations for terms of the lease. Some relevant other facts:

1. Morgan wants to take possession of the machine at the end of the initial lease term.
2. The term may run from four to five years, at Gocker's discretion.
3. Morgan estimates the machine will have no residual value, and Gocker will not purchase it at the end of the lease term.
4. The present value of minimum lease payments on the machine is $890,000.

I Requirements

1. What is (are) the ethical issue(s) in this case?
2. Who are the stakeholders? Analyze the consequences for each stakeholder from the following standpoints: (a) economic, (b) legal, and (c) ethical.
3. How should Gocker structure the lease agreement?

---

[5]For a discussion of preference shares, see Chapter 9.

Focus on Financials: ■ Nokia Corporation

Refer to **Nokia**'s consolidated financial statements in Appendix A at the end of this book.

1. Did accounts payable for Nokia increase or decrease in 2008? What was the amount? What might have caused this change?
2. Examine Note 11—Income Taxes—in the Notes to the Consolidated Financial Statements. What was Nokia's income tax expense in 2008? What does "deferred tax" refer to?
3. Did Nokia borrow more or pay off more long-term debt during 2008? How can you tell? (Challenge)
4. Examine Note 29—Commitments and Contingencies—in the Notes to Consolidated Financial Statements. Describe some of Nokia's contingent liabilities as of December 31, 2008.
5. How would you rate Nokia's overall debt position—risky, safe, or average? Compute the ratio at December 31, 2008, that answers this question.
6. Refer to Note 27 – Provisions. What kind of provisions does Nokia have? Why does it need them? What do you understand by the term "provision", and how is it different from "contingent liabilities"?

Group Projects

Project 1. Consider three different businesses:

1. A bank
2. A magazine publisher
3. A department store

For each business, list all of its liabilities—both current and long-term. Then compare the three lists to identify the liabilities that the three businesses have in common. Also identify the liabilities that are unique to each type of business.

Project 2. Alcenon Corporation leases the majority of the assets that it uses in operations. Alcenon prefers operating leases (versus capital leases) in order to keep the lease liability off its balance sheet and maintain a low debt ratio.

Alcenon is negotiating a 10-year lease on an asset with an expected useful life of 15 years. The lease requires Alcenon to make 10 annual lease payments of $20,000 each, with the first payment due at the beginning of the lease term. The leased asset has a market value of $135,180. The lease agreement specifies no transfer of title to the lessee and includes no bargain purchase option.

Write a report for Alcenon's management to explain what conditions must be present for Alcenon to be able to account for this lease as an operating lease.

Quick Check Answers

1. *d*
2. *e*
3. *b* ($450,000 × 0.01 = $4,500)
4. *c* [900 × 0.04 × $25 = warranty expense of $900; repaired $25 × 15 = $375; year-end liability = $525 ($900 - $375)]
5. *e*
6. *b*
7. *d*
8. *c*
9. *c*
10. *d*
11. *a*
12. *a* ($512,408 × 0.08 × 6/12 = $20,496)
13. *c* [Int. exp. = $20,496 Int. payment = $19,250 ($550,000 × 0.07 × 6/12) $20,496 – $19,250 = $1,246]
14. *b* ($550,000 × 0.07 = $38,500)
15. *a* (See Amortization Schedule)

Date	Interest Payment	Interest Expense	Discount Amortiz.	Bond Carry Amt.
1/1/2011				$512,408
7/1/2011	$19,250	$20,496	$1,246	513,654
1/1/2012	19,250	20,546	1,296	514,950

16. *d* {$512,408 + [($550,000 – $512,408) × 1/10] = $516,167}

9
Shareholders' Equity

SPOTLIGHT: Alibaba.com

Jack Ma, a former English teacher from Hangzhou, China, started **Alibaba.com** with 17 other founders in 1999 as a trading platform for smaller manufacturers to sell their wares. Since then, Alibaba.com has grown into the premier online marketplace for small and medium-size companies around the world to identify potential trading partners and interact with each other to conduct business online.

Alibaba.com's Initial Public Offering (IPO) on the Hong Kong Shares Exchange in November 2007 raised USD 1.7 billion. As at March 2010, Alibaba.com has over 47.7 million users, 6.8 million storefronts and over 7,600 product categories.

(Source: Alibaba.com Limited's Corporate Overview, March 2010)

The management's goal is to maximize the firm's value for the shareholders. But the separation between owners and managers may create problems. Corporate officers may run the business for their own benefit and not for the shareholders. For example, the CEO of **Tyco Corporation** was accused of looting Tyco of $600 million. The CFO of **Enron Corporation** set up outside partnerships and paid himself millions to manage the partnerships—unknown to Enron shareholders. Both men went to prison.

Corporate Taxation. Proprietorships and partnerships pay no business income tax. Instead, the business' tax falls solely on the owners. On the other hand, corporations are separate taxable entities. Just like individuals, they have to pay taxes, usually referred to as *corporate tax*. In some countries, corporations may be subject to federal and state income taxes. The specific rules on taxation would naturally vary from country to country. In general, not everything on the corporation's income statement may be subject to tax, or they may be subject to tax at a different rate. For example, many countries have offered additional tax deductions for spending on research and development, or allow companies to claim an accelerated method of depreciation for tax purposes. Many accounting graduates also work in the area of taxation. If this is an area that is of interest to you, you may find courses on corporate taxation beneficial.

Government Regulation. Because shareholders have only limited liability for corporation debts, outsiders doing business with the corporation can look no further than the corporation if it fails to pay. To protect a corporation's creditors and shareholders, governments monitor corporations. In general, as a company becomes larger, the more rules and regulations it will have to comply. For example, a public company (that raises funds from the public) will be subject to more regulatory oversight than a private company with a small number of shareholders. Similarly, a company that is listed on a stock exchange will be expected to follow the exchange's listing rules. The regulations mainly ensure that corporations disclose the information that investors and creditors need to make informed decisions. Accounting provides much of this information.

Exhibit 9-1 summarizes the advantages and disadvantages of the corporate form of business organization.

EXHIBIT 9-1 | Advantages and Disadvantages of the Corporation

Advantages	Disadvantages
1. Can raise more capital than a proprietorship or partnership can	1. Separation of ownership and management
2. Continuous life	2. Corporate taxation
3. Ease of transferring ownership	3. Government regulation
4. Limited liability of shareholders	

ORGANIZING A CORPORATION

The creation of a corporation begins when its organizers apply for registration as a company with the relevant authority. The local requirements vary from one jurisdiction to another, but would typically require the entity to have a constitution, charter, or memorandum (and articles) of association. The constitution includes the authorization for the corporation to issue a certain number of shares. A share is the basic unit of ownership for a corporation. Once the registration requirements are met, the corporation then comes into existence.

Ultimate control of the corporation rests with the shareholders who elect a **board of directors** that sets company policy and appoints officers. The board elects a chairperson, who usually is the most influential person in the organization. The chairperson of the board of directors, or chairman of the board, may be involved in the running of the corporation as the chief executive officer (CEO), or he/she may be an independent chairman who appoints someone else to be the CEO. The board may also designate a chief operating officer (COO) to be in charge of day-to-day operations. Most corporations also have directors or officers in charge of sales, manufacturing, accounting and finance (the chief financial officer, or CFO), and other key areas. Exhibit 9-2 shows the typical authority structure in a corporation. Note that the local practices in your country may use different titles than those listed below.

EXHIBIT 9-2 | Authority Structure in a Corporation

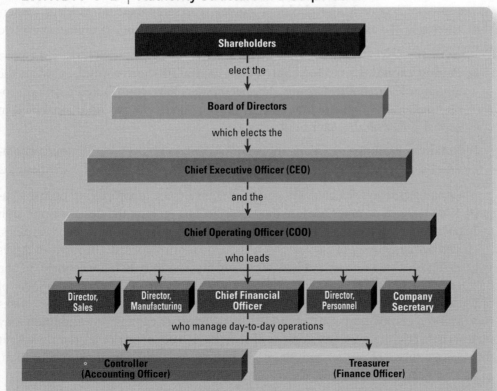

Shareholders' Rights

Ownership of shares entitles shareholders to four basic rights, unless a specific right is withheld by agreement with the shareholders:

1. *Vote.* The right to participate in management by voting on matters that come before the shareholders, usually in an annual general meeting (AGM). This is the shareholder's sole voice in the management of the corporation. A shareholder gets one vote for each share owned, unless otherwise specified in the company's constitution.

2. *Dividends.* The right to receive a proportionate part of any dividend. Each share in a particular class receives an equal dividend.

3. *Liquidation.* The right to receive a proportionate share of any assets remaining after the corporation pays its liabilities in liquidation. Liquidation means to go out of business, sell the assets, pay all liabilities, and distribute any remaining cash to the owners.

4. *Preemption.* The right to maintain one's proportionate ownership in the corporation. Suppose you own 5% of a corporation's shares. If the corporation issues 100,000 new shares, it must offer you the opportunity to buy 5% (5,000) of the new shares. This right, called the *preemptive right*, may be required by law or incorporated into the company's constitution.

Shareholders' Equity

As we saw in Chapter 1, **shareholders' equity** represents the shareholders' ownership interest in the assets of a corporation. Shareholders' equity is divided into two main parts:

1. **Paid-in capital**, also called **contributed capital** or **share capital.** This is the amount of shareholders' equity the shareholders have contributed to the corporation. Paid-in capital includes the share's par-values and any additional paid-in capital (more on this later in the chapter).

2. **Retained earnings.** This is the amount of shareholders' equity the corporation has earned through profitable operations and has not used for dividends.

Companies report shareholders' equity by source. They report paid-in capital separately from retained earnings because most jurisdictions prohibit the declaration of cash dividends from paid-in capital. Thus, cash dividends are declared from retained earnings.

The owners' equity of a corporation is divided into shares. A corporation issues *share certificates* to its owners when the company receives their investment in the business—usually cash. Many countries adopt electronic share certificates in favor of physical share certificates that requires manual handling and storage. Because shares represent the corporation's capital, it is often called share capital. A corporation may issue a share certificate for any number of shares—1, 100, or any other number—but the total number of authorized shares is limited by the company's constitution. Exhibit 9-3 shows an example of a share certificate.

EXHIBIT 9-3 | Share Certificate

Company name → CENTRAL JERSEY BANCORP

Shareholder name →

Number of shares →

Par value of $2.50 →

Shares in the hands of a shareholder is said to be *outstanding*. The total number of shares outstanding at any time represents 100% ownership of the corporation.

Classes of Shares

Corporations issue different types of shares to appeal to a variety of investors. The shares of a corporation may be either:

- Ordinary shares or preference shares
- With or without par-values

Ordinary and Preference Shares. Every corporation issues **ordinary shares**, the basic form of share capital. Unless designated otherwise, the word *share* is understood to mean "ordinary share." Ordinary shareholders have the four basic rights of share ownership, unless a right is specifically withheld. The ordinary shareholders are the owners of the corporation. They stand to benefit the most if the corporation succeeds because they take the most risk by investing in ordinary shares. Sometimes you may see ordinary shares labeled "common stock" in US companies' financial statements.

    Preference shares give their owners certain advantages over ordinary shareholders. Preference shareholders receive dividends before the ordinary shareholders and they also receive assets before the ordinary shareholders if the corporation enters into liquidation. Owners of preference shares also have the four basic shareholder rights, unless a right is specifically denied. Companies may issue different classes of preference shares (Class A and Class B, or Series A and Series B, for example). Each class of preference shares is recorded in a separate account. The preference shareholders expect to earn a fixed dividend on their investments.

A preference share is somewhat a hybrid between ordinary shares and long-term debt. Like interest on debt, preference shares pay a fixed dividend. But unlike interest on debt, the dividend is not required to be paid unless the board of directors declares the dividend. Also, companies have no obligation to pay back true preference shares, unless they are designated as redeemable preference shares. Preference share that must be redeemed (paid back) by the corporation is a liability masquerading as a share!

TECHNICAL UPDATE

Consistent with the IFRS Framework's principle of "substance over form", *FRS32 – Financial Instruments: Presentation* requires redeemable preference shares that have the characteristics of a liability to be shown on the financial statements as a liability, even though the legal form of the instrument is that of equity.

Preference shares are rare. A recent survey of 600 corporations revealed that only 7% of them had preference shares.

EXHIBIT 9-4 | Preference Shares

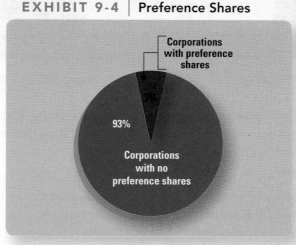

Exhibit 9-5 shows some of the similarities and differences among ordinary shares, preference shares, and long-term debt.

EXHIBIT 9-5 | Comparison of Ordinary Shares, Preference Shares, and Long-Term Debt

	Ordinary Share	Preference Share	Long-Term Debt
1 Obligation to repay principal	No	No	Yes
2 Dividends/interest	Dividends are not tax-deductible	Dividends are not tax-deductible	Interest expense is tax-deductible
3 Obligation to pay dividends/interest	Only after declaration	Only after declaration	At fixed rates and dates

Par-Value and No-Par Shares.   Shares may be par-value shares or no-par shares, depending on the applicable regulatory framework. **Par-value** is an arbitrary nominal amount assigned by a company to its share. Most companies set the par-value of their shares low to avoid legal difficulties from issuing their shares below par. In Exhibit 9-3, you saw that each **Central Jersey Bancorp** share has a par-value of USD 2.50 per share. In the same survey of 600 corporations mentioned earlier, less than 9% of the 600 companies use no-par-value shares.

Let's have a look now at Alibaba.com's share capital. It only has one class of shares, ordinary shares with par-value.

EXCERPTS FROM ALIBABA.COM'S NOTES TO THE 2008 FINANCIAL STATEMENTS

	Number of ordinary shares	Nominal value of ordinary shares HKD	Equivalent nominal value of ordinary shares RMB'000
Issued and fully paid			
Issue of ordinary shares in preparation for the initial public offering of the shares of the Company	4,825,000,000	$482,500	464
Issue of ordinary shares in connection with the initial public offering of the shares of the Company	227,356,500	$22,736	22
As of December 31, 2007	5,052,356,500	$505,236	486

The Company issued 227,356,500 ordinary shares of par-value of HK$0.0001 each pursuant to the initial public offering of the shares of the Company on November 6, 2007.

Voting Rights.   Companies may have different classes of shares with different voting rights. Here's an example from Warren Buffet's **Berkshire Hathaway Inc**.

EXCERPTS FROM BERKSHIRE HATHAWAY'S NOTES TO THE 2009 FINANCIAL STATEMENTS

Each share of Class B Ordinary Shares has dividend and distribution rights equal to one-thirtieth (1/30) of such rights of a Class A share. ... Each share of Class A Ordinary Shares is convertible, at the option of the holder, into thirty shares of Class B Ordinary Shares. Class B Ordinary Shares are not convertible into Class A Ordinary Shares. Each share of Class B Ordinary Shares possesses voting rights equivalent to one-two-hundredth (1/200) of the voting rights of a share of Class A Ordinary Shares. Class A and Class B Ordinary Shares vote together as a single class.

Sometimes, due to national interests on certain industries of significant importance, you may see "special shares" with very special rights. For example, **Singapore Airlines** has the following share structure.

EXCERPTS FROM SINGAPORE AIRLINE'S NOTES TO THE 2009 FINANCIAL STATEMENTS

	The Group and the Company			
	Number of shares		Amount (in million SGD)	
	2009	2008	2009	2008
Issued and fully paid share capital Ordinary shares				
Balance at 31 March	1,186,547,790	1,186,334,147	1,684.8	1,682.0
Special share				
Balance at 1 April and 31 March	1	1	*	*

* The value is $0.50

The Company's ability to operate its existing route network and flight frequency is derived solely from and dependent entirely on the Air Service Agreements ("ASAs") concluded between the Government of Singapore and the governments of other countries. ASAs are therefore critical to the Company's operations. In almost all the ASAs, it is a condition that the Company must at all times be "effectively controlled" and "substantially owned" by Singapore nationals for the tenure of the respective ASAs.

In order to comply with the above requirement, one non-tradable Special Share was issued to the Ministry of Finance. The Special Share enjoys all the rights attached to ordinary shares. In addition, pursuant to Article 3A of the Articles of Association, no resolution may be passed on certain matters without prior written approval of the Special Member.

ISSUING SHARES

Large corporations such as Alibaba.com, **BASF**, and **SAP** need huge quantities of money to operate. Corporations may sell shares directly to the shareholders or use the service of an underwriter, such as the investment banking firms **UBS** and **Goldman Sachs**. Companies often advertise the issuance of their shares to attract investors. The *Wall Street Journal* is the most popular medium for such advertisements, especially for IPOs in the United States. These advertisements are colloquially called "tombstones". Exhibit 9-6 is a reproduction of such a tombstone. **IHOP** is one of the largest full-service franchise restaurant companies in the world.

EXHIBIT 9-6 | **Announcement of Public Offering of IHOP Shares (Adapted)**

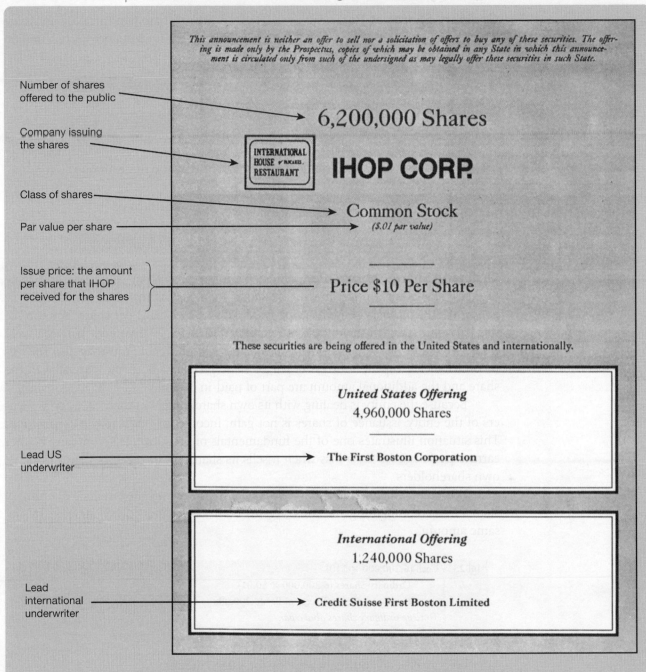

This announcement is neither an offer to sell nor a solicitation of offers to buy any of these securities. The offering is made only by the Prospectus, copies of which may be obtained in any State in which this announcement is circulated only from such of the undersigned as may legally offer these securities in such State.

Number of shares offered to the public

6,200,000 Shares

Company issuing the shares

INTERNATIONAL HOUSE OF PANCAKES RESTAURANT

IHOP CORP.

Class of shares

Par value per share

Common Stock
(*$.01 par value*)

Issue price: the amount per share that IHOP received for the shares

Price $10 Per Share

These securities are being offered in the United States and internationally.

Lead US underwriter

United States Offering
4,960,000 Shares

The First Boston Corporation

Lead international underwriter

International Offering
1,240,000 Shares

Credit Suisse First Boston Limited

The lead underwriter of IHOP's public offering was **First Boston Corporation**. Outside the United States, **Credit Suisse First Boston Limited** led the way. Several other US domestic brokerage firms and investment bankers sold IHOP shares to their clients. In its initial public offering, IHOP sought to raise $62 million of capital (6.2 million shares at the offering price of $10 per share). Let's see how a shares issuance works.

Ordinary Shares

Ordinary Shares at Par.

Suppose IHOP's ordinary share had carried a par-value equal to its issuance price of $10 per share. The entry for issuance of 6.2 million shares of ordinary shares at par would be:

Jul 23	Cash (6,200,000 × $10)	62,000,000	
	Ordinary shares		62,000,000
	To issue ordinary shares.		

IHOP's assets and shareholders' equity increase by the same amount.

Assets	=	Liabilities	+	Shareholders' Equity
+ 62,000,000	=	0	+	+ 62,000,000

Ordinary Shares above Par.

Most corporations set par-value low and issue ordinary shares for a price above par. Rather than $10 as in the assumed example above, IHOP's ordinary share has a par-value of $0.01 (1 cent) per share. You can see this par-value stated at the middle of Exhibit 9-6. The $9.99 difference between issue price ($10) and par-value ($0.01) is *additional paid-in capital*. You may also see this account labeled *capital in-excess of par* or *share premium*. Both the par-value of the share and the additional amount are part of paid-in capital.

Because the entity is dealing with its own shareholders in their capacity as owners of the entity, issuance of shares is not gain, income, or profit to the corporation. This situation illustrates one of the fundamentals of accounting: A company neither earns a profit nor incurs a loss when it sells its shares to, or buys its shares from, its own shareholders.

With par-value of $0.01, IHOP's actual entry to record the issuance of ordinary shares looked something like this. Again, both assets and equity increase by the same amount.

Jul 23	Cash (6,200,000 × $10)	62,000,000	
	Ordinary Shares (6,200,000 × $0.01)		62,000
	Paid-in Capital in Excess of Par (6,200,000 × $9.99)		
	To issue ordinary shares above par.		61,938,000

Both assets and equity increase by the same amount.

Assets	=	Liabilities	+	Shareholders' Equity
+ 62,000,000	=	0	+	+ 62,000
				+ 61,938,000

All the transactions in this section include a receipt of cash by the corporation as it issues new shares. The transactions we illustrate are different from those mergers and acquisitions reported in the daily news. In those transactions, one shareholder sold shares to another investor. The corporation doesn't record those transactions because they were between two outside parties.

STOP & THINK...

Examine Alibaba.com's balance sheet on page 538, along with excerpts from Note 22 to Alibaba.com's 2008 financial statements on page 545.

1. What was Alibaba.com's total paid-in capital at December 31, 2008?
2. Assume that the share premium account at December 31, 2007 was all related to Alibaba.com's IPO in November 2007, and propose the journal entry Alibaba.com would have performed for the IPO share issuance. Use the account titles as shown on Alibaba.com's balance sheet. What is the impact of the issuance on the accounting equation?

Answers:

1. Total paid-capital includes both the share capital and additional paid in capital (in this case, Alibaba.com uses the term "share premium"). Total paid-in capital as at December 31, 2008 is therefore: ¥486 + ¥3,067,924 = ¥3,068,410.
2. Alibaba.com's par-value per share was HK$0.0001 per share. Its IPO issuance of 227,356,500 shares equals to a total par-value of ¥22,000. The share premium account at December 31, 2007 was ¥2,893,132,000. Alibaba.com would have performed the following journal entry in relation to its IPO. Amounts are in thousands RMB.

2007			
Nov	Cash	2,893,154	
	Share Capital		22
	Share Premium		2,893,132
	To record issuance of shares above par.		

Assets	=	Liabilities	+	Shareholders' Equity
+ 2,893,154	=	0	+	+ 22
				+ 2,893,132

Ordinary Shares with No-Par Values. To record the issuance of no-par shares, the company debits the asset received and credits the share capital for the cash value of the asset received. If Alibaba.com's share had been no-par shares, the issuance would be recorded to share capital only.

2007			
Nov	Cash	2,893,154	
	Share Capital		2,893,154
	To record issuance of no-par shares.		

Assets	=	Liabilities	+	Shareholders' Equity
+ 2,893,154	=	0	+	+ 2,893,154

No-Par Shares with a Stated Value. Accounting for no-par shares with a stated value is identical to accounting for par-value shares. The excess over stated value is credited to Additional Paid-in Capital.

Shares Issued for Assets Other than Cash. When a corporation issues shares and receives assets other than cash, the company records the assets received at their current market value and credits the shares capital and additional paid-in capital accounts accordingly. The assets' prior book value isn't relevant because the shareholder will demand shares equal to the market value of the asset given. On November 12, Kahn Corporation issued 15,000 shares of its $1 par ordinary shares for equipment worth $4,000 and a building worth $120,000. Kahn's entry is:

Nov 12	Equipment	4,000	
	Building	120,000	
	Ordinary Shares (15,000 × $1)		15,000
	Paid-in Capital in Excess of Par ($124,000 – $15,000)		109,000
	To issue no-par shares in exchange for equipment and a building.		

Assets and equity both increase by $124,000.

Assets	=	Liabilities	+	Shareholders' Equity
+ 4,000	=	0	+	+ 15,000
+ 120,000				+ 109,000

Ordinary Shares Issued for Services. Sometimes a corporation will issue shares in exchange for services rendered, either by employees or outsiders. In this case, no cash is exchanged. However, the transaction is recognized at fair market value. The corporation usually recognizes an expense for the fair market value of the services rendered. Ordinary share capital is increased for its par-value (if any) and additional paid-in capital is increased for any difference. For example, assume that Kahn Corporation engages an attorney to represent the company on a legal matter. The attorney bills the corporation $25,000 for services, and agrees to accept 2,500 shares of $1 par shares, rather than cash, in settlement of the fee. The fair market value of the share is $10 per share. The journal entry to record the transaction is:

	Legal Expense	25,000	
	Ordinary Shares		2,500
	Paid-in Capital in Excess of Par ($25,000 – $2,500)		22,500

In this case, retained earnings (shareholders' equity) is eventually decreased by $25,000 (when the net profit is closed to retained earnings account), and paid-in capital (shareholders' equity) is increased for the same amount.

Shares Issuance for Other Than Cash Can Create an Ethical Challenge

Accounting standards require a company to record its shares at the fair market value of whatever the corporation receives in exchange for the shares. When the corporation receives cash, there is clear evidence of the value of the shares because cash is worth its face amount. But when the corporation receives an asset other than cash, the value of the asset can create an ethical challenge.

A computer whiz may start a new company by investing in computer software. The software may be market-tested or it may be new. The software may be worth millions or worthless. The corporation must record the asset received and the shares exchanged with a journal entry such as the following:

Software	500,000	
Share Capital		500,000
Issued shares in exchange for software.		

If the software is really worth $500,000, the accounting records are okay. But if the software is new and untested, the assets and equity may be overstated.

Suppose your computer-whiz friend now invites you to invest in the new business and shows you this balance sheet:

Gee-Whiz Computer Solutions, Ltd.
Balance Sheet
December 31, 2011

Assets		Liabilities	
Computer software	$500,000		$ -0-
		Shareholders' Equity	
		Share capital.................................	500,000
Total assets...........................	$500,000	Total liabilities and equity............	$500,000

Companies like to report large asset and equity amounts on their balance sheets. That makes them look prosperous and creditworthy. Gee-Whiz looks debt-free and appears to have a valuable asset. Will you invest in this new business? Here are two takeaway lessons:

- Some accounting values are more solid than others.
- Not all financial statements mean exactly what they say—an audit by an independent CPA lends more credibility to the financial reporting process.

Preference Shares

Accounting for preference shares follows the same pattern we illustrated for ordinary shares. When a company issues preference shares, it credits Preference Share account at its par-value, with any excess credited to Paid-in Capital in Excess of Par—Preference Shares. There may be separate accounts for paid-in capital in excess of par for preference shares. Many companies combine paid-in capital in excess of par from both preference and ordinary share transactions into one account. Accounting for no-par preference shares follows the pattern for no-par ordinary shares.

In Chapter 8 we saw how to account for convertible bonds payable (p. 493). Companies also issue convertible preference shares. The preference shares are usually convertible into the company's ordinary shares at the discretion of the preference shareholders.

For example, let's assume that in November 2011, Alibaba.com issued 30,000 preference shares of ¥1 par-value per share for ¥50,000. Each of these preference shares is convertible into 100 Alibaba.com's ordinary share at a par-value of ¥0.01 per share. Suppose these preference shares are converted in November 2013. The journal entries to record this series of transactions would be:

2011			
Nov	Cash	50,000	
	Preference Share Capital		30,000
	Share Premium		20,000
	To record issuance of preference shares after par.		

2013			
Nov	Preference Share Capital	30,000	
	Ordinary Share Capital		30,000
	To record conversion of preference shares into ordinary shares.		

As you can see, we merely remove Preference Share Capital from the books and increase Ordinary Share Capital by the book value of the preference shares.

MID-CHAPTER SUMMARY PROBLEM

1. Test your understanding of the first half of this chapter by deciding whether each of the following statements is true or false.
   a. The policy-making body in a corporation is called the board of directors.
   b. The owner of 100 preference shares has greater voting rights than the owner of 100 ordinary shares.
   c. Par-value shares are worth more than no-par shares.
   d. Issuance of 1,000 $5 par-value shares at $12 increases contributed capital by $12,000.
   e. The issuance of no-par shares with a stated value is fundamentally different from issuing par-value shares.
   f. A corporation issues its preference shares in exchange for land and a building with a combined market value of $200,000. This transaction increases the corporation's owners' equity by $200,000 regardless of the assets' prior book values.
   g. Preference shares are a riskier investment than ordinary shares.

2. Adolfo Company has two classes of ordinary shares. Only the Class A ordinary shares are entitled to vote. The company's balance sheet included the following presentation:

Shareholders' Equity

Share capital:	
Class A ordinary share, voting, $1 par-value,	
authorized and issued 1,260,000 shares.................	$ 1,260,000
Class B ordinary share, non-voting, no par-value,	
authorized and issued 46,200,000 shares................	11,000,000
	12,260,000
Additional paid-in capital...	2,011,000
Retained earnings...	872,403,000
	$886,674,000

Requirements

a. Record the issuance of the Class A ordinary shares. Use the Adolfo account titles.
b. Record the issuance of the Class B ordinary shares. Use the Adolfo account titles.
c. How much of Adolfo's shareholders' equity was contributed by the shareholders? How much was provided by profitable operations? Does this division of equity suggest that the company has been successful? Why or why not?
d. Write a sentence to describe what Adolfo's shareholders' equity means.

Answers

1. a. True   b. False   c. False   d. True   e. False   f. True   g. False
2. a.

Cash		3,271,000	
	Class A Ordinary Shares		1,260,000
	Additional Paid-in Capital		2,011,000
	To record issuance of Class A ordinary shares.		

Creative Technology, one of the world leaders in digital entertainment products, has one class of shares with no par-value. Excerpts of its share capital and treasury share movements are provided below.

	Number of ordinary shares		Amount	
	Issued share capital '000	Treasury shares '000	Share capital US$'000	Treasury shares US$'000
Group and Company 2009				
Beginning of financial year	83,626	(6,981)	300,100	(32,113)
Purchase of treasury share	–	(7,756)	–	(22,719)
Utilisation of treasury share for shares issued under employee options plans	–	2	–	10
Cancellation of treasury shares	(8,626)	8,626	(33,347)	33,347
End of financial year	75,000	(6,109)	266,753	(21,475)

Let's start with purchases of treasury shares. Treasury shares are recorded at cost (the market value of the share on the purchased date) without regard to the share's par-value. The treasury share account is a *contra shareholders' equity* account. Therefore, the treasury share account carries a debit balance, the opposite of the other equity accounts. It is reported on the balance sheet as a negative amount.

Creative bought 7,756 shares amounting to $22,719 during 2009. This would be recorded as below:

2009	Treasury Shares	22,719	
	Cash		22,719
	To record purchased treasury shares.		

Assets	=	Liabilities	+	Shareholders' Equity
– 22,719	=	0	+	– 22,719

Notice that treasury shares are recorded at cost, which is the market price of the shares on the day Creative purchased them (at an average of $2.93 per share). The financial statement impact of the transaction is to decrease cash as well as shareholders' equity by $22,719.

In summary, the purchase of treasury shares has the opposite effect of issuing shares:

- Issuing shares *grows* assets and equity.
- Purchasing treasury shares *shrinks* assets and equity.

Resale of Treasury Shares

Reselling treasury shares grows assets and equity exactly as issuing new shares does. The sale increases assets and equity by the full amount of cash received. Notice that the company **never records gains or losses on transactions involving its own treasury shares**. Rather, amounts received in excess of amounts originally paid for treasury shares are recorded as paid-in capital from treasury shares transactions, thus bypassing the income statement. If the proceeds from the resale of treasury shares were less than the amounts originally paid to acquire them, the difference would be debited to paid-in capital.

Creative did not resale any treasury shares during 2009. Let's assume it actually sold 1,000 of the treasury shares it bought at $2 for $3. Creative would record:

2009	Cash	3,000	
	Treasury Shares		2,000
	Share Capital		1,000
	To record resale of treasury shares.		

The impact of this resale would be:

Assets	=	Liabilities	+	Shareholders' Equity
+ 3,000	=	0	+	+ 2,000
				+ 1,000

On the other hand, what if Creative sold the 1,000 treasury shares at $1.50?

2009	Cash	1,500	
	Share Capital	500	
	Treasury Shares		2,000
	To record resale of treasury shares.		

Assets	=	Liabilities	+	Shareholders' Equity
+ 1,500	=	0	+	− 500
				+ 2,000

In both cases, note that any difference is not recognized as a gain or loss on the income statement, but recognized directly in share capital (or additional paid-in capital, if any).

Issuing Treasury Shares as Compensation

This is probably the most common use of treasury shares. Creative used 2,000 treasury shares (at $5 per share) as part of its employee share option compensation. It would have recorded the following:

2009	Share Option Compensation	10,000	
	Treasury Shares		10,000
	To record reissuance of treasury shares *for employee share options.*		

Retiring Treasury Shares

A corporation may purchase its own shares and retire it by canceling the shares. The retired shares cannot be reissued. Creative cancelled 8,626 shares amounting to $33,347 during 2009.

2009	Share Capital	33,347	
	Treasury Shares		33,347
	To record cancellation of shares from treasury shares.		

Note that this cancellation permanently reduces the amount of outstanding shares. At the end of the 2009 financial year, Creative's issued shares are therefore 83,626 or $300,100 and its outstanding shares are 68,891 shares (75,000 less 6,109) or $245,278 ($266,753 less $21,475).

RETAINED EARNINGS, DIVIDENDS, AND SPLITS

The Retained Earnings account carries the balance of the business's net income, less its net losses and less any declared dividends that have been accumulated over the corporation's lifetime. *Retained* means "held onto". Successful companies grow by reinvesting back into the business the assets they generate through profitable operations.

Let's look at Alibaba.com again. Take another look at its shareholders' equity as of December 31, 2008 (p. 538). Notice that the Retained Earnings account grew from ¥635,278 to ¥1,709,951. You would remember that retained earnings are increased by the net profit for the year and decreased by the amount of dividends paid out. Alibaba's net income for the year was ¥1,205,186 but it actually didn't pay any dividends for 2008. Why would the retained earnings account be less than ¥1,840,464 (¥635,278 + ¥1,205,186)? This is because companies in the People's Republic of China (PRC) are required to set aside some amount to their Statutory Reserves account, which cannot be distributable or transferable in the form of loans, advances or cash dividends. Alibaba.com transferred ¥130,513 to its statutory reserve account during 2009.

The Retained Earnings account is not a reservoir of cash for paying dividends to the shareholders. In fact, the corporation may have a large balance in Retained Earnings but not have enough cash to pay a dividend. Cash and Retained Earnings are two entirely separate accounts with no particular relationship. Retained Earnings says nothing about the company's Cash balance. A credit balance in Retained Earnings is normal, indicating that the corporation's lifetime earnings exceed lifetime losses and dividends. A debit balance in Retained Earnings arises when a corporation's lifetime losses and dividends exceed lifetime earnings. Called a *deficit*, this amount is subtracted to determine total shareholders' equity. In a recent survey of 600 companies, 15.5% had a retained earnings deficit (sometimes labeled "accumulated losses").

EXHIBIT 9-7 | Retained Earnings

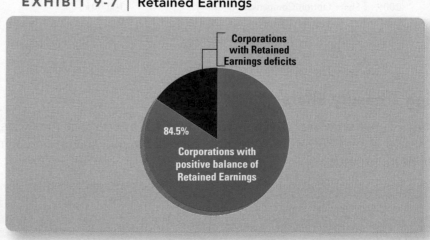

Corporations with Retained Earnings deficits

84.5%

Corporations with positive balance of Retained Earnings

Should the Company Declare and Pay Cash Dividends?

A **dividend** is a distribution by a corporation to its shareholders, usually based on earnings. Dividends usually take one of three forms:

OBJECTIVE

4 Account for dividends

- Cash
- Shares
- Non-cash assets

In this section we focus on cash dividends and share dividends because non-cash dividends are rare. For a non-cash asset dividend, debit Retained Earnings and credit the asset (for example, Long-Term Investment) for the current market value of the asset given.

Cash Dividends

Most dividends are cash dividends. Finance courses discuss how a company decides on its dividend policy. Accounting tells a company if it can pay a dividend. To do so, a company must have both:

- Enough Retained Earnings   and
  to *declare* the dividend

- Enough Cash to *pay*
  the dividend

A corporation declares a dividend before paying it. A company may pay dividends once a year, twice a year, or sometimes every quarter. Usually, the largest dividend is the one that follows the end of the financial year when financial results are published and the corporation's annual general meeting (AGM) is held. This is called the "final dividend". Other dividends during the financial year are thus called "interim dividends".

Interim dividends are declared by the board of directors and become payable immediately. The final dividend is recommended by the board but requires shareholder approval in an AGM and is not payable until the shareholders vote to do so. Thus, the dividend paid during one financial year typically starts with the prior year's final dividends plus the current year's interim dividends, if any.

There are three relevant dates for dividends (using assumed amounts and dates):

1. **Declaration date, June 19.**   On the declaration date, the board of directors announces the dividend. If it is for an interim dividend, the declaration of the dividend creates a liability for the corporation. If it is for a final dividend, it will have to be approved by shareholders at the AGM. Declaration (or shareholder approval, if it is for a final dividend) is recorded by debiting Retained Earnings and crediting Dividends Payable. Assume a $50,000 dividend was declared and approved.

Jun 19	Retained Earnings[3]	50,000	
	Dividends Payable		50,000
	Declared a cash dividend.		

Liabilities increase, and equity goes down.

Assets	=	Liabilities	+	Shareholders' Equity
0	=	+ 50,000	+	− 50,000

---

[3] In the early part of this book, we debited a Dividends account to clearly identify the purpose of the payment. From here on, we follow the more common practice of debiting the Retained Earnings account for dividend declarations.

2. **Date of record, July 1.** As part of the declaration, the corporation announces the record date (or book closure date), which follows the declaration date by a few weeks. The shareholders on the record date will receive the dividend. You don't need to own shares of a company for a whole period receive the dividends for the period. You just have to make sure you own the share at book closure date! There is no journal entry for the date of record.

3. **Payment date, July 10.** Payment of the dividend usually follows the record date by a week or two. Payment is recorded by debiting Dividends Payable and crediting Cash.

Jul 10	Dividends Payable	50,000	
	Cash		50,000
	Paid cash dividend.		

Both assets and liabilities decrease.

Assets	=	Liabilities	+	Shareholders' Equity
− 50,000	=	− 50,000	+	0

The net effect of a dividend declaration and its payment, as shown in steps 1, 2, and 3, is a decrease in assets and a corresponding decrease in shareholders' equity.

Dividends on Preference Shares

When a company issues both preference and ordinary shares, the preference shareholders receive their dividends first. The ordinary shareholders receive dividends only if the total dividend is large enough to pay the preference shareholders first.

Dividends for preference shares are usually described as a percentage of par-value. For example, preference shares may be labeled "6%" which means that owners of the preference shares receive an annual dividend equal to 6% of the preference share's par-value. If the preference shares are no-par shares, then it will be based on the share's issuance price.

Consider this example. Avant Garde, Inc., has 100,000 2% preference shares (par-value of $100) outstanding in addition to its ordinary shares. The 2% designation means that the preference shareholders receive an annual cash dividend of 2% x $100 par-value per share. In 2010, Avant Garde declares an annual dividend of $500,000. The allocation to preference and ordinary shareholders is:

Preference dividend (100,000 shares × 20% per share)	$200,000
Ordinary dividend (remainder: $500,000 – $200,000).............	300,000
Total dividend...	$500,000

If Avant Garde declares only a $250,000 dividend, preference shareholders receive $200,000, and the ordinary shareholders get the remainder, $50,000 ($250,000 − $200,000).

Dividends on Cumulative and Non-cumulative Preference Shares

Preference shareholders are typically promised a fixed return for their investments. What happens if the company was not able to make payments for the preference dividends? Corporations sometimes fail to pay a dividend to preference shareholders. This is called *passing the dividend*, and the passed dividends are said to be *in arrears*.

In some jurisdictions, preference shares are automatically "cumulative", unless its constitution specifically declares them to be non-cumulative. This means that the owners of **cumulative preference shares** must receive all dividends in arrears plus the current year's dividend before any dividends go to the ordinary shareholders. In this sense, cumulative dividends almost take on the flavor of accrued interest on long-term debt, but not quite. Although cumulative dividends must be paid before other dividends, they must still be declared by the company's board of directors. In contrast, interest on long-term debt doesn't have to go through a formal approval process by the board.

Here's an example of how cumulative dividends work. The preference shares of Avant Garde, Inc., is cumulative. Suppose Avant Garde passed the preference dividend of $200,000 in 2010. Before paying dividends to common stock in 2011, Avant Garde must first pay preference dividends of $200,000 for both 2010 and 2011, a total of $400,000. On September 6, 2011, Avant Garde declares a $500,000 dividend. The entry to record the declaration is

Sep 6	Retained Earnings	500,000	
	Dividends Payable, Preference ($200,000 × 2)		400,000
	Dividends Payable, Ordinary ($500,000 − $400,000)		100,000
	To declare a cash dividend.		

If the preference share is non-cumulative, the corporation is not obligated to pay dividends in arrears—until the board of directors declares the dividend.

Share Dividends

A **shares dividend** is a proportional distribution by a corporation of its own shares to its shareholders. Share dividends increase the Share Capital account and decrease Retained Earnings (alternatively, additional paid-in capital or share premium account). Total equity is unchanged, and no asset or liability is affected.

The corporation distributes share dividends to shareholders in proportion to the number of shares they already own. If you own 1,000 shares of Alibaba.com's ordinary shares and Alibaba.com distributes a 10% ordinary share dividend, you get 100 (1,000 x 0.10) additional shares. You would then own 1,100 shares. All other Alibaba.com's shareholders would also receive 10% more shares, leaving all shareholders' ownership unchanged.

In distributing share dividends, the corporation gives up no assets. Why, then, do companies issue share dividends? A corporation may choose to distribute share dividends for these reasons:

1. *To continue dividends but conserve cash.* A company may need to conserve cash and yet wish to continue dividends in some form. So the corporation may distribute shares as dividends instead.

2. *To reduce the market price of its share.* Distribution of a share dividend usually causes the share's market price to fall because of the increased number of outstanding shares that result from it. The objective is to make the shares less expensive and therefore attractive to more investors.

Let's continue with our example. Suppose sometime in 2012, Alibaba.com declared the 10% share dividend when the share is trading at $10 per share. Assuming that there are 20,000,000 shares outstanding at the time of the share dividend, Alibaba.com would record the share dividend as follows:

2012			
Retained Earnings[4] (20,000,000 shares outstanding × 0.10 share dividend × $10 market value per share)		20,000,000	
Ordinary Share (20,000,000 × 0.10 × $0.01 par value per share)			20,000
Paid-in Capital in Excess of Par			19,980,000
Distributed a 10% share dividend.			

The accounting equation clearly shows that a share dividend has no effect on total assets, liabilities, or equity. The increases in equity offset the decreases, and the net effect is zero.

Assets	=	Liabilities	+	Shareholders' Equity
				− 20,000,000
0	=	0	+	+ 20,000
				+ 19,980,000

Stock Splits

A **stock split** is an increase in the number of shares authorized, issued, and outstanding, coupled with a proportionate reduction in the share's par-value. For example, if the company splits its shares 2 for 1, the number of outstanding shares is doubled and each share's par-value is halved. A stock split, like a large share dividend, decreases the market price of the share—with the intention of making the share more attractive in the market. Stock splits are usually undertaken by companies that feel a lower share price would enable more investors to participate in the company's shares. A lower share price also allows a more active or liquid market. Nothing really changes with the company; it still makes the same profit and it still has the same assets. All that changes is the denomination of shares. It is not much different than you changing a $10 note into 10 $1 notes.

Stock splits are more popular with North American companies than companies in other parts of the world. For example, **Microsoft**, **Nike**, **Research in Motion** (makers of Blackberry), **NVIDIA Corp** (makers of computer graphic cards), **Porsche**, **Danone**, all have carried out some stock splits in the recent years.

---

[4]Many companies debit Additional Paid-in Capital for their shares dividends.

The market price of a Danone share is approximately $50. Assume that Danone wishes to decrease the market price to approximately $25 per share. Danone can split its shares 2 for 1, and the share price will fall to around $25. A 2-for-1 stock split means that:

- the company will have twice as many shares authorized, issued, and outstanding after the split as it had before.
- each share's par-value will be cut in half.

Before the split, Danone had approximately 250 million shares of €0.50 par ordinary shares issued and outstanding. Compare Danone's shareholders' equity before and after a 2-for-1 stock split:

Danone's Shareholders' Equity (Adapted)			
Before **2-for-1 Stock Split**	(In millions)	After **2-for-1 Stock Split**	(In millions)
Ordinary share, €0.50 par, 500 shares authorized, 250 shares issued.........	€ 125	Ordinary share, €0.25 par, 1,000 shares authorized, 500 shares issued.........	€ 125
Additional paid-in capital..................	643	Additional paid-in capital..................	643
Retained earnings..............................	4,304	Retained earnings..............................	4,304
Other equity......................................	260	Other......................................	260
Total shareholders' equity..................	€5,332	Total shareholders' equity..................	€5,332

All account balances are the same after the stock split as before. Only three Danone items are affected:

- Par value per share drops from €0.50 to €0.25.
- Shares *authorized* double from 500 to 1,000 (both in millions).
- Shares *issued* double from 250 to 500 (both in millions).

Total equity doesn't change, nor do any assets or liabilities.

A stock split does not require any journal entry. The record of the split will be a note in the company's corporate action log and share registry.

Summary of the Effects on Assets, Liabilities, and Shareholders' Equity

We've seen how to account for the basic shareholders' equity transactions:

- Issuance of shares—ordinary and preference shares
- Purchase and sale of treasury shares
- Cash dividends
- Share dividends and stock splits

How do these transactions affect assets, liabilities, and equity? Exhibit 9-8 provides a helpful summary.

EXHIBIT 9-8 | **Effects on Assets, Liabilities, and Equity**

	Effect on Total				
Transaction	Assets	=	Liabilities	+	Shareholders' Equity
Issuance of share—ordinary and preference shares	Increase		No effect		Increase
Purchase of treasury share	Decrease		No effect		Decrease
Sale of treasury share	Increase		No effect		Increase
Declaration of cash dividend	No effect		Increase		Decrease
Payment of cash dividend	Decrease		Decrease		No effect
Share dividend	No effect		No effect		No effect*
Stock split	No effect		No effect		No effect

*The share capital account increases and retained earnings decreases by offsetting amounts that net to zero.

MEASURING THE VALUE OF SHARES

OBJECTIVE

5 Use shares values in decision making

The business community measures *share values* in various ways, depending on the purpose of the measurement. These values include market value, redemption value, liquidation value, and book value.

Market, Redemption, Liquidation, and Book Value

A share's **market value**, or *market price*, is the price a person can buy or sell one share of the shares for. Market value varies with the corporation's net income, financial position, and future prospects, and with general economic conditions. *In almost all cases, shareholders are more concerned about a share's market value than any other share value.*

Alibaba.com's market price is about 18 HKD (about USD 2.3 or EUR 1.7) in March 2010. Multiply this price per share with the shares outstanding, we can say that the **market capitalization** of Alibaba.com is about 86 billion HKD.

A preference share that requires the company to redeem the share at a set price is called a redeemable preference share. The company is obligated to redeem (pay to retire) the *preference shares*. As we discussed earlier, redeemable preference shares are really not equity, but a liability. The price the corporation agrees to pay for the share, set when the share is issued, is called the **redemption value**. **Liquidation value** is the amount that a company must pay a preference shareholder in the event the company liquidates (sells out) and goes out of business.

The book value per ordinary share is the amount of owners' equity on the company's books for each ordinary share. If the company has only ordinary share outstanding, its book value is computed by dividing total equity by the number of shares of ordinary shares *outstanding*. Recall that outstanding shares issued shares minus treasury shares, if any. For example, a company with shareholders' equity of $150,000 and 5,000 ordinary shares outstanding has a book value of $30 per share ($150,000 ÷ 5,000 shares).

If the company has both preference and ordinary shares outstanding, the preference shareholders have the first claim to owners' equity. Preference shares often have a specified redemption value. The preference component of equity is its redemption value plus any cumulative preference dividends in arrears. The book value per share of ordinary shares is then computed as follows:

$$\text{Book value per ordinary share} = \frac{\text{Total shareholders' equity} - \text{Preference equity}}{\text{Number of ordinary shares outstanding}}$$

Crusader Corporation's balance sheet reports the following amounts:

Shareholders' Equity	
Preference shares, 5%, $100 par, 400 shares issued, redemption value $130 per share............................	$ 40,000
Ordinary shares, $10 par, 5,500 shares issued...............	55,000
Additional paid-in capital—ordinary shares	72,000
Retained earnings...	88,000
Treasury share, 500 ordinary shares at cost..................	(15,000)
Total shareholders' equity	$240,000

Assume Crusader's cumulative preference dividends are in arrears for four years (including the current year). Crusader's preference share has a redemption value of $130 per share. The book-value-per-share computations for Crusader Corporation are:

Preference Equity	
Redemption value (400 shares × $130)	$52,000
Cumulative dividends ($40,000 × 0.05 × 4 years)	8,000
Preference equity..	$60,000*
Ordinary Equity	
Total shareholders' equity..	$240,000
Less preference equity	(60,000)
Ordinary equity...	$180,000
Book value per share [$180,000 ÷ 5,000 shares outstanding (5,500 shares issued minus 500 treasury shares)]	$ 36.00

*If the preference share had no redemption value, then preference equity would be $40,000 + preference dividends in arrears.

Some investors search for shares whose market price is below book value. They believe this indicates a good buy. Financial analysts often shy away from companies with a share price at or below book value. To these investors, such a company is in trouble. As you can see, not all investors agree on a share's value. In fact, wise investors base their decisions on more than a single ratio. Later in Chapter 13, you'll see the full range of financial ratios, plus a few more analytical techniques.

Relating Profitability to a Company's Shares

OBJECTIVE

6 Compute return on assets and return on equity

Investors search for companies whose shares are likely to increase in value.

They're constantly comparing companies. But a comparison of Alibaba.com with a new Internet start-up may not be meaningful. Alibaba.com's profits run into the millions, which far exceed a new company's net income. Does this automatically make Alibaba.com a better investment? Not necessarily. To compare companies of different size, investors use some standard profitability measures, including:

- return on assets
- return on equity

Return on Assets. The **rate of return on total assets**, or simply **return on assets (ROA)**, measures a company's use of its assets to earn income for the two groups who finance the business:

- Creditors to whom the corporation owes money. Creditors want interest.
- Shareholders who own the corporation's shares. Shareholders want net income.

The sum of interest expense and net income is the return to the two groups who finance a corporation. This sum is the numerator of the return-on-assets ratio. The denominator is average total assets. ROA is computed as follows, using actual data from the 2008 annual report of Alibaba.com:

$$\text{Rate of return on total assets} = \frac{\text{Net income} + \text{Interest expense}}{\text{Average total assets}}$$

$$= \frac{\$1,205,186 + 0}{\$(7,892,930 + 6,053,469)/2} = 0.017 = 17\%$$

Net income and interest expense come from the income statement. Average total assets is computed from the beginning and ending balance sheets. Notice that Alibaba.com does not have any interest-bearing loans and liabilities, making the interest expense zero. Total assets have increased about 30%. Alibaba.com's ROA for 2008 is therefore about 17%.

What is a good rate of return on total assets? Ten percent is considered strong in most industries. However, rates of return vary by industry. Some high technology companies earn much higher returns than utility companies, grocery sellers, and manufacturers of consumer goods such as toothpaste and paper towels. Alibaba.com's return on assets (17%) can be considered high. Alibaba.com is able to utilize its assets effectively in generating profits.

Return on Equity.   **Rate of return on ordinary equity**, often called **return on equity (ROE)**, shows the relationship between net income available to average ordinary shareholders' equity. Return on equity is computed only on ordinary equity because the return to preference shareholders is the specified dividend (for example, 5%).

The numerator of return on equity is net income minus preference dividends, if any. The denominator is *average ordinary shareholders' equity*—total shareholders' equity minus preference equity. Alibaba.com's ROE for 2008 is computed as follows:

$$\text{Rate of return on ordinary shareholder's equity} = \frac{\text{Net income} - \text{Preference dividends}}{\text{Average ordinary shareholders' equity}}$$

$$= \frac{\$1,205,186 - 0}{\$(4,968,409 + 3,613,081)/2} = 0.28 = 28\%$$

As Alibaba.com does not have preference shares, we have no preference dividends to subtract from net income on the numerator. Similarly, the denominator is simply total shareholders' equity. Alibaba.com's ROE is a very strong 28%. Alibaba.com is generating very generous returns for the money invested by its shareholders.

ROE is always higher than ROA for a successful company in the long run. Shareholders take a lot more investment risk than bondholders, so the shareholders demand that ROE exceeds ROA. They expect the return on their investment to exceed the amount they have to pay their creditors for borrowed funds. You can see that in this case, ROE of 28% is indeed much higher than ROA of 17%.

Investors and creditors use ROE in much the same way they use ROA—to compare companies. The higher the rate of return, the more successful the company. In many industries, 15% is considered a good ROE.

The Decision Guidelines feature (p. 569) offers suggestions for what to consider when investing in shares.

REPORTING SHAREHOLDERS' EQUITY TRANSACTIONS

OBJECTIVE

7 **Report** equity transactions on the statement of cash flows

Statement of Cash Flows

Many of the transactions we've covered are reported on the statement of cash flows. Equity transactions are *financing* activities because the company is dealing with its owners. Financing transactions that affect both cash and equity fall into three main categories:

- issuance of shares
- treasury shares
- dividends

Issuances of Shares.   During 2007, Alibaba.com's IPO generated a significant cash inflow to the company, amounting to close to RMB 3 billion. This is as a financing activity, as shown in Exhibit 9-9. In 2008, it did not issue any new shares.

EXHIBIT 9-9 | Alibaba.com's Statement of Cash Flows

Alibaba.com
Consolidated Cash Flow Statement (Partial, adapted)
Financial Year Ended December 31

(in thousands ¥ Chinese Renminbi)	2009	2008
Cash flows from operating activities	¥ 1,580,924	¥1,409,217
Cash flows from investing activities	(3,101,782)	(101,947)
Cash flows from financing activities:		
Payments for share issuance costs	(66,472)	(112,249)
Payments for repurchase of issued ordinary shares	(12,401)	–
Proceeds from issuance of ordinary shares	–	2,935,079
Dividends paid	–	(195,909)
	(78,873)	2,626,921
Net cash flows	¥(1,599,731)	¥3,934,191

Treasury Share.   During 2008, Alibaba.com purchased treasury shares and reported the payment as a financing activity. Alibaba.com spent RMB 12.4 million to repurchase issued ordinary shares.

Dividends.   Most companies, including Alibaba.com, pay cash dividends to their shareholders. Dividend payments are a type of financing transaction because the company is paying its shareholders for the use of their money. Share dividends are not reported in the statement of cash flows because the company pays no cash for them.

In Exhibit 9-9, cash receipts appear as positive amounts and cash payments as negative amounts, denoted by parentheses.

DECISION GUIDELINES

INVESTING IN SHARES

Suppose you've saved $5,000 to invest. You visit a nearby **Standard Chartered Bank** office, where the broker probes for your risk tolerance. Are you investing mainly for dividends or for growth in the share price? You must make some key decisions.

Investor Decision	Guidelines
Which category of shares to buy for:	
■ A safe investment?	Preference shares are safer than ordinary share, but for even more safety, invest in high-grade corporate bonds or government securities.
■ Steady dividends?	Cumulative preference shares. However, the company is not obligated to declare preference dividends, and the dividends are unlikely to increase.
■ Increasing dividends?	Ordinary shares, as long as the company's net income is increasing and the company has adequate cash flow to pay a dividend after meeting all obligations and other cash demands.
■ Increasing share price?	Ordinary shares, but again only if the company's net income and cash flow are increasing.
How to identify a good share to buy?	There are many ways to pick share investments. One strategy that works reasonably well is to invest in companies that consistently earn higher rates of return on assets and on equity than competing firms in the same industry. Also, select industries that are expected to grow.

END-OF-CHAPTER SUMMARY PROBLEM

1. The balance sheet of Trendline Corp. reported the following at December 31, 2010.

Shareholders' Equity	
Preference share, 4%, $10 par, 10,000 shares authorized and issued (redemption value, $110,000)................	$100,000
Ordinary share, no-par, $5 stated value, 100,000 shares authorized, 50,000 shares issued.............................	250,000
Paid-in capital in excess of par or stated value:	
Ordinary share...	239,500
Retained earnings..	395,000
Less: Treasury share, Ordinary (1,000 shares)..............	(8,000)
Total shareholders' equity	$976,500

▌Requirements

    a. Is the preference share cumulative or non-cumulative? How can you tell?

    b. What is the total amount of the annual preference dividend?

    c. How many ordinary shares are outstanding?

    d. Compute the book value per share of the ordinary share. No preference dividends are in arrears, and Trendline has not yet declared the 2010 dividend.

2. Use the following accounts and related balances to prepare the classified balance sheet of Whitehall, Inc., at September 30, 2011. Use the account format of the balance sheet.

Ordinary share, $1 par, 50,000 shares authorized, 20,000 shares issued..................	20,000	Long-term note payable	80,000
		Inventory......................................	85,000
Dividends payable.........................	4,000	Property, plant and equipment, net	226,000
Cash..	9,000	Accounts receivable, net..............	23,000
Accounts payable	28,000	Preference share, $3.75, no-par, 10,000 shares authorized,	
Paid-in capital in excess of par—Ordinary share..............	115,000	2,000 shares issued..................	24,000
Treasury share, Ordinary,		Accrued liabilities........................	3,000
1,000 shares at cost...................	6,000	Retained earnings........................	75,000

Answers

  1. **a.** The preference shares are cumulative because they are not specifically labeled otherwise.

      b. Total annual preference dividend: $4,000 ($100,000 × 0.04).

c. Ordinary shares outstanding: 49,000 (50,000 issued – 1,000 treasury).
d. Book value per share of ordinary share:

Ordinary:		
Total shareholders' equity	$976,500	
Less shareholders' equity allocated to preference................	(114,000)*	
Shareholders' equity allocated to ordinary	$862,500	
Book value per share ($862,500 ÷ 49,000 shares)	$17.60	

*Redemption value	$110,000	
Cumulative dividend ($100,000 × 0.04)...	4,000	
Shareholders' equity allocated to preference...	$114,000	

2.

Whitehall, Inc.
Balance Sheet
September 30, 2011

Assets		Liabilities	
Current		**Current**	
Cash	$ 9,000	Account payable	$ 28,000
Accounts receivable, net..............	23,000	Dividends payable.......................	4,000
Inventory....................................	85,000	Accrued liabilities	3,000
Total current assets	117,000	Total current liabilities	35,000
Property, plant and equipment, net	226,000	Long-term note payable	80,000
		Total liabilities	115,000
		Shareholders' Equity	
		Preference share, $3.75, no par,	
		10,000 shares authorized,	
		2,000 shares issued	$ 24,000
		Ordinary share, $1 par,	
		50,000 shares authorized,	
		20,000 shares issued	20,000
		Paid-in capital in excess of	
		par—ordinary shares	115,000
		Retained earnings............................	75,000
		Treasury share, ordinary,	
		1,000 shares at cost	(6,000)
		Total shareholders' equity...........	228,000
		Total liabilities and	
Total assets.......................................	$343,000	shareholders' equity....................	$343,000

REVIEW SHAREHOLDERS' EQUITY

Quick Check (Answers are given on page 605.)

1. Lurvey Company is authorized to issue 50,000 shares of $25 par ordinary share. On May 30, 2010, Lurvey issued 20,000 shares at $45 per share. Lurvey's journal entry to record these facts should include a
   a. credit to ordinary shares for $500,000.
   b. debit to ordinary shares for $900,000.
   c. credit to Paid-in Capital in Excess of Par for $900,000.
   d. both a and c.

Questions 2–5 use the following account balances of Machado Co. at August 31, 2010:

Dividends Payable	$ 12,500	Cash	$111,000
Preference Shares, $150 par	375,000	Ordinary Shares, $5 par	600,000
Paid-in Capital in Excess of Par—		Retained Earnings	325,000
Ordinary Shares	60,000		

2. How many ordinary shares has Machado issued?
   a. 111,000
   b. 660,000
   c. 120,000
   d. Some other amount

3. Machado's total paid-in capital at August 31, 2010, is
   a. $1,347,500.
   b. $1,022,500.
   c. 1,458,500.
   d. $1,035,000.

4. Machado's total shareholders' equity as of August 31, 2010, is
   a. $1,035,000.
   b. $1,347,500.
   c. $1,458,500.
   d. $1,360,000.

5. What would Machado's total shareholders' equity be if Machado had $10,000 of treasury shares?
   a. $1,448,500
   b. $1,025,000
   c. $1,350,000
   d. $1,337,500

6. Syracuse Corporation purchased treasury shares in 2010 at a price of $15 per share and resold the treasury share in 2011 at a price of $35 per share. What amount should Syracuse report on its income statement for 2011?
   a. $20 gain per share
   b. $15 gain per share
   c. $35 gain per share
   d. $0

7. The shareholders' equity section of a corporation's balance sheet reports

	Discount on Bonds Payable	Treasury Shares
a.	No	Yes
b.	Yes	No
c.	No	No
d.	Yes	Yes

8. The purchase of treasury shares
   a. decreases total assets and increases total shareholders' equity.
   b. decreases total assets and decreases total shareholder's equity.
   c. has no effect on total assets, total liabilities, or total shareholders' equity.
   d. increases one asset and decreases another asset.

9. When does a cash dividend become a legal liability?
   a. It never becomes a liability because it is paid.
   b. On date of payment.
   c. On date of record.
   d. On date of declaration and approval.

10. When do dividends increase shareholders' equity?
   a. On date of declaration.   c. Never.
   b. On date of payment.   d. On date of record.

11. Maple Tree Mall, Inc., has 2,500 shares of 2%, $25 par cumulative preference shares and 125,000 shares of $2 par ordinary shares outstanding. At the beginning of the current year, preference dividends were four years in arrears. Maple Tree's board of directors wants to pay a $2.50 cash dividend on each share of outstanding ordinary shares in the current year. To accomplish this, what total amount of dividends must Maple Tree declare?
   a. $250,000   c. $256,250
   b. $255,000   d. Some other amount

12. Share dividends
   a. have no effect on total shareholders' equity.
   b. increase the corporation's total liabilities.
   c. reduce the total assets of the company.
   d. are distributions of cash to shareholders.

13. What is the effect of a share dividend and a stock split on total assets?

	Shares dividend	Stock split
a.	No effect	Decrease
b.	Decrease	Decrease
c.	No effect	No effect
d.	Decrease	No effect

14. A 2-for-1 stock split has the same effect on the number of shares being issued as a
   a. 50% share dividend.   c. 100% share dividend.
   b. 200% share dividend.   d. 20% share dividend.

15. The numerator for computing the rate of return on total assets is
   a. net income.
   b. net income minus preference dividends.
   c. net income minus interest expense.
   d. net income plus interest expense.

16. The numerator for computing the rate of return on ordinary equity is
   a. net income.
   b. net income minus interest expense.
   c. net income minus preference dividends.
   d. net income plus preference dividends.

Accounting Vocabulary

authorized share (p. 554) Maximum number of shares a corporation can issue under its constitution.

board of directors (p. 539) Group elected by the shareholders to set policy for a corporation and to appoint its officers.

book value (of a share) (p. 564) Amount of owners' equity on the company's books for each share.

chairperson (p. 541) Elected by a corporation's board of directors, usually the most influential person in the corporation.

ordinary share (p. 543) The most basic form of capital shares. The ordinary shareholders own a corporation.

contributed capital (p. 542) The amount of shareholders' equity that shareholders have contributed to the corporation. Also called *paid-in capital*.

cumulative preference share (p. 561) Preference share whose owners must receive all dividends in arrears before the corporation can pay dividends to the ordinary shareholders.

deficit (p. 558) Debit balance in the Retained Earnings account.

dividend (p. 558) Distribution (usually cash) by a corporation to its shareholders.

issued share (p. 554) Number of shares a corporation has issued to its shareholders.

limited liability (p. 539) No personal obligation of a shareholder for corporation debts. A shareholder can lose no more on an investment in a corporation's share than the cost of the investment.

liquidation value (p. 564) The amount a corporation must pay a preference shareholder in the event the company liquidates and goes out of business.

market capitalization (p. 564) A measure of the size of a listed company, equal to the share price multiplied by the number of shares outstanding.

market value (of a share) (p. 564) Price for which a person could buy or sell a share.

outstanding share (p. 554) Share in the hands of shareholders calculated as issued shares less treasury shares, if any.

paid-in capital (p. 542) The amount of shareholders' equity that shareholders have contributed to the corporation. Also called *contributed capital*.

par-value (p. 545) Arbitrary amount assigned by a company to a share.

preference share (p. 552) Share that gives its owners certain advantages, such as the priority to receive dividends before the ordinary shareholders and the priority to receive assets before the ordinary shareholders if the corporation liquidates.

rate of return on ordinary shareholders' equity (p. 567) Net income minus preference dividends, divided by average ordinary shareholders' equity. A measure of profitability. Also called *return on equity*.

rate of return on total assets (p. 566) Net income plus interest expense divided by average total assets. This ratio measures a company's success in using its assets to earn income for the persons who finance the business. Also called *return on assets*.

redeemable preference shares (p. 564) A corporation reserves the right to buy an issue of shares back from its shareholders, with the intent to retire the share.

redemption value (p. 564) The price a corporation agrees to eventually pay for its redeemable preference shares, set when the share is issued.

retained earnings (p. 542) The amount of shareholders' equity that the corporation has earned through profitable operation of the business and has not given back to shareholders.

return on assets (ROA) (p. 566) Another name for *rate of return on total assets*.

return on equity (ROE) (p. 567) Another name for *rate of return on common shareholders' equity*.

share (p. 542) Share into which the owners' equity of a corporation is divided.

shareholder (p. 539) A person who owns share in a corporation.

stated value (p. 549) An arbitrary amount assigned to no-par share; similar to par-value.

share dividend (p. 561) A proportional distribution by a corporation of its own shares to its shareholders.

shareholders' equity (p. 542) The shareholders' ownership interest in the assets of a corporation.

stock split (p. 562) An increase in the number of authorized, issued, and outstanding shares of share coupled with a proportionate reduction in the share's par-value and market price per share.

treasury share (p. 555) A corporation's own share that it has issued and later reacquired.

ASSESS YOUR PROGRESS

Short Exercises

S9-1 (*Learning Objective 1: Explaining advantages and disadvantages of a corporation*) What are two main advantages that a corporation has over a proprietorship and a partnership? What are two main disadvantages of a corporation?

S9-2 (*Learning Objective 1: Describing the authority structure in a corporation*) Consider the authority structure in a corporation, as illustrated in Exhibit 9-2.

1. What group holds the ultimate power in a corporation?
2. Who is the most influential person in the corporation? What's the abbreviation of this person's title?
3. Who's in charge of day-to-day operations? What's the abbreviation of this person's title?
4. Who's in charge of accounting and finance? What's the abbreviation of this person's title?

S9-3 (*Learning Objective 1: Describing characteristics of preference and ordinary shares*)   Answer the following questions about the characteristics of a corporation's shares:

1. Who are the real owners of a corporation?
2. What privileges do preference shareholders have over ordinary shareholders?
3. Which class of shareholders reap greater benefits from a highly profitable corporation? Explain.

S9-4 (*Learning Objective 1: Organizing a corporation*)   Karen Scanlon and Jennifer Shaw are opening a Submarine's deli. Scanlon and Shaw need outside capital, so they plan to organize the business as a corporation. They come to you for advice. Write a memorandum informing them of the steps in forming a corporation. Identify specific documents used in this process, and name the different parties involved in the ownership and management of a corporation.

S9-5 (*Learning Objective 2: Describing the effect of a shares issuance on paid-in capital*)   SHOE received $73,000,000 for the issuance of its shares on April 24. The par-value of the SHOE shares was only $73,000. Was the excess amount of $72,927,000 a profit to SHOE? If not, what was it?

Suppose the par-value of the SHOE share had been $2 per share, $12 per share, or $15 per share. Would a change in the par-value of the company's share affect SHOE's total paid-in capital? Give the reason for your answer.

S9-6 (*Learning Objective 2: Issuing shares—par-value share and no-par share*)   At fiscal year-end 2010, Horris Printer and Delectable Doughnuts reported these adapted amounts on their balance sheets (amounts in millions):

Horris Printer:		
Ordinary shares, 1 cent par value, 2,300		$ 23
shares issued		
Additional paid-in capital		17,100

Delectable Doughnuts:		
Ordinary shares, no par value, 63 shares issued		$ 292

Assume each company issued its shares in a single transaction. Journalize each company's issuance of its shares, using its actual account titles. Explanations are not required.

S9-7 (*Learning Objective 2: Issuing shares to finance the purchase of assets*)   This short exercise demonstrates the similarity and the difference between two ways to acquire PPE.

Case A—Issue share and buy the assets in separate transactions:

Ashley, Inc., issued 12,000 shares of its $20 par ordinary shares for cash of $800,000. In a separate transaction, Ashley used the cash to purchase a building for $550,000 and equipment for $250,000. Journalize the two transactions.

Case B—Issue share to acquire the assets in a single transaction:

Ashley, Inc., issued 12,000 shares of its $20 par ordinary shares to acquire a building valued at $550,000 and equipment worth $250,000. Journalize this transaction.

Compare the balances in all the accounts after making both sets of entries. Are the account balances similar or different?

S9-8 (*Learning Objective 2: Preparing the shareholders' equity section of a balance sheet*)   The financial statements of Mountainpeak Employment Services, Inc., reported the following accounts (adapted, with dollar amounts in thousands except for par-value):

Paid-in capital in excess of par	$196	Total revenues	$1,340
Other shareholders' equity (negative)	(22)	Accounts payable	440
Ordinary share, $0.01 par		Retained earnings	647
400 shares issued	4	Other current liabilities	2,569
Long-term debt	27	Total expenses	806

Prepare the shareholders' equity section of Mountainpeak's balance sheet. Net income has already been closed to Retained Earnings.

S9-9 (*Learning Objective 2: Using shareholders' equity data*)   Use the Mountainpeak Employment Services data in Short Exercise 9-8 to compute Mountainpeak's:

    a. Net income.

    b. Total liabilities.

    c. Total assets (use the accounting equation).

S9-10 (*Learning Objective 3: Accounting for the purchase and sale of treasury shares*)   Genius Marketing Corporation reported the following shareholders' equity at December 31 (adapted and in millions):

Ordinary share	$ 225
Additional paid-in capital	245
Retained earnings	2,149
Treasury share	(621)
Total shareholders' equity	$1,998

During the next year, Genius Marketing purchased treasury shares at a cost of $29 million and resold treasury shares for $8 million (this treasury share had cost Genius Marketing $2 million). Record the purchase and resale of Genius Marketing's treasury shares. Overall, how much did shareholders' equity increase or decrease as a result of the two treasury share transactions?

S9-11 (*Learning Objective 3: Purchasing treasury share to fight off a takeover of the corporation*)   Susan Smith Exports, Inc., is located in Birmingham, Alabama. Smith is the only company with reliable sources for its imported gifts. The company does a brisk business with specialty stores such as Bloomingdale's. Smith's recent success has made the company a prime target for a takeover. An investment group in Mobile is attempting to buy 52% of Smith's outstanding share against the wishes of Smith's board of directors. Board members are convinced that the Mobile investors would sell the most desirable pieces of the business and leave little of value.

At the most recent board meeting, several suggestions were advanced to fight off the hostile takeover bid. The suggestion with the most promise is to purchase a huge quantity of treasury shares. Smith has the cash to carry out this plan.

❙ Requirements

   1. Suppose you are a significant shareholder of Susan Smith Exports, Inc. Write a memorandum to explain to the board how the purchase of treasury shares would make it difficult for the Mobile group to take over Smith. Include in your memo a discussion of the effect that purchasing treasury shares would have on shares outstanding and on the size of the corporation.

2. Suppose Smith's management is successful in fighting off the takeover bid and later sells the treasury shares at prices greater than the purchase price. Explain what effect these sales will have on assets, shareholders' equity, and net income.

S9-12 (*Learning Objective 4: Accounting for cash dividends*) Greentea Corporation earned a net income of $95,000 during the year ended December 31, 2010. On December 15, Greentea declared the annual cash dividend on its 6% preference shares (11,000 shares with total par-value of $110,000) and a $1.00 per share cash dividend on its ordinary shares (45,000 shares with total par-value of $450,000). Greentea then paid the dividends on January 4, 2011.

Journalize for Greentea Corporation:

a. Declaring the cash dividends on December 15, 2010.
b. Paying the cash dividends on January 4, 2011.

Did Retained Earnings increase or decrease during 2010? By how much?

S9-13 (*Learning Objective 4: Dividing cash dividends between preference and ordinary share*) Access Garde, Inc., has 200,000 shares of $1.80 preference share outstanding in addition to its ordinary shares. The $1.80 designation means that the preference shareholders receive an annual cash dividend of $1.80 per share. In 2010, Access Garde declares an annual dividend of $500,000. The allocation to preference and ordinary shareholders is:

Preference dividend, (200,000 shares × $1.80 per share)	$360,000
Ordinary dividend (remainder: $500,000 – $360,000)	140,000
Total dividend	$500,000

Answer these questions about Access Garde's cash dividends.

1. How much in dividends must Access Garde declare each year before the ordinary shareholders receive any cash dividends for the year?
2. Suppose Access Garde, Inc., declares cash dividends of $400,000 for 2010. How much of the dividends goes to preference? How much goes to ordinary?
3. Is Access Garde's preference shares cumulative or non-cumulative? How can you tell?
4. Access Garde, Inc., passed the preference dividend in 2009 and 2010. Then in 2011, Access Garde declares cash dividends of $1,500,000. How much of the dividends goes to preference? How much goes to ordinary?

S9-14 (*Learning Objective 4: Recording a small share dividend*) Centerville Bancshares has 13,000 shares of $3 par ordinary shares outstanding. Suppose Centerville distributes a 15% shares dividend when the market value of its shares is $25 per share.

1. Journalize Centerville's distribution of the share dividend on May 11. An explanation is not required.
2. What was the overall effect of the share dividend on Centerville's total assets? On total liabilities? On total shareholders' equity?

S9-15 (*Learning Objective 5: Computing book value per share*) Fools Gold, Inc., has the following shareholders' equity:

Preference share, 4%, $5 par,	
33,000 shares authorized and issued	$ 195,000
Ordinary share, $2 par, 100,000 shares authorized	
63,000 shares issued	126,000
Additional paid-in capital	2,170,000
Retained earnings	1,700,000
Less treasury share, ordinary share (1,400 shares at cost)	(45,000)
Total shareholders' equity	$4,146,000

That company has passed its preference dividends for three years including the current year. Compute the book value per share of the company's ordinary shares.

S9-16 (*Learning Objective 6: Computing and explaining return on assets and return on equity*)   Give the formula for computing (a) rate of return on total assets (ROA) and (b) rate of return on ordinary shareholders' equity (ROE). Then answer these questions about the rate-of-return computations.

1. Why is interest expense added to net income in the computation of ROA?
2. Why are preference dividends subtracted from net income to compute ROE?

S9-17 (*Learning Objective 6: Computing return on assets and return on equity for a leading company*)   Godhi Corporation's 2010 financial statements reported the following items, with the 2009 figures given for comparison (adapted and in millions).

	2010	2009
Balance Sheet		
Total assets	¥10,624	¥9,515
Total liabilities	¥ 7,412	¥6,637
Total shareholders' equity (all ordinary)	3,212	2,878
Total liabilities and equity	¥10,624	¥9,515
Income Statement		
Revenues and other income	¥ 7,633	
Operating expense	7,286	
Interest expense	31	
Other expense	196	
Net income	¥ 120	

Compute Godhi's return on assets and return on ordinary equity for 2011. Evaluate the rates of return as strong or weak.

S9-18 (*Learning Objectives 1, 2, 5: Explaining the features of a corporation's shares*)   McGahan Corporation is conducting a special meeting of its board of directors to address some concerns raised by the shareholders. Shareholders have submitted the following questions. Answer each question.

1. Why are ordinary shares and retained earnings shown separately in the shareholders' equity section of the balance sheet?
2. Linda Leary, a McGahan shareholder, proposes to transfer some land she owns to the company in exchange for share of the company shares. How should McGahan Corporation determine the number of shares to issue for the land?
3. Preference shares generally are preference with respect to dividends and in the event of our liquidation. Why would investors buy our ordinary shares when preference shares are available?
4. What does the redemption value of our preference shares require us to do?
5. One of our shareholders owns 200 shares of McGahan share and someone has offered to buy her share for their book value. Our shareholder asks us the formula for computing the book value of her share.

S9-19 (*Learning Objective 7: Measuring cash flows from financing activities*)   During 2010, Dwyer Corporation earned net income of $5.8 billion and paid off $2.4 billion of long-term notes payable. Dwyer raised $1.1 billion by issuing ordinary shares, paid $3.5 billion to purchase treasury shares, and paid cash dividends of $1.6 billion. Report Dwyer's *cash flows from financing* activities on the statement of cash flows for 2010.

Exercises

All of the A and B exercises can be found within MyAccountingLab, an online homework and practice environment. Your instructor may ask you to complete these exercises using MyAccountingLab.

(Group A)

E9-20A *(Learning Objective 2: Issuing shares and reporting shareholders' equity)* Bread & Butter, Inc., is authorized to issue 120,000 shares of ordinary shares and 7,000 shares of preference shares. During its first year, the business completed the following share issuance transactions:

Jan 19	Issued 12,000 shares of $2.00 par ordinary shares for cash of $6.00 per share.
Apr 3	Issued 400 shares of $1.00 no-par preference shares for $54,000 cash.
11	Received inventory valued at $16,000 and equipment with market value of $9,500 for 3,700 shares of the $2.00 par ordinary share.

❙ Requirements

1. Journalize the transactions. Explanations are not required.
2. Prepare the shareholders' equity section of Bread & Butter's balance sheet. The ending balance of retained earnings is a deficit of $43,000.

E9-21A *(Learning Objective 2: Preparing shareholders' equity section of a balance sheet)* Army Navy Sporting Goods is authorized to issue 10,000 preference shares and 19,000 ordinary shares. During a two-month period, Army Navy completed these shares-issuance transactions:

Apr 23	Issued 1,700 shares of $1.50 par ordinary share for cash of $16.50 per share.
May 2	Issued 600 shares of $2.50, no-par preference share for $22,000 cash.
12	Received inventory valued at $19,000 and equipment with market value of $41,000 for 3,300 shares of the $1.50 par ordinary share.

❙ Requirement

1. Prepare the shareholders' equity section of the Army Navy Sporting Goods' balance sheet for the transactions given in this exercise. The Retained Earnings account currently has a balance of $45,000. Journal entries are not required.

E9-22A *(Learning Objective 2: Measuring the paid-in capital of a corporation)* Travel Publishing was recently organized. The company issued ordinary shares to an attorney who provided legal services worth $23,000 to help organize the corporation. Travel also issued ordinary shares to an inventor in exchange for his patent with a market value of $82,000. In addition, Travel received cash both for the issuance of 2,000 shares of its preference shares at

$120 per share and for the issuance of 22,000 of its ordinary shares at $1 per share. During the first year of operations, Travel earned a net income of $50,000 and declared a cash dividend of $29,000. Without making journal entries, determine the total paid-in capital created by these transactions.

E9-23A (*Learning Objectives 2, 3: Preparing shareholders' equity section of a balance sheet*) Patterson Software had the following selected account balances at December 31, 2010 (in thousands, except par-value per share).

Inventory..	$ 651	Ordinary share, $0.75 par	
Property, plant and		per share, 800 shares	
equipment, net	900	authorized, 320 shares	
Paid-in capital in excess of par	899	issued	$ 240
Treasury shares,		Retained earnings..............	2,220
100 shares at cost......................	1,150	Accounts receivable, net	1,000
Other shareholders' equity	(730)*	Notes payable	1,100

*Debit balance

Requirements

1. Prepare the shareholders' equity section of Patterson's balance sheet (in thousands).
2. How can Patterson have a larger balance of treasury shares than the sum of ordinary shares and Paid-in Capital in Excess of Par?

E9-24A (*Learning Objectives 2, 3: Recording treasury shares transactions and measuring their effects on shareholders' equity*) Journalize the following transactions of Aliant Productions:

Jan 17	Issued 2,200 shares of $2.50 par ordinary share at $10 per share.
May 23	Purchased 300 shares of treasury share at $12 per share.
Jul 11	Sold 200 shares of treasury share at $20 per share.

What was the overall effect of these transactions on Aliant's shareholders' equity?

E9-25A (*Learning Objectives 2, 3, 4: Recording share issuance, treasury share, and dividend transactions*) At December 31, 2010, Northeast Corporation reported the shareholders' equity accounts shown here (with dollar amounts in millions, except per share amounts).

Ordinary share $2.00 par value per share,	
2,100 million shares issued................	$ 4,200
Capital in excess of par value................	8,400
Retained earnings.................................	250
Treasury share, at cost	(70)
Total shareholders' equity................	$12,780

Northeast's 2011 transactions included the following:

  a. Net income, $446 million.
  b. Issuance of 8 million shares of ordinary share for $13.50 per share.
  c. Purchase of 2 million shares of treasury share for $16 million.
  d. Declaration and payment of cash dividends of $31 million.

I *Requirement*

1. Journalize Northeast's transactions in **b**, **c**, and **d**. Explanations are not required.

E9-26A *(Learning Objectives 2, 3, 4: Reporting shareholders' equity after a sequence of transactions)* Use the Northeast Corporation data in Exercise 9-25A to prepare the shareholders' equity section of the company's balance sheet at December 31, 2011.

E9-27A *(Learning Objectives 2, 3, 4, 5: Inferring transactions from a company's shareholders' equity)* Theta Products Company reported the following shareholders' equity on its balance sheet:

Shareholders' Equity (Dollars and shares in millions)	December 31, 2011	December 31, 2010
Convertible Preference share—$0.50 par value; authorized 30 shares; issued and outstanding: 2011 and 2010— 6 and 12 shares, respectively	$ 3	$ 6
Ordinary share —$2 per share par value; authorized 1,400 shares; issued: 2011 and 2010—300 and 200 shares, respectively	600	400
Additional paid-in capital	1,950	1,200
Retained earnings	6,270	5,066
Treasury share, ordinary share —at cost 2011—52 shares; 2010—12 shares	(1,144)	(228)
Total shareholders' equity	7,679	6,444
Total liabilities and shareholders' equity	$48,299	$45,294

I *Requirements*

1. What caused Theta's preference shares to decrease during 2011? Cite all possible causes.
2. What caused Theta's ordinary shares to increase during 2011? Identify all possible causes.
3. How many shares of Theta's ordinary shares were outstanding at December 31, 2011?
4. Theta's net income during 2011 was $1,380 million. How much were Theta's dividends during the year?
5. During 2011, Theta sold no treasury shares. What average price per share did Theta pay for the treasury shares the company purchased during the year?

E9-28A *(Learning Objective 4: Computing dividends on preference and ordinary share)* Huron Manufacturing, Inc., reported the following:

Shareholders' Equity	
Preference share, cumulative, $0.50 par, 9%, 40,000 shares issued....	$ 20,000
Ordinary share, $0.10 par, 9,170,000 shares issued	917,000

Huron Manufacturing has paid all preference dividends through 2007.

I *Requirement*

1. Compute the total amounts of dividends to both preference and ordinary shares for 2010 and 2011 if total dividends are $60,000 in 2010 and $120,000 in 2011.

E9-29A (*Learning Objective 4: Recording a share dividend and reporting shareholders' equity*)   The shareholders' equity for Heavenly Desserts Drive-Ins (HD) on December 31, 2010, is as follows:

Shareholders' Equity	
Ordinary share, $0.80 par, 2,600,000 shares authorized, 300,000 shares issued......................	$ 240,000
Paid-in capital in excess of par—ordinary..............	307,200
Retained earnings..	7,122,000
Other equity...	(200,000)
Total shareholders' equity.................................	$7,469,200

On May 11, 2011, the market price of HD's ordinary shares was $19 per share. Assume HD distributed a 15% share dividend on this date.

❚ Requirements

1. Journalize the distribution of the share dividend.
2. Prepare the shareholders' equity section of the balance sheet after the share dividend.
3. Why is the total shareholders' equity unchanged by the share dividend?
4. Suppose HD had a cash balance of $560,000 on May 12, 2011. What is the maximum amount of cash dividends HD can declare?

E9-30A (*Learning Objectives 2, 3, 4: Measuring the effects of share issuance, dividends, and treasury shares transactions*)   Identify the effects—both the direction and the dollar amount—of these assumed transactions on the total shareholders' equity of Athol Corporation. Each transaction is independent.

   a. Declaration of cash dividends of $78 million.
   b. Payment of the cash dividend in **a**.
   c. A 25% shares dividend. Before the dividend, 70 million shares of $2.00 par ordinary share were outstanding; the market value was $8.250 at the time of the dividend.
   d. Purchase of 1,900 shares of treasury shares (par-value $2.00) at $5.25 per share.
   e. Sale of 900 shares of the treasury shares for $7.00 per share. Cost of the treasury share was $5.25 per share.
   f. A 2-for-1 stock split. Prior to the split, 70 million shares of $2.00 par ordinary shares were outstanding.

E9-31A (*Learning Objective 4: Reporting shareholders' equity after a stock split*)   Clublink Corp. had the following shareholders' equity at October 31 (dollars in millions, except par-value per share):

Shareholders' Equity	
Ordinary share, $1.50 par, 750 million shares authorized, 420 million shares issued.................	$ 630
Additional paid-in capital...	318
Retained earnings..	2,399
Other equity...	(148)
Total shareholders' equity.................................	$3,199

On December 6, Clublink split its $1.50 par ordinary share 3-for-1.

❙ Requirement

1. Prepare the shareholders' equity section of the balance sheet immediately after the split.

E9-32A *(Learning Objective 5: Measuring the book value per share of ordinary share)*   The balance sheet of Luxury Rug Company reported the following:

Redeemable preference share, 4%, $60 par value,	
redemption value $45,000; outstanding 500 shares...............	$30,000
Ordinary shareholders' equity:	
6,000 shares issued and outstanding	66,000
Total shareholders' equity	$96,000

❙ Requirements

1. Compute the book value per share for an ordinary share, assuming all preference dividends are fully paid up (none in arrears).
2. Compute the book value per share of the ordinary shares, assuming that three years' cumulative preference dividends including the current year, are in arrears.
3. Luxury Rug's ordinary shares recently traded at a market price of $6.00 per share. Does this mean that Luxury Rug's shares are a good buy at $6.00?

E9-33A *(Learning Objective 6: Evaluating profitability)*   Luna Inns reported these figures for 2011 and 2010 (in millions):

	2011	2010
Balance sheet		
Total assets	$15,906	$13,700
Ordinary share and additional paid-in capital...............	44	390
Retained earnings	11,522	16,490
Other equity	(3,010)	(9,044)
Income statement		
Operating income	$ 4,023	$ 3,818
Interest expense	222	269
Net income	1,525	1,549

❙ Requirement

1. Compute Luna's return on assets and return on ordinary shareholders' equity for 2011. Do these rates of return suggest strength or weakness? Give your reason.

E9-34A *(Learning Objective 6: Evaluating profitability)*   Littleton Company included the following items in its financial statements for 2010, the current year (amounts in millions):

Payment of long-term debt..........	$17,060	Dividends paid	$ 230
Proceeds from issuance		Interest expense:	
of ordinary share.....................	8,500	Current year.....................	1,439
Total liabilities:		Preceding year.................	601
Current year-end....................	32,315	Net income:	
Preceding year-end	38,025	Current year.....................	1,878
Total shareholders' equity:		Preceding year.................	2,003
Current year-end....................	23,475	Operating income:	
Preceding year-end	14,033	Current year.....................	4,884
Borrowings..............................	6,580	Preceding year.................	4,006

❙ *Requirement*

1. Compute Littleton's return on assets and return on ordinary equity during 2010 (the current year). Littleton has no preference shares outstanding. Do the company's rates of return look strong or weak? Give your reason.

E9-35A *(Learning Objective 7: Reporting cash flows from financing activities)*   Use the Littleton Company data in Exercise E9-34A to show how the company reported cash flows from financing activities during 2010 (the current year). List items in descending order from largest to smallest dollar amount.

(Group B)

E9-36B *(Learning Objective 2: Issuing share and reporting shareholders' equity)*   Sweet & Sour, Inc., is authorized to issue 110,000 shares of ordinary shares and 5,000 shares of preference shares. During its first year, the business completed the following share issuance transactions:

Aug	19	Issued 15,000 shares of $3.50 par ordinary share for cash of $7.50 per share.
Nov	3	Issued 400 shares of $2.00 no-par preference share for $55,000 cash.
	11	Received inventory valued at $18,000 and equipment with market value of $10,500 for 4,000 shares of the $3.50 par ordinary share.

❙ *Requirements*

1. Journalize the transactions. Explanations are not required.
2. Prepare the shareholders' equity section of Sweet & Sour's balance sheet. The ending balance of retained earnings is a deficit of $47,000.

E9-37B *(Learning Objective 2:   Preparing shareholders' equity section of a balance sheet)*   Honcho Sporting Goods is authorized to issue 7,000 preference shares and 16,000 ordinary shares. During a two-month period, Honcho completed these share-issuance transactions:

Jun	23	Issued 1,500 shares of $2.00 par ordinary share for cash of $17.50 per share.
Jul	2	Issued 400 shares of $5.50, no-par preference share for $30,000 cash.
	12	Received inventory valued at $15,000 and equipment with market value of $44,000 for 3,700 shares of the $2.00 par ordinary share.

❙ *Requirement*

1. Prepare the shareholders' equity section of the Honcho Sporting Goods balance sheet for the transactions given in this exercise. The Retained Earnings account currently has a balance of $45,000. Journal entries are not required.

E9-38B *(Learning Objective 2: Measuring the paid-in capital of a corporation)*   Journey Publishing was recently organized. The company issued ordinary shares to an attorney who provided legal services worth $24,000 to help organize the corporation. Journey also issued ordinary shares to an inventor in exchange for his patent with a market value of $85,000. In addition, Journey received cash both for the issuance of 3,000 shares of its preference shares at $90 per share and for the issuance of 17,000 shares of its ordinary shares at $18 per share. During the first year of operations, Journey earned a net income of $65,000 and declared a cash dividend of $23,000. Without making journal entries, determine the total paid-in capital created by these transactions.

E9-39B (*Learning Objectives 2, 3: Shareholders' equity section of a balance sheet*)   Bukala Software had the following selected account balances at December 31, 2010 (in thousands, except par-value per share):

Inventory..	$ 705	Ordinary share, $0.50 par	
Property, plant and		per share, 900 shares	
equipment, net	903	authorized, 300 shares	
Paid-in capital in excess of par	897	issued	$ 150
Treasury share,		Retained earnings...............	2,270
140 shares at cost......................	1,610	Accounts receivable, net......	200
Other shareholders' equity	(726)*	Notes payable	1,166

*Debit balance

I Requirements

1. Prepare the shareholders' equity section of Bukala Software's balance sheet (in thousands).
2. How can Bukala have a larger balance of treasury shares than the sum of ordinary shares and Paid-in Capital in Excess of Par?

E9-40B (*Learning Objectives 2, 3: Recording treasury share transactions and measuring their effects on shareholders' equity*)   Journalize the following assumed transactions of Applebug Productions:

Mar 16	Issued 2,400 shares of $1.50 par ordinary share at $7 per share.
Apr 20	Purchased 800 shares of treasury share at $16 per share.
Aug 8	Sold 600 shares of treasury share at $17 per share.

What was the overall effect of these transactions on Applebug's shareholders' equity?

E9-41B (*Learning Objectives 2, 3, 4: Recording share issuance, treasury share, and dividend transactions*)   At December 31, 2010, Eastern Corporation reported the shareholders' equity accounts shown here (with dollar amounts in millions, except per share amounts).

Ordinary share $1.50 par value per share,	
1,700 million shares issued................	$ 2,550
Capital in excess of par value................	7,650
Retained earnings.................................	260
Treasury share, at cost	(10)
Total shareholders' equity................	$10,450

E9-47B (*Learning Objective 4: Reporting shareholders' equity after a stock split*) Griffin Corp. had the following shareholders' equity at March 31 (dollars in millions, except par-value per share):

Shareholders' Equity	
Ordinary share, $0.30 par, 500 million shares authorized, 450 million shares issued	$ 135
Additional paid-in capital	315
Retained earnings	2,393
Other equity	(146)
Total shareholders' equity	$2,697

On May 3, Griffin split its $0.30 par ordinary share 3-for-1.

I *Requirement*

1. Prepare the shareholders' equity section of the balance sheet immediately after the split.

E9-48B (*Learning Objective 5: Measuring the book value per share of ordinary share*) The balance sheet of Eclectic Rug Company reported the following:

Redeemable preference share, 10%, $30 par value, redemption value $25,000; outstanding 700 shares	$ 21,000
Ordinary shareholders' equity:	
10,000 shares issued and outstanding	100,000
Total shareholders' equity	$121,000

I *Requirements*

1. Compute the book value per share for the ordinary shares, assuming all preference dividends are fully paid up (none in arrears).
2. Compute the book value per share of the ordinary shares, assuming that three years' cumulative preference dividends, including the current year, are in arrears.
3. Eclectic Rug's ordinary shares recently traded at a market price of $7.10 per share. Does this mean that Eclectic Rug's shares are a good buy at $7.10?

E9-49B (*Learning Objective 6: Evaluating profitability*) LaSalle Inns reported these figures for 2011 and 2010 (in millions):

	2011	2010
Balance sheet		
Total assets	$16,000	$13,790
Ordinary share and additional paid-in capital	38	384
Retained earnings	11,528	16,530
Other equity	(2,962)	(9,112)
Income statement		
Operating income	$ 4,022	$ 3,815
Interest expense	219	273
Net income	1,530	1,544

I *Requirement*

1. Compute LaSalle's return on assets and return on ordinary shareholders' equity for 2011. Do these rates of return suggest strength or weakness? Give your reason.

E9-50B *(Learning Objective 6: Evaluating profitability)* Lawrence Company included the following items in its financial statements for 2010, the current year (amounts in millions):

Payment of long-term debt..........	$17,100	Dividends paid.....................	$ 215
Proceeds from issuance		Interest expense:	
of ordinary share....................	8,495	Current year....................	1,443
Total liabilities:		Preceding year................	603
Current year-end....................	32,315	Net income:	
Preceding year-end.................	38,031	Current year....................	1,872
Total shareholders' equity:		Preceding year................	1,993
Current year-end....................	23,477	Operating income:	
Preceding year-end.................	14,043	Current year....................	4,876
Borrowings...........................	6,590	Preceding year................	3,996

I *Requirement*

1. Compute Lawrence's return on assets and return on ordinary equity during 2010 (the current year). Lawrence has no preference shares outstanding. Do the company's rates of return look strong or weak? Give your reason.

E9-51B *(Learning Objective 7: Reporting cash flows from financing activities)* Use the Lawrence data in Exercise E9-50B to show how the company reported cash flows from financing activities during 2010 (the current year). List items in descending order from largest to smallest dollar amount.

Challenge Exercises

E9-52 *(Learning Objectives 2, 3, 4: Reconstructing transactions from the financial statements)* D-4 Networking Solutions began operations on January 1, 2010, and immediately issued its shares, receiving cash. D-4's balance sheet at December 31, 2010, reported the following shareholders' equity:

Ordinary share, $1 par.....................	$ 51,000
Additional paid-in capital.................	102,000
Retained earnings.............................	35,000
Treasury share, 850 shares...............	(7,650)
Total shareholders' equity............	$180,350

During 2010, D-4

a. Issued shares for $3 per share.
b. Purchased 950 shares of treasury shares, paying $9 per share.
c. Resold some of the treasury shares.
d. Earned net income of $58,000 and declared and paid cash dividends. Revenues were $172,000 and expenses totaled $114,000.

I *Requirement*

1. Journalize all of D-4's shareholders' equity transactions during the year. D-4's entry to close net income to Retained Earnings was:

Revenues	172,000	
Expenses		114,000
Retained Earnings		58,000

Use the following information for Questions Q9-62 to Q9-64:

These account balances at December 31 relate to Sportworld, Inc.:

Accounts Payable	$ 51,500	Paid-in Capital in Excess	
Accounts Receivable	81,550	of Par—Ordinary Share	$220,000
Ordinary Share	317,000	Preference share, 10%, $100 Par	85,000
Treasury Share	5,200	Retained Earnings	71,300
Bonds Payable	3,800	Notes Receivable	12,100

Q9-62 What is total paid-in capital for Sportworld, Inc.?

a. $634,445
b. $622,000
c. $641,345

d. $693,300
e. None of the above

Q9-63 What is total shareholders' equity for Sportworld, Inc.?

a. $688,100
b. $641,345
c. $693,300

d. $698,500
e. None of the above

Q9-64 Sportworld's net income for the period is $119,100 and beginning ordinary shareholders' equity is $681,500. Calculate Sportworld's return on ordinary shareholders' equity.

a. 17.2%
b. 16.4%

c. 18.2%
d. 19.3%

Q9-65 A company paid $24 per share to purchase 600 shares of its ordinary shares as treasury shares. The shares were originally issued at $16 per share. The journal entry to record the purchase of the treasury shares is:

a.	Treasury Shares	14,400	
	Cash		14,400
b.	Treasury Shares	9,600	
	Retained Earnings	4,800	
	Cash		14,400
c.	Treasury Shares	7,200	
	Paid-in Capital in Excess of Par	7,200	
	Cash		14,400
d.	Ordinary Shares	14,000	
	Cash		14,000

Q9-66 When treasury shares are sold for less than its cost, the entry should include a debit to:

a. Paid-in Capital in Excess of Par.
b. Retained Earnings.

c. Gain on Sale of Treasury Shares.
d. Loss on Sale of Treasury Shares.

Q9-67 A company purchased 100 shares of its ordinary shares at $50 per share. It then sells 35 of the treasury shares at $56 per share. The entry to sell the treasury shares includes a

a. credit to Paid-in Capital, Treasury Shares for $210.
b. debit to Retained Earnings for $210.
c. credit to Retained Earnings for $600.
d. credit to Treasury Shares for $1,960.
e. credit to Cash for $1,960.

Q9-68 Shareholders are eligible for a dividend if they own the share on the date of

a. record.

c. declaration.

b. issuance.

d. payment.

Q9-69 Luca's Foods has outstanding 600 shares of 7% preference shares, $100 par-value, and 1,600 shares of ordinary shares, $30 par-value. Luca's declares dividends of $15,800. The correct entry is:

a.	Dividends Payable, Preference	4,200	
	Dividends Payable, Ordinary	11,600	
	Cash		15,800
b.	Dividends Expense	15,800	
	Cash		15,800
c.	Retained Earnings	15,800	
	Dividends Payable, Preference		4,200
	Dividends Payable, Ordinary		11,600
d.	Retained Earnings	15,800	
	Dividends Payable, Preference		7,900
	Dividends Payable, Ordinary		7,900

Q9-70 A corporation has 40,000 shares of 10% preference share outstanding. Also, there are 40,000 shares of ordinary share outstanding. Par value for each is $100. If a $500,000 dividend is paid, how much goes to the preference shareholders?

a. None

d. $380,000

b. $400,000

e. $500,000

c. $50,000

Q9-71 Assume the same facts as in question 70. What is the amount of dividends per share on ordinary share?

a. $1.00

d. $12.50

b. $5.50

e. None of these

c. $2.50

Q9-72 Which of the following is *not* true about a 10% share dividend?

a. The market value of the share is needed to record the share dividend.

b. Total shareholders' equity remains the same.

c. Paid-in Capital increases.

d. Retained Earnings decreases.

e. Par value decreases.

Q9-73 A company declares a 5% share dividend. The debit to Retained Earnings is an amount equal to

a. the excess of the market price over the original issue price of the shares to be issued.

b. the market value of the shares to be issued.

c. the par-value of the shares to be issued.

d. the book value of the shares to be issued.

Q9-74 Which of the following statements is *not* true about a 3-for-1 stock split?

a. The market price of each share will decrease.

b. Total shareholders' equity increases.

c. A shareholder with 10 shares before the split owns 30 shares after the split.

d. Par value is reduced to one-third of what it was before the split.

e. Retained Earnings remains the same.

P9-80A *(Learning Objectives 2, 3, 4: Accounting for shares issuance, dividends, and treasury shares)* Moscow Jewelry Company reported the following summarized balance sheet at December 31, 2010:

Assets	
Current assets...	$ 33,600
Property and equipment, net	74,000
Total assets...	$107,600
Liabilities and Equity	
Liabilities	$ 37,300
Shareholders' equity:	
$0.70 cumulative preference share, $5 par, 300 shares issued ...	1,500
Ordinary share, $4 par, 6,500 shares issued........................	26,000
Paid-in capital in excess of par	17,800
Retained earnings..	25,000
Total liabilities and equity...	$107,600

During 2011, Moscow completed these transactions that affected shareholders' equity:

Feb	13	Issued 5,400 ordinary shares for $5 per share.
Jun	7	Declared the regular cash dividend on the preference share.
	24	Paid the cash dividend.
Aug	9	Distributed a 10% share dividend on the ordinary share. Market price of the ordinary share was $6 per share.
Oct	26	Reacquired 500 shares of ordinary share as treasury share, paying $7 per share.
Nov	20	Sold 200 shares of the treasury shares for $11 per share.

❚ Requirements

1. Journalize Moscow's transactions. Explanations are not required.
2. Report Moscow's shareholders' equity at December 31, 2011. Net income for 2011 was $28,000.

P9-81A *(Learning Objectives 3, 4: Measuring the effects of dividend and treasury share transactions on a company)* Assume Dessert Destination of Montana, Inc., completed the following transactions during 2010, the company's 10th year of operations:

Feb	3	Issued 15,000 ordinary shares ($1.00 par) for cash of $435,000.
Mar	19	Purchased 2,600 shares of the company's own ordinary share at $24 per share.
Apr	24	Sold 1,300 shares of treasury share – ordinary for $32 per share.
Aug	15	Declared a cash dividend on the 18,000 shares of $0.40 no-par preference shares.
Sep	1	Paid the cash dividends.
Nov	22	Distributed a 8% share dividend on the 92,000 shares of $1.00 par ordinary share outstanding. The market value of the ordinary share was $26 per share.

▌ Requirement

1. Analyze each transaction in terms of its effect on the accounting equation of Dessert Destination of Montana, Inc.

P9-82A *(Learning Objectives 3, 6: Preparing a corporation's balance sheet; measuring profitability)* The following accounts and related balances of Seagull Designers, Inc., as of December 31, 2010, are arranged in no particular order.

Cash...	$55,000	Interest expense..........................	$ 15,600
Accounts receivable, net................	34,000	Property, plant and	
Paid-in capital in excess		equipment, net	364,000
of par—ordinary........................	20,000	Ordinary share, $2 par,	
Accrued liabilities..........................	24,000	600,000 shares authorized,	
Long-term note payable	99,000	116,000 shares issued.............	232,000
Inventory......................................	93,000	Prepaid expenses	13,000
Dividends payable.........................	6,000	Ordinary shareholders'	
Retained earnings..........................	?	equity, December 31, 2009	222,000
Accounts payable	136,000	Net income.................................	32,000
Trademarks, net.............................	4,000	Total assets,	
Preference share, $0.50,		December 31, 2009................	493,000
no-par, 11,000 shares		Treasury share,	
authorized and issued................	29,700	21,000 shares at cost.............	24,000
Goodwill......................................	13,000		

▌ Requirements

1. Prepare Seagull's classified balance sheet in the account format at December 31, 2010.
2. Compute rate of return on total assets and rate of return on ordinary shareholders' equity for the year ended December 31, 2010.
3. Do these rates of return suggest strength or weakness? Give your reason.

P9-83A *(Learning Objective 7: Analyzing the statement of cash flows)* The statement of cash flows of Frappe, Inc., reported the following (adapted) for the year ended December 31, 2010:

Cash flows from financing activities (amounts in millions)	
Cash dividends paid	$(1,890)
Issuance of ordinary shares at par value.................................	1,234
Proceeds from issuance of long-term notes payable...............	58
Purchases of treasury share	(3,080)
Payments of long-term notes payable.....................................	(162)

▌ Requirement

1. Make the journal entry that Frappe would use to record each of these transactions.

(Group B)

P9-84B *(Learning Objective 2: Recording corporate transactions and preparing the shareholders' equity section of the balance sheet)* The partners who own Liard Canoes Co. wished to avoid the unlimited personal liability of the partnership form of

During 2011, London completed these transactions that affected shareholders' equity:

Feb	13	Issued 5,200 ordinary shares for $6 per share.
Jun	7	Declared the regular cash dividend on the preference share.
	24	Paid the cash dividend.
Aug	9	Distributed a 20% share dividend on the ordinary share. Market price of the ordinary share was $7 per share.
Oct	26	Reacquired 900 ordinary shares as treasury shares, paying $8 per share.
Nov	20	Sold 600 shares of the treasury shares for $12 per share.

❙ Requirements

1. Journalize London's transactions. Explanations are not required.
2. Report London's shareholders' equity at December 31, 2011. Net income for 2011 was $25,000.

P9-89B (*Learning Objectives 3, 4: Measuring the effects of dividend and treasury share transactions on a company*)   Assume Cookie Corner of Wisconsin, Inc., completed the following transactions during 2010, the company's 10th year of operations:

Feb	4	Issued 14,000 shares ($1.00 par) for cash of $350,000.
Mar	20	Purchased 2,200 shares of the company's own ordinary share at $21 per share.
Apr	25	Sold 900 shares of treasury shares—ordinary for $30 per share.
Aug	17	Declared a cash dividend on the 14,000 shares of $0.80 no-par preference shares.
Sep	4	Paid the cash dividends.
Nov	28	Distributed a 5% share dividend on the 99,000 shares of $1.00 par ordinary share outstanding. The market value of the ordinary share was $22 per share.

❙ Requirement

1. Analyze each transaction in terms of its effect on the accounting equation of Cookie Corner of Wisconsin, Inc.

P9-90B (*Learning Objectives 3, 6: Preparing a corporation's balance sheet; measuring profitability*)   The following accounts and related balances of Hawk Designers, Inc., as of December 31, 2010, are arranged in no particular order.

Cash	$43,000	Interest expense	$ 16,000
Accounts receivable, net	22,000	Property, plant and	
Paid-in capital in excess		equipment, net	359,000
of par—ordinary	17,000	Ordinary share, $2 par,	
Accrued liabilities	27,000	300,000 shares authorized,	
Long-term note payable	96,000	117,000 shares issued	234,000
Inventory	94,000	Prepaid expenses	16,000
Dividends payable	12,000	Ordinary shareholders'	
Retained earnings	?	equity, December 31, 2009	225,000
Accounts payable	133,000	Net income	30,000
Trademarks, net	10,000	Total assets,	
Preference share, $.50,		December 31, 2009	496,000
no-par, 12,000 shares		Treasury share, ordinary,	
authorized and issued	32,400	19,000 shares at cost	22,000
Goodwill	11,000		

Requirements

1. Prepare Hawk's classified balance sheet in the account format at December 31, 2010.
2. Compute rate of return on total assets and rate of return on ordinary shareholders' equity for the year ended December 31, 2010.
3. Do these rates of return suggest strength or weakness? Give your reason.

P9-91B *(Learning Objective 7: Analyzing the statement of cash flows)*   The statement of cash flows of Smoothie, Inc., reported the following (adapted) for the year ended December 31, 2010:

Cash flows from financing activities (amounts in millions)	
Cash dividends paid	$(1,890)
Issuance of ordinary shares at par value	1,234
Proceeds from issuance of long-term notes payable	58
Purchases of treasury share	(3,080)
Payments of long-term notes payable	(162)

Requirement

1. Make the journal entry that Smoothie would use to record each of these transactions.

APPLY YOUR KNOWLEDGE

Decision Cases

Case 1. *(Learning Objective 2: Evaluating alternative ways of raising capital)* Nate Smith and Darla Jones have written a computer program for a video game that may rival Playstation and Xbox. They need additional capital to market the product, and they plan to incorporate their business. Smith and Jones are considering alternative capital structures for the corporation. Their primary goal is to raise as much capital as possible without giving up control of the business. Smith and Jones plan to receive 50,000 of the corporation's ordinary shares in return for the net assets of their old business. After the old company's books are closed and the assets adjusted to current market value, Smith's and Jones' capital balances will each be $25,000.

writing assignment ■

The corporation's plans for a constitution include an authorization to issue 10,000 preference shares and 500,000 shares of $1 par ordinary shares. Smith and Jones are uncertain about the most desirable features for the preference shares. Prior to incorporating, Smith and Jones are discussing their plans with two investment groups. The corporation can obtain capital from outside investors under either of the following plans:

- *Plan 1.* Group 1 will invest $80,000 to acquire 800 shares of 6%, $100 par nonvoting, preference shares.
- *Plan 2.* Group 2 will invest $55,000 to acquire 500 shares of $5, no-par preference shares and $35,000 to acquire 35,000 ordinary shares. Each preference share receives 50 votes on matters that come before the shareholders.

Requirements

Assume that the business is now incorporated.

1. Journalize the issuance of ordinary shares to Smith and Jones. Debit each person's capital account for its balance.
2. Journalize the issuance of shares to the outsiders under both plans.
3. Assume that net income for the first year is $120,000 and total dividends are $30,000. Prepare the shareholders' equity section of the corporation's balance sheet under both plans.
4. Recommend one of the plans to Smith and Jones. Give your reasons. (Challenge)

2. Refer to the Consolidated Balance Sheets and the Consolidated Statements of Changes in Equity. (Note: The Statement of Changes in Equity is discussed in detail in Chapter 11.) How many shares of treasury shares did the company purchase during the year ended December 31, 2008? How much did it pay for it in total? How much per share?

3. Examine Nokia's consolidated statement of shareholders' equity. Analyze the change that occurred in the company's Retained Earnings account during the year ended December 31, 2008. Can you link the changes to any of its other financial statements?

4. Create the T-account for Nokia's Retained Earnings and show the beginning and ending balances, as well as all related activity for the year ended 31 December 2008. Journalize the transactions relating to profit, dividends and the cancellation of treasury shares.

5. Compute Nokia's return on equity and return on assets for 2008. Which is larger? Is this a sign of financial strength or weakness? Explain.

Group Project in Ethics

The global economic recession that started in 2007 has impacted every business, but it was especially hard on banks, automobile manufacturing, and retail companies. Banks were largely responsible for the recession. Some of the biggest banks made excessively risky investments collateralized by real estate mortgages, and many of these investments soured when the real estate markets collapsed. When banks had to write these investments down to market values, the regulatory authorities notified them that they had inadequate capital ratios on their balance sheets to operate. Banks stopped loaning money. Because shares prices were depressed, companies could not raise capital by selling shares. With both debt and shares financing frozen, many businesses had to close their doors.

Fearing collapse of the whole economy, the central governments of the United States and several European nations loaned money to banks to prop up their capital ratios and keep them open. The government also loaned massive amounts to the largest insurance company in the United States (AIG), as well as to General Motors and Chrysler, to help them stay in business. When asked why, many in government replied "these businesses were too important to fail." In several cases, the U.S. government has taken an "equity stake" in some banks and businesses by taking preference shares in exchange for the cash infusion.

Because of the recession, corporate downsizing has occurred on a massive scale throughout the world. While companies in the retail sector provide more jobs than the banking and automobile industry combined, the government has not chosen to "bail out" any retail businesses. Each company or industry mentioned in this book has pared down plant and equipment, laid off employees, or restructured operations. Some companies have been forced out of business altogether.

writing assignment ■

I *Requirements*

1. Identify all the stakeholders of a corporation. A *stakeholder* is a person or a group who has an interest (that is, a stake) in the success of the organization.

2. Do you believe that some entities are "too important to fail?" Should a federal government help certain businesses to stay afloat during economic recessions, and allow others to fail?

3. Identify several measures by which a company may be considered deficient and in need of downsizing. How can downsizing help to solve this problem?

4. Debate the bailout issue. One group of students takes the perspective of the company and its shareholders, and another group of students takes the perspective of the other stakeholders of the company (the community in which the company operates and society at large).

5. What is the problem with the government taking an equity position such as preference shares in a private enterprise?

For online homework, exercises, and problems that provide you with immediate feedback, please visit www.myaccountinglab.com.

Quick Check Answers

1. *a* (20,000 shares × $25 = $500,000)
2. *c* ($600,000/$5 par = 120,000 shares)
3. *d* ($375,000 + $60,000 + $600,000)
4. *d* ($375,000 + $60,000 + $600,000 + $325,000)
5. *c* ($1,360,000 − $10,000)
6. *d* [No gain or loss (for the income statement) on treasury shares transactions]
7. *a*
8. *b*
9. *d*
10. *c*
11. *d* [First, annual preference dividend = $1,250 (2,500 × $25 × 0.02)]. Five years of preference dividends must be paid (four in arrears plus the current year).
    [($1,250 × 5) + ($125,000 × $2.50 per share ordinary dividend) = $318,750]
12. *a*
13. *c*
14. *c*
15. *d*
16. *c*

10

Long-Term Investments & International Operations

SPOTLIGHT: Vivendi

What do Activision Blizzard (producer of games such as World of Warcraft, Guitar Hero, Diablo and Call of Duty), Universal Music (with artists such as U2, Lady Gaga, Black-Eyed Peas), SFT, Maroc Telecom and GBVT (leading telecommunication companies in Europe, Morocco and Brazil, respectively), Canal+ (Pay TV with over 10 million subscribers) and NBC Universal (with popular TV series such as Heroes, movies from Universal Pictures and Universal Studios theme parks) have in common? They are all related companies! **Vivendi** is either an owner of, or investor in, all these companies. You'll also learn how companies like Vivendi do business across international borders, and the impact that business has on their financial statements.

Vivendi
Consolidated Balance Sheet (Partial, adapted)
As at December 31

(in millions € Euros)	2009	2008
1 Current assets:		
2 Short-term financial assets	€ 464	€ 287
3 Non-current assets:		
4 Investment in equity affiliates......................	4,146	4,441
5 Non-current financial assets.......................	476	709
6 Sub-total investment related accounts	5,086	5,437
7 Total assets..	€58,125	€56,497

Vivendi
Company Balance Sheet (Partial, adapted)
As at December 31

(in millions € Euros)	2009	2008
8 Current assets: Marketable securities	€ 210	€ 75
9 Non-current assets: Long-term investments....	38,151	39,033
10 Sub-total investment related accounts	38,361	39,108
11 Total assets...	€42,166	€41,920

You might still be wondering how all those companies are related to Vivendi. This is why inter-corporate investments is an important element in your study of accounting. It is a challenging topic, but all the companies you have seen so far, from **Carrefour**, **Nestlé** to **Lenovo** have subsidiaries and investments in other companies. The first of the two balance sheets above are investment-related accounts for the Vivendi group. As you can see, Vivendi has some short-term financial assets, investment in equity affiliates and non-current financial assets, totaling about €5.1 billion (line 6), out of total assets of €58.1 billion (line 7). How could this relatively small amount of investments be the connecting factors of all the businesses of Vivendi?

Financial performance and financial position of all the companies in a group are consolidated at a group level. The consolidated balance sheet is what the Vivendi group collectively has in terms of investments and will not show the investments in its own subsidiaries. The second balance sheet extract is for the "parent" entity only. You can see that the parent entity's overwhelming majority of its €42.2 billion total assets (line 11) are in the form of "long-term investments" of about €38.4 billion (line 9). This is the account that connects all the Vivendi subsidiaries.

One of your learning goals should be to develop the ability to analyze whatever you encounter in real-company statements. This chapter will help you advance toward that goal. The first half of this chapter shows how to account for long-term investments, including a brief overview of consolidated financial statements. The second half of the chapter covers accounting for international operations.

LEARNING OBJECTIVES

1 **Account** for available-for-sale investments

2 **Use** the equity method for investments

3 **Understand** consolidated financial statements

4 **Account** for long-term investments in bonds

5 **Account** for international operations

6 **Report** investing transactions on the statement of cash flows

SHARE INVESTMENTS: AN OVERVIEW

Investments come in all sizes and shapes—from a few shares to a controlling interest in multiple companies. In earlier chapters, we discussed shares and bonds from the perspective of the company that issued the securities. In this chapter, we examine *long-term* investments.

To consider investments, we need to define two key terms. The entity that owns the shares of a corporation is the investor. The corporation that issued the shares is the investee. If you own Vivendi shares, you are an investor and Vivendi is the investee. Similarly, a company may also own shares of another company. Vivendi, for example, owns 100% of **Universal Music Group** and **Canal**, over half of **Activision Blizzard** and **SFR**, and 20% of **NBC Universal**.

EXHIBIT 10-1 | **Vivendi and its Major Subsidiaries**

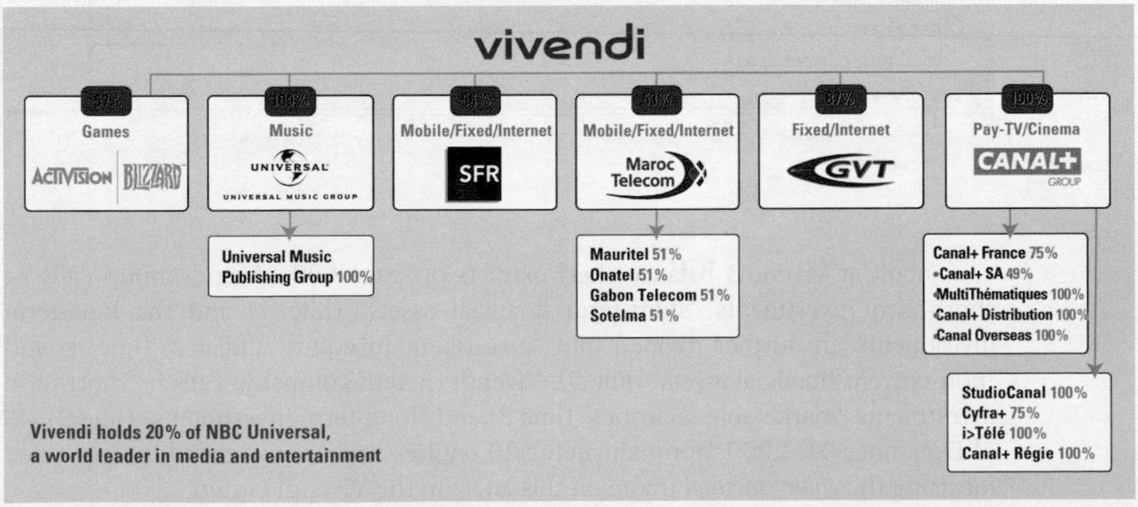

Source: http://www.vivendi.com/vivendi/Simplified-Organisation-Chart

You can log onto the Internet to learn Vivendi's current share price. Some companies provide share information directly on their website, but for some others, you may have to visit the actual stock exchange where the company is listed to see "live" prices. For Vivendi, you can visit http://www.vivendi.com/vivendi/Share-price and check out its share price information and charts.

Reporting Investments on the Balance Sheet

An investment is an asset to the investor. The investment may be short-term or long-term. **Short-term investments** in marketable securities are current assets. They can be classified as either *trading*, *held-to-maturity*, or *available for sale*, depending on management's intent and ability to hold them until they mature. We saw how to account for short-term investments in Chapter 5.

Investments that aren't short-term are listed as **long-term investments**, a category of non-current assets. Long-term investments include shares and bonds that the investor expects to hold for longer than one year. Exhibit 10-2 below shows where short-term and long-term investments typically appear on the balance sheet.

EXHIBIT 10-2 | **Reporting Investments on the Balance Sheet**

Current Assets:		
Cash	$X	
Short-term investments	X	
Account receivables	X	
Inventories	X	
Prepaid expenses	X	
Total current assets		X
Non-current Assets:		
Long-term investments [or simply Investments]	X	
Property, plant and equipment	X	
Intangible assets	X	
Other assets	X	
Total non-current assets		X
Total Assets		X

Look at Vivendi's balance sheet extracts on page 608. Vivendi group calls its short-term investments "short-term financial assets" (line 2) and the long-term investments are further divided into "investment in equity affiliates" (line 4) and "non-current financial assets" (line 5). Vivendi (parent company) calls its short-term investments "marketable securities" (line 8) and "long-term investments" (line 9). As of December 31, 2009, approximately 520 entities were consolidated or accounted for using the *equity method* (more on this later) in the Vivendi Group.

The accounting rules for long-term investments in shares usually depends on the percentage of ownership by the investor. The accounting methods and relevant accounting standards typically used are shown in Exhibit 10-3. We have already covered short-term investments (trading, held-to-maturity) in Chapter 5.

EXHIBIT 10-3 | Typical Accounting Methods for Long-Term Investments Based on Level of Ownership

Percentage Ownership by the Investor	Accounting Treatment	IFRS
Up to 20% (when classified Available-for-Sale)	Fair Market Value	IAS39
Up to 20% (when classified as Held-to-Maturity)	Amortized Cost	IAS39
Between 20–50%	Equity Method	IAS28
Greater than 50%	Consolidation	IAS27

TECHNICAL UPDATE

Percentage of ownership is a good indicator of the accounting treatment above, but the underlying principle is more important than the actual percentage of ownership. *IAS28 – Investment in Associates* states that the equity method is to be used when an entity has "significant influence" over its investee. Significant influence is the power to participate in the financial and operating policy decisions of the investee but is not in control or joint control over those policies. While this usually exists when the shareholding exceeds 20%, it is not always the case.

Similarly, consolidation is usually performed when an entity holds more than 50% of an investee. *IAS27 – Consolidated and Separate Financial Statements* states that the primary determinant of whether an entity is consolidated or not is the existence of "control". Control is the power to govern the financial and operating policies of an investee so as to obtain benefits from its activities. For example, even if share holding is below 50%, but if an entity is able to elect a majority of the members of the investee's board of directors and thus control the investee, the investee is still considered a subsidiary and will be consolidated.

IASB is in the process of rewriting *IAS39*. This is expected to be completed in three stages. The new *IFRS9 – Financial Instruments* (stage one of the *IAS39* rewrite) was issued in November 2009 and will only be mandatorily effective in 2013, but early adaptation is permitted. The new *IFRS9*, when effective in your jurisdiction, will change some of the accounting treatment discussed in this chapter.

An investment of up to 20% may be classified as available-for-sale if it does not fit in the other categories outlined in Chapter 5. Available-for-sale investments are usually shown as non-current or long-term assets because the entity intends on making them available for sale in periods beyond the end of the fiscal year. Held-to-maturity investments are accounted for using amortized cost (p. 626). It is classified non-current when the maturity date is beyond the next financial year. In general, investments below 20% are called "passive investments" because the investor does not play an active role or exert much influence on the investee.

On the other hand, ownership between 20% and 50% provides the investor with the opportunity to significantly influence the investee's operating decisions and policies over the long run. These investees are usually called "associates" or "equity affiliates". An investment above 50% allows the investor a great deal of long-term influence and control over the investee company, and these investees are said to be "subsidiaries" of the parent company. Let's see how these methods apply to long-term investments in shares.

AVAILABLE-FOR-SALE INVESTMENTS

Available-for-sale investments are share investments other than trading securities. They are classified as current assets if the business expects to sell them within the next year. All other available-for-sale investments are classified as long term.

Accounting for Available-for-Sale Investments

Available-for-sale investments are accounted for at fair market value because the company expects to sell the investment at its market price. *Cost* is used only as the initial amount for recording the investments. These investments are reported on the balance sheet at current **fair market values**. Let's see what Vivendi says in its accounting policies on available-for-sale investments. Note 1.3.5.8 of Vivendi's 2009 annual report states:

EXCERPTS (ADAPTED) FROM VIVENDI'S NOTES TO THE 2009 FINANCIAL STATEMENTS

Available-for-sale securities consist of unconsolidated interests and other securities not qualifying for classification in the other financial asset categories... Unrealized gains and losses on available-for-sale securities are recognized in equity until the financial asset is sold... at which time the accumulated gain or loss previously reported in equity is expensed in other financial charges and income.

Suppose Vivendi purchases 1,000 **Siemens** shares at the market price of €44.00 per share. Vivendi intends to hold this investment for longer than a year and decides to treat it as an available-for-sale investment. Vivendi's entry to record the investment is:

2010			
Oct 23	Long-Term Investment (1,000 × €44)	44,000	
	Cash		44,000
	Purchased investment.		

Assets	=	Liabilities	+	Shareholders' Equity
+ 44,000	=	0	+	0
− 44,000				

Assume that Vivendi receives a €0.20 cash dividend on the Siemens shares. Vivendi's entry to record receipt of the dividend is:

2010			
Nov 14	Cash (1,000 × €0.20)	200	
	Dividend Income		200
	Received cash dividend.		

Assets	=	Liabilities	+	Shareholders' Equity	
+200	=	0	+	+200	(Dividend income)

Receipt of a *share dividend* (or stock dividend) is different from receipt of a cash dividend. For a share dividend, the investor records no dividend income. Instead, the investor makes a memorandum entry in the accounting records to denote the new number of shares held as an investment. Because the number of shares held has increased, the investor's cost per share decreases. To illustrate, suppose Vivendi receives a 10%-share dividend from Siemens. Vivendi would receive 100 shares (10% of 1,000 shares previously held) and make this memorandum entry in its accounting records:

> **MEMORANDUM–Receipt of share dividend: Received 100 shares of Siemens share capital in 10% share dividend. New cost per share is €40.00 (cost of €44,000 ÷ 1,000 shares).**

In all future transactions affecting this investment, Vivendi's cost per share is now €40.00.

Which Value of an Investment Is Most Relevant?

IAS39 – Financial Instruments: Recognition and Measurement requires that financial assets categorized as available-for-sale to be measured at fair value on the balance sheet, with the with value changes recognized in other comprehensive income. Like many other assets, available for sale investments are also subject to impairment testing (*IAS36*). If fair value of an available-for-sale asset cannot be measured reliably, the investment is then carried at cost.

Fair market value is the amount that a seller would receive on the sale of an investment to a willing purchaser on a given date. Because of the relevance of fair market values for decision making, available-for-sale investments in shares are usually reported on the balance sheet at their fair market values. On the balance-sheet date we therefore adjust available-for-sale investments from their last carrying amount to current fair market value. Assume that the fair market value of the Siemens ordinary shares is €46,500 on December 31, 2010. Remember that Vivendi bought these shares for €44,000 on October 23, 2010. In this case, Vivendi makes the following entry to bring the investment to fair market value.

2010			
Dec 31	Market Value Adjustments (€46,500 − €44,000)	2,500	
	Unrealized Gain on Investment		2,500
	Adjusted investment to fair market value.		

The increase in the investment's fair market value creates additional equity for the investor.

Assets	=	Liabilities	+	Shareholders' Equity	
+ 2,500	=	0	+	+ 2,500	(through other comprehensive income)

The Market Value Adjustment (MVA) account is a companion account to Long-Term Investment. This account can also be called Fair Value Adjustments or other titles of similar nature. In this case, the investment's cost (€44,000) plus the Adjustment (€2,500) equals the investment fair market value carrying amount (€46,500), as follows:

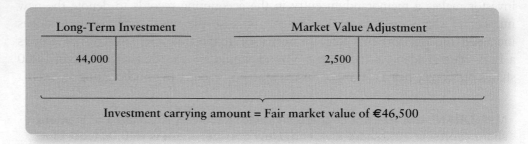

Here the Adjustment account has a debit balance because the fair market value of the investment increased. If the investment's fair market value declines, the Adjustment is credited. In that case the carrying amount is its cost minus the Adjustment.

The other side of this adjustment entry is a credit to Unrealized Gain on Investment. If the fair market value of the investment declines, the company debits Unrealized Loss on Investment. *Unrealized* gains and losses result from changes in fair market value, not from sales of investments. For available-for-sale investments, the Unrealized Gain account or the Unrealized Loss account is reported as other comprehensive income (or recognized directly in equity).

TECHNICAL UPDATE

Recall that *IAS1*'s requirements for Other Comprehensive Income may not yet be effective in your country, which means the changes in value of available for sale investments would be recognized directly in equity (and appears in the statement of changes in equity).

The following display shows how Vivendi could report its investment and the related unrealized gain in its financial statements at the end of 2010 (all other figures are assumed for this illustration):

Balance sheet		Income statement		
Assets:				
Total current assets	€ XXX	Revenues......................................		€50,000
Long-term investments —		Expenses, including		
at market value (€44,000 + €2,500)....	46,500	income tax		36,000
Property, plant and equipment, net	XXX	Net income.................................		€14,000
Shareholders' equity:		Other comprehensive income:		
Share capital...	10,000	Unrealized gain on investments	€ 2,500	
Retained earnings.................................	20,000	Less Income tax 40%	(1,000)	1,500
Comprehensive income	2,500	Comprehensive income		€15,500
Total shareholders' equity.......................	€32,500			

The preceding example assumes that the investor holds an investment in only one security of another company. Usually companies invest in a portfolio of securities (more than one). In this case, the periodic adjustment to fair market value must be made for the portfolio as a whole. See the "Stop & Think" exercise at the end of this section for an example.

Selling an Available-for-Sale Investment

The sale of an available-for-sale investment usually results in a *realized* gain or loss. Realized gains and losses measure the difference between the amount received from the sale and the cost of the investment.

Suppose Vivendi sells its investment in Siemens shares for €43,000 during 2011. Vivendi would record the sale as follows:

2011	Cash	43,000	
May 19	Loss on Sale of Investment	1,000	
	Long-Term Investment (cost)		44,000
	Sold investment.		

Assets	=	Liabilities	+	Shareholders' Equity	
+ 43,000 − 44,000	=	0	+	− 1,000	(loss on sale of investment)

Vivendi would report Loss on Sale of Investments as an "other" item on the income statement. Vivendi must also make adjusting entries to update the Market Value Adjustment account and the Unrealized Gain on Investment accounts to their current balances (in this case, these accounts have been reduced to zero since the entire investment was sold). These adjustments are covered in intermediate accounting courses.

STOP & THINK...

Suppose Vivendi holds the following available-for-sale securities as long-term investments at December 31, 2011:

Available for sale (Investments)	Cost	Current Fair Market Value
Bayer...	€85,000	€71,000
Phillips......................................	16,000	12,000

Show how Vivendi will report long-term investments on its December 31, 2011, balance sheet.

Answer:

Assets	
Long-term investments, at fair market value	€83,000

When Should We Sell an Investment?

Companies control when they sell investments, and that helps them control when they record gains and losses. Suppose a bad year hits and Vivendi holds an investment that has appreciated in value. Vivendi can sell the investment, raise cash, record the gain, and boost reported income.

The cost principle of accounting provides this opportunity to "manage" earnings. If companies had to account for all investments at pure market value, there would be no gain or loss on the sale. Instead, all gains and losses would be recorded when the market value of the asset changes. That would eliminate part of management's ability to "manage" earnings. But the business community and general users of financial statements may not be ready to fully embrace fair-market-value accounting.

EQUITY-METHOD INVESTMENTS

OBJECTIVE

2 Use the equity method for investments

We use the **equity method** to account for investments in which the investor typically owns 20% to 50% of the investee's shares.

Buying a Large Stake in Another Company

An investor with a shareholding between 20% and 50% of the investee's voting share may significantly influence the investee. Such an investor can probably affect dividend policy, product lines, and other important matters.

Vivendi holds equity-method investments in NBC Universal. *IAS28 – Investment in Associates* refers to these investee companies as associates (but you may see the term "affiliates" used in practice sometimes). An associate is an entity over which the investor has significant influence and that is neither a subsidiary nor an interest in a joint venture, thus NBC Universal is an affiliate of Vivendi. And because Vivendi has a voice in shaping the policy and operations of NBC Universal, some measure of NBC Universal's profits and losses should be included in Vivendi's income.

Accounting for Equity-Method Investments

IAS28 provides a quick summary of the equity method: a method of accounting whereby the investment is initially recognized at cost and adjusted thereafter for the post-acquisition change in the investor's share of net assets of the investee. The profit or loss of the investor includes the investor's share of the profit or loss of the investee. Let's continue our example with Vivendi and NBC Universal.

Investments accounted for by the equity method are recorded initially at cost. Suppose Vivendi pays €400 million for 20% of the ordinary shares of NBC Universal. Vivendi's entry to record the purchase of this investment follows (in millions):

2010			
Jan 6	Long-Term Investment	400	
	Cash		400
	To purchase equity–method investment.		

Assets	=	Liabilities	+	Shareholders' Equity
+ 400 − 400	=	0	+	0

The Investor's Percentage of Investee Income. Under the equity method, Vivendi, as the investor, applies its percentage of ownership—20%, in our example—in recording its share of the investee's net income and dividends. If NBC Universal reports net income of €250 million for the year, Vivendi records 20% of this amount as follows (in millions):

2010			
Dec 31	Long-Term Investment (€250 × 0.20)	50	
	Income from Associates		50
	To record investment revenue.		

Assets	=	Liabilities	+	Shareholders' Equity	
+ 50	=	0	+	+ 50	(equity-method income)

Because of the close relationship between Vivendi and NBC Universal, Vivendi the investor, increases the Investment account and records Income from Associates when NBC Universal the investee, reports income. As NBC Universal's equity increases, so does the Investment account on Vivendi's books. This was what *IAS28* terms "the investor's share of net assets of the investee." The equity earnings that appear on the investor's income statement may be labeled by other terms such as "share of profits of associates". Vivendi uses the term "income from equity affiliates."

If the affiliate made a loss during the financial year, the investor would also have to share the loss of the associate.

Receiving Dividends Under the Equity Method. Vivendi records its proportionate part of cash dividends received from NBC Universal. When NBC Universal declares and pays a cash dividend of €100 million, Vivendi receives 20% of this dividend and records this entry (in millions):

2010			
Dec 31	Cash (€100 × 0.20)	20	
	Long-Term Investment		20
	To receive cash dividend on equity-method investment.		

Assets	=	Liabilities	+	Shareholders' Equity
+ 20				
	=	0	+	0
− 20				

The Investment account is *decreased* for the receipt of a dividend on an equity-method investment. Why? Because the dividend decreases the investee's owners' equity and thus the investor's investment.

After the preceding entries are posted, Vivendi's Investment account at December 31, 2010, shows Vivendi's equity in the net assets of NBC Universal (in millions):

Long-Term Investment					
Jan 6	Purchase	400	Dec 31	Dividends	20
Dec 31	Net income	50			
Dec 31	Balance	430			

Vivendi would report the long-term investment on the balance sheet and the income from associates on the income statement as follows:

	Millions
Balance sheet (partial):	
Assets	
Total current assets..	€XXX
Long-term investments, at equity......................	430
Property, plant and equipment, net....................	XXX
Income statement (partial):	
Income from operations.....................................	€XXX
Other revenue:	
Income from associates	50
Net income..	€XXX

Gain or loss on the sale of an equity-method investment is measured as the difference between the sale proceeds and the carrying amount of the investment. For example, Vivendi's sale all of its 20% holding in NBC Universal for €425 million would be recorded as follows:

2011			
Feb 13	Cash	425	
	Loss on Sale of Investment	5	
	Long-Term Investment		430
	Sold investment in affiliate.		

Assets	=	Liabilities	+	Shareholders' Equity	
+ 425 – 430	=	0	+	– 5	(loss on sale of investment)

Summary of the Equity Method. The following T-account illustrates the accounting for equity-method investments:

Equity-Method Investment	
Original cost	Share of losses
Share of income	Share of dividends
Balance	

CONSOLIDATED SUBSIDIARIES

Companies buy a significant stake in another company in order to *influence* the other company's operations. In this section we cover the situation in which a corporation buys enough of another company to actually *control* that company.

Why Buy Another Company?

Most large corporations own controlling interests in other companies. A **controlling** (or **majority**) **interest** is typically indicated by the ownership of more than 50% of the investee's voting shares. The investor is called the "**parent company**," and the investee company is called the "**subsidiary**." For example, Activision Blizzard, Universal Music Group, and Canal+ are subsidiaries of Vivendi, the parent. Therefore, the shareholders of Vivendi control Activision Blizzard, Universal Music Group, and Canal+ (and many others) as diagrammed in Exhibit 10-4.

EXHIBIT 10-4 | **Ownership Structure of Vivendi and Key Subsidiaries**

Consolidation Accounting

Consolidation accounting is a method of combining the financial statements of all the companies controlled by the same shareholders. This method reports a single set of financial statements for the consolidated entity, which carries the name of the parent company.

Consolidated statements combine the balance sheets, income statements, and cash-flow statements of the parent company with those of its subsidiaries. The result is a single set of statements as if the parent and its subsidiaries were one company. Investors can gain a better perspective on total operations than they could by examining the reports of the parent and each individual subsidiary.

In consolidated statements the assets, liabilities, revenues, and expenses of each subsidiary are added to the parent's accounts. For example, the Cash account balances in Activision Blizzard and Canal+ and all other subsidiaries are added to Vivendi's (the parent company) own Cash balance. The sum of all of the cash amounts is presented as a single amount in Vivendi's consolidated balance sheet. Each account balance of a subsidiary, such as UMG or SFR, loses its identity in the consolidated statements, which bear the name of the parent, Vivendi. In turn, these subsidiaries may be even be parents of other subsidiaries! For example, UMG is the parent of **Polygram Holding**, **Centenary Music International**, **Universal Entertainment**, and many more. Modern business structures make very complicated family trees!

Exhibit 10-5 demonstrates a corporate structure for a parent corporation that owns controlling interests in five subsidiaries and an equity-method investment in another investee company.

EXHIBIT 10-5 | **Parent Company with Consolidated Subsidiaries and an Equity-Method Investment**

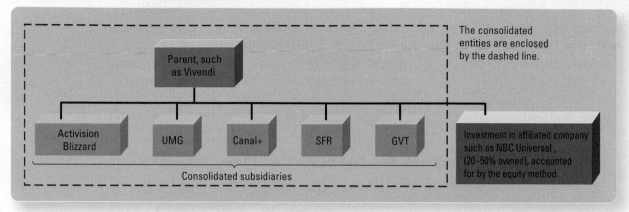

The Consolidated Balance Sheet and the Related Worksheet

Vivendi owns all (100%) the outstanding shares of Universal Music Group (UMG). Both Vivendi and UMG keep separate sets of books. Vivendi, the parent company, uses a worksheet to prepare the consolidated statements of Vivendi and its consolidated subsidiaries. Then Vivendi's consolidated balance sheet shows the combined assets and liabilities of both Vivendi and all its subsidiaries. Exhibit 10-6 below shows how the parent's balances are consolidated with those of the subsidiary, and the resulting consolidated balance sheet.

EXHIBIT 10-6 | **Consolidation of a Wholly-Owned Subsidiary**

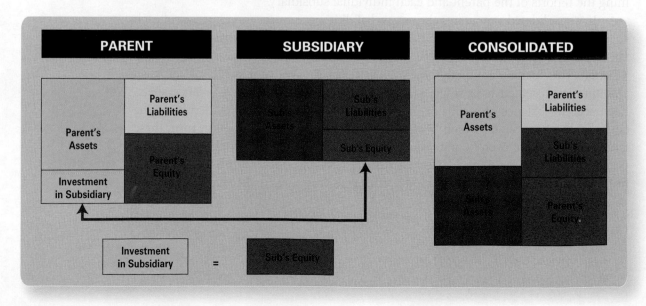

EXHIBIT 10-7 | Worksheet for a Consolidated Balance Sheet

	Parent Corporation	Subsidiary Corporation	Eliminations Debit	Eliminations Credit	Parent and Subsidiary Consolidated Amounts
Assets					
Cash	12,000	18,000			30,000
Note receivable from Subsidiary	80,000	—		(b) 80,000	—
Inventory	104,000	91,000			195,000
Investment in Subsidiary	150,000	—		(a) 150,000	—
Other assets	218,000	138,000			356,000
Total	564,000	247,000			581,000
Liabilities and Shareholders' Equity					
Accounts payable	43,000	17,000			60,000
Notes payable	190,000	80,000	(b) 80,000		190,000
Share Capital	176,000	100,000	(a) 100,000		176,000
Retained earnings	155,000	50,000	(a) 50,000		155,000
Total	564,000	247,000	230,000	230,000	581,000

Exhibit 10-7 shows the worksheet for consolidating the balance sheets of Parent Corporation and Subsidiary Corporation at the date of acquisition. We use these hypothetical entities to illustrate the consolidation process. Consider elimination entry (a) for the parent-subsidiary ownership accounts. Entry (a) credits the parent's Investment account to eliminate its debit balance. Entry (a) also eliminates the subsidiary's shareholders' equity accounts by debiting the subsidiary's share capital and retained earnings for their full balances. Without this elimination, the consolidated financial statements would include both the parent company's investment in the subsidiary and the subsidiary company's equity. But these accounts represent the same thing—Subsidiary's equity—and so they must be eliminated from the consolidated totals. If they weren't, the same resources would be counted twice.

The resulting Parent and Subsidiary consolidated balance sheet (far-right column) reports no Investment in Subsidiary account. Moreover, the consolidated totals for share capital and retained earnings are those of Parent Corporation only. Study the final column of the consolidation worksheet.

In this example, Parent Corporation has an $80,000 note receivable from Subsidiary, and Subsidiary has a note payable to Parent. The parent's receivable and the subsidiary's payable represent the same resources—all entirely within the consolidated entity. Both, therefore, must be eliminated and entry (b) accomplishes this.

- The $80,000 credit in the Elimination column of the worksheet zeros out Parent's Note Receivable from Subsidiary.
- The $80,000 debit in the Elimination column zeros out the Subsidiary's note payable to Parent.
- The resulting consolidated amount for notes payable is the amount owed to creditors outside the consolidated entity, which is appropriate.

After the worksheet is complete, the consolidated amount for each account represents the total asset, liability, and equity amounts controlled by Parent Corporation.

deducting share of the profits for non-controlling interest (line 6), the consolidated net income attributable to equity holders of the parent is €0.8 billion.

EXHIBIT 10-11 | Vivendi's Income Statement

Vivendi Consolidated Income Statement (Partial, adapted) Financial Year ended December 31		
(in millions € Euros)	2009	2008
1 Revenues..	€27,132	€25,392
2 ⋮	⋮	⋮
3 Income from equity affliates..........................	171	260
4 ⋮	⋮	⋮
5 Net profit..	2,086	3,699
6 Attributable to non-controlling interest..........	(1,256)	(1,096)
7 Attributable to equity holders of parent.........	€830	€2,603

Suppose Parent Company owns all the shares of Subsidiary S-1 and 60% of the shares of Subsidiary S-2. During the year just ended, Parent earned net income of $330,000, S-1 earned $150,000, and S-2 had a net loss of $100,000. Parent Company would report net income of $420,000, computed as follows:

	Net Income (Net Loss) of Each Company		Parent's Ownership of Each Company		Parent's Consolidated Net Income (Net Loss)
Parent Company	$330,000	×	100%	=	$330,000
Subsidiary S-1	150,000	×	100%	=	150,000
Subsidiary S-2	(100,000)	×	60%	=	(60,000)
Consolidated net income..........					$420,000

TECHNICAL UPDATE

Since consolidated financial statements are presented as if the parent and all its subsidiaries are one economic entity, it makes sense that transactions between members of the group need special attention. You have seen in Exhibit 10-7 that any amounts owing to and by members of the group must be eliminated. Similarly, if one member of the consolidated entity sells goods or services to another member of the same entity, this transaction would have to be eliminated as well. For example, if Activision Blizzard licenses some music from UMG for its video games, revenue is earned by UMG and expenses are incurred by Activision Blizzard. However, from a consolidated perspective, this transaction should not exist (you can't make money from yourself!) and will be eliminated from the consolidated income statement. More complicated transactions would include sale of a PPE from a subsidiary to another subsidiary. As the transaction is deemed void from a consolidated perspective, numerous adjustments would have to be made on the consolidation worksheet. If you are doing an accounting major, you are likely to cover this topic in your advanced accounting courses.

COOKING THE BOOKS
with Investments and Debt

Enron Corporation

In 2000, Enron Corporation in Houston, Texas, employed approximately 22,000 people and was one of the world's leading electricity, natural gas, pulp and paper, and communications companies, with reported revenues of nearly $101 billion. *Fortune* had named Enron "America's Most Innovative Company" for six consecutive years. To many outside observers, Enron was the model corporation.

Enron's financial statements showed that the company was making a lot of money, but in reality, most of its profits were merely on paper. Rather than from operations, the great majority of the cash Enron needed to operate on a day-to-day basis came from bank loans. It was very important, therefore, that Enron keep its debt ratio (discussed in Chapter 8) as well as its return on assets (ROA, discussed in Chapter 9) at acceptable levels, so the banks would continue to view the company as creditworthy. Enron's balance sheets contained large misstatements in the liabilities and shareholders' equity sections over a period of years. Many of the offsetting misstatements were in long-term assets. Specifically, Enron owned numerous long-term investments, including power plants, water, broadband cable, and sophisticated, complex, and somewhat dubious derivative financial instruments in such unusual things as the weather! Many of these investments actually had questionable value, but Enron had abused fair market value accounting to estimate them at grossly inflated values.

To create paper profits, Andrew Fastow, Enron's chief financial officer, created a veritable maze of "special purpose entities" (SPEs), financed with bank debt. He then "sold" the dubious investments to the SPEs to get them off Enron's books. Enron recorded millions of dollars in "profits" from these transactions. Fastow then used Enron shares to collateralize the bank debt of the SPEs, making the transactions entirely circular. Unknown to Enron's board of directors, Fastow or members of his own family owned most of these entities, making them related parties to Enron. Enron was, in fact, the owner of the assets, and was, in fact, obligated for the debts of the SPEs since those debts were collateralized with Enron shares. When Enron's fraud was discovered in late 2001, the company was forced to consolidate the assets of the SPEs, as well as all of their bank debt, into its own financial statements. The end result of the restatement so depressed Enron's debt ratio and ROA that the banks refused to loan the company any more money to operate. Enron's energy trading business virtually dried up overnight, and it was bankrupt within 60 days. An estimated $60 billion in shareholder value, and 22,000 jobs, were lost. Enron's CEO, Jeffrey Skilling, its CFO, Andrew Fastow, and Board Chairman Kenneth Lay were all convicted of fraud. Skilling and Fastow both went to prison. Lay died suddenly of a heart attack before being sentenced.

Enron's audit firm, Arthur Andersen, was accused of trying to cover up its knowledge of Enron's practices by shredding documents. The firm was indicted by the U.S. Justice Department in March 2002. Because of the indictment, Andersen lost all of its public clients and was forced out of business. As a result, over 58,000 persons lost their jobs worldwide. A U.S. Supreme Court decision in 2005 eventually led to withdrawal of the indictment, but it came much too late for the once "gold plated" CPA firm. Allegations about the quality of its work on Enron, as well as other well-publicized cases such as Waste Management and WorldCom, who were also clients, doomed Arthur Andersen.

Decision Case 1 in Chapter 8 and Decision Case 3 in Chapter 9 illustrate the financial statement impact of Enron's fraudulent transactions.

MID-CHAPTER SUMMARY PROBLEMS

1. Identify the appropriate accounting method for each of the following situations:
   a. Investment in 25% of investee's shares
   b. 10% investment in shares
   c. Investment in more than 50% of investee's shares
2. At what amount should the following available-for-sale investment portfolio be reported on the December 31 balance sheet? All the investments are less than 5% of the investee's shares.

Investments	Investment Cost	Current Market Value
DuPont	$ 5,000	$ 5,500
ExxonMobil	61,200	53,000
Procter & Gamble	3,680	6,230

Journalize any adjusting entry required by these data.

3. Investor paid $67,900 to acquire a 40% equity-method investment in the share capital of Investee. At the end of the first year, Investee's net income was $80,000, and Investee declared and paid cash dividends of $55,000. What is Investor's ending balance in its Equity-Method Investment account? Use a T-account to answer.

4. Parent company paid $85,000 for all the shares of Subsidiary Company, and Parent owes Subsidiary $20,000 on a note payable. Complete the consolidation worksheet below.

	Parent Company	Subsidiary Company	Eliminations Debit	Eliminations Credit	Consolidated Amounts
Assets					
Cash	7,000	4,000			
Note receivable					
from Parent.........................	—	20,000			
Investment in					
Subsidiary...........................	85,000	—			
Other assets............................	108,000	99,000			
Total......................................	200,000	123,000			
Liabilities and Shareholders' Equity					
Accounts payable....................	15,000	8,000			
Notes payable.........................	20,000	30,000			
Share capital...........................	120,000	60,000			
Retained earnings	45,000	25,000			
Total.......................................	200,000	123,000			

Answers

1. **a.** Equity   **b.** Available-for-sale   **c.** Consolidation
2. Report the investments at market value: $64,730, as follows:

Investments	Investment Cost	Current Market Value
DuPont	$ 5,000	$ 5,500
ExxonMobil	61,200	53,000
Procter & Gamble	3,680	6,230
Totals	$69,880	$64,730

Adjusting entry:

Depreciation Expense ($10,000/10 years × 9/12)		5,150	
Accumulated Depreciation—Equipment			5,150
To update depreciation.			

3.

Equity-Method Investment			
Cost	67,900	Dividends	22,000**
Income	32,000*		
Balance	77,900		

* $80,000 × 0.40 = $32,000
** $55,000 × 0.40 = $22,000

4. Consolidation worksheet:

	Parent Company	Subsidiary Company	Eliminations Debit	Eliminations Credit	Consolidated Amounts
Assets					
Cash	7,000	4,000			11,000
Note receivable from Parent ...	—	20,000		(a) 20,000	—
Investment in Subsidiary.........	85,000	—		(b) 85,000	—
Other assets	108,000	99,000			207,000
Total	200,000	123,000			218,000
Liabilities and Shareholders' Equity					
Accounts payable....................	15,000	8,000			23,000
Notes payable.........................	20,000	30,000	(a) 20,000		30,000
Share capital	120,000	60,000	(b) 60,000		120,000
Retained earnings	45,000	25,000	(b) 25,000		45,000
Total	200,000	123,000	105,000	105,000	218,000

Accounting for International Operations

OBJECTIVE

5 Account for international operations

In this globalized world, many companies earn revenue beyond its national boundaries. Accounting for business activities across national boundaries involves foreign currencies and exchange rates. Transactions may be expressed in currencies other than the company's local currency. This is the subject of *IAS21 – The Effects of Changes in Foreign Exchange Rates*.

Foreign Currencies and Exchange Rates

Most countries use their own national currency, usually denoted by their three letter currency codes. For example, the United States uses United States Dollars (USD), South Africa uses South African Rand (ZAR), Malaysia uses Malaysian Ringgit (MYR) and Indonesia uses Rupiah (IDR). An exception is the European Union nations; France, Germany, Italy, Belgium, Netherlands and others use a common currency, the Euro (€ or EUR).

The price of one nation's currency can be stated in terms of another country's monetary unit. This measure of one currency against another is called the **foreign-currency exchange rate**. In Exhibit 10-12, you can see cross rates of major currencies in the world.

EXHIBIT 10-12 | Foreign-Currency Exchange Rates

	USD	EUR	JPY	GBP	CHF	CAD	AUD	HKD
HKD	7.7692	10.6032	0.0865	12.1211	7.2285	7.3339	6.8743	—
AUD	1.1302	1.5425	0.0126	1.7633	1.0515	1.0669	—	1.1455
CAD	1.0594	1.4458	0.0118	1.6527	0.9856	—	0.9373	0.1364
CHF	1.0748	1.4669	0.012	1.6768	—	1.0146	0.951	0.1383
GBP	0.641	0.8748	0.0071	—	0.5964	0.6051	0.5671	0.0825
JPY	89.77	122.5163	—	140.0547	83.5225	84.7405	79.4294	11.5546
EUR	0.7327	—	0.0082	1.1432	0.6817	0.6917	0.6483	0.0943
USD	—	1.3648	0.0111	1.5602	0.9304	0.944	0.8848	0.1287

Currency keys: USD = U.S. Dollar; EUR = Euro; JPY = Japanese Yen; GBP = British Pound; CHF = Swiss Franc; CAD = Canadian Dollar; AUD = Australian Dollar; HKD = Hong Kong Dollar. Source: Bloomberg, 12 February 2010

For example, 1 EUR is equal to 1.3648 USD, 1 HKD = 11.5546 JPY. Obviously, exchange rates move all the time, so the actual rates at any time may be different from the cross rates table above. We call this conversion a *translation*. Suppose an item costs 400 euros. To compute its cost in Australian dollar (AUD), we multiply the euro amount by the conversion rate: EUR 400 × AUD 1.5425 = AUD 617.

Two main factors affect the price (the exchange rate) of a particular currency:

1. the ratio of a country's imports to its exports, and

2. the rate of return available in the country's capital markets.

The Import/Export Ratio. Japanese exports often exceed Japan's imports. Customers of Japanese companies must buy yen (the Japanese unit of currency) to pay for their purchases. This strong demand drives up the price of the yen. In contrast, the United States imports more goods than it exports. Americans must sell dollars to buy the foreign currencies needed to pay for the foreign goods. As the supply of dollars increases (including new notes printed to support the economic bailouts during the financial crisis), the price of the dollar falls.

The Rate of Return. The rate of return available in a country's capital markets affects the amount of investment funds flowing into the country. When rates of return are high in a politically stable country such as Singapore and Switzerland, international investors buy shares, bonds, and real estate in that country. This activity increases the demand for the nation's currency and drives up its exchange rate. Similarly, when there is a lot of political uncertainty in countries such as Thailand, its share market and currency may be affected unfavorably.

Currencies are often described as "strong" or "weak." The exchange rate of a **strong currency** is rising relative to other nations' currencies. The exchange rate of a **weak currency** is falling relative to other currencies. For example, Bloomberg listed the conversion rate for USD to JPY (Japanese yen) at 89.77 on February 12, 2010. The rate may rise to 90.00 the next day, and we would say that US dollar has strengthened against the yen. Or the rate may drop to 88.00 and we would say US dollar has weakened against the yen.

Accounting for Foreign Currency Transactions

International transactions are common. Many businesses buy and sell in currencies other than their local currency. In accounting for transactions involving foreign currencies, *IAS21 – The Effects of Changes in Foreign Exchange Rates* requires the determination of "functional currency," which is the currency of the primary economic environment in which the business operates. In most cases, we can assume that the business's local currency is the functional currency. All foreign currency items are then translated into the functional currency at initial recognition using transaction-date exchange rates.

Let's use **Qian Hu**, an ornamental fish farmer and retailer, as a working example. Qian Hu sells various kinds of ornamental fish and pet accessories from its base in Singapore to other Asian countries and Europe. Its sales outside Singapore are over 70% of its total revenue in 2008. Your local pet stores may be selling Qian Hu's fish!

Let's be a little more specific in our example. Suppose Qian Hu supplies a pet store in Europe and makes some of its sales in euros and buys some of its breeding equipment from Japan and pays for them in Japanese yen.

Consider Qian Hu's sale of ornamental fish and aquariums to FishyTales, a pet store in Europe, on a 30-day credit term, on June 10, 2010. The sale can be conducted in Singapore dollars (SGD) or in euros (EUR), or even in other currencies such as US dollars. If FishyTales agrees to pay in SGD, Qian Hu avoids the complication of dealing in a foreign currency, and the transaction is treated the same way as sales of ornamental fish across town in Singapore. But suppose FishyTales orders EUR 1,000 worth of fish and aquariums from Qian Hu. Further suppose FishyTales would like to pay in euros and Qian Hu agrees to receive euros instead of Singapore dollars.

On initial recognition of the sale, Qian Hu would have recorded in its books sales of EUR 1,000 and a receivable of the same amount. This would be entered using transaction date exchange rates. Suppose that the exchange rate on June 10, 2010, the day of the sale, is 1 EUR for 2.00 SGD. Qian Hu would thus record:

2010			
Jun 10	Accounts Receivable—Fishy Tales	2,000	
	Sales Revenue		2,000
	Sale on account (€1,000 × 2.00).		

Assets	=	Liabilities	+	Shareholders' Equity	
+ 2,000	=	0	+	+ 2000	(sales revenue)

When Qian Hu receives payment of EUR 1,000 from FishyTales on July 10, 2010, it may or may not translate to the amount recognized at initial measurement of SGD 2,000. The prevailing exchange rate on the payment date will determine how much SGD Qian Hu actually receives. If the exchange rate on July 10, 2010 is 1 EUR for 2.10 SGD (in other words, the euro has strengthened against the Singapore dollar), Qian Hu would collect more in Singapore dollar terms. Qian Hu would collect SGD 2,100 (EUR 1,000 × 2.10), resulting in a "translation gain" of SGD 100.

2010			
Jul 10	Cash	2,100	
	Accounts Receivables—Fishy Tales		2,000
	Translation Gain		100
	Collection of account (€1,000 × 2.10).		

Assets	=	Liabilities	+	Shareholders' Equity	
+ 2,100 − 2,000	=	0	+	+ 100	(translation gain)

Conversely, had the euro weakened against Singapore dollar, Qian Hu would have recognized a translation loss. Suppose the exchange rate on July 10 was 1 EUR = 1.95 SGD instead of 2.10 SGD. The EUR 1,000 payment from FishyTales would translate to SGD 1,950 in settlement of an account receivable of SGD 2,000. Qian Hu would process this journal entry instead:

2010			
Jul 10	Cash	1,950	
	Translation Loss	50	
	Accounts Receivables—Fishy Tales		2,000
	Collection of account (€1,000 × 1.95).		

Assets	=	Liabilities	+	Shareholders' Equity	
+ 1,950 − 2,000	=	0	+	− 50	(translation loss)

TECHNICAL UPDATE

What if Qian Hu's financial year-end was June 30, 2010? How should the transaction be reported on the financial statements?

Subsequent to initial measurement, *IAS21* requires entities to distinguish between "monetary" and "non-monetary" items. The key distinction between the two categories is whether or not there is a right to receive (or obligation to deliver) a fixed or determinable number of units of currency. For example, FishyTales receivable is a monetary item because it is deliverable in the fixed amount of EUR 1,000. At the end of each reporting period, *IAS21* requires monetary assets to be retranslated using the closing rate. Non-monetary assets carried at historical costs continue to be measured using historical transaction date exchange rates.

If Qian Hu's financial year end was June 30, 2010, it will be required to re-measure the FishyTale receivables using the closing exchange rate on June 30, 2010. Any gains (or losses) on the balance sheet date are recognized in the income statement.

Reporting Gains and Losses on the Income Statement

The Foreign-Currency Translation Gain/Loss account holds gains and losses on transactions settled in foreign currencies. The net amount of the gains and losses are reported on the income statement as Other Revenues and Gains, or Other Expenses and Losses, as the case may be. For example, Qian Hu may report the net impact of its translation gains and losses as follows:

Other Expenses and Losses:	
Foreign-currency transaction loss, net	$2,600

Should We Hedge Our Foreign-Currency-Transaction Risk?

One way for companies to avoid foreign-currency transaction losses is to insist that international transactions be settled in the local currency. This requirement puts the burden of currency translation on the foreign party. But this approach may not always work and may even alienate customers and decrease sales. Another way for a company to protect itself is by hedging. **Hedging** means to protect oneself from losing money in one transaction by engaging in a counter-balancing transaction.

A company selling goods to be collected in a foreign currency expects to receive a fixed number of foreign currency units. If the foreign currency weakens, the company would receive the agreed amounts in foreign currency units, but this would translate to a lower local currency, resulting in a foreign currency translation loss.

A company may have accumulated a number or receivables and payables expressed in foreign currencies. Losses on one currency may be offset by gains on another. Most companies do not have equal amounts of receivables and payables in foreign currency. To obtain a more precise hedge, companies can buy futures contracts. These are contracts for foreign currencies to be received in the future. Futures contracts can create a payable to exactly offset a receivable, and vice versa. Many companies that do business internationally use hedging techniques to minimize their foreign currency exposure.

IMPACT OF INVESTING ACTIVITIES ON THE STATEMENT OF CASH FLOWS

OBJECTIVE

6 Report investing transactions on the statement of cash flows

Investing activities include many types of transactions. In Chapter 7, we covered the purchase and sale of long-term assets such as Property, Plant and Equipment (PPE). In this chapter, we examine investments in shares and bonds.

Exhibit 10-14 provides excerpts from Vivendi's 2009 consolidated statement of cash flows. During 2008, Vivendi made additional investments in consolidated companies and equity affiliates totaling €3.85 billion (lines 3 and 4). It also sold a small amount shares in some other consolidated companies and equity affiliates (lines 7 and 8). These actual investing activities relate directly to the topics you studied in this chapter.

EXHIBIT 10-14 | Vivendi's Statement of Cash Flows

Vivendi		
Consolidated Statement of Cash Flows (Partial, adapted)		
Financial Year Ended December 31		
(in millions € Euros)	2009	2008
1 Cash flows provided by (used for) investing activities:		
2 Purchase of PPEs...	€(2,648)	€(2,105)
3 Purchase of consolidated companies	(2,682)	(3,735)
4 Investment in equity affiliates.................................	(9)	(114)
5 Increase in financial assets......................................	(359)	(98)
6 Proceeds from disposal of PPE and intangible	86	104
7 Proceeds from states of consolidated companies	15	(6)
8 Disposal of equity affiliates.....................................	–	18
9 Decrease in financial assets......................................	82	340
10 Other terms (summarized).......................................	310	299
11 Net cash flows from investing activities..................	€(5,205)	€(5,297)

END-OF-CHAPTER SUMMARY PROBLEM

Translate the balance sheet of the Brazilian subsidiary of **Unilever**, a European company, into euros. When **Unilever** acquired this subsidiary, the exchange rate of the Brazilian currency, the real, was €0.40. The average exchange rate applicable to retained earnings is €0.41. The real's current exchange rate is €0.43.

Before performing the translation, predict whether the translation adjustment will be positive or negative. Does this situation generate a foreign-currency translation gain or loss? Give your reasons.

	Reals
Assets..	900,000
Liabilities	600,000
Shareholders' equity:	
Share capital................................	30,000
Retained earnings........................	270,000
	900,000

Answer

Translation of foreign-currency balance sheet:

This situation will generate a *positive* translation adjustment, which is like a gain. The gain occurs because the real's current exchange rate, which is used to translate net assets (assets minus liabilities), exceeds the historical exchange rates used for shareholders' equity. The calculation follows.

	Reals	Exchange Rate	Euros
Assets......................................	900,000	0.43	387,000
Liabilities	600,000	0.43	258,000
Shareholders' equity:			
Share capital........................	30,000	0.40	12,000
Retained earnings................	270,000	0.41	110,700
Accumulated other comprehensive income:			
Foreign-currency translation adjustment	—		6,300
	900,000		387,000

I Requirement

1. Prepare the investing activities section of Frosted Doughnuts' statement of cash flows. Based solely on Frosted Doughnuts investing activities, does it appear that the company is growing or shrinking? How can you tell?

E10-34B *(Learning Objective 6: Using the statement of cash flows)* At the end of the year, Elite Properties' statement of cash flows reported the following for investment activities:

Elite Properties Consolidated Statement of Cash Flows (Partial)	
Cash flows from Investing Activities:	
Notes receivable collected	$ 3,113,000
Purchases of short-term investments	(3,453,000)
Proceeds from sales of equipment	1,529,000*
Proceeds from sales of investments (cost of $490,000)	498,000
Expenditures for property and equipment	(1,720,000)
Net used for investing activities	$ (33,000)

*Cost $5,200,000; Accumulated depreciation, $3,671,000.

I Requirement

1. For each item listed, make the journal entry that placed the item on Elite's statement of cash flows.

Challenge Exercises

E10-35 *(Learning Objectives 1, 2, 3, 5: Accounting for various types of investments)* Suppose ChatNow owns the following investments at December 31, 2010:

a. 100% of the ordinary shares of ChatNow United Kingdom, which holds assets of £1,400,000 and owes a total of £1,200,000. At December 31, 2010, the current exchange rate of the pound (£) is £1 = $2.01. The translation rate of the pound applicable to share-holders' equity is £1 = $1.64. During 2010, ChatNow United Kingdom earned net income of £120,000 and the average exchange rate for the year was £1 = $1.92. ChatNow United Kingdom paid cash dividends of £20,000 during 2010.

b. Investments that ChatNow is holding to sell. These investments cost $1,500,000 and declined in value by $350,000 during 2010, but they paid cash dividends of $23,000 to ChatNow. One year ago, at December 31, 2009, the market value of these investments was $1,500,000.

c. 45% of the ordinary shares of ChatNow Financing Associates. During 2010, ChatNow Financing earned net income of $500,000 and declared and paid cash dividends of $25,000. The carrying amount of this investment was $500,000 at December 31, 2009.

I Requirements

1. Which method is used to account for each investment?
2. By how much did each of these investments increase or decrease ChatNow's net income during 2010?
3. For investments b and c, show how ChatNow would report these investments on its balance sheet at December 31, 2010.

E10-36 (*Learning Objectives 1, 6: Explaining and analyzing accumulated other comprehensive income*)   In-the-Box Retail Corporation reported shareholders' equity on its balance sheet at December 31, as follows:

In-the-Box Retail
Balance Sheet (Partial)

Shareholder's Equity:
  Ordinary shares, $1.00 par value—
    600 million shares authorized,
    200 shares issued .... $ 200
  Additional paid-in capital 1,080
  Retained earnings.. 6,350
  Accumulated other comprehensive (loss)................ (?)
  Less: Treasury shares, at cost................................. (60)

I **Requirements**

1. Identify the two components that typically make up accumulated other comprehensive income.
2. For each component of accumulated other comprehensive income, describe the event that can cause a *positive* balance. Also describe the events that can cause a *negative* balance for each component.
3. At December 31, 2010, In-the-Box Retail's accumulated other comprehensive loss was $54 million. Then during 2011, In-the-Box Retail had a positive foreign-currency translation adjustment of $24 million and an unrealized loss of $11 million on available-for-sale investments. What was In-the-Box Retail's balance of accumulated other comprehensive income (loss) at December 31, 2011?

Quiz

Test your understanding of long-term investments and international operations by answering the following questions. Select the best choice from among the possible answers given.

Questions 37–39 use the following data:

Assume that Clear Networks owns the following long-term available-for-sale investments:

Company	Number of Shares	Cost per Share	Current Market Value per Share	Dividend per Share
ABC Corp.	1,200	$60	$74	$2.10
Good Food, Inc.	150	11	13	1.40
Lesley Ltd.	700	22	26	0.80

At year-end, the fair market values of Noram's investments are: Canton, $26,600; Rockaway, $698,000.

❙ Requirements

1. Record the transactions in the journal of Noram Corporation.
2. Post entries to the T-account for Long-Term Investment in Rockaway and determine its balance at December 31.
3. Show how to report the Long-Term Available-for-Sale Investments and the Long-Term Investment in Rockaway accounts on Noram's balance sheet at December 31.

P10-51A (*Learning Objective 3: Analyzing consolidated financial statements*) This problem demonstrates the dramatic effect that consolidation accounting can have on a company's ratios. Fixed Motor Company (Fixed) owns 100% of Fixed Motor Credit Corporation (FMCC), its financing subsidiary. Fixed's main operations consist of manufacturing automotive products. FMCC mainly helps people finance the purchase of automobiles from Fixed and its dealers. The two companies' individual balance sheets are adapted and summarized as follows (amounts in billions):

	Fixed (Parent)	FMCC (Subsidiary)
Total assets	$89.7	$170.7
Total liabilities	$65.1	$156.6
Total shareholders' equity	24.6	14.1
Total liabilities and equity	$89.7	$170.7

Assume that FMCC's liabilities include $1.2 billion owed to Fixed, the parent company.

❙ Requirements

1. Compute the debt ratio of Fixed Motor Company considered alone.
2. Determine the consolidated total assets, total liabilities, and shareholders' equity of Fixed Motor Company after consolidating the financial statements of FMCC into the totals of Fixed, the parent company.
3. Recompute the debt ratio of the consolidated entity. Why do companies prefer not to consolidate their financing subsidiaries into their own financial statements?

■ spreadsheet

P10-52A (*Learning Objective 3: Consolidating a wholly owned subsidiary*) Assume Rose, Inc., paid $453,000 to acquire all the share capital of Mountain Corporation, and Mountain owes Rose $175,000 on a note payable. Immediately after the purchase on September 30, 2010, the two companies' balance sheets follow.

	Rose	Mountain
Assets		
Cash	$ 60,000	$ 59,000
Accounts receivable, net	194,000	86,000
Note receivable from Mountain	175,000	—
Inventory	305,000	458,000
Investment in Mountain	453,000	—
PPE, net	403,000	524,000
Total	$1,590,000	$1,127,000
Liabilities and Shareholders' Equity		
Accounts payable	$ 122,000	$ 67,000
Notes payable	410,000	312,000
Other liabilities	216,000	295,000
Share capital	556,000	268,000
Retained earnings	286,000	185,000
Total	$1,590,000	$1,127,000

Requirement

1. Prepare the worksheet for the consolidated balance sheet of Rose, Inc.

P10-53A (*Learning Objective 4: Accounting for a bond investment purchased at a premium*) Insurance companies and pension plans hold large quantities of bond investments. Sea Insurance Corp. purchased $2,400,000 of 4.0% bonds of Sheehan, Inc., for 110 on January 1, 2010. These bonds pay interest on January 1 and July 1 each year. They mature on January 1, 2014. At October 31, 2010, the market price of the bonds is 108.

Requirements

1. Journalize Sea's purchase of the bonds as a long-term investment on January 1, 2010 (to be held to maturity), receipt of cash interest, and amortization of the bond investment at July 1, 2010. The straight-line method is appropriate for amortizing the bond investment.
2. Show all financial statement effects of this long-term bond investment on Sea Insurance Corp.'s balance sheet and income statement at October 31, 2010.

P10-54A (*Learning Objective 5: Recording foreign-currency transactions and reporting the transaction gain or loss*) Suppose Turquoise Corporation completed the following international transactions:

■ **general ledger**

May	1	Sold inventory on account to Fiat, the Italian automaker, for €65,000. The exchange rate of the euro was $1.32, and Fiat demands to pay in euros.
	10	Purchased supplies on account from a Canadian company at a price of Canadian $59,000. The exchange rate of the Canadian dollar was $0.77, and the payment will be in Canadian dollars.
	17	Sold inventory on account to an English firm for 134,000 British pounds. Payment will be in pounds, and the exchange rate of the pound was $1.97.
	22	Collected from Fiat. The exchange rate is €1 = $1.35.
Jun	18	Paid the Canadian company. The exchange rate of the Canadian dollar is $0.76.
	24	Collected from the English firm. The exchange rate of the British pound was $1.94.

Requirements

1. Record these transactions in Turquoise's journal and show how to report the transaction gain or loss on the income statement.
2. How will what you learned in this problem help you structure international transactions?

P10-55A (*Learning Objective 5: Measuring and explaining the foreign-currency translation adjustment*) Assume that Folgate has a subsidiary company based in Japan.

Requirements

1. Translate into dollars the foreign-currency balance sheet of the Japanese subsidiary of Folgate.

	Yen
Assets	480,000,000
Liabilities	115,000,000
Shareholders' equity:	
Share capital	40,000,000
Retained earnings	325,000,000
	480,000,000

When Folgate acquired this subsidiary, the Japanese yen was worth $0.0095. The current exchange rate is $0.0110. During the period when the subsidiary earned its income, the average exchange rate was $0.0100 per yen. Before you perform the foreign-currency translation calculations, indicate whether Folgate has experienced a positive or a negative translation adjustment. State whether the adjustment is a gain or a loss, and show where it is reported in the financial statements.

2. To which company does the foreign-currency translation adjustment "belong"? In which company's financial statements will the translation adjustment be reported?

(Group B)

P10-56B (*Learning Objectives 1, 2: Reporting investments on the balance sheet and the related revenue on the income statement*) Colorado Exchange Company completed the following long-term investment transactions during 2010:

2010	
May 12	Purchased 18,200 shares, which make up 40% of the ordinary shares of Brentwood Corporation at total cost of $330,000.
Jul 9	Received annual cash dividend of $1.24 per share on the Brentwood investment.
Sep 16	Purchased 900 shares of Bangkok, Inc., ordinary shares as an available-for-sale investment, paying $42.00 per share.
Oct 30	Received cash dividend of $0.33 per share on the Bangkok investment.
Dec 31	Received annual report from Brentwood Corporation. Net income for the year was $530,000.

At year-end the fair market value of the Bangkok shares is $30,300. The fair market value of the Brentwood shares is $655,000.

I Requirements

1. For which investment is fair market value used in the accounting? Why is fair market value used for one investment and not the other?
2. Show what Colorado would report on its year-end balance sheet and income statement for these investment transactions. It is helpful to use a T-account for the Long-Term Investment in Brentwood Share account. Ignore income tax.

P10-57B (*Learning Objectives 1, 2: Accounting for available-for-sale and equity-method investments*) The beginning balance sheet of Segui Corporation included the following:

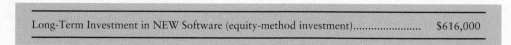

Long-Term Investment in NEW Software (equity-method investment)......................	$616,000

Segui completed the following investment transactions during the year:

Mar 16	Purchase 1,600 shares of Hubbardston, Inc., ordinary share as a long-term available-for-sale investment, paying $12.75 per share.
May 21	Received cash dividend of $1.50 per share on the Hubbardston investment.
Aug 17	Received cash dividend of $85,000 from NEW Software.
Dec 31	Received annual reports from NEW Software, net income for the year was $500,000. Of this amount Segui's proportion is 23%.

At year-end, the fair market values of Segui's investments are: Hubbardston, $26,100; NEW, $701,000.

Requirements

1. Record the transactions in the journal of Segui Corporation.
2. Post entries to the T-account for Long-Term Investment in NEW and determine its balance at December 31.
3. Show how to report the Long-Term Available-for-Sale Investments and the Long-Term Investment in NEW accounts on Segui's balance sheet at December 31.

P10-58B (*Learning Objective 3: Analyzing consolidated financial statements*)   This problem demonstrates the dramatic effect that consolidation accounting can have on a company's ratios. Space Motor Company (Space) owns 100% of Space Motor Credit Corporation (SMCC), its financing subsidiary. Space's main operations consist of manufacturing automotive products. SMCC mainly helps people finance the purchase of automobiles from Space and its dealers. The two companies' individual balance sheets are adapted and summarized as follows (amounts in billions):

	Space (Parent)	SMCC (Subsidiary)
Total assets	$89.5	$170.8
Total liabilities	$65.7	$156.1
Total shareholders' equity	23.8	14.7
Total liabilities and equity	$89.5	$170.8

Assume that SMCC's liabilities include $1.7 billion owed to Space, the parent company.

Requirements

1. Compute the debt ratio of Space Motor Company considered alone.
2. Determine the consolidated total assets, total liabilities, and shareholders' equity of Space Motor Company after consolidating the financial statements of SMCC into the totals of Space, the parent company.
3. Recompute the debt ratio of the consolidated entity. Why do companies prefer not to consolidate their financing subsidiaries into their own financial statements?

P10-59B (*Learning Objective 3: Consolidating a wholly owned subsidiary*)   Assume Ronny, Inc., paid $346,000 to acquire all the share capital of Dinette Corporation, and Dinette owes Ronny $192,000 on a note payable. Immediately after the purchase on September 30, 2010, the two companies' balance sheets follow.

■ **spreadsheet**

	Ronny	Dinette
Assets		
Cash	$ 54,000	$ 52,000
Accounts receivable, net	195,000	89,000
Note receivable from Dinette	192,000	—
Inventory	278,000	452,000
Investment in Dinette	346,000	—
PPE, net	397,000	457,000
Total	$1,462,000	$1,050,000
Liabilities and Shareholders' Equity		
Accounts payable	$ 127,000	$ 79,000
Notes payable	399,000	329,000
Other liabilities	249,000	296,000
Share capital	577,000	259,000
Retained earnings	110,000	87,000
Total	$1,462,000	$1,050,000

I Requirement

1. Prepare the worksheet for the consolidated balance sheet of Ronny, Inc.

P10-60B (*Learning Objective 4: Accounting for a bond investment purchased at a premium*) Insurance companies and pension plans hold large quantities of bond investments. Safe Insurance Corp. purchased $2,700,000 of 8.0% bonds of Sherman, Inc., for 118 on January 1, 2010. These bonds pay interest on January 1 and July 1 each year. They mature on January 1, 2014. At October 31, 2010, the market price of the bonds is 104.

I Requirements

1. Journalize Safe's purchase of the bonds as a long-term investment on January 1, 2010 (to be held to maturity), receipt of cash interest, and amortization of the bond investment at July 1, 2010. The straight-line method is appropriate for amortizing the bond investment.
2. Show all financial statement effects of this long-term bond investment on Safe Insurance Corp.'s balance sheet and income statement at October 31, 2010.

■ **general ledger**

P10-61B (*Learning Objective 5: Recording foreign-currency transactions and reporting the transaction gain or loss*) Suppose Lavender Corporation completed the following international transactions:

May	1	Sold inventory on account to Palermo, the Italian automaker, for €60,000. The exchange rate of the euro was $1.38, and Palermo demands to pay in euros.
	10	Purchased supplies on account from a Canadian company at a price of Canadian $57,000. The exchange rate of the Canadian dollar was $0.78, and the payment will be in Canadian dollars.
	17	Sold inventory on account to an English firm for 148,000 British pounds. Payment will be in pounds, and the exchange rate of the pound was $1.94.
	22	Collected from Palermo. The exchange rate is €1 = $1.41.
Jun	18	Paid the Canadian company. The exchange rate of the Canadian dollar is $0.77.
	24	Collected from the English firm. The exchange rate of the British pound was $1.91.

I Requirements

1. Record these transactions in Lavender's journal and show how to report the transaction gain or loss on the income statement.
2. How will what you learned in this problem help you structure international transactions?

P10-62B (*Learning Objective 5: Measuring and explaining the foreign-currency translation adjustment*) Assume that Mason has a subsidiary company based in Japan.

I Requirements

1. Translate into dollars the foreign-currency balance sheet of the Japanese subsidiary of Mason.

	Yen
Assets	410,000,000
Liabilities	100,000,000
Shareholders' equity:	
Share capital	18,000,000
Retained earnings	292,000,000
	410,000,000

When Mason acquired this subsidiary, the Japanese yen was worth $0.0075. The current exchange rate is $0.0090. During the period when the subsidiary earned its income, the average exchange rate was $0.0088 per yen. Before you perform the foreign-currency translation calculations, indicate whether Mason has experienced a positive or a negative translation adjustment. State whether the adjustment is a gain or a loss, and show where it is reported in the financial statements.

2. To which company does the foreign-currency translation adjustment "belong"? In which company's financial statements will the translation adjustment be reported?

APPLY YOUR KNOWLEDGE

Decision Cases

Case 1. (*Learning Objectives 1, 5: Making an investment decision*) Infografix Corporation's consolidated sales for 2010 were $26.6 billion, and expenses totaled $24.8 billion. Infografix operates worldwide and conducts 37% of its business outside the United States. During 2010, Infografix reported the following items in its financial statements (amounts in billions):

Foreign-currency translation adjustments...	$(202)
Unrealized holding _____ on available-for-sale investments.............	(328)

As you consider an investment in Infografix shares, some concerns arise. Answer each of the following questions:

1. What do the parentheses around the two dollar amounts signify?
2. Are these items reported as assets, liabilities, shareholders' equity, revenues, or expenses? Are they normal-balance accounts, or are they contra accounts?
3. Did Infografix include these items in net income? in retained earnings? In the final analysis, how much net income did Infografix report for 2010?
4. Should these items scare you away from investing in Infografix shares? Why or why not? (Challenge)

Case 2. (*Learning Objectives 1, 2, 4: Making an investment sale decision*) Cathy Talbert is the general manager of Barham Company, which provides data-management services for physicians in the Columbus, Ohio, area. Barham Company is having a rough year. Net income trails projections for the year by almost $75,000. This shortfall is especially important. Barham plans to issue shares early next year and needs to show investors that the company can meet its earnings targets.

Barham holds several investments purchased a few years ago. Even though investing in shares is outside Barham's core business of data-management services, Talbert thinks these investments may hold the key to helping the company meet its net income goal for the year. She is considering what to do with the following investments:

1. Barham owns 50% of the ordinary shares of Ohio Office Systems, which provides the business forms that Barham uses. Ohio Office Systems has lost money for the past two years but still has a retained earnings balance of $550,000. Talbert thinks she can get Ohio's treasurer to declare a $160,000 cash dividend, half of which would go to Barham.
2. Barham owns a bond investment purchased eight years ago for $250,000. The purchase price represents a discount from the bonds' maturity value of $400,000. These bonds mature two years from now, and their current market value is $380,000. Ms. Talbert has checked with a Charles Schwab investment representative, and Talbert is considering selling the bonds. Schwab would charge a 1%-commission on the sale transaction.

3. Barham owns 5,000 Microsoft's shares valued at $53 per share. One year ago, Microsoft's share was worth only $28 per share. Barham purchased the Microsoft shares for $37 per share. Talbert wonders whether Barham should sell the shares.

▌ Requirement

1. Evaluate all three actions as a way for Barham Company to generate the needed amount of income. Recommend the best way for Barham to achieve its net income goal.

Ethical Issue

writing assignment ▪

Media One owns 18% of the voting shares of Web Talk, Inc. The remainder of the Web Talk shares are held by numerous investors with small holdings. Austin Cohen, president of Media One and a member of Web Talk's board of directors, heavily influences Web Talk's policies.

Under the market value method of accounting for investments, Media One's net income increases as it receives dividend revenue from Web Talk. Media One pays President Cohen a bonus computed as a percentage of Media One's net income. Therefore, Cohen can control his personal bonus to a certain extent by influencing Web Talk's dividends.

A recession occurs in 2010, and Media One's income is low. Cohen uses his power to have Web Talk pay a large cash dividend. The action requires Web Talk to borrow in order to pay the dividend.

▌ Requirements

1. What are the ethical issues in the Media One case?
2. Who are the stakeholders? What are the possible consequences to each?
3. What are the alternatives for Austin Cohen to consider? Analyze each alternative from the following standpoints: (a) economic, (b) legal, (c) ethical.
4. If you were Cohen, what would you do?
5. Discuss how using the equity method of accounting for investment would decrease Cohen's potential for manipulating his bonus.

Focus on Financials: ▪ Nokia Corporation

The consolidated financial statements of **Nokia**, are given in Appendix A at the end of this book.

▌ Requirements

1. How does Nokia account for its available-for-sale investments? Does it adjust for periodic changes in fair market value of these investments? If so, where do these adjustments appear?
2. Continue looking in Note 1, under the caption Foreign Currency Translation. Describe the nature of Nokia's business dealings with foreign currencies. What has been the impact of this activity on its financial statements? On which financial statement is the impact of this activity reflected?
3. What indicates that Nokia owns foreign subsidiaries? Identify the item that proves your point and the financial statement on which the item appears.
4. Which currency, the Euro, or the currencies of foreign countries in which Nokia did business, was stronger in each fiscal year 2008, 2007 and 2006? Give the evidence to support each answer.
5. At December 31, 2008, did Nokia have a cumulative net gain or a cumulative net loss from translating its foreign subsidiaries' financial statements into dollars? How can you tell?
6. What do you understand by the "Equity method"? Under what circumstances would we use it? How much income did Nokia recognize in 2008 from its associated companies? Show the journal entry for recording income from associates. Look at Note 14. A deduction of $239m was made from the investments in associated companies account in 2008. Explain what happened.

7. Open a T-account and label it "investments in associated companies." Enter $325 million as the opening amount on 1 January 2008. Show all the relevant movements in the account. Enter the following transactions:

   a. Additions: 24 million
   b. Deductions: 239 million
   c. Impairment: 8 million
   d. Share of results: 6 million
   e. Dividends: 6 million
   f. Other movements: (6) million

Group Project

Pick a share from The *Wall Street Journal* or other database or publication. Assume that your group purchases 1,000 shares of the shares as a long-term investment and that your 1,000 shares are less than 20% of the company's outstanding shares. Research the share in *Value Line*, *Moody's Investor Record*, or other source to determine whether the company pays cash dividends and, if so, how much and at what intervals.

▌*Requirements*

1. Track the share for a period assigned by your professor. Over the specified period, keep a daily record of the price of the share to see how well your investment has performed. Each day, search the Corporate Dividend News in The *Wall Street Journal* to keep a record of any dividends you've received. End the period of your analysis with a month end, such as September 30 or December 31.
2. Journalize all transactions that you have experienced, including the share purchase, dividends received (both cash dividends and share dividends), and any year-end adjustment required by the accounting method that is appropriate for your situation. Assume you will prepare financial statements on the ending date of your study.
3. Show what you will report on your company's balance sheet, income statement, and statement of cash flows as a result of your investment transactions.

For online homework, exercises, and problems that provide you with immediate feedback, please visit www.myaccountinglab.com.

Quick Check Answers

1. *a*
2. *b* (1,500 shares x $27 = $40,500)
3. *d*
4. *c* ($45,000 − $36,000)

5. *d* [$180,000 + 0.30 ($50,000 − $20,000) = $189,000]
6. *c* {$200,000 + 0.70 [$64,000 + 0.70($55,000)] = $271,750}

7. *d*
8. *c*
9. *d* ($1,600,000 Canadian × $0.90 = $1,440,000)
10. *a*

11

The Income Statement & the Statement of Changes in Equity

SPOTLIGHT: Marks & Spencer

Marks & Spencer (M&S) is one of the world's leading retailers known for its quality clothing, food and home products. From its humble beginning in 1884, M&S started as a penny bazaar stall, to now having over 700 stores in UK and over 320 International stores in 42 territories around the world.

Sir Stuart Rose, CEO of M&S, in an Harvard Business Review article said "On January 9, 2008… our share price fell 18%, taking 1.6 billion off the value of our business. In light of increased business uncertainty and fragile consumer confidence, it might have been tempting to quietly shelve Plan A, our 100-point, five-year eco-plan. We could have heeded critics who said, 'Times are tought, best ditch the fluffy stuff.' But we didn't."

Having survived two world wars and numerous recessions over its 125-year history, how is M&S weathering the latest financial crisis? We will examine M&S's income statements to better understand how quality of earnings matters when you evaluate a company'a performance.

This chapter will round up your coverage of a corporate income statement. After studying this chapter, you will have seen all the types of items that typically appear on an income statement, including the new statement of comprehensive income and its link to the statement of changes in equity. You'll study the components of *net income from continuing operations*, which is the basis for many analysts' predictions about companies' future operations, as well as their current values. You'll also learn about earnings per share, the most often-mentioned statistic in business. Finally, you'll learn more about the statement of changes in equity, the analysis of changes in retained earnings and other equity items. The knowledge you get from this chapter will help you analyze financial statements and use the information in decision making. Chapter 13 will further elaborate on analysis of financial statements.

We begin with a basic question: How do we evaluate the quality of a company's earnings? The term *quality of earnings* refers to the characteristics of an earnings number that make it most useful for decision making.

LEARNING OBJECTIVES

1 **Analyze** a corporate income statement

2 **Account** for a corporation's income tax

3 **Analyze** a statement of shareholders' equity

4 **Understand** managers' and auditors' responsibilities for the financial statements

EVALUATING THE QUALITY OF EARNINGS

A corporation's net income (including earnings per share) receives more attention than any other item in the financial statements. To shareholders, the larger the net income, the greater the likelihood of dividends. In addition, an upward trend in net income generally translates sooner or later to a higher share price.

Suppose you are considering investing in either the share of Marks & Spencer, or LVMH (Louis Vuitton Moët Hennessy). How do you make the decision? A knowledgeable investor will want to assess each company's **earnings quality**. The higher the quality of earnings in the current period as compared to its recent past, the more likely it is that the company is executing a successful business strategy to generate healthy earnings in the future, which is a key component in its share price.

There are many components of earnings quality. Among the most prominent ones are (1) proper revenue and expense recognition, (2) high and recurring gross, operating, and net profit ratios, and (3) absence of changes in accounting policies, assumptions and estimates to boost earning. To explore the makeup and the quality of earnings, let's examine its various sources. Exhibit 11-1 shows the Consolidated Income Statement of Marks & Spencer (M&S) for financial years 2009, 2008, and 2007. We'll use this statement as a basis for our discussion of earnings quality and support it with examples from other companies.

EXHIBIT 11-1 | M&S's Consolidated Income Statement

Marks & Spencer Group Plc
Consolidated Income Statement (Partial, adapted)

(in millions £ pounds)	52 Weeks Ended		
	March 28, 2009	March 29, 2008	March 31, 2007
1 Revenue	£9,062.1	£9,022.0	£8,588.1
2 Cost of sales	(5,690.2)	(5,535.2)	(5,246.9)
3 Gross profit	3,371.9	3,486.8	3,341.2
4 Selling and marketing expenses	(2,074.4)	(1,912.7)	(1,779.2)
5 Administrative expense	(570.1)	(534.5)	(584.1)
6 Other operating income	41.5	49.7	68.1
7 Profit on property disposals	6.4	27.0	1.9
8 Exceptional items	95.4	95.0	–
9 Operating profit	870.7	1,211.3	1,045.9
10 Finance income	50.0	64.4	33.8
11 Finance costs	(214.5)	(146.6)	(143.0)
12 Profit on ordinary activities before taxation	706.2	1,129.1	936.7
13 Income tax expense	(199.4)	(308.1)	(277.5)
14 Profit from discontinued operations	–	–	0.7
15 Profit for the year	506.8	821.0	669.9
16 Attributable for equity shareholders of the company	508.0	821.7	659.9
17 Attributable for non-controlling interests	(1.2)	(0.7)	–
18 Basic earnings per share (in pence per share)	32.3	49.2	39.1
19 Diluted earnings per share (in pence per share)	£ 32.3	£ 48.7	£ 38.5

Revenue Recognition

The first component of earnings quality, and the top line of the income statement, is proper recognition of net revenue, or net sales. You learned many aspects of revenue in Chapters 3 through 6. The *revenue recognition principle*, discussed in Chapter 3 states that, under accrual accounting, revenue should be recognized when it is earned—that is, when the selling business has done everything it has to do to either deliver the product or the service to the customer. To recap, in recognizing revenue from sales of goods, *IAS18* requires that (a) the entity has transferred to the buyer the significant risks and rewards of ownership of the goods, (b) the entity retains neither continuing managerial involvement to the degree usually associated with ownership nor effective control over the goods sold, (c) the amount of revenue can be measured reliably, (d) it is probable that the economic benefits associated with the transaction will flow to the entity, and (e) the costs incurred or to be incurred in respect of the transaction can be measured reliably. In Chapter 4, you learned the process by which cash collected over the counter is entered into the accounting system. In Chapter 5, you learned that credit sales, or sales on account, have to go through the process of collection, that some would ultimately not be collectible, and that a company must make allowances for doubtful accounts. In Chapter 6, you studied the concept of *free on board* (F.O.B.) terms, which governs the issue of who owns the goods during the shipment process, and therefore the timing of revenue. You must understand all of these concepts in order to grasp the meaning of revenue recognition.

Proper revenue recognition in a retail business, like M&S, is relatively straightforward. M&S revenue recognition policy, as outlined in its Notes states:

EXCERPTS FROM M&S'S NOTES TO THE 2009 FINANCIAL STATEMENTS

Revenue comprises sales of goods to customers outside the Group less an appropriate deduction for actual and expected returns, discounts and loyalty scheme voucher costs, and is stated net of Value Added Tax and other sales taxes. Sales of furniture and online sales are recorded on delivery to the customer.

M&S recognizes revenue, as well as related cost of goods sold, at the time customers receive the products. In the stores, revenue is recognized at the cash registers when the customers receive and pay for merchandise. As the transfer of significant risks and rewards of ownership of furniture and online sales will require delivery of goods to customers, revenue is not recognized until the goods are actually delivered to customers. For both over-the-counter and Internet sales, the company estimates an allowance for returns, discounts and loyalty scheme voucher costs, and deducts them from gross sales, to report net sales.

COOKING THE BOOKS
with Revenue

The Deloitte Forensic Center[i], published a report on financial statement fraud schemes alleged by the United States' Securities and Exchange Commission (SEC) in enforcement releases issued from 2000 to 2008. Revenue recognition was the most susceptible area to fraud, accounting for almost 40% of the financial statement frauds alleged during the period. The two most common alleged methods of cheating on revenue recognition identified in the SEC enforcement releases were recording fictitious revenue and recognition of revenue when products or services are not yet delivered, delivery is incomplete or delivered without customer acceptance.

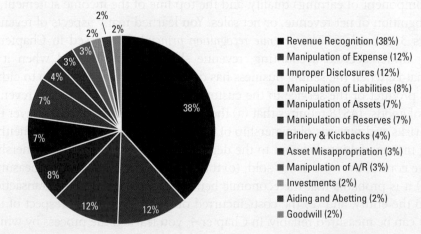

- ■ Revenue Recognition (38%)
- ■ Manipulation of Expense (12%)
- ■ Improper Disclosures (12%)
- ■ Manipulation of Liabilities (8%)
- ■ Manipulation of Assets (7%)
- ■ Manipulation of Reserves (7%)
- ■ Bribery & Kickbacks (4%)
- ■ Asset Misappropriation (3%)
- ■ Manipulation of A/R (3%)
- ■ Investments (2%)
- ■ Aiding and Abetting (2%)
- ■ Goodwill (2%)

Proportion of financial statement fraud schemes represented by each alleged fraud scheme in SEC enforcement releases from 2000 through 2008

---

[i] The Deloitte Forensic Center is a think tank aimed at exploring new approaches for mitigating the costs, risks and effects of fraud, corruption and other issues facing the global business community. The Center aims to advance the state of thinking in areas such as fraud and corruption by exploring issues from the perspective of forensic accountants, corporate leaders, and other professionals involved in forensic matters. The Deloitte Forensic Center is sponsored by Deloitte Financial Advisory Services LLP. For more information, visit www.deloitte.com/forensiccenter.

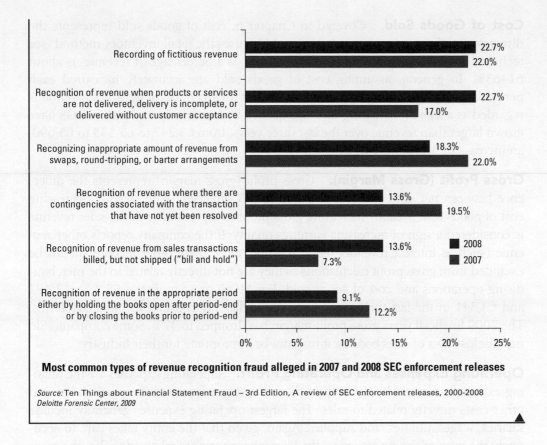

Most common types of revenue recognition fraud alleged in 2007 and 2008 SEC enforcement releases

Source: Ten Things about Financial Statement Fraud – 3rd Edition, A review of SEC enforcement releases, 2000-2008
Deloitte Forensic Center, 2009

Let's examine Exhibit 11-1 and analyze the trend in M&S's net sales revenue (line 1). Notice that, over the past three years, net sales for the company have been relatively stagnant (£9,062, £9,022 and £8,588, respectively). M&S attributed this to "Group revenue was up 0.4% to just over £9bn. UK sales were down 1.7% and were clearly impacted by the difficult market conditions" and "reflecting the deterioration in market conditions and consumer spending". The decline in UK domestic sales was partially offset by a 25% growth in M&S's overseas revenues, which constituted 10% of group revenue. M&S has said in its annual report that it aims to increase its international segment revenue to between 15 to 20% of total group revenues by 2012.

Cost of Goods Sold, Gross Profit, Operating Profit and Net Profit

After revenue, the next two important components in earnings quality are cost of goods sold and resulting gross profit. Before we get to these components, however, it is important to emphasize that, just as it is important to avoid premature or improper revenue recognition, it is equally important to make sure that *all expenses are accurately, completely, and transparently included* in the computation of net income. We saw with the example of the WorldCom fraud in Chapter 7 what can happen when a company manipulates reported earnings by deliberately understating expenses. Without the integrity that comes through full and complete disclosures of all existing expenses, and without matching those expenses against the revenues they are incurred to earn, trends in earnings are at best meaningless, and at worst, downright misleading.

Cost of Goods Sold. Covered in Chapter 6, cost of goods sold represents the direct cost of the goods sold to customers. M&S uses the retail inventory method (see technical update, Chapter 6, page 350). COGS, as a percentage of revenue, is about 61–63%. In general, assuming cost of goods sold are accurately measured each period, steadily decreasing cost of goods sold as a percentage of net sales revenue is regarded as a sign of increasing earnings quality. Unfortunately for M&S, COGS have grown larger than revenue over the last three years, from £5,247 to £5,535 to £5,690, an increase of 5.5% and 2.80%.

Gross Profit (Gross Margin). Gross profit (gross margin) represents the difference between net sales and cost of goods sold. Conversely, with steadily decreasing cost of goods sold, steadily increasing gross profit as a percentage of net sales revenue is considered a sign of increasing earnings quality. If the company reports other revenue (such as interest revenue, rental revenue, etc.), these other income should be excluded from gross profit calculations as they are not directly related to the merchandising operations and cost of goods sold. For M&S, gross profits of £3,372, £3,487 and £3,341 in the last three years have been relatively constant in monetary terms. The 2009 financial year's gross profit margin has dropped to 37%. Some companies do not disclose cost of sales because it may not be appropriate for their industry.

Operating Expenses and Operating Profit. Operating expenses are the ongoing expenses incurred by the entity, other than direct expenses for merchandise and other costs directly related to sales. The largest operating expenses generally include salaries, wages, utilities, and supplies. Again, given that the entity takes care to accurately measure operating expenses, the lower these costs are relative to sales, the more efficient the business operations, resulting in higher profitability. M&S grouped its expenses into functional categories and reported expenses for selling and marketing expenses and administrative expenses (lines 4 and 5). Recall from Chapter 3 (page 167) that this is a **function of expense** method of reporting expenses. *IAS1* requires companies using the function method to provided additional disclosure on the nature of expenses, which M&S shows below.

EXCERPTS (ADAPTED) FROM M&S'S NOTES TO THE 2009 FINANCIAL STATEMENTS

(in millions £ pounds)	Function of expense		
	Selling and marketing expenses	Administrative expenses	Total
Nature of expense:			
Employee costs	923.2	231.1	1,154.3
Occupancy costs	439.2	77.5	516.7
Repairs, renewals and maintenance of property	76.6	19.1	95.7
Depreciation	343.5	38.2	381.7
Amortisation	24.6	2.7	27.3
Other costs	267.3	201.5	468.8
Operating expenses	2,074.4	570.1	2,644.5

M&S's income statement (p. 663) also shows two lines that require readers' further attention. Lines 7 and 8 are disclosed separately because they may be relevant when readers evaluate M&S's profitability. As you can see from line 7, profit on property disposals clearly depends on the presence or absence of actual PPE transactions during the year. Note that 2008's operating profit is boosted by the £27 million profit, whereas 2008 and 2006 had much smaller amounts of profit from disposal of properties.

Line 8 contains "exceptional items". M&S's notes to the account explained the nature of the exceptional items.

EXCERPTS FROM M&S'S NOTES TO THE 2009 FINANCIAL STATEMENTS

Exceptional income and charges are those items that are one-off in nature and create significant volatility in reported earnings and are therefore reported separately in the income statement. This includes costs relating to strategy changes that are not regular running costs of the underlying business and pension credits arising on changes to the UK defined benefit scheme.

As you analyze M&S's performance, you must remember that these profits are likely to be non-recurring for future years.

M&S's operating profits for the last three financial years were £871, £1,211 and £1,046 million, respectively. Expressed as a percentage of total revenue, operating profit margin for M&S was about 10% in 2009. Whilst revenue has remained constant, there has been a marked decrease in operating profits. It increased from 2007 to 2008 (16%) and then dropped 28% from 2008 to 2009. This is undoubtedly a real impact of the global financial crisis in 2008.

TECHNICAL UPDATE

Sometimes you may see companies that disclose "extraordinary items" on the income statement, usually defined as significant items (gains or losses) that are both unusual and infrequent that impact the results of an entity. Gains and losses due to lawsuits, restructuring, and the sale of PPEs are not extraordinary items. These gains and losses are considered normal business occurrences and are reported as Other Gains and Losses. Typical examples quoted for extraordinary items include unexpected natural disasters (a severe cold frost in Iceland will not qualify, but a severe snow storm in Thailand would!) and expropriation of assets (by government decrees).

IAS1 prohibits the use of this category of item in financial reporting under IFRS. It encourages entities to disclose any additional line items that may be needed to fairly present the entity's results of operations. Some companies, like M&S, label these items "exceptional".

However, other accounting regimes outside IFRS may still allow the use of "extraordinary items", but it is becoming rare and difficult for a gain or loss to qualify as an extraordinary item. For example, whilst extraordinary items are still allowed under US GAAP, even the most catastrophic events in the last decade (September 11 and Hurricane Katrina) are deemed "non-extraordinary".

Net Profit. After operating profit, you will see a few more important items before arriving at net profit. First, let's look at lines 10 and 11 of Exhibit 11-1. Interest expense and interest income represent the charges for borrowed money, and the return earned on invested money. Line 10 shows that on average, finance income (i.e. interest revenue) hovers about £50 million each year. You would probably worry more about line 11 (finance cost or interest expense). M&S's interest expense has increased quite substantially from £143 in 2007 to £215 in 2009, a 50% increase over the two-year period. A quick check on the balance sheet shows that total borrowings and other financial liabilities (both short and long-term) have increased from £3,703 in 2007 to £5,070 in 2009 (a 37% increase). This would be a worrying trend if the economy remains depressed for long periods.

The next important ingredient in determining net income is corporate income tax expense, which must be subtracted in arriving at net profit or net income for the year. M&S's income tax expense (line 13) is about 28% of profit before taxation. This is in line with the United Kingdom's corporate tax rate. In general, income tax rate for corporations in developed economies in Asia is about 20%, 30% in Europe, and 40% in United States (inclusive of state income taxes). Effective tax planning, both by in-house tax staff, and externally, through the counsel of the company's independent outside accountants and attorneys, can help lower the company's tax burden, and can contribute substantially to improved operating profits.

Lastly, line 17 deserves some further examination. Profit from discontinued operations (*IFRS5 – Non-current Assets Held for Sale and Discontinued Operations*) is singled out because it represents parts of the entity that will no longer be held for use, but are intended for sale. Whilst profit from discontinued operations is very small for M&S (£0.7 million in 2007 only), it can be quite substantial in other companies. **Financial analysts typically do *not* include discontinued operations in predictions of future corporate income because the discontinued segments will not continue to generate income for the company.**

M&S's net profit has increased almost 25% from 2007 (£660) to 2008 (£821), but declined 38% in 2009 (£507). As a percentage of total revenue, M&S's net profit margin in 2009 was slightly less than 6%. Remember that revenue had held steady in the last three years, so the overall net profit decline is likely to be because of higher expenses or lower margins from sale. M&S offered the following reasoning for its clothing segment:

EXCERPTS (ADAPTED) FROM M&S'S 2008 ANNUAL REPORT

Our Marketplace

The clothing market faced a difficult year. In this highly competitive sector several factors are driving shopping trends on the High Street. Older customers, who are more cautious about spending, are increasingly buying on a 'needs' basis or replacing staples with investment pieces. They are looking for clothing that lasts beyond the current season, which can be dressed up or down and accessorized. Additionally, the economic climate has forced customers to consider carefully before buying, prompting retailers to introduce promotions and discounts to entice them in, especially during Christmas. This resulted in customers widening their store choice so they could cherry pick the best offers, and use deals to 'trade up' to better quality items for less money.

Evaluating Performance with Peers/Benchmarks

Are the results of 37% gross profit margin, 10% operating profit margin, and 6% net profit margin, good or bad? Well, it is worse than what M&S achieved in 2007 and 2008. But unless you make comparisons to M&S's peers, it is difficult to say if any of these ratios are good numbers or disappointing ones. A quick check on some other selected retailers shows the following gross margins:

Retailers	Financial Year End	GPM (%)	OPM (%)	NPM (%)
Carrefour (France)	Dec 31, 2008	20.99	3.79	1.77
Macy's (US)	Jan 31, 2009	39.70	-17.95	-19.30
Next (UK)	Jan 24, 2009	20.65	14.61	9.23
Saks Fifth Avenue (US)	Jan 31, 2009	31.93	-4.47	-5.11
Wal-Mart (US)	Jan 31, 2009	23.70	5.68	3.34
Averages from selected peers/benchmarks		27.39	0.41	-2.01

Obviously you will never find a company exactly like M&S, with the exact same product mix, same location mix, same marketing strategy, etc. Each company is unique; all we can say is that the companies above are competing in the same broad retail space as M&S. Some are more volume based (such as Walmart and Carrefour), some are more high-end (Saks Fifth Avenue). In any case, the companies above seem to be good benchmarks in terms of giving context to the M&S results. You can see that M&S's 37% gross profit margin, 10% operating profit margin and 6% net profit margin, are very respectable! Only its competitor in the UK (Next) has done better in terms of operating profit and net profit margins.

Which Income Number Predicts Future Profits?

How is net profit or net income used in investment analysis? Suppose Darren Lim, an investment banker with **Hongkong and Shanghai Banking Corporation (HSBC)**, is estimating the value of Marks & Spencer's shares. Darren believes that M&S can earn annual income each year equal to £924 million, its average income over the last three years (£706, £1,129 and £937).

To estimate the value of M&S's shares, financial analysts determine the present value (present value means the value *today*) of M&S's stream of future income. Darren must use some interest rate to compute the present value. Assume that an appropriate interest rate (*i*) for the valuation of M&S is 12%. This rate is based on the risk that M&S might not be able to earn its expected annual income of £924 million for the indefinite future. The rate is also called the **investment capitalization rate** because it is used to estimate the value of an investment. The higher the risk, the higher the rate, and vice versa. The computation of the estimated value of M&S's shares is:

$$\text{Estimated value of Marks \& Spencer's shares} = \frac{\text{Estimated annual income in the future}}{\text{Investment capitalization rate}} = \frac{£924 \text{ million}}{0.12} = £7,700 \text{ million}$$

Darren thus estimates that M&S, as a company, is worth $7.7 billion. He then computes the company's market capitalization. M&S's balance sheet at March 28, 2009, reports that the company has about 1,578 million ordinary shares outstanding. The market price of M&S's ordinary shares on March 30, 2009 was about £2.65 per share. The current market value of M&S, as a company (market capitalization) is thus:

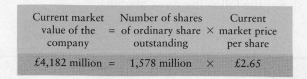

Current market value of the company	=	Number of shares of ordinary share outstanding	×	Current market price per share
£4,182 million	=	1,578 million	×	£2.65

The investment decision rule may then be formulated as follows:

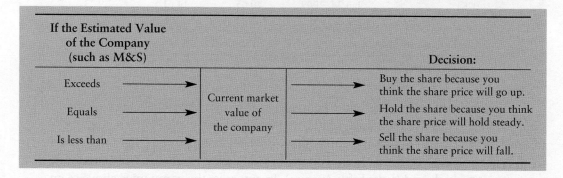

If the Estimated Value of the Company (such as M&S)			Decision:
Exceeds	→	Current market value of the company	→ Buy the share because you think the share price will go up.
Equals	→		→ Hold the share because you think the share price will hold steady.
Is less than	→		→ Sell the share because you think the share price will fall.

In this case,

			Decision:
Estimated Value of M&S £7,700 million	Is more than	Current market value of M&S £4,182 million	→ Buy the share
£4.88 per share*	Is more than	£2.65 per share	

*£7,700 million / 1,878 million = £4.88 per share

Darren believes M&S's share price should rise above its current market value of £2.65 to somewhere in a range near £4.88. Based on this analysis, HSBC would recommend that investors buy M&S's shares as they are undervalued. Do remember that March 2009 is probably the trough of the recession, with many share markets reporting record lows and having recovered significantly since then. M&S's share price at the end of December 2009 is about £4.01, and had you invested back in March 2009, you would have increased your investment by 50%! But, obviously, investment is easy when you have hindsight, investing in real life (and real time) is a lot more challenging due to the uncertainty of future events.

This is just a simple example of how net income can be used in investment analysis. There are many other financial models and techniques that help investors assess share prices such as price-earnings multiples and discounted cash flows.

Accounting Changes

Companies sometimes change from one accounting method to another, such as from double-declining-balance (DDB) to straight-line depreciation, or from first-in, first-out (FIFO) to average cost for inventory. An accounting change makes it difficult to compare one period with preceding periods. Without detailed information, investors can be misled into thinking that the current year is better or worse than the preceding year, when in fact the only difference is a change in accounting method. As noted in Chapter 7, changes in accounting policies should only be effected if such change is required by an accounting pronouncement or if the change results in reliable and more relevant information. The primary source of authority for accounting changes is *IAS8 – Accounting Policies, Changes in Accounting Estimates and Errors*. Accounting policies are defined as the specific principles, bases, conventions, rules and practices applied by an entity in preparing and presenting financial statements.

There are three types of accounting changes are relevant to us:

a. *Changes due to new accounting standards or pronouncements*. Accounting standards do evolve, and from time to time, an entity would need to apply new or updated accounting standards. Such changes should be done in accordance with the specific transitional provisions in the new IFRS.

b. *Changes in accounting estimates* include changing the estimated life of a building or equipment and the collectability of receivables. For these changes, companies report amounts for the current and future periods on the new basis, i.e. prospectively. There is no looking back to the past, but a disclosure of the impact of the change is required (see **Lenovo**'s disclosure on page 428).

c. *Changes in accounting principles* include most changes in accounting methods, such as from FIFO to average cost (see pages 358-359) and from one recognition method to another for a revenue or an expense. For these changes, the company reports figures for all periods presented in the income statement—past as well as current—on the new basis. The company *retrospectively applies* (looks back and reapplies) all prior-period amounts that are presented for comparative purposes with the current year, as though the new accounting method had been in effect all along. This lets investors compare all periods that are presented on the same accounting basis. If an accounting change impacts periods prior to the earliest one presented in the current income statement, an adjustment to retained earnings must be made. *IAS8* contains additional provisions when the retrospective application is "impractical". For our purpose, prior period adjustments can be made to beginning retained earnings.

Watch out for voluntary accounting changes that increase reported income. Investment analysts follow companies to see if they meet their forecasted earnings targets. And managers sometimes take drastic action to increase reported earnings. Assume it's late in November and our earnings may fall below the target for the year. A reasonable thing to do is to try to increase sales and net income. Managers can also cut expenses. These actions are ethical and honest. Profits earned by these corrective actions are real. Managers can take another action that is technically legal, but its ethics could be questionable. Suppose the company has been using the double-declining-balance method for depreciation. Changing to straight-line depreciation can increase reported income. Remember that in accounting, not everything that is legally allowed is ethical.

Accounting changes are a quick-and-dirty way to create profits when the company can't earn enough from continuing operations. This is why accounting standards require companies to report all accounting changes, along with their effects on earnings—to let investors know where the income came from.

Correcting retained earnings. Occasionally, a company fails to properly record an element of the financial statement. *IAS8* refers to these as "prior-period errors", which may be caused by omissions from, and misstatements in, the entity's financial statements for one or more prior-periods arising from a failure to use, or misuse of, reliable information. These errors include the effects of arithmetic mistakes, mistakes in applying accounting policies, oversights or misinterpretations of facts, and fraud. All material prior-period errors require retrospective restatement, either by restating the opening balances of assets, liabilities and equity for the earliest prior-period presented in a set of financial statements, or if impractical, through a **prior-period adjustment**" to the beginning retained earnings in the statement of changes in equity.

Assume that MWS Corporation incorrectly recorded an expense as $30,000, but the correct amount was $40,000. This error understated expenses by $10,000 and overstated net income by $10,000. Let's assume we will correct this accounting error using a prior-period adjustment. Prior-period adjustments are not reported on the income statement because they relate to an earlier accounting period. This prior-period adjustment would appear on the statement of changes in equity earnings, as shown in Exhibit 11-2, with all amounts assumed:

EXHIBIT 11-2 | Reporting a Prior-Period Adjustment

MWS Corporation
Statement of Changes in Equity
Year Ended December 31, 2011

Total shareholder equity, December 31, 2010		$490,000
Share capital..	$100,000	
Retained earnings balance, December 31, 2010,		
as originally reported	390,000	
Prior-period adjustment—debit to correct error in		
recording expense...	(10,000)	
Retained earnings balance, December 31, 2010, as adjusted......	380,000	
Net income for 2011..	110,000	
Dividends for 2011	(40,000)	
Retained earnings balance, December 31, 2011	450,000	
Total shareholder equity, December 31, 2011		$550,000

Reporting Comprehensive Income

All companies report net income or net loss on their income statements. As we saw in Chapter 10, companies with unrealized gains and losses on certain investments and foreign-currency translation adjustments also report another income figure. Comprehensive income is the company's change in total shareholders' equity from all sources other than from the owners of the business. **Comprehensive income** includes net income or loss (from the income statement) plus items of all other items of income and expense that are not recognized in profit or loss as required or permitted by other IFRSs, such as:

- changes in revaluation surplus (if the revaluation model is elected under *IAS16 – Property, Plant and Equipment* and *IAS38 – Intangible Assets*)
- actuarial gains and losses on defined benefit plans (under *IAS19 – Employee Benefits*)
- gains and losses arising from translating the financial statements of a foreign operation (under *IAS21 – The Effects of Changes in Foreign Exchange Rates*)
- gains and losses on re-measuring available-for-sale financial assets (under *IAS39 – Financial Instruments: Recognition and Measurement*)
- the effective portion of gains and losses on hedging instruments in a cash flow hedge (also under *IAS39*).

Note that most of these other comprehensive income items are more complex in nature and may be covered in your advanced accounting courses. **These items do not enter into the determination of net income as we have covered in this course.**

IAS1 permits statement of comprehensive income to be presented in two ways:

- in a single statement, or
- in two statements: a separate income statement, followed by a second statement of comprehensive income which begins with the profit for the year from the separately disclosed income statement.

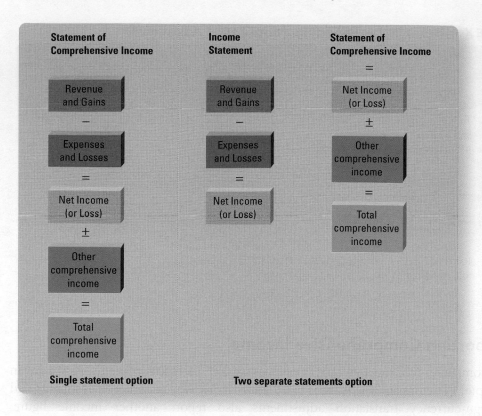

You may encounter companies using a single statement of comprehensive income or a two-separate statements format. M&S uses the latter and calls it "Consolidated Statement of Recognized Income and Expenses". Exhibit 11-3 shows this statement for M&S for the last three financial years. You will notice that line 1 starts with the Profit for the Year, which is exactly the profit in M&S's income statements (line 15 of Exhibit 11-1). Lines 2–7 are other comprehensive income items, and line 8 is their tax effect. The total comprehensive income (loss) for M&S is thus (£72), £1,232 and £667 million for the years ending with March 28, 2009, 2008 and 2007 respectively. As you can see, other comprehensive income items can swing a "profit" in income statement into a "loss" in total comprehensive income, (and vice versa).

EXHIBIT 11-3 | **M&S's Statement of Comprehensive Income**

	52 Weeks Ended		
(in millions £ pounds)	**March 28, 2009**	**March 29, 2008**	**March 31, 2007**
1 Profit for the year.....................	£506.8	£ 821.0	£659.9
2 Foreign currency translation differences.....................	33.1	21.3	(14.0)
3 Actuarial (losses)/gains on retirement benefit schemes.................	(927.1)	605.4	(8.6)
4 Cash flow and net investment hedges:			
5 – fair value movements in equity.....................	304.8	(33.5)	(7.4)
6 – recycled and reported in net profit.....................	(206.8)	1.3	10.7
7 – amount recognized in inventories.....................	(8.6)	2.4	2.1
8 Tax on items taken directly to equity.....................	225.8	(185.7)	24.5
9 Net (losses)/gains not recognized in the income statement...........	(578.8)	411.2	7.3
10 Total recognized income and expense for the year	£ (72.0)	£1,232.2	£667.2

Marks & Spencer Group Plc
Consolidated Statement of Recognized Income & Expense (Partial, adapted)

Earnings per Share

The final segment of the income statement reports earnings per share. **Earnings per share (EPS)** is the amount of a company's net income per share of its *outstanding ordinary shares*. EPS is a key measure of a business's success because it shows how much income the company earned for each share. Share prices are quoted at an amount per share, and investors buy a certain number of shares. EPS is used to help determine the value of a share. EPS is computed as follows:

$$\text{Earnings per share} = \frac{\text{Net income} - \text{Preferred dividends}}{\text{Average number of ordinary shares outstanding}}$$

The corporation lists its various sources of income separately: continuing operations, discontinued operations, and so on. It also lists the EPS figure for each element of net income. Consider the EPS of M&S. The final section of Exhibit 11-1 (lines 18 and 19) shows how companies report EPS. Notice that two EPS computations are made: one for "basic" (the currently outstanding shares) and one for "diluted" (which takes into account potential increases in outstanding shares). Companies must first compute a weighted average number of shares outstanding. This computation takes into account the changes that might occur in the number of shares outstanding during the year from such things as treasury share purchases or reissuances and is only possible if you have access to the detailed daily outstanding ordinary shares of the company, As an example, assume M&S has 1,500 million ordinary shares outstanding at the start of the financial year, and three months before the financial year ends, it issued an additional 100 million shares and the ending shares outstanding at year-end is 1,600 million shares. Weighted average of shares outstanding for M&S can thus be calculated as:

First 9 months = 1,500 million × 9/12 =	1,125 million shares
Last 3 months = 1,600 million × 3/12 =	400 million shares
Weighted average outstanding shares =	1,525 million shares

Effect of Preference Dividends on Earnings per Share.

Recall that that EPS is earnings per share of ordinary shares. But the holders of preference shares have first claim on dividends. Therefore, preference dividends must be subtracted from net income to compute EPS. Preference dividends are not subtracted from discontinued operations.

M&S has only one class of ordinary shares outstanding. Since there is no preference shares, there is no corresponding preference dividend. Let's see how this would work for a company with preference shares. Assume MWS Corporation (Exhibit 11-2) has $110,000 net income for the 2011 financial year and the weighted average number of ordinary shares outstanding is calculated as 1 million shares. Half of MWS's capital is in the form of preference shares which pay 5% preference dividends per year. Basic EPS for MWS can therefore be calculated as follows.

$$\text{Earnings per share} = \frac{\$110,000 - (5\% \times 50,000)}{1 \text{ million shares}} = \frac{107,500}{1,000,000} = 10.75 \text{ cents per ordinary share}$$

Earnings per Share Dilution. Some corporations have *convertible preference shares*, which may be exchanged for ordinary shares. Others may have share options outstanding, or convertible debt securities, all of which may potentially increase the number of shares outstanding. A company may not yet issue any new ordinary shares (arising from exercise of share options or conversions preference shares), but could, at some date in the future. When this happens, we say the EPS is *diluted*—reduced— because net income is shared by more shares accordingly. Corporations with complex capital structures present two sets of EPS figures:

- EPS based on actual outstanding ordinary shares (*basic* EPS)
- EPS based on outstanding ordinary shares plus the *potential additional shares that may arise* from conversion of the preference shares, debt securities into ordinary shares or exercise of share options (*diluted* EPS)

Let's examine M&S's disclosure on basic and diluted EPS. Partial extracts of M&S's Notes to the Financial Statements are provided below.

EXCERPTS FROM M&S'S NOTES TO THE 2009 FINANCIAL STATEMENTS

The calculation of earnings per ordinary share is based on earnings after tax and the weighted average number of ordinary shares in issue during the year. For diluted earnings per share, the weighted average number of ordinary shares in issue is adjusted to assume conversion of all dilutive potential ordinary shares. The Group has only one class of dilutive potential ordinary shares being those share options granted to employees where the exercise price is less than the average market price of the Company's ordinary shares during the year.

	2009 £m	2008 £m
1 Earnings after tax	508.0	821.7
	million	million
2 Weighted average number of ordinary shares in issue	1,573.2	1,671.3
3 Potentially dilutive share options under Group's share option schemes	0.8	16.0
4 Weighted average number of diluted ordinary shares	1,574.0	1,687.3
	pence	pence
5 Basic earnings per share	32.3	49.2
6 Diluted earnings per share	32.3	48.7

M&S's basic EPS is calculated by line 1 divided by line 2, whereas diluted EPS is calculated dividing the same earning number (line 1) by line 4 (sum of line 2 and line 3). Further details on calculating EPS are available in *IAS33 – Earnings per Share*.

Earnings from Operations Versus Cash Flow from Operations

Two key figures used in financial analysis are:

- net income (or income from continuing operations), and
- cash flow from operations.

For a given period, M&S's net income and net cash flow from operating activities may chart different paths. Accounting income arises from the accrual process as follows:

> Total revenues and gains – Total expenses and losses = Net income (or Net loss)

As we have seen, revenues and gains are recorded when they occur, regardless of when the company receives or pays cash.

Net cash flow, on the other hand, is based solely on cash receipts and cash payments. During any financial year, a company may have lots of revenues and expenses and a hefty net income. But the company may have weak cash flow because it cannot collect from customers. The reverse may also be true: A company may have abundant cash but little income (for example, having collected cash in advance of earning the revenue).

The income statement and the cash flows statement often paint different pictures of the company. Which statement provides better information? Neither: Both statements are needed, along with the balance sheet and statement of changes in equity, for an overall view of the business. In Chapter 12 we'll cover the statement of cash flows in detail.

ACCOUNTING FOR CORPORATE INCOME TAXES

Corporations pay income tax as individuals do, but corporate and personal tax rates usually differ in many jurisdictions. As you read earlier in this chapter, in general, income tax rate for corporations in developed economies in Asia is about 20%, 30% in Europe and 40% in United States (inclusive of state income taxes).

To account for income tax, the corporation measures:

OBJECTIVE

2 **Account** for a corporation's income tax

- *Income tax expense*, an expense on the income statement. Income tax expense is used in determining net income.
- *Income tax payable*, a current liability on the balance sheet. Income tax payable is the amount of tax to pay the government in the next period.

Accounting for income tax usually follows the principles of accrual accounting. Suppose at the end of financial year 2010, M&S reports net income before tax (also called **pre-tax accounting income**) of £1 billion. M&S's income tax rate is close to 30%. To start this discussion, assume income tax expense and income tax payable are the same. Then M&S would record income tax for the year as follows (amounts in millions):

2011			
Mar 28	Income Tax Expense (£1,000 × 0.30)	300	
	Income Tax Payable		300
	Recorded income tax for the year.		

M&S's financial statements for fiscal 2010 would report these figures (partial, in millions):

Income statement		Balance sheet	
Income before income tax	£1,000	Current liabilities:	
Income tax expense	(300)	Income tax payable	£300
Net income.................................	£ 700		

In general, income tax expense and income tax payable can be computed as follows:*

Income tax expense	=	Income before income tax (from the income statement)	×	Income tax rate		Income tax payable	=	Taxable income (from the *income tax return* filed with tax authorities)	×	Income tax rate

*The authors thank Jean Marie Hudson for suggesting this presentation.

The income statement and the income tax return are entirely separate documents:

- The *income statement* reports the results of operations.
- The *income tax return* is filed with the tax authority to measure how much tax to pay the government in the current period.

For most companies, tax expense and tax payable differ. Some revenues and expenses affect income differently for accounting and for tax purposes. One of the most common differences between accounting income and **taxable income** occurs when a corporation uses straight-line depreciation in its financial statements and accelerated depreciation for the tax return. Another difference is when a corporation has an expense in its income statement that is not allowed for tax purposes. Conversely, most government bonds pay tax-free interest, so whilst interest income from such investments may be recognized in the income statement, they are not subject to tax. *IAS12 – Income Taxes* covers this area of accounting, but it is outside the scope of this text.

Continuing with the M&S illustration, suppose for fiscal 2010 that it had:

- pre-tax accounting income of £1 billion on its income statement, and
- taxable income of £800 million on its income tax return.

Taxable income is less than accounting income because M&S uses:

- straight-line depreciation for accounting purposes (say £100 million), and
- accelerated depreciation for tax purposes (say £300 million).

M&S would record income tax for fiscal 2010 as follows (amounts in millions and an income tax rate of 30%):

2011			
Mar 28	Income Tax Expense (£1,000 × 0.30)	300	
	Income Tax Payable (£800 × 0.30)		240
	Deferred Tax Liability		60
	Recorded income tax for the year.		

Deferred Tax Liability is usually a long-term liability.

M&S's financial statements for fiscal 2010 will report the following:

Income statement		Balance sheet	
Income before income tax	£1,000	Current liabilities:	
Income tax expense	(300)	Income tax payable	£240
Net income	£ 700	Long-term liabilities:	
		Deferred tax liability	60*

*Assuming that the beginning balance of Deferred tax liability was zero.

In March 2011, M&S would pay income tax payable of £240 million because this is a current liability (and the tax authority would like to have its tax assessment paid!). The deferred tax liability will be settled in future.

For a given year, Income Tax Payable can exceed Income Tax Expense. This occurs when, because of differences in revenue and expenses for book and tax purposes, taxable income exceeds book income. When that occurs, the company debits a deferred tax asset. Further discussion on this topic (covered in *IAS12 – Income Taxes*) is reserved for a more advanced course.

ANALYZING THE STATEMENT OF CHANGES IN EQUITY

The **statement of changes in equity** reports the reasons for all the changes in the shareholders' equity section of the balance sheet during the period.

OBJECTIVE

3 Analyze a statement of changes in equity

EXHIBIT 11-4 | **M&S's Statements of Changes in Equity**

	Marks & Spencer Group Plc Statement of Changes in Equity (Adapted) 52 Weeks Ended March 28, 2009						
(in millions £ pounds)	Ordinary Share Capital	Share Premium Account	Capital Redemption Reserve	Hedging Reserve	Other Reserve	Retained Earnings	Total
1 As at March 30, 2008...............	£396.6	£231.4	£2,199.9	£(36.9)	£(6,542.2)	£5,707.9	£1,956.7
2 Profit for the year attributable to shareholers........................						508.0	508.0
3 Other comprehensive income*				71.7		(650.5)	(578.8)
4 Dividends..................................						(354.6)	(354.6)
5 Shares issued on exercise of share options........................	0.5	4.8					5.3
6 Shares bought back..................	(2.7)		2.7			(40.9)	(40.9)
7 Other equity transactions*				27.8		558.2	586.0
8 As at March 28, 2009..............	£394.4	£236.2	£2,202.6	£ 62.6	£(6,542.2)	£5,728.1	£2,081.7

Summarized

Take another look at Exhibit 11-4, the Consolidated Statements of Changes in Equity for M&S. Study its format. There is a column for each element of equity, starting with Ordinary Share Capital on the left. Recall from Chapter 9 that some companies have shares with par values and others have shares with no par values. One of the telltale signs of having shares with par values is the share premium or additional paid-in capital account, which is shown in the second column. Columns 3–5 are other components of equity that are beyond our scope. The Retained Earning account is where most transactions in equity take place. The column on the far right reports the total of the various components of equity.

The top row (line 1) reports beginning balances as of March 30, 2008, taken from the previous period's statement of changes in equity. The rows then report the various transactions that affected equity, starting with net earnings (line 2). The statement ends with the March 28, 2009 balances (line 8). All the amounts on the bottom line appear on the ending balance sheet, given in Exhibit 11-5 on the next page.

Let's examine the changes in M&S's shareholders' equity during the financial year ended March 28, 2009.

Net Income (Line 2).   During financial year, M&S earned net income (net earnings) of £508 million, which increased Retained Earnings. Trace net income from the consolidated income statements (Exhibit 11-1) to the consolidated statements of changes in equity (Exhibit 11-4). You will note that the net profit that enters retained earnings is the profit attributable to shareholders of the Company (that is the parent company), not net profit for the year.

Other Comprehensive Income (Line 3).   You saw from Exhibit 11-3 (p. 676 , line 9) that total other comprehensive income (loss) was (£578.8). This is recognized directly in equity even though it was not included in the calculation of net income. Because other comprehensive income was negative, it reduces retained earnings (and hedging reserves because some of the comprehensive income items relate to cash flow hedges).

Dividends (Line 4).   M&S paid a total of £354.6 million dividends during the year. This was recorded as a reduction of retained earnings.

Issuance and Cancellation of Shares (Lines 5 and 6).   During the financial year, M&S issued some shares and bought some shares for cancellation. Share options are usually granted to key employees as a form of employee compensation. Share option holders are given the rights to purchase shares at a certain price (called the exercise or strike price) at some time in the future. If the share price is above the exercise price, share option holders would exercise their options, pay the exercise price and obtain the shares at a lower than market price. The issuance of shares due to the exercise of share options increases ordinary share capital and share premium account. Similarly, when M&S bought back shares for cancellation, share capital is reduced.

Other equity transactions (Line 7).   Line 7 contains a few transactions that are beyond the scope of introductory accounting. It contains two items, charges for share-based payments (in accordance with *IFRS2 – Share-based payments*) and de-recognition of financial liabilities (*IAS39 – Financial Instruments: Recognition and Measurement*).

    The ending equity tallies with M&S's balance sheet as at March 28, 2009, shown in Exhibit 11-5 below.

EXHIBIT 11-5 | M&S's Balance Sheet

Marks & Spencer Group Plc
Consolidated Balance Sheet (Partial, adapted)

(in millions £ pounds)	March 28, 2009	March 29, 2008	March 31, 2007
1 Total assets	£7,258.1	£7,161.0	£5,381.0
2 Total liabilities	5,157.5	5,197.0	3,732.8
3 Equity			
4 Share capital	394.4	396.6	424.9
5 Share premium account	236.2	231.4	202.9
6 Capital redemption reserve	2,202.6	2,199.9	2,168.5
7 Hedgeing reserve	62.6	(36.9)	(4.4)
8 Other reserve	(6,542.2)	(6,542.2)	(6,542.2)
9 Retained earnings	5,728.1	5,707.9	5,397.1
10 Total shareholders equity	2,081.7	1,966.7	1,646.8
11 Minority interests in equtiy	18.9	7.3	1.4
12 Total equity	2,100.6	1,964.1	1,648.2
13 Total liabilities and equity	£7,258.1	£7,161.0	£5,381.0

RESPONSIBILITY FOR THE FINANCIAL STATEMENTS
Management's Responsibility

Management issues a report on accountability and audit, along with the company's financial statements. Exhibit 11-6 is an excerpt from the report of management for M&S.

EXHIBIT 11-6 | **Excerpt from Management's Responsibility for Financial Reporting**

Accountability and audit

The Board's objective is to achieve success for M&S by building a sustainable business for the long term, generating shareholder value through consistent profitable growth, whilst making sure that our customers can always trust us to do the right thing. In doing so, the directors recognize that creating value is the reward for taking acceptable risks. The Board has overall accountability for the Group's approach to assessing systems of internal control and risk, and for monitoring their effectiveness. Independent assurance is provided by the external auditors and internal audit, who present their findings regularly to the Audit Committee on behalf of the Board. Internal control and risk assessment are designed to manage, rather than eliminate, the risk of failure to achieve corporate objectives. Accordingly, they can only provide reasonable but not absolute assurance against material misstatement or loss.

Directors' responsibilities

The directors are responsible for preparing the Annual Report, the Remuneration report and the financial statements in accordance with applicable law and regulations. Company law requires the directors to prepare financial statements for each financial year. Under that law the directors have prepared the Group and Company financial statements in accordance with International Financial Reporting Standards (IFRSs) as adopted by the EU. The financial statements are required by law to give a true and fair view of the state of affairs of the Company and the Group and of the profit of the Company and Group for that period.

In preparing those financial statements, the directors are required to:
– select suitable accounting policies and then apply them consistently;
– make judgments and estimates that are reasonable and prudent;
– state that the financial statements comply with IFRSs as adopted by the EU; and
– prepare the financial statements on the going concern basis, unless it is inappropriate to presume that the Group will continue in business, in which case there should be supporting assumptions or qualifications as necessary.

The directors confirm that, to the best of their knowledge:
– the Group and Company financial statements, which have been prepared in accordance with IFRSs as adopted by the EU, give a true and fair view of the assets, liabilities, financial position and profit of the Group and the Company; and
– the Business review contained in this report includes a fair review of the development and performance of the business and the position of the Group and the Company, together with a description of the principal risks and uncertainties that it faces.

Recall from Chapter 4 that internal control is a plan of organization and a system of procedures implemented by company management and the board of directors, and designed to safeguard assets, encourage employees to follow company policy, promote operational efficiency, ensuring accurate and reliable accounting records, and comply with legal requirements. Management declares its responsibility for the internal controls over financial. Management also states that it has monitored the effectiveness of these controls, including assurances from both internal and external auditors. In some jurisdictions, you may find additional requirements regarding management responsibilities. For example, in the United States, the Sarbanes-Oxley Act (SOX) requires companies to make a formal assessment of the effectiveness of internal controls. Similar provisions exist in Japan and China (colloquially termed J-SOX and C-SOX). A brief review of SOX was covered in Chapter 4 (p. 238).

Audit Report

The requirement for audit of financial statements is legally placed by respective jurisdiction's corporation or company law. Companies engage external auditors who are certified public accountants to examine their financial statements (and other aspects of the financial report as required, such as internal controls, director's report, remuneration report, etc.). The independent auditors express an opinion on whether the company's financial statements comply with the applicable accounting standards and regulations. Exhibit 11-7 contains excerpts of the auditor's report for M&S and its subsidiaries.

An audit report is usually addressed to the board of directors and shareholders of the company. A partner of the auditing firm signs the firm's name to the report. In this case, the auditing firm is the London office of **PricewaterhouseCoopers** (one of the "Big 4" accounting firms, along with **Deloitte & Touche**, **Ernst & Young** and **KPMG**). The audit report on financial statements typically contains four sections:

- The first section identifies the audited financial statements as well as the company being audited.
- The second section outlines the respective responsibility of the company's management as well as the auditor's responsibilities.
- The third section describes how the audit was performed in accordance with generally accepted auditing standards of the jurisdiction (in this case, it is the UK and Ireland's International Standards on Auditing issued by the Auditing Practices Board). These are the standards used by auditors as the benchmark for evaluating audit quality.
- The last section expresses the auditor's combined opinion on the entity's financial statements, remuneration report and director's report. This may be different in different jurisdictions, depending on the local requirements. You may see assessment of internal controls reported in some companies. PricewaterhouseCoopers is expressing an **unqualified (clean) opinion**. The unqualified opinion is the highest statement of assurance that an independent certified public accountant can express. Unqualified means the auditors did not qualify the opinion with matters that require the readers' attention. Qualified opinion may be given if there is one or more areas where the financial statements may not comply with applicable accountings standards. If the auditors are of the opinion that the financial statements are materially misstated, they may issue an adverse opinion. In very rare cases, auditors may not even be able to express an opinion due to their inability to complete the audit procedures as required.

EXHIBIT 11-7 | **Excerpt of Report of Independent Registered Public Accounting Firm**

Independent auditors' report to the members of Marks & Spencer Group plc

We have audited the Group and parent company financial statements (the 'financial statements') of Marks & Spencer Group plc for the year ended March 28, 2009 which comprise the Consolidated and Company income statements, the Consolidated and Company balance sheets, the Consolidated and Company cash flow statements, the Consolidated statement of recognized income and expense, the Company statement of changes in shareholders' equity and the related Group and parent company notes. These financial statements have been prepared under the accounting policies set out therein. We have also audited the information in the Remuneration report that is described as having been audited.

Respective responsibilities of directors and auditors
The directors' responsibilities for preparing the Annual Report, the Remuneration report and the financial statements in accordance with applicable law and International Financial Reporting Standards (IFRSs) as adopted by the European Union are set out in the Statement of directors' responsibilities.

Our responsibility is to audit the financial statements and the part of the Remuneration report to be audited in accordance with relevant legal and regulatory requirements and International Standards on Auditing (UK and Ireland). ... We report to you our opinion as to whether the financial statements give a true and fair view and whether the financial statements and the part of the Remuneration report to be audited have been properly prepared in accordance with the Companies Act 1985 and, as regards the Group financial statements, Article 4 of the IAS Regulation. We also report to you whether in our opinion the information given in the Directors' report is consistent with the financial statements. ... In addition we report to you if, in our opinion, the Company has not kept proper accounting records, if we have not received all the information and explanations we require for our audit, or if information specified by law regarding directors' remuneration and other transactions is not disclosed. ...

Basis of audit opinion
We conducted our audit in accordance with International Standards on Auditing (UK and Ireland) issued by the Auditing Practices Board. An audit includes examination, on a test basis, of evidence relevant to the amounts and disclosures in the financial statements and the part of the Remuneration report to be audited. It also includes an assessment of the significant estimates and judgments made by the directors in the preparation of the financial statements, and of whether the accounting policies are appropriate to the Group's and Company's circumstances, consistently applied and adequately disclosed.

We planned and performed our audit so as to obtain all the information and explanations which we considered necessary in order to provide us with sufficient evidence to give reasonable assurance that the financial statements and the part of the Remuneration report to be audited are free from material misstatement, whether caused by fraud or other irregularity or error. In forming our opinion we also evaluated the overall adequacy of the presentation of information in the financial statements and the part of the Remuneration report to be audited.

Opinion
In our opinion:
- the financial statements give a true and fair view, in accordance with IFRSs as adopted by the European Union, of the state of the Group's and the parent company's affairs as at March 28, 2009 and of the Group's and the parent company's profit and cash flows for the year then ended;
- the financial statements and the part of the Remuneration report to be audited have been properly prepared in accordance with the Companies Act 1985 and, as regards the Group financial statements, Article 4 of the IAS Regulation; and
- the information given in the Directors' report is consistent with the financial statements.

PricewaterhouseCoopers LLP
Chartered Accountants and Registered Auditors
London
May 18, 2009

DECISION GUIDELINES

USING THE INCOME STATEMENT AND RELATED NOTES IN INVESTMENT ANALYSIS

Suppose you've completed your studies, taken a job, and been fortunate to save $10,000. Now you are ready to start investing. These guidelines provide a framework for using accounting information for investment analysis.

Decision	Factors to Consider		Decision Variable or Model
Which measure of profitability should be used for investment analysis?	Are you interested in accounting income? →	Income, including all revenues, expenses, gains, and losses?	Net income (bottom line)
		Income that can be → expected to repeat from year to year?	Income from continuing operations
	Are you interested in cash flows? →		Cash flows from operating activities (Chapter 12)

Note: A conservative strategy may use both income and cash flows and compare the two sets of results.

What is the estimated value of the share?	If you believe the company can earn the income (or → cash flow) indefinitely	$$\text{Estimated value} = \frac{\text{Annual income}}{\text{Investment capitalization rate}}$$
	If you believe the company can earn the income (or → cash flow) for a finite number of years	$$\text{Estimated value} = \text{Annual income} \times \begin{array}{l}\text{Present value of annuity}\\ \text{(See Appendix B)}\end{array}$$
How does risk affect the value of the share?	If the investment is high risk →	Increase the investment capitalization rate
	If the investment is low risk →	Decrease the investment capitalization rate

END-OF-CHAPTER SUMMARY PROBLEM

The following information was taken from the ledger of Maxim, Inc.:

Prior-period adjustment—		Treasury shares, ordinary	
credit to Retained Earnings	$ 5,000	(5,000 shares at cost)	$ 25,000
Gain on sale of PPE..........................	21,000	Selling expenses.................................	78,000
Cost of goods sold...........................	380,000	Ordinary share, no par,	
Income tax expense (saving):		45,000 shares issued.....................	180,000
Continuing operations.................	32,000	Sales revenue	620,000
Discontinued operations..............	8,000	Interest expense.................................	30,000
Preference share, 8%, $100 par,		Income from discontinued	
500 shares issued..........................	50,000	operations	20,000
Dividends.......................................	16,000	Loss due to lawsuit............................	11,000
Retained earnings, beginning,		General expenses..............................	62,000
as originally reported	103,000		

I Requirement

1. Prepare an income statement (with all revenues and gains grouped together) and a statement of changes in equity for Maxim, Inc., for the current year ended December 31, 2010. Include the earnings-per-share presentation and show computations. Assume no changes in the number of shares outstanding during the year.

7. Never Lost Systems earned income before tax of $190,000. Taxable income was $165,000, and the income tax rate was 35%. Never Lost recorded income tax with this journal entry:

a.	Income Tax Expense	66,500	
	Income Tax Payable		57,750
	Deferred Tax Liability		8,750
b.	Income Tax Expense	66,500	
	Income Tax Payable		66,500
c.	Income Tax Payable	66,500	
	Income Tax Expense		57,750
	Deferred Tax Liability		8,750
d.	Income Tax Expense	57,750	
	Income Tax Payable		57,750

8. Deferred Tax Liability is usually

	Type of Account	Reported on the
a.	Long-term	Income statement
b.	Long-term	Balance sheet
c.	Short-term	Statement of changes in equity
d.	Short-term	Income statement

9. The main purpose of the statement of changes in equity is to report
   a. reasons for changes in the equity accounts.
   b. results of operations.
   c. financial position.
   d. comprehensive income.

10. An audit report by independent accountants
    a. gives investors assurance that the company's financial statements conform to GAAP.
    b. is ultimately the responsibility of the management of the client company.
    c. ensures that the financial statements are error-free.
    d. gives investors assurance that the company is a safe investment.

Accounting Vocabulary

clean opinion (p. 682) An *unqualified opinion.*

comprehensive income (p. 673) A company's change in total shareholders' equity from all sources other than from the owners of the business.

earnings per share (EPS) (p. 675) Amount of a company's net income per share of its outstanding ordinary shares.

earnings quality (p. 662) The characteristics of an earnings number that make it most useful for decision making. The degree to which earnings are an accurate reflection of underlying economic events for both revenues and expenses, and the extent to which earnings from a company's core operations are improving over time. Assuming that revenues and expenses are measured accurately, high-quality earnings are reflected in steadily improving sales and steadily declining costs over time, so that income from continuing operations follows a high and improving pattern over time.

extraordinary items (p. 667) An *extraordinary gain or loss.* These gains and losses are both unusual for the company and infrequent. Not allowed under IFRS.

investment capitalization rate (p. 669) An earnings rate used to estimate the value of an investment in shares.

pretax accounting income (p. 677) Income before tax on the income statement.

prior-period adjustment (p. 672) A correction to beginning balance of retained earnings for an error of an earlier period.

statement of changes in equity (p. 679) Reports the changes in all categories of shareholders' equity during the period.

taxable income (p. 678) The basis for computing the amount of tax to pay the government.

unqualified (clean) opinion (p. 682) An audit opinion stating that the financial statements are reliable.

ASSESS YOUR PROGRESS

Short Exercises

S11-1 (*Learning Objective 1: Analyzing a corporate income statement*) Research has shown that about 40% of financial statement frauds are committed by companies that improperly recognize revenue. What does this mean? Describe the most common ways companies improperly recognize revenue.

S11-2 (*Learning Objective 1: Analyzing items on an income statement*) Study the 2010 (not 2011) income statement of Household Imports, Inc., and answer the following questions about the company:

writing assignment ■

Household Imports, Inc. Consolidated Income Statement of Operations (Adapted)		
	Year Ended	
(In thousands except per share amounts)	**2010**	**2009**
1 Net sales...	$1,825,775	$1,806,293
Operating costs and expenses:		
2 Cost of sales (including buying and store occupancy costs).................	1,121,697	1,045,380
3 Selling, general, and administrative expenses..........................	549,250	526,550
4 Depreciation and amortization...	55,275	48,750
	1,726,222	1,620,680
5 Operating income (loss)...	99,553	185,613
Nonoperating (income) and expenses:		
6 Interest and investment income.......................................	(2,665)	(2,760)
7 Interest expense...	1,785	1,610
	(880)	(1,150)
8 Income (loss) from continuing operations before income taxes...............	100,433	186,763
9 Provision (benefit) for income taxes..................................	36,384	69,515
10 Income (loss) from continuing operations............................	64,049	117,248
11 Discontinued operations:		
12 Income (loss) from discontinued operations (including write down of assets held for sale of $7,993 in 2011)...........................	(2,500)	270
13 Income tax savings..	—	—
14 Income (loss) from discontinued operations...........................	(2,500)	270
15 Net income (loss)...	$ 61,549	$ 117,518
16 Basic Earnings (loss) per share from continuing operations:	$ 0.69	$ 1.52
17 Basic Earnings (loss) per share from discontinued operations:	$ (0.06)	$ 0.00
18 Basic Earnings (loss) per share:	$ 0.63	$ 1.52

1. How much gross profit did Household earn on the sale of its products? How much was income from continuing operations? Net income?
2. At the end of 2010, what dollar amount of net income would most sophisticated investors use to predict Household's net income for 2011 and beyond? Name this item, give its amount, and state your reason.

1. How much cash did the issuance of ordinary shares bring in during 2010?
2. What was the effect of the share dividends on Mason's retained earnings? On total paid-in capital? On total shareholders' equity? On total assets?
3. What was the cost of the treasury shares that Mason purchased during 2010? What was the cost of the treasury shares that Mason sold during the year? For how much did Mason sell the treasury shares during 2010?

writing assignment ■

S11-12 (*Learning Objective 4: Identifying responsibility and standards for the financial statements*)   The annual report of Ashburnham Computer, Inc., included the following:

Management's Annual Report on Internal Control over Financial Reporting

The Company's management is responsible for establishing and maintaining adequate control over financial reporting [....] Management conducted an evaluation of the effectiveness of the Company's internal control over financial reporting [....] Based on this evaluation, management has concluded that the Company's internal control over financial reporting was effective as of September 30, 2010....

Report of Independent Registered Public Accounting Firm
The Board of Directors and Shareholders
Ashburnham Computer, Inc.:

We have audited the accompanying consolidated balance sheets of Ashburnham Computer, Inc., and subsidiaries (the Company) as of September 30, 2010, and September 30, 2009, and the related consolidated statements of operations, shareholders' equity, and cash flows for each of the years in the three-year period ended September 30, 2010. These consolidated financial statements are the responsibility of the Company's management. Our responsibility is to express an opinion on these consolidated financial statements based on our audits.
We conducted our audits in accordance with the standards of the Public Company Accounting Oversight Board (United States)....
In our opinion, the consolidated financial statements referred to above present fairly, in all material respects, the financial position of the Company as of September 30, 2010, and September 30, 2009, and the results of their operations and their cash flows for each of the years in the three-year period ended September 30, 2010, in conformity with accounting principles generally accepted in the United States of America.

/S/ SLMA LLP

Portage, Michigan
December 28, 2010

---

1. Who is responsible for Ashburnham's financial statements?
2. By what accounting standard are the financial statements prepared?
3. Identify one concrete action that Ashburnham management takes to fulfill its responsibility for the reliability of the company's financial information.
4. Which entity gave an outside, independent opinion on the Ashburnham financial statements? Where was this entity located, and when did it release its opinion to the public?
5. Exactly what did the audit cover? Give names and dates.
6. By what standard did the auditor conduct the audit?
7. What was the auditor's opinion of Ashburnham's financial statements?

Exercises

All of the A and B exercises can be found within MyAccountingLab, an online homework and practice environment. Your instructor may ask you to complete these exercises using MyAccountingLab.

(Group A)

E11-13A *(Learning Objective 1: Preparing and using a complex income statement)* Suppose Dighton Cycles, Inc., reported a number of special items on its income statement. The following data, listed in no particular order, came from Dighton's financial statements (amounts in thousands):

Income tax expense (saving):		Net sales...	$14,000
Continuing operations.................	$295	Foreign-currency translation	
Discontinued operations..............	56	adjustment	320
Unrealized gain on		Income from discontinued operations	280
available-for-sale investments.......	35	Dividends declared and paid	600
Short-term investments....................	25	Total operating expenses.......................	12,800

Requirement

1. Show how Dighton Cycles Inc.'s income statement for the year ended September 30, 2010 should appear. Omit earnings per share.

E11-14A *(Learning Objective 1: Preparing and using a complex income statement)* The Regan Books Company accounting records include the following for 2010 (in thousands):

■ **spreadsheet**

Other revenues...	$ 2,400
Income tax expense—exceptional gain..	1,600
Income tax expense—income from continuing operations...........	2,880
Exceptional gain..	4,000
Sales revenue..	102,000
Total operating expenses..	97,200

Requirements

1. Prepare Regan Books's income statement for the year ended December 31, 2010, including EPS. Regan Books had 1,800 thousand shares of ordinary shares and no preference share outstanding during the year.
2. Assume investors capitalize Regan Books's earnings at 5%. Estimate the price of one Regan Books's share.

Requirements

1. Determine the December 31, 2010, balances in Clean Water's shareholders' equity accounts and total shareholders' equity on this date.
2. Clean Water's total liabilities on December 31, 2010, are $8,000. What is Clean Water's debt ratio on this date?
3. Was there a profit or a loss for the year ended December 31, 2010? How can you tell?
4. At what price per share did Clean Water issue ordinary shares during 2010?

(Group B)

E11-23B (*Learning Objective 1: Preparing and using a complex income statement*) Suppose Searstown Cycles, Inc., reported a number of special items on its income statement. The following data, listed in no particular order, came from Searstown's financial statements (amounts in thousands):

Income tax expense (saving):			Net sales....................................	$13,300
Continuing operations..................	$300		Foreign-currency translation	
Discontinued operations..............	(62)		adjustment	330
Unrealized gain on			Income from discontinued operations	310
available-for-sale investments.......	38		Dividends declared and paid	610
Short-term investments..................	50		Total operating expenses.......................	12,400

Requirement

1. Show how Searstown Cycles Inc.'s income statement for the year ended September 30, 2010 should appear. Omit earnings per share.

E11-24B (*Learning Objective 1: Preparing and using a complex income statement*) The Beemer Books Company accounting records include the following for 2010 (in thousands):

Other revenues..	$ 2,100
Income tax expense—exceptional gain	1,440
Income tax expense—income from continuing operations............	4,840
Exceptional gain..	3,600
Sales revenue..	107,000
Total operating expenses..	97,000

Requirements

1. Prepare Beemer Books' income statement for the year ended December 31, 2010, including EPS. Beemer Books had 1,500 thousand ordinary shares and no preference share outstanding during the year.
2. Assume investors capitalize Beemer Books earnings at 6%. Estimate the price of the company's share.

E11-25B (*Learning Objective 1: Using income data for investment analysis*) During 2010, Doppler, Inc., had sales of $7.36 billion, operating profit of $2.10 billion, and net income of $3.10 billion. EPS was $4.20. On April 12, 2011, one Doppler ordinary share was priced at $54.40 on the New York Stock Exchange.

What investment capitalization rate did investors appear to be using to determine the value of one Doppler share? The formula for the value of one share uses EPS in the calculation.

E11-26B *(Learning Objective 1: Computing earnings per share)* Tidepool Loan Company's balance sheet reports the following:

Preference shares, $40 par value, 4%, 9,000 shares issued...........	$ 360,000
Ordinary shares, $2.00 par, 1,000,000 shares issued	2,000,000
Treasury shares, 200,000 shares at cost	1,200,000

During 2010 Tidepool earned net income of $6,000,000. Compute Tidepool's earnings per ordinary share for 2010. (Round EPS to two decimal places.)

E11-27B *(Learning Objective 1: Computing and using earnings per share)* Helenic Holding Company operates numerous businesses, including motel, auto rental, and real estate companies. Year 2010 was interesting for Helenic, which reported the following on its income statement (in millions):

Net revenues	$3,934
Total expenses and other...	3,357
Income from continuing operations..............................	577
Discontinued operations, net of tax.............................	88
Income before exceptional item and cumulative...........	
effect of accounting change, net of tax...............	665
Exceptional gain, net of tax..	10
Net income...	$ 675

During 2010, Helenic had the following (in millions, except for par value per share):

Ordinary share, $0.30 par value, 600 shares issued................	$ 180
Treasury share, 200 shares at cost...	(3,542)

I Requirement

1. Show how Helenic should report earnings per share for 2010. (Round EPS to the nearest cent.)

E11-28B *(Learning Objective 2: Accounting for income tax by a corporation)* For 2010, its first year of operations, Johnson Advertising earned pre-tax accounting income (on the income statement) of $750,000. Taxable income (on the tax return filed with the tax authority) is $650,000. The income tax rate is 35%. Record Johnson's income tax for the year. Show what Johnson will report on its 2010 income statement and balance sheet for this situation. Start the income statement with income before tax.

E11-29B *(Learning Objective 2: Accounting for income tax by a corporation)* During 2010, Florimax Heights Corp. income statement reported income of $410,000 before tax. The company's income tax return filed with the tax authorily showed taxable income of $360,000. During 2010, Florimax Heights was subjected to an income tax rate of 32%.

I Requirements

1. Journalize Florimax Heights's income taxes for 2010.
2. How much income tax did Florimax Heights have to pay for the year 2010?
3. At the beginning of 2010, Florimax Heights's balance of Deferred Tax Liability was $34,000. How much Deferred Tax Liability did Florimax Heights report on its balance sheet at December 31, 2010?

Q11-41 Use the Copyhouse Corporation data in question 39. At the end of its first year of operations, Copyhouse's deferred tax liability is

a. $12,000.   c. $36,000.
b. $20,000.   d. $28,000.

Q11-42 Which of the following items is most closely related to prior-period adjustments?

a. Preference share dividends   c. Accounting changes
b. Retained earnings   d. Earnings per share

Q11-43 Examine the statement of changes in equity of Mason Electronics Corporation.

| | | | | | Accumulated Other Comprehensive Income | | |
	Ordinary Share $2 Par	Additional Paid-in Capital	Retained Earnings	Treasury share	Unrealized Gain (Loss) on Investments	Foreign-Currency Translation Adjustment	Total Shareholders' Equity
	Mason Electronics Corporation Statement of Changes in Equity Year Ended December 31, 2010						
1 Balance, December 31, 2009.....	$20,000	$ 140,000	$185,000	$(24,000)	$21,000	$(11,000)	$ 331,000
2 Issuance of share......................	40,000	1,100,000					1,140,000
3 Net income			93,000				93,000
4 Cash dividends.........................			(23,000)				(23,000)
5 Share dividend—10%..............	6,000	78,000	(84,000)				0
6 Purchase of treasury share				(8,000)			(8,000)
7 Sale of treasury share...............		7,000		5,000			12,000
8 Unrealized gain on investments					6,000		6,000
9 Foreign-currency translation adj.......................						3,000	3,000
10 Balance, December 31, 2010	$66,000	$1,325,000	$171,000	$ 27,000	$27,000	$ (8,000)	$1,554,000

What was the market value of each share that Mason gave its shareholders in the share dividend?

a. $3,000   c. $42,000
b. $28   d. $56

Q11-44 Which statement is true?

a. Independent auditors prepare the financial statements.
b. Management audits the financial statements.
c. GAAP governs the form and content of the financial statements.
d. A qualified opinion is one that is issued by qualified CPA.

Problems

All of the A and B problems can be found within MyAccountingLab, an online homework and practice environment. Your instructor may ask you to complete these problems using MyAccountingLab.

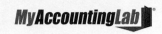

(Group A)

P11-45A *(Learning Objective 1: Preparing a complex income statement)*   The following information was taken from the records of Daughtry Cosmetics, Inc., at December 31, 2010:

Prior-period adjustment—			Dividends on ordinary share	$24,000
debit to Retained Earnings.............	$	1,000	Interest expense.................................	30,000
Income tax expense (saving):			Gain on lawsuit settlement................	14,000
Continuing operations		33,980	Dividend revenue	20,000
Income from discontinued			Treasury share, ordinary	
operations.....................................		8,680	(3,000 shares at cost)...............	17,000
Exceptional loss............................		(12,280)	General expenses...............................	85,000
Loss on sale of PPE		15,000	Sales revenue.....................................	610,000
Income from discontinued			Retained earnings, beginning,	
operations.....................................		21,000	as originally reported...............	195,000
Preference share, 4%, $20 par,			Selling expenses.................................	105,000
3,000 shares issued		60,000	Ordinary share, no par,	
Exceptional loss		29,400	25,000 shares authorized	
Cost of goods sold.................................		324,000	and issued...............................	400,000

▌Requirements

1. Prepare Daughtry Cosmetics's income statement, which lists all revenues together and all expenses together, for the fiscal year ended December 31, 2010. Include earnings-per-share data.
2. Evaluate income for the year ended December 31, 2010. Daughtry's top managers hoped to earn income from continuing operations equal to 12% of sales.

P11-46A *(Learning Objective 3: Preparing a statement of changes in equity)*   Use the data in Problem P11-45A to prepare the Daughtry Cosmetics statement of changes in equity for the year ended December 31, 2010. Use the Statement of Changes in Equity for Maxim, Inc., in the End-of-Chapter Summary Problem as a model.

P11-47A *(Learning Objective 1: Using income data to make an investment decision)*   Daughtry Cosmetics in Problem P11-45A holds significant promise for carving a niche in its industry. A group of Irish investors is considering purchasing the company's outstanding ordinary shares. Daughtry shares are currently selling for $43 per share.

A *BetterLife Magazine* story predicted the company's income is bound to grow. It appears that Daughtry can earn at least its current level of income for the indefinite future. Based on this information, the investors think that an appropriate investment capitalization rate for estimating the value of Daughtry's ordinary shares is 5%. How much will this belief lead the investors to offer for Daughtry Cosmetics? Will Daughtry's existing shareholders be likely to accept this offer? Explain your answers.

P11-48A (*Learning Objective 1: Computing earnings per share and estimating the price of a share*)   Overhaul Experts, Ltd., (OEL) specializes in taking underperforming companies to a higher level of performance. OEL's capital structure at December 31, 2009, included 11,000 shares of $2.30 preference share and 125,000 ordinary shares. During 2010, OEL issued ordinary shares and ended the year with 131,000 ordinary shares outstanding. Average ordinary shares outstanding during 2010 were 128,000. Income from continuing operations during 2010 was $220,000. The company discontinued a segment of the business at a loss of $67,000, and an exceptional item generated a gain of $50,000. All amounts are after income tax.

I Requirements

1. Compute OEL's earnings per share. Start with income from continuing operations.
2. Analysts believe OEL can earn its current level of income for the indefinite future. Estimate the market price of a share of OEL ordinary shares at investment capitalization rates of 10%, 12%, and 14%. Which estimate presumes an investment in OEL is the most risky? How can you tell?

P11-49A (*Learning Objective 1: Preparing a corrected income statement, including comprehensive income*)   Jim Heller, accountant for Perfect Pie Foods, was injured in an auto accident. Another employee prepared the following income statement for the fiscal year ended June 30, 2010:

Perfect Pie Foods, Inc.
Income Statement
June 30, 2010

Revenue and gains:		
Sales		$896,000
Paid-in capital in excess of par		15,000
Total revenues and gains		911,000
Expenses and losses:		
Cost of goods sold	$387,000	
Selling expenses	101,000	
General expenses	93,000	
Sales returns	23,000	
Unrealized loss on available-for-sale investments	13,000	
Dividends paid	16,000	
Sales discounts	12,000	
Income tax expense	35,000	
Total expenses and losses		680,000
Income from operations		231,000
Other gains and losses:		
Exceptional loss	(42,000)	
Income from discontinued operations	27,000	
Total other gains (losses)		(15,000)
Net income		$216,000
Earnings per share		$ 10.80

The individual *amounts* listed on the income statement are correct. However, some *accounts* are reported incorrectly, and some accounts do not belong on the income statement at all. Also, income tax (40%) has not been applied to all appropriate figures. Perfect Pie Foods issued 24,000 ordinary shares back in 2004 and held 4,000 shares as treasury shares all during the fiscal year 2010.

I Requirement

1. Prepare a corrected income statement including comprehensive income, for fiscal year 2010. Include earnings per share.

P11-50A *(Learning Objective 2: Accounting for a corporation's income tax)* The accounting (not the income tax) records of Crowley Publications, Inc., provide the comparative income statement for 2010 and 2011, respectively:

	2010	2011
Total revenue	$930,000	$1,020,000
Expenses:		
Cost of goods sold	$410,000	$ 440,000
Operating expenses	290,000	300,000
Total expenses before tax	700,000	740,000
Pretax accounting income	$230,000	$ 280,000

Taxable income for 2010 includes these modifications from pre-tax accounting income:

a. Additional taxable income of $18,000 for accounting income earned in 2011 but taxed in 2010.
b. Additional depreciation expense of $30,000 for tax depreciation purposes.

The income tax rate is 30%.

I Requirements

1. Compute Crowley's taxable income for 2010.
2. Journalize the corporation's income taxes for 2010.
3. Prepare the corporation's income statement for 2010.

P11-51A *(Learning Objective 3: Using a statement of changes in equity)* Falmouth Food Specialties, Inc., reported the following statement of changes in equity for the year ended October 31, 2010:

Falmouth Food Specialties, Inc.
Statement of Changes in Equity
For the Year Ended October 31, 2010

(In millions)	Ordinary Share	Additional Paid-in Capital	Retained Earnings	Treasury share	Total
Balance, October 31, 2009	$450	$1,670	$ 911	$(114)	$2,917
Net income			280		280
Cash dividends			(197)		(197)
Issuance of share (25 shares)	50	200			250
Dividend	100	400	(500)		—
Sale of treasury share		12		13	25
Balance, October 31, 2010	$600	$2,282	$ 494	$(101)	$3,275

❙ Requirements

Answer these questions about Falmouth Food Specialties' shareholders' equity transactions.

1. The income tax rate is 30%. How much income before income tax did Falmouth Food Specialties report on the income statement?
2. What is the par value of the company's ordinary shares?
3. At what price per share did Falmouth Food Specialties issue its ordinary shares during the year?
4. What was the cost of treasury shares sold during the year? What was the selling price of the treasury shares? What was the increase in total shareholders' equity?
5. Falmouth Food Specialties' statement of changes in equity lists the share transactions in the order in which they occurred. What was the percentage of the share dividend? (Round to the nearest percentage.)

(Group B)

P11-52B (*Learning Objective 1: Preparing a complex income statement*)   The following information was taken from the records of Ahern Cosmetics, Inc., at December 31, 2010:

Prior-period adjustment—			Dividends on ordinary share	$23,000
debit to Retained Earnings	$ 3,000		Interest expense	25,000
Income tax expense (saving):			Gain on lawsuit settlement	9,000
Continuing operations	24,450		Dividend revenue	15,000
Income from discontinued			Treasury share, ordinary	
operations	7,190		(4,000 shares at cost)	12,000
Exceptional loss	(12,910)		General expenses	80,000
Loss on sale of PPE	13,000		Sales revenue	560,000
Income from discontinued			Retained earnings, beginning,	
operations	18,000		as originally reported	193,000
Preference share, 10%, $15 par,			Selling expenses	90,000
500 shares issued	7,500		Ordinary shares, no par,	
Exceptional loss	32,000		27,000 shares authorized	
Cost of goods sold	314,000		and issued	380,000

❙ Requirements

1. Prepare Ahern Cosmetics's income statement, for the fiscal year ended December 31, 2010. Include earnings-per-share data.
2. Evaluate income for the year ended December 31, 2010. Ahern's top managers hoped to earn income from continuing operations equal to 14% of sales.

P11-53B (*Learning Objective 3: Preparing a statement of changes in equity*)   Use the data in Problem P11-52B to prepare Ahern Cosmetics's statement of changes in equity for the year ended December 31, 2010. Use the Statement of Changes in Equity for Maxim, Inc., in the End-of-Chapter Summary Problem as a model.

P11-54B (*Learning Objective 1: Using income data to make an investment decision*)   Ahern Cosmetics in Problem P11-52B holds significant promise for carving a niche in its industry. A group of Swedish investors is considering purchasing the company's outstanding ordinary shares. Ahern's shares are currently selling for $19 per share.

A *Dollars and Sense* story predicted the company's income is bound to grow. It appears that Ahern can earn at least its current level of income for the indefinite future. Based on this information, the investors think that an appropriate investment capitalization rate for estimating the value of Ahern's ordinary shares is 10%. How much will this belief lead the investors to offer for Ahern Cosmetics? Will Ahern's existing shareholders be likely to accept this offer? Explain your answers.

P11-55B (*Learning Objective 1: Computing earnings per share and estimating the price of a share*)   New Ventures Ltd. (NVL) specializes in taking underperforming companies to a higher level of performance. NVL's capital structure at December 31, 2009, included 12,000 shares of $2.20 preference share and 130,000 ordinary shares. During 2010, NVL issued ordinary shares and ended the year with 138,000 ordinary shares outstanding. Average ordinary shares outstanding during 2010 were 134,000. Income from continuing operations during 2010 was $225,000. The company discontinued a segment of the business at a loss of $66,000, and an exceptional item generated a gain of $48,000. All amounts are after income tax.

I Requirements

1. Compute NVL's earnings per share. Start with income from continuing operations.
2. Analysts believe NVL can earn its current level of income for the indefinite future. Estimate the market price of a share of NVL ordinary shares at investment capitalization rates of 9%, 11%, and 13%. Which estimate presumes an investment in NVL is the most risky? How can you tell?

P11-56B (*Learning Objective 1: Preparing a corrected income statement, including comprehensive income*)   Jack Hodges, accountant for Edible Pie Foods, was injured in an auto accident. Another employee prepared the following income statement for the fiscal year ended June 30, 2010:

Edible Pie Foods, Inc.		
Income Statement		
June 30, 2010		
Revenue and gains:		
Sales..		$894,000
Paid-in capital in excess of par..		14,000
Total revenues and gains...		908,000
Expenses and losses:		
Cost of goods sold..	$382,000	
Selling expenses...	106,000	
General expenses..	95,000	
Sales returns...	26,000	
Unrealized loss on available-for-sale investments.................	12,000	
Dividends paid	17,000	
Sales discounts	14,000	
Income tax expense..	33,000	
Total expenses and losses..		685,000
Income from operations		223,000
Other gains and losses:		
Exceptional gain..	40,000	
Loss on discontinued operations	(26,000)	
Total other gains (losses)..		14,000
Net income..		$237,000
Earnings per share		$ 23.70

The individual *amounts* listed on the income statement are correct. However, some *accounts* are reported incorrectly, and some accounts do not belong on the income statement at all. Also, income tax (30%) has not been applied to all appropriate figures. Edible Pie Foods issued 13,000 ordinary shares back in 2004 and held 3,000 shares as treasury shares all during the fiscal year 2010.

I *Requirement*

1. Prepare a corrected income statement including comprehensive income for 2010. Include earnings per share.

P11-57B (*Learning Objective 2: Accounting for a corporation's income tax*) The accounting (not the income tax) records of Consolidated Publications, Inc., provide the comparative income statement for 2010 and 2011, respectively:

	2010	2011
Total revenue	$920,000	$1,010,000
Expenses:		
Cost of goods sold	$470,000	$ 500,000
Operating expenses	270,000	280,000
Total expenses before tax	740,000	780,000
Pretax accounting income	$180,000	$ 230,000

Taxable income for 2010 includes these modifications from pre-tax accounting income:

a. Additional taxable income of $13,000 for accounting income earned in 2011 but taxed in 2010.
b. Additional depreciation expense of $40,000 for tax depreciation purposes.

The income tax rate is 35%.

I *Requirements*

1. Compute Consolidated's taxable income for 2010.
2. Journalize the corporation's income taxes for 2010.
3. Prepare the corporation's income statement for 2010.

P11-58B (*Learning Objective 3: Using a statement of changes in equity*) Franklin Food Specialties Inc. reported the following statement of changes in equity for the year ended October 31, 2010:

Franklin Food Specialties, Inc.
Statement of Change in Equity
For the Year Ended October 31, 2010

(In millions)	Ordinary Share	Additional Paid-in Capital	Retained Earnings	Treasury Share	Total
Balance, October 31, 2009	$440	$1,680	$ 907	$(114)	$2,913
Net income			420		420
Cash dividends			(190)		(190)
Issuance of share (10 shares)	10	220			230
Share dividend	45	990	(1,035)		—
Sale of treasury share		16		11	27
Balance, October 31, 2010	$495	$2,906	$ 102	$(103)	$3,400

I *Requirements*

Answer these questions about Franklin Food Specialties's shareholders' equity transactions.

1. The income tax rate is 40%. How much income before income tax did Franklin Food Specialties report on the income statement?

2. What is the par value of the company's ordinary shares?
3. At what price per share did Franklin Food Specialties issue its ordinary shares during the year?
4. What was the cost of treasury shares sold during the year? What was the selling price of the treasury shares sold? What was the increase in total shareholders' equity?
5. Franklin Food Specialties's statement of changes in equity lists the share transactions in the order in which they occurred. What was the percentage of the share dividend? (Round to the nearest percent).

APPLY YOUR KNOWLEDGE

Decision Cases

Case 1. (*Learning Objective 1: Evaluating the components of income*) Prudhoe Bay Oil Co. is having its initial public offering (IPO) of its shares. To create public interest, Prudhoe Bay's chief financial officer has blitzed the media with press releases. One, in particular, caught your eye. On November 19, Prudhoe Bay announced unaudited earnings per share (EPS) of $1.19, up 89% from last year's EPS of $0.63. An 89% increase in EPS is outstanding!

Before deciding to buy Prudhoe Bay shares, you investigated further and found that the company omitted several items from the determination of unaudited EPS, as follows:

- Unrealized loss on available-for-sale investments, $0.06 per share
- Gain on sale of building, $0.05 per share
- Prior-period adjustment, increase in retained earnings $1.10 per share
- Restructuring expenses, $0.29 per share
- Loss on settlement of lawsuit begun five years ago, $0.12 per share
- Loss on income due to employee labor strike, $0.24 per share
- Income from discontinued operations, $0.09 per share

Wondering how to treat these "special items," you called your stockbroker. She thinks that these items are nonrecurring and outside Prudhoe Bay's core operations. Furthermore, she suggests that you ignore the items and consider Prudhoe Bay's earnings of $1.19 per share to be a good estimate of long-term profitability.

❚ Requirement

1. What EPS number will you use to predict Prudhoe Bay's future profits? Show your work, and explain your reasoning for each item.

Case 2. (*Learning Objective 1: Using the financial statements in investment analysis*) Mike Magid Toyota is an automobile dealership. Magid's annual report includes Note 1— Summary of Significant Accounting Policies as follows:

> **Income Recognition**
>
> **Sales are recognized when cash payment is received or, in the case of credit sales, which represent the majority of . . . sales, when a down payment is received and the customer enters into an installment sales contract. These installment sales contracts . . . are normally collectible over 36 to 60 months. . . .**
>
> **Revenue from auto insurance policies sold to customers are recognized as income over the life of the contracts.**

Bay Area Nissan, a competitor of Mike Magid Toyota, includes the following note in its Summary of Significant Accounting Policies:

> **Accounting Policies for Revenues**
>
> Sales are recognized when cash payment is received or, in the case of credit sales, which represent the majority of . . . sales, when the customer enters into an installment sales contract. Customer down payments are rare. Most of these installment sales contracts are normally collectible over 36 to 60 months. . . . Revenue from auto insurance policies sold to customers are recognized when the customer signs an insurance contract. Expenses arerecognized over the life of the insurance contracts.

Suppose you have decided to invest in an auto dealership and you've narrowed your choices to Magid and Bay Area. Which company's earnings are of higher quality? Why? Will their accounting policies affect your investment decision? If so, how? Mention specific accounts in the financial statements that will differ between the two companies. (Challenge)

Ethical Issue

The income statement of Royal Bank of Singapore reported the following results of operations:

Earnings before income taxes and exceptional gain	$187,046
Income tax expense	72,947
Earnings before exceptional gain	114,099
Exceptional gain, net of income tax	419,557
Net earnings	$533,656

Suppose Royal Bank's management, in violation of International Financial Reporting Standards (IFRS), had reported the company's results of operations in this manner:

Earnings before income taxes	$847,111
Income tax expense	352,651
Net earnings	$494,460

I Requirements

1. Identify the ethical issue in this situation.
2. Who are the stakeholders?
3. Evaluate the issue from the standpoint of (a) economic, (b) legal or regulatory, and (c) ethical dimensions. What are the possible effects on all stakeholders you identified?
4. Put yourself in the position of the controller of the bank. Your boss, the CEO, tries to pressure you to make the disclosure that violates IFRS. What would you do? What are the potential consequences?

Focus on Financials: ■ Nokia Corporation

Refer to **Nokia**'s consolidated financial statements in Appendix A at the end of this book.

❚ Requirements

1. What is your evaluation of the quality of Nokia's earnings in 2008? Explain how you formed your opinion.
2. Unscrupulous management can perform certain accounting tricks to hide bad performance and poor earnings. Give 3 examples of red flags in financial statements and briefly explain why they are a cause for concern.
3. Take the role of an investor and suppose you are determining the price to pay for a share of Nokia shares. Assume you are considering three investment capitalization rates that depend on the risk of an investment in Nokia: 5%, 6%, and 7%. Compute your estimated value of a share of Nokia's share using each of the three capitalization rates. Which estimated value would you base your investment strategy on if you rate Nokia, risky? If you consider Nokia, a safe investment? Use basic earnings per share for 2008.
4. Go to Nokia's Web site and compare your computed estimates to its actual share price. Which of your prices is most realistic? (Challenge)

Group Project

Select a company and research its business. Search the Internet for articles about this company. Obtain its latest available annual report from the company's Web site.

❚ Requirements

1. Based on your group's analysis, come to class prepared to instruct the class on six interesting facts about the company that can be found in its financial statements and the related notes. Your group can mention only the obvious, such as net sales or total revenue, net income, total assets, total liabilities, total shareholders' equity, and dividends, in conjunction with other terms. Once you use an obvious item, you may not use that item again.
2. The group should write a paper discussing the facts that it has uncovered. Limit the paper to two double-spaced word-processed pages.

For online homework, exercises, and problems that provide you with immediate feedback, please visit www.myaccountinglab.com.

Quick Check Answers

1. *d*
2. *b*
3. *d* ($5.12/.04)
4. *d* (($60,000)/(.40)) (rounding causes slight differences for computations of other lines)
5. *a*
6. *a*
7. *a*
8. *b*
9. *a*
10. *a*

12
The Statement of Cash Flows

SPOTLIGHT: Philips

Royal Philips Electronics (**Philips**) of the Netherlands is a diversified health and well-being company, and a world leader in healthcare, lifestyle and lighting. Philips's sales revenue in 2009 financial year was over €23 billion. The worldwide recession has hurt its bottom line hard. Net income was €4,880 million in 2007, but it registered a €92 million loss in 2008. With the recovery in the second half of 2009, Philips returned to profitability, making €424 million in 2009.

In periods of economic hardship, managing cash flows is extremely important. At the same time, with a cash balance of almost €9 billion dollars at the start of 2008, Philips also continued to look for strategic business opportunities.

What did Philips do in terms of its cash flows from operating, investing and financing activities? Let's find out!

Philips
Consolidated Statement of Cash Flows (Adapted)
Financial Year Ended December 31

(in millions € Euros)	2009	2008	2007
1 Income for the period	€ 424	€ (92)	€4,880
2 Income (loss) from discontinued operations	0	(3)	138
3 Depreciation and amortization	1,469	1,528	1,083
4 Impairment	2	1,509	39
5 Net gain on sale of assets	(140)	(1,536)	(3,385)
6 Income and dividends received from equity investments, net	12	(26)	(323)
7 (Increase) decrease in receivables	496	234	(435)
8 (Increase) decrease in inventories	687	(9)	(348)
9 Increase (decrease) in payables, accruals and provisions	(1,091)	335	(17)
10 (Increase) decrease in other current assets and liabilities	(314)	(292)	(76)
11 Proceeds from sales of trading securities	0	0	196
12 Net cash provided by operating activities	1,545	1,648	1,752
13 Purchase of intangible assets	(96)	(121)	(118)
14 Expenditure on development assets	(188)	(154)	(233)
15 Capital expenditures on property, plant and equipment	(524)	(770)	(658)
16 Proceeds from disposals of property, plant and equipment	126	170	81
17 Cash from (used for) derivatives and securities	(39)	337	385
18 Purchase of other non-current financial assets	(6)	0	(17)
19 Proceeds from other non-current financial assets	718	2,576	4,105
20 Purchase of businesses net of cash acquired	(294)	(5,316)	(1,485)
21 Proceeds from sales of interests in businesses	84	24	1,640
22 Net cash provided by (used for) investing activities	(219)	(3,254)	3,700
23 Principal payments of loans and borrowings	(252)	(1,726)	(313)
24 Proceeds from loans and borrowings	312	2,106	29
25 Treasury shares transactions	29	(3,257)	(1,448)
26 Dividends paid	(634)	(698)	(639)
27 Net cash provided used for financing activities	(545)	(3,575)	(2,371)
28 Net cash flows	781	(5,181)	3,081
29 Other adjustments (exchange rates, discontinued operations)	(15)	(76)	(227)
30 Cash and cash equivalents at the beginning of the year	3,620	8,877	6,023
31 Cash and cash equivalents at the end of the year	€4,386	€3,620	€8,877

In preceding chapters, we covered cash flows as they related to various topics: receivables, property, plant and equipment (PPE), and so on. In this chapter, we show you how to prepare and use the statement of cash flows.

We begin with the statement format used by the vast majority of companies, called the indirect method. We end with the alternate format of the statement of cash flows, the direct method.

We start with an introduction, and proceed to discuss the cash flow from operating (using the indirect method), investing and financing activities. For courses that require materials on the preparation of cash flow from operating activities using direct method, it starts on page 733. After working through this chapter, you can analyze the actual cash flows of companies.

LEARNING OBJECTIVES

1 **Identify** the purposes of the statement of cash flows

2 **Distinguish** among operating, investing, and financing cash flows

3 **Prepare** cash flows from operating activities using the indirect method

4 **Prepare** cash flows from investing activities

5 **Prepare** cash flows from financing activities

6 **Prepare** cash flows from operating activities using the direct method

OVERVIEW OF STATEMENT OF CASH FLOWS

The balance sheet reports financial position, and balance sheets from two periods show whether cash had increased or decreased. But that doesn't tell us *why* the cash balance had changed. The income statement reports net income and offers clues about cash, but the income statement doesn't tell *why* cash increased or decreased. We need a third financial statement.

The **statement of cash flows** reports **cash flows**—cash receipts and cash payments—in other words, where cash came from (receipts) and how it was spent (payments). The statement covers a span of time and therefore is labeled "Financial Year Ended December 31, 2010" or "Month Ended June 30, 2011".

IAS7 – Cash Flow Statements is the primary accounting standard that provides guidance on this financial statement. The statement of cash flows serves these purposes:

1. *Predicts future cash flows.*   Past cash receipts and payments are reasonably good predictors of the timing, amount and certainty of future cash flows. For example, shareholders want dividends on their investments and creditors demand interest and principal on their loans. The statement of cash flows reports on an entity's ability to make these payments.

2. *Evaluates management decisions.*   An entity's ability to adapt to changing circumstances and opportunities depends on its ability to generate funds from operations and raise funding from shareholders and creditors. It also enhances comparability of different entities as it reduces the effects of using different accounting treatments for the same transactions and events.

3. *Shows the relationship of net income to cash flows.*   An entity's performance is measured using accrual accounting. Under accrual accounting, cash transfers are neither a prerequisite nor evidence of the revenue generation process. Therefore, it is important to understand the relationship between income and cash flows generated over a period time.

On a statement of cash flows, *cash* means more than just cash in the bank. It includes **cash equivalents**, which are highly liquid short-term investments that can be converted into known amounts of cash readily and not subject to significant risk of changes in its value. Examples include money-market accounts and investments in government securities. It may also include bank overdrafts, when used as an integral part of day-to-day cash management of the entity. Throughout this chapter, the term "cash" refers to cash and cash equivalents. Philips provided this explanation about its cash and cash equivalents.

OBJECTIVE

1 **Identify** the purposes of the statement of cash flows

> **EXCERPTS FROM PHILIPS'S NOTES TO THE 2009 FINANCIAL STATEMENTS**
>
> Cash and cash equivalents include all cash balances and short-term highly liquid investments with an original maturity of three months or less that are readily convertible into known amounts of cash. They are stated at face value, which approximates fair value.

Have a look again at Philips's consolidated statement of cash flows on page 712. Let's see some common features of a cash flow statement:

1. It reports inflows and outflows across three categories: operating activities (lines 1–12), investing activities (lines 13–22) and financing activities (lines 23–27). Inflows are shown as positive numbers, and outflows in shown in brackets to indicate negative numbers.
2. The net cash flow (line 28) is the sum of the three cash flow subtotals (lines 12, 22 and 27).
3. Net cash flow (line 28), plus some other adjustment beyond the scope of this textbook (in Philips's case, they were actually impact of changes in foreign currency and discontinued operations), explains the changes in cash and cash equivalent at the beginning of the year (line 30) and at the end of the year (line 31).

How's Your Cash Flow? Telltale Signs of Financial Difficulty

Companies want to earn net income because profit measures success. Without net income, a business sinks. There will be no dividends, and the share price suffers. High net income attracts investors, but you can't pay bills with net income. That requires cash.

A company needs both net income and strong cash flow. Income and cash flow usually move together because net income generates cash. Sometimes, however, net income and cash flow take different paths. To illustrate, consider Fastech Company:

Fastech Company Income Statement Year Ended December 31, 2010	
Sales revenue	$100,000
Cost of goods sold	30,000
Operating expenses	10,000
Net income	$ 60,000

Fastech Company Balance Sheet December 31, 2010			
Cash	$ 3,000	Total current liabilities	$ 50,000
Receivables	37,000	Long-term liabilities	20,000
Inventory	40,000		
PPE, net	60,000	Shareholders' equity	70,000
Total assets	$140,000	Total liabilities and equity	$140,000

What can we glean from Fastech's income statement and balance sheet?

- Fastech is profitable. Net income is 60% of revenue. Fastech's profitability looks outstanding.
- The current ratio is 1.6, and the debt ratio is only 50%. These measures suggest little trouble in paying bills.
- But Fastech is on the verge of bankruptcy. Can you spot the problem? Can you see what is causing the problem? Three trouble spots leap out to a financial analyst.

1. The cash balance is very low. Three thousand dollars isn't enough cash to pay the bills of a company with sales of $100,000.

2. Fastech isn't selling inventory fast enough. Fastech turned over its inventory only 0.75 times during the year. As we saw in Chapter 6, inventory turnover rates of 3–8 times a year are common. A turnover ratio of 0.75 times means it takes Fastech far too long to sell its inventory, and that delays cash collections.

3. Fastech's days' sales in receivables ratio is 135 days (see Chapter 5). Very few companies can wait that long to collect from customers.

The takeaway lesson from this discussion is this:

- You need both net income and strong cash flow to succeed in business.

Let's turn now to the different categories of cash flows.

Operating, Investing, and Financing Activities

A business engages in three types of business activities:

- Operating activities
- Investing activities
- Financing activities

OBJECTIVE

2 Distinguish among operating, investing, and financing cash flows

The statement of cash flows shows the cash receipts and payments related to these three activities. The major classes of cash receipts and payments are shown in Exhibit 12-1 on the following page.

Operating activities create revenues, expenses, gains, and losses—*net income*, which is a product of accrual-basis accounting. The cash flow from operating activities thus reports these principal revenue-generating activities, i.e. transactions and other events that enter into the determination of profit or loss of an entity. Operating activities are the most important of the three categories because they reflect the core of the organization. *A successful business must generate most of its cash from operating activities.*

Investing activities increase and decrease non-current assets, such as PPE, intangible assets and investments in other companies. Purchases and sales of these assets are investing activities. Investing activities are important for a company's medium- and long-term operations, as they represent the extent to which investments have been made for resources intended to generate future income and cash flows.

Financing activities obtain cash from, and pay cash to, investors and creditors. Issuing shares, borrowing money, buying and selling treasury shares, and paying cash dividends are financing activities. Paying off a loan is another example. Financing cash flows relate to non-current liabilities and shareholders' equity. These activities are important to help readers predict claims on future cash flows by providers of capital to the entity.

EXHIBIT 12-1 | **Major Classes of Cash Receipts and Cash Payments on the Statement of Cash Flows**

CASH RECEIPTS	Business Activity	CASH PAYMENTS
Collections from customers		Payments to suppliers
Receipts of interest and dividends		Payments to employees
Sale of short-term investments	Operating Activities	Payments of interest and income tax
Other operating receipts		Purchase of short-term investments
		Other operating payments
Sale of PPE		Acquisition of PPE
Sale of long-term investments	Investing Activities	Purchase of long-term investments
Collections of loans from others		Making loans to others
Issuance of shares		Payment of dividends
Sale of treasury shares		Repurchase of shares
Proceeds from loans and borrowing	Financing Activities	Purchase of treasury shares
		Payment of principal amounts of debts

STOP & THINK...

Royal Dutch Shell borrowed €1 billion from **Rabobank**. The term of the loan requires Shell to make a full payment in three years' time amounting €1.1 billion, inclusive of interest. How should the cash outflow of €1.1 billion be reported on Shell's cash flow statement?

Answers:

a. The €1.1 billion outflow actually consists of two components, €1 billion for the loan principal repayment and €0.1 billion for the interest payment. Shell would report a cash outflow of €1 billion under cash flows from financing activities and €0.1 billion interest payments under cash flows from operations.

Exhibit 12-2 shows how operating, investing, and financing activities relate to the various parts of the balance sheet.

EXHIBIT 12-2 | **How Operating, Investing, and Financing Cash Flows Affect the Balance Sheet**

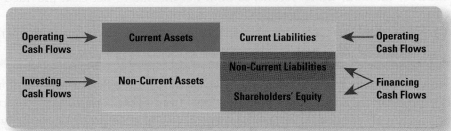

Philips's statement of cash flows reports cash flows under these three headings, as shown on page 714. For the year ended December 31, 2009, Philips generated €1.5 billion from operating activities, used €219 and €545 million for investing and financing activities, respectively. You can also see the pattern of cash flows over the three years provided. These figures show that:

- Operations consistently are Philips's largest source of cash inflows and they have been very resilient over the three years, despite great fluctuations on net income.
- Philips is consistently investing in the future, with its biggest cash flow item over the three years being the purchase of businesses amounting to over €5 billion.
- Philips is still able to repay some loans and maintain its dividend payments despite tough economic conditions.

TECHNICAL UPDATE

You may see some companies' cash flow items not being categorized in the same way we have done it in Exhibit 12-1, which is the most common way of classifying cash flow items. *IAS7* allows for alternatives classifications, "in a manner which is most appropriate to its business ... in a consistent manner". *IAS7* provides guidance on some of these alternatives:

- Interest paid, usually categorized as an operating cash flow item, may be classified as financing cash flow items.
- Interest and dividends received, usually classified as operating cash flow items, may be classified as investing cash flow items.
- Dividends paid, usually categorized as a financing cash flow item, may be classified as cash flow from operations.

For the purposes of learning cash flow items, we will use the "usual" classifications of cash flow items, i.e. interest paid, interest and dividends received as operating cash flows, and dividends paid as financing cash flows. But remember that when you look at companies' real financial statements, you may see alternative placements of these items.

Two Formats for Operating Activities

IAS7 requires an entity to report cash flows from operating activities using one of two methods:

- **Indirect method**, which reconciles from net income to net cash provided by operating activities.
- **Direct method**, which reports all cash receipts and cash payments from operating activities are disclosed.

How do the two methods differ? The two methods use different computations, but they produce the same figure for cash flows from *operating activities*. The two methods do not affect *investing* or *financing activities*, which are prepared similarly to the direct method, by the reporting of major classes of cash receipts and payments in their respective activities.

A simple analogy provides a good explanation of the two methods. Suppose you are given a series of numbers: 2, 3, 5, 7, and 8, which totals 25. You are then asked to sum the prime numbers in the sequence. There are clearly two methods of doing this. You could identify the prime numbers, in this case 2, 3, 5 and 7 and sum them, the answer would be 17. This is the direct method, where you identify the items (or cash flows) and then sum them. Alternatively, since you know the total of the sequence was 25, and 8 is the only number that is not a prime number, you could arrive at the same answer by making use of this total, i.e. 25 − 8 = 17. The indirect method make use of a total (in cash flow terms, it would be your net income, a total of revenues less expenses in your income statement) and adjust for items that are not prime, to arrive at the same answer. Note that 25 is not prime, neither is 8, but yet you get the 17 as the sum of prime numbers in the sequence.

IAS7 actually advocates for the direct method because it provides information which may be useful in estimating future cash flows that is not available under the indirect method. However, this is not heeded by most companies which mostly prepare their cash flow statements using the indirect method.

The following table summarizes the differences between the indirect and direct methods:

Indirect Method		Direct Method	
Net income..................................	$600	Collections from customers..........	$2,000
Adjustments:		*Deductions:*	
Depreciation, etc.	300	Payments to suppliers, etc.	(1,100)
Net cash provided by		Net cash provided by	
operating activities..............	$900	operating activities...............	$ 900
		same	

We shall begin with the indirect method since it is the more common method that you are likely to see in financial reports. Philips's cash flow from operations was prepared using the indirect format. To illustrate the statement of cash flows, we use **The Roadster Factory, Inc. (TRF)**, a dealer in auto parts for sports cars. TRF's balance sheet and income statement are shown on the next page in Exhibit 12-3 and 12-4, respectively.

EXHIBIT 12-3 | **TRF's Income Statement**

The Roadster Factory, Inc. (TRF)
Income Statement
Year Ended December 31, 2011

(In thousands)

Revenues and gains:

Sales revenue	$303	
Interest revenue	2	
Gain on sale of PPE	8	
Total revenues and gains		$313

Expenses:

Cost of goods sold	$150	
Salary and wage expense	56	
Depreciation expense	18	
Other operating expense	17	
Income tax expense	15	
Interest expense	7	
Total expenses		263
Net income		$ 50

EXHIBIT 12-4 | **TRF's Balance Sheet**

The Roadster Factory, Inc. (TRF)
Comparative Balance Sheets
December 31, 2011 and 2010

(In thousands)	2011	2010	Increase (Decrease)
Assets			
Current:			
Cash	$ 34	$ 42	$ (8)
Accounts receivable	96	81	15
Inventory	35	38	(3)
Prepaid expenses	8	7	1
Notes receivable	21	—	21
PPE, net	343	219	124
Total	$537	$387	$150
Liabilities			
Current:			
Accounts payable	$ 91	$ 57	$ 34
Salary and wage payable	4	6	(2)
Accrued liabilities	1	3	(2)
Long-term debt	160	77	83
Shareholders' Equity			
Ordinary share capital	162	158	4
Retained earnings	119	86	33
Total	$537	$387	$150

Preparing Cash Flows from Operating Activities: Indirect Method

OBJECTIVE

3 **Prepare** cash flows from operating activities using the indirect method

You read earlier that *IAS7* describes operating activities as principal revenue-generating activities, i.e. transactions and other events that enter into the determination of profit or loss of an entity. Under the indirect method, this is exactly how we start cash flows from operating activities. The operating section begins with the net income, taken from the income statement (see Exhibit 12-3) and is followed by "Adjustments to reconcile net income to net cash provided by operating activities". These adjustments include items that are **not** cash flows, just like our simple analogy earlier uses number 8 (from the series of 2, 3, 5, 7, 8) to determine the sum of the prime numbers. Let's discuss these adjustments.

To make it easier for our discussion, let's have a look at a template for the preparation of cash flow from operating activities using the indirect method.

EXHIBIT 12-5 | **Template for Cash Flows from Operating Activities: Indirect Method**

The Roadster Factory, Inc. (TRF)
Statement of Cash Flows (Partial)
Year Ended December 31, 2011

Cash flows from operating activities

Net income

Adjustments to reconcile net income to net cash provided by operating activities:

+ Depreciation/depletion/amortization expense

+ Loss on sale of long-term assets

− Gain on sale of long-term assets

− Increases in current assets other than cash

+ Decreases in current assets other than cash

+ Increases in current liabilities

− Decreases in current liabilities

Net cash provided by (used for) operating activities

Proceed as follows to prepare the cash flow from the operating activities (usually referred to as the "CFO" for short) section of the statement of cash flows by using the indirect method:

Step 1 Start with net income from the income statement (Exhibit 12-3). The indirect method always starts with a summary number from the income statement. We use net income in our example here, but sometimes you may see companies using pre-tax income. If a company starts the indirect method with profit before tax, it will need to show a separate line on "income taxes paid" after Step 5 below.

Step 2 From the income statement (Exhibit 12-3), add back depreciation, depletion, and amortization expense, and remove any gains (or add back losses) on the sale of long-term assets.

Step 3 Examine the balance sheet (Exhibit 12-4), identify changes in current assets and current liabilities (usually referred to as "changes in working capital"), except for cash and cash equivalents.

Step 4 Deduct increases in current assets other than cash and add decreases in current assets other than cash.

Step 5 Deduct decreases in current liabilities and add increases in current liabilities.

If you have completed the five steps using the exhibits above, you will probably have obtained something like Exhibit 12-6 below.

EXHIBIT 12-6 | **Statement of Cash Flows—Operating Activities by the Indirect Method**

The Roadster Factory, Inc. (TRF)
Statement of Cash Flows (Partial, Indirect Method)
For the Year Ended December 31, 2011

(In thousands)

	Cash flows from operating activities:		
	Net income		$50
	Adjustments to reconcile net income to net cash provided by operating activities:		
Ⓐ*	Depreciation	$ 18	
Ⓑ	Gain on sale of PPE...	(8)	
	Increase in accounts receivable...................................	(15)	
	Decrease in inventory...	3	
Ⓒ	Increase in prepaid expenses	(1)	
	Increase in accounts payable	34	
	Decrease in salary and wage payable...........................	(2)	
	Decrease in accrued liabilities....................................	(2)	27
	Net cash provided by operating activities.............		$77

*Adjustments A, B, and C are explained in the following section.

Understanding Reconciliation of Net Income to Cash Flows from Operations

Ⓐ **Depreciation, Depletion, and Amortization Expenses.**   These expenses are added back to net income to convert net income to cash flow. Let's see why. Depreciation is recorded as follows:

Depreciation Expense	18,000	
Accumulated Depreciation		18,000

Depreciation has no effect on cash. But depreciation, like all other expenses, decreases net income. Therefore, to convert net income to cash flows, we add depreciation back to net income. The add-back cancels the earlier deduction.

Example: Suppose you had only two transactions, a $1,000 cash sale and depreciation expense of $300. Cash flow from operations is $1,000, and net income is $700 ($1,000 – $300). To go from net income ($700) to cash flow ($1,000), we add back the depreciation ($300). Depletion and amortization are treated like depreciation.

⑧ Gains and Losses on the Sale of Long-term Assets.

The proceeds from disposal of long-term assets are reported in the cash flow from investing activities (see Exhibit 12-1, line 16). However, the resulting gains (or losses) from the disposal have been included in the determination of income. Therefore, to avoid double counting, we will need to adjust the net income. Losses are added back to net income and gains are deducted from net income.

© Changes in the Current Asset and Current Liability Accounts.

Most current assets and current liabilities result from operating activities. For example, accounts receivable result from sales, inventory relates to cost of goods sold, and so on. Changes in the current accounts are adjustments to net income under the indirect method. The reasoning follows:

1. *An increase in another current asset decreases cash.* It takes cash to acquire assets. Suppose you make a sale on account. Accounts receivable are increased, but cash isn't affected yet. Exhibit 12-4 reports that during 2011, The Roadster Factory's Accounts Receivable increased by $15,000. To compute cash flow from operations, we must subtract the $15,000 increase in Accounts Receivable, as shown in Exhibit 12-6. The reason is this: We have *not* collected this $15,000 in cash. Similar logic applies to all the other current assets. If they increase, cash decreases.

2. *A decrease in another current asset increases cash.* Suppose TRF's Accounts Receivable balance decreased by $4,000. Cash receipts caused Accounts Receivable to decrease, so we add decreases in Accounts Receivable and the other current assets to net income.

3. *A decrease in a current liability decreases cash.* Payment of a current liability decreases both cash and the liability, so we subtract decreases in current liabilities from net income. In Exhibit 12-6, the $2,000 decrease in Accrued Liabilities is *subtracted* to compute net cash provided by operations.

4. *An increase in a current liability increases cash.* The Roadster Factory's Accounts Payable increased. That can occur only if cash was not spent to pay this debt. Cash payments are therefore less than expenses and TRF has more cash on hand. Thus, increases in current liabilities increase cash.

Evaluating Cash Flows from Operating Activities.

Let's step back and evaluate The Roadster Factory's operating cash flows during 2011. TRF's operations provided net cash flow of $77,000. This amount exceeds net income, which is one sign of a healthy company.

If you want to immediately compare the indirect method above with the direct method, you can take a detour to pages 733-738 then return here to continue with the other cash flow activities.

EVALUATING CASH FLOWS FROM OPERATING ACTIVITIES

Cash flows from investing activities (or "CFI") basically revolve around the cash inflows and outflows related to long-term assets of the entity. Exhibit 12-1 showed us that the major classes of cash receipts include sale of PPE and other non-current assets, sale of long-term investments and collections of loans to others; and the outflows are typically for acquisition of PPE and other non-current assets, purchase of long-term investments, and making loans to others.

Most of the data for this section are from the TRF's balance sheet (refer to Exhibit 12-4 earlier). Let's calculate the cash flow items under this category (remember, you don't have shortcuts like the CFO's indirect method for CFI).

Computing Purchases and Sales of PPE.   Companies keep a separate account for each item of PPE. But for computing cash flows, it is helpful to combine all the PPE into a single summary account. Also, we subtract accumulated depreciation and use the net figure. It's easier to work with a single PPE account.

To illustrate, observe that The Roadster Factory's:

- balance sheet reports beginning PPE, net of accumulated depreciation, of $219,000. The ending balance is $343,000 (Exhibit 12-4).
- income statement shows a depreciation expense of $18,000 and an $8,000 gain on sale of PPE (Exhibit 12-3).

TRF's purchases of PPE during the year totaled $196,000 (we shall take this as given). How much, then, are the proceeds from the sale of PPE? To do this, you must remember that (1) proceeds less book value of assets sold equal to gain on disposal, and (2) the change in net PPE is caused by addition of new PPE, depreciation charge for the period and the book value of PPE sold. So, let's first determine the book value of the PPE sold, as follows:

PPE, Net								
Beginning balance	+	Acquisitions	−	Depreciation	−	Book value of assets sold	=	Ending balance
$219,000	+	$196,000	−	$18,000		−X	=	$343,000
						−X	=	$343,000 − $219,000 − $196,000 + $18,000
						X	=	$54,000

The sale proceeds are $62,000, determined as follows:

Sale proceeds	=	Book value of assets sold	+	Gain	−	Loss
X	=	$54,000	+	$8,000	−	$0
X	=	$62,000				

The PPE T-account provides another look at the computation of the book value of the assets sold.

PPE, Net			
Beginning balance	219,000	Depreciation	18,000
Acquisitions	196,000	Book value of assets sold	54,000
Ending balance	343,000		

OBJECTIVE

4 Prepare cash flows from investing activities

If the sale had resulted in a loss of $3,000 instead, the sale proceeds would be $51,000 ($54,000 – $3,000), and the statement of cash flows would report $51,000 as a cash receipt from this investing activity.

Computing Purchases and Sales of Investments, and Loans and Collections. The cash amounts of investment transactions can be computed in the manner illustrated for PPE. Investments are easier because there is no depreciation, as shown in the following equation:

Investments (amounts assumed for illustration only)

Beginning balance	+	Purchases	–	Book value of investments sold	=	Ending balance
$100,000	+	$50,000		–X	=	$140,000
				–X	=	$140,000 – $100,000 – $50,000
				X	=	$10,000

The Investments T-account provides another look (amounts assumed).

Investments			
Beginning balance	100		
Purchases	50	Book value of investments sold	10
Ending balance	140		

The Roadster Factory has a long-term receivable, and the cash flows from loan transactions on notes receivable can be determined as follows (data from Exhibit 12-4):

Notes Receivable

Beginning balance	+	New loans made	–	Collections	=	Ending balance
$0	+	X	–	–0	=	$21,000
		X			=	$21,000

Notes Receivable			
Beginning balance	0		
New loans made	21	Collections	0
Ending balance	21		

EXHIBIT 12-7 | **Statement of Cash Flows—Investing Activities**

The Roadster Factory, Inc. (TRF) Statement of Cash Flows (Partial) For the Year Ended December 31, 2011

(In thousands)

Cash flows from investing activities:

Acquisition of PPE	$(196)
Loan to another company	(21)
Proceeds from sale of PPE	62
Net cash used for investing activities	(155)

Exhibit 12-8 summarizes the cash flows from investing activities, highlighted in color.

EXHIBIT 12-8 | **Computing Cash Flows from Investing Activities**

Receipts

From sale of PPE	Beginning PPE, net	+	Acquisition cost	−	Depreciation	−	Book value of assets sold	=	Ending PPE, net
	Cash received	=	Book value of assets sold	+ or −	Gain on sale Loss on sale				
From sale of investments	Beginning investments	+	Purchase cost of investments	−	Cost of investments sold	=	Ending investments		
	Cash received	=	Cost of investments sold	+ or −	Gain on sale Loss on sale				
From collection of notes receivable	Beginning notes receivable	+	New loans made	−	Collections	=	Ending notes receivable		

Payments

For acquisition of PPE	Beginning PPE, net	+	Acquisition cost	−	Depreciation	−	Book value of assets sold	=	Ending PPE, net
For purchase of investments	Beginning investments	+	Purchase cost of investments	−	Cost of investments sold	=	Ending investments		
For new loans made	Beginning notes receivable	+	New loans made	−	Collections	=	Ending notes receivable		

PREPARING CASH FLOWS FROM FINANCING ACTIVITIES

Cash flows from financing activities (or "CFF" for short) are those that relate to the capital structure and owners of the entity. Financing activities affect long-term liabilities and equity accounts such as Notes Payable, Bonds Payable, Long-Term Debt, Share Capital, Paid-in Capital in Excess of Par, Treasury Shares, and Retained Earnings. Most of the data come from the balance sheet (see Exhibit 12-4).

Exhibit 12-1 showed us that the major classes of cash receipts include issuance of shares, proceeds from selling treasury shares, loans and borrowings; and the outflows include repurchase of shares ("share buy-back") either for cancellation or treasury, and repayment of loans and borrowings. Let's work out TRF's cash flows from financing activities.

OBJECTIVE

5 **Prepare** cash flows from financing activities

Computing Issuances and Payments of Long-Term Debt. The beginning and ending balances of Long-Term Debt, Notes Payable, or Bonds Payable come from the balance sheet. If either new issuances or payments are known, the other amount can be computed. The Roadster Factory's new debt issuances total $94,000 (take this amount as given). Debt payments are computed from the Long-Term Debt account (see Exhibit 12-4).

Long-Term Debt (Notes Payable, Bonds Payable)								
Beginning balance	+	Issuance of new debt	−	Payments of debt	=	Ending balance		
$77,000	+	$94,000		−X	=	$160,000		
				−X	=	$160,000 − $77,000 − $94,000		
				X	=	$11,000		

Long-Term Debt

		Beginning balance	77,000
Payments	11,000	Issuance of new debt	94,000
		Ending balance	160,000

If the $94,000 new debt issuance information was not given, we would have naturally assumed that the TRF had simply borrowed an additional $83,000 (i.e. $160,000 ending balance less $77,000 beginning balance).

Computing Issuances of Shares and Purchases of Treasury Shares. These cash flows can be determined from the share capital accounts. For example, cash received from issuing shares is computed from Share Capital and Capital in Excess of Par. We use a single summary Share Capital account as we do for PPE. The Roadster Factory data are

Share Capital

Beginning balance	+	Issuance of new shares	=	Ending balance
$158,000	+	$4,000	=	$162,000

Share Capital

		Beginning balance	158,000
		Issuance of new shares	4,000
		Ending balance	162,000

This $4,000 would have been the net impact of the issuances and repurchases of shares. You could have been told in the question that the issuance of shares for the period was $20,000. You would have noticed that TRF must have bought back some shares, otherwise $158,000 + $20,000 would not equal $162,000. In such situations, TRF must have bought back $16,000 worth of shares, either for treasury or cancellation.

Computing Dividend Declarations and Payments. If dividend declarations and payments are not given elsewhere, they can be computed. For The Roadster Factory, this computation is

Retained Earnings

Beginning balance	+	Net income	–	Dividend payments	=	Ending balance
$86,000	+	$50,000		–X	=	$119,000
				–X	=	$119,000 – $86,000 – $50,000
				X	=	$17,000

The T-account also shows the dividend computation.

Retained Earnings

Dividend payments	17,000	Beginning balance	86,000
		Net income	50,000
		Ending balance	119,000

Our completed cash flows from financing would look something like

EXHIBIT 12-9 | Statement of Cash Flows—Investing Activities

The Roadster Factory, Inc. (TRF)
Statement of Cash Flows (Partial)
For the Year Ended December 31, 2011

(In thousands)

Cash flows from financing activities:	
Proceeds from issuance of long-term debt	$ (94)
Proceeds from issuance of shares	4)
Payment of long-term debt	(11)
Payment of dividends	(17)
Net cash provided by financing activities	70

Exhibit 12-10 summarizes the cash flows from financing activities, highlighted in color.

EXHIBIT 12-10 | Computing Cash Flows from Financing Activities

Receipts

From borrowing—issuance of long-term debt	Beginning long-term debt	+	Cash received from issuance of long-term debt	−	Payment of debt	=	Ending long-term debt
From issuance of share	Beginning share capital	+	Cash received from issuance of new shares	−	Share cancellations	=	Ending share capital

Payments

Of long-term debt	Beginning long-term debt	+	Cash received from issuance of long-term debt	−	Payment of debt	=	Ending long-term debt
To purchase treasury share	Beginning treasury share	+	Purchase cost of treasury shares			=	Ending treasury share
Of dividends	Beginning retained earnings	+	Net income	−	Dividend payment	=	Ending retained earnings

STOP & THINK...

Classify each of the following as an operating activity, an investing activity, or a financing activity as reported on the statement of cash flows prepared by the *indirect* method.

a. Issuance of shares
b. Borrowing
c. Sales revenue
d. Payment of dividends
e. Purchase of land
f. Purchase of treasury shares

g. Paying bonds payable
h. Interest expense
i. Sale of equipment
j. Cost of goods sold
k. Purchase of another company
l. Making a long-term loan to another company

Answers:

a. Financing
b. Financing
c. Operating
d. Financing

e. Investing
f. Financing
g. Financing
h. Operating

i. Investing
j. Operating
k. Investing
l. Investing

Completing the Statement of Cash Flows (Indirect CFO)

Now that we have prepared all the three categories of cash flow activities, it is time to complete the cash flow statement. Let's assemble what we have done into one single statement and calculate the net cash flows from the three cash flow activities. This is often a very stressful time, because if we have done our work carefully, we sure want our net cash flows to reconcile the change in cash on the balance sheet.

EXHIBIT 12-11 | Statement of Cash Flows—Indirect Method

The Roadster Factory, Inc. (TRF)
Statement of Cash Flows
For the Year Ended December 31, 2011

(In thousands)

Cash flows from operating activities:			
Net income			$ 50
Adjustments to reconcile net income to net cash provided by operating activities:			
Ⓐ Depreciation		$ 18	
Ⓑ Gain on sale of PPE		(8)	
Increase in accounts receivable		(15)	
Decrease in inventory		3	
Ⓒ Increase in prepaid expenses		(1)	
Increase in accounts payable		34	
Decrease in salary and wage payable		(2)	
Decrease in accrued liabilities		(2)	27
Net cash provided by operating activities			77
Cash flows from investing activities:			
Acquisition of PPE		$(196)	
Loan to another company		(21)	
Proceeds from sale of PPE		62	
Net cash used for investing activities			(155)
Cash flows from financing activities:			
Proceeds from issuance of long-term debt		$ 94	
Proceeds from issuance of shares		4	
Payment of long-term debt		(11)	
Payment of dividends		(17)	
Net cash provided by financing activities			70
Net (decrease) in cash			$ (8)
Cash balance, December 31, 2010			42
Cash balance, December 31, 2011			$ 34

As you can see, we did a pretty a good job! The net cash flows for the period shows a decrease of $8,000, which explains why TRF's cash went from $42,000 to $34,000. What does the statement of cash flow tell us? TRF was able to generate cash flow from operating activities, which is used (together with some borrowings) to expand its investments in new PPE. Reflect on TRF's financial position (its balance sheet, Exhibit 12-4) and financial performance (its income statement, Exhibit 12-5). Whilst they were your source data for the cash flow statement, the insights you get from the cash flow statement clearly supplements what you already have.

Non-cash Investing and Financing Activities

Companies sometimes make investments that do not require cash. They may also obtain financing other than cash. Our examples have included none of these transactions. Now suppose The Roadster Factory issued shares valued at $300,000 to acquire a warehouse. TRF would journalize this transaction as follows:

Warehouse Building	300,000	
Share Capital		300,000

This transaction would not be reported as a cash payment because TRF paid no cash. But the investment in the warehouse and the issuance of shares are important. These non-cash investing and financing activities can be reported in a separate schedule under the statement of cash flows. Exhibit 12-12 illustrates non-cash investing and financing activities (all amounts are assumed).

EXHIBIT 12-12 | **Non-cash Investing and Financing Activities (All Amounts Assumed)**

	Thousands
Noncash Investing and Financing Activities:	
Acquisition of building by issuing shares	$300
Acquisition of land by issuing note payable	70
Payment of long-term debt by issuing shares	100
Total noncash investing and financing activities	$470

At the end of its cash flow statements, Philips disclosed that it has non-cash transactions amounting to €148 million ("assets received in lieu of cash from the sale of its businesses"). Examine the Excerpts from Note 28 below.

EXCERPTS (ADAPTED) FROM PHILIPS'S NOTES TO THE 2009 FINANCIAL STATEMENTS

In 2007 and 2009, the Company received only cash as consideration in connection with the sale of businesses.

In April 2008, the Company acquired 64.5 million shares in Pace Micro Technology (Pace) in exchange for the transfer of the Company's Set-Top Boxes and Connectivity Solutions activities, which represented a value of EUR 74 million at the date of the closing of that transaction.

In August 2008, Philips transferred its 69.5% ownership in MedQuist to CBAY. A part of the consideration was settled through the issuance of a convertible bond by CBAY which represented a fair value of EUR 53 million at the date of the closing of the transaction.

In September 2008, Philips acquired a 33.5% interest in Prime Technology Ventures III in exchange for the transfer of seven incubator activities which represented a value of EUR 21 million at the date of the closing of that transaction.

Now let's apply what you've learned about the statement of cash flows prepared by the indirect method.

MID-CHAPTER SUMMARY PROBLEM

Lucas Corporation reported the following income statement and comparative balance sheets, along with transaction data for 2011:

Lucas Corporation
Income Statement
Year Ended December 31, 2011

Sales revenue		$662,000
Cost of goods sold		560,000
Gross profit		102,000
Operating expenses		
Salary expenses	$46,000	
Depreciation expense— equipment	7,000	
Amortization expense— patent	3,000	
Rent expense	2,000	
Total operating expenses		58,000
Income from operations		44,000
Other items:		
Loss on sale of equipment		(2,000)
Income before income tax		42,000
Income tax expense		16,000
Net income		$ 26,000

Lucas Corporation
Comparative Balance Sheets
December 31, 2011 and 2010

Assets	2011	2010	Liabilities	2011	2010
Current:			Current:		
Cash and equivalents	$ 19,000	$ 3,000	Accounts payable	$ 35,000	$ 26,000
Accounts receivable	22,000	23,000	Accrued liabilities	7,000	9,000
Inventories	34,000	31,000	Income tax payable	10,000	10,000
Prepaid expenses	1,000	3,000	Total current liabilities	52,000	45,000
Total current assets	76,000	60,000	Long-term note payable	44,000	—
Long-term investments	18,000	10,000	Bonds payable	40,000	53,000
Equipment, net	67,000	52,000	Owners' Equity		
Patent, net	44,000	10,000	Share capital	52,000	20,000
			Retained earnings	27,000	19,000
			Less: Treasury shares	(10,000)	(5,000)
Total assets	$205,000	$132,000	Total liabilities and equity	$205,000	$132,000

Transaction Data for 2011:

Purchase of equipment	$ 98,000	Issuance of long-term note payable	
Payment of cash dividends	18,000	to purchase patent	$ 37,000
Issuance of shares to retire bonds		Issuance of long-term note payable to	
payable	13,000	borrow cash	7,000
Purchase of long-term investment	8,000	Issuance of shares for cash	19,000
Purchase of treasury shares	5,000	Sale of equipment (book value, $76,000)	74,000

I *Requirement*

1. Prepare Lucas Corporation's statement of cash flows (indirect method) for the year ended December 31, 2011. Follow the four steps outlined below. For Step 4, prepare a T-account to show the transaction activity in each long-term balance sheet account. For each PPE, use a single account, net of accumulated depreciation (for example: Equipment, Net).

Step 1 Lay out the template of the statement of cash flows.

Step 2 From the comparative balance sheet, determine the increase in cash during the year, $16,000.

Step 3 From the income statement, take net income, depreciation, amortization, and the loss on sale of equipment to the statement of cash flows.

Step 4 Complete the statement of cash flows. Account for the year-to-year change in each balance sheet account.

Answer

Lucas Corporation Statement of Cash Flows Year Ended December 31, 2011		
Cash flows from operating activities:		
Net income		$ 26,000
Adjustments to reconcile net income to net cash provided by operating activities:		
Depreciation	$ 7,000	
Amortization...	3,000	
Loss on sale of equipment	2,000	
Decrease in accounts receivable..................	1,000	
Increase in inventories................................	(3,000)	
Decrease in prepaid expenses	2,000	
Increase in accounts payable	9,000	
Decrease in accrued liabilities......................	(2,000)	19,000
Net cash provided by operating activities.............		45,000
Cash flows from investing activities:		
Purchase of equipment	$(98,000)	
Sale of equipment..	74,000	
Purchase of long-term investment	(8,000)	
Net cash used for investing activities....................		(32,000)
Cash flows from financing activities:		
Issuance of shares...	$ 19,000	
Payment of cash dividends	(18,000)	
Issuance of long-term note payable	7,000	
Purchase of treasury shares	(5,000)	
Net cash provided by financing activities.............		3,000
Net increase in cash.......................................		16,000
Cash balance, December 31, 2010		3,000
Cash balance, December 31, 2011		$ 19,000
Noncash investing and financing activities:		
Issuance of long-term note payable to purchase patent...		$ 37,000
Issuance of shares to retire bonds payable		13,000
Total noncash investing and financing activities.........		$ 50,000

	Long-Term Investments	
Bal	10,000	
	8,000	
Bal	18,000	

	Equipment, Net	
Bal	52,000	
	98,000	76,000
		7,000
Bal	67,000	

	Patent, Net	
Bal	10,000	
	37,000	3,000
Bal	44,000	

	Long-Term Note Payable	
		Bal 0
		37,000
		7,000
		Bal 44,000

	Bonds Payable	
		Bal 53,000
	13,000	
		Bal 40,000

	Share Capital	
		Bal 20,000
		13,000
		19,000
		Bal 52,000

	Retained Earnings	
		Bal 19,000
	18,000	26,000
		Bal 27,000

	Treasury Shares	
Bal	5,000	
Bal	5,000	
Bal	10,000	

Using the Statement of Cash Flows

Analysts find the statement of cash flows more helpful for spotting weaknesses than for gauging successes. Why? Because a *shortage* of cash can throw a company into bankruptcy, but lots of cash doesn't ensure success. What do you think of the following statement of cash flows?

Enix Corporation
Statement of Cash Flows
Year Ended June 30, 2010

(In millions)

Operating activities:		
Net income		$ 35,000
Adjustments for noncash items:		
Depreciation	$ 14,000	
Net increase in current assets other than cash	(24,000)	
Net increase in current liabilities	8,000	(2,000)
Net cash provided by operating activities		33,000
Investing activities:		
Sale of property, plant and equipment	$ 91,000	
Net cash provided by investing activities		91,000
Financing activities:		
Borrowing	$ 22,000	
Payment of long-term debt	(90,000)	
Purchase of treasury shares	(9,000)	
Payment of dividends	(23,000)	
Net cash used for financing activities		(100,000)
Increase (decrease) in cash		$ 24,000

Perhaps some of your observations include the following points:

- Enix's operations provide less cash than net income. That's strange. Ordinarily, cash provided by operations exceeds net income because of the add-back of depreciation and amortization. The increases in current assets and current liabilities should cancel out over time. For Enix Corporation, current assets increased far more than current liabilities during the year. This may be harmless. But it may signal difficulty in collecting receivables or selling inventory. Either event will cause trouble.

- The sale of PPE is Enix's major source of cash. This is okay if this is a one-time situation. Enix may be shifting from one line of business to another, and it may be selling off old assets. But if the sale of long-term assets is the major source of cash for several periods, Enix will face a cash short-age. A company can't sell off its PPE forever. Soon it will go out of business.

- The only strength shown by the statement of cash flows is that Enix paid off more long-term debt than it did new borrowing. This will improve the debt ratio and Enix's credit standing.

Here are some cash-flow signs of a healthy company:

- Operations are the major *source* of cash (not a *use* of cash).
- Investing activities include more purchases than sales of long-term assets.
- Financing activities are not dominated by new loans and borrowings.

PREPARING CASH FLOWS FROM OPERATING ACTIVITIES: DIRECT METHOD

The direct method is the method advocated by *IAS7* because it provides clearer information about the sources and uses of cash. But very few companies use this method because it requires more computations than the indirect method.

We shall use the same example, The Roadster Factory (TRF), to illustrate the preparation of cash flow from operating activities using the direct method. The direct method will require you to actually calculate each (major class of) cash inflow and cash outflow.

OBJECTIVE

6 **Prepare** cash flows from operating activities using the direct payment method

Computing Operating Cash Flows by the Direct Method

To compute operating cash flows by the direct method, we use the income statement and the *changes* in the balance sheet accounts. Exhibit 12-13 illustrates the process. We reproduce The Roadster Factory's income statement in Exhibit 12-14 and its comparative balance sheet in Exhibit 12-15.

EXHIBIT 12-13 | Direct Method of Computing Cash Flows from Operating Activities

RECEIPTS / PAYMENTS	Income Statement Account	Change in Related Balance Sheet Account	
RECEIPTS:			
From customers	Sales Revenue	+ Decrease in Accounts Receivable − Increase in Accounts Receivable	
Of interest	Interest Revenue	+ Decrease in Interest Receivable − Increase in Interest Receivable	
PAYMENTS:			
To suppliers	Cost of Goods Sold	+ Increase in Inventory − Decrease in Inventory	+Decrease in Accounts Payable −Increase in Accounts Payable
	Operating Expense	+ Increase in Prepaids − Decrease in Prepaids	+Decrease in Accrued Liabilities −Increase in Accrued Liabilities
To employees	Salary (Wage) Expense	+ Decrease in Salary (Wage) Payable − Increase in Salary (Wage) Payable	
For interest	Interest Expense	+ Decrease in Interest Payable − Increase in Interest Payable	
For income tax	Income Tax Expense	+ Decrease in Income Tax Payable − Increase in Income Tax Payable	

*We thank Professor Barbara Gerrity for suggesting this exhibit.

EXHIBIT 12-14 | TRF's Income Statement

The Roadster Factory, Inc. (TRF)
Income Statement
Year Ended December 31, 2011

(In thousands)

Revenues and gains:		
Sales revenue	$303	
Interest revenue	2	
Gain on sale of PPE	8	
Total revenues and gains		$313
Expenses:		
Cost of goods sold	$150	
Salary and wage expense	56	
Depreciation expense	18	
Other operating expense	17	
Income tax expense	15	
Interest expense	7	
Total expenses		263
Net income		$ 50

EXHIBIT 12-15 | **TRF's Balance Sheets**

The Roadster Factory, Inc. (TRF)
Comparative Balance Sheets
December 31, 2011 and 2010

(In thousands)	2011	2010	Increase (Decrease)
Assets			
Current:			
Cash..	$ 34	$ 42	$ (8)
Accounts receivable................	96	81	15
Inventory	35	38	(3)
Prepaid expenses	8	7	1
Notes receivable.........................	21	—	21
PPE, net.....................................	343	219	124
Total	$537	$387	$150
Liabilities			
Current:			
Accounts payable	$ 91	$ 57	$ 34
Salary and wage payable	4	6	(2)
Accrued liabilities....................	1	3	(2)
Long-term debt	160	77	83
Shareholders' Equity			
Ordinary share capital................	162	158	4
Retained earnings........................	119	86	33
Total	$537	$387	$150

Computing Cash Collections from Customers.

Collections start with sales revenue (an accrual-basis amount). The Roadster Factory's income statement (Exhibit 12-14) reports sales of $303,000. Accounts receivable increased from $81,000 at the beginning of the year to $96,000 at year-end, a $15,000 increase (Exhibit 12-15). Based on those amounts, cash collections equal $288,000, as follows. We must solve for cash collections (X):

Accounts Receivable					
Beginning balance	+	Sales	−	Collections	=	Ending balance
$81,000	+	$303,000		−X	=	$96,000
				−X	=	$96,000 − $81,000 − $303,000
				X	=	$288,000

The T-account for Accounts Receivable provides another view of the same computation.

Accounts Receivable			
Beginning balance	81,000		
Sales	303,000	Collections	288,000
Ending balance	96,000		

Accounts Receivable increased, so collections must be less than sales. All collections of receivables are computed this way. Let's turn now to cash receipts of interest revenue. In our example, The Roadster Factory earned interest revenue and collected cash of $2,000 (because there was no interest receivable in the beginning and at the end of the period). The amounts of interest revenue and cash receipts of interest often differ and Exhibit 12-13 shows how to make this computation, when necessary.

Computing Payments to Suppliers. This computation includes two parts:

- Payments for inventory
- Payments for operating expenses (other than interest and income tax)

Payments for inventory are computed by converting cost of goods sold to the cash basis. We use Cost of Goods Sold, Inventory, and Accounts Payable. First, we must solve for purchases. All the amounts come from Exhibits 12-14 and 12-15.

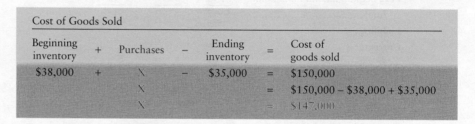

Cost of Goods Sold							
Beginning inventory	+	Purchases	−	Ending inventory	=	Cost of goods sold	
$38,000	+	X	−	$35,000	=	$150,000	
		X			=	$150,000 − $38,000 + $35,000	
		X			=	$147,000	

Now we can compute cash payments for inventory (Y), as follows:

Accounts Payable							
Beginning balance	+	Purchases	−	Payments for inventory	=	Ending balance	
$57,000	+	$147,000	−	Y	=	$91,000	
				Y	=	$91,000 − $57,000 − $147,000	
				Y	=	$113,000	

The T-accounts show where the data come from. Start with Cost of Goods Sold.

Cost of Goods Sold			
Beg inventory	38,000	End inventory	35,000
Purchases	147,000		
Cost of goods sold	150,000		

Accounts Payable			
Payments for inventory	113,000	Beg bal	57,000
		Purchases	147,000
		End bal	91,000

Accounts Payable increased, so payments for inventory are less than purchases.

Computing Payments for Operating Expenses. Payments for operating expenses other than interest and income tax are computed from three accounts: Prepaid Expenses, Accrued Liabilities, and Other Operating Expenses. All The Roadster Factory data come from Exhibits 12-14 and 12-15.

We can assume that the beginning prepayments will be used in the period and the ending prepayment is what we paid for during the year. Similarly, we can assume that the beginning accrued liabilities will be paid for during the year, and the ending balance will remain owing.

Prepaid Expenses

Beginning balance	−	Expiration of prepaid expense	+	Payments	=	Ending balance
$7,000	−	$7,000	+	X	=	$8,000
				X	=	$8,000 − $7,000 + $7,000
				X	=	$8,000

Accrued Liabilities

Beginning balance	−	Payments	+	Accrual of expense at year-end	=	Ending balance
$3,000	−	X	+	$1,000	=	$1,000
		−X			=	$1,000 − $3,000 − $1,000
		X			=	$3,000

Other Operating Expenses

Accrual of expense at year-end	+	Expiration of prepaid expense	+	Payments	=	Ending balance
$1,000	+	$7,000	+	X	=	$17,000
				X	=	$17,000 − $1,000 − $7,000
				X	=	$9,000
	Total payments for operating expenses		=	$8,000 + $3,000 + $9,000		
			=	$20,000		

The T-accounts give another picture of the same data.

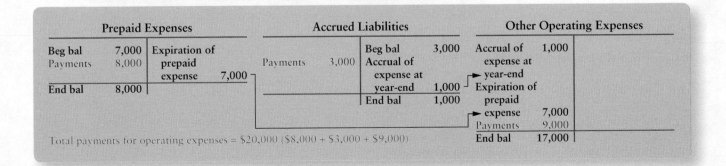

Prepaid Expenses				Accrued Liabilities			Other Operating Expenses		
Beg bal	7,000	Expiration of				Beg bal 3,000	Accrual of	1,000	
Payments	8,000	prepaid		Payments 3,000		Accrual of	expense at		
		expense 7,000				expense at	year-end		
End bal	8,000					year-end 1,000	Expiration of		
						End bal 1,000	prepaid		
							expense	7,000	
							Payments	9,000	
Total payments for operating expenses = $20,000 ($8,000 + $3,000 + $9,000)							End bal	17,000	

Now we can compute Payments to Suppliers as follows:

Payments to Suppliers	=	Payments for Inventory	+	Payments for Operating Expenses
$133,000	=	$113,000	+	$20,000

Computing Payments to Employees. It is convenient to combine all payments to employees into one account, Salary and Wage Expense. We then adjust the expense for the change in Salary and Wage Payable, as shown here:

Salary and Wage Payable					
Beginning balance	+	Salary and wage expense	− Payments	=	Ending balance
$6,000	+	$56,000	−X	=	$4,000
			−X	=	$4,000 − $6,000 − $56,000
			X	=	$58,000

Salary and Wage Payable			
		Beginning balance	6,000
Payments to employees	58,000	Salary and wage expense	56,000
		Ending balance	4,000

Computing Payments of Interest and Income Taxes. The Roadster Factory's expense and payment amounts are the same for interest and income tax (because interest payable and tax payable balances are zero), so no analysis is required. If the expense and the payment differ, the payment can be computed as shown in Exhibit 12-13.

Let's put the direct method of cash flow from operations all together.

The Roadster Factory, Inc. (TRF)
Statement of Cash Flows (Partial, Direct Method)
For Year Ended December 31, 2011

(In thousands)

Cash flows from operating activities:		
Receipts:		
Collections from customers....................................	$ 288	
Interest received	2	
Total cash receipts		$ 290
Payments:		
To suppliers...	$(133)	
To employees	(58)	
For income tax...	(15)	
For interest..	(7)	
Total cash payments		(213)
Net cash provided by operating activities...............		77

As you can see, the cash flow from operating activities is $77,000, the same as how it was prepared under indirect method (Exhibit 12-6). Remember both methods give you the same cash flows from operating activities, they are just calculated differently.

STOP & THINK...

Fidelity Company reported the following for 2011 and 2010 (in millions):

At December 31,	2011	2010
Receivables, net	$3,500	$3,900
Inventory	5,200	5,000
Accounts payable	900	1,200
Income taxes payable	600	700

Year Ended December 31,	2011
Revenues	$23,000
Cost of goods sold	14,100
Income tax expense	900

Based on these figures, how much cash did
- **Fidelity collect from customers during 2011?**
- **Fidelity pay for inventory during 2011?**
- **Fidelity pay for income taxes during 2011?**

Answers

		Beginning Receivables	+	Revenues	−	Collections	=	Ending Receivables
Collections from customers	= $23,400:	$3,900	+	$23,000	−	$23,400	=	$3,500

		Cost of Goods Sold	+	Increase in Inventory	+	Decrease in Accounts Payable	=	Payments
Payments for inventory	= $14,600:	$14,100	+	($5,200 − $5,000)	+	($1,200 − $900)	=	$14,600

		Beginning Income Taxes Payable	+	Income Tax Expense	−	Payment	=	Ending Income Taxes Payable
Payment of income taxes	= $1,000:	$700	+	$900	−	$1,000	=	$600

MEASURING CASH ADEQUACY: FREE CASH FLOW

Throughout this chapter, we have focused on cash flows from operating, investing, and financing activities. Some investors want to know how much cash a company can "free up" for new opportunities. **Free cash flow** is the amount of cash available from operations after paying for capital expenditures (i.e. investments in new PPE). Free cash flow can be computed as follows:

Free cash flow =	Net cash provided by operating activities	−	Cash payments for investments in PPE

Shell uses free cash flow to manage its operations. Suppose Shell expects net cash inflow of $2.3 billion from operations. Assume Shell plans to spend $1.9 billion to modernize its bottling plants. In this case, Shell's free cash flow would be $0.4 billion ($2.3 billion – $1.9 billion). If a good investment opportunity comes along, Shell should have $0.4 billion to invest in the other company. A large amount of free cash flow is generally preferable because it means that a lot of cash is available for new investments.

Let's have a look at Philips's cash flow statement again on page 714. Its CFO for 2009 was €1,545 million and its capital expenditures on PPE were €524 million. Philip's free cash flow is thus €1,021 million.

EXAMINING CASH FLOW PATTERNS

A company's cash flows should be examined over a period of time, not just at the end of one financial year. One simple but insightful cash flow analysis is to simply plot the cash flow patterns over a number of years. Exhibit 12-16 below shows Philips's cash flow patterns for the last four years. We have also plotted net profit for the year for comparison.

EXHIBIT 12-14 | **Philips's Cash Flow Patterns 2006-2009**

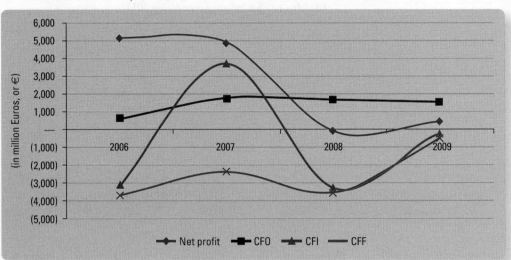

STOP & THINK...

What observations do you make out of Philips's cash flow patterns from 2006 to 2009?

Answers:

- Philips's CFO has always been positive, even with a significant drop in profit in 2008.
- Generally, CFI should be negative, but Philips must have sold something in 2007 that caused a large spike in CFI (upon further investigation it was "proceeds from other non-current financial assets" of over €4 billion). This gave Philips a large cash cushion as it entered into tough market conditions in 2008 and 2009.
- Philips seemed to be conserving cash in 2008 and 2009, with CFI and CFF becoming much smaller.

The Decision Guidelines that follow show some ways to use cash-flow and income data for investment and credit analysis.

DECISION GUIDELINES

INVESTORS' AND CREDITORS' USE OF CASH-FLOW AND RELATED INFORMATION

Jan Childres is a private investor. Through years of experience she has devised some guidelines for evaluating both share investments and bond investments. Childres uses a combination of accrual-accounting data and cash-flow information. Here are her decision guidelines for both investors and creditors.

INVESTORS

Questions	Factors to Consider	Financial Statement Predictor/Decision Model*
1. How much in dividends can I expect to receive from an investment in shares?	Expected future net income	Income from continuing operations**
	Expected future cash balance	Net cash flows from (in order): ■ Operating activities ■ Investing activities ■ Financing activities
	Future dividend policy	Current and past dividend policy
2. Is the share price likely to increase or decrease?	Expected future net income	Income from continuing operations**
	Expected future cash flows from operating activities	Income from continuing operations** Net cash flow from operating activities
3. What is the future share price likely to be?	Expected future income from: ■ continuing operations, and ■ net cash flow from operating activities	$$\text{Expected future price of one share} = \frac{\text{Net cash flow from operations per share}}{\text{Investment capitalization rate**}}$$ $$\text{Expected future price of one share} = \frac{\text{Expected future earnings per share**}}{\text{Investment capitalization rate**}}$$

CREDITORS

Questions	Factors to Consider	Financial Statement Predictor
Can the company pay the interest and principal at the maturity of a loan?	Expected future net cash flow from operating activities	Income from continuing operations** Net cash flow from operating activities

*There are many other factors to consider in making these decisions. These are some of the more common ores.

**See Chapter 11.

END-OF-CHAPTER SUMMARY PROBLEM

Adeva Health Foods, Inc., reported the following comparative balance sheet and income statement for 2011.

Adeva Health Foods, Inc.
Comparative Balance Sheets
December 31, 2011 and 2010

	2011	2010
Cash....................................	$ 19,000	$ 3,000
Accounts receivable...............	22,000	23,000
Inventories	34,000	31,000
Prepaid expenses	1,000	3,000
Equipment, net......................	90,000	79,000
Intangible assets	9,000	9,000
	$175,000	$148,000
Accounts payable	$ 14,000	$ 9,000
Accrued liabilities..................	16,000	19,000
Income tax payable	14,000	12,000
Notes payable	45,000	50,000
Share capital..........................	31,000	20,000
Retained earnings..................	64,000	40,000
Treasury shares	(9,000)	(2,000)
	$175,000	$148,000

Adeva Health Foods, Inc.
Income Statement
Year Ended December 31, 2011

Sales revenue	$190,000
Gain on sale of equipment..................	6,000
Total revenue and gains	196,000
Cost of goods sold..............................	85,000
Depreciation expense	19,000
Other operating expenses...................	36,000
Total expenses	140,000
Income before income tax	56,000
Income tax expense............................	18,000
Net income...	$ 38,000

Assume that **Berkshire Hathaway Inc.** is considering buying Adeva. Berkshire Hathaway requests the following cash-flow data for 2011. There were no non-cash investing and financing activities.

a. Collections from customers
b. Cash payments for inventory
c. Cash payments for operating expenses
d. Cash payment for income tax
e. Cash received from the sale of equipment (Adeva paid $40,000 for new equipment during the year.)

f. Issuance of shares
g. Issuance of notes payable (Adeva paid off $20,000 during the year.)
h. Cash dividends (There were no share dividends.)

Provide the requested data. Show your working.

Answers

a. Analyze Accounts Receivable (let X = Collections from customers):

Beginning	+	Sales	−	Collections	=	Ending
$23,000	+	$190,000	−	X	=	$22,000
				X	=	$191,000

b. Analyze Inventory and Accounts Payable (let X = Purchases, and let Y = Payments for inventory):

Beginning Inventory	+	Purchases	−	Ending Inventory	=	Cost of Goods Sold
$31,000	+	X	−	$34,000	=	$85,000
		X			=	$88,000

Beginning Accounts Payable	+	Purchases	−	Payments	=	Ending Accounts Payable
$9,000	+	$88,000	−	Y	=	$14,000
				Y	=	$83,000

c. Start with Other Operating Expenses, and adjust for the changes in Prepaid Expenses and Accrued Liabilities:

Other Operating Expenses	− Decrease in Prepaid Expenses	+ Decrease in Accrued Liabilities	=	Payments for Operating Expenses
$36,000	− $2,000	+ $3,000	=	$37,000

d. Analyze Income Tax Payable (let X = Payment of income tax):

Beginning	+	Income Tax Expense	−	Payments	=	Ending
$12,000	+	$18,000	−	X	=	$14,000
				X	=	$16,000

e. Analyze Equipment, Net (let X = Book value of equipment sold. Then combine with the gain or loss to compute cash received from the sale.)

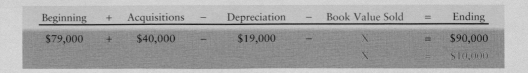

Beginning	+	Acquisitions	−	Depreciation	−	Book Value Sold	=	Ending
$79,000	+	$40,000	−	$19,000	−	X	=	$90,000
						X	=	$10,000

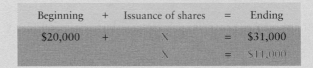

Cash Received from Sale	=	Book Value Sold	+	Gain on Sale
$16,000	=	$10,000	+	$6,000

f. Analyze Share Capital (let X = Issuance) of shares

Beginning	+	Issuance of shares	=	Ending
$20,000	+	X	=	$31,000
		X	=	$11,000

g. Analyze Notes Payable (let X = Issuance) of notes payable:

Beginning	+	Issuance of notes payable	−	Payment	=	Ending
$50,000	+	X	−	$20,000	=	$45,000
		X			=	$15,000

h. Analyze Retained Earnings (let X = Dividends) payments

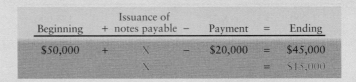

Beginning	+	Net Income	−	Dividends	=	Ending
$40,000	+	$38,000	−	X	=	$64,000
				X	=	$14,000

REVIEW STATEMENT OF CASH FLOWS

Quick Check (Answers are given on page 782.)

1. All of the following activities are reported on the statement of cash flows except
   a. marketing activities.
   b. investing activities.
   c. operating activities.
   d. financing activities.

2. Activities that create long-term liabilities are usually
   a. financing activities.
   b. operating activities.
   c. non-cash investing and financing activities.
   d. investing activities.

3. Activities affecting long-term assets are
   a. financing activities.
   b. marketing activities.
   c. operating activities.
   d. investing activities.

4. In 2010, PMW Corporation borrowed $110,000, paid dividends of $34,000, issued 10,000 shares for $45 per share, purchased land for $240,000, and received dividends of $10,000. Net income was $150,000, and depreciation for the year totaled $8,000. How much should be reported as net cash provided by operating activities by the indirect method?
   a. $194,000   c. $234,000
   b. $158,000   d. $134,000

5. Activities that obtain the cash needed to launch and sustain a company are
   a. marketing activities.   c. investing activities.
   b. income activities.   d. financing activities.

6. The exchange of shares for land would be reported as
   a. Exchanges are not reported on the statement of cash flows.
   b. financing activities.
   c. non-cash investing and financing activities.
   d. investing activities.

Use the following Montana Company information for questions 7–10.

Net income..	$50,000	Increase in accounts payable	$ 9,000
Depreciation expense	10,000	Acquisition of equipment	35,000
Payment of dividends............................	1,000	Sale of treasury shares...............	4,000
Increase in accounts receivable...........	8,000	Payment of long-term debt.........	16,000
Collection of long-term notes receivable..........	5,000	Proceeds from sale of land..........	40,000
Loss on sale of land.............................	15,000	Decrease in inventories..............	3,000

7. Under the indirect method, net cash provided by operating activities would be
   a. $84,000.   c. $79,000.
   b. $76,000.   d. $89,000.

8. Net cash provided by (used for) investing activities would be
   a. $20,000.   c. $(15,000).
   b. $10,000.   d. $(10,000).

9. Net cash provided by (used for) financing activities would be
   a. $3,000.   c. $(21,000).
   b. $(13,000).   d. $1,000.

10. The cost of land must have been
    a. $40,000.
    b. $55,000.
    c. $25,000.
    d. cannot be determined from the data given.

11. Sweet Treat Ice Cream began the year with $60,000 in accounts receivable and ended the year with $50,000 in accounts receivable. If sales for the year were $700,000, the cash collected from customers during the year amounted to
    a. $690,000.   c. $750,000.
    b. $760,000.   d. $710,000.

12. Nassau Farms, Ltd., made sales of $750,000 and had cost of goods sold of $410,000. Inventory decreased by $10,000 and accounts payable decreased by $12,000. Operating expenses were $180,000. How much was Nassau Farms's net income for the year?
    a. $150,000   c. $148,000
    b. $160,000   d. $340,000

13. Use the Nassau Farms data from question 12. How much cash did Nassau Farms pay for inventory during the year?
    a. $410,000   c. $422,000
    b. $400,000   d. $412,000

Accounting Vocabulary

cash equivalents (p. 713) Highly liquid short-term investments that can be converted into cash immediately.

cash flows (p. 713) Cash receipts and cash payments (disbursements).

direct method (p. 718) Format of the operating activities section of the statement of cash flows; lists the major categories of operating cash receipts (collections from customers and receipts of interest and dividends) and cash disbursements (payments to suppliers, to employees, for interest and income taxes).

financing activities (p. 716) Activities that obtain from investors and creditors the cash needed to launch and sustain the business; a section of the statement of cash flows.

free cash flow (p. 739) The amount of cash available from operations after paying for planned investments in PPE.

indirect method (p. 718) Format of the operating activities section of the statement of cash flows; starts with net income and reconciles to cash flows from operating activities.

investing activities (p. 715) Activities that increase or decrease the long-term assets available to the business; a section of the statement of cash flows.

operating activities (p. 715) Activities that create revenue or expense in the entity's major line of business; a section of the statement of cash flows. Operating activities affect the income statement.

statement of cash flows (p. 713) Reports cash receipts and cash payments classified according to the entity's major activities: operating, investing, and financing.

ASSESS YOUR PROGRESS

Short Exercises

S12-1 (*Learning Objectives 1, 2, 3: Explaining the purposes of the statement of cash flows*) State how the statement of cash flows helps investors and creditors perform each of the following functions:

    a. Predict future cash flows.
    b. Evaluate management decisions.

writing assignment ■

S12-2 (*Learning Objectives 1, 2, 3: Explaining the purposes of the statement of cash flows*) Rondeau Ltd., has experienced an unbroken string of nine years of growth in net income. Nevertheless, the company is facing bankruptcy. Creditors are calling all of Rondeau's loans for immediate payment, and the cash is simply not available. It is clear that the company's top managers overemphasized profits and gave too little attention to cash flows.

▌Requirement

    1. Write a brief memo, in your own words, to explain to the managers of Rondeau Ltd., the purposes of the statement of cash flows.

S12-3 (*Learning Objective 3: Evaluating operating cash flows—indirect method*)   Examine the statement of cash flows of Clock, Inc.

Clock, Inc. Consolidated Statement of Cash Flows (Adapted; in millions) Year Ended December 31, 2010		
Cash Flows from Operating Activities		
Net income..	$ 983	
Adjustment to reconcile net income to net cash provided by operating activities:		
Depreciation and amortization	278	
Change in assets and liabilities, net of acquired businesses:		
Accounts receivable..	(587)	
Other current assets..	(200)	
Accounts payable	(98)	
Accrued expenses and other liabilities	(298)	
Unearned revenue..	31	
Income taxes payable	(333)	
Other, net	33	
Net cash used in operating activities.............................		(191)
Cash Flows from Investing Activities		
Purchase of property and equipment.................................	$ (1,991)	
Purchase of investments..	(26,603)	
Sale of investments..	24,108	
Acquisitions of other companies	(454)	
Net cash used in investing activities.............................		(4,940)
Cash Flows from Financing Activities		
Proceeds from the issuance of shares, net...........................	$ 1,043	
Other, net...	473	
Net cash provided by financing activities......................		1,516
Other, net...		22
Net increase (decrease) in cash and cash equivalents		(3,593)
Cash and cash equivalents at beginning of year.................		5,194
Cash and cash equivalents at end of year...........................		$ 1,601

Suppose Clock's operating activities *provided*, rather than *used*, cash. Identify three things under the indirect method that could cause operating cash flows to be positive.

S12-4 (*Learning Objectives 1, 2: Using cash-flow data to evaluate performance*)   Top managers of Tranquility Inns are reviewing company performance for 2010. The income statement reports a 25% increase in net income over 2009. However, most of the increase resulted from an exceptional gain from a lawsuit Tranquility Inns has last won against a competitor. The balance sheet shows a large increase in receivables. The cash flows statement, in summarized form, reports the following:

writing assignment ■

Net cash used for operating activities......................	$(50,000)
Net cash provided by investing activities.................	30,000
Net cash provided by financing activities	25,000
Increase in cash during 2010...................................	$ 5,000

I *Requirement*

1. Write a memo giving Tranquility Inns's managers your assessment of 2010 operations and your outlook for the future. Focus on the information content of the cash flows data.

S12-5 (*Learning Objective 3: Reporting cash flows from operating activities—indirect method*) Beautiful Atlantic Transportation (BAT) began 2010 with accounts receivable, inventory, and prepaid expenses totaling $58,000. At the end of the year, BAT had a total of $55,000 for these current assets. At the beginning of 2010, BAT owed current liabilities of $20,000, and at year-end current liabilities totaled $32,000.

Net income for the year was $12,000. Included in net income were a $2,000 loss on the sale of land and depreciation expense of $8,000.

Show how BAT should report cash flows from operating activities for 2010. BAT uses the *indirect* method.

S12-6 (*Learning Objectives 2, 3: Identifying items for reporting cash flows from operations—indirect method*) Campbell Clinic, Inc., is preparing its statement of cash flows (*indirect* method) for the year ended March 31, 2010. Consider the following items in preparing the company's statement of cash flows. Identify each item as an operating activity—addition to net income (O+) or subtraction from net income (O-), an investing activity (I), a financing activity (F), or an activity that is not used to prepare the cash flows statement by the indirect method (N). Place the appropriate symbol in the blank space.

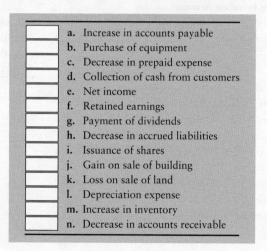

	a. Increase in accounts payable
	b. Purchase of equipment
	c. Decrease in prepaid expense
	d. Collection of cash from customers
	e. Net income
	f. Retained earnings
	g. Payment of dividends
	h. Decrease in accrued liabilities
	i. Issuance of shares
	j. Gain on sale of building
	k. Loss on sale of land
	l. Depreciation expense
	m. Increase in inventory
	n. Decrease in accounts receivable

S12-7 (*Learning Objective 3: Computing operating cash flows—indirect method*) Ethan Corporation accountants have assembled the following data for the year ended June 30, 2010.

Net income......................	$?	Cost of goods sold...................	$116,000
Payment of dividends..............	5,600	Other operating expenses.........	33,000
Proceeds from the issuance		Purchase of equipment.............	43,000
of shares.......................	26,000	Increase in current liabilities.....	7,000
Sales revenue...........................	228,000	Payment of note payable..........	32,000
Decrease in current assets		Proceeds from sale of land........	29,000
other than cash...............	35,000	Depreciation expense..............	11,000
Purchase of treasury shares......	6,000		

Prepare the *operating activities section* of Ethan's statement of cash flows for the year ended June 30, 2010. Ethan uses the *indirect* method for operating cash flows.

S12-8 (*Learning Objective 3, 4, 5: Preparing a statement of cash flows—indirect method*) Use the data in Short Exercise 12-7 to prepare Ethan Corporation's statement of cash flows for the year ended June 30, 2010. Ethan uses the *indirect* method for operating activities.

S12-9 (*Learning Objective 4: Computing investing cash flows*) Motorsports of Munich, reported the following financial statements for 2010:

Motorsports of Munich
Income Statement
Year Ended December 31, 2010

(In thousands)	
Service revenue............................	$770
Cost of goods sold....................	330
Salary expense............................	40
Depreciation expense	30
Other expenses..........................	170
Total expenses..........................	570
Net income	$200

Motorsports of Munich
Comparative Balance Sheets
December 31, 2010 and 2009

(In thousands)					
Assets	**2010**	**2009**	**Liabilities**	**2010**	**2009**
Current:			Current:		
Cash.......................................	$ 28	$ 11	Accounts payable	$ 48	$ 43
Accounts receivable............	54	43	Salary payable....................	26	24
Inventory.............................	77	89	Accrued liabilities..............	16	19
Prepaid expenses	6	5	Long-term notes payable........	69	54
Long-term investments...........	54	79			
PPE, net..................................	229	188	**Shareholders' Equity**		
			Share capital..........................	48	38
			Retained earnings...................	241	237
Total	$448	$415	Total	$448	$415

Compute the following investing cash flows: (Enter all amounts in thousands.)

a. Acquisitions of PPE (all were for cash). Motorsports of Munich sold no PPE.

b. Proceeds from the sale of investments. Motorsports of Munich purchased no investments.

S12-10 (*Learning Objective 5: Computing financing cash flows*) Use the Motorsports of Munich data in Short Exercise 12-9 to compute the following: (Enter all amounts in thousands.)

a. New borrowing or payment of long-term notes payable. Motorsports of Munich had only one long-term note payable transaction during the year.

b. Issuance of share capital or retirement of shares. Motorsports of Munich had only one share capital during the year.

c. Payment of cash dividends (same as dividends declared).

S12-11 (*Learning Objective 6: Computing operating cash flows—direct method*) Use the Motorsports of Munich data in Short Exercise 12-9 to compute the following: (Enter all amounts in thousands.)

    a. Collections from customers

    b. Payments for inventory

S12-12 (*Learning Objective 6: Computing operating cash flows—direct method*) Use the Motorsports of Munich data in Short Exercise 12-9 to compute the following: (Enter all amounts in thousands).

    a. Payments to employees

    b. Payments of other expenses

S12-13 (*Learning Objective 4, 5, 6: Preparing a statement of cash flows—direct method*) Horse Heaven Farm, began 2010 with cash of $170,000. During the year, Horse Heaven earned service revenue of $590,000 and collected $480,000 from customers. Expenses for the year totaled $320,000, with $310,000 paid in cash to suppliers and employees. Horse Heaven also paid $136,000 to purchase equipment and a cash dividend of $49,000 to shareholders. During 2010, Horse Heaven borrowed $26,000 by issuing a note payable. Prepare the company's statement of cash flows for the year. Format operating activities by the *direct* method.

S12-14 (*Learning Objective 6: Computing operating cash flows—direct method*) Middleton Golf Club, has assembled the following data for the year ended September 30, 2010:

Cost of goods sold...........................	$104,000	Payment of dividends........................	$ 8,000
Payments to suppliers......................	90,000	Proceeds from issuance	
Purchase of equipment	42,000	of shares	16,000
Payments to employees...................	75,000	Sales revenue.....................................	211,000
Payment of note payable	15,000	Collections from customers...............	203,000
Proceeds from sale of land...............	61,000	Payment of income tax......................	14,000
Depreciation expense	6,000	Purchase of treasury shares	5,700

Prepare the *operating activities section* of Middleton Golf Club's statement of cash flows for the year ended September 30, 2010. Middleton uses the *direct* method for operating cash flows.

S12-15 (*Learning Objective 4, 5, 6: Preparing a statement of cash flows—direct method*) Use the data in Short Exercise 12-14 to prepare Middleton Golf Club's statement of cash flows for the year ended September 30, 2010. Middleton uses the *direct* method for operating activities.

Exercises

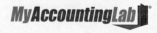

> All of the A and B exercises can be found within MyAccountingLab, an online homework and practice environment. Your instructor may ask you to complete these exercises using MyAccountingLab.

(Group A)

E12-16A (*Learning Objectives 2, 3: Identifying activities for the statement of cash flows—indirect method*) Tucker-Breen Investments specializes in low-risk government bonds. Identify each of Tucker-Breen's transactions as operating (O), investing (I), financing (F), non-cash investing and financing (NIF), or a transaction that is not reported on the statement of cash flows (N). Indicate whether each item increases (+) or decreases (−) cash. The *indirect* method is used for operating activities.

	a. Sale of long-term investment
	b. Issuance of long-term note payable to borrow cash
	c. Increase in prepaid expenses
	d. Payment of cash dividend
	e. Loss of sale of equipment
	f. Decrease in merchandise inventory
	g. Acquisition of equipment by issuance of note payable
	h. Increase in accounts payable
	i. Amortization of intangible assets
	j. Net income
	k. Payment of long-term debt
	l. Accrual of salary expense
	m. Cash sale of land
	n. Purchase of long-term investment
	o. Acquisition of building by cash payment
	p. Purchase of treasury shares
	q. Issuance of shares for cash
	r. Decrease in accrued liabilities
	s. Depreciation of equipment

E12-17A (*Learning Objectives 2, 3: Classifying transactions for the statement of cash flows—indirect method*)   Indicate whether each of the following transactions records an operating activity, an investing activity, a financing activity, or a non-cash investing and financing activity.

a.	Depreciation Expense	11,000		h.	Cash	50,000	
	Accumulated Depreciation		11,000		Accounts Receivable	9,000	
b.	Treasury Shares	7,800			Service Revenue		59,000
	Cash		7,800	i.	Bonds Payable	47,000	
c.	Land	83,000			Cash		47,000
	Cash		83,000	j.	Cash	74,000	
d.	Equipment	19,000			Share Capital		11,000
	Cash		19,000		Capital in Excess of Par		63,000
e.	Salary Expense	24,000		k.	Dividends Payable	17,100	
	Cash		24,000		Cash		17,100
f.	Furniture and Fixtures	24,200		l.	Loss on Disposal of Equipment	1,200	
	Cash		24,200		Equipment, Net		1,200
g.	Building	159,000		m.	Cash	6,900	
	Note Payable, Long-Term		159,000		Long-Term Investment		6,900

E12-18A (*Learning Objective 3: Computing cash flows from operating activities—indirect method*)   The accounting records of North East Distributors, Inc., reveal the following: **writing assignment ■**

Net income...............................	$38,000	Depreciation.................................	$17,000
Collection of dividend revenue..........	7,800	Decrease in current liabilities..........	19,000
Payment of interest............................	11,000	Increase in current assets	
Sales revenue.....................................	13,000	other than cash...........................	24,000
Loss on sale of land..........................	22,000	Payment of dividends.....................	7,800
Acquisition of land	42,000	Payment of income tax...................	15,000

▌Requirement

1. Compute cash flows from operating activities by the *indirect* method. Use the format of the operating activities section of Exhibit 12-6. Also evaluate the operating cash flow of North East Distributors. Give the reason for your evaluation.

E12-19A (*Learning Objective 3: Computing cash flows from operating activities—indirect method*) The accounting records of Wilderness Fruit Traders include these accounts:

Cash				Accounts Receivable				Inventory			
May 1	90,000			May 1	1,000			May 1	3,000		
Receipts	440,000	Payments	445,000	Receipts	540,000	Collections	440,000	Purchases	438,000	Cost of sales	336,000
May 31	85,000			May 31	101,000			May 31	105,000		

Equipment				Accumulated Deprec.—Equipment				Accounts Payable			
May 1	185,000					May 1	55,000			May 1	14,500
Acquisition	5,000					Depreciation	5,000	Payments	327,000	Purchases	438,000
May 31	190,000					May 31	60,000			May 31	125,500

Accrued Liabilities				Retained Earnings			
		May 1	19,000	Quarterly		May 1	63,000
Payments	32,000	Receipts	26,000	Dividend	16,000	Net Income	20,000
		May 31	13,000			May 31	67,000

❙ Requirement

1. Compute Wilderness net cash provided by (used for) operating activities during May. Use the *indirect* method. Does Wilderness have trouble collecting receivables or selling inventory? How can you tell?

writing assignment ■

E12-20A (*Learning Objective 3, 4, 5: Preparing the statement of cash flows—indirect method*) The income statement and additional data of Newbury Travel Products, Inc., follow:

Newbury Travel Products, Inc.
Income Statement
Year Ended December 31, 2010

Revenues:		
Service revenue	$283,000	
Dividend revenue	8,000	$291,000
Expenses:		
Cost of goods sold	103,000	
Salary expense	78,000	
Depreciation expense...............	26,000	
Advertising expense	4,500	
Interest expense	2,600	
Income tax expense..................	8,000	222,100
Net income		$ 68,900

Additional data:

a. Acquisition of PPE was $212,000. Of this amount, $160,000 was paid in cash and $52,000 by signing a note payable.

b. Proceeds from sale of land totaled $27,000.

c. Proceeds from issuance of shares totaled $80,000.

d. Payment of long-term note payable was $17,000.

e. Payment of dividends was $13,000.

f. From the balance sheets:

	December 31,	
	2010	2009
Current Assets:		
Cash	$30,000	$10,800
Accounts receivable	42,000	59,000
Inventory.............................	30,000	91,000
Prepaid expenses...................	9,400	8,700
Current Liabilities:		
Accounts payable...................	$38,000	$27,000
Accrued liabilities	18,000	99,000

❙ Requirements

1. Prepare Newbury's statement of cash flows for the year ended December 31, 2010, using the *indirect* method.
2. Evaluate Newbury's cash flows for the year. In your evaluation, mention all three categories of cash flows and give the reason for your evaluation.

E12-21A (*Learning Objective 3, 4, 5: Interpreting a statement of cash flows—indirect method*)   Consider three independent cases for the cash flows of 579 Pavilion Shoes. For each case, identify from the statement of cash flows how 579 Pavilion Shoes generated the cash to acquire new PPE. Rank the three cases from the most healthy financially to the least healthy.

	Case A	Case B	Case C
Cash flows from operating activities			
Net income	$ 20,000	$ 20,000	$ 20,000
Depreciation and amortization	9,000	9,000	9,000
Increase in current assets	(22,000)	(2,000)	(11,000)
Decrease in current liabilities	(10,000)	(4,000)	(1,000)
	(3,000)	23,000	17,000
Cash flows from investing activities:			
Acquisition of PPE.........................	(83,000)	(83,000)	(83,000)
Sales of PPE	9,000	37,000	90,000
	(74,000)	(46,000)	7,000
Cash flows from financing activities:			
Issuance of shares	97,000	62,000	15,000
Payment of debt.............................	(22,000)	(38,000)	(23,000)
	75,000	24,000	(8,000)
Net increase (decrease) in cash	$ (2,000)	$ 1,000	$ 16,000

E12-22A (*Learning Objectives 4, 5: Computing investing and financing amounts for the statement of cash flows*)   Compute the following items for the statement of cash flows:

a. Beginning and ending PPE, Net, are $110,000 and $106,000, respectively. Depreciation for the period was $9,000, and purchases of new PPE were $33,000. PPE were sold at a $4,000 loss. What were the cash proceeds of the sale?

b. Beginning and ending Retained Earnings are $49,000 and $74,000, respectively. Net income for the period was $58,000, and dividends were $7,000. How much were cash dividends?

E12-23A (*Learning Objective 6: Computing cash flows from operating activities—direct method*) The accounting records of Princeton Pharmaceuticals, Inc., reveal the following:

Payment of salaries		Net income..................................	$60,000
and wages.........................	$35,000	Payment of income tax..............	24,000
Depreciation...............................	20,000	Collection of dividend	
Decrease in current		revenue	10,000
liabilities..........................	22,000	Payment of interest....................	17,000
Increase in current assets		Cash sales..................................	33,000
other than cash...............	23,000	Loss on sale of land	6,000
Payment of dividends...............	7,000	Acquisition of land	38,000
Collection of accounts		Payment of accounts	
receivable.........................	50,000	payable	58,000

❙ Requirement

1. Compute cash flows from operating activities by the *direct* method. Also evaluate Princeton's operating cash flow. Give the reason for your evaluation.

E12-24A (*Learning Objective 4, 5, 6: Identifying items for the statement of cash flows—direct method*) Selected accounts of Ashley Antiques show the following:

Salary Payable			
		Beginning balance	10,000
Payments	30,000	Salary expense	28,000
		Ending balance	8,000

Buildings			
Beginning balance	80,000	Depreciation	20,000
Acquisitions	120,000	Book value of building sold	119,000*
Ending balance	61,000		

*Sale price was 150,000.

Notes Payable			
		Beginning balance	234,000
Payments	67,000	Issuance of note payable for cash	74,000
		Ending balance	241,000

❙ Requirement

1. For each account, identify the item or items that should appear on a statement of cash flows prepared by the *direct* method. State where to report the item.

E12-25A (*Learning Objective 4, 5, 6: Preparing the statement of cash flows—direct method*)   The income statement and additional data of Cobbs Hill, Inc., follow: **writing assignment ■**

Cobbs Hill, Inc.
Income Statement
Year Ended April 30, 2010

Revenues:		
Sales revenue......................	$232,000	
Dividend revenue...............	11,000	$243,000
Expenses:		
Cost of goods sold..............	108,000	
Salary expense	46,000	
Depreciation expense..........	31,000	
Advertising expense	11,500	
Interest expense	2,100	
Income tax expense.............	9,000	207,600
Net income		$ 35,400

Additional data:

   a. Collections from customers are $13,000 more than sales.

   b. Payments to suppliers are $1,300 less than the sum of cost of goods sold plus advertising expense.

   c. Payments to employees are $2,000 more than salary expense.

   d. Dividend imcome, interest expense, and income tax expense equal their cash amounts.

   e. Acquisition of PPE is $143,000. Of this amount, $100,000 is paid in cash and $43,000 by signing a note payable.

   f. Proceeds from sale of land total $28,000.

   g. Proceeds from issuance of shares total $93,000.

   h. Payment of long-term note payable is $17,000.

   i. Payment of dividends is $8,500.

   j. Cash balance, April 30, 2009, was $21,000.

I Requirements

1. Prepare Cobbs Hill, Inc.'s statement of cash flows and accompanying schedule of non-cash investing and financing activities. Report operating activities by the *direct* method.

2. Evaluate Cobbs Hill's cash flows for the year. In your evaluation, mention all three categories of cash flows and give the reason for your evaluation.

E12-26A (*Learning Objective 4, 5, 6: Computing amounts for the statement of cash flows—direct method*)   Compute the following items for the statement of cash flows:

   a. Beginning and ending Accounts Receivable are $25,000 and $20,000, respectively. Credit sales for the period total $62,000. How much are cash collections from customers?

   b. Cost of goods sold is $79,000. Beginning Inventory was $26,000, and ending Inventory balance is $29,000. Beginning and ending Accounts Payable are $11,000 and $9,000, respectively. How much are cash payments for inventory?

(Group B)

E12-27B (*Learning Objectives 2, 3: Identifying activities for the statement of cash flows—indirect method*) Burke-Cassidy Investments specializes in low-risk government bonds. Identify each of Burke-Cassidy's transactions as operating (O), investing (I), financing (F), non-cash investing and financing (NIF), or a transaction that is not reported on the statement of cash flows (N). Indicate whether each item increases (+) or decreases (–) cash. The *indirect* method is used for operating activities.

	a. Acquisition of building by cash payment
	b. Decrease in merchandise inventory
	c. Depreciation of equipment
	d. Decrease in accrued liabilities
	e. Payment of cash dividend
	f. Purchase of long-term investment
	g. Issuance of long-term note payable to borrow cash
	h. Increase in prepaid expenses
	i. Accrual of salary expense
	j. Acquisition of equipment by issuance of note payable
	k. Sale of long-term investment
	l. Issuance of shares for cash
	m. Increase in accounts payable
	n. Amortization of intangible assets
	o. Loss of sale of equipment
	p. Payment of long-term debt
	q. Cash sale of land
	r. Purchase of treasury shares
	s. Net income

E12-28B (*Learning Objectives 2, 3: Classifying transactions for the statement of cash flows—indirect method*) Indicate whether each of the following transactions records an operating activity, an investing activity, a financing activity, or a non-cash investing and financing activity.

a.	Cash	85,000		g.	Equipment	15,600	
	Share Capital		14,000		Cash		15,600
	Capital in Excess of Par		71,000	h.	Dividends Payable	18,200	
b.	Furniture and Fixtures	25,600			Cash		18,200
	Cash		25,600	i.	Salary Expense	19,400	
c.	Cash	72,000			Cash		19,400
	Accounts Receivable	15,000		j.	Building	146,000	
	Service Revenue		87,000		Note Payable—Long-Term		146,000
d.	Cash	9,100		k.	Dividends Payable	17,100	
	Long-Term Investment		9,100		Cash		17,100
e.	Loss on Disposal of Equipment	1,500		l.	Depreciation Expense	7,000	
	Equipment, Net		1,500		Accumulated Depreciation		7,000
f.	Land	20,300		m.	Bonds Payable	49,000	
	Cash		20,300		Cash		49,000

E12-29B (*Learning Objective 3: Computing cash flows from operating activities—indirect*   <u>**writing assignment** ■</u>
method)   The accounting records of Central Distributors, Inc., reveal the following:

Net income..	$40,000	Depreciation....................................	$15,000
Collection of dividend revenue..........	6,900	Increase in current liabilities...........	23,000
Payment of interest............................	14,000	Decrease in current assets	
Sales revenue.....................................	12,000	other than cash..........................	28,000
Loss on sale of land...........................	19,000	Payment of dividends....................	7,200
Acquisition of land	43,000	Payment of income tax..................	12,000

❙ Requirement

1. Compute cash flows from operating activities by the *indirect* method. Use the format of the operating activities section of Exhibit 12-6. Also evaluate the operating cash flow of Central Distributors. Give the reason for your evaluation.

E12-30B (*Learning Objective 3: Computing cash flows from operating activities—indirect method*)   The accounting records of Lawrence Fruit Traders include these accounts:

Cash			
Oct 1	11,000		
Receipts	537,000	Payments	446,000
Oct 31	102,000		

Accounts Receivable			
Oct 1	8,000		
Receipts	538,000	Collections	537,000
Oct 31	9,000		

Inventory			
Oct 1	4,000		
Purchases	437,000	Cost of sales	434,000
Oct 31	7,000		

Equipment	
Oct 1	188,000
Acquisition	7,000
Oct 31	195,000

Accumulated Deprec.—Equipment			
		Oct 1	52,000
		Depreciation	9,000
		Oct 31	61,000

Accounts Payable			
		Oct 1	14,000
Payments	328,000	Purchases	437,000
		Oct 31	123,000

Accrued Liabilities			
		Oct 1	12,000
Payments	28,000	Receipts	22,000
		Oct 31	6,000

Retained Earnings			
Quarterly		Oct 1	66,000
Dividend	18,000	Net Income	35,000
		Oct 31	83,000

❙ Requirement

1. Compute Lawrence's net cash provided by (used for) operating activities during October. Use the *indirect* method. Does Lawrence have trouble collecting receivables or selling inventory? How can you tell?

E12-31B (*Learning Objective 3, 4, 5: Preparing the statement of cash flows—indirect method*) The income statement and additional data of Norton Travel Products, Inc., follow:

Norton Travel Products, Inc.
Income Statement
Year Ended December 31, 2010

Revenues:		
Service revenue	$235,000	
Dividend revenue	8,300	$243,300
Expenses:		
Cost of goods sold	102,000	
Salary expense	62,000	
Depreciation expense	33,000	
Advertising expense	4,300	
Interest expense	2,400	
Income tax expense	7,000	210,700
Net income		$ 32,600

Additional data:

a. Acquisition of PPE was $170,000. Of this amount, $140,000 was paid in cash and $30,000 by signing a note payable.
b. Proceeds from sale of land totaled $48,000.
c. Proceeds from issuance of shares totaled $31,000.
d. Payment of long-term note payable was $16,000.
e. Payment of dividends was $10,000.
f. From the balance sheets:

	December 31,	
	2010	2009
Current Assets:		
Cash	$32,000	$13,300
Accounts receivable	41,000	57,000
Inventory	48,000	87,000
Prepaid expenses	9,100	8,200
Current Liabilities:		
Accounts payable	$32,000	$17,000
Accrued liabilities	14,000	43,000

❙ Requirements

1. Prepare Norton's statement of cash flows for the year ended December 31, 2010, using the *indirect* method.
2. Evaluate Norton's cash flows for the year. In your evaluation, mention all three categories of cash flows and give the reason for your evaluation.

E12-32B *(Learning Objective 3, 4, 5: Interpreting a statement of cash flows—indirect method)*
Consider three independent cases for the cash flows of 424 Promenade Shoes. For each case, identify from the statement of cash flows how 424 Promenade Shoes generated the cash to acquire new PPE. Rank the three cases from the most healthy financially to the least healthy.

	Case A	Case B	Case C
Cash flows from operating activities			
Net income	$ 10,000	$ 10,000	$ 10,000
Depreciation and amortization	12,000	12,000	12,000
Increase in current assets	1,000	(5,000)	2,000
Decrease in current liabilities	2,000	(19,000)	3,000
	25,000	(2,000)	27,000
Cash flows from investing activities:			
Acquisition of PPE..........................	(99,000)	(99,000)	(99,000)
Sales of PPE	104,000	20,000	33,000
	5,000	(79,000)	(66,000)
Cash flows from financing activities:			
Issuance of shares	18,000	105,000	73,000
Payment of debt..............................	(27,000)	(20,000)	(32,000)
	(9,000)	85,000	41,000
Net increase (decrease) in cash	$ 21,000	$ 4,000	$ 2,000

E12-33B *(Learning Objectives 4, 5: Computing investing and financing amounts for the statement of cash flows)*   Compute the following items for the statement of cash flows:

a. Beginning and ending PPE, Net, are $102,000 and $97,000, respectively. Depreciation for the period was $12,000, and purchases of new PPE were $30,000. PPE were sold at a $5,000 gain. What were the cash proceeds of the sale?

b. Beginning and ending Retained Earnings are $46,000 and $70,000, respectively. Net income for the period was $48,000, and dividends were $11,000. How much were cash dividends?

E12-34B *(Learning Objective 6: Computing cash flows from operating activities—direct method)*   The accounting records of One Stop Pharmaceuticals, Inc., reveal the following:

writing assignment ■

Payment of salaries and wages..........................	$40,000	Net income.................................	$20,000
Depreciation...............................	25,000	Payment of income tax...............	8,000
Increase in current liabilities..........................	27,000	Collection of dividend revenue............................	7,000
		Payment of interest....................	13,000
Increase in current assets other than cash	28,000	Cash sales....................................	36,000
		Gain on sale of land	2,000
Payment of dividends...............	6,000	Acquisition of land	35,000
Collection of accounts receivable.........................	80,000	Payment of accounts payable	51,000

❙ Requirement

1. Compute cash flows from operating activities by the *direct* method. Also evaluate One Stop's operating cash flow. Give the reason for your evaluation.

E12-35B (*Learning Objective 4, 5, 6: Identifying items for the statement of cash flows—direct method*) Selected accounts of Elizabeth Antiques show the following:

Salary Payable

		Beginning balance	14,000
Payments	20,000	Salary expense	42,000
		Ending balance	36,000

Buildings

Beginning balance	100,000	Depreciation	22,000
Acquisitions	155,000	Book value of building sold	117,000*
Ending balance	116,000		

*Sale price was 160,000.

Notes Payable

		Beginning balance	244,000
Payments	72,000	Issuance of note payable for cash	90,000
		Ending balance	262,000

Requirement

1. For each account, identify the item or items that should appear on a statement of cash flows prepared by the *direct* method. State where to report the item.

E12-36B (*Learning Objective 4, 5, 6: Preparing the statement of cash flows—direct method*) The income statement and additional data of Happy Life, Inc., follow:

Happy Life, Inc.
Income Statement
Year Ended November 30, 2010

Revenues:		
Sales revenue......................	$223,000	
Dividend income.................	10,500	$233,500
Expenses:		
Cost of goods sold..............	102,000	
Salary expense	42,000	
Depreciation expense..........	19,000	
Advertising expense	14,000	
Interest expense	4,500	
Income tax expense.............	8,000	189,500
Net income		$ 44,000

Additional data:

a. Collections from customers are $16,500 more than sales.

b. Payments to suppliers are $1,200 more than the sum of cost of goods sold plus advertising expense.

c. Payments to employees are $1,700 less than salary expense.
d. Dividend income, interest expense, and income tax expense equal their cash amounts.
e. Acquisition of PPE is $154,000. Of this amount, $108,000 is paid in cash and $46,000 by signing a note payable.
f. Proceeds from sale of land total $21,000.
g. Proceeds from issuance of shares total $86,000.
h. Payment of long-term note payable is $13,000.
i. Payment of dividends is $9,000.
j. Cash balance, November 30, 2009, was $23,000.

❙ Requirements

1. Prepare Happy Life, Inc.'s statement of cash flows and accompanying schedule of non-cash investing and financing activities. Report operating activities by the *direct* method.
2. Evaluate Happy Life's cash flows for the year. In your evaluation, mention all three categories of cash flows and give the reason for your evaluation.

E12-37B (*Learning Objective 4, 5, 6: Computing amounts for the statement of cash flows—direct method*)   Compute the following items for the statement of cash flows:

a. Beginning and ending Accounts Receivable are $20,000 and $17,000, respectively. Credit sales for the period total $61,000. How much are cash collections from customers?
b. Cost of goods sold is $79,000. Beginning Inventory balance is $28,000, and ending Inventory balance is $24,000. Beginning and ending Accounts Payable are $12,000 and $13,000, respectively. How much are cash payments for inventory?

Challenge Exercises

E12-38 (*Learning Objectives 3, 6: Computing cash-flow amounts*)   Tip Top, Inc., reported the following in its financial statements for the year ended May 30, 2010 (in thousands):

	2010	2009
Income Statement		
Net sales	$23,984	$21,674
Cost of sales	18,026	15,432
Depreciation	266	227
Other operating expenses	3,875	4,254
Income tax expense	536	488
Net income	$ 1,281	$ 1,273
Balance Sheet		
Cash and equivalents	$ 16	$ 15
Accounts receivable	603	614
Inventory	3,140	2,872
Property and equipment, net	4,346	3,436
Accounts payable	1,551	1,371
Accrued liabilities	935	632
Income tax payable	197	193
Long-term liabilities	480	468
Share capital	515	445
Retained earnings	4,427	3,828

I Requirement

1. Determine the following cash receipts and payments for Tip Top, Inc., during 2010:
(Enter all amounts in thousands.)
   a. Collections from customers
   b. Payments for inventory
   c. Payments for other operating expenses
   d. Payment of income tax
   e. Proceeds from issuance of shares
   f. Payment of cash dividends

E12-39 *(Learning Objective 3: Using the balance sheet and the statement of cash flows together)* Delorme Specialties reported the following at December 31, 2010 (in thousands):

	2010	2009
From the comparative balance sheet:		
Property and equipment, net..	$10,950	$9,630
Long-term notes payable..	4,500	3,040
From the statement of cash flows:		
Depreciation	$ 1,950	
Capital expenditures...	(4,090)	
Proceeds from sale of property and equipment	740	
Proceeds from issuance of long-term note payable........	1,250	
Payment of long-term note payable...............................	(80)	
Issuance of shares	389	

I Requirement

1. Determine the following items for Delorme Specialties during 2010:
   a. Gain or loss on the sale of property and equipment
   b. Amount of long-term debt issued for something other than cash

Quiz

Test your understanding of the statement of cash flows by answering the following questions. Select the best choice from among the possible answers given.

Q12-40 Paying off bonds payable is reported on the statement of cash flows under
a. non-cash investing and financing activities.   c. operating activities.
b. investing activities.   d. financing activities.

Q12-41 The sale of inventory for cash is reported on the statement of cash flows under
a. financing activities.   c. investing activities.
b. non-cash investing and financing activities.   d. operating activities.

Q12-42 Selling equipment is reported on the statement of cash flows under
a. financing activities.   c. non-cash investing and financing activities.
b. investing activities.   d. operating activities.

Q12-43 Which of the following terms appears on a statement of cash flows—indirect method?
a. Cash receipt of interest revenue   c. Depreciation expense
b. Collections from customers   d. Payments to suppliers

Q12-44 On an indirect method statement of cash flows, an increase in a prepaid insurance would be
a. added to increases in current assets.   c. deducted from net income.
b. included in payments to suppliers.   d. added to net income.

Q12-45 On an indirect method statement of cash flows, an increase in accounts payable would be
a. reported in the financing activities section.
b. reported in the investing activities section.
c. added to net income in the operating activities section.
d. deducted from net income in the operating activities section.

Q12-46 On an indirect method statement of cash flows, a gain on the sale of PPE would be
a. reported in the investing activities section.
b. added to net income in the operating activities section.
c. deducted from net income in the operating activities section.
d. ignored, since the gain did not generate any cash.

Q12-47 Select an activity for each of the following transactions:
1. Paying cash dividends is a/an _____ activity.
2. Receiving cash dividends is a/an _____ activity.

Q12-48 Click Camera Co. sold equipment with a cost of $21,000 and accumulated depreciation of $9,000 for an amount that resulted in a gain of $1,000. What amount should Click report on the statement of cash flows as "proceeds from sale of PPE"?
a. $10,000
b. $20,000
c. $13,000
d. Some other amount

Questions 49–57 use the following data. Sheehan Corporation formats operating cash flows by the *indirect* method.

Sheehan's Income Statement for 2010

Sales revenue	$177,000	
Gain on sale of equipment	9,000*	$186,000
Cost of goods sold	114,000	
Depreciation	6,500	
Other operating expenses	24,000	144,500
Net income		$ 41,500

*The book value of equipment sold during 2010 was $21,000.

Sheehan's Comparative Balance Sheet at the end of 2010

	2010	2009		2010	2009
Cash	$ 5,500	$ 3,000	Accounts payable	$ 8,000	$ 9,000
Accounts receivable	5,000	13,000	Accrued liabilities	6,000	4,000
Inventory	11,000	10,000	Share capital	18,000	9,000
Plant and equipment, net	97,000	71,000	Retained earnings	86,500	75,000
	$118,500	$97,000		$118,500	$97,000

Q12-49 How many items enter the computation of Sheehan's net cash provided by operating activities?
a. 3
b. 2
c. 7
d. 5

Q12-50 How do Sheehan's accrued liabilities affect the company's statement of cash flows for 2010?

a. Increase in cash used by investing activities.

b. Increase in cash provided by operating activities.

c. Increase in cash used by financing activities.

d. They don't because the accrued liabilities are not yet paid.

Q12-51 How do accounts receivable affect Sheehan's cash flows from operating activities for 2010?

a. Decrease in cash provided by operating activities.

b. Decrease in cash used by investing activities.

c. Increase in cash provided by operating activities.

d. They don't because accounts receivable result from investing activities.

Q12-52 Sheehan's net cash provided by operating activities during 2010 was

a. $53,000.

b. $50,000.

c. $47,000.

d. $44,000.

Q12-53 How many items enter the computation of Sheehan's net cash flow from investing activities for 2010?

a. 5

b. 3

c. 7

d. 2

Q12-54 The book value of equipment sold during 2010 was $21,000. Sheehan's net cash flow from investing activities for 2010 was

a. net cash used of $23,500.

b. net cash used of $53,000.

c. net cash used of $50,000.

d. net cash used of $44,000.

Q12-55 How many items are included the computation of Sheehan's net cash flow from financing activities for 2010?

a. 7

b. 3

c. 5

d. 2

Q12-56 Sheehan's largest financing cash flow for 2010 resulted from

a. payment of dividends.

b. sale of equipment.

c. purchase of equipment.

d. issuance of shares.

Q12-57 Sheehan's net cash flow from financing activities for 2010 was

a. net cash used of $21,000.

b. net cash used of $50,000.

c. net cash provided of $9,000.

d. net cash used of $44,000.

Q12-58 Sales totaled $820,000, accounts receivable increased by $50,000, and accounts payable decreased by $30,000. How much cash did the company collect from customers?

a. $800,000

b. $820,000

c. $770,000

d. $870,000

Q12-59 Income Tax Payable was $4,500 at the end of the year and $3,000 at the beginning. Income tax expense for the year totaled $59,500. What amount of cash did the company pay for income tax during the year?

a. $62,500

b. $58,000

c. $61,000

d. $59,500

Problems

All of the A and B problems can be found within MyAccountingLab, an online homework and practice environment. Your instructor may ask you to complete these problems using MyAccountingLab.

(Group A)

P12-60A (*Learning Objectives 2, 3, 4, 5: Preparing an income statement, balance sheet, and statement of cash flows—indirect method*)   Antique Automobiles of Dubai, Inc., was formed on January 1, 2010. The following transactions occurred during 2010:

On January 1, 2010, Antique issued its shares for $440,000. Early in January, Antique made the following cash payments:

- **a.** $180,000 for equipment
- **b.** $203,000 for inventory (seven cars at $29,000 each)
- **c.** $17,000 for 2010 rent on a store building

In February, Antique purchased two cars for inventory on account. Cost of this inventory was $80,000 ($40,000.00 each). Before year-end, Antique paid $56,000 of this debt. Antique uses the FIFO method to account for inventory.

During 2010, Antique sold eight vintage autos for a total of $488,000. Before year-end, Antique collected 80% of this amount.

The business employs five people. The combined annual payroll is $125,000, of which Antique owes $7,000 at year-end. At the end of the year, Antique paid income tax of $12,600.

Late in 2010, Antique declared and paid cash dividends of $12,000.

For equipment, Antique uses the straight-line depreciation method, over five years, with zero residual value.

❚ *Requirements*

1. Prepare Antique Automobiles of Dubai, Inc.'s income statement for the year ended December 31, 2010.
2. Prepare Antique's balance sheet at December 31, 2010.
3. Prepare Antique's statement of cash flows for the year ended December 31, 2010. Format cash flows from operating activities by using the *indirect* method.

P12-61A (*Learning Objectives 2, 4, 5, 6: Preparing an income statement, balance sheet, and statement of cash flows—direct method*)   Use the Antique Automobiles of Dubai, Inc., data from Problem 12-60A.

❚ *Requirements*

1. Prepare Antique's income statement for the year ended December 31, 2010.
2. Prepare Antique's balance sheet at December 31, 2010.
3. Prepare Antique's statement of cash flows for the year ended December 31, 2010. Format cash flows from operating activities by using the *direct* method.

P12-62A (*Learning Objectives 2, 3, 4, 5: Preparing the statement of cash flows—indirect method*) Morgensen Software Corp. has assembled the following data for the years ending December 31, 2010 and 2009.

	December 31,	
	2010	2009
Current Accounts:		
Current assets:		
Cash and cash equivalents	$120,400	$30,000
Accounts receivable	69,900	64,400
Inventories...	8,600	80,000
Prepaid expenses..............................	3,100	1,500
Current liabilities:		
Accounts payable..............................	$ 57,200	$55,800
Income tax payable..........................	18,600	16,700
Accrued liabilities	15,500	27,200

Transaction Data for 2010:			
Acquisition of land by issuing		Purchase of treasury shares....	$10,700
long-term note payable	$201,000	Loss on sale of equipment	5,000
Dividends..............................	31,400	Payment of cash dividends	9,300
Collection of loan..................	10,600	Issuance of long-term note	
Depreciation expense	17,000	payable to borrow cash.....	34,500
Purchase of building..............	97,000	Net income..........................	6,500
Retirement of bonds payable		Issuance of ordinary shares	
by issuing ordinary shares ...	64,000	for cash	36,500
Purchase of long-term		Proceeds from sale of	
investment.........................	44,600	equipment	81,000
		Amortization expense..........	5,000

❙ Requirement

1. Prepare Morgensen Software Corp.'s statement of cash flows using the *indirect* method to report operating activities. Include an accompanying schedule of non-cash investing and financing activities.

writing assignment ■

■ spreadsheet

P12-63A (*Learning Objectives 2, 3, 4, 5: Preparing the statement of cash flows—indirect method*) The comparative balance sheets of Maynard Movie Theater Company at June 30, 2010 and 2009, reported the following:

	June 30,	
	2010	2009
Current assets:		
Cash and cash equivalents	$52,600	$17,000
Accounts receivable	14,500	21,600
Inventories...	63,500	61,100
Prepaid expenses..............................	3,100	8,000
Current liabilities:		
Accounts payable..............................	$57,800	$56,200
Accrued liabilities	37,300	17,300
Income tax payable..........................	9,100	10,100

Maynard Movie Theater's transactions during the year ended June 30, 2010, included the following:

Acquisition of land		Sale of long-term investment....	$12,700
by issuing note payable	$100,000	Depreciation expense	15,700
Amortization expense............	9,000	Cash purchase of building.....	44,000
Payment of cash dividend......	29,000	Net income..........................	54,000
Cash purchase of		Issuance of share for cash......	24,000
equipment	79,000	Dividend	11,000
Issuance of long-term note			
payable to borrow cash.....	42,000		

▎Requirements

1. Prepare Maynard Movie Theater Company's statement of cash flows for the year ended June 30, 2010, using the *indirect* method to report cash flows from operating activities. Report non-cash investing and financing activities in an accompanying schedule.
2. Evaluate Maynard Movie Theater's cash flows for the year. Mention all three categories of cash flows and give the reason for your evaluation.

P12-64A (*Learning Objectives 2, 3, 4, 5: Preparing the statement of cash flows—indirect method*)   The 2010 and 2009 comparative balance sheets and 2010 income statement of Affordable Supply Corp. follow:

■ **spreadsheet**

writing assignment ■

Affordable Supply Corp.
Comparative Balance Sheets

	December 31, 2010	December 31, 2009	Increase (Decrease)
Current assets:			
Cash and cash equivalents	$ 17,300	$ 4,000	$ 13,300
Accounts receivable	45,700	44,500	1,200
Inventories...................................	61,400	47,000	14,400
Prepaid expenses..........................	1,800	3,900	(2,100)
PPE:			
Land.......................................	69,100	22,600	46,500
Equipment, net	53,100	49,500	3,600
Total assets.................................	$248,400	$171,500	$ 76,900
Current liabilities:			
Accounts payable..........................	$ 35,200	$ 26,900	$ 8,300
Salary payable	24,000	13,100	10,900
Other accrued liabilities.................	22,100	23,700	(1,600)
Long-term liabilities:			
Notes payable.............................	51,000	34,000	17,000
Shareholders' equity:			
Share capital, no-par.....................	88,600	65,900	22,700
Retained earnings	27,500	7,900	19,600
Total liabilities and shareholders' equity.....	$248,400	$171,500	$ 76,900

Affordable Supply Corp.
Income Statement
Year Ended December 31, 2010

Revenues:		
Sales revenue		$446,000
Expenses:		
Cost of goods sold	$186,600	
Salary expense	76,000	
Depreciation expense	17,700	
Other operating expense	49,700	
Interest expense	24,100	
Income tax expense	29,000	
Total expenses		383,100
Net income		$ 62,900

Affordable Supply had no non-cash investing and financing transactions during 2010. During the year, there were no sales of land or equipment, no payment of notes payable, no retirements of shares, and no treasury shares transactions.

❚ Requirements

1. Prepare the 2010 statement of cash flows, formatting operating activities by using the *indirect* method.
2. How will what you learned in this problem help you evaluate an investment?

writing assignment ■

■ spreadsheet

P12-65A (*Learning Objectives 2, 4, 5, 6: Preparing the statement of cash flows—direct method*) Use the Affordable Supply Corp. data from Problem 12-64A.

❚ Requirements

1. Prepare the 2010 statement of cash flows by using the *direct* method.
2. How will what you learned in this problem help you evaluate an investment?

writing assignment ■

P12-66A (*Learning Objectives 2, 4, 5, 6: Preparing the statement of cash flows—direct method*) Ramirez Furniture Gallery, Inc., provided the following data from the company's records for the year ended May 31, 2010:

a. Credit sales, $584,500
b. Loan to another company, $12,300
c. Cash payments to purchase PPE, $72,100
d. Cost of goods sold, $312,400
e. Proceeds from issuance of ordinary shares, $7,000
f. Payment of cash dividends, $48,300
g. Collection of interest, $4,600
h. Acquisition of equipment by issuing short-term note payable, $16,000
i. Payments of salaries, $78,000
j. Proceeds from sale of PPE, $22,600, including $6,900 loss
k. Collections on accounts receivable, $428,500
l. Interest revenue, $3,500
m. Cash receipt of dividend income, $8,900
n. Payments to suppliers, $368,000

o. Cash sales, $191,300
p. Depreciation expense, $40,100
q. Proceeds from issuance of note payable, $24,500
r. Payments of long-term notes payable, $83,000
s. Interest expense and payments, $13,400
t. Salary expense, $75,800
u. Loan collections, $11,900
v. Proceeds from sale of investments, $9,500, including $4,400 gain
w. Payment of short-term note payable by issuing long-term note payable, $94,000
x. Amortization expenses, $3,100
y. Income tax expense and payments, $38,300
z. Cash balance: May 31, 2009, $19,100; May 31, 2010, $14,500

Requirements

1. Prepare Ramirez Furniture Gallery, Inc.'s statement of cash flows for the year ended May 31, 2010. Use the *direct* method for cash flows from operating activities. Include an accompanying schedule of non-cash investing and financing activities.
2. Evaluate 2010 from a cash-flows standpoint. Give your reasons.

P12-67A (*Learning Objectives 3, 4, 5, 6: Preparing the statement of cash flows—direct and indirect methods*)   To prepare the statement of cash flows, accountants for Daisy Electric Company have summarized 2010's activities in two accounts as follows:

■ **spreadsheet**

Cash

Beginning balance	49,600	Payments on accounts payable	402,000
Sale of long-term investment	14,600	Payments of dividends	47,900
Collections from customers	661,800	Payments of salaries and wages	143,600
Issuance of shares	61,000	Payments of interest	26,600
Receipts of dividends	16,900	Purchase of equipment	31,000
		Payments of operating expenses	34,500
		Payment of long-term note payable	41,500
		Purchase of treasury shares	22,400
		Payment of income tax	17,000
Ending Balance	37,400		

Share Capital

Beginning balance	74,200
Issuance for cash	61,000
Issuance to acquire land	80,800
Issuance to retire note payable	20,000
Ending balance	236,000

Daisy's 2010 income statement and balance sheet data follow:

Daisy Electric Company
Income Statement
Year Ended December 31, 2010

Revenues:		
Sales revenue		$689,200
Dividend income		16,900
Total revenue		706,100
Expenses and losses:		
Cost of goods sold	$334,000	
Salary and wage expense	135,800	
Depreciation expense	19,000	
Other operating expense	23,700	
Interest expense	29,100	
Income tax expense	14,500	
Loss on sale of investments	22,100	
Total expenses and losses		578,200
Net income		$127,900

Daisy Electric Company
Selected Balance Sheet Data
December 31, 2010

	Increase (Decrease)
Current assets:	
Cash and cash equivalents	$(12,200)
Accounts receivable	27,400
Inventories	59,700
Prepaid expenses	600
Long-term investments	(36,700)
Equipment, net	12,000
Land	80,800
Current liabilities:	
Accounts payable	(8,300)
Interest payable	2,500
Salary payable	(7,800)
Other accrued liabilities	(10,200)
Income tax payable	(2,500)
Long-term note payable	(61,500)
Share capital	161,800
Retained earnings	80,000
Treasury shares	(22,400)

▌Requirements

1. Prepare the statement of cash flows of Daisy Electric Company for the year ended December 31, 2010, using the *direct* method to report operating activities. Also prepare the accompanying schedule of non-cash investing and financing activities.
2. Use Daisy's 2010 income statement and balance sheet to prepare a supplementary schedule of cash flows from operating activities by using the *indirect* method.

P12-68A *(Learning Objectives 3, 4, 5, 6: Preparing the statement of cash flows—indirect and direct methods)* The comparative balance sheets of Stephen Summers Design Studio, Inc., at June 30, 2010 and 2009, and transaction data for fiscal 2010 are as follows:

Stephen Summers Design Studio
Comparative Balance Sheets

	June 30, 2010	June 30, 2009	Increase (Decrease)
Current assets:			
Cash	$ 28,900	$ 21,000	$ 7,900
Accounts receivable	48,800	31,700	17,100
Inventories	78,400	80,700	(2,300)
Prepaid expenses	3,100	2,200	900
Long-term investment	10,300	5,600	4,700
Equipment, net	74,000	73,300	700
Land	33,100	94,500	(61,400)
	$276,600	$309,000	$(32,400)
Current liabilities:			
Notes payable, short-term	$ 14,000	$19,000	$(5,000)
Accounts payable	29,400	40,400	(11,000)
Income tax payable	13,200	14,400	(1,200)
Accrued liabilities	3,700	9,400	(5,700)
Interest payable	3,400	2,400	1,000
Salary payable	1,000	4,400	(3,400)
Long-term note payable	47,200	94,000	(46,800)
Share capital	59,400	52,000	7,400
Retained earnings	105,300	73,000	32,300
	$276,600	$309,000	$(32,400)

Transaction data for the year ended June 30, 2010:

a. Net income, $80,700

b. Depreciation expense on equipment, $13,900

c. Purchased long-term investment, $4,700

d. Sold land for $54,900, including $6,500 loss

e. Acquired equipment by issuing long-term note payable, $14,600

f. Paid long-term note payable, $61,400

g. Received cash for issuance of shares, $2,400

h. Paid cash dividends, $48,400

i. Paid short-term note payable by issuing shares, $5,000

❙ Requirements

1. Prepare the statement of cash flows of Stephen Summers Design Studio, Inc., for the year ended June 30, 2010, using the *indirect* method to report operating activities. Also prepare the accompanying schedule of non-cash investing and financing activities. All current accounts except short-term notes payable result from operating transactions.
2. Prepare a supplementary schedule showing cash flows from operations by the *direct* method. The accounting records provide the following: collections from customers, $241,700; interest received, $1,700; payments to suppliers, $118,600; payments to employees, $41,900; payments for income tax, $12,900; and payment of interest, $4,900.

(Group B)

P12-69B *(Learning Objectives 2, 3, 4, 5: Preparing an income statement, balance sheet, and statement of cash flows—indirect method)* Sweet Automobiles of Dubai, Inc., was formed on January 1, 2010. The following transactions occurred during 2010:

On January 1, 2010, Sweet issued its shares for $350,000. Early in January, Sweet made the following cash payments:

    a. $140,000 for equipment
    b. $175,000 for inventory (five cars at $35,000 each)
    c. $19,000 for 2010 rent on a store building

In February, Sweet purchased six cars for inventory on account. Cost of this inventory was $282,000 ($47,000 each). Before year end, Sweet paid $197,400 of this debt. Sweet uses the FIFO method to account for inventory.

    During 2010, Sweet sold six vintage autos for a total of $426,000. Before year-end, Sweet collected 90% of this amount.

    The business employs three people. The combined annual payroll is $90,000, of which Sweet owes $5,000 at year-end. At the end of the year, Sweet paid income tax of $14,000.

    Late in 2010, Sweet declared and paid cash dividends of $16,000.

    For equipment, Sweet uses the straight-line depreciation method, over five years, with zero residual value.

❙ Requirements

1. Prepare Sweet Automobiles of Dubai, Inc.'s income statement for the year ended December 31, 2010.
2. Prepare Sweet's balance sheet at December 31, 2010.
3. Prepare Sweet's statement of cash flows for the year ended December 31, 2010. Format cash flows from operating activities by using the *indirect* method.

P12-70B *(Learning Objectives 2, 4, 5, 6: Preparing an income statement, balance sheet, and statement of cash flows—direct method)* Use the Sweet Automobiles of Dubai, Inc., data from Problem 12-69B.

❙ Requirements

1. Prepare Sweet's income statement for the year ended December 31, 2010.
2. Prepare Sweet's balance sheet at December 31, 2010.
3. Prepare Sweet's statement of cash flows for the year ended December 31, 2010. Format cash flows from operating activities by using the *direct* method.

P12-71B *(Learning Objectives 2, 3, 4, 5: Preparing the statement of cash flows—indirect method)* Neighbor Software Corp. has assembled the following data for the year ended December 31, 2010:

	December 31,	
	2010	2009
Current Accounts:		
Current assets:		
Cash and cash equivalents	$60,000	$26,000
Accounts receivable	22,000	64,100
Inventories..	88,500	85,000
Prepaid expenses..............................	3,200	2,400
Current liabilities:		
Accounts payable.............................	57,700	55,500
Income tax payable..........................	29,000	16,900
Accrued liabilities	15,500	7,600

Transaction Data for 2010:

Acquisition of land by issuing		Purchase of treasury shares....	$14,400
long-term note payable	$198,000	Loss on sale of equipment	3,000
Dividends..............................	31,600	Payment of cash dividends	18,800
Collection of loan..................	11,000	Issuance of long-term note	
Depreciation expense	17,000	payable to borrow cash.....	34,000
Purchase of building..............	159,000	Net income..........................	58,000
Retirement of bonds payable		Issuance of ordinary shares	
by issuing ordinary shares ...	71,000	for cash	74,200
Purchase of long-term		Proceeds from sale of	
investment........................	49,900	equipment	12,900
		Amortization expense..........	6,000

Requirement

1. Prepare Neighbor Software Corp.'s statement of cash flows using the *indirect* method to report operating activities. Include an accompanying schedule of non-cash investing and financing activities.

P12-72B (*Learning Objectives 2, 3, 4, 5: Preparing the statement of cash flows—indirect method*)   The comparative balance sheets of Medford Movie Theater Company at June 30, 2010 and 2009, reported the following:

writing assignment ∎

∎ spreadsheet

	June 30,	
	2010	2009
Current assets:		
Cash and cash equivalents	$ 5,800	$16,000
Accounts receivable	14,000	21,700
Inventories..	63,000	60,800
Prepaid expenses..............................	17,200	8,000
Current liabilities:		
Accounts payable.............................	$58,000	$55,900
Accrued liabilities	57,400	47,400
Income tax payable..........................	6,500	10,500

Medford's transactions during the year ended June 30, 2010, included the following:

Acquisition of land		Sale of long-term investment....	$13,400
by issuing note payable	$115,000	Depreciation expense	15,600
Amortization expense............	6,000	Cash purchase of building.....	59,000
Payment of cash dividend......	34,000	Net income..........................	50,000
Cash purchase of		Issuance of shares	
equipment	45,600	for cash	13,000
Issuance of long-term note		Dividend	9,000
payable to borrow cash.....	26,000		

Requirements

1. Prepare Medford Movie Theater Company's statement of cash flows for the year ended June 30, 2010, using the *indirect* method to report cash flows from operating activities. Report non-cash investing and financing activities in an accompanying schedule.
2. Evaluate Medford's cash flows for the year. Mention all three categories of cash flows and give the reason for your evaluation.

writing assignment ■

■ **spreadsheet**

P12-73B (*Learning Objectives 2, 3, 4, 5: Preparing the statement of cash flows—indirect method*)   The 2010 and 2009 comparative balance sheets and 2010 income statement of King Supply Corp. follow:

King Supply Corp. Comparative Balance Sheets			
	December 31,		**Increase**
	2010	**2009**	**(Decrease)**
Current assets:			
Cash and cash equivalents	$ 17,600	$ 5,000	$ 12,600
Accounts receivable	45,500	44,500	1,000
Inventories...................................	79,100	67,500	11,600
Prepaid expenses...........................	2,100	6,000	(3,900)
PPE:			
Land...	69,100	21,900	47,200
Equipment, net	53,100	49,200	3,900
Total assets....................................	$266,500	$194,100	$ 72,400
Current liabilities:			
Accounts payable..........................	$ 35,800	$ 25,600	$ 10,200
Salary payable	22,000	15,600	6,400
Other accrued liabilities................	22,900	24,200	(1,300)
Long-term liabilities:			
Notes payable.............................	50,000	37,000	13,000
Shareholders' equity:			
Share capital, no-par.....................	88,600	64,300	24,300
Retained earnings	47,200	27,400	19,800
Total liabilities and shareholders' equity.....	$266,500	$194,100	$ 72,400

King Supply Corp.
Income Statement
Year Ended December 31, 2010

Revenues:		
Sales revenue		$445,000
Expenses:		
Cost of goods sold	$185,100	
Salary expense	76,400	
Depreciation expense	17,400	
Other operating expense	49,800	
Interest expense	24,800	
Income tax expense	29,500	
Total expenses...........................		383,000
Net income...................................		$ 62,000

King Supply had no non-cash investing and financing transactions during 2010. During the year, there were no sales of land or equipment, no payment of notes payable, no retirements of shares, and no treasury shares transactions.

I Requirements

1. Prepare the 2010 statement of cash flows, formatting operating activities by using the *indirect* method.
2. How will what you learned in this problem help you evaluate an investment?

P12-74B (*Learning Objectives 2, 4, 5, 6: Preparing the statement of cash flows—direct method*)   Use the King Supply Corp. data from Problem P12-73B.

writing assignment ■

■ spreadsheet

I Requirements

1. Prepare the 2010 statement of cash flows by using the *direct* method.
2. How will what you learned in this problem help you evaluate an investment?

P12-75B (*Learning Objectives 2, 4, 5, 6: Preparing the statement of cash flows—direct method*)   Dunleavy Furniture Gallery, Inc., provided the following data from the company's records for the year ended December 31, 2010:

writing assignment ■

a. Credit sales, $567,000
b. Loan to another company, $12,800
c. Cash payments to purchase PPE, $59,900
d. Cost of goods sold, $382,700
e. Proceeds from issuance of ordinary shares, $7,000
f. Payment of cash dividends, $48,000
g. Collection of interest, $4,200
h. Acquisition of equipment by issuing short-term note payable, $16,500
i. Payments of salaries, $93,700
j. Proceeds from sale of PPE, $22,300, including $7,000 loss
k. Collections on accounts receivable, $406,000
l. Interest revenue, $3,300
m. Cash receipt of dividend income, $4,000
n. Payments to suppliers, $387,200

o. Cash sales, $201,000
p. Depreciation expense, $40,100
q. Proceeds from issuance of note payable, $19,300
r. Payments of long-term notes payable, $69,000
s. Interest expense and payments, $13,700
t. Salary expense, $91,600
u. Loan collections, $12,100
v. Proceeds from sale of investments, $11,200, including $3,800 gain
w. Payment of short-term note payable by issuing long-term note payable, $68,000
x. Amortization expenses, $3,200
y. Income tax expense and payments, $36,800
z. Cash balance: December 31, 2009, $40,000; December 31, 2010, $6,000

❙ Requirements

1. Prepare Dunleavy Furniture Gallery, Inc.'s statement of cash flows for the year ended December 31, 2010. Use the *direct* method for cash flows from operating activities. Include an accompanying schedule of non-cash investing and financing activities.
2. Evaluate 2010 from a cash-flows standpoint. Give your reasons.

■ **spreadsheet**

P12-76B (*Learning Objectives 3, 4, 5, 6: Preparing the statement of cash flows—direct and indirect methods*)   To prepare the statement of cash flows, accountants for Spencer Electric Company have summarized 2010 activity in two accounts as follows:

Cash			
Beginning balance	71,500	Payments on accounts payable	399,500
Sale of long-term investment	20,000	Payments of dividends	27,600
Collections from customers	661,600	Payments of salaries and wages	143,300
Issuance of shares	22,200	Payments of interest	27,100
Receipts of dividends	16,800	Purchase of equipment	31,700
		Payments of operating expenses	34,900
		Payment of long-term note payable	41,300
		Purchase of treasury shares	26,300
		Payment of income tax	18,600
Ending Balance	41,800		

Share Capital		
	Beginning balance	73,200
	Issuance for cash	22,200
	Issuance to acquire land	61,700
	Issuance to retire note payable	17,000
	Ending balance	174,100

Spencer's 2010 income statement and balance sheet data follow:

Spencer Electric Company
Income Statement
Year Ended December 31, 2010

Revenues:		
Sales revenue		$647,200
Dividend income		16,800
Total revenue		664,000
Expenses and losses:		
Cost of goods sold	$404,600	
Salary and wage expense	150,500	
Depreciation expense	16,400	
Other operating expense	30,500	
Interest expense	24,900	
Income tax expense	16,100	
Loss on sale of investments	16,700	
Total expenses and losses		659,700
Net income		$ 4,300

Spencer Electric Company
Selected Balance Sheet Data
December 31, 2010

	Increase (Decrease)
Current assets:	
Cash and cash equivalents	$(29,700)
Accounts receivable	(14,400)
Inventories	(12,900)
Prepaid expenses	(6,000)
Long-term investments	(36,700)
Equipment, net	15,300
Land	61,700
Current liabilities:	
Accounts payable	(7,800)
Interest payable	(2,200)
Salary payable	7,200
Other accrued liabilities	(10,400)
Income tax payable	(2,500)
Long-term note payable	(58,300)
Share capital	100,900
Retained earnings	(23,300)
Treasury shares	(26,300)

Requirements

1. Prepare the statement of cash flows of Spencer Electric Company for the year ended December 31, 2010, using the *direct* method to report operating activities. Also prepare the accompanying schedule of non-cash investing and financing activities.
2. Use Spencer's 2010 income statement and balance sheet to prepare a supplementary schedule of cash flows from operating activities by using the *indirect* method.

P12-77B (*Learning Objectives 3, 4, 5, 6: Preparing the statement of cash flows—indirect and direct methods*) The comparative balance sheets of Franny Franklin Design Studio, Inc., at June 30, 2010 and 2009, and transaction data for fiscal 2010 are as follows:

Franny Franklin Design Studio
Comparative Balance Sheets

	June 30, 2010	June 30, 2009	Increase (Decrease)
Current assets:			
Cash	$ 28,900	$ 2,400	$ 26,500
Accounts receivable	59,000	22,300	36,700
Inventories	98,200	40,400	57,800
Prepaid expenses	3,500	2,500	1,000
Long-term investment	10,000	5,000	5,000
Equipment, net	74,900	73,600	1,300
Land	58,100	98,900	(40,800)
	$332,600	$245,100	$ 87,500
Current liabilities:			
Notes payable, short-term	$ 13,200	$20,200	$ (7,000)
Accounts payable	42,300	41,300	1,000
Income tax payable	13,300	14,400	(1,100)
Accrued liabilities	97,400	9,300	88,100
Interest payable	3,500	2,500	1,000
Salary payable	400	3,100	(2,700)
Long-term note payable	48,700	94,200	(45,500)
Share capital	79,700	51,600	28,100
Retained earnings	34,100	8,500	25,600
	$332,600	$245,100	$ 87,500

Transaction data for the year ended June 30, 2010:

  a. Net income, $73,400
  b. Depreciation expense on equipment, $13,900
  c. Purchased long-term investment, $5,000
  d. Sold land for $33,800, including $7,000 loss
  e. Acquired equipment by issuing long-term note payable, $15,200
  f. Paid long-term note payable, $60,700
  g. Received cash for issuance of shares, $21,100
  h. Paid cash dividends, $47,800
  i. Paid short-term note payable by issuing shares, $7,000

I *Requirements*

  1. Prepare the statement of cash flows of Franny Franklin Design Studio, Inc., for the year ended June 30, 2010, using the *indirect* method to report operating activities. Also prepare the accompanying schedule of non-cash investing and financing activities. All current accounts except short-term notes payable result from operating transactions.
  2. Prepare a supplementary schedule showing cash flows from operations by the *direct* method. The accounting records provide the following: collections from customers, $272,300; interest received, $1,400; payments to suppliers, $130,900; payments to employees, $40,000; payments for income tax, $12,500; and payment of interest, $5,200.

APPLY YOUR KNOWLEDGE

Decision Cases

Case 1. *(Learning Objective 3, 4, 5: Preparing and using the statement of cash flows to evaluate operations)* The 2011 income statement and the 2011 comparative balance sheet of T-Bar-M Camp, Inc., have just been distributed at a meeting of the camp's board of directors. The directors raise a fundamental question: Why is the cash balance so low? This question is especially troublesome since 2011 showed record profits. As the controller of the company, you must answer the question.

writing assignment ■

T-Bar-M Camp, Inc.
Income Statement
Year Ended December 31, 2011

(In thousands)		
Revenues:		
Sales revenue		$436
Expenses:		
Cost of goods sold	$221	
Salary expense	48	
Depreciation expense	46	
Interest expense	13	
Amortization expense	11	
Total expenses		339
Net income		$ 97

T-Bar-M Camp, Inc.
Comparative Balance Sheets
December 31, 2011 and 2010

(In thousands)	2011	2010
Assets		
Cash	$ 17	$ 63
Accounts receivable, net	72	61
Inventories	194	181
Long-term investments	31	0
Property, plant and equipment	369	259
Accumulated depreciation	(244)	(198)
Patents	177	188
Totals	$ 616	$ 554
Liabilities and Owners' Equity		
Accounts payable	$ 63	$ 56
Accrued liabilities	12	17
Notes payable, long-term	179	264
Share capital, no par	149	61
Retained earnings	213	156
Totals	$ 616	$ 554

I *Requirements*

1. Prepare a statement of cash flows for 2011 in the format that best shows the relationship between net income and operating cash flow. The company sold no PPE or long-term investments and issued no notes payable during 2011. There were *no* non-cash investing and financing transactions during the year. Show all amounts in thousands.
2. Answer the board members' question: Why is the cash balance so low? Point out the two largest cash payments during 2011. (Challenge)
3. Considering net income and the company's cash flows during 2011, was it a good year or a bad year? Give your reasons.

writing assignment ■

Case 2. *(Learning Objectives 1, 2: Using cash-flow data to evaluate an investment)* Applied Technology, Inc., and Four-Star Catering are asking you to recommend their shares to your clients. Because Applied and Four-Star earn about the same net income and have similar financial positions, your decision depends on their statements of cash flows, summarized as follows:

	Applied		Four–Star	
Net cash provided by operating activities:......................		$ 30,000		$ 70,000
Cash provided by (used for) investing activities:				
Purchase of PPE..	$(20,000)		$(100,000)	
Sale of PPE	40,000	20,000	10,000	(90,000)
Cash provided by (used for) financing activities:				
Issuance of shares		—		30,000
Paying off long-term debt		(40,000)		—
Net increase in cash...		$ 10,000		$10,000

Based on their cash flows, which company looks better? Give your reasons. (Challenge)

Ethical Issue

writing assignment ■

Copenhagen Motors is having a bad year. Net income is only $37,000. Also, two important overseas customers are falling behind in their payments to Copenhagen, and Copenhagen's accounts receivable are ballooning. The company desperately needs a loan. The board of directors is considering ways to put the best face on the company's financial statements. Copenhagen's bank closely examines cash flow from operations. Daniel Peavey, Copenhagen's controller, suggests reclassifying as long-term the receivables from the slow-paying clients. He explains to the board that removing the $80,000 rise in accounts receivable from current assets will increase net cash provided by operations. This approach may help Copenhagen get the loan.

I *Requirements*

1. Using only the amounts given, compute net cash provided by operations, both without and with the reclassification of the receivables. Which reporting makes Copenhagen look better?
2. Identify the ethical issue(s).
3. Who are the stakeholders?
4. Analyze the issue from the (a) economic, (b) legal, and (c) ethical standpoints. What is the potential impact on all stakeholders?
5. What should the board do?
6. Under what conditions would the reclassification of the receivables be considered ethical?

Focus on Financials: ■ Nokia Corporation

<u>**writing assignment**</u> ■

Use **Nokia's** consolidated statement of cash flows along with the company's other consolidated financial statements, all in Appendix A at the end of the book, to answer the following questions.

I *Requirements*

1. By which method does Nokia report cash flows from operating activities? How can you tell?
2. Suppose Nokia reported net cash flows from operating activities by using the direct method. Compute these amounts for the year ended December 31, 2008 (ignore the statement of cash flows, and use only Nokia's income statement and balance sheet).

   a. Collections from vendors, customers, and others. Assume that all sales are on account.
   b. Payments to suppliers. Nokia calls its Cost of Goods Sold "Cost of Sales." Assume all inventory is purchased on account, and that all cash payments to suppliers are made from accounts payable.

3. What is Nokia's main source of cash? Is this good news or bad news to Nokia managers, shareholders, and creditors? What is Nokia's main use of cash? Good news or bad news? Explain all answers in detail.
4. Calculate Nokia's Free Cash Flow ratios for 2007 and 2008.

Group Projects

Project 1.   Each member of the group should obtain the annual report of a different company. Select companies in different industries. Evaluate each company's trend of cash flows for the most recent two years. In your evaluation of the companies' cash flows, you may use any other information that is publicly available—for example, the other financial statements (income statement, balance sheet, statement of changes in equity, and the related notes) and news stories from magazines and newspapers. Rank the companies' cash flows from best to worst and write a two-page report on your findings.

Project 2.   Select a company and obtain its annual report, including all the financial statements. Focus on the statement of cash flows and, in particular, the cash flows from operating activities. Specify whether the company uses the direct method or the indirect method to report operating cash flows. As necessary, use the other financial statements (income statement, balance sheet, and statement of changes in equity) and the notes to prepare the company's cash flows from operating activities by using the *other* method.

For online homework, exercises, and problems that provide you with immediate feedback, please visit www.myaccountinglab.com.

Quick Check Answers

1. *a*
2. *a*
3. *d*
4. *b* ($150,000 + $8,000)
5. *d*
6. *c*
7. *c* ($50,000 + $10,000 − $8,000 + $15,000 + $9,000 + $3,000)
8. *b* ($5,000 − $35,000 + $40,000)
9. *b* (− $1,000 + $4,000 − $16,000)
10. *b* ($40,000 + $15,000)
11. *d* ($60,000 + $700,000 − $50,000)
12. *b* ($750,000 − $410,000 − $180,000)
13. *d* ($410,000 − $10,000 + $12,000)

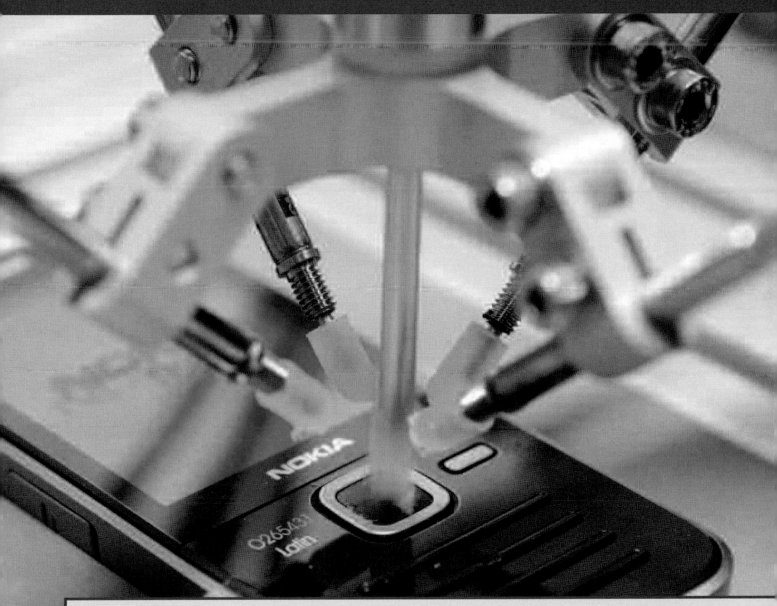

13
Financial Statement Analysis

SPOTLIGHT: Nokia

What do a paper mill, cable and rubber companies have in common? Probably very little. But did you know that **Nokia Corporation**, one of the biggest mobile telecommunication companies in the world, was formed by a merger of Nokia Ab, Finnish Cable Works and Finnish Rubber Works in 1967?

The objective of financial reporting, through financial statements and other disclosures, is to help users make economic decisions. One of the primary tools available to you is a process we call financial statement analysis. This includes examining year-on-year changes, component and common-size analysis, as well as using the common financial ratios to help you make an economic decision on the financial position and financial performance of an entity.

In this chapter, we cover this process, using the financial statements of Nokia Corporation, whose annual report is in Appendix A.

Nokia Corporation
Consolidated Profit and Loss Accounts (Adapted)
Financial Year Ended December 31

(in millions € Euros)	2008	2007	2006
Net sales	€50,710	€51,058	€41,121
Cost of sales	(33,337)	(33,781)	(27,742)
Gross profit	17,373	17,277	13,379
Research and development expenses	(5,968)	(5,636)	(3,897)
Selling and marketing expenses	(4,380)	(4,379)	(3,314)
Administrative and general expenses	(1,284)	(1,165)	(666)
Other income	420	2,312	522
Other expenses	(1,195)	(424)	(536)
Operating profit	4,966	7,985	5,488
Share of results of associated companies	6	44	28
Financial income and expenses	(2)	239	207
Profit before tax	4,970	8,268	5,723
Tax	(1,081)	(1,522)	(1,357)
Profit for the year	3,889	6,746	4,366
Basic earnings per share	€ 1.07	€ 1.85	€ 1.06

This chapter covers the basic tools of financial analysis. The first part of the chapter shows how to evaluate Nokia Corporation from year to year and how to compare Nokia to other companies that are in the same lines of business. For this comparison we use another mobile phone specialist, **Research in Motion**, the maker of the Blackberry line of phones. The second part of the chapter discusses the most widely used financial ratios. You have seen many of these ratios in earlier chapters—the current ratio, days' sales in receivables, and inventory turnover, return on assets, and return on equity.

By studying all these ratios together:

- You will learn the basic tools of financial analysis.
- You will enhance your ability to assess operations of a business.

Regardless of your chosen field—marketing, management, finance, entrepreneurship, or accounting—you will find these analytical tools useful as you move through your career.

LEARNING OBJECTIVES

1 **Perform** a horizontal analysis of financial statements

2 **Perform** a vertical analysis of financial statements

3 **Prepare** common-size financial statements

4 **Compute** the standard financial ratios

5 **Measure** the economic value added by operations

How Does an Investor Evaluate a Company?

Investors and creditors cannot evaluate a company by examining only one year's data. This is why *IAS1 – Presentation of Financial Statements* requires all financial statements to have comparative figures, that is, they cover at least two periods, like Nokia's consolidated profit and loss accounts, shown at the beginning of this chapter. In fact, most financial analysis covers trends of three to five years. Since one of the goals of financial analysis is to predict the future performance of an entity, it makes sense to start by mapping the trends of the past. You saw an example of this with Philips' cash flow trends in Chapter 12 (page 740). This is particularly true of income statement data such as net sales and net income.

The graphs in Exhibit 13-1 show Nokia's three-year trend of net sales and income from operations.

EXHIBIT 13-1 | **Representative Financial Data of Nokia Corp.**

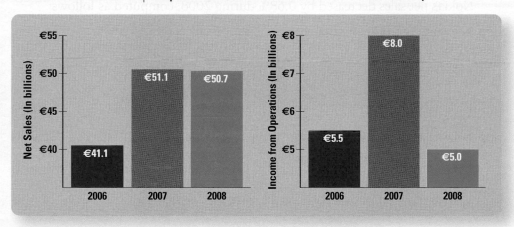

Nokia's net sales has increased from €41 billion in 2006 to €51 billion in 2008. Sales growth seemed to have stagnated, and operating profit has dropped much more than the decline in sales. How would you predict Nokia's net sales and income from operations for 2009 and beyond? The global financial crisis would probably cause a further decline in Nokia's sales and profitability. Let's examine some financial analysis tools. We begin with horizontal analysis.

HORIZONTAL ANALYSIS

Many decisions hinge on the trend of revenues, expenses, income from operations, and so on. Have revenues increased from last year? By how much? Suppose net sales have increased by $50,000. Considered alone this fact is not very helpful, but knowing the long-term percentage change in net sales helps a lot. It's better to know that net sales have increased by 20% than to know that the increase is $50,000. It's even better to know that *percentage increases* in net sales for the past several years have been rising year over year.

The study of percentage changes from year to year is called **horizontal analysis**. Computing a percentage change takes two steps:

1. Compute the dollar amount of the change from one period (the base period) to the next.

2. Divide the dollar amount of change by the base-period amount.

Illustration: Nokia Corporation

Horizontal analysis is illustrated for Nokia, as follows (using the 2007 and 2008 figures, in millions of euros):

	2008	2007	Increase (Decrease)	
			Amount	Percentage
Net sales................	€50,710	€51,058	(€348)	(0.68%)

Nokia's net sales decreased by 0.68% during 2008, computed as follows:

Step 1 Compute the amount of change from 2007 to 2008:

2008		2007		Decrease
€50,710	–	€51,058	=	(€348)

Step 2 Divide the amount of change by the base-period amount. This computes the percentage change for the period:

$$\text{Percentage change} = \frac{\text{Amount of change}}{\text{Base-year amount}}$$

$$= \frac{(€348)}{€51,058} = (0.68\%)$$

Exhibits 13-2 and 13-3 are detailed horizontal analysis for Nokia. In Exhibit 13-2, the comparative consolidated profit and loss accounts show that net sales decreased marginally (0.68%) during 2008. It seems that Nokia was able to maintain its sales in a very competitive mobile communication market, with strong competition from **Apple**'s iPhone and Research in Motion's Blackberry and many others. Nokia was able to control its cost of sales in 2008 and the savings were larger than reduction in sales, thus there was a slight increase in Nokia's 2008 gross margin.

EXHIBIT 13-2 | Horizontal Analysis—Income Statement

Nokia Corporation
Consolidated Profit and Loss Accounts (Adapted)
Financial Year Ended December 31

(in millions € Euros)	2008	2007	Increase (decrease) Amount	Percentage
Net sales	€50,710	€51,058	€ (348)	-0.68%
Cost of sales	(33,337)	(33,781)	(444)	-1.31%
Gross profit	17,373	17,277	96	0.56%
Research and development expenses	(5,968)	(5,636)	332	5.89%
Selling and marketing expenses	(4,380)	(4,379)	1	0.02%
Administrative and general expenses	(1,284)	(1,165)	119	10.21%
Other income	420	2,312	(1,892)	-81.83%
Other expenses	(1,195)	(424)	771	181.84%
Operating profit	4,966	7,985	(3,019)	-37.81%
Share of results of associated companies	6	44	(38)	-86.36%
Financial income and expenses	(2)	239	(237)	-99.16%
Profit before tax	4,970	8,268	(3,298)	-39.89%
Tax	(1,081)	(1,522)	(441)	-28.98%
Profit for the year	3,889	6,746	(2,857)	-42.35%
Basic earnings per share	€ 1.07	€ 1.85	€(0.78)	-42.16%

However, Nokia's net income on the bottom line dropped by 42%. Why the difference? If gross margins are roughly the same, the explanation must be in other operating expenses. R&D expenses increased by 5%, whilst selling and marketing expenses did not change, and there was a 10% increase in administrative and general expenses. But the big items were a two-sided hit on other income and other expenses. Other income decreased by 82% and other expenses increased by over 180%. These two items are the primary reason why Nokia's bottom line performance in 2008 was almost half that of 2007.

Horizontal analysis does not provide you with answers as to why other incomes increase (and other expenses increase). You will need to carefully study the notes to the financial statements and make an assessment if these 2008 amounts are likely to repeat in 2009. It does look that 2007's other income was significantly higher than in 2008 and 2006, and might have involved a one-time gain that skewed our analysis in 2008. Similarly, 2008's other expenses seem to be much higher than in 2007 and 2006. As an investor, you would want to assess if these items are likely to have further impact in future operations!

Studying changes in balance sheet accounts can also enhance our total understanding of the current and long-term financial position of the entity. Let's look at a few balance sheet changes that transpired in 2008 for Nokia as shown in Exhibit 13-3 on the following page.

EXHIBIT 13-3 | Horizontal Analysis—Balance Sheet

Nokia Corporation
Consolidated Balance Sheet (Adapted)
As at December 31

(in millions € Euros)	2008	2007	Increase (decrease) Amount	Percentage
Current assets				
Bank, cash and cash equivalents...........................	€ 5,548	€ 6,850	€(1,302)	-19.01%
Short-term investments	1,272	4,903	(3,631)	-74.06%
Other financial assets..	1,034	239	795	332.64%
Current portion of long-term loans receivables	101	156	(55)	-35.26%
Prepare expenses and accrued income	4,538	3,070	1,468	47.82%
Accounts receivable, net.......................................	9,444	11,200	(1,756)	-15.68%
Inventories	2,533	2,876	(343)	-11.93%
	24,470	29,294	(4,824)	-16.47%
Non-current assets				
Capitalized development costs.....	244	378	(134)	-35.45%
Goodwill..	6,257	1,384	4,873	352.10%
Other intangible assets	3,913	2,358	1,565	66.95%
Property plant and equipment..............................	2,090	1,912	178	9.31%
Investment in associated companies.....	96	325	(229)	-70.46%
Available-for-sale investments	512	341	171	60.15%
Deferred tax assets	1,963	1,553	410	26.40%
Long-term loans receivable	27	10	17	170.00%
Other non-current assets.....	10	44	(34)	-77.27%
	15,112	8,305	6,807	81.96%
Total assets..	39,582	37,599	1,983	5.27%
Liabilities				
Current liabilities				
Current portion of long-term loans.....	13	173	(160)	-92.49%
Short-term borrowings...	3,578	714	2,864	401.12%
Other financial liabilities.....................................	924	184	740	402.17%
Accounts payable	5,225	7,074	(1,849)	-26.14%
Accrued expenses	7,023	7,114	(91)	-1.28%
Provision...	3,592	3,717	(125)	-3.36%
	20,355	18,976	1,379	7.27%
Non-current liabilities				
Long-term interest-bearing liabilities....................	861	203	658	324.14%
Deferred tax liabilities...	1,787	963	824	85.57%
Other long-term liabilities....................................	69	119	(60)	-42.02%
	2,717	1,285	1,432	111.44%
Total liabilities	23,072	20,261	2,811	13.87%
Shareholders Equity..				
Share capital	246	246	–	0.00%
Share issue premium	442	644	(202)	-31.37%
Treasury share at cost	(1,881)	(3,146)	(1,265)	-40.21%
Reserves..	3,709	3,159	560	17.41%
Retained earnings..	11,692	13,870	(2,178)	-15.70%
Minority interests..	2,302	2,565	(263)	-10.25%
Total shareholders equity.....................................	€16,510	€17,338	€ (828)	-4.78%

From a total assets perspective, Nokia actually has gotten a little bigger in 2008, from €37,599 to €39,582 billion. However, there was a large drop in cash and cash equivalent, as well as short-term investments. Accounts receivable has also decreased by €1.8 billion or 16%. This could either mean Nokia was more effective in its collection or experienced a slow-down in sales. We saw in Exhibit 13-2 that the 2008 sales were similar to 2007, so the drop in receivables is likely because Nokia has been able to collect the receivables faster in 2008.

The drop in current assets was surpassed by a larger growth in non-current assets. One item that clearly stood out was goodwill, it increased by almost €5 billion (or 352% from 2007's balance), and other intangibles also increased 67%. Nokia must have made a large acquisition during 2008, paying a premium above the fair value of identifiable net assets of the entity purchased.

Of some concern would be Nokia's increased borrowings. Nokia's total borrowings (short-term and long-term) increased from €917 million to €4,439 million, an increase of about 385%. It is likely that the increased borrowings were necessary to fund its acquisitions in 2008.

Overall, it appears that 2008 was a challenging year for Nokia, but it has made some acquisitions, financed by internal resources and additional borrowings, that will hopefully contribute to the company's overall performance in the future. The year 2009 would likely to be just as challenging, with the economic downturn around the corner.

STOP & THINK. . .

Have another look at Exhibits 13-2 and 13-3. Are the biggest percentage items always the most important items that cause changes in income statement or balance sheet from one year to another? Can you always ignore small changes, such as anything that is less than 5%?

Answer:

The largest percentage change in Nokia's income statement was "other expenses" at 182%, and "other financial liabilities" at 402% for Nokia's balance sheet. Whilst these are good indicators, they are not always the most important things in horizontal analysis. Percentage change depends on the base, so large fluctuations may result simply because of a small base. These fluctuations would not cause alarm because the dollar amount of the category is relatively small to begin with, causing year over year percentage changes to look very large. A smaller percentage change on a larger base may be more important than a larger percentage change on a small base. For example, a 5% change in net sales would have been bigger (in amounts and importance) than some other larger percentage changes.

Trend Percentages

Trend percentages are a form of horizontal analysis. Trends indicate the direction a business is taking. How have revenues changed over a five-year period? What trend does net income show? These questions can be answered by trend percentages over a representative period, such as the most recent five years.

Trend percentages are computed by selecting a base year whose amounts are set equal to 100%. The amount for each following year is stated as a percentage of the base amount. To compute a trend percentage, divide an item for a later year by the base-year amount.

$$\text{Trend \%} = \frac{\text{Any year \$}}{\text{Base year \$}}$$

Recall that, in Chapter 11, we established that income from operations or operationing income is often viewed as the primary measure of a company's earnings quality. This is because operating income represents a company's best predictor of the future net inflows from its core business units. Net income from operations is often used in estimating the current value of the business.

Nokia showed income from operations for 2004-2008 as follows:

(In millions, €)	2008	2007	2006	2005	Base 2004
Operating profit............................	€4,966	€7,985	€5,488	€4,639	€4,326

We want to calculate a trend for the five-year period 2004 through 2008. The first year in the series (2004) is set as the base year. Trend percentages are computed by dividing each year's amount by the 2004 amount. The resulting trend percentages follow (2004 = 100%):

	2008	2007	2006	2005	Base 2004
Operating profit............................	115	185	127	107	100

Nokia's income from operations has grown since 2004, with the biggest jump in the 2007 financial year. However, this was followed by a very deep drop in operating profit in 2008. The 2008 operating profit level is somewhere between what Nokia achieved back in 2005-2006, effectively wiping out three years of operating profit growth.

You can perform a trend analysis on any item you consider important. Trend analysis using income statement data is widely used for predicting the future. Horizontal analysis highlights changes over time. However, no single technique can give you a complete picture of a business.

VERTICAL ANALYSIS

OBJECTIVE

2 Perform a vertical analysis of financial statements

Vertical analysis (or component analysis) shows the relationship of financial-statement items relative to a total, which is the 100% figure. All items on the particular financial statement are reported as a percentage of the base. For the income statement, total revenue (sales) is usually the base. Suppose under normal conditions a company's net income is 8% of revenue. A drop to 6% may cause the company's share price to fall.

Illustration: Nokia Corporation

Exhibit 13-4 shows the vertical analysis of Nokia's income statement as a percentage of revenue (net sales). In this case,

$$\text{Vertical analysis } \% = \frac{\text{Each income statement item}}{\text{Total revenue}}$$

EXHIBIT 13-4 | **Vertical Analysis—Income Statement**

Nokia Corporation
Consolidated Profit and Loss Accounts (Adapted)
Financial Year Ended December 31

(in millions € Euros)	2008	% of total	2007	% of total
Net sales	€50,710	100.0%	€51,058	100.0%
Cost of sales	(33,337)	-65.7%	(33,781)	-66.2%
Gross profit	17,373	34.3%	17,277	33.8%
Research and development expenses	(5,968)	-11.8%	(5,636)	-11.0%
Selling and marketing expenses	(4,380)	-8.6%	(4,379)	-8.6%
Administrative and general expenses	(1,284)	-2.5%	(1,165)	-2.3%
Other income	420	0.8%	2,312	4.5%
Other expenses	(1,195)	-2.4%	(424)	-0.8%
Operating profit	4,966	9.8%	7,985	15.6%
Share of results of associated companies	6	0.0%	44	0.1%
Financial income and expenses	(2)	0.0%	239	0.5%
Profit before tax	4,970	9.8%	8,268	16.2%
Tax	(1,081)	-2.1%	1,622	-3.0%
Profit for the year	€ 3,889	7.7%	€ 6,746	13.2%

For Nokia, in 2008, the vertical-analysis percentage shows us:

- Cost of sales only took 65.7% of revenue, compared to 66.2% in 2007. This cost saving directly translated to higher gross profit in 2008.
- Most operating expenses took the same percentage of revenue in 2007 and 2008. R&D expenses were about 11-12% of sales, selling and marketing expenses about 8-9% of sales, and administrative and general expenses about 2.5%.
- Other income added only 0.8% to net profit, as opposed to 4.5% in 2008, and other expenses took a much larger share of revenue in 2008 (2.5%) versus 0.8% in 2007.
- In 2008, for every euro of sales, Nokia booked a net profit of 7.7 cents, very much lesser than 13.2 cents in 2007.

STOP & THINK...

Perform a vertical analysis for the common-size percentages for the following income statement:

Net sales.................................	$150,000
Cost of goods sold.................	60,000
Gross profit............................	90,000
Operating expense..................	40,000
Operating income...................	50,000
Income tax expense...............	15,000
Net income.............................	$ 35,000

Answer:

Net sales.................................	100%	(= $150,000 ÷ $150,000)
Cost of goods sold.................	40	(= $ 60,000 ÷ $150,000)
Gross profit............................	60	(= $ 90,000 ÷ $150,000)
Operating expense..................	27	(= $ 40,000 ÷ $150,000)
Operating income...................	33	(= $ 50,000 ÷ $150,000)
Income tax expense...............	10	(= $ 15,000 ÷ $150,000)
Net income.............................	23%	(= $ 35,000 ÷ $150,000)

We could do similar vertical analysis on the balance sheet. If you want to see composition of total assets, then let total assets be 100% and express all assets as a percentage of total assets. However, if you are zooming in on the composition of current assets, then let current assets be 100% and examine only components of current assets. Here's an example of component analysis of Nokia's current liabilities using a pie chart (we have combined short-term portion of long-term loans with other financial liabilities as "others" as the amounts are small).

EXHIBIT 13-5 | **Vertical Analysis using Pie Chart**

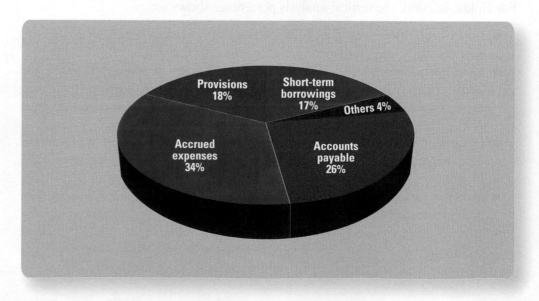

BENCHMARKING

Benchmarking simply means comparing one entity to another. Usually benchmarks are selected as because they are either direct competitors in the same industry or market, peers in the broader market, or just any other "aspiration" entities. You may be running a small retail shop, but if you aspire to do just as well as **Marks & Spencer**, then go ahead, you can always benchmark your own company's performance against M&S. The most important aspect of benchmarking, however, is that it gives you context in which you could interpret one data.

Suppose you are a financial analyst for **Citigroup**, a large investment bank. You are considering investing in one of two different companies in the same industry, say Nokia or RIM. A direct numerical comparison of these companies' financial statements is not meaningful, in part because Nokia is so much larger than RIM. One of the techniques you could use, called common-size financial statements, is basically an extension of vertical analysis. You convert the companies' income statements to common size and compare the percentages. This comparison is meaningful, as we shall see.

How Do We Compare One Company to Another?

Exhibits 13-4 and 13-5 can be modified to report only percentages (no currency amounts). When compared side-by-side, such financial statements are called **common-size statements**. A common-size financial statement aids the comparison of different companies because all amounts are stated in percentages, thus expressing the financial results of each comparative company in terms of a common denominator. Currency and size differences are eliminated when you do a common-size comparison.

Exhibit 13-6 on the following page presents the common-size income statements of Nokia and RIM. There may be other mobile phone companies you can compare Nokia to, but other companies may have businesses outside mobile phones, making direct comparison a little more difficult (for example, **Samsung**, **LG**, **Apple**, and **Sony**). To make common-size comparison meaningful, you often have to synchronize the items in the two (or more) financial statements. For example, Nokia separates selling and marketing expenses from administrative expenses, but RIM combines them. We would then have to combine Nokia's two expense items into one, to make it more comparable to RIM. Another difference is RIM separately discloses revenue (and its associated cost of sales) into two components: devices and other, and services and software, but Nokia does not. So, we aggregate the two components back to net sales and cost of sales.

OBJECTIVE

3 **Prepare** common-size financial statements

EXHIBIT 13-6 | Common-size Income Statements—Nokia and RIM

	Nokia	RIM
Financial year ended	Dec 31, 2008	Feb 28, 2009
Net sales	100.0%	100.0%
Cost of sales	−65.7%	−53.9%
Gross profit	34.3%	46.1%
Research and development expenses	−11.8%	−6.2%
Selling, marketing and administrative expenses	−11.2%	−13.5%
Other income	0.8%	0.7%
Other expenses	−2.4%	−1.8%
Operating profit	9.8%	25.3%
Tax	−2.1%	−8.2%
Profit for the year	7.7%	17.1%

As you can see, the above comparison tells us that RIM enjoys a higher margin than Nokia. Its R&D cost is lower (as a percentage of sales), but it spends more on selling, marketing and administrative expenses than Nokia. For every euro and dollar of sales, Nokia makes a net profit of 7.7 cents and RIM 17.1 cents respectively. Our common-size analysis seems to indicate that RIM has better profitability than Nokia.

MID-CHAPTER SUMMARY PROBLEM

Perform a horizontal analysis and a vertical analysis of the comparative income statement of Hard Rock Products, Inc., which makes metal detectors. State whether 2011 was a good year or a bad year, and give your reasons.

Hard Rock Products, Inc. Comparative Income Statements Years Ended December 31, 2011 and 2010		
	2011	2010
Total revenues	$275,000	$225,000
Expenses:		
Cost of goods sold	194,000	165,000
Engineering, selling, and administrative expenses	54,000	48,000
Interest expense	5,000	5,000
Income tax expense	9,000	3,000
Other expense (income)	1,000	(1,000)
Total expenses	263,000	220,000
Net income	$ 12,000	$ 5,000

Answer

The horizontal analysis shows that total revenues increased 22.2%. This was greater than the 19.5% increase in total expenses, resulting in a 140% increase in net income.

Hard Rock Products, Inc.
Horizontal Analysis of Comparative Income Statements
Years Ended December 31, 2011 and 2010

	2011	2010	Increase (Decrease) Amount	Percent
Total revenues	$275,000	$225,000	$50,000	22.2%
Expenses:				
Cost of goods sold	194,000	165,000	29,000	17.6
Engineering, selling, and				
administrative expenses.......	54,000	48,000	6,000	12.5
Interest expense	5,000	5,000	—	—
Income tax expense.................	9,000	3,000	6,000	200.0
Other expense (income)	1,000	(1,000)	2,000	—*
Total expenses....................	263,000	220,000	43,000	19.5
Net income.................................	$ 12,000	$ 5,000	$ 7,000	140.0%

*Percentage changes are typically not computed for shifts from a negative to a positive amount and vice versa.

The vertical analysis on the next page shows decreases in the percentages of net sales consumed by the cost of goods sold (from 73.3% to 70.5%) and by the engineering, selling, and administrative expenses (from 21.3% to 19.6%). Because these two items are Hard Rock's largest dollar expenses, their percentage decreases are quite important. The relative reduction in expenses raised 2011 net income to 4.4% of sales, compared with 2.2% the preceding year. The overall analysis indicates that 2011 was significantly better than 2010.

Hard Rock Products, Inc.
Vertical Analysis of Comparative Income Statements
Years Ended December 31, 2011 and 2010

	2011 Amount	Percent	2010 Amount	Percent
Total revenues	$275,000	100.0 %	$225,000	100.0 %
Expenses:				
Cost of goods sold	194,000	70.5	165,000	73.3
Engineering, selling, and				
administrative expenses........	54,000	19.6	48,000	21.3
Interest expense	5,000	1.8	5,000	2.2
Income tax expense.................	9,000	3.3	3,000	1.4**
Other expense (income)	1,000	0.4	(1,000)	(0.4)
Total expenses.....................	263,000	95.6	220,000	97.8
Net income.................................	$ 12,000	4.4 %	$ 5,000	2.2 %

**Number rounded up.

Using Ratios to Make Business Decisions

OBJECTIVE

4 Compute the standard financial ratios

Financial ratios are a major tool of financial analysis. We have discussed the use of many ratios in financial analysis in various chapters throughout the book. A ratio expresses the relationship of one number to another. Suppose your balance sheet shows current assets of $100,000 and current liabilities of $50,000. The ratio of current assets to current liabilities is $100,000 to $50,000. We can express this ratio as 2 to 1, or 2:1. The current ratio is 2.0.

Many companies include ratios in a special section of their annual reports. Nokia, for example, provided the following on its 2008 annual report. Investment services—**Moody's, Standard & Poor's, Risk Management Association**, and others—report these ratios. You can visit http://www.reuters.com/finance/stocks/financialHighlights?symbol=NOK.N for a sample of Reuter ratios for Nokia, along with comparable ratios for the technology sector and communication equipment industry.

EXHIBIT 13-8 | Sample Ratios from Nokia's 2008 Annual Report

Key ratios and economic indicators	2008	2007	2006	2005	2004
Return on capital employed, %	27.2	54.8	46.1	36.5	31.5
Return on equity, %	27.5	53.9	35.5	27.1	21.5
Equity ratio, %	41.2	45.5	52.6	56.4	64.6
Net debt to equity, %	−14	−62	−69	−77	−78

The Limitations of Ratio Analysis

Business decisions are made in a world of uncertainty. As useful as financial ratios are, they aren't a cure-all. Consider a physician's use of a thermometer. A reading of 40° Celsius (or 104.0° Fahrenheit) tells a doctor something is wrong with the patient, but that doesn't indicate what the problem is or how to cure it.

In financial analysis, a sudden drop in any ratio may signal that something is wrong, but that doesn't identify the problem. A manager must analyze the figures to learn what caused the ratio to fall. The manager must evaluate all the ratios in the light of factors such as increased competition or a slowdown in the economy.

Legislation, international affairs, scandals, and other factors can turn profits into losses. To be useful, ratios should be analyzed over a period of years to consider all relevant factors. Any one year, or even any two years, may not represent the company's performance over the long term.

Financial Ratios

The ratios we discuss in this chapter are classified as follows:

1. Ability to pay current liabilities
2. Cash conversion cycle
3. Ability to pay long-term debt
4. Profitability
5. Analyze shares as an investment

Sometimes you may find different ratio classifications and even slightly different formulas for the ratios we are about to discuss. Don't be alarmed by any differences, as long as you calculate the ratios consistently, there is always value to financial statement analysis. A ruler that is imperfect can still tell you who is the tallest amongst a group of people!

Exhibit 13-9 gives the income statement and balance sheet data of Palisades Furniture, an independent furniture and home wares retailer. We will work with this exhibit as our running example on how to perform financial statement analysis.

EXHIBIT 13-9 | **Comparative Financial Statements**

Palisades Furniture, Inc.
Comparative Income Statements
Years Ended December 31, 2011 and 2010

	2011	2010
Net sales	$858,000	$803,000
Cost of goods sold	513,000	509,000
Gross profit	345,000	294,000
Operating expenses:		
Selling expenses	126,000	114,000
General expenses	118,000	123,000
Total operating expenses	244,000	237,000
Income from operations	101,000	57,000
Interest revenue	4,000	—
Interest (expense)	(24,000)	(14,000)
Income before income taxes	81,000	43,000
Income tax expense	33,000	17,000
Net income	$ 48,000	$ 26,000

(Exhibit 13-9 continued on next page)

Palisades Furniture, Inc.
Comparative Balance Sheets
December 31, 2011 and 2010

	2011	2010
Assets		
Current Assets:		
Cash	$ 29,000	$ 32,000
Accounts receivable, net	114,000	85,000
Inventories	113,000	111,000
Prepaid expenses	6,000	8,000
Total current assets	262,000	236,000
Long-term investments	18,000	9,000
Property, plant and equipment, net	507,000	399,000
Total assets	$787,000	$644,000
Liabilities		
Current Liabilities:		
Notes payable	$ 42,000	$ 27,000
Accounts payable	73,000	68,000
Accrued liabilities	27,000	31,000
Total current liabilities	142,000	126,000
Long-term debt	289,000	198,000
Total liabilities	431,000	324,000
Shareholders' Equity		
Share capital, no par	186,000	186,000
Retained earnings	170,000	134,000
Total shareholders' equity	356,000	320,000
Total liabilities		
and shareholders' equity	$787,000	$644,000

Measuring Ability to Pay Current Liabilities

Working capital is defined as follows:

Working capital = Current assets – Current liabilities

Working capital measures the ability to pay current liabilities with current assets. In general, the larger the working capital, the better the ability to pay debts. Recall that capital is total assets minus total liabilities. Working capital is like a "current" version of total capital. Consider two companies with equal working capital:

	Company	
	Jones	Smith
Current assets	$100,000	$200,000
Current liabilities	50,000	150,000
Working capital	$ 50,000	$ 50,000

Both companies have working capital of $50,000, but Jones' working capital is as large as its current liabilities. Smith's working capital is only one-third as large as current liabilities. Jones is in a better position because its working capital is a higher percentage of current liabilities. Two decision-making tools based on working-capital data are the *current ratio* and the *acid-test ratio*.

Current Ratio.   The most common ratio evaluating current assets and current liabilities is the **current ratio**, which is current assets divided by current liabilities. As discussed in Chapter 3, the current ratio measures the ability to pay current liabilities with current assets.

The current ratios of Palisades Furniture, Inc., at December 31, 2011 and 2010, follow, along with the average for the retail furniture industry:

Formula	Palisades' Current Ratio		Industry Average
	2011	2010	
Current ratio = $\dfrac{\text{Current assets}}{\text{Current liabilities}}$	$\dfrac{\$262,000}{\$142,000} = 1.85$	$\dfrac{\$236,000}{\$126,000} = 1.87$	1.50

The current ratio decreased slightly but not significantly during 2011. In general, a higher current ratio indicates a stronger financial position. The business has sufficient current assets to maintain its operations. Palisades Furniture's current ratio of 1.85 compares favorably with the current ratios of some well-known companies:

Company	Current Ratio
Wal-Mart	0.80
Hewlett-Packard Company	0.98
eBay	1.70

Note: These figures show that ratio values vary widely from one industry to another.

What is an acceptable current ratio? The answer depends on the industry. The norm for companies in most industries is around 1.50, as reported by the Risk Management Association. Palisades Furniture's current ratio of 1.85 is better than average.

Acid-Test Ratio.   As discussed in Chapter 5, the acid-test (or quick) ratio tells us whether the entity could pass the acid test of paying all its current liabilities if they came due immediately. The acid-test ratio uses a narrower base to measure liquidity than the current ratio does.

To compute the acid-test ratio, we add cash, short-term investments, and net current receivables (accounts and notes receivable, net of allowances) and divide by current liabilities. Inventory and prepaid expenses are excluded because they are less liquid. A business may be unable to convert inventory to cash immediately. This is why sometimes you see this short-cut in measuring quick ratio: (Current Assets − Inventory) ÷ Current Liabilities.

Palisades Furniture's acid-test ratios for 2011 and 2010 follow:

		Palisades' Acid-Test Ratio		Industry
	Formula	2011	2010	Average
Acid-test ratio =	$\dfrac{\text{Cash + Short-term investments + Net current receivables}}{\text{Current liabilities}}$	$\dfrac{\$29,000 + \$0 + \$114,000}{\$142,000} = 1.01$	$\dfrac{\$32,000 + \$0 + \$85,000}{\$126,000} = 0.93$	0.40

The company's acid-test ratio improved during 2011 and is significantly better than the industry average. Compare Palisades' acid test ratio with the values of some leading companies.

Company	Acid-Test Ratio
Best Buy	0.30
DineEquity (IHOP).........	1.41
Foot Locker, Inc.	0.98

An acid-test ratio of 0.90 to 1.00 is acceptable in most industries. How can a company such as Best Buy function with such a low acid-test ratio? Best Buy prices its inventory to turn it over quickly. And most of Best Buy's sales are for cash or credit cards, so the company collects cash quickly. This points us to the next two ratios.

Measuring Ability to Sell Inventory and Collect Receivables

The ability to sell inventory and collect receivables is critical. In this section, we discuss a number of ratios that measure an entity's ability to collect cash.

Inventory Turnover. Companies generally strive to sell their inventory as quickly as possible. The faster inventory sells, the sooner cash comes in. Inventory turnover, discussed in Chapter 6, measures the number of times a company sells its average level of inventory during a year. A fast turnover indicates ease in selling inventory; a low turnover indicates difficulty. A value of 6 means that the company's average level of inventory has been sold six times during the year, and that's usually better than a turnover of three times. But too high a value can mean that the business is not keeping enough inventory on hand, which can lead to lost sales if the company can't fill orders. Therefore, a business strives for the most profitable rate of turnover, not necessarily the *highest* rate.

To compute inventory turnover, divide cost of goods sold by the average inventory for the period. We use the cost of goods sold—not sales—in the computation because both cost of goods sold and inventory are stated at cost. Palisades Furniture's inventory turnover for 2011 is:

	Formula	Palisades' Inventory Turnover	Industry Average
Inventory turnover =	$\dfrac{\text{Cost of goods sold}}{\text{Average inventory}}$	$\dfrac{\$513,000}{\$112,000} = 4.6$	1.50

Cost of goods sold comes from the income statement (Exhibit 13-9). Average inventory is the average of beginning ($111,000) and ending inventory ($113,000). (See the balance sheet, Exhibit 13-9.) Inventory turnover varies widely with the nature of the business. For example, a fast food chain restaurant such as **Pizza Hut**, **Taco Bell**, **KFC**, and **Long John Silver's**, would likely to have a high turnover ratio because they turn around their inventory into sales in a short time. This may be a necessity because food spoils quickly. On the other hand, a furniture retailer turns its inventory over only a few times a year as most of the inventory are kept for a while on shop floors and warehouses, waiting for customers to purchase them. To evaluate inventory turnover, compare the ratio over time. A sharp decline suggests the need for corrective action.

Inventory turnover can also be expressed in number of days. If you divide 365 days by Palisades' inventory turnover ratio of 4.6, this is equal to about 79 days. This ratio is called **inventory resident period**.

Accounts Receivable Turnover. **Receivable turnover** measures the ability to collect cash from customers. In general, the higher the ratio, the better. However, a receivable turnover that is too high may indicate that credit is too tight, and that may cause you to lose sales to good customers.

To compute accounts receivable turnover, divide net sales by average net accounts receivable. The ratio tells how many times during the year average receivables were turned into cash. Palisades Furniture's accounts receivable turnover ratio for 2011 is:

Formula		Palisades' Accounts Receivable Turnover	Industry Average
Accounts payable turnover	$-\dfrac{\text{COGS}}{\text{Average net accounts payable}}$	$\dfrac{\$513,000}{\$70,500} = 7.3$	10.5

Average net accounts receivable can be derived by adding beginning ($85,000) and ending receivables ($114,000), then dividing by 2. Palisades' receivable turnover of 8.6 times per year is much slower than the industry average. Why the slow collection? Palisades may be a hometown store that sells to local people who pay bills over a period of time.

Similarly, we can also convert receivable turnover into days. The days'-sales-in-receivables ratio, also discussed in Chapter 6, shows how many days' sales remain in accounts receivable. This ratio is usually called **receivables collection period**. For Palisades, on average, it takes 42 days to collect cash from its receivables.

Accounts Payable Turnover. Businesses buy their supplies and raw materials on credit, and take time to pay their accounts payable. A high **account payable turnover** ratio means a business pays its suppliers very quickly, and a low payable turnover means a longer time period for payments to suppliers. Generally, a lower payable turnover is better than a higher one as the business is making full use of the credit terms extended by its creditors. However, it can't stretch the payable period too far because no one would supply the business if it continues to be delinquent on its payments.

To compute payable turnover, divide cost of goods sold by the average accounts payable for the period. Average accounts payable for the period is $73,000 + $60,000 divided by 2. Palisades Furniture's payable turnover for 2011 is:

Formula		Palisades' Accounts Receivable Turnover	Industry Average
Accounts payable turnover	$= \dfrac{\text{COGS}}{\text{Average net accounts payable}}$	$\dfrac{\$513,000}{\$70,500} = 7.3$	10.5

It seems that Palisades pays its creditors slower than the industry average. If we express this ratio into days, the **payables outstanding period** is about 50 days (365/7.3), whereas the industry average is about 35 days (365/10.5).

Cash Conversion Cycle. If we put the three ratios (inventory resident period, receivables collection period and payable collection period) together, we can speculate on how long it takes for a business to sell its inventory, collect payments, and less the time it takes to make its own payments to suppliers. This is what we call the **cash conversion cycle**. In general, a shorter cycle is better than a longer cycle, in fact it can even be a negative number! Here's an example of **Dell Computers** disclosure on its cash conversion cycle. Note that Dell uses slightly different terminologies than the ones we used in this chapter.

EXCERPTS FROM DELL INC.'S 2009 ANNUAL REPORT

Key Performance Metrics
Although our cash conversion cycle deteriorated from February 1, 2008 and February 2, 2007, our direct business model allows us to maintain an efficient cash conversion cycle, which compares favorably with that of others in our industry. ...

	Jan 30, 2009	Feb 1, 2008	Feb 2, 2007
Days of sales outstanding..........	35	36	31
Days of supply in inventory.......	7	8	5
Days in accounts payable..........	(67)	(80)	(78)
Cash conversion cycle	(25)	(36)	(42)

STOP & THINK...

What is Palisades' cash conversion cycle in 2008? What is your assessment of its cash conversion cycle relative to Dell? What about Nokia's?

Answers:
Palisades' cash conversion cycle is: Receivables collection period + Inventory resident period – Payables outstanding period = 42 + 79 – 50 = 71 days.
Nokia's cash conversion cycle is: [50,710 ÷ (average of 9,444 and 11,200)] + [33,337 ÷ (average of 2,533 and 2,876)] – [2,533 ÷ (average of 5,225 and 7,074)] = 74.3 + 29.6 – 67.3 = 36.6 days.
Palisades' cash conversion cycle is very different from Dell's. It takes Palisades a longer period to collect its receivables and sell its inventory. On the other hand, Palisades pays its supplier faster than Dell. The biggest difference between the two companies is the inventory resident period. Dell's business model allows it to hold very little inventory and sell whatever they have in inventory in a very short period of time.
Nokia takes a longer time to collect its receivables compared to Palisades and Dell, but Nokia takes much shorter time to sell its inventory than Palisades. Nokia's payable outstanding period is similar to that of Dell's.

Measuring Ability to Pay Debts

The ratios discussed so far relate to current assets and current liabilities. They measure the ability to sell inventory, collect receivables, and pay current obligations. Two indicators of the ability to pay total liabilities are the *debt ratio* and the *times-interest-earned ratio*.

Debt Ratio. Suppose you are a bank loan officer and you have received $500,000 loan applications from two similar companies. The first company already owes $600,000, and the second owes only $250,000. Which company gets the loan? All else being equal, you will probably approve the loan application from Company 2, because it owes less.

This relationship between total liabilities and total assets is called the **debt ratio**, which gives an indication of the degree of **leverage** of a company. Discussed in Chapters 3 and 8, the debt ratio tells us the proportion of assets financed with debt. A debt ratio of 1 reveals that debt has financed all the assets. A debt ratio of 0.50 means that debt finances half the assets. The higher the debt ratio, the greater the pressure to pay interest and principal. The lower the ratio, the lower the risk.

The debt ratios for Palisades Furniture in 2011 and 2010 follow:

		Palisades' Debt Ratio		Industry
	Formula	2011	2010	Average
Debt ratio =	$\dfrac{\text{Total liabilities}}{\text{Total assets}}$	$\dfrac{\$431,000}{\$787,000} = 0.55$	$\dfrac{\$324,000}{\$644,000} = 0.50$	0.64

Risk Management Association reports that the average debt ratio for most companies ranges around 0.62, with relatively little variation from company to company. Palisades' 0.55 debt ratio indicates a fairly low-risk debt position compared with the retail furniture industry average of 0.64.

An alternative way to describe the level of an entity's leverage is **debt-to-equity** ratio. Recall that the accounting equation is Assets = Liabilities plus Equity. If you know the debt ratio (i.e. liabilities over assets), you can easily work out an entity's debt-to-equity ratio. If total assets is $787,000 and total liabilities is $431,000, equity must be $356,000. Debt-to-equity ratio is thus $431,000 over $356,000, or 1.21 times. A debt-ratio is 0.55 is equivalent to a debt-to-equity ratio of 1.21.

Times-Interest-Earned Ratio. Analysts use a second ratio—the times-interest-earned ratio (introduced in Chapter 8)—to relate income to interest expense. To compute the times-interest-earned ratio, divide income from operations (operating income) by interest expense. This ratio measures the number of times operating income can cover interest expense and is also called the *interest-coverage ratio*. A high ratio indicates ease in paying interest; a low value suggests difficulty.

Palisades' times-interest-earned ratios are:

		Palisades' Times-Interest-Earned Ratio		Industry
	Formula	2011	2010	Average
Times-interest-earned ratio =	$\dfrac{\text{Income from operations}}{\text{Interest expense}}$	$\dfrac{\$101,000}{\$24,000} = 4.21$	$\dfrac{\$57,000}{\$14,000} = 4.07$	2.80

The company's times-interest-earned ratio increased in 2011. This is a favorable sign.

Measuring Profitability

The fundamental goal of a business is to earn a profit, and so the ratios that measure profitability are reported widely. Profitability ratios may be expressed as numbers or percentages. For example, 0.10 is equal to 10%, 0.25 equals to 25%, etc.

Rate of Return on Sales. In a business, return refers to profitability. Consider the **rate of return on net sales**, or simply *return on sales* (ROS) or *Net Profit Margin* (NPM). This ratio shows the percentage of each sales dollar earned as net income. You could also modify this ratio to measure gross profit margin (gross profit divided by sales) and operating profit margin (operating profit divided by sales). We discussed gross profit margin in Chapter 6.

The return-on-sales ratios for Palisades Furniture are:

Formula	*Palisades' Rate of Return on Sales* 2011	2010	Industry Average
$\dfrac{\text{Rate of return}}{\text{on sales}} = \dfrac{\text{Net income}}{\text{Net sales}}$	$\dfrac{\$48,000}{\$858,000} = 0.056$	$\dfrac{\$26,000}{\$803,000} = 0.032$	0.008

Companies strive for a high rate of return on sales. The higher the percentage, the more profit is being generated by sales dollars. You have actually seen this earlier as the very last line of a vertical analysis (Exhibits 13-4 and 13-6). Palisades Furniture's return on sales is higher than the average furniture store. Compare Palisades' rate of return on sales to the rates of some leading companies:

Company	Rate of Return on Sales
FedEx.....................	0.056
PepsiCo.................	0.119
Intel......................	0.141

Rate of Return on Total Assets. Also introduced in Chapter 9, the **rate of return on total assets**, or simply *return on assets* (ROA), measures a company's success in using assets to earn a profit. Creditors have loaned money, and the interest they receive is their return on investment. Shareholders have bought the company's shares, and net income is their return. The sum of interest expense and net income are the returns to the two groups that have financed the company. This sum is the numerator of the ratio. Average total assets is the denominator. The return-on-assets ratio for Palisades Furniture is:

Formula	*Palisades' 2011 Rate of Return on Total Assets*	Industry Average
$\dfrac{\text{Rate of return}}{\text{on assets}} = \dfrac{\text{Net income} + \text{Interest expense}}{\text{Average total assets}}$	$\dfrac{\$48,000 + \$24,000}{\$715,500} = 0.101$	0.078

To compute average total assets, add the beginning and ending balances and divide by 2. Compare Palisades Furniture's rate of return on assets to the rates of these leading companies:

Company	Rate of Return on Assets
General Electric.................	0.055
Starbucks	0.066
Google	0.108

Rate of Return on Ordinary Shareholders' Equity. A popular measure of profitability is rate of **return on ordinary shareholders' equity**, often shortened to *return on equity* (ROE). Also discussed in Chapter 9, this ratio shows the relationship between net income and ordinary shareholders' investment in the company—how much income is earned for every $1 invested.

To compute this ratio, first subtract preference dividends from net income to measure income available to the ordinary shareholders. Then divide income available to ordinary shareholders by average ordinary equity during the year. Ordinary equity is total equity minus preference equity. The 2011 return on ordinary equity for Palisades Furniture is:

Formula	Palisades' 2011 Rate of Return on Ordinary Shareholders' Equity	Industry Average
$$\text{Rate of return on ordinary shareholders' equity} = \frac{\text{Net income} - \text{Preference dividends}}{\text{Average ordinary shareholders' equity}}$$	$$\frac{\$48{,}000 - \$0}{\$338{,}000} = 0.142$$	0.121

Palisades Furniture has no preference shares and thus has no preference dividends. All of its equity are therefore ordinary. Average equity uses the beginning and ending balances [($320,000 + $356,000)/2 = $338,000].

Observe that Palisades' return on equity (0.142) is higher than its return on assets (0.101). This is a good sign. The difference results from borrowing at one rate—say, 8%—and investing the funds to earn a higher rate, such as the firm's 14.2% return on equity. This practice is called using **leverage**, or **trading on the equity**. The higher the debt ratio, the higher the leverage. Companies that finance operations with debt are said to leverage their positions.

For Palisades Furniture, leverage increases profitability. This is not always the case, because leverage can hurt profits. If revenues drop, debts still must be paid. Therefore, leverage is a double-edged sword. It increases profits during good times but compounds losses during bad times.

Palisades Furniture's rate of return on equity lags behind that of GE, but exceeds those of Google and Starbucks.

Company	Rate of Return on Ordinary Equity
General Electric.................	0.158
Google	0.121
Starbucks	0.132

Earnings per Share of Ordinary Shares. Discussed in Chapters 8 and 11, earnings per ordinary share, or simply earnings per share (EPS), is the amount of net income earned for each outstanding ordinary share. EPS is the most widely quoted of all financial statistics. It's the only ratio that appears on the income statement.

Earnings per share is computed by dividing net income available to ordinary shareholders by the weighted-average number of ordinary shares outstanding during the year. Preference dividends are subtracted from net income because the preference shareholders have a prior claim to their dividends. Palisades Furniture has no preference shares and thus has no preference dividends. The firm's EPS ratios for 2011 and 2010 follow (Palisades has 10,000 ordinary shares outstanding).

		Palisades' Earnings per Share	
	Formula	2011	2010
Earnings per share of share capital	$= \dfrac{\text{Net income} - \text{Preference dividends}}{\text{Weighted-average number of ordinary shares of outstanding}}$	$\dfrac{\$48,000 - \$0}{10,000} = \$4.80$	$\dfrac{\$26,000 - \$0}{10,000} = \$2.60$

Palisades Furniture's EPS increased 85% during 2011, and that's good news. The Palisades shareholders should not expect such a significant boost every year. Most companies strive to increase EPS by 10% to 15% annually.

Analyzing Share Investments

Investors buy shares to earn a return on their investment. This return consists of two parts: (1) gains (or losses) from selling the shares and (2) dividends.

Price/Earnings Ratio. The **price/earnings ratio** shows how much an investor is willing to pay for each unit of earnings. This ratio, abbreviated P/E, appears in every financial section of newspapers and online financial databases. The P/E ratio makes use of the earnings per share (EPS) ratio we calculated earlier.

Calculations for the P/E ratios of Palisades Furniture, Inc., follow. The market price of Palisades' ordinary share was $60 at the end of 2011 and $35 at the end of 2010. Share prices can be obtained from a company's website, a financial publication or website, or a stockbroker.

		Palisades' Price/Earnings Ratio	
	Formula	2011	2010
P/E ratio $=$	$\dfrac{\text{Market price per share of share capital}}{\text{Earnings per share}}$	$\dfrac{\$60.00}{\$4.80} = 12.5$	$\dfrac{\$35.00}{\$2.60} = 13.5$

Given Palisades Furniture's 2011 P/E ratio of 12.5, we would say that the company's share is selling at 12.5 times earnings. Each $1 of Palisades' earnings is worth $12.50 to the stock market. The P/E ratio reflects market's overall expectation of a company's performance. The more optimistic the market is, the higher the P/E ratio.

Dividend Yield. **Dividend yield** is the ratio of dividends per share of stock to the share's market price. This ratio measures the percentage of a share's market value returned annually to the shareholders as dividends.

Palisades Furniture paid annual cash dividends of $1.20 per share in 2011 and $1.00 in 2010. The market prices of the company's ordinary share were $60 in 2011 and $35 in 2010. The firm's dividend yields on ordinary share are:

		Dividend Yield on Palisades' Share Capital	
	Formula	2011	2010
Dividend yield on ordinary share*	= $\dfrac{\text{Dividend per ordinary share}}{\text{Market price per ordinary share}}$	$\dfrac{\$1.20}{\$60.00} = 0.020$	$\dfrac{\$1.00}{\$35.00} = 0.029$

*Dividend yields may also be calculated for preference shares.

Preference shareholders pay special attention to this ratio because they invest primarily to receive dividends. The same formula can be adjusted to calculate dividend yield only for preference shareholders: dividend per preference shares divided by market price per preference share.

An investor who buys Palisades Furniture ordinary shares for $60 can expect to receive around 2% of the investment annually in the form of cash dividends. Dividend yields vary widely, from 5% to 8% for mature, established firms (such as **Procter & Gamble** and **Unilever**) down to the range of 0% to 3% for younger, growth-oriented companies. Google, RIM, and eBay pay no cash dividends.

Book Value per Ordinary Share. Book value per ordinary share is simply ordinary shareholders' equity divided by the number of ordinary shares outstanding. Ordinary equity equals total equity less preference equity.

Palisades Furniture has no preference shares outstanding. Calculations of its book value per ordinary share follow. Recall that 10,000 ordinary shares were outstanding.

		Book Value per Share of Palisades' Share Capital	
	Formula	2011	2010
Book value per ordinary share	= $\dfrac{\text{Total shareholders' equity} - \text{Preference equity}}{\text{Number of ordinary shares outstanding}}$	$\dfrac{\$356,000 - \$0}{10,000} = \$35.60$	$\dfrac{\$320,000 - \$0}{10,000} = \$32.00$

Book value indicates the recorded accounting amount for each ordinary share outstanding. Many experts believe book value is not useful for investment analysis because it bears no relationship to market value and provides little information beyond what's reported on the balance sheet. But some investors base their investment decisions on book value. For example, some investors rank shares by the ratio of market price to book value. The lower the ratio, the more attractive the share. These investors are called "value' investors, as contrasted with "growth" investors, who focus more on trends in net income.

What does the outlook for the future look like for Palisades Furniture? If the company can stay on the same path it has followed for the past two years, it looks bright. It appears that its earnings per share are solid, and its ROS, ROA, and ROE ratios are all above average for its industry. From the standpoint of liquidity and leverage, it also appears to be in good shape, with higher liquidity, excellent debt and interest coverage, and lower debt ratios than its industry. The company's P/E ratio of 12:1 is relatively low, and it pays a 2% dividend. All of these factors make Palisades Furniture shares look like a good investment.

Using the Statement of Cash Flows

You may have noticed that the ratios we described earlier are all based on income statement and balance sheet. What about cash flows? We covered Free Cash Flow in Chapter 12 (see page 739), but in general, cash flow ratios have received less attention and coverage than they deserve. Fortunately, they are not a whole new set of ratios! Cash flow ratios are usually alternative versions of the ratios we discussed earlier, with emphasis changed to cash from operations (CFO). Here are some of the cash flow ratios you could use:

Standard ratios discussed earlier	Cash flow version	Variation from standard ratios
Current ratio	Operating Cash Flow ratio	CFO ÷ Current liabilities
Debt ratio	Cash flow to debt ratio	CFO ÷ total liabilities
Net Profit Margin	Cash flow margin	CFO ÷ net sales
Times-interest-earned	Cash-interest coverage	(CFO + interest paid) ÷ interest paid

OTHER ISSUES IN FINANCIAL STATEMENT ANALYSIS
Economic Value Added (EVA®)

The top managers of **Coca-Cola**, **Quaker Oats**, and other leading companies use **economic value added (EVA®)** to evaluate operating performance. EVA® combines accounting and finance to measure whether operations have increased shareholder wealth. EVA® can be computed as follows:

$$\text{EVA}^® = \text{Net income} + \text{Interest expense} - \text{Capital charge}$$

$$\text{Capital charge} = \left(\underset{\text{(Beginning balances)}}{\underset{\text{payable}}{\text{Notes}} + \underset{\substack{\text{of long-}\\\text{term debt}}}{\underset{\text{of long-}}{\text{Current}\\\text{maturities}}} + \underset{\text{debt}}{\text{Long-term}} + \underset{\text{equity}}{\text{Shareholders'}}} \right) \times \underset{\text{capital}}{\text{Cost of}}$$

All amounts for the EVA® computation, except the **cost of capital**, come from the financial statements. The cost of capital is a weighted average of the returns demanded by the company's shareholders and lenders. Cost of capital varies with the company's level of risk. For example, shareholders would demand a higher return from a start-up company than from Nokia because the new company is untested and therefore more risky. Lenders would also charge the new company a higher interest rate because of its greater risk. Thus, the new company has a higher cost of capital than Nokia.

The cost of capital is a major topic in finance classes. In the following discussions we assume a value for the cost of capital (such as 10%, 12%, or 15%) to illustrate the computation of EVA®.

The idea behind EVA® is that the returns to the company's shareholders (net income) and to its creditors (interest expense) should exceed the company's **capital**

charge. The capital charge is the amount that shareholders and lenders charge a company for the use of their money. A positive EVA® amount suggests an increase in shareholder wealth, and so the company's shares should remain attractive to investors. If EVA® is negative, shareholders will probably be unhappy with the company and sell its shares, resulting in a decrease in the share's price. Different companies tailor the EVA® computation to meet their own needs.

Let's apply EVA® to Nokia Corporation. The company's EVA® for 2008 can be computed as follows, assuming a 10% cost of capital (in million of euros):

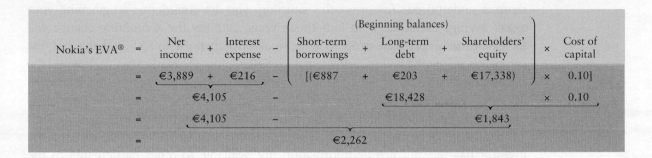

By this measure, Nokia's operations added €2,262 million of value to its shareholders' wealth after meeting the company's capital charge. This performance is considered very strong, especially given the tough economic conditions in 2008.

Red Flags in Financial Statement Analysis

Recent accounting scandals have highlighted the importance of *red flags* in financial statement analysis. The following conditions may mean a company is very risky:

- *Earnings Problems.*   Have income from continuing operations and net income decreased for several years in a row? Has income turned into a loss? This may be okay for a company in a cyclical industry, such as an airline or a home builder, but a company such as Nokia may not be able to survive losses in consecutive years.
- *Decreased Cash Flow.*   Cash flow validates earnings. Is cash flow from operations consistently lower than net income? Are the sales of PPE a major source of cash? If so, the company may be facing a cash shortage.
- *Too Much Debt.*   How does the company's debt ratio compare to that of major competitors and to the industry average? If the debt ratio is much higher than average, the company may be unable to pay debts during tough times.
- *Inability to Collect Receivables.*   Are receivables resident periods growing faster than for other companies in the industry? A cash shortage may be looming.
- *Buildup of Inventories.*   Is inventory turnover slowing down? If so, the company may be unable to move products, or it may be overstating inventory as reported on the balance sheet. Recall from the cost-of-goods-sold model that one of the easiest ways to overstate net income is to overstate ending inventory.
- *Trends of Sales, Inventory, and Receivables.*   Sales, receivables, and inventory generally move together. Increased sales lead to higher receivables and require more inventory in order to meet demand. Strange movements among these items may spell trouble.

Efficient Markets

An **efficient capital market** is one in which market prices fully reflect all information available to the public. Because share prices reflect all publicly accessible data, it can be argued that the stock market is efficient. Market efficiency has implications for management action and for investor decisions. It means that managers cannot fool the market with accounting gimmicks. If the information is available, the market as a whole can set a "fair" price for the company's stock.

Suppose you are the president of Anacomp Corporation. Reported earnings per share are $4, and the stock price is $40—so the P/E ratio is 10. You believe Anacomp's share is underpriced. To correct this situation, you are considering lengthening your assets' average useful life from four to six years. Let's say the accounting change will increase earnings per share to $5. Will the stock price then rise to $50? Probably not; the company's share price will probably remain at $40 because the market can understand the accounting change. After all, the company merely changed its depreciation estimates. There is no effect on Anacomp's cash flows, and the company's economic position is unchanged: An efficient market interprets data in light of their true underlying meaning.

In an efficient market, the search for "underpriced" stock is fruitless unless the investor has relevant *private* information not available to other participants in the market. But it is unlawful as well as unethical to invest on the basis of *inside* information. An appropriate strategy seeks to manage risk, diversify investments, and minimize transaction costs. Financial analysis helps mainly to identify the risks of various stocks and then to manage the risk.

The Decision Guidelines feature summarizes the most widely used ratios.

DECISION GUIDELINES

USING RATIOS IN FINANCIAL STATEMENT ANALYSIS

Lane and Kay Collins operate a financial services firm. They manage other people's money and do most of their own financial statement analysis. How do they measure companies' ability to pay bills, sell inventory, collect receivables, and so on? They use the standard ratios we have covered throughout this book.

Ratio	Computation	Information Provided
Measuring ability to pay current liabilities:		
1. Current ratio	$\dfrac{\text{Current assets}}{\text{Current liabilities}}$	Measures the ability to pay current liabilities with current assets
2. Acid-test (quick) ratio	$\dfrac{\text{Cash} + \dfrac{\text{Short-term}}{\text{investments}} + \dfrac{\text{Net current}}{\text{receivables}}}{\text{Current liabilities}}$	Shows the ability to pay all current liabilities if they come due immediately
Measuring cash conversion cycle:		
3. Inventory turnover	$\dfrac{\text{Cost of goods sold}}{\text{Average inventory}}$	Indicates the saleability of inventory—the number of times a company sells its average level of inventory during a year

Ratio	Computation	Information Provided
4. Accounts receivable turnover	$$\frac{\text{Net credit sales}}{\text{Average net accounts receivable}}$$	Measures the ability to collect cash from credit customers
5. Payable turnover	$$\frac{\text{Cost of goods sold}}{\text{Average payables}}$$	Measures the frequency of payments to trade creditors
6. Cash conversion cycle	Receivables collection period + Inventory resident period − Payable outstanding period	Indicates the speed at which an entity is able to convert cash from its inventory & receivables

Measuring ability to pay long-term debt:

Ratio	Computation	Information Provided
7. Debt ratio	$$\frac{\text{Total liabilities}}{\text{Total assets}}$$	Indicates percentage of assets financed with debt
8. Times-interest-earned ratio (or interest coverage ratio)	$$\frac{\text{Income from operations}}{\text{Interest expense}}$$	Measures the number of times operating income can cover interest expense

Measuring profitability:

Ratio	Computation	Information Provided
9. Rate of return on net sales (or net profit margin)	$$\frac{\text{Net income}}{\text{Net sales}}$$	Shows the percentage of each sales dollar earned as net income
10. Rate of return on total assets	$$\frac{\text{Net income + Interest expense}}{\text{Average total assets}}$$	Measures how profitably a company uses its assets
11. Rate of return on ordinary shareholders' equity	$$\frac{\text{Net income − Preference dividends}}{\text{Average ordinary shareholders' equity}}$$	Gauges how much income is earned with the money invested by the ordinary shareholders
12. Earnings per ordinary share	$$\frac{\text{Net income − Preference dividends}}{\text{Weighted-average number of ordinary shares outstanding}}$$	Gives the amount of net income earned for each share of the company's ordinary shares outstanding

Analyzing shares as an investment:

Ratio	Computation	Information Provided
13. Price/earnings ratio	$$\frac{\text{Market price per ordinary share}}{\text{Earnings per share}}$$	Indicates the market price of 1 currency unit of earnings
14. Dividend yield	$$\frac{\text{Dividend per ordinary share (or preference)}}{\text{Market price per ordinary share (or preference)}}$$	Shows the percentage of a share's market value returned as dividends to shareholders each period
15. Book value per ordinary share	$$\frac{\text{Total shareholders' equity − Preference equity}}{\text{Number of ordinary shares outstanding}}$$	Indicates the recorded accounting amount for each ordinary share outstanding

END-OF-CHAPTER SUMMARY PROBLEM

The following financial data are adapted from the annual reports of Lampeer Corporation:

Lampeer Corporation
Four-Year Selected Financial Data
Years Ended January 31, 2010, 2009, 2008, and 2007

Operating Results*	2010	2009	2008	2007
Net Sales	$13,848	$13,673	$11,635	$9,054
Cost of goods sold and occupancy				
expenses excluding depreciation				
and amortization......................	9,704	8,599	6,775	5,318
Interest expense	109	75	45	46
Income from operations...............	338	1,445	1,817	1,333
Net earnings (net loss)	(8)	877	1,127	824
Cash dividends.............................	76	75	76	77
Financial Position				
Merchandise inventory................	1,677	1,904	1,462	1,056
Total assets	7,591	7,012	5,189	3,963
Current ratio................................	1.48:1	0.95:1	1.25:1	1.20:1
Shareholders' equity....................	3,010	2,928	2,630	1,574
Average number of ordinary				
shares outstanding				
(in thousands)	860	879	895	576

*Dollar amounts are in thousands.

Requirement

1. Compute the following ratios for 2008 through 2010, and evaluate Lampeer's operating results. Are operating results strong or weak? Did they improve or deteriorate during the three-year period? Your analysis will reveal a clear trend.

a. Gross profit margin*

b. Net income as a percentage of sales

c. Earnings per share

d. Inventory turnover

e. Times-interest-earned ratio

f. Rate of return on shareholders' equity

*Refer to Chapter 6 if necessary.

Answer

	2010	2009	2008
1. Gross profit margin	$\dfrac{\$13{,}848 - \$9{,}704}{\$13{,}848} = 29.9\%$	$\dfrac{\$13{,}673 - \$8{,}599}{\$13{,}673} = 37.1\%$	$\dfrac{\$11{,}635 - \$6{,}775}{\$11{,}635} = 41.8\%$
2. Net income as a percentage of sales	$\dfrac{\$(8)}{\$13{,}848} = (0.06)\%$	$\dfrac{\$877}{\$13{,}673} = 6.4\%$	$\dfrac{\$1{,}127}{\$11{,}635} = 9.7\%$
3. Earnings per share	$\dfrac{\$(8)}{860} = \$(0.01)$	$\dfrac{\$877}{879} = \$1.00$	$\dfrac{\$1{,}127}{895} = \$1.26$

4. Inventory turnover	$\dfrac{\$9,704}{(\$1,677 + \$1,904)/2} = 5.4$ times		$\dfrac{\$8,599}{(\$1,904 + \$1,462)/2} = 5.1$ times		$\dfrac{\$6,775}{(\$1,462 + \$1,056)/2} = 5.4$ times
5. Times-interest- earned ratio	$\dfrac{\$338}{\$109} = 3.1$ times		$\dfrac{\$1,445}{\$75} = 19.3$ times		$\dfrac{\$1,817}{\$45} = 40.4$ times
6. Rate of return on shareholders' equity	$\dfrac{\$(8)}{(\$3,010 + \$2,928)/2} = (0.3\%)$		$\dfrac{\$877}{(\$2,928 + \$2,630)/2} = 31.6\%$		$\dfrac{\$1,127}{(\$2,630 + \$1,574)/2} = 53.6\%$

Evaluation: During this period, Lampeer's operating results deteriorated on all these measures except inventory turnover. The gross profit percentage is down sharply, as are the times-interest-earned ratio and all the return measures. From these data it is clear that Lampeer could sell its merchandise, but not at the markups the company enjoyed in the past. The final result, in 2010, was a net loss for the year.

REVIEW FINANCIAL STATEMENT ANALYSIS

Quick Check (Answers are given on page 848.)

Analyze the Oullette Company financial statements by answering the questions that follow. Oullette owns a chain of restaurants.

Oullette Company
Consolidated Statements of Income (Adapted)
Years Ended December 31, 2011 and 2010

(In millions, except per share data)	2011	2010
Revenues..		
Sales by Company-operated restaurants....................................	$13,200	$11,100
Revenues from franchised and affiliated restaurants................	4,500	3,700
Total revenues..	17,700	14,800
Food and paper (Cost of goods sold)...	3,300	3,108
Payroll and employee benefits..	3,200	3,000
Occupancy and other operating expenses...............................	2,900	2,800
Franchised restaurants—occupancy expenses.........................	949	850
Selling, general, and administrative expenses.........................	1,820	1,730
Other operating expense, net..	510	855
Total operating expenses..	12,679	12,343
Operating income...	5,021	2,457
Interest expense...	370	345
Other nonoperating expense, net..	140	168
Income before income taxes..	4,511	1,944
Income tax expense..	1,820	820
Net income..	$ 2,691	$ 1,124
Per ordinary-share basic:		
Net income..	$ 2.69	$ 1.15
Dividends per ordinary share	$ 0.50	$ 0.24

Oulette Company
Consolidated Balance Sheets
December 31, 2011 and 2010

(In millions, except per share data)	2011	2010
Assets		
Current Assets		
Cash and equivalents	$ 690	$ 455
Accounts and notes receivable	780	840
Inventories	140	120
Prepaid expense and other current assets	580	440
Total current assets	2,190	1,855
Other Assets		
Investments in affiliates	1,150	1,055
Goodwill, net	1,780	1,590
Miscellaneous	990	1,100
Total other assets	3,920	3,745
Property and Equipment		
Property and equipment, at cost	28,800	26,500
Accumulated depreciation and amortization	(8,850)	(7,900)
Net property and equipment	19,950	18,600
Total assets	$26,060	$24,200
Liabilities and Shareholders' Equity		
Current liabilities		
Accounts payable	$ 520	$ 675
Income taxes	70	14
Other taxes	230	180
Accrued interest	189	196
Accrued restructuring and restaurant closing costs	110	385
Accrued payroll and other liabilities	890	795
Current maturities of long-term debt	365	305
Total current liabilities	2,374	2,550
Long-term debt	8,700	9,500
Other long-term liabilities and minority interests	690	520
Deferred income taxes	1,005	1,015
Shareholders' Equity		
Preference shares, no par value; authorized—140.0 million shares; issued—none	—	—
Ordinary shares, $0.01 par value; authorized—2.0 billion shares; issued—1,400 million shares	14	14
Additional paid-in capital	1,786	1,662
Unearned ESOP compensation	(85)	(101)
Retained earnings	21,741	19,550
Accumulated other comprehensive income (loss)	(815)	(1,570)
Ordinary shares in treasury, at cost; 400 and 420 million shares	(9,350)	(8,940)
Total shareholders' equity	13,291	10,615
Total liabilities and shareholders' equity	$26,060	$24,200

1. Horizontal analysis of Oullette's income statement for 2011 would show which of the following for Selling, General, and Administrative expenses?
   a. 0.95
   b. 1.05
   c. 0.68
   d. None of the above

2. Vertical analysis of Oullette's income statement for 2011 would show which of the following for Selling, General, and Administrative expenses?
   a. 0.103
   b. 0.144
   c. 0.138
   d. None of the above

3. Which item on Oullette's income statement has the most favorable trend during 2010–2011?
   a. Food and paper costs
   b. Total revenues
   c. Payroll and employee benefits
   d. Net income

4. On Oullette's common-size balance sheet, Goodwill would appear as
   a. $1,780 million.
   b. up by 11.9%.
   c. 0.068.
   d. 10.06% of total revenues.

5. A good benchmark for Oullette Company would be
   a. Volvo.
   b. Microsoft.
   c. Whataburger.
   d. All of the above.

6. Oullette's inventory turnover for 2011 was
   a. 17 times.
   b. 61 times.
   c. 25 times.
   d. 72 times.

7. Oullette's acid-test ratio at the end of 2011 was
   a. 0.62.
   b. 2.83.
   c. 0.92.
   d. 0.06.

8. Oullette's average collection period for accounts and notes receivables is
   a. 32 days.
   b. 2 days.
   c. 17 days.
   d. 1 day.

9. The average debt ratio for most companies is 0.64. Oullette's total debt position looks
   a. risky.
   b. middle-ground.
   c. safe.
   d. cannot tell from the financials.

10. Oullette's return on total revenues for 2011 was
    a. $2.69.
    b. $1.16.
    c. 10.33%.
    d. 15.2%.

11. Oullette's return on shareholders' equity for 2011 was
    a. 15.2%.
    b. 22.5%.
    c. 10.33%.
    d. $2,691 million.

12. On May 31, 2011, Oullette's ordinary shares sold for $30 per share. At that price, how much did investors say $1 of the company's net income was worth?
    a. $1.00
    b. $30.00
    c. $11.15
    d. $10.99

13. On May 31, 2011, Oullette's ordinary shares sold for $30 per share and dividends per share were $0.50. Compute Oullette's dividend yield during 2011.
    a. 2.9%
    b. 4.1%
    c. 1.7%
    d. 5.0%

14. How much EVA® did Oullette generate for investors during 2011? Assume the cost of capital was 5%.
    a. $2,040 million
    b. $1,943 million
    c. $3,061 million
    d. $2,691 million

Accounting Vocabulary

acid-test ratio (p. 799) Ratio of the sum of cash plus short-term investments plus net current receivables to total current liabilities. Tells whether the entity can pay all its current liabilities if they come due immediately. Also called the *quick ratio*.

benchmarking (p. 793) The comparison of an entity to another entity (competitor or peer), with the objective of providing context to the evaluation of the entity.

book value per ordinary share (p. 807) Ordinary shareholders' equity divided by the number of ordinary shares outstanding. The recorded amount for each ordinary share outstanding.

capital charge (p. 808) The amount that shareholders and lenders charge a company for the use of their money. Calculated as beginning balances of (Notes payable + Loans payable + Long-term debt + Shareholders' equity) × Cost of capital.

common-size statement (p. 793) A financial statement that reports only percentages (no dollar amounts).

cash conversion cycle (p. 802) The length of time it takes a company to convert cash from its inventory purchases and receivables. Calculated as inventory resident period plus receivables collection period less payables outstanding period.

cost of capital (p. 808) A weighted average of the returns demanded by the company's shareholders and lenders.

current ratio (p. 799) Current assets divided by current liabilities. Measures a company's ability to pay current liabilities with current assets.

debt ratio (p. 803) Ratio of total liabilities to total assets. States the proportion of a company's assets that is financed with debt.

dividend yield (p. 806) Ratio of dividends per share to the share's market price. Tells the percentage of a share's market value that the company returns to shareholders as dividends.

earnings per share (EPS) (p. 805) Amount of a company's net income earned for each ordinary share outstanding.

economic value added (EVA®) (p. 808) Used to evaluate a company's operating performance. EVA combines the concepts of accounting income and corporate finance to measure whether the company's operations have increased shareholder wealth. EVA = Net income + Interest expense – Capital charge.

efficient capital market (p. 809) A capital market in which market prices fully reflect all information available to the public.

horizontal analysis (p. 786) Study of percentage changes in comparative financial statements.

inventory resident period (p. 801) The average length of time (in days) to sell inventory, based on *inventory turnover*. Part of *cash conversion cycle*.

inventory turnover (p. 800) Ratio of cost of goods sold to average inventory. Indicates how rapidly inventory is sold. Can also be expressed in days (*inventory resident period*).

leverage (p. 803) The degree of external financing of an entity. Earning more income on borrowed money than the related interest expense, thereby increasing the earnings for the owners of the business. Also called *trading on the equity*.

payable outstanding period (p. 802) The average length of time (in days) to pay account payables, based on *payable turnover*. Part of *cash conversion cycle*.

payable turnover (p. 801). Ratio of cost of goods sold to average payables. Indicates how quick trade creditors are paid. Can also be expressed in days (payables outstanding period).

price/earnings ratio (p. 806) Ratio of the market price of an ordinary share to the company's earnings per share. Measures the value that the share market places on 1 currency unit of a company's earnings.

quick ratio (p. 799) Another name for the *acid-test ratio*.

receivable collection period (p. 801) The average length of time (in days) to collect receivables, based on *receivable turnover*. Part of *cash conversion cycle*.

rate of return on ordinary shareholders' equity (p. 805) Net income minus preference dividends, divided by average ordinary shareholders' equity. A measure of profitability. Also called *return on equity*.

rate of return on net sales (p. 804) Ratio of net income to net sales. A measure of profitability. Also called *return on sales or net profit margin*.

rate of return on total assets (p. 804) Net income plus interest expense, divided by average total assets. This ratio measures a company's success in using its assets to earn income for the persons who finance the business. Also called *return on assets*.

return on equity (p. 805) Another name for rate of return on ordinary shareholders' equity.

return on sales (p. 804) Another name for rate of return on ordinary shareholders' equity.

receivables turnover (p. 801). Ratio of sales to average receivables. Indicates how rapidly receivables are collected. Can also be expressed in days (*receivables collection period*).

times-interest-earned ratio (p. 803) Ratio of income from operations to interest expense. Measures the number of times that operating income can cover interest expense. Also called the *interest-coverage ratio*.

trading on the equity (p. 803) Another name for *leverage*.

trend percentages (p. 789) A form of horizontal analysis that indicates the direction a business is taking.

vertical analysis (p. 790) Analysis of a financial statement that reveals the relationship of each statement item to a specified base, which is the 100% figure.

working capital (p. 798) Current assets minus current liabilities; measures a business's ability to meet its short-term obligations with its current assets.

ASSESS YOUR PROGRESS

Short Exercises

S13-1 (*Learning Objective 1: Performing horizontal analysis of revenues and net income*) Fitzgerald Corporation reported the following amounts on its 2010 comparative income statement:

(In thousands)	2010	2009	2008
Revenues	$10,473	$9,998	$9,111
Total expenses	5,822	5,422	5,110

Perform a horizontal analysis of revenues and net income—both in dollar amounts and in percentages—for 2010 and 2009.

S13-2 (*Learning Objective 1: Performing trend analysis of sales and net income*) Fenton, Inc., reported the following sales and net income amounts:

(In thousands)	2010	2009	2008	2007
Sales	$10,020	$8,960	$8,740	$8,490
Net income	620	530	420	330

Show Fenton's trend percentages for sales and net income. Use 2007 as the base year.

S13-3 (*Learning Objective 2: Performing vertical analysis to correct a cash shortage*) Craft Software reported the following amounts on its balance sheets at December 31, 2010, 2009, and 2008:

	2010	2009	2008
Cash	$ 7,500	$ 2,195	$ 1,990
Receivables, net	35,000	21,950	23,880
Inventory	260,000	193,160	147,260
Prepaid expenses	10,000	17,560	11,940
Property, plant and equipment, net	187,500	204,135	212,930
Total assets	$500,000	$439,000	$398,000

Sales and profits are high. Nevertheless, Craft is experiencing a cash shortage. Perform a vertical analysis of Craft Software's assets at the end of years 2010, 2009, and 2008. Use the analysis to explain the reason for the cash shortage.

S13-4 (*Learning Objective 3: Comparing common-size income statements of two companies*) Hartigan, Inc., and Pintal Corporation are competitors. Compare the two companies by converting their condensed income statements to common size.

(In millions)	Hartigan	Pintal
Net sales	$10,800	$8,752
Cost of goods sold	6,469	6,065
Selling and administrative expenses	3,110	1,698
Interest expense	54	35
Other expenses	32	44
Income tax expense	432	210
Net income	$ 703	$ 700

Which company earned more net income? Which company's net income was a higher percentage of its net sales? Explain your answer.

S13-5 (*Learning Objective 4: Evaluating the trend in a company's current ratio*) Examine the financial data of Jacob Corporation.

Year Ended December 31	2010	2009	2008
Operating Results			
Net income	$ 220	$ 120	$ 119
Per ordinary share	$1.23	$0.93	$0.63
Percent of sales	15.6%	17.6%	19.6%
Return on average shareholders' equity	14.0	17.0	20.0
Financial Position			
Current assets	$ 550	$ 445	$ 435
Current liabilities	$ 360	$ 333	$ 356
Working capital	$ 190	$ 112	$ 79
Current ratio	1.53	1.34	1.22

Show how to compute Jacob's current ratio for each year 2008 through 2010. Is the company's ability to pay its current liabilities improving or deteriorating?

S13-6 (*Learning Objective 4: Evaluating a company's acid-test ratio*) Use the Gagnon, Inc., balance sheet data on the following page.

❙ Requirements

1. Compute Gagnon, Inc.'s acid-test ratios at December 31, 2010 and 2009.
2. Use the comparative information from the table on the bottom of the following page for Horner, Inc., Isaacson Company, and Jona Companies Limited. Are Gagnon, Inc.'s acid-test ratios for 2010 and 2009 strong, average, or weak in comparison?

Gagnon, Inc.
Balance Sheets (Adapted)
December 31, 2010 and 2009

(Dollar amounts in millions)	2010	2009	Increase (Decrease) Amount	Percentage
Assets				
Current Assets				
Cash and cash equivalents	$1,203	$ 903	$ 300	33.2 %
Short-term investments	7	84	(77)	(91.7)
Receivables, net	246	256	(10)	(3.9)
Inventories	91	81	10	12.3
Prepaid expenses and other assets	203	343	(140)	(40.8)
Total current assets	1,750	1,667	83	5.0
Property, plant and equipment, net	3,619	3,396	223	6.6
Intangible assets	1,089	841	248	29.5
Other assets	824	718	106	14.8
Total assets	$7,282	$6,622	$ 660	10.0 %
Liabilities and Shareholders' Equity				
Current Liabilities				
Accounts payable	$ 977	$ 884	$ 93	10.5 %
Income tax payable	39	69	(30)	(43.5)
Short-term debt	121	115	6	5.2
Other	70	73	(3)	(4.1)
Total current liabilities	1,207	1,141	66	5.8
Long-term debt	3,544	2,982	562	18.8
Other liabilities	1,177	1,046	131	12.5
Total liabilities	5,928	5,169	759	14.7
Shareholders' Equity				
Share capital	—	—	—	—
Retained earnings	1,513	1,629	(116)	(7.1)
Accumulated other comprehensive (loss)	(159)	(176)	17	9.7
Total shareholders' equity	1,354	1,453	(99)	(6.8)
Total liabilities and shareholders' equity	$7,282	$6,622	$ 660	10.0 %

Company	Acid-Test Ratio
Horner, Inc. (Utility)	0.73
Isaacson Company (Department store)	0.68
Jona Companies Limited (Grocery store)	0.72

S13-7 (*Learning Objectives 4: Computing and evaluating inventory turnover and receivables resident period*)   Use the Gagnon 2010 income statement below and balance sheet from Short Exercise 13-6 to compute the following:

Gagnon, Inc. Statements of Income (Adapted) Year Ended December 31, 2010 and 2009		
(Dollar amounts in millions)	2010	2009
Revenues	$9,500	$9,068
Expenses:		
Food and paper (Cost of goods sold)	2,200	2,236
Payroll and employee benefits	2,138	2,001
Occupancy and other operating expenses	2,778	2,745
General and administrative expenses	1,171	1,135
Interest expense	150	133
Other expense (income), net	11	(29)
Income before income taxes	1,052	847
Income tax expense	273	251
Net income	$ 779	$ 596

   a. Gagnon's rate of inventory turnover for 2010.
   b. Receivables resident period. (Round dollar amounts to one decimal place.)

Do these measures look strong or weak? Give the reason for your answer.

S13-8 (*Learning Objective 4: Measuring ability to pay long-term debt*)   Use the financial statements of Gagnon, Inc., in Short Exercises 13-6 and 13-7.

❙ Requirements

  1. Compute the company's debt ratio at December 31, 2010.
  2. Compute the company's times-interest-earned ratio for 2010. For operating income, use income before both interest expense and income taxes. You can simply add interest expense back to income before taxes.
  3. Is Gagnon's ability to pay liabilities and interest expense strong or weak? Comment on the value of each ratio computed for questions 1 and 2.

S13-9 (*Learning Objective 4: Measuring profitability*)   Use the financial statements of Gagnon, Inc., in Short Exercises 13-6 and 13-7 to compute these profitability measures for 2010. Show each computation.

   a. Rate of return on sales.
   b. Rate of return on total assets.
   c. Rate of return on ordinary shareholders' equity.

S13-10 (*Learning Objective 4: Computing EPS and the price/earnings ratio*)   The annual report of Tri-State Cars, Inc., for the year ended December 31, 2010, included the following items (in millions):

Preference share outstanding, 6%	$400
Net income	$500
Number of ordinary shares outstanding	100

▌Requirements

1. Compute earnings per share (EPS) and the price/earnings ratio for Tri-State Cars' shares. Round to the nearest cent. The price of a share of Tri-State Car shares is $57.12.
2. How much does the stock market say $1 of Tri-State Cars' net income is worth?

S13-11 (*Learning Objective 4: Using ratio data to reconstruct an income statement*)   A skeleton of Athol Country Florist's income statement appears as follows (amounts in thousands):

Income Statement	
Net sales	$7,500
Cost of goods sold	(a)
Selling expenses	1,511
Administrative expenses	328
Interest expense	(b)
Other expenses	154
Income before taxes	1,046
Income tax expense	(c)
Net income	$ (d)

Use the following ratio data to complete Athol Country Florist's income statement:

a. Inventory turnover was 4 (beginning inventory was $784; ending inventory was $762).
b. Rate of return on sales is 0.10.

S13-12 (*Learning Objective 4: Using ratio data to reconstruct a balance sheet*)   A skeleton of Athol Country Florist's balance sheet appears as follows (amounts in thousands):

Balance Sheet			
Cash	$ 85	Total current liabilities	$1,900
Receivables	(a)	Long-term debt	(e)
Inventories	762	Other long-term liabilities	720
Prepaid expenses	(b)		
Total current assets	(c)		
PPE	(d)	Share capital	185
Other assets	2,100	Retained earnings	3,465
Total assets	$7,300	Total liabilities and equity	$ (f)

Use the following ratio data to complete Athol Country Florist's balance sheet:

a. Debt ratio is 0.50.
b. Current ratio is 1.30.
c. Acid-test ratio is 0.40.

writing assignment ∎

S13-13 (*Learning Objective 4: Analyzing a company based on its ratios*) Take the role of an investment analyst at Merrimack Lowell. It is your job to recommend investments for your client. The only information you have is the following ratio values for two companies in the graphics software industry.

Ratio	Graphit.net	Data Doctors
Days' sales in receivables	44	50
Inventory turnover	6	10
Gross profit percentage	69%	60%
Net income as a percent of sales	13%	14%
Times interest earned	17	11
Return on equity	36%	28%
Return on assets	15%	20%

Write a report to the Merrimack Lowell investment committee. Recommend one company's shares over the other. State the reasons for your recommendation.

S13-14 (*Learning Objective 5: Measuring economic value added*) Compute economic value added (EVA®) for Beverly Software. The company's cost of capital is 5%. Net income was $770 thousand, interest expense $409 thousand, beginning long-term debt $700 thousand, and beginning shareholders' equity was $3,060 thousand. Round all amounts to the nearest thousand dollars.

Should the company's shareholders be happy with the EVA®?

Exercises

> All of the A and B exercises can be found within MyAccountingLab, an online homework and practice environment. Your instructor may ask you to complete these exercises using MyAccountingLab.

(Group A)

E13-15A (*Learning Objective 1: Computing year-to-year changes in working capital*) What were the dollar amount of change and the percentage of each change in Wilderness Lodge's working capital during 2010 and 2009? Is this trend favorable or unfavorable?

	2010	2009	2008
Total current assets	$270,000	$320,000	$340,000
Total current liabilities	125,000	160,000	170,000

∎ spreadsheet

E13-16A (*Learning Objective 1: Performing horizontal analysis of an income statement*) Prepare a horizontal analysis of the comparative income statements of Sensible Music Co. Round percentage changes to the nearest one-tenth percent (three decimal places).

Sensible Music Co.
Comparative Income Statements
Years Ended December 31, 2010 and 2009

	2010	2009
Total revenue	$852,000	$912,000
Expenses:		
Cost of goods sold	$402,000	$408,000
Selling and general expenses	232,000	261,000
Interest expense	9,200	10,500
Income tax expense	83,000	84,000
Total expenses	726,200	763,500
Net income	$125,800	$148,500

E13-17A (*Learning Objective 1: Computing trend percentages*)   Compute trend percentages for Palm Valley Sales & Service's total revenue, and net income for the following five-year period, using year 0 as the base year. Round to the nearest full percent.

(In thousands)	Year 4	Year 3	Year 2	Year 1	Year 0
Total revenue	$1,414	$1,203	$1,101	$999	$1,020
Net income	104	99	86	74	88

Which grew faster during the period, total revenue or net income?

E13-18A (*Learning Objective 2: Performing vertical analysis of a balance sheet*)   Fore Golf Company has requested that you perform a vertical analysis of its balance sheet to determine the component percentages of its assets, liabilities, and shareholders' equity.

Fore Golf Company
Balance Sheet
December 31, 2010

Assets	
Total current assets	$ 43,000
Property, plant and equipment, net	117,000
Other assets	38,000
Total assets	$198,000
Liabilities	
Total current liabilities	$ 49,000
Long-term debt	109,000
Total liabilities	158,000
Shareholders' Equity	
Total shareholders' equity	40,000
Total liabilities and shareholders' equity	$198,000

E13-19A (*Learning Objective 3: Preparing a common-size income statement*)   Prepare a comparative common-size income statement for Sensible Music Co., using the 2010 and 2009 data of Exercise 13-16A and rounding to four decimal places.

■ **spreadsheet**

E13-20A *(Learning Objective 3: Preparing a common-size income statement)* Compare the year 2010 common-size income statement you performed earlier in E13-19A. How does this compare to Nokia vertical analysis in Exhibit 13-4? You may need to combine a few line items to make the common-size statements comparable.

California Fruit Growers, Inc.
Statement of Cash Flows
For the Current Year

Operating activities:		
Income from operations...		$ 61,000
Add (subtract) noncash items:		
Depreciation	$ 11,000	
Net increase in current assets other than cash	(52,000)	
Net decrease in current liabilities		
exclusive of short-term debt..........................	(19,000)	(60,000)
Net cash provided by operating activities.........		1,000
Investing activities:		
Sale of property, plant, and equipment		115,000
Financing activities:		
Issuance of bonds payable	$ 113,000	
Payment of short-term debt	(174,000)	
Payment of long-term debt	(86,000)	
Payment of dividends..	(38,000)	
Net cash used for financing activities...............		(185,000)
Increase (decrease) in cash		$ (69,000)

E13-21A *(Learning Objective 4: Computing five ratios)*   The financial statements of Smith News, Inc., include the following items:

	Current Year	Preceding Year
Balance sheet:		
Cash	$ 26,000	$ 32,000
Short-term investments	14,000	20,000
Net receivables	50,000	73,000
Inventory......................................	94,000	76,000
Prepaid expenses.........................	9,000	8,000
Total current assets	193,000	209,000
Total current liabilities................	129,000	96,000
Income statement:		
Net credit sales	$490,000	
Cost of goods sold	274,000	

❙ Requirement

1. Compute the following ratios for the current year:

   a. Current ratio
   b. Acid-test ratio
   c. Inventory turnover

   d. Accounts receivable turnover
   e. Receivables resident period
   f. Cash conversion cycle

(Round your answers to **a** through **d** to two decimal points. Round your answer to **e** and **f** to the nearest whole number.)

E13-22A (*Learning Objective 4: Analyzing the ability to pay current liabilities*) Dorman Furniture Company has requested that you determine whether the company's ability to pay its current liabilities and long-term debts improved or deteriorated during 2010. To answer this question, compute the following ratios for 2010 and 2009:

writing assignment ■

■ **spreadsheet**

    a. Current ratio   **c.** Debt ratio

    b. Acid-test ratio   **d.** Times-interest-earned ratio

Summarize the results of your analysis in a written report.

	2010	2009
Cash	$ 21,000	$ 53,000
Short-term investments	32,000	15,000
Net receivables	117,000	127,000
Inventory	243,000	272,000
Prepaid expenses	18,000	4,000
Total assets	500,000	531,000
Total current liabilities	247,000	312,000
Long-term debt	27,000	134,000
Income from operations	191,000	160,000
Interest expense	39,000	45,000

E13-23A (*Learning Objectives 4: Analyzing profitability*) Compute four ratios that measure the ability to earn profits for Harmon Decor, Inc., whose comparative income statements follow:

Harmon Decor, Inc. Comparative Income Statements Years Ended December 31, 2010 and 2009		
	2010	2009
Net sales	$100,000	$90,000
Cost of goods sold	53,000	46,000
Gross profit	47,000	44,000
Selling and general expenses	20,000	18,000
Income from operations	27,000	26,000
Interest expense	3,000	2,000
Income before income tax	24,000	24,000
Income tax expense	8,000	7,000
Net income	$ 16,000	$17,000

Additional data:

	2010	2009	2008
Total assets	$104,000	$100,000	$83,000
Ordinary shareholders' equity	$ 72,000	$ 70,000	$69,000
Preference dividends	$ 3,000	$ 2,000	$ 1,000
Ordinary shares outstanding during the year	10,000	9,000	4,000

Did the company's operating performance improve or deteriorate during 2010?

E13-24A (*Learning Objectives 4: Evaluating a share as an investment*) Evaluate the ordinary share of Regal Distributing Company as an investment. Specifically, use the three ordinary share ratios to determine whether the ordinary share increased or decreased in attractiveness during the past year.

	2010	2009
Net income..	$ 83,000	$ 60,000
Dividends to ordinary shares.............................	22,000	23,000
Total shareholders' equity at year-end...............	300,000	510,000
(includes 90,000 ord. shares)		
Preference shares, 5%	80,000	80,000
Market price per ordinary share		
at year-end..	$ 24.50	$ 17.50

E13-25A (*Learning Objective 5: Using economic value added to measure corporate performance*) Two companies with different economic-value-added (EVA®) profiles are Barton Oil Pipeline Incorporated and Crompton Bank Limited. Adapted versions of the two companies' financial statements are presented here (in millions):

	Barton Oil Pipeline Inc.	Crompton Bank Limited
Balance sheet data:		
Total assets	$ 4,338	$14,000
Interest-bearing debt	$ 1,257	$ 13
All other liabilities...........................	2,675	2,605
Shareholders' equity........................	406	11,382
Total liabilities and equity...............	$ 4,338	$14,000
Income statement data:		
Total revenue	$11,007	$ 3,819
Interest expense...............................	76	7
Net income......................................	$ 180	$ 1,219

❙ Requirements

1. Before performing any calculations, which company do you think represents the better investment? Give your reason.
2. Compute the EVA® for each company and then decide which company's shares you would rather hold as an investment. Assume both companies' cost of capital is 8.5%.

(Group B)

E13-26B (*Learning Objective 1: Computing year-to-year changes in working capital*) What were the dollar amount of change and the percentage of each change in Ricardo Lodge's working capital during 2010 and 2009? Is this trend favorable or unfavorable?

	2010	2009	2008
Total current assets	$400,000	$300,000	$240,000
Total current liabilities	190,000	150,000	120,000

E13-27B (*Learning Objective 1: Performing horizontal analysis of an income statement*) Prepare a horizontal analysis of the comparative income statements of Fashion Music Co. Round percentage changes to the nearest one-tenth percent (three decimal places).

Fashion Music Co.
Comparative Income Statements
Years Ended December 31, 2010 and 2009

	2010	2009
Total revenue	$1,080,000	$919,000
Expenses:		
Cost of goods sold	$ 479,000	$400,450
Selling and general expenses	289,000	269,000
Interest expense	24,500	14,500
Income tax expense	106,500	86,850
Total expenses	899,000	770,800
Net income	$181,000	$148,200

E13-28B (*Learning Objective 1: Computing trend percentages*)   Compute trend percentages for Andover Valley Sales & Service's total revenue, and net income for the following five-year period, using year 0 as the base year. Round to the nearest full percent.

(in thousands)	Year 4	Year 3	Year 2	Year 1	Year 0
Total revenue	$1,433	$1,251	$1,067	$1,008	$1,022
Net income	120	112	81	69	83

Which grew faster during the period, total revenue or net income?

E13-29B (*Learning Objective 2: Performing vertical analysis of a balance sheet*)   Epsilon Golf Company has requested that you perform a vertical analysis of its balance sheet to determine the component percentages of its assets, liabilities, and shareholders' equity.

Epsilon Golf Company
Balance Sheet
December 31, 2010

Assets	
Total current assets	$ 45,000
Property, plant and equipment, net	210,000
Other assets	42,000
Total assets	$297,000
Liabilities	
Total current liabilities	$ 53,000
Long-term debt	111,000
Total liabilities	164,000
Shareholders' Equity	
Total shareholders' equity	133,000
Total liabilities and shareholders' equity	$297,000

E13-30B (*Learning Objective 3: Preparing a common-size income statement*)   Prepare a comparative common-size income statement for Fashion Music Co. using the 2010 and 2009 data of Exercise 13-27B and rounding to four decimal places.

■ **spreadsheet**

writing assignment ■

E13-31B (*Learning Objective 3: Preparing a common-size income statement*) Compare the year 2010 common-size income statement you performed earlier in E13-21B. How does this compare to Nokia vertical analysis in Exhibit 13-4? You may need to combine a few line items to make the common-size statements comparable.

Massachusetts Chowder Distributors, Inc.
Statement of Cash Flows
For the Current Year

Operating activities:		
Income from operations..		$ 77,000
Add (subtract) noncash items:		
Depreciation	$ 30,000	
Net increase in current assets other than cash	(61,000)	
Net decrease in current liabilities		
exclusive of short-term debt..........................	(22,000)	(53,000)
Net cash provided by operating activities.........		24,000
Investing activities:		
Sale of property, plant and equipment		126,000
Financing activities:		
Issuance of bonds payable	$ 99,000	
Payment of short-term debt	(166,000)	
Payment of long-term debt	(90,000)	
Payment of dividends...	(50,000)	
Net cash used for financing activities..............		(207,000)
Increase (decrease) in cash		$ (57,000)

■ spreadsheet

E13-32B (*Learning Objective 4: Computing five ratios*)   The financial statements of Advent News, Inc., include the following items:

	Current Year	Preceding Year
Balance sheet:		
Cash	$ 65,000	$ 91,000
Short-term investments	13,000	25,000
Net receivables	79,000	82,000
Inventory......................................	93,000	75,000
Prepaid expenses..........................	6,000	12,000
Total current assets	256,000	285,000
Total current liabilities.................	133,000	97,000
Income statement:		
Net credit sales	$494,000	
Cost of goods sold	277,000	

❚ Requirement

1. Compute the following ratios for the current year:

   a. Current ratio   **d.** Accounts receivable turnover
   b. Acid-test ratio   **e.** Receivables resident period
   c. Inventory turnover   **f.** Cash conversion cycle

(Round your answers to **a** through **d** to two decimal points. Round your answer to **e** and **f** to the nearest whole number.)

E13-33B (*Learning Objectives 4: Analyzing the ability to pay current liabilities*)   Jalbert
Furniture Company has requested that you determine whether the company's ability to pay its current liabilities and long-term debts improved or deteriorated during 2010. To answer this question,
compute the following ratios for 2010 and 2009. (Round your answers to two decimal places.)

a. Current ratio
b. Acid-test ratio

c. Debt ratio
d. Times-interest-earned ratio

Summarize the results of your analysis in a written report.

	2010	2009
Cash	$ 27,000	$ 47,000
Short-term investments	33,000	4,000
Net receivables	120,000	135,000
Inventory	238,000	271,000
Prepaid expenses	22,000	8,000
Total assets	590,000	510,000
Total current liabilities	187,000	332,000
Long-term debt	147,000	84,000
Income from operations	191,000	169,000
Interest expense	41,000	43,000

E13-34B (*Learning Objectives 4: Analyzing profitability*)   Compute four ratios that measure
the ability to earn profits for Jarvis Decor, Inc., whose comparative income statements follow:

Jarvis Decor, Inc.
Comparative Income Statements
Years Ended December 31, 2010 and 2009

	2010	2009
Net sales	$254,000	$217,000
Cost of goods sold	125,000	111,000
Gross profit	129,000	106,000
Selling and general expenses	50,000	46,000
Income from operations	79,000	60,000
Interest expense	7,000	6,000
Income before income tax	72,000	54,000
Income tax expense	25,000	19,000
Net income	$ 47,000	$ 35,000

Additional data:

	2010	2009	2008
Total assets	$249,000	$239,000	$227,000
Ordinary shareholders' equity	$106,000	$104,000	$102,000
Preference dividends	$ 17,000	$ 15,000	$ 13,000
Ordinary shares outstanding during the year	19,000	17,000	11,000

Did the company's operating performance improve or deteriorate during 2010?

E13-35B (*Learning Objectives 4: Evaluating a share as an investment*) Evaluate the ordinary share of Basic Distributing Company as an investment. Specifically, use the three ordinary share ratios to determine whether the ordinary share increased or decreased in attractiveness during the past year.

	2010	2009
Net income...	$ 91,000	$ 99,000
Dividends to ordinary shares..............................	28,000	13,000
Total shareholders' equity at year-end...............	565,000	515,000
(includes 80,000 ordinary shares)		
Preference shares, 6%	90,000	90,000
Market price per ordinary share		
at year-end...	$ 24.00	$ 25.16

E13-36B (*Learning Objective 5: Using economic value added to measure corporate performance*) Two companies with different economic-value-added (EVA®) profiles are Houle Oil Pipeline, Inc., and Johnson Bank Limited. Adapted versions of the two companies' financial statements are presented here (in millions):

	Houle Oil Pipeline, Inc.	Johnson Bank Limited
Balance sheet data:		
Total assets	$ 4,338	$14,451
Interest-bearing debt	$ 1,250	$ 5
All other liabilities.............................	2,900	2,585
Shareholders' equity.........................	188	11,861
Total liabilities and equity................	$ 4,338	$14,451
Income statement data:		
Total revenue	$10,991	$ 3,697
Interest expense................................	80	7
Net income...	$ 200	$ 1,197

▌Requirements

1. Before performing any calculations, which company do you think represents the better investment? Give your reason.
2. Compute the EVA® for each company and then decide which company's share you would rather hold as an investment. Assume both companies' cost of capital is 11.0%. (Round your EVA® calculation to the nearest whole number.)

Challenge Exercises

E13-37 *(Learning Objectives 2, 3, 4: Using ratio data to reconstruct a company's balance sheet)*   The following data (dollar amounts in millions) are taken from the financial statements of Floor 1 Industries, Inc.:

Total liabilities	$12,600
Pref. share	$ 0
Total current assets	$11,900
Accumulated depreciation	$ 1,700
Debt ratio	60%
Current ratio	1.70

❙ Requirement

1. Complete the following condensed balance sheet. Report amounts to the nearest million dollars.

	(In millions)
Current assets	☐
Property, plant and equipment ☐	
Less: Accumulated depreciation ☐	☐
Total assets	☐
Current liabilities	☐
Long-term liabilities	☐
Shareholders' equity	☐
Total liabilities and shareholders' equity	☐

E13-38 *(Learning Objectives 2, 3, 4: Using ratio data to reconstruct a company's income statement)*   The following data (dollar amounts in millions) are from the financial statements of County Corporation:

Average shareholders' equity	$3,400
Interest expense	$ 800
Preference shares	$ 0
Operating income as a percent of sales	20%
Rate of return on shareholders' equity	10%
Income tax rate	30%

I Requirement

1. Complete the following condensed income statement. Report amounts to the nearest million dollars.

Sales...	☐
Operating expense..................	☐
Operating income..................	☐
Interest expense......................	☐
Pretax income	☐
Income tax expense................	☐
Net income.............................	☐

Quiz

Use the Hialeah Bell Corporation financial statements that follow to answer questions 13–39 through 13–50.

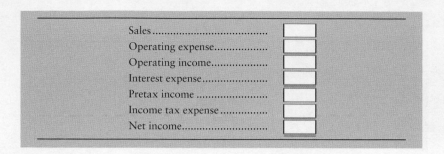

Hialeah Bell Corporation Consolidated Statements of Income (In millions, except per share amounts)			
	Year ended December 31,		
	2010	**2009**	**2008**
Net revenue...	$42,788	$35,299	$30,968
Cost of goods sold...	34,000	29,111	26,061
Gross profit	8,788	6,188	4,907
Operating expenses:			
Selling, general, and administrative......	3,341	3,000	2,581
Research, development, and			
engineering.....................................	574	556	542
Special charges...................................	—	—	502
Total operating expenses	3,915	3,556	3,625
Operating income...........................	4,873	2,632	1,282
Investment and other income (loss), net	170	212	(78)
Income before income taxes................	5,043	2,844	1,204
Income tax expense.....................................	1,100	912	472
Net income	$ 3,943	$ 1,932	$ 732
Earnings per ordinary share:			
Basic..	$ 1.33	$ 0.94	$ 0.42

Hialeah Bell Corporation
Consolidated Statements of Financial Position

(In millions)	December 31, 2010	2009
Assets		
Current assets:		
Cash and cash equivalents..................................	$ 4,301	$ 4,138
Short-term investments......................................	830	512
Accounts receivable, net	3,402	2,401
Inventories	427	410
Other..	1,638	1,213
Total current assets	10,598	8,674
Property, plant and equipment, net	1,517	932
Investments..	6,613	5,323
Other noncurrent assets.....................................	301	144
Total assets..	$19,029	$15,073
Liabilities and Shareholders' Equity		
Current liabilities:		
Accounts payable	$ 7,702	$ 6,002
Accrued and other	3,676	3,044
Total current liabilities....................................	11,378	9,046
Long-term debt...	301	302
Other noncurrent liabilities................................	1,701	1,167
Commitments and contingent liabilities (Note 7)......	—	—
Total liabilities	13,380	10,515
Shareholders' equity:		
Preference share and capital in excess of $0.02 par value; shares issued and outstanding: none	—	—
Ordinary share and capital in excess of $0.05 par value; shares authorized: 6,000; shares issued: 3,240 and 2,989, respectively...........	7,801	7,004
Treasury share, at cost; 175 and 124 shares, respectively..	(6,333)	(4,404)
Retained earnings...	4,321	2,054
Other comprehensive loss.................................	(104)	(50)
Other..	(36)	(46)
Total shareholders' equity..	5,649	4,558
Total liabilities and shareholders' equity	$19,029	$15,073

Q13-39 During 2010, Hialeah Bell's total assets

a. increased by $9,390 million.

b. increased by 26.2%.

c. both a and b.

d. increased by 20.8%.

Q13-40 Hialeah Bell's current ratio at year end 2010 is closest to

a. 1.2.

b. 9,390.

c. 20.8.

d. 0.9.

Q13-41 Hialeah Bell's acid-test ratio at year-end 2010 is closest to

a. $0.68.

b. $0.75.

c. $8,533 million.

d. 0.45.

Q13-42 What is the largest single item included in Hialeah Bell's debt ratio at December 31, 2010?

a. Cash and cash equivalents

b. Investments

c. Accounts payable

d. Share capital

Q13-43 Using the earliest year available as the base year, the trend percentage for Hialeah Bell's net revenue during 2010 was

a. 121%.

b. up by 21.2%.

c. up by $11,820 million.

d. 138%.

Q13-44 Hialeah Bell's common-size income statement for 2010 would report cost of goods sold as

a. 79.5%.

b. Up by 16.8%.

c. 130.5%.

d. $34,000 million.

Q13-45 Hialeah Bell's cash conversion cycle during 2010 was

a. 102.80 days

b. 44.31 days

c. 91.03 days

d. 100.95 days

Q13-46 Hialeah Bell's days' sales in average receivables during 2010 was

a. 29 days.

b. 117 days.

c. 21 days.

d. 25 days.

Q13-47 Hialeah Bell's long-term debt bears interest at 11%. During the year ended December 31, 2010, Bell's times-interest-earned ratio was

a. 137 times.

b. 144 times.

c. 147 times.

d. 150 times.

Q13-48 Hialeah Bell's trend of return on sales is

a. worrisome.

b. declining.

c. improving.

d. stuck at 20.8%.

Q13-49 How many shares of ordinary share did Hialeah Bell have outstanding, on average, during 2010? Hint: Compute earnings per share.

a. 2,947 million

b. 5,258 million

c. 5,244 million

d. 2,965 million

Q13-50 Book value per share of Hialeah Bell's ordinary share outstanding at December 31, 2010, was

a. $5,649.

b. $1.84.

c. $1.96.

d. $2.08.

Problems

All of the A and B problems can be found within MyAccountingLab, an online homework and practice environment. Your instructor may ask you to complete these problems using MyAccountingLab.

(Group A)

■ **spreadsheet**

P13-51A (*Learning Objectives 1, 4: Computing trend percentages, return on sales, and comparison with the industry*)   Net sales, net income, and total assets for Amble Shipping, Inc., for a five-year period follow:

(In thousands)	2010	2009	2008	2007	2006
Net sales..................	$902	$800	$492	$313	$303
Net income................	42	39	15	39	33
Total assets	305	268	256	221	203

I *Requirements*

1. Compute trend percentages for each item for 2007 through 2010. Use 2006 as the base year and round to the nearest percent.

2. Compute the rate of return on net sales for 2008 through 2010, rounding to three decimal places.

3. How does Amble Shipping's return on net sales compare with that of the industry? In the shipping industry, rates above 5% are considered good, and rates above 7% are outstanding.

P13-52A (*Learning Objectives 3, 4: Preparing common-size statements; analyzing profitability; making comparisons with the industry*) Top managers of McDonough Products, Inc., have asked for your help in comparing the company's profit performance and financial position with the average for the industry. The accountant has given you the company's income statement and balance sheet and also the following data for the industry:

writing assignment ■

■ **spreadsheet**

McDonough Products, Inc.
Income Statement Compared with Industry Average
Year Ended December 31, 2010

	McDonough	Industry Average
Net sales..................................	$700,000	100.0%
Cost of goods sold.................	490,000	57.3
Gross profit............................	210,000	42.7
Operating expenses	175,000	29.4
Operating income...................	35,000	13.3
Other expenses.......................	7,000	2.5
Net income	$ 28,000	10.8%

McDonough Products, Inc.
Balance Sheet Compared with Industry Average
December 31, 2010

	McDonough	Industry Average
Current assets...........................	$471,200	72.1%
PPE, net....................................	114,700	19.0
Intangible assets, net	21,080	4.8
Other assets.............................	13,020	4.1
Total	$620,000	100.0%
Current liabilities	$240,560	47.2%
Long-term liabilities	135,160	21.0
Shareholders' equity................	244,280	31.8
Total	$620,000	100.0%

I *Requirements*

1. Prepare a common-size income statement and balance sheet for McDonough Products. The first column of each statement should present McDonough Products' common-size statement, and the second column should show the industry averages.

2. For the profitability analysis, compute McDonough Products' (a) ratio of gross profit to net sales (b) ratio of operating income to net sales, and (c) ratio of net income to net sales. Compare these figures with the industry averages. Is McDonough Products' profit performance better or worse than the average for the industry?

3. For the analysis of financial position, compute McDonough Products' (a) ratios of current assets and current liabilities to total assets and (b) ratio of shareholders' equity to total assets. Compare these ratios with the industry averages. Is McDonough Products' financial position better or worse than the average for the industry?

P13-53A (*Learning Objective 4: Calculating cash conversion cycle*). You are analyzing the effectiveness of the trading operations of AVN Limited. Extracts of its financial statements are provided below.

AVN Limited
Selected information from financial statements

	2011	2010
Sales	$175,000	$140,000
Cost of sales	82,000	63,000
Receivables, net	24,000	18,000
Inventory	16,000	12,000
Payables	20,000	16,000

❙ Requirement

1. Calculate AVN's cash conversion cycle for 2011. What is your assessment of AVN's cash conversion cycle?

P13-54A (*Learning Objectives 4: Computing effects of business transactions on selected ratios*) Financial statement data of Greatland Engineering include the following items:

Cash	$ 25,000	Accounts payable	$101,000
Short-term investments	38,000	Accrued liabilities	37,000
Accounts receivable, net	82,000	Long-term notes payable	160,000
Inventories	149,000	Other long-term liabilities	37,000
Prepaid expenses	6,000	Net income	96,000
Total assets	674,000	Number of ordinary	
Short-term notes payable	41,000	shares outstanding	52,000

❙ Requirements

1. Compute Greatland's current ratio, debt ratio, and earnings per share. (Round all ratios to two decimal places.)
2. Compute the three ratios after evaluating the effect of each transaction that follows. Consider each transaction *separately*.
   a. Borrowed $135,000 on a long-term note payable.
   b. Issued 40,000 ordinary shares, receiving cash of $360,000.
   c. Paid short-term notes payable, $28,000.
   d. Purchased merchandise of $44,000 on account, debiting Inventory.
   e. Received cash on account, $16,000.

P13-55A (*Learning Objectives 4: Using ratios to evaluate a share investment*)   Comparative
financial statement data of Bloomfield Optical Mart follow:

Bloomfield Optical Mart Comparative Income Statements Years Ended December 31, 2010 and 2009		
	2010	2009
Net sales	$690,000	$590,000
Cost of goods sold	375,000	283,000
Gross profit	315,000	307,000
Operating expenses	126,000	141,000
Income from operations	189,000	166,000
Interest expense	36,000	50,000
Income before income tax	153,000	116,000
Income tax expense	40,000	53,000
Net income	$113,000	$ 63,000

Bloomfield Optical Mart Comparative Balance Sheets December 31, 2010 and 2009			
	2010	2009	2008*
Current assets:			
Cash	$ 38,000	$ 40,000	
Current receivables, net	217,000	149,000	$140,000
Inventories	298,000	285,000	181,000
Prepaid expenses	9,000	25,000	
Total current assets	562,000	499,000	
Property, plant and equipment, net	284,000	276,000	
Total assets	$846,000	$775,000	710,000
Total current liabilities	$281,000	$267,000	
Long-term liabilities	241,000	236,000	
Total liabilities	522,000	503,000	
Preference shareholders' equity, 5%, $10 par	70,000	70,000	
Ordinary shareholders' equity, no par	254,000	202,000	195,000
Total liabilities and shareholders' equity	$846,000	$775,000	

*Selected 2008 amounts.

Other information:
1. Market price of Bloomfield ordinary share: $82.20 at December 31, 2010, and $52.96 at
   December 31, 2009.
2. Ordinary shares outstanding: 20,000 during 2010 and 18,000 during 2009.
3. All sales on credit.

❙ *Requirements*

1. Compute the following ratios for 2010 and 2009:
   a. Current ratio
   b. Inventory turnover
   c. Times-interest-earned ratio
   d. Return on assets
   e. Return on common shareholders' equity
   f. Earnings per share of share capital
   g. Price/earnings ratio
2. Decide whether (a) Bloomfield's financial position improved or deteriorated during 2010 and (b) the investment attractiveness of Bloomfield's ordinary shares appears to have increased or decreased.
3. How will what you learned in this problem help you evaluate an investment?

writing assignment ■

P13-56A *(Learning Objectives 4,5: Using ratios to decide between two share investments; measuring economic value added)* Assume that you are considering purchasing shares as an investment. You have narrowed the choice to DVR.com and Express Shops and have assembled the following data.

Selected income statement data for the current year:

	DVR	Express
Net sales (all on credit).................	$602,000	$517,000
Cost of goods sold.........................	449,000	382,000
Income from operations	88,000	73,000
Interest expense.............................	—	16,000
Net income......................................	61,000	39,000

Selected balance sheet and market price data at *end* of current year:

	DVR	Express
Current assets:		
Cash	$ 22,000	$ 38,000
Short-term investments	10,000	14,000
Current receivables, net	182,000	167,000
Inventories..	210,000	181,000
Prepaid expenses..	21,000	8,000
Total current assets	445,000	408,000
Total assets...	981,000	935,000
Total current liabilities	362,000	333,000
Total liabilities	673,000	700,000
Preference shares, 5%, $150 par............................		30,000
Ordinary shares, $1 par (100,000 shares)...............	100,000	
$5 par (15,000 shares).................		75,000
Total shareholders' equity..	308,000	235,000
Market price per ordinary	$ 6.10	$ 55.00

Selected balance sheet data at *beginning* of current year:

	DVR	Express
Balance sheet:		
Current receivables, net...	$144,000	$195,000
Inventories	205,000	199,000
Total assets..	853,000	908,000
Long-term debt	–	299,000
Preference share, 5%, $150 par..................................		30,000
Ordinary share, $1 par (100,000 shares)	100,000	
$5 par (15,000 shares)		75,000
Total shareholders' equity	260,000	221,000

Your strategy is to invest in companies that have low price/earnings ratios but appear to be in good shape financially. Assume that you have analyzed all other factors and that your decision depends on the results of ratio analysis.

I Requirements

1. Compute the following ratios for both companies for the current year and decide which company's shares better fits your investment strategy.
   a. Acid-test ratio
   b. Inventory turnover
   c. Receivables resident period
   d. Debt ratio
   e. Times-interest-earned ratio
   f. Return on ordinary shareholders' equity
   g. Earnings per ordinary share
   h. Price/earnings ratio
2. Compute each company's economic-value-added (EVA®) measure and determine whether the companies' EVA®s confirm or alter your investment decision. Each company's cost of capital is 10%.

(Group B)

P13-57B (*Learning Objectives 1, 4: Computing trend percentages, return on sales equity, and comparison with the industry*)   Net sales, net income, and total assets for Amaze Shipping, Inc., for a five-year period follow:

■ **spreadsheet**

(In thousands)	2010	2009	2008	2007	2006
Net sales..	$616	$503	$358	$309	$300
Net income...	33	30	45	34	27
Total assets..	300	268	255	231	204

I Requirements

1. Compute trend percentages for each item for 2007 through 2010. Use 2006 as the base year and round to the nearest percent.
2. Compute the rate of return on net sales for 2008 through 2010, rounding to three decimal places.
3. How does Amaze Shipping's return on net sales compare with that of the industry? In the shipping industry, rates above 5% are considered good, and rates above 7% are outstanding.

writing assignment ■

■ spreadsheet

P13-58B (*Learning Objectives 3, 4: Preparing common-size statements; analyzing profitability; making comparisons with the industry*)   Top managers of Walsh Products, Inc., have asked for your help in comparing the company's profit performance and financial position with the average for the industry. The accountant has given you the company's income statement and balance sheet and also the following data for the industry:

Walsh Products, Inc.
Income Statement Compared with Industry Average
Year Ended December 31, 2010

	Walsh	Industry Average
Net sales..................................	$900,000	100.0%
Cost of goods sold.................	648,000	57.3
Gross profit............................	252,000	42.7
Operating expenses	216,000	29.4
Operating income...................	36,000	13.3
Other expenses.......................	13,500	2.5
Net income	$ 22,500	10.8%

Walsh Products, Inc.
Balance Sheet Compared with Industry Average
December 31, 2010

	Walsh	Industry Average
Current assets............................	$408,100	72.1%
PPE, net.....................................	99,640	19.0
Intangible assets, net	20,140	4.8
Other assets...............................	2,120	4.1
Total	$530,000	100.0%
Current liabilities	$205,640	47.2%
Long-term liabilities	112,360	21.0
Shareholders' equity.................	212,000	31.8
Total	$530,000	100.0%

❙ Requirements

1. Prepare a common-size income statement and balance sheet for Walsh Products. The first column of each statement should present Walsh Products' common-size statement, and the second column should show the industry averages.
2. For the profitability analysis, compute Walsh Products' (a) ratio of gross profit to net sales (b) ratio of operating income to net sales, and (c) ratio of net income to net sales. Compare these figures with the industry averages. Is Walsh Products' profit performance better or worse than the average for the industry?
3. For the analysis of financial position, compute Walsh Products' (a) ratios of current assets and current liabilities to total assets and (b) ratio of shareholders' equity to total assets. Compare these ratios with the industry averages. Is Walsh Products' financial position better or worse than the average for the industry?

P13-59B *(Learning Objective 4: Calculating cash conversion cycle).* You are analyzing the effectiveness of the trading operations of CMI Limited. Extracts of its financial statements are provided below.

CMI Limited Selected information from financial statements		
	2012	**2011**
Sales...	$1,542,000	$1,356,000
Cost of sales.....................................	850,000	720,000
Receivables, net................................	104,000	107,000
Inventory...	89,000	75,000
Payables	93,000	69,000

❚ Requirement

1. Calculate CMI's cash conversion cycle for 2012. What is your assessment of CMI's cash conversion cycle?

P13-60B *(Learning Objectives 4: Computing effects of business transactions on selected ratios)*   Financial statement data of Trinton Engineering include the following items:

Cash	$ 26,000	Accounts payable	$106,000
Short-term investments..............	34,000	Accrued liabilities.....................	34,000
Accounts receivable, net	87,000	Long-term notes payable...........	165,000
Inventories	145,000	Other long-term liabilities	32,000
Prepaid expenses	8,000	Net income................................	98,000
Total assets	677,000	Number of ordinary	
Short-term notes payable...........	48,000	shares outstanding	47,000

❚ Requirements

1. Compute Trinton's current ratio, debt ratio, and earnings per share. (Round all ratios to two decimal places.)
2. Compute the three ratios after evaluating the effect of each transaction that follows. Consider each transaction *separately*.
   a. Borrowed $115,000 on a long-term note payable.
   b. Issued 20,000 shares of ordinary shares, receiving cash of $365,000.
   c. Paid short-term notes payable, $26,000.
   d. Purchased merchandise of $45,000 on account, debiting Inventory.
   e. Received cash on account, $19,000.

P13-61B (*Learning Objectives 4: Using ratios to evaluate a share investment*) Comparative financial statement data of Rourke Optical Mart follow:

Rourke Optical Mart Comparative Income Statements Years Ended December 31, 2010 and 2009		
	2010	2009
Net sales...	$688,000	$593,000
Cost of goods sold...........................	376,000	283,000
Gross profit......................................	312,000	310,000
Operating expenses	131,000	144,000
Income from operations	181,000	166,000
Interest expense...............................	31,000	50,000
Income before income tax	150,000	116,000
Income tax expense.........................	42,000	47,000
Net income	$108,000	$ 69,000

Rourke Optical Mart Comparative Balance Sheets December 31, 2010 and 2009			
	2010	2009	2008*
Current assets:			
Cash	$ 32,000	$ 36,000	
Current receivables, net	211,000	154,000	$134,000
Inventories...	291,000	288,000	188,000
Prepaid expenses...	6,000	30,000	
Total current assets	540,000	508,000	
Property, plant and equipment, net	288,000	278,000	
Total assets...	$828,000	$786,000	704,000
Total current liabilities	$280,000	$293,000	
Long-term liabilities	240,000	231,000	
Total liabilities	520,000	524,000	
Preference shareholders' equity, 3%, $5 par..................	65,000	65,000	
Ordinary shareholders' equity, no par..........................	243,000	197,000	198,000
Total liabilities and shareholders' equity	$828,000	$786,000	

*Selected 2008 amounts.

Other information:
1. Market price of Rourke ordinary share: $78.12 at December 31, 2010, and $59.10 at December 31, 2009.
2. Ordinary shares outstanding: 19,000 during 2010 and 17,000 during 2009.
3. All sales on credit.

I *Requirements*

1. Compute the following ratios for 2010 and 2009:
   a. Current ratio
   b. Inventory turnover
   c. Times-interest-earned ratio
   d. Return on ordinary shareholders' equity
   e. Earnings per ordinary share
   f. Price/earnings ratio

2. Decide whether (a) Rourke's financial position improved or deteriorated during 2010 and (b) the investment attractiveness of Rourke's ordinary shares appears to have increased or decreased.

3. How will what you learned in this problem help you evaluate an investment?

P13-62B *(Learning Objectives 4, 5: Using ratios to decide between two share investments; measuring economic value added)*   Assume that you are considering purchasing shares as an investment. You have narrowed the choice to CDROM.com and E-shop Stores and have assembled the following data.   **writing assignment ■**

Selected income statement data for current year:

	CDROM	E-Shop
Net sales (all on credit).................	$597,000	$516,000
Cost of goods sold........................	455,000	388,000
Income from operations	89,000	70,000
Interest expense...........................	—	13,000
Net income	68,000	39,000

Selected balance sheet and market price data at the *end* of the current year:

	CDROM	E-Shop
Current assets:		
Cash	$ 24,000	$ 41,000
Short-term investments	5,000	15,000
Current receivables, net	185,000	165,000
Inventories...	219,000	187,000
Prepaid expenses..	21,000	11,000
Total current assets	454,000	419,000
Total assets...	978,000	928,000
Total current liabilities	363,000	332,000
Total liabilities	663,000	693,000
Preference shares, 6%, $150 par.........................		30,000
Ordinary shares, $1 par (100,000 shares)..............	100,000	
$5 par (10,000 shares).................		50,000
Total shareholders' equity	315,000	235,000
Market price per ordinary share...........................	$ 8.84	$ 70.68

Selected balance sheet data at the *beginning* of the current year:

	CDROM	E-Shop
Balance sheet:		
Current receivables, net...	$143,000	$190,000
Inventories	202,000	195,000
Total assets...	843,000	914,000
Long-term debt	—	300,000
Preference share, 6%, $150 par..............................		30,000
Ordinary share, $1 par (100,000 shares)................	100,000	
$5 par (10,000 shares).................		50,000
Total shareholders' equity......................................	259,000	220,000

Your strategy is to invest in companies that have low price/earnings ratios but appear to be in good shape financially. Assume that you have analyzed all other factors and that your decision depends on the results of ratio analysis.

Requirements

1. Compute the following ratios for both companies for the current year and decide which company's shares better fits your investment strategy.
   a. Acid-test ratio
   b. Inventory turnover
   c. Receivables resident period
   d. Debt ratio
   e. Times-interest-earned ratio
   f. Return on ordinary shareholders' equity
   g. Earnings per share of ordinary share
   h. Price/earnings ratio

2. Compute each company's economic-value-added (EVA®) measure and determine whether the companies' EVA®s confirm or alter your investment decision. Each company's cost of capital is 12%.

APPLY YOUR KNOWLEDGE

Decision Cases

Case 1. (*Learning Objective 5: Assessing the effects of transactions on a company*) Suppose **AOL Time Warner, Inc.**, is having a bad year in 2014, as the company has incurred a $4.9 billion net loss. The loss has pushed most of the return measures into the negative column and the current ratio dropped below 1.0. The company's debt ratio is still only 0.27. Assume top management of AOL Time Warner is pondering ways to improve the company's ratios. In particular, management is considering the following transactions:

1. Sell off the cable television segment of the business for $30 million (receiving half in cash and half in the form of a long-term note receivable). Book value of the cable television business is $27 million.
2. Borrow $100 million on long-term debt.
3. Purchase treasury share for $500 million cash.
4. Write off one-fourth of goodwill carried on the books at $128 million.
5. Sell advertising at the normal gross profit of 60%. The advertisements run immediately.
6. Purchase trademarks from **NBC**, paying $20 million cash and signing a one-year note payable for $80 million.

❙ Requirements

1. Top management wants to know the effects of these transactions (increase, decrease, or no effect) on the following ratios of AOL Time Warner:
   a. Current ratio
   b. Debt ratio
   c. Times-interest-earned ratio (measured as [net income + interest expense]/interest expense)
   d. Return on equity
   e. Book value per ordinary share
2. Some of these transactions have an immediate positive effect on the company's financial condition. Some are definitely negative. Others have an effect that cannot be judged as clearly positive or negative. Evaluate each transaction's effect as positive, negative, or unclear. (Challenge)

writing assignment ■

Case 2. (*Learning Objective 4: Analyzing the effects of an accounting difference on the ratios*) Assume that you are a financial analyst. You are trying to compare the financial statements of **CNH Global**, an international company that uses international financial reporting standards (IFRS) to those of **Caterpillar, Inc.**, which uses US GAAP. Caterpillar, Inc., uses the last-in, first-out (LIFO) method to account for its inventories. IFRS does not permit CNH Global to use LIFO. Analyze the effect of this difference in accounting method on the two companies' ratio values. For each ratio discussed in this chapter, indicate which company will have the higher (and the lower) ratio value. Also identify those ratios that are unaffected by the FIFO/LIFO difference. Ignore the effects of income taxes, and assume inventory costs are increasing. Then, based on your analysis of the ratios, summarize your conclusions as to which company looks better overall.

writing assignment ■

Case 3. (*Learning Objectives 2, 4: Identifying action to cut losses and establish profitability*) Suppose you manage Outward Bound, Inc., a Vermont sporting goods store that lost money during the past year. To turn the business around, you must analyze the company and industry data for the current year to learn what is wrong. The company's data follow:

Outward Bound, Inc.
Common-Size Balance Sheet Data

	Outward Bound	Industry Average
Cash and short-term investments	3.0%	6.8%
Trade receivables, net	15.2	11.0
Inventory	64.2	60.5
Prepaid expenses	1.0	0.0
Total current assets	83.4%	78.3%
Fixed assets, net	12.6	15.2
Other assets	4.0	6.5
Total assets	100.0%	100.0%
Notes payable, short-term, 12%	17.1%	14.0%
Accounts payable	21.1	25.1
Accrued liabilities	7.8	7.9
Total current liabilities	46.0	47.0
Long-term debt, 11%	19.7	16.4
Total liabilities	65.7	63.4
Ord. shareholders' equity	34.3	36.6
Total liabilities and shareholders' equity	100.0%	100.0%

Outward Bound, Inc.
Common-Size Income Statement Data

	Outward Bound	Industry Average
Net sales	100.0%	100.0%
Cost of sales	(68.2)	(64.8)
Gross profit	31.8	35.2
Operating expense	(37.1)	(32.3)
Operating income (loss)	(5.3)	2.9
Interest expense	(5.8)	(1.3)
Other revenue	1.1	0.3
Income (loss) before income tax	(10.0)	1.9
Income tax (expense) saving	4.4	(0.8)
Net income (loss)	(5.6)%	1.1%

❙ Requirement

1. On the basis of your analysis of these figures, suggest four courses of action Outward Bound might take to reduce its losses and establish profitable operations. Give your reason for each suggestion. (Challenge)

Ethical Issue

Turnberry Golf Corporation's long-term debt agreements make certain demands on the business. For example, Turnberry may not purchase treasury share in excess of the balance of retained earnings. Also, long-term debt may not exceed shareholders' equity, and the current ratio may not fall below 1.50. If Turnberry fails to meet any of these requirements, the company's lenders have the authority to take over management of the company.

Changes in consumer demand have made it hard for Turnberry to attract customers. Current liabilities have mounted faster than current assets, causing the current ratio to fall to 1.47. Before releasing financial statements, Turnberry's management is scrambling to improve the current ratio. The controller points out that the company owns an investment that is currently classified as long-term. The investment can be classified as either long-term or short-term, depending on management's intention. By deciding to convert an investment to cash within one year, Turnberry can classify the investment as short-term—a current asset. On the controller's recommendation, Turnberry's board of directors votes to reclassify long-term investments as short-term.

writing assignment ■

❙ Requirements

1. What is the accounting issue in this case? What ethical decision needs to be made?
2. Who are the stakeholders?
3. Analyze the potential impact on the stakeholders from the following standpoints: (a) economic, (b) legal, and (c) ethical.
4. Shortly after the financial statements are released, sales improve; so, too, does the current ratio. As a result, Turnberry's management decides not to sell the investments it had reclassified as short term. Accordingly, the company reclassifies the investments as long term. Has management acted unethically? Give the reasoning underlying your answer.

writing assignment ■

Focus on Financials: ■ Nokia Corporation

Refer to **Nokia's** consolidated financial statements in Appendix A at the end of this book.

❙ Requirements

Use the consolidated financial statements and the data in Nokia's annual report (Appendix A at the end of the book) to evaluate the company's comparative performance for 2008 versus 2007.

1. Does the company appear to be improving or declining in the following dimensions?
   a. The ability to pay its current liabilities
   b. The ability to sell inventory and collect receivables (2006 Inventory: 1,554 million; 2006 Accounts Receivables: 5,888 million)
   c. The ability to pay long-term debts
   d. Profitability
   e. Cash flows from operations
   f. The potential of the company's shares as a long-term investment (Challenge) (Share price at 31st December 2007: $38.39, 31st December 2008: $15.60)
2. What is your opinion of the company's outlook for the future? Would you buy the company's share as an investment? Why or why not? (Challenge)

writing assignment ■

Group Projects

Project 1. Select an industry you are interested in, and use the leading company in that industry as the benchmark. Then select two other companies in the same industry. For each category of ratios in the Decision Guidelines feature on pages 812 and 813, compute at least two ratios for all three companies. Write a two-page report that compares the two companies with the benchmark company.

writing assignment ■

Project 2. Select a company and obtain its financial statements. Convert the income statement and the balance sheet to common size and compare the company you selected to the industry average. Risk Management Association's *Annual Statement Studies*, Dun & Bradstreet's *Industry Norms & Key Business Ratios*, and Prentice Hall's *Almanac of Business and Industrial Financial Ratios* by Leo Troy, publish common-size statements for most industries.

For online homework, exercises, and problems that provide you with immediate feedback, please visit www.myaccountinglab.com.

Quick Check Answers

1. *b* ($1,820/$1,730)
2. *a* ($1,820/$17,700)
3. *d* ($2,691 − $1,124)/$1,124 = 139.4%
4. *c* ($1,780/$26,060)
5. *c*
6. *c* $\left[\dfrac{\$3,300}{(\$140 + \$120)/2}\right]$ = 25.4 ≈ 25 times
7. *a* [($690 + $780)/ $2,374 = 0.62]
8. *c* $\left[\dfrac{\$780 + \$840/2}{\$17,700/365}\right]$ = 16.9 ≈ 17 days
9. *c* (Debt ratio is ($26,060 − $13,291)/$26,060 = 0.49. This debt ratio is lower than the average for most companies, given in the chapter as 0.64.)
10. *d* ($2,691/$17,700 = 0.152)
11. *b* $\left[\dfrac{\$2,691}{(\$13,291 + \$10,615)/2}\right]$ = 0.225
12. *c* ($30/$2.69)
13. *c* ($0.50/$30)
14. *a* [$2,691 + $370 − ($305 + $9,500 + $10,615) × 0.05] = $2,040

Appendix A

2 0 0 8

NOKIA CORPORATION

ANNUAL REPORT

Consolidated profit and loss accounts, IFRS

Financial year ended December 31	Notes	2008 EURm	2007 EURm	2006 EURm
Net sales		**50 710**	51 058	41 121
Cost of sales		−33 337	−33 781	−27 742
Gross profit		**17 373**	17 277	13 379
Research and development expenses		−5 968	−5 636	−3 897
Selling and marketing expenses		−4 380	−4 379	−3 314
Administrative and general expenses		−1 284	−1 165	−666
Other income	6	420	2 312	522
Other expenses	6, 7	−1 195	−424	−536
Operating profit	2–9, 22	**4 966**	7 985	5 488
Share of results of associated companies	14, 31	6	44	28
Financial income and expenses	10	−2	239	207
Profit before tax		**4 970**	8 268	5 723
Tax	11	−1 081	−1 522	−1 357
Profit before minority interests		**3 889**	6 746	4 366
Minority interests		99	459	−60
Profit attributable to equity holders of the parent		**3 988**	7 205	4 306

Earnings per share (for profit attributable to the equity holders of the parent)	28	2008 EUR	2007 EUR	2006 EUR
Basic		**1.07**	1.85	1.06
Diluted		**1.05**	1.83	1.05

Average number of shares (1 000 shares)	28	2008	2007	2006
Basic		3 743 622	3 885 408	4 062 833
Diluted		3 780 363	3 932 008	4 086 529

See Notes to consolidated financial statements.

Consolidated balance sheets, IFRS

December 31	Notes	2008 EURm	2007 EURm
ASSETS			
Non-current assets			
Capitalized development costs	12	244	378
Goodwill	12	6 257	1 384
Other intangible assets	12	3 913	2 358
Property, plant and equipment	13	2 090	1 912
Investments in associated companies	14	96	325
Available-for-sale investments	15	512	341
Deferred tax assets	24	1 963	1 553
Long-term loans receivable	16, 35	27	10
Other non-current assets		10	44
		15 112	8 305
Current assets			
Inventories	17, 19	2 533	2 876
Accounts receivable, net of allowances for doubtful accounts (2008: EUR 415 million, 2007: EUR 332 million)	19, 35	9 444	11 200
Prepaid expenses and accrued income	18	4 538	3 070
Current portion of long-term loans receivable	35	101	156
Other financial assets	35	1 034	239
Available-for-sale investments, liquid assets	15, 35	1 272	4 903
Available-for-sale investments, cash equivalents	15, 32, 35	3 842	4 725
Bank and cash	32, 35	1 706	2 125
		24 470	29 294
Total assets		39 582	37 599
SHAREHOLDERS' EQUITY AND LIABILITIES			
Capital and reserves attributable to equity holders of the parent			
Share capital	21	246	246
Share issue premium		442	644
Treasury shares, at cost		−1 881	−3 146
Translation differences		341	−163
Fair value and other reserves	20	62	23
Reserve for invested non-restricted equity		3 306	3 299
Retained earnings		11 692	13 870
		14 208	14 773
Minority interests		2 302	2 565
Total equity		16 510	17 338
Non-current liabilities			
Long-term interest-bearing liabilities	23, 35	861	203
Deferred tax liabilities	24	1 787	963
Other long-term liabilities		69	119
		2 717	1 285
Current liabilities			
Current portion of long-term loans	35	13	173
Short-term borrowings	35	3 578	714
Other financial liabilities	26, 35	924	184
Accounts payable	35	5 225	7 074
Accrued expenses	25	7 023	7 114
Provisions	27	3 592	3 717
		20 355	18 976
Total shareholders' equity and liabilities		39 582	37 599

Consolidated cash flow statements, IFRS

Financial year ended December 31	Notes	2008 EURm	2007 EURm	2006 EURm
Cash flow from operating activities				
Profit attributable to equity holders of the parent		3 988	7 205	4 306
Adjustments, total	32	3 469	1 269	1 857
Change in net working capital	32	-2 546	605	-793
Cash generated from operations		4 911	9 079	5 370
Interest received		416	362	235
Interest paid		-155	-59	-18
Other financial income and expenses, net received		-195	-43	54
Income taxes paid, net received		-1 780	-1 457	-1 163
Net cash from operating activities		3 197	7 882	4 478
Cash flow from investing activities				
Acquisition of Group companies, net of acquired cash		-5 962	253	-517
Purchase of current available-for-sale investments, liquid assets		-669	-4 798	-3 219
Purchase of non-current available-for-sale investments		-121	-126	-88
Purchase of shares in associated companies		-24	-25	-15
Additions to capitalized development costs		-131	-157	-127
Long-term loans made to customers		—	-261	-11
Proceeds from repayment and sale of long-term loans receivable		129	163	56
Recovery of impaired long-term loans made to customers		—	—	276
Proceeds from (+) / payment of (–) other long-term receivables		-1	5	-3
Proceeds from (+) / payment of (–) short-term loans receivable		-15	-119	199
Capital expenditures		-889	-715	-650
Proceeds from disposal of shares in associated companies		3	6	1
Proceeds from disposal of businesses		41	—	—
Proceeds from maturities and sale of current available-for-sale investments, liquid assets		4 664	4 930	5 058
Proceeds from sale of non-current available-for-sale investments		10	50	17
Proceeds from sale of fixed assets		54	72	29
Dividends received		6	12	—
Net cash from (+)/used in (–) investing activities		-2 905	-710	1 006
Cash flow from financing activities				
Proceeds from stock option exercises		53	987	46
Purchase of treasury shares		-3 121	-3 819	-3 371
Proceeds from long-term borrowings		714	115	56
Repayment of long-term borrowings		-34	-16	-7
Proceeds from (+) / repayment of (–) short-term borrowings		2 891	661	-137
Dividends paid		-2 048	-1 760	-1 553
Net cash used in financing activities		-1 545	-3 832	-4 966
Foreign exchange adjustment		-49	-15	-51
Net increase (+) / decrease (–) in cash and cash equivalents		-1 302	3 325	467
Cash and cash equivalents at beginning of period		6 850	3 525	3 058
Cash and cash equivalents at end of period		5 548	6 850	3 525
Cash and cash equivalents comprise of:				
Bank and cash		1 706	2 125	1 479
Current available-for-sale investments, cash equivalents	15, 35	3 842	4 725	2 046
		5 548	6 850	3 525

Consolidated statements of changes in shareholders' equity, IFRS (continued)

EURm	Number of shares (1 000's)	Share capital	Share issue premium	Treasury shares	Translation differences	Fair value and other reserves	Reserve for invested non-restricted equity	Retained earnings	Before minority interests	Minority interests	Total
Balance at December 31, 2007	3 845 950	246	644	-3 146	-163	23	3 299	13 870	14 773	2 565	17 338
Tax benefit on stock options exercised			4						4		4
Excess tax benefit on share-based compensation			-121						-121		-121
Translation differences					595				595	—	595
Net investment hedge losses, net of tax					-91				-91		-91
Cash flow hedges, net of tax						42			42		42
Available-for-sale investments, net of tax						-3			-3		-3
Other increase, net								46	46		46
Profit								3 988	3 988	-99	3 889
Total recognized income and expense	—		-117	—	504	39	—	4 034	4 460	-99	4 361
Stock options exercised	3 547							51	51		51
Stock options exercised related to acquisitions			1						1		1
Share-based compensation			74						74		74
Settlement of performance shares	5 622		-179	154				-44	-69		-69
Acquisition of treasury shares	-157 390			-3 123					-3 123		-3 123
Reissuance of treasury shares	143			2					2		2
Cancellation of treasury shares				4 232				-4 232	—		—
Dividend								-1 992	-1 992	-35	-2 027
Acquisitions and other changes in minority interests									—	-129	-129
Vested portion of share-based payment awards related to acquisitions			19						19		19
Acquisition of Symbian								12	12		12
Total of other equity movements	—		-85	1 265	—	—	7	-6 212	-5 025	-164	-5 189
Balance at December 31, 2008	3 697 872	246	442	-1 881	341	62	3 306	11 692	14 208	2 302	16 510

Notes to the consolidated financial statements

1. Accounting principles

Basis of presentation

The consolidated financial statements of Nokia Corporation ("Nokia" or "the Group"), a Finnish public limited liability company with domicile in Helsinki, in the Republic of Finland, are prepared in accordance with International Financial Reporting Standards as issued by the International Accounting Standards Board ("IASB") and in conformity with IFRS as adopted by the European Union (collectively "IFRS"). The consolidated financial statements are presented in millions of euros ("EURm"), except as noted, and are prepared under the historical cost convention, except as disclosed in the accounting policies below. The notes to the consolidated financial statements also conform to Finnish Accounting legislation. On March 5, 2009, Nokia's Board of Directors authorized the financial statements for issuance and filing.

As described in Note 8 the Group completed the acquisition of all of the outstanding equity of NAVTEQ Corporation ("NAVTEQ") on July 10, 2008 and a transaction to form Nokia Siemens Networks on April 1, 2007. The NAVTEQ and the Nokia Siemens Networks business combinations have had a material impact on the consolidated financial statements and associated notes.

Adoption of pronouncements under IFRS

In the current year, the Group has adopted all of the new and revised standards, amendments and interpretations to existing standards issued by the IASB that are relevant to its operations and effective for accounting periods commencing on or after January 1, 2008.

» IFRS 8, Operating Segments requires the segment information to be presented on the same basis as that used for internal reporting purposes. Under IFRS 8, segments are components of the entity that are regularly reviewed by the chief operating decision-maker in order to allocate resources to a segment and to evaluate its performance.

» IFRIC 11, IFRS 2–Group and Treasury Share Transactions clarifies how IFRS 2 should be applied to share-based payment arrangements involving treasury shares, and arrangements involving grant of the entity's own equity instruments or equity instruments of another entity within the same group.

» IFRIC 14 and IAS 19, The Limit on a Defined benefit Asset, Minimum Funding Requirements and their Interaction addresses when refunds or reductions in future contributions should be regarded as available when measuring a pension asset and how a minimum funding requirement might affect the availability of reductions in future contributions.

» IAS 39 and IFRS 7 (Amendments), Reclassification of Financial Instruments allow an entity to reclassify non-derivative financial assets out of the fair value through profit or loss and available-for-sale categories in particular circumstances and require additional disclosures for the reclassifications.

The adoption of each of the above mentioned standards did not have a material impact to the Group's balance sheet, profit and loss or cash flows.

Principles of consolidation

The consolidated financial statements include the accounts of Nokia's parent company ("Parent Company"), and each of those companies over which the Group exercises control. Control over an entity is presumed to exist when the Group owns, directly or indirectly through subsidiaries, over 50% of the voting rights of the entity, the Group has the power to govern the operating and financial policies of the entity through agreement or the Group has the power to appoint or remove the majority of the members of the board of the entity.

The Group's share of profits and losses of associated companies is included in the consolidated profit and loss account in accordance with the equity method of accounting. An associated company is an entity over which the Group exercises significant influence. Significant influence is generally presumed to exist when the Group owns, directly or indirectly through subsidiaries, over 20% of the voting rights of the company.

All inter-company transactions are eliminated as part of the consolidation process. Minority interests are presented separately as a component of net profit and they are shown as a component of shareholders' equity in the consolidated balance sheet.

Profits realized in connection with the sale of fixed assets between the Group and associated companies are eliminated in proportion to share ownership. Such profits are deducted from the Group's equity and fixed assets and released in the Group accounts over the same period as depreciation is charged.

The companies acquired during the financial periods presented have been consolidated from the date on which control of the net assets and operations was transferred to the Group. Similarly the result of a Group company divested during an accounting period is included in the Group accounts only to the date of disposal.

Business combinations

The purchase method of accounting is used to account for acquisitions of separate entities or businesses by the Group. The cost of an acquisition is measured as the aggregate of the fair values at the date of exchange of the assets given, liabilities incurred, equity instruments issued and costs directly attributable to the acquisition. Identifiable assets, liabilities and contingent liabilities acquired or assumed by the Group are measured separately at their fair value as of the acquisition date. The excess of the cost of the acquisition over the Group's interest in the fair value of the identifiable net assets acquired is recorded as goodwill.

Assessment of the recoverability of long-lived and intangible assets and goodwill

For the purposes of impairment testing, goodwill is allocated to cash-generating units that are expected to benefit from the synergies of the acquisition in which the goodwill arose.

The Group assesses the carrying value of goodwill annually or more frequently if events or changes in circumstances indicate that such carrying value may not be recoverable. The Group assesses the carrying value of identifiable intangible assets and long-lived assets if events or changes in circumstances indicate that such carrying value may not be recoverable. Factors that trigger an impairment review include underperformance relative to historical or projected future results, significant changes in the manner of the use of the acquired assets or the strategy for the overall business and significant negative industry or economic trends.

The Group conducts its impairment testing by determining the recoverable amount for the asset or cash-generating unit. The recoverable amount of an asset or a cash-generating unit is the higher of its fair value less costs to sell and its value in use. The recoverable amount is then compared to its carrying amount and an impairment loss is recognized if the recoverable amount is less than the carrying amount. Impairment losses are recognized immediately in the profit and loss account.

Foreign currency translation

Functional and presentation currency

The financial statements of all Group entities are measured using the currency of the primary economic environment in which the entity operates (functional currency). The consolidated financial statements are presented in Euro, which is the functional and presentation currency of the Parent Company.

Transactions in foreign currencies

Transactions in foreign currencies are recorded at the rates of exchange prevailing at the dates of the individual transactions. For practical reasons, a rate that approximates the actual rate at the date of the transaction is often used. At the end of the accounting period, the unsettled balances on foreign currency receivables and liabilities are valued at the rates of exchange prevailing at the year-end. Foreign exchange gains and losses arising from balance sheet items, as well as fair value changes in the related hedging instruments, are reported in Financial Income and Expenses.

Foreign Group companies

In the consolidated accounts all income and expenses of foreign subsidiaries are translated into Euro at the average foreign exchange rates for the accounting period. All assets and liabilities of foreign Group companies are translated into Euro at the year-end foreign exchange rates with the exception of goodwill arising on the acquisition of foreign companies prior to the adoption of IAS 21 (revised 2004) on January 1, 2005, which is translated to Euro at historical rates. Differences resulting from the translation of income and expenses at the average rate and assets and liabilities at the closing rate are treated as an adjustment affecting consolidated shareholders' equity. On the disposal of all or part of a foreign Group company by sale, liquidation, repayment of share capital or abandonment, the cumulative amount or proportionate share of the translation difference is recognized as income or as expense in the same period in which the gain or loss on disposal is recognized.

Revenue recognition

Sales from the majority of the Group are recognized when the significant risks and rewards of ownership have transferred to the buyer, continuing managerial involvement usually associated with ownership and effective control have ceased, the amount of revenue can be measured reliably, it is probable that economic benefits associated with the transaction will flow to the Group and the costs incurred or to be incurred in respect of the transaction can be measured reliably. An immaterial part of the revenue from products sold through distribution channels is recognized when the reseller or distributor sells the products to the end users. The Group records reductions to revenue for special pricing agreements, price protection and other volume based discounts. Service revenue is generally recognized on a straight line basis over the service period unless there is evidence that some other method better represents the stage of completion. License fees from usage are recognized in the period in which the customer reports them to the Group.

The Group enters into transactions involving multiple components consisting of any combination of hardware, services and software. The commercial effect of each separately identifiable component of the transaction is evaluated in order to reflect the substance of the transaction. The consideration received from these transactions is allocated to each separately identifiable component based on the relative fair value of each component. The Group determines the fair value of each component by taking into consideration factors such as the price when the component or a similar component is sold separately by the Group or a third party. The consideration allocated to each component is recognized as revenue when the revenue recognition criteria for that component have been met. If the Group is unable to reliably determine the fair value attributable to the separately identifiable undelivered components, the Group defers revenue until the revenue recognition criteria for the undelivered components have been met.

In addition, sales and cost of sales from contracts involving solutions achieved through modification of complex telecommunications equipment are recognized using the percentage of completion method when the outcome of the contract can be estimated reliably. A contract's outcome can be estimated reliably when total contract revenue and the costs to complete the contract can be estimated reliably, it is probable that the economic benefits associated with the contract will flow to the Group and the stage of contract completion can be measured reliably. When the Group is not able to meet those conditions, the policy is to recognize revenues only equal to costs incurred to date, to the extent that such costs are expected to be recovered.

Progress towards completion is measured by reference to cost incurred to date as a percentage of estimated total project costs, the cost-to-cost method.

The percentage of completion method relies on estimates of total expected contract revenue and costs, as well as dependable measurement of the progress made towards completing a particular project. Recognized revenues and profits are subject to revisions during the project in the event that the assumptions regarding the overall project outcome are revised. The cumulative impact of a revision in estimates is recorded in the period such revisions become likely and estimable. Losses on projects in progress are recognized in the period they become probable and estimable.

Shipping and handling costs

The costs of shipping and distributing products are included in cost of sales.

Research and development

Research and development costs are expensed as they are incurred, except for certain development costs, which are capitalized when it is probable that a development project will generate future economic benefits, and certain criteria, including commercial and technological feasibility, have been met. Capitalized development costs, comprising direct labor and related overhead, are amortized on a systematic basis over their expected useful lives between two and five years.

Capitalized development costs are subject to regular assessments of recoverability based on anticipated future revenues, including the impact of changes in technology. Unamortized capitalized development costs determined to be in excess of their recoverable amounts are expensed immediately.

Other intangible assets

Acquired patents, trademarks, licenses, software licenses for internal use, customer relationships and developed technology are capitalized and amortized using the straight-line method over their useful lives, generally 3 to 6 years, but not exceeding 20 years. Where an indication of impairment exists, the carrying amount of any intangible asset is assessed and written down to its recoverable amount.

Pensions

The Group companies have various pension schemes in accordance with the local conditions and practices in the countries in which they operate. The schemes are generally funded through payments to insurance companies or to trustee-administered funds as determined by periodic actuarial calculations.

In a defined contribution plan, the Group has no legal or constructive obligation to make any additional contributions if the party receiving the contributions is unable to pay the pension obligations in question. The Group's contributions to defined contribution plans, multi-employer and insured plans are recognized in the profit and loss account in the period to which the contributions relate.

All arrangements that do not fulfill these conditions are considered defined benefit plans. If a defined benefit plan is funded through an insurance contract where the Group does not retain any legal or constructive obligations, such a plan is treated as a defined contribution plan.

For defined benefit plans, pension costs are assessed using the projected unit credit method: The pension cost is recognized in the profit and loss account so as to spread the service cost over the service lives of employees. The pension obligation is measured as the present value of the estimated future cash outflows using interest rates on high quality corporate bonds with appropriate maturities. Actuarial gains and losses outside the corridor are recognized over the average remaining service lives of employees. The corridor is defined as ten percent of the greater of the value of plan assets or defined benefit obligation at the beginning of the respective year.

Past service costs are recognized immediately in income, unless the changes to the pension plan are conditional on the employees remaining in service for a specified period of time (the vesting period). In this case, the past service costs are amortized on a straight-line basis over the vesting period.

The liability (or asset) recognized in the balance sheet is pension obligation at the closing date less the fair value of plan assets, the share of unrecognized actuarial gains and losses, and past service costs.

Property, plant and equipment

Property, plant and equipment are stated at cost less accumulated depreciation. Depreciation is recorded on a straight-line basis over the expected useful lives of the assets as follows:

Buildings and constructions	20–33 years
Production machinery, measuring and test equipment	1–3 years
Other machinery and equipment	3–10 years

Land and water areas are not depreciated.

Maintenance, repairs and renewals are generally charged to expense during the financial period in which they are incurred. However, major renovations are capitalized and included in the carrying amount of the asset when it is probable that future economic benefits in excess of the originally assessed standard of performance of the existing asset will flow to the Group. Major renovations are depreciated over the remaining useful life of the related asset. Leasehold improvements are depreciated over the shorter of the lease term or useful life.

Gains and losses on the disposal of fixed assets are included in operating profit/loss.

Leases

The Group has entered into various operating leases, the payments under which are treated as rentals and recognized in the profit and loss account on a straight-line basis over the lease terms unless another systematic approach is more representative of the pattern of the user's benefit.

Inventories

Inventories are stated at the lower of cost or net realizable value. Cost is determined using standard cost, which approximates actual cost on a FIFO basis. Net realizable value is the amount that can be realized from the sale of the inventory in the normal course of business after allowing for the costs of realization.

In addition to the cost of materials and direct labor, an appropriate proportion of production overhead is included in the inventory values.

An allowance is recorded for excess inventory and obsolescence based on the lower of cost or net realizable value.

Financial assets

The Group has classified its financial assets as one of the following categories: available-for-sale investments, loans and receivables, bank and cash and financial assets at fair value through profit or loss.

Available-for-sale investments
The Group classifies the following investments as available for sale based on the purpose for acquiring the investments as well as ongoing intentions: (1) highly liquid, interest-bearing investments with maturities at acquisition of less than 3 months, which are classified in the balance sheet as current available-for-sale investments, cash equivalents, (2) similar types of investments as in category (1), but with maturities at acquisition of longer than 3 months, classified in the balance sheet as current available-for-sale investments, liquid assets, (3) investments in technology related publicly quoted equity shares, or unlisted private equity shares and unlisted funds, classified in the balance sheet as non-current available-for-sale investments.

Current fixed income and money-market investments are fair valued by using quoted market rates, discounted cash flow analyses and other appropriate valuation models at the balance sheet date. Investments in publicly quoted equity shares are measured at fair value using exchange quoted bid prices. Other available-for-sale investments carried at fair value include holdings in unlisted shares. Fair value is estimated by using various factors, including, but not limited to: (1) the current market value of similar instruments, (2) prices established from a recent arm's length financing transaction of the target companies, (3) analysis of market prospects and operating performance of the target companies taking into consideration the public market of comparable companies in similar industry sectors. The remaining available-for-sale investments are carried at cost less impairment, which are technology related investments in private equity shares and unlisted funds for which the fair value cannot be measured reliably due to non-existence of public markets or reliable valuation methods against which to value these assets. The investment and disposal decisions on these investments are business driven.

All purchases and sales of investments are recorded on the trade date, which is the date that the Group commits to purchase or sell the asset.

The fair value changes of available-for-sale investments are recognized in fair value and other reserves as part of shareholders' equity, with the exception of interest calculated using effective interest method and foreign exchange gains and losses on monetary assets, which are recognized directly in profit and loss. Dividends on available-for-sale equity instruments are recognized in profit and loss when the Group's right to receive payment is established. When the investment is disposed of, the related accumulated fair value changes are released from shareholders' equity and recognized in the profit and loss account. The weighted average method is used when determining the cost-basis of publicly listed equities being disposed of. FIFO (First-in First-out) method is used to determine the cost basis of fixed income securities being disposed of. An impairment is recorded when the carrying amount of an available-for-sale investment is greater than the estimated fair value and there is objective evidence that the asset is impaired including but not limited to counterparty default and other factors causing a reduction in value that can be considered permanent. The cumulative net loss relating to that investment is removed from equity and recognized in the profit and loss account for the period. If, in a subsequent period, the fair value of the investment in a non-equity instrument increases and the increase can be objectively related to an event occurring after the loss was recognized, the loss is reversed, with the amount of the reversal included in the profit and loss account.

Loans receivable
Loans receivable include loans to customers and suppliers and are measured at amortized cost using the effective interest method less impairment. Loans are subject to regular and thorough review as to their collectability and as to available collateral; in the event that any loan is deemed not fully recoverable, a provision is made to reflect the shortfall between the carrying amount and the present value of the expected cash flows. Interest income on loans receivable is recognized by applying the effective interest rate. The long term portion of loans receivable is included on the balance sheet under long-term loans receivable and the current portion under current portion of long-term loans receivable.

Bank and cash
Bank and cash consist of cash at bank and in hand.

Accounts receivable
Accounts receivable are carried at the original amount invoiced to customers, which is considered to be fair value, less allowances for doubtful accounts based on a periodic review of all outstanding amounts including an analysis of historical bad debt, customer concentrations, customer creditworthiness, current economic trends and changes in our customer payment terms. Bad debts are written off when identified as uncollectible.

Financial liabilities

Loans payable
Loans payable are recognized initially at fair value, net of transaction costs incurred. Any difference between the fair value and the proceeds received is recognized in profit and loss at initial recognition. In the subsequent periods, they are stated at amortized cost using the effective interest method. The long term portion of loans payable is included on the balance sheet under long-term interest-bearing liabilities and the current portion under current portion of long-term loans.

Accounts payable
Accounts payable are carried at the original invoiced amount, which is considered to be fair value due to the short-term nature.

Derivative financial instruments

All derivatives are initially recognized at fair value on the date a derivative contract is entered into and are subsequently remeasured at their fair value. The method of recognizing the resulting gain or loss varies according to whether the derivatives are designated and qualify under hedge accounting or not.

Derivatives not designated in hedge accounting relationships carried at fair value through profit and loss
Fair values of forward rate agreements, interest rate options, futures contracts and exchange traded options are calculated based on quoted market rates at each balance sheet date. Discounted cash flow analyses are used to value interest rate and currency swaps. Changes in the fair value of these contracts are recognized in the profit and loss account.

Fair values of cash settled equity derivatives are calculated by revaluing the contract at each balance sheet date end quoted market rates. Changes in fair value are recognized in the profit and loss account.

Forward foreign exchange contracts are valued at the market forward exchange rates. Changes in fair value are measured by comparing these rates with the original contract forward rate. Currency options are valued at each balance sheet date by using the Garman & Kohlhagen option valuation model. Changes in the fair value on these instruments are recognized in the profit and loss account.

Embedded derivatives are identified and monitored by the Group and fair valued as at each balance sheet date. In assessing the fair value of embedded derivatives, the Group employs a variety of methods including option pricing models and discounted cash flow analysis using assumptions that are based on market conditions existing at each balance sheet date. The fair value changes are recognized in the profit and loss account.

Hedge accounting

Cash flow hedges: Hedging of anticipated foreign currency denominated sales and purchases
The Group applies hedge accounting for "Qualifying hedges". Qualifying hedges are those properly documented cash flow hedges of the foreign exchange rate risk of future anticipated foreign currency denominated sales and purchases that meet the requirements set out in IAS 39. The cash flow being hedged must be "highly probable" and must present an exposure to variations in cash flows that could ultimately affect profit or loss. The hedge must be highly effective both prospectively and retrospectively.

The Group claims hedge accounting in respect of certain forward foreign exchange contracts and options, or option strategies, which have zero net premium or a net premium paid, and where the critical terms of the bought and sold options within a collar or zero premium structure are the same and where the nominal amount of the sold option component is no greater than that of the bought option.

For qualifying foreign exchange forwards the change in fair value that reflects the change in spot exchange rates is deferred in shareholders' equity to the extent that the hedge is effective. For qualifying foreign exchange options, or option strategies, the change in intrinsic value is deferred in shareholders' equity to the extent that the hedge is effective. In all cases the ineffective portion is recognized immediately in the profit and loss account as financial income and expenses. Hedging costs, expressed either as the change in fair value that reflects the change in forward exchange rates less the change in spot exchange rates for forward foreign exchange contracts, or changes in the time value for options, or options strategies, are recognized within other operating income or expenses.

Accumulated fair value changes from qualifying hedges are released from shareholders' equity into the profit and loss account as adjustments to sales and cost of sales, in the period when the hedged cash flow affects the profit and loss account. If the hedged

cash flow is no longer expected to take place, all deferred gains or losses are released immediately into the profit and loss account as adjustments to sales and cost of sales. If the hedged cash flow ceases to be highly probable, but is still expected to take place, accumulated gains and losses remain in equity until the hedged cash flow affects the profit and loss account.

Changes in the fair value of any derivative instruments that do not qualify for hedge accounting under IAS 39 are recognized immediately in the profit and loss account. The fair value changes of derivative instruments that directly relate to normal business operations are recognized within other operating income and expenses. The fair value changes from all other derivative instruments are recognized in financial income and expenses.

Cash flow hedges: Hedging of foreign currency risk of highly probable business acquisitions and other transactions
The Group hedges the cash flow variability due to foreign currency risk inherent in highly probable business acquisitions and other future transactions that result in the recognition of non-financial assets. When those non-financial assets are recognized in the balance sheet the gains and losses previously deferred in equity are transferred from equity and included in the initial acquisition cost of the asset. The deferred amounts are ultimately recognized in the profit and loss as a result of goodwill assessments in case of business acquisitions and through depreciation in case of other assets. In order to apply for hedge accounting, the forecasted transactions must be highly probable and the hedges must be highly effective prospectively and retrospectively.

The Group claims hedge accounting in respect of forward foreign exchange contracts, foreign currency denominated loans, and options, or option strategies, which have zero net premium or a net premium paid, and where the terms of the bought and sold options within a collar or zero premium structure are the same.

For qualifying foreign exchange forwards, the change in fair value that reflects the change in spot exchange rates is deferred in shareholders' equity. The change in fair value that reflects the change in forward exchange rates less the change in spot exchange rates is recognized in the profit and loss account within financial income and expenses. For qualifying foreign exchange options the change in intrinsic value is deferred in shareholders' equity. Changes in the time value are at all times recognized directly in the profit and loss account as financial income and expenses. In all cases the ineffective portion is recognized immediately in the profit and loss account as financial income and expenses.

Hedges of net investments in foreign operations
The Group also applies hedge accounting for its foreign currency hedging on net investments.

Qualifying hedges are those properly documented hedges of the foreign exchange rate risk of foreign currency denominated net investments that meet the requirements set out in IAS 39. The hedge must be

effective both prospectively and retrospectively.

The Group claims hedge accounting in respect of forward foreign exchange contracts, foreign currency denominated loans, and options, or option strategies, which have zero net premium or a net premium paid, and where the terms of the bought and sold options within a collar or zero premium structure are the same.

For qualifying foreign exchange forwards, the change in fair value that reflects the change in spot exchange rates is deferred in shareholders' equity. The change in fair value that reflects the change in forward exchange rates less the change in spot exchange rates is recognized in the profit and loss account within financial income and expenses. For qualifying foreign exchange options the change in intrinsic value is deferred in shareholders' equity. Changes in the time value are at all times recognized directly in the profit and loss account as financial income and expenses. If a foreign currency denominated loan is used as a hedge, all foreign exchange gains and losses arising from the transaction are recognized in shareholders' equity. In all cases the ineffective portion is recognized immediately in the profit and loss account as financial income and expenses.

Accumulated fair value changes from qualifying hedges are released from shareholders' equity into the profit and loss account only if the legal entity in the given country is sold, liquidated, repays its share capital or is abandoned.

Income taxes

Current taxes are based on the results of the Group companies and are calculated according to local tax rules.

Deferred tax assets and liabilities are determined, using the liability method, for all temporary differences arising between the tax bases of assets and liabilities and their carrying amounts in the consolidated financial statements. Deferred tax assets are recognized to the extent that it is probable that future taxable profit will be available against which the unused tax losses or deductible temporary differences can be utilized. Deferred tax liabilities are recognized for temporary differences that arise between the fair value and tax base of identifiable net assets acquired in business combinations.

The enacted or substantially enacted tax rates as of each balance sheet date that are expected to apply in the period when the asset is realized or the liability is settled are used in the measurement of deferred tax assets and liabilities.

Deferred taxes are recognized directly in equity, when temporary differences arise on items that are not recognized in the profit and loss.

Provisions

Provisions are recognized when the Group has a present legal or constructive obligation as a result of past events, it is probable that an outflow of resources will be required to settle the obligation and a reliable estimate of the amount can be made. Where the Group expects a provision to be reimbursed, the reimbursement is recognized as an asset only when the reimbursement is virtually certain. At each balance sheet date, the Group assesses the adequacy of its preexisting provisions and adjusts the amounts as necessary based on actual experience and changes in future estimates.

Warranty provisions

The Group provides for the estimated liability to repair or replace products under warranty at the time revenue is recognized. The provision is an estimate calculated based on historical experience of the level of repairs and replacements.

Intellectual property rights (IPR) provisions

The Group provides for the estimated future settlements related to asserted and unasserted IPR infringements based on the probable outcome of potential infringement.

Tax provisions

The Group recognizes a provision for tax contingencies based upon the estimated future settlement amount at each balance sheet date.

Restructuring provisions

The Group provides for the estimated cost to restructure when a detailed formal plan of restructuring has been completed and the restructuring plan has been announced.

Other provisions

The Group recognizes the estimated liability for non-cancellable purchase commitments for inventory in excess of forecasted requirements at each balance sheet date.

The Group provides for onerous contracts based on the lower of the expected cost of fulfilling the contract and the expected cost of terminating the contract.

Share-based compensation

The Group offers three types of equity settled share-based compensation schemes for employees: stock options, performance shares and restricted shares. Employee services received, and the corresponding increase in equity, are measured by reference to the fair value of the equity instruments as of the date of grant, excluding the impact of any non-market vesting conditions. Non-market vesting conditions attached to the performance shares are included in assumptions about the number of shares that the employee will ultimately receive. On a regular basis, the Group reviews the assumptions made and, where necessary, revises its estimates of the number of performance shares that are expected to be settled. Share-based compensation is recognized as an expense in the profit and loss account over the service period. A separate vesting period is defined for each quarterly lot of the

stock options plans. When stock options are exercised, the proceeds received net of any transaction costs are credited to share premium and the reserve for invested non-restricted equity.

Treasury shares

The Group recognizes acquired treasury shares as a deduction from equity at their acquisition cost. When cancelled, the acquisition cost of treasury shares is recognized in retained earnings.

Dividends

Dividends proposed by the Board of Directors are not recorded in the financial statements until they have been approved by the shareholders at the Annual General Meeting.

Earnings per share

The Group calculates both basic and diluted earnings per share. Basic earnings per share is computed using the weighted average number of shares outstanding during the period. Diluted earnings per share is computed using the weighted average number of shares outstanding during the period plus the dilutive effect of stock options, restricted shares and performance shares outstanding during the period.

Use of estimates

The preparation of financial statements in conformity with IFRS requires the application of judgment by management in selecting appropriate assumptions for calculating financial estimates, which inherently contain some degree of uncertainty. Management bases its estimates on historical experience and various other assumptions that are believed to be reasonable under the circumstances, the results of which form the basis for making judgments about the reported carrying values of assets and liabilities and the reported amounts of revenues and expenses that may not be readily apparent from other sources. Actual results may differ from these estimates under different assumptions or conditions.

Set forth below are areas requiring significant judgment and estimation that may have an impact on reported results and the financial position.

Revenue recognition

Sales from the majority of the Group are recognized when the significant risks and rewards of ownership have transferred to the buyer, continuing managerial involvement usually associated with ownership and effective control have ceased, the amount of revenue can be measured reliably, it is probable that economic benefits associated with the transaction will flow to the Group and the costs incurred or to be incurred in respect of the transaction can be measured reliably.

Sales may materially change if management's assessment of such criteria was determined to be inaccurate.

The Group makes price protection adjustments based on estimates of future price reductions and certain agreed customer inventories at the date of the price adjustment. Possible changes in these estimates could result in revisions to the sales in future periods.

Revenue from contracts involving solutions achieved through modification of complex telecommunications equipment is recognized on the percentage of completion basis when the outcome of the contract can be estimated reliably. Recognized revenues and profits are subject to revisions during the project in the event that the assumptions regarding the overall project outcome are revised. Current sales and profit estimates for projects may materially change due to the early stage of a long-term project, new technology, changes in the project scope, changes in costs, changes in timing, changes in customers' plans, realization of penalties, and other corresponding factors.

Customer financing

The Group has provided a limited amount of customer financing and agreed extended payment terms with selected customers. Should the actual financial position of the customers or general economic conditions differ from assumptions, the ultimate collectability of such financings and trade credits may be required to be re-assessed, which could result in a write-off of these balances and thus negatively impact profits in future periods. The Group endeavors to mitigate this risk through the transfer of its rights to the cash collected from these arrangements to third party financial institutions on a non-recourse basis in exchange for an upfront cash payment.

Allowances for doubtful accounts

The Group maintains allowances for doubtful accounts for estimated losses resulting from the subsequent inability of customers to make required payments. If the financial conditions of customers were to deteriorate, resulting in an impairment of their ability to make payments, additional allowances may be required in future periods.

Inventory-related allowances

The Group periodically reviews inventory for excess amounts, obsolescence and declines in market value below cost and records an allowance against the inventory balance for any such declines. These reviews require management to estimate future demand for products. Possible changes in these estimates could result in revisions to the valuation of inventory in future periods.

Warranty provisions

The Group provides for the estimated cost of product warranties at the time revenue is recognized. The Group's warranty provision is established based upon best estimates of the amounts necessary to settle future and existing claims on products sold as of each balance sheet date. As new products incorporating complex technologies are continuously introduced, and as local laws, regulations and practices may change, changes in these estimates could result in additional allowances or changes to recorded allowances being required in future periods.

Provision for intellectual property rights, or IPR, infringements

The Group provides for the estimated future settlements related to asserted and unasserted IPR infringements based on the probable outcome of potential infringement. IPR infringement claims can last for varying periods of time, resulting in irregular movements in the IPR infringement provision. The ultimate outcome or actual cost of settling an individual infringement may materially vary from estimates.

Legal contingencies

Legal proceedings covering a wide range of matters are pending or threatened in various jurisdictions against the Group. Provisions are recorded for pending litigation when it is determined that an unfavorable outcome is probable and the amount of loss can be reasonably estimated. Due to the inherent uncertain nature of litigation, the ultimate outcome or actual cost of settlement may materially vary from estimates.

Capitalized development costs

The Group capitalizes certain development costs when it is probable that a development project will generate future economic benefits and certain criteria, including commercial and technological feasibility, have been met. Should a product fail to substantiate its estimated feasibility or life cycle, material development costs may be required to be written-off in future periods.

Business combinations

The purchase method of accounting is used to account for acquisitions of separate entities or businesses by the Group. The cost of an acquisition is measured as the aggregate of the fair values at the date of exchange of the assets given, liabilities incurred, equity instruments issued and costs directly attributable to the acquisition. Identifiable assets, liabilities and contingent liabilities acquired or assumed by the Group are measured separately at their fair value as of the acquisition date. The excess of the cost of the acquisition over the Group's interest in the fair value of the identifiable net assets acquired is recorded as goodwill.

The allocation of fair values to the identifiable assets acquired and liabilities assumed is based on various assumptions requiring management judgment. Actual results may differ from the forecasted amounts and the difference could be material.

Assessment of the recoverability of long-lived assets, intangible assets and goodwill

The recoverable amounts for long-lived assets, intangible assets and goodwill have been determined based on value in use calculations. Value in use is calculated based on the expected future cash flows attributable to the asset or cash-generating unit discounted to present value. The key assumptions applied in the determination of the value in use include the discount rate, length of the explicit forecast period and estimated growth rates, profit margins and level of operational and capital investment. Amounts estimated could differ materially from what will actually occur in the future.

Fair value of derivatives and other financial instruments

The fair value of financial instruments that are not traded in an active market (for example, unlisted equities, currency options and embedded derivatives) are determined using various valuation techniques. The Group uses judgment to select an appropriate valuation methodology as well as underlying assumptions based on existing market practice and conditions. Changes in these assumptions may cause the Group to recognize impairments or losses in future periods.

Income taxes

Management judgment is required in determining provisions for income taxes, deferred tax assets and liabilities and the extent to which deferred tax assets can be recognized. If the final outcome of these matters differs from the amounts initially recorded, differences may impact the income tax and deferred tax provisions in the period in which such determination is made.

Pensions

The determination of pension benefit obligation and expense for defined benefit pension plans is dependent on the selection of certain assumptions used by actuaries in calculating such amounts. Those assumptions include, among others, the discount rate, expected long-term rate of return on plan assets and annual rate of increase in future compensation levels. A portion of plan assets is invested in equity securities which are subject to equity market volatility. Changes in assumptions and actuarial conditions may materially affect the pension obligation and future expense.

Share-based compensation

The Group operates various types of equity settled share-based compensation schemes for employees. Fair value of stock options is based on certain assumptions, including, among others, expected volatility and expected life of the options. Non-market vesting conditions attached to performance shares are included in assumptions about the number of shares that the employee will ultimately receive relating to projections of net sales and earnings per share. Significant differences in equity market performance, employee option activity and the Group's projected and actual net sales and earnings per share performance, may materially affect future expense.

New accounting pronouncements under IFRS

The Group will adopt the following new and revised standards, amendments and interpretations to existing standards issued by the IASB that are expected to be relevant to its operations:

Amendment to IFRS 2, Share-based payment, Group and Treasury Share Transactions, clarifies the definition of different vesting conditions, treatment of all non-vesting conditions and provides further guidance on the accounting treatment of cancellations by parties other than the entity.

IAS 1 (Revised), Presentation of financial statements, prompts entities to aggregate information in the financial statements on the basis of shared characteristics. All non-owner changes in equity (i.e. comprehensive income) should be presented either in one statement of comprehensive income or in a separate income statement and statement of comprehensive income.

Amendment to IAS 20, Accounting for government grants and disclosure of government assistance, requires that the benefit of a below-market rate government loan is measured as the difference between the carrying amount in accordance with IAS 39 and the proceeds received, with the benefit accounted for in accordance with IAS 20.

Amendment to IAS 23, Borrowing costs, changes the treatment of borrowing costs that are directly attributable to an acquisition, construction or production of a qualifying asset. These costs will consequently form part of the cost of that asset. Other borrowing costs are recognized as an expense.

Under the amended IAS 32 Financial Instruments: Presentation, the Group must classify puttable financial instruments or instruments or components thereof that impose an obligation to deliver to another party, a pro-rata share of net assets of the entity only on liquidation, as equity. Previously, these instruments would have been classified as financial liabilities.

IFRIC 13, Customer Loyalty Programs addresses the accounting surrounding customer loyalty programs and whether some consideration should be allocated to free goods or services provided by a company. Consideration should be allocated to award credits based on their fair value, as they are a separately identifiable component.

IFRIC 16, Hedges of a Net Investment in a Foreign Operation clarifies the accounting treatment in respect of net investment hedging. This includes the fact that net investment hedging relates to differences in functional currency not presentation currency, and hedging instruments may be held anywhere in the group.

IFRIC 18 Transfers of Assets from Customers clarifies the requirements for agreements in which an entity receives an item of property, plant and equipment or cash it is required to use to construct or acquire an item of property, plant and equipment that must be used to provide access to a supply of goods or services.

IFRS 3 (revised) Business Combinations replaces IFRS 3 (as issued in 2004). The main changes brought by IFRS 3 (revised) include immediate recognition of all acquisition-related costs in profit or loss, recognition of subsequent changes in the fair value of contingent consideration in accordance with other IFRSs and measurement of goodwill arising from step acquisitions at the acquisition date.

IAS 27 (revised), "Consolidated and Separate Financial Statements" clarifies presentation of changes in parent-subsidiary ownership. Changes in a parent's ownership interest in a subsidiary that do not result in the loss of control must be accounted for exclusively within equity. If a parent loses control of a subsidiary it shall derecognize the consolidated assets and liabilities, and any investment retained in the former subsidiary shall be recognized at fair value at the date when control is lost. Any differences resulting from this shall be recognized in profit or loss. When losses attributed to the minority (non-controlling) interests exceed the minority's interest in the subsidiary's equity, these losses shall be allocated to the non-controlling interests even if this results in a deficit balance.

In addition, there are a number of other amendments that form part of the IASB's annual improvement project, which will be adopted by the Group on January 1, 2009.

The Group will adopt the amendments to IFRS 2, IAS 1, IAS 20, IAS 23, IAS 32, IFRIC 13, IFRIC 16 and IFRIC 18 as well as the additional amendments that form part of the IASB's annual improvement project on January 1, 2009. The Group does not expect that the adoption of these revised standards, interpretations and amendments will have a material impact on the financial condition and results of operations.

The Group is required to adopt both IFRS 3 (revised) and IAS 27 (revised) on January 1, 2010 with early adoption permitted. The Group is currently evaluating the impact of these standards on the Group's accounts.

7. Impairment

EURm	2008	2007	2006
Property, plant and equipment	77	—	—
Inventories	13	—	—
Available-for-sale investments	43	29	18
Investments in associated companies	8	7	—
Capitalized development costs	—	27	—
Other intangible assets	—	—	33
Other non-current assets	8	—	—
Total, net	149	63	51

Property, plant and equipment and inventories

In conjunction with the Group's decision to discontinue the production of mobile devices in Germany, an impairment loss was recognized amounting to EUR 55 million. The impairment loss related to the closure and sale of production facilities at Bochum, Germany during 2008 and was included in Devices & Services segment.

In 2008, Nokia Siemens Networks recognized an impairment loss amounting to EUR 35 million relating to the sale of its manufacturing site in Durach, Germany. The impairment loss was determined as the excess of the book value of transferring assets over the fair value less costs to sell for the transferring assets. The impairment loss was allocated to property, plant and equipment and inventories.

Available-for-sale investments

The Group's investment in certain equity securities held as non-current available-for-sale suffered a permanent decline in fair value resulting in an impairment charge of EUR 43 million (EUR 29 million in 2007, EUR 18 million in 2006).

Investments in associated companies

After application of the equity method, including recognition of the associate's losses, the Group determined that recognition of an impairment loss of EUR 8 million in 2008 (EUR 7 million in 2007) was necessary to adjust the Group's net investment in the associate to its recoverable amount.

Capitalized development costs

During 2007, Nokia Siemens Networks recorded an impairment charge on capitalized development costs of EUR 27 million. The impairment loss was determined as the full carrying amount of the capitalized development programs costs related to products that will not be included in future product portfolios. This impairment amount is included within research and development expenses in the consolidated profit and loss statement.

Other intangible assets

In connection with the restructuring of its CDMA business, the Group recorded an impairment charge of EUR 33 million during 2006 related to an acquired CDMA license. The impaired CDMA license was included in Devices & Services segment.

Goodwill

Goodwill is allocated to the Group's cash-generating units (CGU) for the purpose of impairment testing. The allocation is made to those cash-generating units that are expected to benefit from the synergies of the business combination from which the goodwill arose.

The recoverable amounts of each CGU are determined based on a value in use calculation. The pre-tax cash flow projections employed in the value in use calculation are based on financial plans approved by management. These projections are consistent with external sources of information, wherever available. Cash flows beyond the explicit forecast period are extrapolated using an estimated terminal growth rate that does not exceed the long-term average growth rates for the industry and economies in which the CGU operates.

Rapid deterioration in the macroeconomic environment during 2008 has negatively affected cash flow expectations for all of the Group's CGUs. The global slowdown in consumer spending, unprecedented currency volatility and reductions in the availability of credit have dampened growth and profitability expectations during the short to medium term.

Goodwill of EUR 1 106 million has been allocated to the Devices & Services CGU for the purpose of impairment testing. The impairment testing has been carried out based on Management's expectation of moderate market share growth and stable profit margins in the medium to long term.

Goodwill amounting to EUR 905 million has been allocated to the NSN CGU. The impairment testing has been carried out based on Management's expectation of a constant market share, and a declining total market value in the shorter term, stabilizing on the longer term. Tight focus on profitability and cash collection is expected to improve operating cash flow.

Goodwill amounting to EUR 4 119 million has been allocated to the NAVTEQ CGU. The impairment testing has been carried out based on Management's expectation of longer term strong growth in mobile device navigation services with increased volumes driving profitability. The recoverable amount of the NAVTEQ CGU is less than 1% higher than its carrying amount. A reasonably possible change of 1% in the valuation assumptions for long-term growth rate and pre-tax discount rate would give rise to an impairment loss.

The aggregate carrying amount of goodwill allocated across multiple CGUs amounts to EUR 127 million and the amount allocated to each individual CGU is not individually significant.

The key assumptions applied in the value-in-use calculation for each CGU are presented in the table below:

| | Cash-generating unit | | |
%	Devices & Services	NSN	NAVTEQ
Terminal growth rate	2.28	1.00	5.00
Pre-tax discount rate	12.35	14.86	10.92

The goodwill impairment testing analyses conducted for each of the Group's CGUs for the years ended December 31, 2008, 2007 and 2006 have not resulted in any impairment charges.

9. Depreciation and amortization

EURm	2008	2007	2006
Depreciation and amortization by function			
Cost of sales	297	303	279
Research and development [1]	778	523	312
Selling and marketing [2]	368	232	9
Administrative and general	174	148	111
Other operating expenses	—	—	1
Total	1 617	1 206	712

1 In 2008, depreciation and amortization allocated to research and development included amortization of acquired intangible assets of EUR 351 million (EUR 136 million in 2007).

2 In 2008, depreciation and amortization allocated to selling and marketing included amortization of acquired intangible assets of EUR 343 million (EUR 214 million in 2007).

10. Financial income and expenses

EURm	2008	2007	2006
Dividend income on available-for-sale financial investments	1	—	—
Interest income on available-for-sale financial investments	353	338	225
Interest income on loans receivables carried at amortized cost	—	1	—
Interest expense on financial liabilities carried at amortized cost	−185	−43	−22
Other financial income	17	43	55
Other financial expenses	−31	−24	−18
Net foreign exchange gains (or losses)			
From foreign exchange derivatives designated at fair value through profit and loss account	432	37	75
From balance sheet items revaluation	−595	−118	−106
Net gains (net losses) on other derivatives designated at fair value through profit and loss account	6	5	−2
Total	−2	239	207

During 2008, Nokia's interest expense increased significantly due to an increase in interest-bearing liabilities mainly related to financing of the NAVTEQ acquisition. Foreign exchange gains (or losses) increased due to a higher cost of hedging and increased volatility on the foreign exchange market.

11. Income taxes

EURm	2008	2007	2006
Income tax expense			
Current tax	−1 514	−2 209	−1 303
Deferred tax	433	687	−54
Total	−1 081	−1 522	−1 357
Finland	−604	−1 323	−941
Other countries	−477	−199	−416
Total	−1 081	−1 522	−1 357

The differences between income tax expense computed at the statutory rate in Finland of 26% and income taxes recognized in the consolidated income statement is reconciled as follows at December 31, 2008:

EURm	2008	2007	2006
Income tax expense at statutory rate	1 292	2 150	1 488
Items without tax benefit/expense	−65	61	12
Non-taxable gain on formation of Nokia Siemens Networks [1]	—	−489	—
Taxes for prior years	−128	20	−24
Taxes on foreign subsidiaries' profits in excess of (lower than) income taxes at statutory rates	−181	−138	−73
Operating losses with no current tax benefit	—	15	—
Net increase in tax provisions	2	50	−12
Change in income tax rate [2]	−22	−114	—
Deferred tax liability on undistributed earnings [3]	220	−37	−3
Other	−37	4	−31
Income tax expense	1 081	1 522	1 357

1 See Note 8.

2 In 2007, the change in income tax rate decreased Group tax expense primarily due to the impact of a decrease in the German statutory tax rate on deferred tax asset balances.

3 The change in deferred tax liability on undistributed earnings mainly relates to changes to tax rates applicable to profit distributions.

12. Intangible assets

EURm	2008	2007
Capitalized development costs		
Acquisition cost January 1	1 817	1 533
Additions during the period	131	157
Acquisitions	—	154
Impairment losses	—	−27
Retirements	−124	—
Disposals during the period	−13	—
Accumulated acquisition cost December 31	1 811	1 817
Accumulated amortization January 1	−1 439	−1 282
Retirements during the period	14	
Disposals during the period	11	
Amortization for the period	−153	−157
Accumulated amortization December 31	−1 567	−1 439
Net book value January 1	378	251
Net book value December 31	244	378
Goodwill		
Acquisition cost January 1	1 384	532
Translation differences	431	−30
Acquisitions	4 482	882
Disposals during the period	−35	—
Other changes	−5	—
Accumulated acquisition cost December 31	6 257	1 384
Net book value January 1	1 384	532
Net book value December 31	6 257	1 384
Other intangible assets		
Acquisition cost January 1	3 218	772
Translation differences	265	−20
Additions during the period	95	102
Acquisitions	2 189	2 437
Retirements during the period	−55	—
Disposals during the period	−214	−73
Accumulated acquisition cost December 31	5 498	3 218
Accumulated amortization January 1	−860	−474
Translation differences	−32	11
Disposals during the period	48	73
Amortization for the period	−741	−470
Accumulated amortization December 31	−1 585	−860
Net book value January 1	2 358	298
Net book value December 31	3 913	2 358

13. Property, plant and equipment

EURm	2008	2007
Land and water areas		
Acquisition cost January 1	73	78
Translation differences	−4	−2
Additions during the period	3	4
Acquisitions	—	5
Impairments during the period	−4	—
Disposals during the period	−8	−12
Accumulated acquisition cost December 31	60	73
Net book value January 1	73	78
Net book value December 31	60	73
Buildings and constructions		
Acquisition cost January 1	1 008	925
Translation differences	−9	−15
Additions during the period	382	97
Acquisitions	28	58
Impairments during the period	−90	—
Disposals during the period	−45	−57
Accumulated acquisition cost December 31	1 274	1 008
Accumulated depreciation January 1	−239	−230
Translation differences	1	3
Impairments during the period	30	—
Disposals during the period	17	25
Depreciation for the period	−159	−37
Accumulated depreciation December 31	−350	−239
Net book value January 1	769	695
Net book value December 31	924	769
Machinery and equipment		
Acquisition cost January 1	4 012	3 707
Translation differences	10	−42
Additions during the period	613	448
Acquisitions	68	264
Impairments during the period	−21	—
Disposals during the period	−499	−365
Accumulated acquisition cost December 31	4 183	4 012
Accumulated depreciation January 1	−3 107	−2 966
Translation differences	−8	34
Impairments during the period	8	—
Disposals during the period	466	364
Depreciation for the period	−556	−539
Accumulated depreciation December 31	−3 197	−3 107
Net book value January 1	905	741
Net book value December 31	986	905
Other tangible assets		
Acquisition cost January 1	20	22
Translation differences	2	−1
Additions during the period	8	2
Disposals during the period	—	−3
Accumulated acquisition cost December 31	30	20
Accumulated depreciation January 1	−9	−7
Translation differences	—	—
Disposals during the period	—	1
Depreciation for the period	−6	−3
Accumulated depreciation December 31	−15	−9
Net book value January 1	11	15
Net book value December 31	15	11

14. Investments in associated companies

EURm	2008	2007
Net carrying amount January 1	325	224
Translation differences	-19	—
Additions	24	19
Acquisitions	—	67
Deductions [1]	-239	-6
Impairment	-8	-7
Share of results	6	44
Dividends	-6	-12
Other movements	13	-4
Net carrying amount December 31	96	325

1 On December 2, 2008, the Group completed its acquisition of 52.1% of the outstanding common stock of Symbian Ltd, a UK-based software licensing company. As a result of this acquisition, the Group's total ownership interest has increased from 47.9% to 100% of the outstanding common stock of Symbian. See Note 8.

Shareholdings in associated companies are comprised of investments in unlisted companies in all periods presented.

15. Available-for-sale investments

Available-for-sale investments included the following:

	2008		2007	
EURm	Current	Non-current	Current	Non-current
Fixed income and money-market investments carried at fair value	5 114	38	9 628	—
Available-for-sale investments in publicly quoted equity shares	—	8	—	10
Other available-for-sale investments carried at fair value	—	225	—	184
Other available-for-sale investments carried at cost less impairment	—	241	—	147
	5 114	512	9 628	341

The current fixed income and money-market investments, carried at fair value, included available for sale liquid assets of EUR 1 272 million (EUR 4 903 million in 2007) and cash equivalents of EUR 3 842 million (EUR 4 725 million in 2007). See Note 35 for details of fixed income and money-market investments.

17. Inventories

EURm	2008	2007
Raw materials, supplies and other	519	591
Work in progress	744	1 060
Finished goods	1 270	1 225
Total	2 533	2 876

19. Valuation and qualifying accounts

Allowances on assets to which they apply:	Balance at beginning of year EURm	Charged to cost and expenses EURm	Deductions [1] EURm	Acquisitions EURm	Balance at end of year EURm
2008					
Allowance for doubtful accounts	332	224	-141		415
Excess and obsolete inventory	417	151	-221	1	348
2007					
Allowance for doubtful accounts	212	38	-72	154	332
Excess and obsolete inventory	218	145	-202	256	417
2006					
Allowance for doubtful accounts	281	70	-139		212
Excess and obsolete inventory	176	353	-311		218

1 Deductions include utilization and releases of the allowances.

25. Accrued expenses

EURm	2008	2007
Social security, VAT and other taxes	1 700	2 024
Wages and salaries	665	865
Advance payments	532	503
Other	4 126	3 722
Total	7 023	7 114

Other operating expense accruals include dererred service revenue, accrued discounts, royalties and marketing expenses as well as various amounts which are individually insignificant.

27. Provisions

EURm	Warranty	Restructuring	IPR infringements	Tax	Other	Total
At January 1, 2007	1 198	65	284	402	437	2 386
Exchange differences	−10	—	—	—	—	−10
Acquisitions	263	—	—	—	134	397
Additional provisions	1 127	744	345	59	548	2 823
Change in fair value	—	—	—	—	16	16
Changes in estimates	−126	−53	−47	−9	−216	−451
Charged to profit and loss account	1 001	691	298	50	348	2 388
Utilized during year	−963	−139	−37	—	−305	−1 444
At December 31, 2007	1 489	617	545	452	614	3 717
At January 1, 2008	1 489	617	545	452	614	3 717
Exchange differences	−16	—	—	—	—	−16
Acquisitions	1	—	3	6	2	12
Additional provisions	1 211	533	266	47	1 136	3 193
Change in fair value	—	—	—	—	−7	−7
Changes in estimates	−240	−211	−92	−45	−185	−773
Charged to profit and loss account	971	322	174	2	944	2 413
Utilized during year	−1 070	−583	−379	—	−502	−2 534
At December 31, 2008	1 375	356	343	460	1 058	3 592

EURm	2008	2007
Analysis of total provisions at December 31:		
Non-current	978	1 323
Current	2 614	2 394

Outflows for the warranty provision are generally expected to occur within the next 18 months. Timing of outflows related to tax provisions is inherently uncertain.

The restructuring provision is mainly related to restructuring activities in Devices & Services and Nokia Siemens Networks segments. The majority of outflows related to the restructuring is expected to occur during 2009.

In conjunction with the Group's decision to discontinue the production of mobile devices in Germany, a restructuring provision of EUR 259 million was recognized. Devices & Services also recognized EUR 52 million charges related to other restructuring activities.

Restructuring and other associated expenses incurred in Nokia Siemens Networks in 2008 totaled EUR 646 million (EUR 1 110 million in 2007) including mainly personnel related expenses as well as expenses arising from the elimination of overlapping functions, and the realignment of product portfolio and related replacement of discontinued products in customer sites. These expenses included EUR 402 million (EUR 318 million in 2007) impacting gross profit, EUR 46 million (EUR 439 million in 2007) research and development expenses, EUR 14 million of reversal of provision (EUR 149 million expenses in 2007) in selling and marketing expenses, EUR 163 million (EUR 146 million in 2007) administrative expenses and EUR 49 million (EUR 58 million in 2007) other operating expenses. EUR 790 million was paid during 2008 (EUR 254 million during 2007).

The IPR provision is based on estimated future settlements for asserted and unasserted past IPR infringements. Final resolution of IPR claims generally occurs over several periods. In 2008, EUR 379 million usage of the provisions mainly relates to the settlements with Qualcomm, Eastman Kodak, Intertrust Technologies and ContentGuard.

Other provisions include provisions for non-cancelable purchase commitments, provision for pension and other social costs on share-based awards and provision for losses on projects in progress.

29. Commitments and contingencies

EURm	2008	2007
Collateral for our own commitments		
Property under mortgages	18	18
Assets pledged	11	29
Contingent liabilities on behalf of Group companies		
Other guarantees	2 896	2 563
Contingent liabilities on behalf of other companies		
Financial guarantees on behalf of third parties	2	130
Other guarantees	1	1
Financing commitments		
Customer finance commitments [1]	197	270
Venture fund commitments [2]	467	251

1 See also note 35 b).
2 See also note 35 a).

The amounts above represent the maximum principal amount of commitments and contingencies.

Property under mortgages given as collateral for our own commitments include mortgages given to the Finnish National Board of Customs as a general indemnity of EUR 18 million in 2008 (EUR 18 million in 2007).

Assets pledged for the Group's own commitments include available-for-sale investments of EUR 10 million in 2008 (EUR 10 million in 2007).

Other guarantees include guarantees of EUR 2 682 million in 2008 (EUR 2 429 million in 2007) provided to certain Nokia Siemens Networks' customers in the form of bank guarantees, standby letters of credit and other similar instruments. These instruments entitle the customer to claim payment as compensation for non-performance by Nokia of its obligations under network infrastructure supply agreements. Depending on the nature of the instrument, compensation is payable either immediately upon request, or subject to independent verification of non-performance by Nokia.

Guarantees for loans and other financial commitments on behalf of other companies were EUR 2 million in 2008 (EUR 130 million in 2007). The amount of 2007 represents guarantees relating to payment by certain Nokia Siemens Networks' customers and other third parties under specified loan facilities between such a customer and other third parties and their creditors. Nokia's obligations under such guarantees are released upon the earlier of expiration of the guarantee or early payment by the customer.

Financing commitments of EUR 197 million in 2008 (EUR 270 million in 2007) are available under loan facilities negotiated mainly with Nokia Siemens Networks' customers. Availability of the amounts is dependent upon the borrower's continuing compliance with stated financial and operational covenants and compliance with other administrative terms of the facility. The loan facilities are primarily available to fund capital expenditure relating to purchases of network infrastructure equipment and services.

Venture fund commitments of EUR 467 million in 2008 (EUR 251 million in 2007) are financing commitments to a number of funds making technology related investments. As a limited partner in these funds Nokia is committed to capital contributions and also entitled to cash distributions according to respective partnership agreements.

The Group is party to routine litigation incidental to the normal conduct of business, including, but not limited to, several claims, suits and actions both initiated by third parties and initiated by Nokia relating to infringements of patents, violations of licensing arrangements and other intellectual property related matters, as well as actions with respect to products, contracts and securities. In the opinion of the management the outcome of and liabilities in excess of what has been provided for relating to these or other proceedings, in aggregate, are not likely to be material to the financial condition or result of operations.

Nokia's payment obligations under the subscriber unit cross-license agreements signed in 1992 and 2001 with Qualcomm Incorporated (Qualcomm) expired on April 9, 2007. The parties entered into negotiations for a new license agreement with the intention of reaching a mutually acceptable agreement on a timely basis. Prior to the commencement of negotiations and as negotiations proceeded, Nokia and Qualcomm were engaged in numerous legal disputes in the United States, Europe and China. On July 24, 2008, Nokia and Qualcomm entered into a new license agreement covering various current and future standards and other technologies, and resulting in a settlement of all litigation between the companies. Under the terms of the 15 year agreement covering various standards and other technologies, Nokia has been granted a license under all Qualcomm's patents for use in Nokia's mobile devices and Nokia Siemens Networks infrastructure equipment, and Nokia has agreed not to use any of its patents directly against Qualcomm. The financial terms included a one-time lump-sum cash payment of EUR 1.7 billion made by Nokia to Qualcomm in the fourth quarter of 2008 and on-going royalty payments to Qualcomm. The lump-sum payment made to Qualcomm will be expensed over the term of the agreement. Nokia also agreed to assign ownership of a number of patents to Qualcomm.

As of December 31, 2008, the Group had purchase commitments of EUR 2 351 million (EUR 2 610 million in 2007) relating to inventory purchase obligations, service agreements and outsourcing arrangements, primarily for purchases in 2009.

32. Notes to cash flow statement

EURm	2008	2007	2006
Adjustments for:			
Depreciation and amortization (Note 9)	1 617	1 206	712
(Profit)/loss on sale of property, plant and equipment and available-for-sale investments	–11	–1 864	–4
Income taxes (Note 11)	1 081	1 522	1 357
Share of results of associated companies (Note 14)	–6	–44	–28
Minority interest	–99	–459	60
Financial income and expenses (Note 10)	2	–239	–207
Impairment charges (Note 7)	149	63	51
Retirements (Note 8, 12)	186	—	—
Share-based compensation (Note 22)	74	228	192
Restructuring charges	448	856	—
Customer financing impairment charges and reversals	—	—	–276
Finnish pension settlement (Note 5)	152	—	—
Other income and expenses	–124	—	—
Adjustments, total	**3 469**	**1 269**	**1 857**
Change in net working capital			
Increase in short-term receivables	–534	–2 146	–1 770
Decrease (+)/increase (–) in inventories	321	–245	84
Decrease (–)/increase (+) in interest-free short-term liabilities	–2 333	2 996	893
Change in net working capital	**–2 546**	**605**	**–793**

The Group did not engage in any material non-cash investing activities in 2008 and 2006. In 2007 the formation of Nokia Siemens Networks was completed through the contribution of certain tangible and intangible assets and certain business interests that comprised Nokia's networks business and Siemens' carrier-related operations. See Note 8.

Nokia shares and shareholders

Shares and share capital

Nokia has one class of shares. Each Nokia share entitles the holder to one vote at General Meetings of Nokia.

On December 31, 2008, the share capital of Nokia Corporation was EUR 245 896 461.96 and the total number of shares issued was 3 800 948 552.

On December 31, 2008, the total number of shares included 103 076 379 shares owned by Group companies representing approximately 2.7% of the share capital and the total voting rights.

Under the the Articles of Association of Nokia, Nokia Corporation does not have minimum or maximum share capital or a par value of a share.

Share capital and shares December 31, 2008	2008	2007	2006	2005	2004
Share capital, EURm	246	246	246	266	280
Shares (1 000)	3 800 949	3 982 812	4 095 043	4 433 887	4 663 761
Shares owned by the Group (1 000)	103 076	136 862	129 312	261 511	176 820
Number of shares excluding shares owned by the Group (1 000)	3 697 872	3 845 950	3 965 730	4 172 376	4 486 941
Average number of shares excluding shares owned by the Group during the year (1 000), basic	3 743 622	3 885 408	4 062 833	4 365 547	4 593 196
Average number of shares excluding shares owned by the Group during the year (1 000), diluted	3 780 363	3 932 008	4 086 529	4 371 239	4 600 337
Number of registered shareholders [1]	122 713	103 226	119 143	126 352	142 095

1   Each account operator is included in the figure as only one registered shareholder.

Appendix B

TIME VALUE OF MONEY: FUTURE VALUE AND PRESENT VALUE

The following discussion of future value lays the foundation for our explanation of present value in Chapter 8 but is not essential. For the valuation of long-term liabilities, some instructors may wish to begin on page 885 of this appendix.

The term *time value of money* refers to the fact that money earns interest over time. *Interest* is the cost of using money. To borrowers, interest is the expense of renting money. To lenders, interest is the revenue earned from lending. We must always recognize the interest we receive or pay. Otherwise, we overlook an important part of the transaction. Suppose you invest $4,545 in corporate bonds that pay 10% interest each year. After one year, the value of your investment has grown to $5,000. The difference between your original investment ($4,545) and the future value of the investment ($5,000) is the amount of interest revenue you will earn during the year ($455). If you ignored the interest, you would fail to account for the interest revenue you have earned. Interest becomes more important as the time period lengthens because the amount of interest depends on the span of time the money is invested.

Let's consider a second example, this time from the borrower's perspective. Suppose you purchase a machine for your business. The cash price of the machine is $8,000, but you cannot pay cash now. To finance the purchase, you sign an $8,000 note payable. The note requires you to pay the $8,000 plus 10% interest one year from the date of purchase, i.e. a total of $8,800. The $800 interest is what you pay for the time value of money you bonds.. Is your cost of the machine $8,000, or is it $8,800 [$8,000 plus interest of $800 ($8,000 × 0.10)]? The cost is $8,000. The additional $800 is interest expense and not part of the cost of the machine.

Future Value

The main application of future value is the accumulated balance of an investment at a future date. In our first example, the investment earned 10% per year. After one year, $4,545 grew to $5,000, as shown in Exhibit B-1.

EXHIBIT B-1 | Future Value: An Example

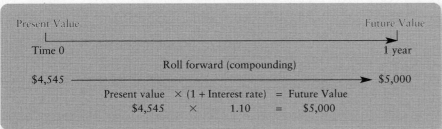

If the money were invested for five years, you would have to perform five such calculations. You would also have to consider the compound interest that your investment is earning. *Compound interest* is not only the interest you earn on your principal amount, but also the interest you receive on the interest you have already earned. Most business applications include compound interest. The following table shows the interest revenue earned on the original $4,545 investment each year for five years at 10%:

End of Year	Interest	Future Value
0	—	$4,545
1	$4,545 × 0.10 = $455	5,000
2	5,000 × 0.10 = 500	5,500
3	5,500 × 0.10 = 550	6,050
4	6,050 × 0.10 = 605	6,655
5	6,655 × 0.10 = 666	7,321

Earning 10%, a $4,545 investment grows to $5,000 at the end of one year, to $5,500 at the end of two years, and $7,321 at the end of five years. Throughout this appendix we round off to the nearest dollar.

Future-Value Tables

The process of computing a future value is called *compounding* because the future value is *more* than the present value. Mathematical tables ease the computational burden. Exhibit B-2, Future Value of $1, gives the future value for a single sum (a present value), $1, invested to earn a particular interest rate for a specific number of periods. Future value depends on three factors: (1) the amount of the investment,

EXHIBIT B-2 | Future Value of $1

Future Value of $1									
Periods	4%	5%	6%	7%	8%	9%	10%	12%	14%	16%
---	---	---	---	---	---	---	---	---	---	---
1	1.040	1.050	1.060	1.070	1.080	1.090	1.100	1.120	1.140	1.160
2	1.082	1.103	1.124	1.145	1.166	1.188	1.210	1.254	1.300	1.346
3	1.125	1.158	1.191	1.225	1.260	1.295	1.331	1.405	1.482	1.561
4	1.170	1.216	1.262	1.311	1.360	1.412	1.464	1.574	1.689	1.811
5	1.217	1.276	1.338	1.403	1.469	1.539	1.611	1.762	1.925	2.100
6	1.265	1.340	1.419	1.501	1.587	1.677	1.772	1.974	2.195	2.436
7	1.316	1.407	1.504	1.606	1.714	1.828	1.949	2.211	2.502	2.826
8	1.369	1.477	1.594	1.718	1.851	1.993	2.144	2.476	2.853	3.278
9	1.423	1.551	1.689	1.838	1.999	2.172	2.358	2.773	3.252	3.803
10	1.480	1.629	1.791	1.967	2.159	2.367	2.594	3.106	3.707	4.411
11	1.539	1.710	1.898	2.105	2.332	2.580	2.853	3.479	4.226	5.117
12	1.601	1.796	2.012	2.252	2.518	2.813	3.138	3.896	4.818	5.936
13	1.665	1.886	2.133	2.410	2.720	3.066	3.452	4.363	5.492	6.886
14	1.732	1.980	2.261	2.579	2.937	3.342	3.798	4.887	6.261	7.988
15	1.801	2.079	2.397	2.759	3.172	3.642	4.177	5.474	7.138	9.266
16	1.873	2.183	2.540	2.952	3.426	3.970	4.595	6.130	8.137	10.748
17	1.948	2.292	2.693	3.159	3.700	4.328	5.054	6.866	9.276	12.468
18	2.026	2.407	2.854	3.380	3.996	4.717	5.560	7.690	10.575	14.463
19	2.107	2.527	3.026	3.617	4.316	5.142	6.116	8.613	12.056	16.777
20	2.191	2.653	3.207	3.870	4.661	5.604	6.728	9.646	13.743	19.461

(2) the length of time between investment and future accumulation, and (3) the interest rate. Future-value and present-value tables are based on $1 because unity (the value 1) is so easy to work with.

In business applications, interest rates are usually stated for the annual period of one year unless specified otherwise. In fact, an interest rate can be stated for any period, such as 3% per quarter or 5% for a six-month period. The length of the period is arbitrary. For example, an investment may promise a return (income) of 3% per quarter for six months (two quarters). In that case, you would be working with 3% interest for two periods. It would be incorrect to use 6% for one period because the interest is 3% compounded quarterly, and that amount differs from 6% compounded semiannually. *Take care in studying future-value and present-value problems to align the interest rate with the appropriate number of periods.*

Let's see how a future-value table like the one in Exhibit B-2 is used. The future value of $1.00 invested at 8% for one year is $1.08 ($1.00 × 1.080, which appears at the junction of the 8% column and row 1 in the Periods column). The figure 1.080 includes both the principal (1.000) and the compound interest for one period (0.080).

Suppose you deposit $5,000 in a savings account that pays annual interest of 8%. The account balance at the end of one year will be $5,400. To compute the future value of $5,000 at 8% for one year, multiply $5,000 by 1.080 to get $5,400. Now suppose you invest in a 10-year, 8% certificate of deposit (CD). What will be the future value of the CD at maturity? To compute the future value of $5,000 at 8% for 10 periods, multiply $5,000 by 2.159 (from Exhibit B-2) to get $10,795. This future value of $10,795 indicates that $5,000, earning 8% interest compounded annually, grows to $10,795 at the end of 10 years. Using Exhibit B-2, you can find any present amount's future value at a particular future date. Future value is especially helpful for computing the amount of cash you will have on hand for some purpose in the future.

Future Value of an Annuity

In the preceding example, we made an investment of a single amount. Other investments, called *annuities*, include multiple investments of an equal periodic amount at fixed intervals over the duration of the investment. Consider a family investing for a child's education. The Dietrichs can invest $4,000 annually to accumulate a college fund for 15-year-old Helen. The investment can earn 7% annually until Helen turns 18—a three-year investment. How much will be available for Helen on the date of the last investment? Exhibit B-3 shows the compounding—a total future value of $12,860.

EXHIBIT B-3 | **Future Value of an Annuity**

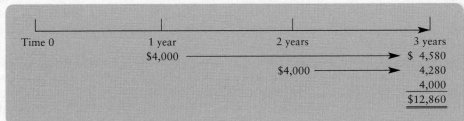

Time 0	1 year	2 years	3 years
	$4,000 ⟶		$ 4,580
		$4,000 ⟶	4,280
			4,000
			$12,860

The first $4,000 invested by the Dietrichs grows to $4,580 over the investment period. The second amount grows to $4,280, and the third amount stays at $4,000 because it has no time to earn interest. The sum of the three future values

($4,580 + $4,280 + $4,000) is the future value of the annuity ($12,860), which can also be computed as follows:

End of Year	Annual Investment	Interest	Increase for the Year	Future Value of Annuity
0	—	—	—	0
1	$4,000	—	$4,000	$ 4,000
2	4,000	+ ($4,000 × 0.07 = $280) =	4,280	8,280
3	4,000	+ ($8,280 × 0.07 = $580) =	4,580	12,860

These computations are laborious. As with the Future Value of $1 (a lump sum), mathematical tables ease the strain of calculating annuities. Exhibit B-4, Future Value of Annuity of $1, gives the future value of a series of investments, each of equal amount, at regular intervals.

What is the future value of an annuity of three investments of $1 each that earn 7%? The answer, 3.215, can be found at the junction of the 7% column and row 3 in Exhibit B-4. This amount can be used to compute the future value of the investment for Helen's education, as follows:

Amount of each periodic investment	×	Future value of annuity of $1 (Exhibit B-4)	×	Future value of investment
$4,000	×	3.215	×	$12,860

EXHIBIT B-4 | Future Value of Annuity of $1

Future Value of Annuity of $1

Periods	4%	5%	6%	7%	8%	9%	10%	12%	14%	16%
1	1.000	1.000	1.000	1.000	1.000	1.000	1.000	1.000	1.000	1.000
2	2.040	2.050	2.060	2.070	2.080	2.090	2.100	2.120	2.140	2.160
3	3.122	3.153	3.184	3.215	3.246	3.278	3.310	3.374	3.440	3.506
4	4.246	4.310	4.375	4.440	4.506	4.573	4.641	4.779	4.921	5.066
5	5.416	5.526	5.637	5.751	5.867	5.985	6.105	6.353	6.610	6.877
6	6.633	6.802	6.975	7.153	7.336	7.523	7.716	8.115	8.536	8.977
7	7.898	8.142	8.394	8.654	8.923	9.200	9.487	10.089	10.730	11.414
8	9.214	9.549	9.897	10.260	10.637	11.028	11.436	12.300	13.233	14.240
9	10.583	11.027	11.491	11.978	12.488	13.021	13.579	14.776	16.085	17.519
10	12.006	12.578	13.181	13.816	14.487	15.193	15.937	17.549	19.337	21.321
11	13.486	14.207	14.972	15.784	16.645	17.560	18.531	20.655	23.045	25.733
12	15.026	15.917	16.870	17.888	18.977	20.141	21.384	24.133	27.271	30.850
13	16.627	17.713	18.882	20.141	21.495	22.953	24.523	28.029	32.089	36.786
14	18.292	19.599	21.015	22.550	24.215	26.019	27.975	32.393	37.581	43.672
15	20.024	21.579	23.276	25.129	27.152	29.361	31.772	37.280	43.842	51.660
16	21.825	23.657	25.673	27.888	30.324	33.003	35.950	42.753	50.980	60.925
17	23.698	25.840	28.213	30.840	33.750	36.974	40.545	48.884	59.118	71.673
18	25.645	28.132	30.906	33.999	37.450	41.301	45.599	55.750	68.394	84.141
19	27.671	30.539	33.760	37.379	41.446	46.018	51.159	63.440	78.969	98.603
20	29.778	33.066	36.786	40.995	45.762	51.160	57.275	72.052	91.025	115.380

This one-step calculation is much easier than computing the future value of each annual investment and then summing the individual future values. In this way, you can compute the future value of any investment consisting of equal periodic amounts at regular intervals. Businesses make periodic investments to accumulate funds for equipment replacement and other uses—an application of the future value of an annuity.

Present Value

Often a person knows a future amount and needs to know the related present value. Recall Exhibit B-1, in which present value and future value are on opposite ends of the same time line. Suppose an investment promises to pay you $5,000 at the *end* of one year. How much would you pay *now* to acquire this investment? You would be willing to pay the present value of the $5,000 future amount.

Like future value, present value depends on three factors: (1) the *amount of payment* (or receipt), (2) the length of *time* between investment and future receipt (or payment), and (3) the *interest rate*. The process of computing a present value is called *discounting* because the present value is *less* than the future value.

In our investment example, the future receipt is $5,000. The investment period is one year. Assume that you demand an annual interest rate of 10% on your investment. With all three factors specified, you can compute the present value of $5,000 at 10% for one year:

$$\text{Present value} = \frac{\text{Future value}}{1 + \text{Interest rate}} = \frac{\$5,000}{1.10} = \$4,545$$

By turning the data around into a future-value problem, we can verify the present-value computation:

Amount invested (present value)	$4,545
Expected earnings ($4,545 × 0.10)	455
Amount to be received one year from now (future value)	$5,000

This example illustrates that present value and future value are based on the same equation:

$$\text{Future value} = \text{Present value} \times (1 + \text{Interest rate})$$

$$\text{Present value} = \frac{\text{Future value}}{1 + \text{Interest rate}}$$

If the $5,000 is to be received two years from now, you will pay only $4,132 for the investment, as shown in Exhibit B-5 on the following page. By turning the data around, we verify that $4,132 accumulates to $5,000 at 10% for two years:

Amount invested (present value)	$4,132
Expected earnings for first year ($4,132 × 0.10)	413
Value of investment after one year	4,545
Expected earnings for second year ($4,545 × 0.10)	455
Amount to be received two years from now (future value)	$5,000

EXHIBIT B-5 | **Present Value: An Example**

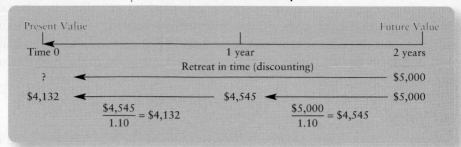

You would pay $4,132—the present value of $5,000—to receive the $5,000 future amount at the end of two years at 10% per year. The $868 difference between the amount invested ($4,132) and the amount to be received ($5,000) is the return on the investment, the sum of the two interest receipts: $413 + $455 = $868.

Present-Value Tables

We have shown the simple formula for computing present value. However, figuring present value "by hand" for investments spanning many years is time-consuming and presents too many opportunities for arithmetic errors. Present-value tables ease our work. Let's reexamine our examples of present value by using Exhibit B-6, Present Value of $1, given below.

EXHIBIT B-6 | **Present Value of $1**

Present Value of $1									
Periods	4%	5%	6%	7%	8%	10%	12%	14%	16%
1	0.962	0.952	0.943	0.935	0.926	0.909	0.893	0.877	0.862
2	0.925	0.907	0.890	0.873	0.857	0.826	0.797	0.769	0.743
3	0.889	0.864	0.840	0.816	0.794	0.751	0.712	0.675	0.641
4	0.855	0.823	0.792	0.763	0.735	0.683	0.636	0.592	0.552
5	0.822	0.784	0.747	0.713	0.681	0.621	0.567	0.519	0.476
6	0.790	0.746	0.705	0.666	0.630	0.564	0.507	0.456	0.410
7	0.760	0.711	0.665	0.623	0.583	0.513	0.452	0.400	0.354
8	0.731	0.677	0.627	0.582	0.540	0.467	0.404	0.351	0.305
9	0.703	0.645	0.592	0.544	0.500	0.424	0.361	0.308	0.263
10	0.676	0.614	0.558	0.508	0.463	0.386	0.322	0.270	0.227
11	0.650	0.585	0.527	0.475	0.429	0.350	0.287	0.237	0.195
12	0.625	0.557	0.497	0.444	0.397	0.319	0.257	0.208	0.168
13	0.601	0.530	0.469	0.415	0.368	0.290	0.229	0.182	0.145
14	0.577	0.505	0.442	0.388	0.340	0.263	0.205	0.160	0.125
15	0.555	0.481	0.417	0.362	0.315	0.239	0.183	0.140	0.108
16	0.534	0.458	0.394	0.339	0.292	0.218	0.163	0.123	0.093
17	0.513	0.436	0.371	0.317	0.270	0.198	0.146	0.108	0.080
18	0.494	0.416	0.350	0.296	0.250	0.180	0.130	0.095	0.069
19	0.475	0.396	0.331	0.277	0.232	0.164	0.116	0.083	0.060
20	0.456	0.377	0.312	0.258	0.215	0.149	0.104	0.073	0.051

For the 10% investment for one year, we find the junction of the 10% column and row 1 in Exhibit B-6. The figure 0.909 is computed as follows: 1/1.10 = 0.909. This work has been done for us, and only the present values are given in the table. To figure the present value for $5,000, we multiply 0.909 by $5,000. The result is $4,545, which matches the result we obtained by hand.

For the two-year investment, we read down the 10% column and across row 2. We multiply 0.826 (computed as 0.909/1.10 = 0.826) by $5,000 and get $4,130, which confirms our earlier computation of $4,132 (the difference is due to rounding in the present-value table). Using the table, we can compute the present value of any single future amount.

Present Value of an Annuity

Return to the investment example near the bottom of page 881 of this appendix. That investment provided the investor with only a single future receipt ($5,000 at the end of two years). *Annuity investments* provide multiple receipts of an equal amount at fixed intervals over the investment's duration.

Consider an investment that promises *annual* cash receipts of $10,000 to be received at the end of three years. Assume that you demand a 12% return on your investment. What is the investment's present value? That is, what would you pay today to acquire the investment? The investment spans three periods, and you would pay the sum of three present values. The computation follows.

Year	Annual Cash Receipt	Present Value of $1 at 12% (Exhibit B-6)	Present Value of Annual Cash Receipt
1	$10,000	0.893	$ 8,930
2	10,000	0.797	7,970
3	10,000	0.712	7,120
Total present value of investment...............			$24,020

The present value of this annuity is $24,020. By paying this amount today, you will receive $10,000 at the end of each of the three years while earning 12% on your investment.

This example illustrates repetitive computations of the three future amounts, a time-consuming process. One way to ease the computational burden is to add the three present values of $1 (0.893 + 0.797 + 0.712) and multiply their sum (2.402) by the annual cash receipt ($10,000) to obtain the present value of the annuity ($10,000 × 2.402 = $24,020).

An easier approach is to use a present-value-of-an-annuity table. Exhibit B-7 on the following page shows the present value of $1 to be received periodically for a given number of periods. The present value of a three-period annuity at 12% is 2.402 (the junction of row 3 and the 12% column). Thus, $10,000 received annually at the end of each of three years, discounted at 12%, is $24,020 ($10,000 × 2.402), which is the present value.

EXHIBIT B-7 | **Present Value Annuity of $1**

						Present Value of Annuity of $1			
Periods	4%	5%	6%	7%	8%	10%	12%	14%	16%
1	0.962	0.952	0.943	0.935	0.926	0.909	0.893	0.877	0.862
2	1.886	1.859	1.833	1.808	1.783	1.736	1.690	1.647	1.605
3	2.775	2.723	2.673	2.624	2.577	2.487	2.402	2.322	2.246
4	3.630	3.546	3.465	3.387	3.312	3.170	3.037	2.914	2.798
5	4.452	4.329	4.212	4.100	3.993	3.791	3.605	3.433	3.274
6	5.242	5.076	4.917	4.767	4.623	4.355	4.111	3.889	3.685
7	6.002	5.786	5.582	5.389	5.206	4.868	4.564	4.288	4.039
8	6.733	6.463	6.210	5.971	5.747	5.335	4.968	4.639	4.344
9	7.435	7.108	6.802	6.515	6.247	5.759	5.328	4.946	4.608
10	8.111	7.722	7.360	7.024	6.710	6.145	5.650	5.216	4.833
11	8.760	8.306	7.887	7.499	7.139	6.495	5.938	5.453	5.029
12	9.385	8.863	8.384	7.943	7.536	6.814	6.194	5.660	5.197
13	9.986	9.394	8.853	8.358	7.904	7.103	6.424	5.842	5.342
14	10.563	9.899	9.295	8.745	8.244	7.367	6.628	6.002	5.468
15	11.118	10.380	9.712	9.108	8.559	7.606	6.811	6.142	5.575
16	11.652	10.838	10.106	9.447	8.851	7.824	6.974	6.265	5.669
17	12.166	11.274	10.477	9.763	9.122	8.022	7.120	6.373	5.749
18	12.659	11.690	10.828	10.059	9.372	8.201	7.250	6.467	5.818
19	13.134	12.085	11.158	10.336	9.604	8.365	7.366	6.550	5.877
20	13.590	12.462	11.470	10.594	9.818	8.514	7.469	6.623	5.929

Present Value of Bonds Payable

The present value of a bond—its market price—is the present value of the future principal amount at maturity plus the present value of the future stated interest payments. The principal is a *single amount* to be paid at maturity. The interest is an *annuity* because it occurs periodically.

Let's compute the present value of the assumed 9% five-year bonds of **Unilever** (discussed on pages 483–484). The face value of the bonds is $100,000, and they pay 4½%—stated (cash) interest semiannually (that is, twice a year).[1] At issuance, the market interest rate is expressed as 10% annually, but it is computed at 5% semiannually. Therefore, the effective interest rate for each of the 10 semiannual periods is 5%. We thus use 5% in computing the present value (PV) of the maturity and of the interest. The market price of these bonds is $96,149, as follows:

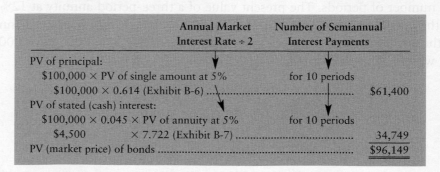

	Annual Market Interest Rate ÷ 2	Number of Semiannual Interest Payments	
PV of principal:			
$100,000 × PV of single amount at 5%		for 10 periods	
$100,000 × 0.614 (Exhibit B-6)			$61,400
PV of stated (cash) interest:			
$100,000 × 0.045 × PV of annuity at 5%		for 10 periods	
$4,500 × 7.722 (Exhibit B-7)			34,749
PV (market price) of bonds			$96,149

[1] For a definition of stated interest rate, see page 482.

The market price of the Unilever bonds shows a discount because the contract (stated) interest rate on the bonds (9%) is less than the market interest rate (10%).

Let's consider a premium price for the 9% Unilever bonds. Assume that the market interest rate is 8% (rather than 10%) at issuance. The effective interest rate is thus 4% for each of the 10 semiannual periods:

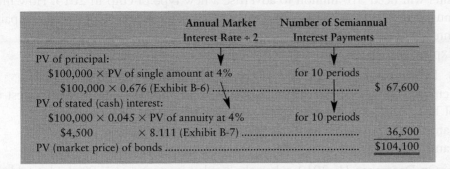

	Annual Market Interest Rate ÷ 2	Number of Semiannual Interest Payments	
PV of principal:			
$100,000 × PV of single amount at 4%		for 10 periods	
$100,000 × 0.676 (Exhibit B-6)			$ 67,600
PV of stated (cash) interest:			
$100,000 × 0.045 × PV of annuity at 4%		for 10 periods	
$4,500 × 8.111 (Exhibit B-7)			36,500
PV (market price) of bonds			$104,100

We discuss accounting for these bonds on pages 485–488. It may be helpful for you to reread this section ("Present Value of Bonds Payable") after you've studied those pages.

Capital Leases

How does a lessee compute the cost of an asset acquired through a capital lease?[2] Consider that the lessee gets the use of the asset but does *not* pay for the leased asset in full at the beginning of the lease. A capital lease is therefore similar to an installment purchase of the leased asset. The lessee must record the leased asset at the present value of the lease liability. The time value of money must be weighed.

The cost of the asset to the lessee is the sum of any payment made at the beginning of the lease period plus the present value of the future lease payments. The lease payments are equal amounts occurring at regular intervals—that is, they are annuity payments.

Consider a 20-year equipment lease that requires 20 annual payments of $10,000 each, with the first payment due immediately.[3] The interest rate in the lease is 10%, and the present value of the 19 future payments is $83,650 ($10,000 × PV of annuity at 10% for 19 periods, or 8.365 from Exhibit B-7). The lessee's cost of the equipment is $93,650 (the sum of the initial payment, $10,000, plus the present value of the future payments, $83,650). The lessee would base its accounting for the leased asset (and the related depreciation) and for the lease liability (and the related interest expense) on the cost of the equipment that we have just computed.

Appendix Problems

PC-1. For each situation, compute the required amount.

a. **Kellogg Corporation** is budgeting for the acquisition of land over the next several years. Kellogg can invest $100,000 today at 9%. How much cash will Kellogg have for land acquisitions at the end of five years? At the end of six years?

b. Davidson, Inc., is planning to invest $50,000 each year for five years. The company's investment adviser believes that Davidson can earn 6% interest without taking on too much risk. What will be the value of Davidson's investment on the date of the last deposit if Davidson can earn 6%? If Davidson can earn 8%?

---

[2]See page 499 for the definition of *capital leases*.
[3]This lease is calculated as *annuity due* where the first payment is made immediately on the signing of the lease. If you are calculating leases based on *ordinary annuity*, the first payment will be made at the end of year 1. This will affect PV calculations.

PC-2. For each situation, compute the required amount.

a. **Intel Corporation** operations are generating excess cash that will be invested in a special fund. During 2009, Intel invests $5,643,341 in the fund for a planned advertising campaign on a new product to be released six years later, in 2015. If Intel's investments can earn 10% each year, how much cash will the company have for the advertising campaign in 2015?

b. Intel will need $10 million to advertise a new type of chip in 2015. How much must Intel invest in 2009 to have the cash available for the advertising campaign? Intel's investments can earn 10% annually.

c. Explain the relationship between your answers to a and b.

PC-3. Determine the present value of the following notes and bonds:

1. Ten-year bonds payable with maturity value of $500,000 and stated interest rate of 12%, paid semiannually. The market rate of interest is 12% at issuance.

2. Same bonds payable as in number 1, but the market interest rate is 14%.

3. Same bonds payable as in number 1, but the market interest rate is 10%.

PC-4. On December 31, 2010, when the market interest rate is 8% Libby, Libby, & Short, a partnership, issues $400,000 of 10-year, 7.25% bonds payable. The bonds pay interest semiannually.

❚ Requirements

1. Determine the present value of the bonds at issuance.

2. Assume that the bonds are issued at the price computed in Requirement 1. Prepare an effective-interest-method amortization table for the first two semiannual interest periods.

3. Using the amortization table prepared in Requirement 2, journalize issuance of the bonds and the first two interest payments and amortization of the bonds.

PC-5. St. Mere Eglise Children's Home needs a fleet of vans to transport the children to singing engagements throughout Normandy. **Renault** offers the vehicles for a single payment of ⟺ 630,000 due at the end of four years. **Peugeot** prices a similar fleet of vans for four annual payments of ⟺150,000 at the end of each year. The children's home could borrow the funds at 6%, so this is the appropriate interest rate. Which company should get the business, Renault or Peugeot? Base your decision on present value, and give your reason.

PC-6. American Family Association acquired equipment under a capital lease that requires six annual lease payments of $40,000. The first payment is due when the lease begins, on January 1, 2010. Future payments are due on January 1 of each year of the lease term. The interest rate in the lease is 16%.

❚ Requirement

1. Compute the association's cost of the equipment.

Answers

PC-1	a. 5 yrs. $153,900		b. 6% $281,850	
	6 yrs. $167,700		8% $293,350	
PC-2	a. $10,000,000		b. $5,640,000	
PC-3	1. $500,100	2. $446,820	3. $562,360	
PC-4	1. $379,455	2. Bond		
	carry. amt. at 12-31-11 $380,838			
PC-5	Renault PV €498,960			
	Peugeot PV €519,750			
PC-6	Cost $170,960			

Appendix C

TYPICAL CHARTS OF ACCOUNTS FOR DIFFERENT TYPES OF BUSINESSES

A Simple Service Corporation

Assets	Liabilities	Shareholders' Equity
Cash	Accounts Payable	Share Capital
Accounts Receivable	Notes Payable, Short-Term	Retained Earnings
Allowance for Uncollectible Accounts	Salary Payable	Dividends
Notes Receivable, Short-Term	Wages Payable	**Revenues and Gains**
Interest Receivable	Payroll Taxes Payable	
Supplies	Employee Benefits Payable	Service Revenue
Prepaid Rent	Interest Payable	Interest Revenue
Prepaid Insurance	Unearned Service Revenue	Gain on Sale of Land (Furniture,
Notes Receivable, Long-Term	Notes Payable, Long-Term	Equipment, or Building)
Land		**Expenses and Losses**
Furniture		
Accumulated Depreciation—Furniture		Salary Expense
Equipment		Payroll Tax Expense
Accumulated Depreciation—Equipment		Employee Benefits Expense
Building		Rent Expense
Accumulated Depreciation—Building		Insurance Expense
		Supplies Expense
		Uncollectible Account Expense
		Depreciation Expense

Service Partnership

Same as service corporation, except for owners' equity

Owners' Equity

Partner 1, Capital
Partner 2, Capital
.
.
.
Partner N, Capital

Partner 1, Drawing
Partner 2, Drawing
.
.
.
Partner N, Drawing

A Complex Merchandising Corporation

Assets	Liabilities	Shareholders' Equity	

Assets

Cash
Short-Term Investments
Accounts Receivable
Allowance for Uncollectible
    Accounts
Notes Receivable, Short-Term
Interest Receivable
Inventory
Supplies
Prepaid Rent
Prepaid Insurance
Notes Receivable, Long-Term
Investments in Subsidiaries
Investments in Stock
    (Available-for-Sale
    Securities)
Investments in Bonds (Held-to-
    Maturity Securities)
Other Receivables, Long-Term
Land
Land Improvements
Furniture and Fixtures
Accumulated Depreciation—
    Furniture and Fixtures
Equipment
Accumulated Depreciation—
    Equipment
Buildings
Accumulated Depreciation—
    Buildings
Franchises
Patents
Leaseholds
Goodwill

Liabilities

Accounts Payable
Notes Payable, Short-Term
Current Portion of Bonds
    Payable
Salary Payable
Wages Payable
Payroll Taxes Payable
Employee Benefits Payable
Interest Payable
Income Tax Payable
Unearned Sales Revenue
Notes Payable, Long-Term
Bonds Payable
Lease Liability
Minority Interest

Shareholders' Equity

Preference Shares
Paid-in Capital in Excess of
    Par—Preference Shares
Ordinary Shares
Retained Earnings
    Unrealized Gain (or Loss)
on Investments
Foreign Currency Translation
    Adjustment
Treasury Share

Revenues and Gains

Sales Revenue
Interest Revenue
Dividend Revenue
Equity-Method Investment
    Revenue
Unrealized Holding Gain on
    Trading Investments
Gain on Sale of Investments
Gain on Sale of Land
    (Furniture and Fixtures,
    Equipment, or Buildings)
Discontinued Operations—
    Gain

Expenses and Losses

Cost of Goods Sold
Salary Expense
Wage Expense
Commission Expense
Payroll Tax Expense
Employee Benefits Expense
Rent Expense
Insurance Expense
Supplies Expense
Uncollectible Account Expense
Depreciation Expense
Administrative Expense
Amortization Expense
Income Tax Expense
Unrealized Holding Loss on
    Trading Investments
Loss on Sale of Investments
Loss on Sale (or Exchange) of
    Land (Furniture and
    Fixtures, Equipment, or
    Buildings)
Discontinued Operations—
    Loss

A Manufacturing Corporation

Same as merchandising corporation, except for Assets

Assets

Inventories:
    Materials Inventory
    Work-in-Process Inventory
    Finished Goods Inventory
Factory Wages
Factory Overhead

Appendix D

INTERNATIONAL FINANCIAL REPORTING STANDARDS (IFRSs)

Every technical area has professional associations and regulatory bodies that govern the practice of the profession. Accounting is no exception. Whilst the International Financial Reporting Standards, issued by the International Accounting Standards Board (IASB), are gaining momentum all around the world, they actually have no "legal" authority, unless formally adopted by a country's accounting regulatory body. In some countries, adaption of certain standards may be faster than others. This is why sometimes you see IFRSs relabeled into various names and not always applicable at the same time around the world. Exhibit D-1 below shows the level of IFRS adoption in 2010. Blue areas indicate countries that either require or permit the use of IFRSs, and grey areas indicate countries that are currently seeking convergence with IASB.

EXHIBIT D-1 | **Use of IFRSs around the world**

THE MOMENTUM TOWARDS GLOBAL ADOPTION OF IFRSs

More than 100 countries require or permit the use of International Financial Reporting Standards (IFRSs), or are converging with the IASB's standards.

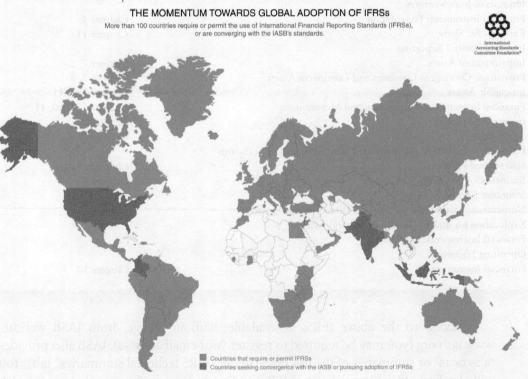

- Countries that require or permit IFRSs
- Countries seeking convergence with the IASB or pursuing adoption of IFRSs

Throughout this textbook, we have used the standards' formal names and they may be a little different from what is applicable in your own country. Standards issued by the predecessor of IASB are labeled IAS and the newer standards are labeled IFRS. There are also interpretations of IFRSs labeled IFRIC (or SIC, under the predecessor to IASB) on the IASB website. Collectively, they are referred to as IFRSs. As of April 2010, the IASB have issued the following standards.

EXHIBIT D-2 | IFRSs as at Jan 1, 2010

Name of Standards	Text Reference
Preface to International Financial Reporting Standards	
IFRS Framework for Preparation and Presentation of Financial Statements	Chapter 1, 3, 8
IAS1 Presentation of Financial Statements	Chapter 1, 3, 10, 11, 13
IAS2 Inventories	Chapter 6
IAS7 Statement of Cash Flows	Chapter 12
IAS8 Accounting Policies, Changes in Accounting Estimates and Errors	Chapter 7, 11
IAS10 Events After the Reporting Period	
IAS11 Construction Contracts	
IAS12 Income Taxes	Chapter 7, 11
IAS14 Segment Reporting	
IAS16 Property, Plant and Equipment	Chapter 7, 11
IAS17 Leases	Chapter 8
IAS18 Revenue	Chapter 3, 6, 11
IAS19 Employee Benefits	Chapter 11
IAS20 Accounting for Government Grants and Disclosure of Government Assistance	
IAS21 The Effects of Changes in Foreign Exchange Rates	Chapter 10, 11
IAS23 Borrowing Costs	Chapter 7
IAS24 Related Party Disclosures	
IAS26 Accounting and Reporting by Retirement Benefit Plans	
IAS27 Consolidated and Separate Financial Statements	Chapter 10
IAS28 Investment in Associates	Chapter 10
IAS29 Financial Reporting in Hyperinflationary Economies	
IAS31 Interests in Joint Ventures	
IAS32 Financial Instrument: Presentation	Chapter 5
IAS33 Earnings Per Share	Chapter 11
IAS34 Interim Financial Reporting	
IAS36 Impairment of Assets	Chapter 7
IAS37 Provisions, Contingent Liabilities and Contingent Assets	Chapter 7, 8
IAS38 Intangible Assets	Chapter 3, 7, 11
IAS39 Financial Instruments: Recognition and Measurement	Chapter 5, 8, 10, 11
IAS40 Investment Property	Chapter 7
IAS41 Agriculture	Chapter 7
IFRS1 First-time Adoption of International Financial Reporting Standards	
IFRS2 Share-based Payment	Chapter 11
IFRS3 Business Combinations	Chapter 7
IFRS4 Insurance Contracts	
IFRS5 Non-current Assets Held for Sale and Discontinued Operations	Chapter 11
IFRS6 Exploration for and Evaluation of Mineral Assets	
IFRS7 Financial Instruments: Disclosures	
IFRS8 Operating Segments	
IFRS9 Financial Instruments	Chapter 10

Access to the above IFRSs is available, without charge, from IASB website, www.iasb.org (you may be required to register your email address). IASB also provides "abstracts" or summaries of the full IFRS (under "IFRS technical summaries" tab). You will also find official translations of IFRSs in Dutch, French, German, Italian, Spanish and Russian. Your instructor may also refer you to the regulatory body that adopts and prescribes the relevant accounting standards for your own country.

Another useful website for IFRS is www.iasplus.com, maintained by **Deloitte**, one of the Big 4 accounting firms. Some of the tools and resources you can find in this website includes: comparison of IFRS to local accounting standards, IFRS summaries in a booklet format ("IFRSs in Your Pocket"), model financial statements and much more.

Company Index

Glindex
A Combined Glossary and Subject Index

FOB. Stands for free on board (or freight on board), a legal term that designates the point at which title passes for goods sold. 346

foreign-currency
exchange rate, 630
foreign-currency translation adjustment, 635
strong currency, 631
weak currency, 631

franchises and licenses. Privileges granted by a private business or a government to sell a product or service in accordance with specified conditions. See *intangible assets.* 438

fraud. An intentional misrepresentation of facts, made for the purpose of persuading another party to act in a way that causes injury or damage to that party. 233
fraud triangle, 236
fraudulent financial reporting, 235
lapping, 234
misappropriation of assets, 235

G

gains. Usually separated from revenues. Part of income and result in an increase in equity. 11

general purpose financial statements. The common set of financial statements prepared for all users of financial statements. 7

generally accepted accounting principles (GAAP). Accounting guidelines, usually in reference to US standards as formulated by the Financial Accounting Standards Board. 6

going concern. An assumption that an entity will remain in operation for the foreseeable future. 11

goodwill. Excess of the cost of an acquired company over the sum of the market values of its net assets (assets minus liabilities). See *intangible assets.* 438

gross profit (margin). Sales revenue minus cost of goods sold. 345
gross profit (margin) method, 364
gross profit (margin) percentage, 361

H

hedging. To protect oneself from losing money in one transaction by engaging in a counterbalancing transaction. 633

held-to-maturity investments. Bonds and notes that an investor intends to hold until maturity. 626

horizontal analysis. Study of percentage changes in comparative financial statements. 786

I

impairment. The condition that exists when the carrying amount of a long-lived asset exceeds its fair value. 439

imprest system. A way to account for petty cash by maintaining a constant balance in the petty cash account, supported by the fund (cash plus payment tickets) totaling the same amount. 260

income. Increases in equity from revenue and gains. 11

income statement. A financial statement listing an entity's revenues, expenses, and net income or net loss for a specific period. Part of *statement of comprehensive income.* 12
function of expense income statement, 168
nature of expense income statement, 168

intangible assets. An asset with no physical form, a special right to current and expected future benefits. 409
amortization, 434
copyright, 437
franchises and licenses, 438
goodwill, 438
patent, 437
trademark (brands), 437

interest. The borrower's cost of renting money from a lender. Interest is revenue for the lender and expense for the borrower. 306

interest-coverage ratio. See *times-interest-earned* ratio. 496

internal control. Organizational plan and related measures adopted by an entity to safeguard assets, encourage adherence to company policies, promote operational efficiency, and ensure accurate and reliable accounting records. 238

International Financial Reporting Standards (IFRS). Accounting guidelines, formulated by the International Accounting Standards Board (IASB). 6

inventory. The merchandise that a company holds for sale to customers. 20, 343
consignment, 346
inventory costing methods, 350
average-cost method (weighted average method), 353
FIFO, 352
LIFO, 352
net realizable value, 359
periodic inventory system, 347
perpetual inventory system, 347
turnover, 362, 800
resident period, 801

investing activities. Activities that increase or decrease the long-term assets available to the business; a section of the *statement of cash flows.* 22, 715

investment capitalization rate. An earnings rate used to estimate the value of an investment in shares. 670

J

journal. The chronological accounting record of an entity's transactions. 78

L

lapping. A fraudulent scheme to steal cash through misappropriating certain customer payments and posting payments from other customers to the affected accounts to cover it up. 234

last-in, first-out (LIFO) cost (method). Inventory costing method by which the last costs into inventory are the first costs out to cost of goods sold. See *inventory.* 352

lease. Rental agreement in which the tenant (lessee) agrees to make rent payments to the property owner (lessor) in exchange for the use of the asset. 497
capital lease, 499
lessee, 497
lessor, 497
operating lease, 498

ledger. The book of accounts and their balances. 79

leverage. The degree of external financing of an entity. See *debt ratio.* 495, 803

liability. An economic obligation payable to an individual or an organization outside the business. 11

limited liability. No personal obligation of a shareholder for corporation debts. A shareholder can lose no more on an investment in a corporation's share than the cost of the investment. 539

liquidation value. The amount a corporation must pay a preference shareholder in the event the company liquidates and goes out of business. 564

liquidity. Measure of how quickly an item can be converted to cash. 166

lock-box system. A system of handling cash receipts by mail whereby customers remit payment directly to the bank, rather than through the entity's mail system. 234

long-term investments. Any investment that does not meet the criteria of a short-term investment; any investment that the investor expects to hold longer than a year or that is not readily marketable. 610